*The Varieties of Religious Repression*

# The Varieties of Religious Repression

## Why Governments Restrict Religion

ANI SARKISSIAN

OXFORD

UNIVERSITY PRESS

# OXFORD
UNIVERSITY PRESS

Oxford University Press is a department of the University of
Oxford. It furthers the University's objective of excellence in research,
scholarship, and education by publishing worldwide.

Oxford   New York
Auckland   Cape Town   Dar es Salaam   Hong Kong   Karachi
Kuala Lumpur   Madrid   Melbourne   Mexico City   Nairobi
New Delhi   Shanghai   Taipei   Toronto

With offices in
Argentina   Austria   Brazil   Chile   Czech Republic   France   Greece
Guatemala   Hungary   Italy   Japan   Poland   Portugal   Singapore
South Korea   Switzerland   Thailand   Turkey   Ukraine   Vietnam

Oxford is a registered trademark of Oxford University Press
in the UK and certain other countries.

Published in the United States of America by
Oxford University Press
198 Madison Avenue, New York, NY 10016

Library of Congress Cataloging-in-Publication Data
Sarkissian, Ani, 1973–
The varieties of religious repression : why governments restrict religion / Ani Sarkissian.
pages cm
Includes bibliographical references and index.
ISBN 978–0–19–934808–4 (hardcover : alk. paper)—ISBN 978–0–19–934809–1
(ebook)—ISBN 978–0–19–934810–7 (ebook)   1. Religion and state.   2. Freedom of
religion.   3. Religious tolerance.   4. Religious discrimination.   I. Title.
BL65.S8S27 2015
323.44'2—dc23
2014016383

1 3 5 7 9 8 6 4 2
Printed in the United States of America
on acid-free paper

*For my mother, and in memory of my father*

# Contents

# Acknowledgments

A PROJECT OF this scope cannot be completed without the help and support of a number of people, and I have been fortunate to have had many patient people in my life over the past several years. I began to think about democratization, human and civil rights, and civil society in graduate school at the University of California, Los Angeles (UCLA). Richard Hovannisian was one of the reasons I decided to attend UCLA, and I will always be grateful for his wise mentorship and unflagging support. Thanks to Daniel Treisman for encouraging me to pursue the topic of religion in relation to democratization and for teaching me not to be afraid to tackle big questions in political science. Ş. İlgü Özler was the first person I met at UCLA, and she continues to be my dear friend and collaborator. Thanks and much love go to the many more good friends I made in Los Angeles, especially Marisa Kellam, Shuhei Kurizaki, Elizabeth Stein, Joel Scanlon, Marty Cohen, and Brian Obach, who have continued to support me through the process of writing this book.

I collected some of the material for this book during fieldwork in the republics of Armenia and Georgia in 2005 and Turkey in 2008 and 2009. I am grateful to the many individuals who were willing to take time to answer my numerous questions about religion and politics in their countries. They remain nameless for reasons of confidentiality. Research in Armenia and Georgia was conducted with support from the National Science Foundation and IREX (IRB#G05-09-104-01). Research in Turkey was supported by the Muslim Studies Program at Michigan State University (IRB#08-400). I am grateful to Jonathan Fox for offering me access to his Religion and State Dataset and to Brian Grim and Juan Carlos Esparza Ochoa at the Pew Research Center for making available detailed data on government restrictions and social hostilities related to religion.

Many of my colleagues in the Department of Political Science at Michigan State University (MSU) have helped me to navigate life as an assistant professor. I am grateful to department chairs Ric Hula and Chuck Ostrom for offering me the time and support I needed to complete this manuscript. For reading and commenting on portions of this book and moral support while I was writing it, I would also like to thank Paul Abramson, Benjamin Appel, Valentina Bali, Cristina Bodea, Michael Bratton, Eric Chang, Michael Colaresi, Jeffrey Conroy-Krutz, Matt Grossmann, Masaaki Higashijima, Christian Houle, Eric Juenke, Steven Kautz, Sarah Reckhow, Joshua Sapotichne, Brian Silver, Corwin D. Smidt, and Jakana Thomas. The Muslim Studies Program at MSU continues to offer opportunities for intellectual growth, and I am fortunate to be a part of such a dynamic and collegial collection of academics. My love and thanks go to my friends Karrin Hanshew, Sean Forner, Denise Demetriou, Mindy Smith, and Suman Seth for many great conversations, meals, and adventures.

I spent a very productive year in Montreal, Canada, writing the bulk of this manuscript. I am grateful to Hudson Meadwell and the Department of Political Science at McGill University for offering me space to work and opportunities to connect with other faculty. Members of the Comparative Politics Workshop graciously invited me to participate and share my research. I am especially grateful to Juan Wang and Erik Kuhonta for being so welcoming and supportive. I also thank Karen Fricker, Stephanie Nutting, Will Straw, and Joanne Sloane for their encouragement and delightful company.

Numerous colleagues in the fields of politics and religion have inspired and encouraged me, helped to refine my ideas, invited me to share my work, and served as collaborators. They include Jonathan Fox, Yasemin Akbaba, Robert Dowd, Paul Kollman, Anthony Gill, William Inboden, Ramazan Kılınç, Corwin Smidt, Ted Jelen, Donald Miller, Cynthia Buckley, Timothy Shah, Thomas Farr, and members of the Religious Freedom Project at Georgetown University's Berkley Center for Religion, Peace & World Affairs; the Melikian Center for Russian, Eurasian, and East European Studies at Arizona State University; Calvin College; and the Comparative Politics Workshop at Yale University. I look forward to many more years of working together in these important fields of research. My heartfelt thanks go to Oxford University Press, and especially Theo Calderara, for taking on this manuscript and guiding it to its fruition.

My family is the source of my strength and happiness. My father, Vahe Sarkissian, passed away in 1998, but I know he would have been proud of my achievements. My mother, Lusik Sarkissian, is the strongest woman I know, and she continues to inspire me to persevere, no matter what obstacles life presents. My sister, Teni Sarkissian, has taught me the importance of generosity and of living life in the present. The Sarkissian and Danoukh families have raised me to be proud of my heritage and to work to be a worthy representative of it. Michell Smith has been an exceptional mother-in-law and friend. I am grateful to the Smiths and Stamms for welcoming me and helping to (further) enlarge my extended family.

Finally, Michael Stamm has supported and encouraged me throughout my intellectual journey. He has given me more happiness than I ever could have imagined. I cannot wait to see what new adventures the future will bring for us.

*The Varieties of Religious Repression*

# *I*

# *Introduction*

## RELIGION, RIGHTS, AND REPRESSION

IN FOURTEENTH-CENTURY (BCE) Egypt, Pharaoh Akhenaten (born Amenhotep IV) introduced monotheism to his kingdom and imposed perhaps the first known instance of state repression of religion. Akhenaten overturned the entire belief system of Egyptian society, replacing the worship of a pantheon of gods with that of Aten, the Sun. Akhenaten diverted subsidies from major temples to those devoted to Aten, abolished festivals to other gods and goddesses, defaced temples to ancient gods, and built a new sacred city. After his death, the boy-king Tutankhamen and his handlers dismantled Akhenaten's legacy and restored worship to the old deities. A later king, Horemheb, sought to destroy all traces of Akhenaten's name and existence, demolishing all of the temples and the city he had built (Engh 2007).

Several examples of state-imposed religious persecution and repression can be found in the ancient world outside Egypt. During the seventh century BCE in the kingdoms of Judah and Israel, under the reign of Josiah, soldiers purged Jerusalem and the countryside of all altars, holy places, and images—killing many priests as well—to remake religious practice according to a particular contract that enumerated how Yahweh (i.e., Jehovah or God) should be worshiped. In ancient Greece, Socrates— among scores of others—was tried by the Athenian court under a charge of impiety, defined as anything that could endanger the city's good relations with the gods. He was convicted on charges of not recognizing the deities of Athens, inventing new deities, and corrupting young people and was sentenced to death. In ancient Rome, the Bacchanalia, a cult known for orgies involving drunkenness, sexual promiscuity, and criminal behavior, was banned by the Senate in 186 BCE, and several thousand of its initiates were imprisoned or executed on the grounds that it was spreading foreign rites and endangering Rome by offending the gods that protected it.

Once Christianity began to spread throughout the Roman Empire, emperors, governors, and generals encountered and suppressed new (and new to them) religions taking hold among different populations. They repressed Christians, Jews, Samaritans, Druids, and others, suspicious of their potential to subvert authority and pose problems for the empire. For instance, Christians were blamed for fires, earthquakes, and other natural disasters and subjected to death by crucifixion, fire, or behead-ing. Those who were not Roman citizens were subjected to the harshest punishment meted out by Roman law: torture and subsequent killing by wild beasts in front of crowds at the arena. During the Great Persecution from 303 to 311, Emperor Diocletian issued a series of edicts ordering the destruction of all Christian churches, the arrest of all Christian clergy, and executions of Christian adherents. However, once Constantine adopted Christianity as the religion of the empire, emperors turned the tables and repressed pagans, Jews, and even other Christians. This included banning non-Christian worship, destroying temples, making conversion away from Christianity illegal, imposing laws discriminating against non-Christians in areas such as property ownership, and impos-ing particular interpretations of Christian dogma.

Persecution of non-Christians and nonconformists by fellow Christians began in the fourth century CE and continued for centuries. During the original Crusades, Christians attempted to reclaim land conquered by Muslims, but later Crusades (starting in the late twelfth century) were fought against Christian heretics. In Europe during the period known as the Inquisition, Christians charged with heresy were forced to repent and subjected to punishments ranging from pilgrimage and confiscation of property to life imprisonment. Those who refused were burned alive at the stake. Official repression of other Christians continued in Europe through the seventeenth century.

Farther east, in the Persian Empire, where Zoroastrianism had been the religion of the rulers and many inhabitants since the sixth century BCE, changes in religious practice and political leadership shifted gover-nance away from the tolerant policies of previous rulers such as Cyrus the Great. From the second to sixth centuries CE, successive Zoroastrian rul-ers of the empire repressed Manichaeans, Christians, Jews, Mazdakites, and other groups before succumbing to Muslim conquerors, who, in turn, repressed Zoroastrians. In Arabia, the Prophet Muhammad himself removed pagan icons from the Ka'aba in Mecca and extended protection only to followers of biblical religions—Jews and Christians—in exchange for a tax. Spreading into India, eleventh-century Muslim rulers destroyed Hindu temples and icons. Like Christians, Muslim rulers have also been known to persecute heretics inhabiting the regions they have ruled, including Sikhs in India, Baha'is in Iran, Hazaras in Afghanistan, and Ahmadiyas in Pakistan.

Although many examples from the premodern era involve violent persecution, in modern times we find religious groups more often targeted with nonviolent repression. For instance, during the French Revolution in the late eighteenth century, leaders of the First Republic—under a purportedly democratic constitution—turned against the Catholic Church and stripped it of its traditionally favored political position. They closed churches and monasteries, seized church property, forced priests to marry, and destroyed religious statues, paintings, and other instruments of worship. Rather than preventing Christians from practicing and attempting to spread their religion by throwing them to wild animals in the arena, governments began to impose laws intended to make it difficult for them to gain political power.

The twentieth century featured no shortage of religious persecution and repression. Political ideologies such as communism and fascism targeted religious believers and groups. In the Soviet Union, state atheism waxed and waned, but authorities consistently repressed religious practice, construction, publishing, and education. At its harsher moments, the Soviet state imprisoned and killed clergy and those who refused to abandon their religious beliefs. In Nazi Germany, of course, Jews were targeted for annihilation. Other religious groups were also besieged. Despite a concordat with the Vatican signed in 1933, the state shut Catholic institutions, oppressed organizations, and imprisoned and murdered thousands of clergy. Jehovah's Witnesses, Protestants, and other minorities were also persecuted for their resistance to the regime. After World War II, religious groups and individuals in Central and Eastern Europe, Asia, Latin America, and Africa continued to face punishments ranging from fines to imprisonment to death.

This brief history illustrates that religious persecution and repression are not new phenomena in any part of the world. This is especially true of the predemocratic period, when suppression of religion was particularly violent and deadly. Although violent religious persecution persists today, what is even more prevalent is lower-intensity repression disguised as legalism. Laws, policies, and executive decrees purport to regulate religion in a neutral manner but are wielded to target particular groups. Sometimes these laws lead to religious conflict and violent persecution. More often, they lead to repression, by which I mean the nonviolent suppression of civil and political rights. Most of the time, they allow politicians to entrench their rule.

The central question of this book is why some countries choose to repress religion while others do not. In addition, I pose and attempt to answer such questions as: What types of policies do states use to repress religious groups? How do political leaders decide which religious groups to repress? Why do some states target small, seemingly nonthreatening religious groups with repression? When does favoritism of some groups lead to repression of others? Several recent studies have established that states do use policy mechanisms to restrict and repress religion, but few delve into why states vary in their policies and why they choose to target specific groups. This book aims to fill this gap.

The idea that religious freedom—including freedom from religion—is a fundamental human right is one of the founding principles of the United Nations and a notion that has been supported by scholars, policymakers, and human rights advocates around the world. Scholars have observed that human rights tend to be better protected in democracies than in nondemocracies, but there is still much to be learned about the relationship of religious freedom to regime type and stability. Those who study religion-state relations around the world note that while democracies do tend to protect religious freedom, many restrict religion as well (Fox 2008). For instance, in France, restrictions on religious attire (Fetzer and Soper 2005) and in Switzerland, a ban on constructing minarets (Ramadan 2010) have been used to target Muslim religious practices. Scholars have also noted a relationship between democracy and the protection of personal integrity rights (i.e., freedom from state violence such as torture, killing, or imprisonment) (Davenport and Armstrong 2004; Keith 2002; Poe and Tate 1994; Regan and Henderson 2002). Yet many studies remain concerned with explaining violent repression rather than denial of individual or group rights that are repressive but not necessarily violent (Grim and Finke 2011). Fewer studies examine civil liberties restrictions, which involve fines, arrests, bans, and other limitations imposed by the state on expression, association, assembly, and beliefs.

At the same time, few realize that levels of both persecution and repression vary across countries that are not fully democratic.[1] Statistics on religious freedom indicate that in 2008 approximately 30 percent of these states had a high level of religious freedom, and the level of religious freedom for about 28 percent of the countries was low or nonexistent.[2] Yet these patterns mask great differences in the types of restrictions imposed on religious individuals and groups in societies lacking democratic governance. They range from preventing Buddhist monks in Burma from speaking out about political issues to, in Iran, banning members of the Baha'i faith and preventing adherents from attending schools and obtaining employment. What these examples illustrate is that the variation in these states involves both the types of restrictions imposed and the groups that are targeted.

While repression of many kinds is common in nondemocratic countries, there are reasons to consider *religious* repression a phenomenon requiring separate treatment. First, religion is an important topic of study for social scientists because it exists across the globe and in every society. Levels of religious affiliation are high across the world, and even many nonaffiliated individuals report holding some belief in the divine.[3] Arguments about the uniqueness of religious freedom are abundant in both scholarly and popular sources and often rest on the assumption that something inherent in human beings drives them toward religious belief. For instance, Timothy Samuel Shah (2012, 12–13) cites findings from cognitive science claiming that religion is a natural part of human development and argues: "Everyone has an interest in religion, for the simple reason that no one can reasonably be indifferent to whether there is a transcendent order of reality and meaning, and to achieving whatever harmony can be achieved with such an order." He concludes that if everyone has an interest in religion, everyone must necessarily be interested in religious freedom.

Second, even if not all people hold religious beliefs, religion is distinct from other types of identity studied by political scientists, including race, language, caste, and tribe. Some scholars of ethnicity dispute this, considering religion to be one of several possible types of identity that are socially constructed and fungible (Chandra 2004; Posner 2005). But even if religious identities are constructed and changeable, they differ from other identities in that they transcend national borders, make demands on every aspect of their members' lives, and are able to withstand secular challenges because of the supernatural claims they make and the stakes they pose for their adherents (Grzymala-Busse 2012). Because religious identities are often exclusive and encompass all aspects of human life, they are intrinsically tied to individual political beliefs and group political behavior.[4] By ignoring religion or incorporating it into analyses of other types of identities, we risk missing the essential role it plays in the politics of many societies. Moreover, because religious associations are widespread and pervasive, their existence and activities are an important topic of study for social scientists interested in investigating different forms of human social organization.

Religious freedom also exists alongside other kinds of freedoms. Governments that protect religious freedom tend to protect other civil liberties and ensure greater political freedom. Brian J. Grim and Roger Finke (2011) present evidence that religious freedom is correlated with freedom of the press and civil liberties, political outcomes such as longevity of democracy and low levels of armed conflict, and economic indicators such as gender empowerment, income equality, and wealth. Yet correlation does not imply causation, and further scholarship is needed to show the paths through which these phenomena are related. Because restrictions on religion target issues of conscience, speech, association, and assembly, states that target religion (and nonreligion) for restrictions are able to limit the ability of individuals and groups to organize and express themselves politically under the guise of protecting their countries from extremism, encouraging national unity, or preserving historical legacies. Examining religious repression in a global context thus allows us to recognize similarities in motivations for and methods of imposing all types of repression. Limiting the study to nondemocratic regimes focuses attention on the ways that leaders are able to manipulate policy to target independent civil society, a realm from which opposition may emerge. Such analysis illuminates the various "democratic" means that nondemocratic rulers use to suppress political opposition.

Comparing 101 nondemocratic countries from around the globe from 1990 through 2010, this book seeks to explain (1) why they vary in their state religion policies and (2) how understanding religious repression informs the study of regimes. Examining the level of competition in the political sphere gives us some clues to why the level of religious repression varies across countries. Nondemocratic regimes can have little to no competition for executive office (e.g., hereditary monarchies) or hold unfree and unfair elections to pick top state officials (e.g., electoral authoritarian states). Therefore, we should expect to find higher levels of religious repression in countries with less competitive politics. In states with few checks and constraints on executive power, incumbent politicians are able to repress with impunity, as there are few institutions or groups able to challenge their authority. On the other hand, greater political competition decreases the repressive capacity of governments, as it requires them to compete for political support and therefore moderate their coercive tendencies.

However, outcomes in the actual world are not as clear-cut. Some nondemocratic states with greater political competition impose high levels of religious restrictions, and others with less competition impose few or no restrictions on religion. Moreover, when we examine more closely the types of repressive policies states impose, we find that states vary significantly in terms of which groups they target. To explain this variation, we must consider the context within which states construct religion policy, namely, the structure of religious divisions in society. A *religiously divided society* is one in which religion acts as an important source of societal cleavage and conflict. It can take many forms, including conflicts over the role that religion should play in the state and politics and competition between different religious groups (or sects within one religious group) for adherents, legitimacy, or influence (Lerner 2013). A religiously divided society may also have unresolved conflicts over the legitimacy of unbelief and conversion, which is especially relevant in areas where the state or state-supported groups enforce some sort of religious orthodoxy.

By focusing on how nondemocratic regimes differ in their treatment of religious groups in civil society, we can also learn about the nature of regimes. Many current studies distinguish regimes based on the freeness and fairness of their elections and the performance of their political institutions, but ratings based on these factors still lead to situations in which countries that are considered to be democratic fail to perform in ways that look very democratic. For instance, Turkey ranks relatively high on commonly used measures of democracy.[5] Yet Turkey remains deficient in its protection of civil and human rights and levels of political pluralism (Özler and Sarkissian 2011). As some scholars of democratization have argued, consolidated democracy requires not only free and fair elections but also a robust civil society that can monitor government and improve its quality (Levitsky and Way 2010; Linz and Stepan 1996). Because of the prevalence of regimes that combine elements of democracy and authoritarianism in the world today, a focus on civil society is vital to understanding the various forms that contemporary regimes can take.

This study therefore turns the focus to civil society, examining the number of groups states target with repression to understand how these regimes differ. Focusing on the number of groups repressed allows us to explain why these states target religion and why they focus that repression on particular groups. This allows us to paint a more holistic picture of regimes that better addresses the issue of competition throughout the various parts of public life. Therefore, by comparing nondemocratic regimes according to their relationship to religion and their methods of controlling independent religious activity, we can improve our understanding of differences and commonalities among the full range of nondemocratic regimes across world regions.

## The State of Current Scholarship on Regimes and Religion

Democratization has been described as proceeding in waves that swallow up neighboring countries in a manner similar to how the domino theory predicted communism would spread during the Cold War (Huntington 1991). Following the collapse of communism and through the Arab Spring that spread protests from North Africa to the Persian Gulf in 2011, analysts and scholars have focused on explaining how, why, when, and where democracy will next take hold. Yet many have been disappointed with the lack of democratic progress, leading to a renewed focus on how to explain the fact that countries that were once expected to turn democratic exist in an in-between state that appears to be quite stable. A variety of terms have been used to describe those hybrid regimes that have both democratic and authoritarian features, including "illiberal democracy" (Zakaria 1997) and "pseudodemocracy" (Diamond 2002) and, for more repressive regimes, "liberalized autocracy" (Brumberg 2002), "competitive authoritarianism" (Levitsky and Way 2010), and "electoral authoritarianism" (Schedler 2010). These terms get at the mixed nature of regimes that often possess democratic institutions on paper but lack democratic procedures in practice. In the past, these types of regimes may have been considered to be transitioning toward democracy, but at present they are acknowledged to form a new type of authoritarianism. Scholars tend to agree that most of these hybrid regimes combine elements of democracy with more authoritarian features. They may hold elections, but those elections may be rigged.

Aside from debates about how to classify nondemocratic regimes, we can also question what determines the durability of authoritarian governments (Brownlee 2007) and how authoritarian leaders use institutions as ruling instruments (Blaydes 2010; Gandhi and Przeworski 2007; Lust-Okar 2005; Magaloni 2006). Recent studies of authoritarianism consider the interests of politicians—primarily the desire to stay in office and reap the rewards that come from such a position—in crafting theories of the ways that these rulers manipulate policies and political processes to their benefit. Yet few scholars mention religion as a policy area that can be manipulated to the benefit of authoritarian leaders. For example, banning religious political parties and preventing religious leaders from becoming involved in politics are two common aspects of religion policy found in some parts of the world, yet they are not often discussed by scholars of authoritarianism as part of a larger toolkit that can be used by political incumbents to preserve their rule. In 2008, 48 countries banned religious political parties, and an additional 15 placed restrictions on them.[6] Moreover, individual rights related to religion can be restricted in a variety of ways to benefit incumbent politicians, another area that has received scant attention from scholars.

Despite near-daily accounts in the popular media of religious interactions with politics, the scholarly study of religion remains largely marginalized in the field of political science. Some scholars of religion attribute the lack of attention to religion to the bias created by the secularization paradigm prevalent in the Western academy since the early twentieth century. Secularization theorists famously predicted the decline of religion in modern society, and thus several generations of academics operated on the assumption that this decline was proceeding and religion would not be a fruitful area of research (Berger 1967).[7] This was especially true in the field of political science. The Iranian revolution in 1979 and subsequent political events forced scholars to contend with a religious resurgence and attempt to understand why religion's predicted death failed to materialize.

As it has become more difficult to ignore religion as a political factor in the last few decades, scholars have presented important work on how religious interests can be accommodated, particularly in democratic settings. They have developed models that explain how religion-state neutrality, separation, or accommodation work in different settings to represent the interests of religious and nonreligious individuals and keep state institutions independent of unelected religious groups (Demerath and Straight 1997; Mazie 2004; Monsma and Soper 1997; Stepan 2000).

Reflecting the discipline's focus on interests, some scholars make use of rational choice theory to explain religious behavior. Applied to religion, the rational choice perspective sees religious behavior as operating in a marketplace full of competing religious groups governed by regulations set by governments. Rodney Stark and Roger Finke (2000, 193) define a religious economy as consisting of "all of the religious activity going on in any society: a 'market' of current and potential adherents, a set of one or more organizations seeking to attract or maintain adherents, and the religious culture offered by the organization(s)." The theory assumes individuals are rational in their religious choices and, as in economics and political science, argues that, given a set of preference constraints, people try to achieve their goals in the least costly manner possible. Proponents argue that such an approach is useful because it allows for explanations of behavior in the event of changing constraints (e.g., a change in religious demographics) (Gill 1998). Because it leaves aside previous ideologically based explanations for religious behavior, it has been referred to as a "new paradigm" in the study of religion and politics (Warner 1993).

Coming from this perspective, Anthony Gill's (2008) book, *The Political Origins of Religious Liberty*, explains the development of religious freedom by focusing on the incentives politicians have for regulating or deregulating religion and how those interact with the interests of religious leaders. Gill argues that the main goals of politicians are political survival, maximizing economic revenue and growth, minimizing civil unrest, and minimizing the costs of ruling and that politicians use their available tools of coercion, patronage, and ideological legitimacy to achieve those goals. According to Gill, of the three tools available, ideological legitimacy is the least costly to attain, as it does not involve funding a costly coercive apparatus or paying off certain groups to get their support. Therefore, he argues, politicians court religious leaders (who have a reputation for being credible guides to what is in the best interests of their constituents in the secular realm) to gain legitimacy. In exchange for such support, politicians can use regulations to benefit those groups or harm others. Which kinds of regulations politicians adopt depends on the particular political and religious environment in question.

The rational choice perspective can thus explain how both politicians and religious leaders will contend with religious regulation. Politicians will make decisions on religious regulations based on their own interests (i.e., retaining political power). Gill argues that while religious deregulation can occur because of shocks such as revolution or military coups, often it is undertaken as a conscious policy platform by politicians hoping to gain the support of religious groups and gain or retain office. However, once their political tenure becomes more secure, politicians will be less likely to enforce regulations that are backed by monopolistic (e.g., majority) religious groups (Gill and Keshavarzian 1999). Because deregulation increases religious pluralism, it also decreases the likelihood that politicians will support regulation that restricts the rights of minority religions. At the same time, the competition created by deregulation increases the religious options available to individuals and thus forces religious groups and their leaders to adjust their strategies to retain current members, attract new adherents, and hold on to the societal or political benefits they enjoy by virtue of being the majority religion.

This book adopts a focus on competing interests in explaining variation in state religion policy but diverges from prior rational choice perspectives in three ways. First, many rational choice studies are concerned with understanding the relationship between the development of religious freedom and liberal democracy. For instance, Gill focuses on conditions leading to *deregulation* of religion, but he does not spend as much time explaining the conditions that lead to *repression* of religion, which studies show has been increasing and which occurs most often in non-democratic states. As new regime types are becoming more entrenched, it is worth shifting the focus away from explaining religious liberty to one that explains how politicians use religious restrictions to coerce political opponents to support the regime or to punish those who refuse to be co-opted. It is also important to explain situations in which politicians largely ignore religion.

Second, rational choice theory does not adequately assess the threat potential of small and heterodox groups or consider non-Western religions. For instance, rational choice theorists argue that it is less costly (and thus more likely) for individuals to reaffiliate (switch to a religious organization within the same religious family) than to convert to a completely different religion (Stark and Finke 2000, 114). Therefore, new religious movements—such as Pentecostalism—are particularly threatening to more traditional Christian denominations such as Catholicism, Orthodox Christianity, and Lutheranism (from which it is easy to convert to other Christian denominations), and the bulk of the scholarship has been based on these religions. Yet these assumptions may not hold for other religious traditions where reaffiliation—even to another sect within the same religious family—is extremely costly. For example, it may be costlier for a Sunni Muslim to join a Muslim sect considered by some jurists to be heterodox (e.g., the Ahmadiya sect) than to become a Christian, as Christians are offered protection as peoples of the book under Islamic law and other religions are considered offensive to Islam (Furman 2000; Yousif 2000). In some instances, such individuals are subject to state-imposed punishments as serious as death. Only a few scholars from the religious economies tradition raise these issues or apply those theories outside the West or in non-Christian societies (Sarkissian, Fox, and Akbaba 2011; Yang 2006).

Third, rational choice theorists focus on the configuration of groups in society (i.e., the number and size of groups) to understand how a government will regulate religion. However, these scholars fail to address the character and severity of religious divisions as a key issue in understanding religious regulations. A great degree of religious pluralism might indicate a situation in which regulations do not favor one group over others, but one cannot assume that the religious pluralism *causes* religious liberty. In fact, it is not hard to imagine that a society with several religious groups might have high levels of repression if these groups are competing with each other for political influence. Moreover, small groups might be more important in understanding repression than has been acknowledged. For instance, Gill (1998, 109) notes that religious groups become threatening to the hegemonic religion when they reach about 5 percent of the population, but this does not explain why groups such as Baha'is, Jehovah's Witnesses, and Ahmadiya Muslims are so severely persecuted in countries where they are less than 1 percent of the population (e.g., Iran, Georgia, and Pakistan). Such situations merit close attention.

An alternative to the rational choice perspective asserts that particular religion-state relations are inherent in certain cultural traditions. Scholars of this school often operate on the assumption that ideal religion-state relations require a separation of the two spheres, a condition they attribute to Western religions and ultimately democracies. Many in the past have argued that Protestant and Catholic doctrines are amenable to democracy, whereas Eastern Christian and Islamic doctrines are hostile to it (with other religious traditions often omitted) (Casanova 2001; Hefner 2000, 2001; Huntington 1996; Lewis 1996; Linz and Stepan 1996; Radu 1998). Explanations for the uniqueness of these societies include their cultural and ideological teachings, as well as the influence of colonialism. For example, Seymour Martin Lipset (1963), drawing on Max Weber, argued that Protestantism holds features that accord with the ideals of democracy, including a focus on individual responsibility, and support for capitalist institutions. Samuel Huntington (1991) argued the same for Catholicism, pointing to changes in the Catholic

Church after 1970 that made it a force opposed to authoritarianism. He concluded that countries with Western Christian religious traditions are more likely to democratize, whereas countries with Islamic traditions were unlikely to, mainly due to the lack of separation of religion and the state in Islam. Adrian Karatnycky (2002) attributes the "democracy gap" between Islamic and non-Islamic countries to several factors, including the idea that Islam relegates women to second-class status and impedes their participation in civic life and the claim that Islamic tradition does not distinguish between the religious and the political. Islam is described as lacking the notion of popular sovereignty, which some claim inhibits Muslim-majority countries from accepting a separation of the religious and political spheres and constitutional government (Fish 2002; Kedourie 1992; Midlarsky 1998).

I acknowledge that cultural factors have a role to play in determining what types of religion-state relations have been practiced in a particular country over its life span. I also acknowledge that the most stable democracies have tended to exist in Western, Christian societies. However, this does not mean that particular religion-state relations are a cultural inevitability or that states outside the West and the reach of Christendom are doomed to authoritarian governance. Instead, I set aside such discussions as beyond the realm of the current study, which accepts that nondemocratic governments exist or have existed in every region of the world. Because such regimes exist, and because all states have policies toward religion, isolating these regimes for study can help us to better understand both the dynamics of nondemocratic rule and the varieties and implications of religion policy. Moreover, it is important to trace the roots of current religion-state relations by considering how religious institutions and the state historically interacted, not by merely grouping states according to their traditional religious identity.

## A Theory of Religious Repression in Nondemocratic Countries

This book uses and elaborates on several insights from the rational choice perspective, including the ideas that politicians regulate religion based on their interest in political survival and that religious regulations hinder pluralism and help to create religious monopolies. It combines these with arguments taken from scholarship on authoritarianism, which has long dealt with issues of repression. Yet because the rational choice perspective on religion does not address differences in the behavior of politicians and religious leaders in democratic versus nondemocratic political settings, and because the scholarship on authoritarianism does not focus on religion, combining elements from the two fields helps to elaborate a new theory of religious regulation and repression in countries governed by nondemocratic regimes.

Both the rational choice perspective on religion and much of the scholarship on regimes assume that the primary goal of politicians in any type of regime is to preserve and prolong their rule. While in democratic countries this is done by appeasing constituents and winning votes, politicians in nondemocratic countries use three tools to hold on to power: repression, co-optation, and legitimation. These tools are not mutually exclusive. For instance, a ruler may be able to repress some groups by co-opting others, and co-optation of popular groups may lend rulers legitimacy. Even though the focus of this book is on religious repression, it necessarily must explore how co-optation and legitimation can be used to repress.

Religion policy in nondemocratic countries is often drafted and implemented in the same manner as in democracies. Most states have clauses in their constitutions or founding documents relating to religious freedom; some identify particular religions as being the religion of the state or enjoying some sort of privileged status by virtue of historical ties between the nation and the religion (Fox and Flores 2009). Aside from constitutional means, both democracies and nondemocratic regimes may use the legislative system to pass laws regulating the practice of religion. Additionally, in both kinds of regimes, the executive often has the power to establish policy, either through executive orders or through government ministries and other bureaucratic agencies tasked with regulating religion. Courts may adjudicate how policies are enacted or whether legislation conforms to constitutional principles. Finally, local authorities often take the reins in enforcing religious restrictions, either as a complement to national policy or sometimes in contradiction to national-level laws.

Yet, nondemocratic regimes differ from democratic ones in significant ways. With regard to their use of political institutions, democracies devise institutions to keep executive power in check. They develop mechanisms to ensure that the executive does not overstep his or her popular mandate and that other parts of government are able to perform their roles without being subsumed under the executive's absolute power. However, as Dan Slater (2003, 82) has argued, the function of institutions in nondemocratic regimes is to "keep political opposition under wraps." Government agencies, electoral rules, and coercive apparatuses are not able to check the power of the executive, which limits their proper functioning and effectiveness. Instead, state institutions give government the tools to "monitor, co-opt, intimidate, and repress potential opponents, both within and outside the regime" (Levitsky and Way 2010, 57). Therefore, we must assume that the logic of authoritarian authority differs from that of democracy (Svolik 2012).[8]

Since all types of institutions in nondemocratic regimes function differently from those of democratic ones, we can assume that religion policy—and the institutions used to enforce it—differs as well. Policies governing religion can include both regulations regarding the interaction of religious groups with the state and regulations concerning individual and group practice of religion. This can lead to the creation of state policies that on their face lack political motivation, such as regulations on religious buildings. Closer examination of how such policies are applied helps to illuminate their political motivations, as subsequent chapters of this book describe.

Understanding the motivations of nondemocratic leaders to repress religion requires considering its costs and benefits. The logic of authoritarianism states that dictators cannot rule by repression (or coercion) alone, as they risk that citizens will pretend to support the ruler even as they collude secretly to overthrow him or her, a situation sometimes referred to as the "dictator's dilemma" (Wintrobe 1998). Both violent persecution and nonviolent repression are costly because they require enforcement. Politicians require administrators, local officials, and police to ensure that restrictions are implemented and target the intended groups. These actors can be difficult to corral and fund. Moreover, persecution and repression may backfire on politicians, galvanizing opposition groups and leading to violent reprisals from extremists. Persecution and repression can also be costly outside the domestic arena. Because many types of religious rights are protected under international law, nondemocratic leaders face potential international sanctions for violating the human rights of their populations. These sanctions are most often imposed in the case of violent persecution, however, as nonviolent repression tends to fly under the radar of groups focused on preventing unfair imprisonment, torture, and death. The laws, regulations, and restrictions that have the effect of suppressing religion receive much less attention because they tend not to involve violence against individuals and groups.

Despite these potential costs, politicians may still benefit from imposing repressive laws and policies. Repression can weaken or silence opposition, contributing to regime stability. Even if repression mobilizes opposition, the nature of that opposition may help nondemocratic leaders gain legitimacy. For instance, leaders who successfully suppress violent opposition may receive credit for preserving societal peace. Moreover, repression in the form of restrictive policies may help politicians avoid resorting to violent persecution, which is costlier to enforce. As Dobson (2012) argues in a recent book, contemporary dictators understand that subtle coercion is a more effective form of political repression than brutal intimidation. They can write broad laws that do not draw attention and then target them to apply only to those groups that threaten their power the most.

Of all possible venues in which to practice repression, why would political leaders choose to target religion specifically? First, religious groups represent potential sites of public and/or political activity. States seeking to control public activity target religious groups to ensure that they do not act in ways contrary to the state's interests. This can include such actions as organizing meetings in opposition to government policies or organizing protests that condemn government actions. Second, religious groups hold the power to influence citizens' perceptions of state or government legitimacy. By restricting the ability of religious groups to express themselves through public speech or publications or by restricting clergy or other religious individuals from participating in the political process, politicians can prevent criticism from the religious sector from being made public. Third, some religious groups (e.g., Jehovah's Witnesses) profess teachings that are antipolitical or that discourage engagement in politics. This may work to the benefit of some politicians, but it can be problematic for nondemocratic regimes claiming popular legitimacy through elections (however flawed). In these cases, groups that teach adherents to refrain from political engagement may threaten the regime's ability to garner enough popular support and establish political legitimacy. Fourth, some religious groups (e.g., sects or heterodox groups) are considered unacceptable or offensive to other, usually larger religions. Politicians may justify repression of these small and seemingly unthreatening groups as a way of protecting orthodox or mainstream religions, some of which serve to prop up political leaders.

Why would nondemocratic leaders decide *not* to repress religion? From a rational choice perspective, we would expect them to ignore religion when their authority is not under attack and their political position is stable. According to Gill (2008), under these conditions, religious groups that lobby politicians for restrictions are no longer useful to them politically, and thus politicians ignore them, a situation that exists most often in stable democracies. But this perspective also presumes that religious restrictions come about because religious groups advocate for them, rather than as a policy tool that politicians wield to control politics. In fact, even in stable authoritarian systems, we find rulers imposing a large variety of religious restrictions to ensure that opposition is suppressed. We even find rulers repressing majority religions (e.g., in Syria), a situation not addressed by rational choice theory, which focuses on favoritism toward majority religious groups. Assuming no politician has complete information about the stability of his or her rule, it is difficult to imagine a situation in which a politician would not be concerned with minimizing potential political competition.

## *Religious Repression and Nondemocratic Regime Variation*

A simple comparison can help to illustrate the relationship between political competition and religious repression. Figure 1.1 plots the level of religious repression in each of the 101 countries included in this study against a commonly used measure of regime type that incorporates competitiveness as one of its main characteristics. The level of religious repression is measured as the number of types of restrictions each country imposed as of 2010 (see chapter 2 and appendix B for details on this measure). The regime score (Polity2) rates regimes on a scale ranging from most autocratic (-10) to most democratic (10) (see appendix A).

The figure shows that, for the most part, less democratic regimes do tend to impose more religious restrictions than more democratic ones. The solid line represents the results of a bivariate regression between the two factors, and its downward slope indicates the direction of the relationship (the correlation of regime score and religious repression (*r*) is −0.6). Points that lie far from the line, in the upper right and lower left quadrants of the figure, do not follow the general pattern of more political competition and less religious repression. For example, Malaysia, Turkey, and Indonesia are rated toward the more democratic end of the regime measure but impose a large number of restrictions on religion. On the other hand, Swaziland, Gambia, and Cameroon are located toward the

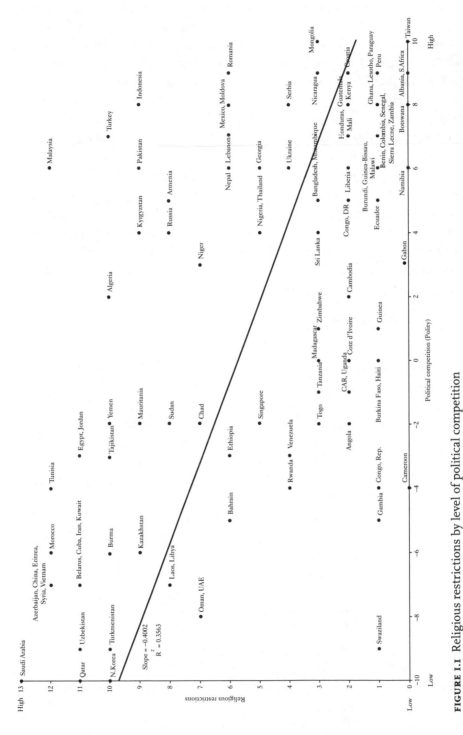

**FIGURE 1.1** Religious restrictions by level of political competition

*Sources*: Political competition is measured with Polity2 regime scores from Marshall and Jaggers (2011). Religious repression scores are the author's calculations.

autocratic end of the regime spectrum, yet they impose few to no restrictions on religion. These examples suggest that differences in levels of authoritarianism (or relative democracy) are not enough to explain how much religious repression we might find in a state. Moreover, focusing solely on the existence of repressive religious regulations does not do much to explain why they are imposed. To uncover the motivations for religious repression, we must focus on its targets. To understand why some groups are targeted with repression, we need to examine the nature of societal divisions.

A religiously divided society may have one or more of a number of characteristics. First, politicians' proreligious or antireligious ideology can lead to conflict between government elites and those in society who do not ascribe to the regime's governing philosophy. Societies governed by antireligious (e.g., communist), aggressively secular (e.g., laicist), or religious (e.g., Islamist) ideologies are likely to experience conflict over the role that religion should play in public life and politics if portions of the population do not subscribe to the ruling ideology. Second, historical religion-state relations can lead to divisions over the status of a preferred church or the legacy of perceived past injustices. Third, demographic factors such as the particular balance of the religious majority and minorities or competition between groups for the same adherents can lead to a divided society ripe for conflict.

A quantitative measure of the nature of religious divisions is difficult to construct because of the complexity of the concept. The closest available measure is the Social Hostilities Index (SHI), compiled by the Pew Research Center's Forum on Religion and Public Life (see appendix A for details). The Pew Forum used multiple sources to measure incidents of tension, harassment, hostility, and violence around religion that were committed by societal (not governmental) actors. The measure therefore captures the level of actual religious conflict in a country between religious groups and does not overlap with the count of state-imposed religious restrictions. It does not take into account divisions between secular and religious ideologies or account for religious demographics in society. However, it can be used to present a rough comparison of the countries in this study with a single readily accessible data source.

Table 1.1 summarizes the differences in regime score and religious repression across the countries according to the level of social hostilities measured by the Pew Research Center, using categories they define (see appendix A). As hypothesized, countries with the lowest levels of

Table 1.1  Average political competition and repression scores by level of
religious divisions in society

| Religious Divisions (SHI, 0–10) | Political Competition (Polity, –10 to +10) | Religious Repression (0–13) |
|---|---|---|
| Low | 1 | 3.1 |
| Moderate | 0 | 6.2 |
| High/very high | 2 | 7.4 |

Compiled from data from the Pew Research Center (2012b) and Marshall and Jaggers (2011).
Religious repression scores were calculated by the author using sources listed in appendix B.

social hostilities have the lowest average levels of religious repression,
and those at the highest levels of hostilities have the highest levels of
repression. Yet the table also shows that the regime score varies only
slightly across different levels of social hostilities. Because these specific
regime scores take into account only institutional measures of authority at the state level, this result is somewhat expected. Yet it also points
to the deficiency of measures that rely only on formal institutions for
capturing the amount of competition and potential conflict in countries.

Despite the fact that quantitative data can provide some preliminary
support for the argument about the role that religious divisions in society play in explaining levels of religious repression, this type of data is
insufficient for capturing the complexity of how religious repression is
practiced around the world. In particular, data on the amount of religious
repression cannot show which groups are being targeted by repressive
policies, knowledge that is vital to understanding the motivations of autocratic politicians who decide to use religious repression as an instrument
of their rule. Case studies in subsequent chapters allow a more expansive
conception of religious divisions in society.

A focus on how many and which groups states choose to repress is
important because it points to a central property of religions: they are
important actors in civil society. Religious groups organize individuals
into associations aimed not only at practicing religious rituals and expe-
riencing the divine but also at educating youths, curing the sick, feeding
the hungry, helping the poor, and—most dangerously for politicians—
changing policies to reflect their beliefs. Because religions perform so
many functions besides the expression of individual conscience, they have
the potential to threaten the political status quo and thus are an important
element of civil society that politicians know they must control.

Exploring the varieties of religious repression in nondemocratic regimes from this perspective puts the focus on how different regime types deal with civil society and can help us to better understand the various types of regime we find on the spectrum between full autocracy and full democracy. By limiting the study to restrictions that constitute prohibitions or severe restrictions against religious groups, we can directly compare states based on how many groups bear the brunt of these harsh restrictions. This focus on the number of groups repressed also helps to reveal their identity. For instance, in a state that restricts all but one religion, it is most often the majority religion of the country (or the religion of the country's leaders) that is spared repression. Identifying which groups are restricted also aids in understanding the motivations for religion policy. Because of the cost of enforcement, politicians are unlikely to seek to regulate religion in the absence of political motivations. Aside from suppressing the potential oppositional capabilities of religious groups, governments may target specific religious groups for repression because they threaten the identity or unity of the society. The mere existence of these groups may question what it means to be a Christian, Russian, Muslim, or Turk, thus contributing to existential anxiety among a country's population and the impetus by its leaders to control how identity is framed and expressed. Although some may argue that nationalist appeals are excuses autocrats use to suppress potentially threatening groups of people, these types of appeals are too prevalent worldwide to dismiss as mere rhetoric.[9]

Figure 1.2 summarizes the argument and shows how political competition and religious divisions in society explain how states should target repression. We expect to find countries with the lowest levels of political competition (i.e., full autocracies) and high religious divisions in society targeting repression at all religious groups. High levels of religious division make these countries more susceptible to group-based conflict. Low levels of political competition make it easier for the state to repress as many groups as possible to avoid that conflict. States will not only target dangerous groups but also maintain strict control over groups friendly to them to avoid the potential for these groups to gain enough power to destabilize the government in power.

At the opposite end of the spectrum, countries with the highest levels of political competition (i.e., full or partial democracies) and societies that are not religiously divided should commit little religious repression. If religion is not a significant societal cleavage, the potential for conflict

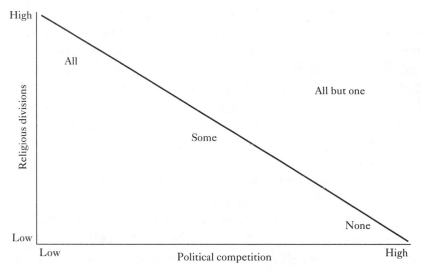

**FIGURE I.2** Hypothesized number of targets of religious repression by levels of political competition and religious divisions in society

along religious lines is also low, and religious groups do not pose a political threat. Furthermore, if higher levels of competition characterize politics in a country, then even those currently in power will find it hard to wield repression as a governing tool without sacrificing legitimacy, influence, and votes.

Countries located in the middle should exhibit more selective state repression of religion, targeting only some groups. The exact number and identity of groups will depend on circumstances specific to each country's religious arena. Yet because political competition is constrained in these countries, state leaders are able to apply laws selectively to certain groups in society without facing the negative consequences we would expect from such behavior by more competitive regimes. For instance, since most of the regimes in this middle part of the spectrum hold elections, politicians must be able to build winning coalitions. At the same time, because these elections are not fully free or fair, it is possible for those in power to selectively apply restrictions to those groups perceived to be the most threatening to the persistence of their rule.

Among those states that focus repression on only some religious groups, that repression may be targeted at all but one group, which I define as a unique category. We should find this situation in countries combining higher levels of political competition with religious divisions that primarily involve ideology and religion-state relations, but not major competition among religious groups. Even though these societies may not have much religious heterogeneity, they do tend to have a history of close religion-state cooperation that has privileged one religious group while excluding all others from state favor. We find this legacy affecting contemporary regimes and contributing to their legitimacy. When these countries hold elections for higher office, politicians need to win allies from the religious sector for political support against competitors. If a society has one clear majority religious group, it easy for the state to ally with that group and target restrictions against others to prevent those smaller groups from mounting opposition against the government in power and its largest supporter. Therefore, while this book is about state-imposed religious repression, religious groups are sometimes complicit in it. Countries with a similar pattern of religious divisions but lower levels of political competition would be more likely to get away with imposing strict state control (which is also repression) on all religious groups—even the majority—as they would not be subject to elections or other expressions of popular support to maintain power.

## *Scope and Plan of the Book*

This study examines all countries in the world with populations over 1 million that had or adopted nondemocratic regimes *at any time* between 1990 and 2010.[10] This includes countries that were fully authoritarian during the period (e.g., Saudi Arabia and China), as well as countries with some democratic elements but little ability for opposition parties to compete seriously for power. It includes the full range of nondemocratic regimes because differences in authority relations can account for some of the differences we see in religion policy. At the same time, it excludes from the analysis countries that were fully democratic during the entire time period, as this study is concerned with political dynamics that differ in important ways from those in fully free and competitive regimes. Although politicians may be able to use religious regulations to restrict competition in democracies as well, their set of regulatory options is limited by constitutional, institutional, and societal checks on government power. However, politicians in nondemocratic regimes have a unique "menu of manipulation," (Schedler 2002) which they can use to support their own hold on power.

I used a number of indicators to select the countries to be included in this study (see appendix A). As is to be expected, there are disagreements among data sources and coding schemes regarding regime classification. These disagreements tend to cluster in the middle ranges of regimes, as has been pointed out previously by Axel Hadenius and Jan Teorell (2005) in their comparative assessment of democratic indices. It can be difficult to find agreement on these ambiguous regimes using indices that measure different aspects of government functions. For instance, while some scholars rely on elections to determine the presence or absence of democracy, others also consider the protection of a variety of rights (including belief, media, and property) or the distribution of power in a regime. I am not concerned with determining which dataset is most appropriate for measuring regime type. Instead, I use a variety of sources to compile a list of countries considered by at least some scholars to have been nondemocratic at any time from 1990 to 2010.

I am particularly interested in those countries for which scholars disagree on regime classification (e.g., Georgia, Indonesia, and Turkey). Including those countries that are classified as electoral democracies by some and electoral authoritarian by others helps to illustrate the importance of looking at rights policies for distinguishing regime types. Examining religion policy in these ambiguous regimes can contribute to understanding their political systems. Moreover, by including the full range of nondemocratic regimes—from monarchies to partial democracies—we can explore how different configurations of power allow leaders to repress or not repress religion, and why or when they choose to do so.

I use the best available sources of empirical data on religious repression, religious divisions in society, and regime type to conduct my analyses. Repression, religion, and regimes are notoriously difficult concepts to quantify, but several scholars have made notable efforts to do so, which I employ in chapter 2 to test the theory outlined here (and illustrated in figure 1.2). Yet quantitative measurements can go only so far in capturing the complexities of the relationship between state power and societal structures that I specify in my theory. The remainder of the study (chapters 3 to 6) uses comparative case studies to examine the historical and structural characteristics of 16 states and societies with a view to understanding how they affect contemporary levels of religious repression and regime type. The cases chosen provide a wide range of spatial and cultural variation to test a general theory about the sources of variation in religious repression. The evidence presented in the case studies relies largely on primary documentation and secondary sources but is supplemented with interviews I conducted in 2005 in the Republic of Georgia and in 2008 and 2009 in Turkey.

This book aims to explain why politicians in nondemocratic states use religious repression as an instrument of their rule and also why they do not. To answer this question, we must first understand what constitutes religious repression and the many varieties it can take. It is to this endeavor that we turn in the next chapter.

## 2

## *Varieties of Religious Repression*

THIS BOOK EXPLAINS the variation in the level, types, and targets of religious repression across nondemocratic countries between 1990 and 2010. In the previous chapter, I argued and demonstrated—using quantitative data—that less politically competitive states do not necessarily repress religion more. In fact, the data reveal that religious repression occurs at high levels across the range of nondemocratic regime types. I presented an explanation for the variation in religious repression that depends on the interaction of the level of political competition in a state with the structure of religious divisions in society. Furthermore, I introduced the idea that to understand how religious repression varies, we must not only examine the degree of repression but also the number and character of groups that are targeted with it. This perspective incorporates the character of civil society into theoretical discussions of the role that political competition plays in determining and distinguishing regimes from each other.

The current chapter turns the focus to the types and targets of religious repression across nondemocratic regimes. First, the chapter presents a definition of religious repression and elaborates on the various ways in which it can be imposed on religious individuals and groups. Presenting examples of repression as it has been recently applied around the world, this discussion highlights the importance of understanding why certain types of restrictions are adopted and which groups they are intended to suppress. Second, the chapter presents empirical evidence for the theoretical propositions posed in the previous chapter and explains how the countries in the present study array themselves in terms of the number of religious groups targeted with repression. It concludes with a discussion of how a focus on the number of groups targeted with state repression helps to inform and advance the study of nondemocratic regimes.

## *What Is Repression?*

All governments regulate religion to some extent. Religious *regulation* can be defined broadly to include all laws and rules that are enacted to govern religious affairs in a state, those that both support and oppose religion. This book focuses on regulations intended to *repress* religion and therefore on policies that *restrict* it. Such regulations include requiring religious groups to register with the state to legally practice their religion, restrictions on property ownership by religious groups, and restrictions against religious group participation in politics. All of these types of regulation—along with others outlined later—constitute attempts by the state to restrict and therefore repress religion.

Regulations can also support or favor some or all religions with such policies as government funding for religious buildings and activities, government subsidies for clerical salaries, and government support for religious education. It is possible for such policies to constitute religious repression, for support that is targeted at particular groups to the exclusion of others often results in discrimination or restrictions against those who do not benefit from the government support (Stark and Finke 2000). For example, when government funds construction of religious buildings for only one group, those not eligible for funding may face greater difficulty growing their ranks if they are not able to construct enough buildings to minister to their adherents. Yet favoring a particular religious group may also be intended to restrict the group itself. For instance, the government may pay the clerical salaries of a particular religious group but also retain authority over the group's clerical appointments. Funding religious personnel may constitute a great benefit to a religious group, yet surrendering authority over its own appointment process constitutes a restriction of it. Although government favoritism of religion is often correlated with restriction, it is not necessarily so (Grim and Finke 2011, 206–210). Disentangling these relationships requires close study of particular cases.

Although the number of individual types of regulation of religion is large, I group them into categories capturing a range of restrictions that function to repress the public expression of religion by individuals and groups (appendix B). These categories incorporate restrictions that violate the 1948 United Nations Universal Declaration of Human Rights, as well as the International Covenant on Civil and Political Rights (ICCPR).[1] This treaty entered into force in 1976 and has 74 signatories and 168 parties, making it an important source articulating international standards for human rights protection. In addition to violations of these rights, direct restrictions on the political activities of religious individuals and groups are also considered. Studies have demonstrated that in many societies, religious participation encourages political participation, which many nondemocratic leaders may fear (McKenzie 2004; Verba, Scholzman, and Brady 1995). By limiting what religious leaders and organizations are able to say and do in the public sphere, restrictions target political contestation. Restrictions on organizing into political parties and civic organizations are the most apparent efforts at constraining the potential political power of religious groups. What these restrictions all have in common are efforts to prevent the formation of groups in society that may challenge the hegemony of those holding power or those groups that prop them up. This chapter outlines the range of restrictions states can impose on religion and discusses patterns across the 101 countries included in this study. Later chapters present more detailed studies of a number of countries, tracing the motivations and political outcomes that result from particular types of restrictions on religious groups.

## *Repression of Religious Expression and Association*

One of the most obvious ways to repress religion is to prevent individuals from exercising their faith through religious services. Although most states do not have the means or ability to prevent individuals from praying in private, there are a number of ways states can restrict *individual or group observance of religious services, festivals, or holidays in public or private.* This first set of restrictions refers specifically to worship during religious services such as Christian mass or Islamic daily prayer. They can include services that are performed by groups in private residences, as often occurs for small groups or those that do not have access to religious buildings (see later). For instance, in Saudi Arabia, non-Muslims are allowed to practice their religion only in private, and the law requires that all citizens be Muslims.[2] In Iran, non-Muslims are not allowed to engage in public acts of religious expression among Muslims, and Christians report that the government places security cameras outside churches to confirm that no Muslims attend religious services. Government surveillance of minority group religious services has also been reported in Belarus, Jordan, and Uzbekistan, among other countries.

Restricting individual or group observance of religious festivals and holidays is another way the state can prevent individuals from practicing their faith. These restrictions can include requiring or denying permits for celebrations held outside religious edifices or denying individuals the right to uphold the Sabbath. For instance, in Kuwait, the government does not allow Shia Muslims to perform public reenactments of the martyrdom of Hussein or to conduct public marches commemorating Ashura, an important holiday. In Burma, the government frequently has denied requests from Christian and Muslim groups to gather to celebrate holidays and restricted the number of people who could gather, targeting Muslims specifically for such restrictions. In Armenia, Seventh-Day Adventists have reported that employers and schools frequently denied members the ability to observe the Sabbath on Saturday.[3]

Governments may also restrict specific groups of people from participating in religious services. For instance, in the Kyrgyz Republic, minors are not allowed to participate in religious organizations or wear religious clothing in public schools. In Tajikistan, women have been barred from praying in mosques since 2004, and in some areas, children are also prohibited from attending mosques.

Like demonstrations or rallies, individual or group observance of religious services, holidays, or festivals can be a means for religious groups to publicly display the amount of support they have in society. Politicians may be compelled to restrict these activities if they fear such groups threaten their legitimacy or their ability to rule. In addition, by imposing limits on the location or number of participants in celebrations, governments can maintain control over religious groups and ensure that threatening groups are not able to amass in large numbers. Yet limitations on celebrations of a religious nature differ from those placed on secular demonstrations because they deny religion a fundamental source of its expression. By taking away the ability to gather together to celebrate religious events, restrictions target the group nature of religious practice and thus identify it as a potential locus for other sorts of activities.

Another way that states can prevent individuals from practicing their faith is by placing *restrictions on places of worship*. In some countries, groups face restrictions in trying to construct new buildings. Since 2006 in Indonesia, several requirements must be met before religious groups can build houses of worship. First, the group must obtain signatures of 90 of its own members. Next, the group must obtain signatures of 60 members of other religious groups in the community stating they support construction. Finally, the group must get approval from the local religious affairs office.

Other countries make religious observance difficult for minority groups by restricting where they are allowed to practice legally. In Belarus, it is illegal to hold religious services in private homes, yet regulations make it difficult to convert residential property to religious use through legal means. Similarly, in Laos, worshiping in homes is illegal, yet Christian groups face difficulty in obtaining permits to build new churches. Other countries impose restrictions on the number of religious buildings that can exist in certain areas. For instance, in Libya before the overthrow of Muammar Gaddafi in 2011, Christian denominations were allowed only one place of worship per city. In Tajikistan, the religion law limits the number of mosques that may be registered within a given population area. In Sri Lanka, informal rules allow local authorities to prevent Christian groups from building churches. These rules include requiring approval from a majority of a town's residents for construction, which was difficult to obtain in many majority Buddhist areas.

Several countries restrict the use of religious buildings for anything other than religious services. In Algeria, mosques cannot be used as meeting places outside of regular prayer hours. In Azerbaijan and Mauritania, religious facilities cannot be used for political purposes. In Bahrain, places of worship cannot be used for political campaigning. In Yemen, the government reportedly attempted to stop the growth of the popularity of the minority Houthi group by limiting the hours that mosques were open to the public.

In several postcommunist countries, restitution of property seized by the previous regime remains a problem. In Georgia, all groups other than the majority Georgian Orthodox Church have complained of difficulties in regaining property and in obtaining permits to construct new religious facilities. In Romania, several minority religious groups have unresolved restitution claims, as is the case in Russia, Serbia, and Ukraine as well.

Restricting places of worship is motivated by similar reasons as restricting religious practice. Because religious facilities can be used as meeting places for potential opposition groups, authoritarian politicians have an interest in limiting access to them. Limiting where religious groups can meet can limit their growth, making it an important tool politicians can use if they want to suppress a group. The type of restrictions imposed can allow specific groups to be targeted. Restrictions on new buildings target the growth of small, often foreign, religious minorities. Restrictions on the hours that religious buildings can be used target politicized religious groups—as is often found in countries that have Islamist movements.

Delaying the return of property seized by a previous regime to groups helps the government favor particular denominations and assert its authority over the religious sector. These and other methods of regulating places of worship can be very effective ways of restricting religious groups from meeting to promote opposition to the government or its policies.

Another way that governments can intervene in the practice of faith is by *restricting people's ability to observe the laws of their own religion or forcing individuals to observe the laws of another religious group*. Many states allow religious groups to have some authority to perform marriage rites or manage other matters related to personal law; others require that the state be in charge of these things exclusively. Recent debates over Islamic headscarves in both the West and the Middle East involve the ability of individuals to follow the dictates of their religion in public settings. For instance, wearing the headscarf in public settings such as government offices and universities has been a long-standing issue in Turkey, with only recent changes to laws and accepted practices relaxing the restriction.[4]

Another issue related to restricting observance of religious laws is adoption of alternative service laws in countries that require military service. For some religious groups, military service goes against their religious beliefs. Thus, providing civilian alternatives to military service that do not impose longer terms or discriminatory conditions is considered necessary to protect their religious freedom. This has been an important issue for Jehovah's Witnesses in postcommunist countries. In Armenia, several Jehovah's Witnesses remain imprisoned for their objection to military service.[5] In Turkmenistan, the government does not offer alternative military service for conscientious objectors, and they are subject to up to two years of imprisonment for refusing service.[6] Although international organizations such as the Organization for Security and Cooperation in Europe (OSCE) have been trying to convince these states to adopt forms of civilian service that allow individuals to fulfill their obligations of citizenship without violating their own religious beliefs, many states have been slow to adopt and enforce more lenient regulations.[7]

Allowing religious laws to be part of the laws of a country, either alone or alongside secular/civil law, is a controversial issue. On the one hand, opponents argue that having different legal systems in one country violates constitutional clauses guaranteeing citizens' equality. On the other hand, religious freedom proponents argue for allowing parallel religious legal systems on the grounds of protecting free exercise. The debate is especially strong in Muslim-majority countries. Senegal's fight over revising its family code is one example of this controversy (see chapter 6). Other examples include apostasy laws that make converting away from a particular religion illegal and laws that enforce or prohibit certain types of religious clothing.

The ability to choose one's religion (or to reject having a religion) is one of the central aspects of the concept of religious freedom. *Restricting, forcing, or otherwise coercing conversion* is an uncommon but effective tool that states can use to enforce citizen compliance to a particular religion or to prevent a favored group from losing adherents or being subjected to competition from other groups. Few states engage in forced coercion of individuals to other religions, but some do restrict the ability of individuals to convert. The latter is especially true in states that incorporate Islamic (Sharia) law into their legal codes. For example, in Egypt (prior to the ouster of Hosni Mubarak in 2011), the government did not recognize conversion of Muslims to other religions, which was enforced by not allowing such conversions to be recorded on identity documents that contained one's religious affiliation. In the United Arab Emirates and Yemen, Muslims are not allowed to change their religion. In Iran, Muslim citizens are not allowed to change or renounce their faith, and apostasy can be punished by death.

Some states do not practice forced coercion but make it clear that advancement in politics is closely tied to religious affiliation. For instance, in Burma, the government has moved away from a campaign of forced conversion to Buddhism. However, there is some evidence that other means have been used to entice individuals to convert, including the opportunity to advance in the ranks of the military.

Proselytizing is the act of attempting to induce others to change their religion. If the rights to express and to change one's religion are protected under the concept of religious freedom, then proselytism qualifies as a protected right. Moreover, some religions include doctrine that mandates the attempt to convert nonbelievers, if it is believed that the religion is the one true path to salvation for all individuals. In practice, however, there can be arguments for *restricting proselytizing* in a society: protection of the dominant religious tradition or political ideology, preservation of public order, and regulation of the religious marketplace to ensure fairness and encourage informed religious choices (Stahnke 1999).

There is an important distinction between prohibiting all proselytizing and prohibiting only certain groups from proselytizing. In Armenia, proselytizing is referred to as "soul hunting" and prohibited by law, and it applies to all groups, including the majority and established Armenian Apostolic Church (which is not traditionally a proselytizing faith). Conversely, in many Muslim-majority countries, proselytizing to Muslims is illegal, while Muslims proselytizing to members of other religions is not. For example, in Malaysia, Mauritania, Somalia, Tunisia, the United Arab Emirates (UAE), and Yemen, non-Muslims are prohibited from proselytizing Muslims. In Qatar, the practice is illegal and carries prison sentences of 5 to 10 years. In other countries, laws do not specifically forbid proselytizing, but practices by local officials act as de facto restrictions. For example, in Egypt as of 2010, there was no legal ban on proselytizing Muslims, but in practice it was restricted through police harassment and detention of suspected proselytizers, as well as expulsion of foreigners suspected of engaging in the practice.

Governments can also repress religious groups by *restricting the formation of religious communities through discriminatory registration or monitoring requirements, including surveillance of or bans on groups.* Registration requirements, one of the most commonly used restrictions against religious groups, can be found across the globe. They vary according to the number of groups they target and the types of restrictions they impose. Having the status of a legal entity can provide religious groups with a number of advantages—including protection under the law, the ability to purchase property, and the right to form affiliated organizations—but registration requirements hinder groups when they are applied differentially or are onerous (Langlaude 2010). Moreover, if registration is required for groups to congregate and penalties are involved in operating as an unregistered religious group, this is repression. Aside from registration requirements, some countries impose outright bans on particular religious groups. Often these are justified on the basis of the alleged threat the group poses to society. However, it is not difficult in many cases to identify the political threat that these groups pose to states and their leaders.

Some states impose threshold requirements for groups to register, making it difficult for smaller or new groups to operate legally. For instance, in Angola, the 2004 Law on Religion requires any group to have more than 100,000 members and be present in 12 of the 18 provinces to gain legal status. No new organizations have been registered since the law was implemented. Most notably, the government does not recognize any Islamic organization, which gives the government the authority to close mosques, schools, and community centers. In other states, threshold requirements categorize groups into tiers of recognition, with accompanying benefits and restrictions applying to each tier. In Belarus, there are three tiers of official recognition for religious groups. Romania and Russia also have tiered registration systems, with higher tiers enjoying more rights and privileges. In Croatia since 2003, groups are required to have 500 members and to have been registered as an association for at least five years to be able to register as a religious community.

Sometimes states pass laws requiring reregistration when more lenient previous laws were seen as granting legal status to too many undesirable groups. In Belarus, a law passed in 2002 required all groups to reregister (with difficult requirements) by 2004 and bans all activities by unregistered groups, with penalties including heavy fines and imprisonment. In Azerbaijan, reregistration was compelled in January 2010, imposing additional requirements that resulted in many groups being denied registration. In Ethiopia, all groups except the Ethiopian Orthodox Church and the Ethiopian Islamic Affairs Supreme Council are required to register with the Ministry of Justice and renew their registrations every three years.

The structure of registration laws can make it difficult for smaller groups to register. For example, in Bosnia, evangelical groups have difficulty registering because officials tried to fit them into the categories outlined for the four main religious communities already defined by law. In Eritrea, a 2002 government decree forbids all religious practice outside of four officially recognized religions. Religious facilities of unregistered groups were forcibly closed.

Some countries impose outright bans on specific religious denominations and penalties for belonging to banned groups. In China, groups including Guan Yin and Falun Gong are banned by law, and individual members have been imprisoned and subjected to "Reeducation through Labor." Several Islamic countries, including Iran and Jordan, ban or deny recognition to the Baha'i religion. Other minority Islamic (or related) sects banned or restricted in Muslim-majority countries include the Ahmadiya (Indonesia, Pakistan), some Sufi orders (Libya, Turkey), and Salafist organizations (Syria, Tajikistan).

Imposing discriminatory registration requirements is a less obvious way of restricting religious groups than banning or otherwise making them illegal. Yet because such requirements have the veneer of following the rule of law, they can be manipulated to target specific groups that states find undesirable without having to justify outlawing any particular group.

Aside from restricting individuals or groups from practicing their religion in public, states can also attempt to assert control over the internal operation of religious organizations, thus taking away the independence of religious groups. One way to control religious organizations is by *restricting or controlling clerical appointments.* By maintaining state control over who is authorized to lead a religious group and represent it officially to laypeople, states can pick sympathetic leaders and censor critical ones.

Many of the instances of state restriction or control over clerical appointments occur in majority-Muslim states, where one or more state-affiliated agencies are put in charge of a number of religious matters, including hiring, approving, and training clergy. For instance, in Algeria, imams are hired and trained by the state. In Egypt, the government appoints the imams who lead prayers in mosques and pays their salaries. In Jordan, the Ministry of Religious Affairs and Awqaf appoints imams and manages clerical training. In Kazakhstan, the Spiritual Association of Muslims administers examinations and background checks for imams. Imams who are not affiliated with the official organization are pressured to join. In Tunisia, the 1988 Law on Mosques allows only government-appointed personnel to lead activities in mosques. In a more blatant use of state power to control religiously associated dissent, in Yemen in 2010, the government reassigned imams it thought were radical and monitored mosque sermons. In the north of the country, the government replaced Zaydi imams (a Shia sect suspected of sympathizing with rebel groups) with Sunni ones.

*Restricting religious speech* can be seen as a restriction of religious practice or of the political role of religion, depending on the type of restriction that is imposed and the kinds of speech that are restricted. For instance, states may prohibit all or some religious groups from purchasing broadcasting licenses. States may also prohibit printing and distributing religious materials or any materials produced by religious groups. The content does not have to be expressly political for the laws to target preventing future political organization. Regulation of religious speech can include censorship of speech that is deemed to be antireligious, antiregime, or otherwise offensive. While laws banning speech or publications deemed antireligious or blasphemous can be seen as government support for religion, they can also be used as a means of repressing minority religions or groups that are hostile to a state-supported or state-affiliated religion.

States may repress religious publications by restricting printing or distribution of religious materials. For example, in Laos, the government does not allow Bibles to be printed and requires groups to get special permission to have them imported. In Malaysia, the distribution of Malay-language Bibles is restricted, and those that are distributed must have the words "Not for Muslims" on the cover. In Mauritania, it is illegal to print and distribute non-Islamic religious materials, although possession is legal. In Tunisia, Christians were generally not given government permission to print religious materials in Arabic, but they could circulate materials printed in other languages. In the UAE, the government prohibits the distribution of non-Islamic literature.

Other states ban publications by minority groups or submit them to government censorship. Kazakhstan bans publications by the Jehovah's Witnesses. In Singapore under the Undesirable Publications Act, the government bans publications by several groups, including the Jehovah's Witnesses and the Unification Church. In Iran, religious minorities were required to submit their annual calendar to state censors before printing and distributing them (Sanasarian 2000). In Tajikistan, religious organizations must submit literature to the ministry of culture for approval one month prior to delivery. In Russia, the 2002 Law on Countering Extremist Activity has allowed the government to ban publications by religious groups such as the Jehovah's Witnesses, Scientology, Falun Gong, and followers of Muslim preacher Said Nursi.

An increasingly common occurrence in majority-Muslim countries is government control over the content of sermons. In Algeria, the government has the right to prescreen and approve Friday sermons. More often, however, it provides preapproved sermon topics to clergy prior to Friday prayers. In Bahrain, the government censors sermons. In Egypt, the government monitored the sermons of its own appointed clergy. In Tajikistan, the Council of Ulemo drafts and approves topics for Friday sermons. In Uzbekistan, the muftiate (which is controlled by the government) controls the content of sermons and the substance of published Islamic materials.

Some states repress religion by *restricting or banning private religious education*. Debates continue in democratic societies about the appropriateness of state funding for religious education. They have been resolved in various ways, spanning from no state funds for religious schools and no teaching of religion in public schools to equal state funding for religious and secular schools and religious instruction within public schools. While the question is debatable, allowing non-state-funded, private religious education enables religious groups to educate their children outside state educational structures according to their own customs and beliefs (although most states require these schools to meet certain standards). Restricting private religious education is rare; when practiced, it occurs in states with antireligious ideologies or a deep suspicion of the potential political power of religion.

Banning religious instruction in schools may be a result of a policy of official state secularism. For example, in Ethiopia, the government does not allow religious instruction in any school, whether public or private. It claims this is a part of the constitutional provision that requires separation of religion and state. Restricting religious education can also result from state hostility toward religion. In Uzbekistan, the private teaching of religion is prohibited, and religious subjects are also banned in public schools. In Vietnam, religious groups are not permitted to operate schools beyond preschool and kindergarten.

## Repression of the Political Expression of Religion

One of the most obvious means of repressing religious involvement in politics is by *restricting or banning religious political parties*. In many countries, bans on such parties are included among bans on other types of identity-based parties. For example, the elections law in Kazakhstan prohibits political parties based on ethnicity, gender, or religious affiliation. Similarly, the constitution of Togo prohibits the establishment of political parties based on religion, ethnic group, or region. In other countries, religious parties are specifically identified as illegal. For example, in Ethiopia, Tunisia, Turkey, Uganda, and Uzbekistan, the law prohibits the creation of political parties based on religion or formed by religious groups. Bans against religious parties are often justified on the basis of either preserving the secular character of a state or avoiding potential hostilities between groups in multireligious states. This book does not consider bans of parties that promote extremism or violence to constitute religious repression.

In some countries, laws against religious political parties are aimed at specific organizations. Before the overthrow of Hosni Mubarak, Egyptian law prohibited political parties or conducting political activities on a religious basis, a law intended to target the Muslim Brotherhood specifically, which was outlawed in 1954. As of the end of 2010, several thousand people remained imprisoned because of alleged support for or membership in Islamist groups seeking to overthrow the government.

The constitution of the Kyrgyz Republic prohibits religious parties or the pursuit of political goals by religious organizations. The Supreme Court has banned several groups, including Hizb ut-Tahrir, the Islamic Party of Turkestan, the Organization for Freedom of Eastern Turkestan, and the Eastern Turkestan Islamic Party, claiming they have extremist agendas.

Restriction of religious political parties is not a purely authoritarian tactic. Sylvie Langlaude (2010) notes that OSCE states are given wide latitude in deciding whether religious political parties are legal. However, Portugal is the only Western democracy that does not allow religious parties. Langlaude indicates that there is little international case law on the issue, and the leading case on the matter remains *Refah Partisi (the Welfare Party) and Others v. Turkey*, where the European Court of Human Rights upheld the Turkish Supreme Court's dissolution of the Welfare Party for being against the country's secular principles, outlined in its constitution. Thus, whether religious groups have the right to form political parties remains questionable within international law as well. Nevertheless, many examples point to the usefulness of bans on religious political parties to nondemocratic regimes hoping to restrict opposition they face from organized religious movements. Such parties can threaten the secular basis on which some of these regimes originally established the legitimacy of their rule, or they can galvanize popular opposition to repressive leaders.

In addition to political parties, states can also *restrict nongovernmental associations that are affiliated with religious groups*, including trade unions, professional associations, and a variety of voluntary groups that fall outside of official state institutions. By preventing religious groups from forming such associations or by allowing only officially sanctioned groups to operate, governments are able to control sites of potential political organization and opposition. Although many such associations have no explicit political purpose or goals, self-interested politicians know the potential danger of allowing like-minded individuals to gather and share views. By tightly controlling the associational sector, governments can quell upstart groups.

Some states restrict religious groups from forming organizations related to political or social issues generally or subject them to close state monitoring. For example, in China, faith-based charities are required to register with the government and be sponsored by a local religious affairs bureau. Often, the charities are also required to affiliate with one of the country's "patriotic religious associations." In Libya under the regime of

Muammar Gaddafi, independent associations were prohibited, and only groups that were in line with the regime's policies were allowed to exist. In Morocco, government authorities suppress the activities of political groups that are religiously oriented. In Tanzania, religious organizations are banned from involvement in politics. In Turkey, groups have the opportunity to register as an association or foundation but not on religious grounds.

In other states, the government bans organizations or associations it considers to be extremist, often under specific antiextremism legislation. This can be considered repressive when banned groups do not actually promote or engage in extremist activity. For example, in Uzbekistan, religious groups are prohibited from forming social movements, and the government bans a variety of Islamic organizations. The Ugandan government monitors the activities of nongovernmental organizations (NGOs) it considers to be cults.

Other restrictions focus on religious individuals, often clergy or other religious officials, but sometimes lay members of religious organizations as well. States may *restrict the political activities and/or speech of religious leaders or individuals*, either through formal laws or informal harassment. Often these restrictions target members of the majority religion. For example, in Burma, members of the Buddhist community (sangha) were not allowed to preach sermons pertaining to politics, and words, phrases, or stories reflecting political views in religious lectures were banned. Members of the sangha were barred from running for public office and instructed by the regime to distance themselves from politics. In Zimbabwe, government officials reportedly harassed religious leaders who were critical of government policies and who organized public rallies that centered on political and social issues.

States can also restrict what clergy can say in the media or the content of religious media, such as newspapers or radio stations. For instance, in Eritrea, religious media do not have the right to comment on political matters. In Iran, the Special Clerical Courts, an institution not specified in the constitution but set up to investigate offenses committed by clerics, are used to prosecute clerics for expressing political ideas that are controversial and for participating in nonreligious activities.

Moreover, states can repress religion by *restricting access to political office based on religious identity or position*. Some states prohibit religious officials from running for or holding state office. This is different from states that impose reserved government positions for unelected religious officials, a situation considered undemocratic by many scholars (Dahl 1971; Stepan 2001). For example, in Azerbaijan, religious leaders are not allowed to serve in public office while they hold religious positions. In Honduras, the constitution states that only laypersons may be elected to congress.

Other states restrict political office to members of certain religious groups, often excluding religious minorities from formal participation in government. For instance, in Algeria, non-Muslims are prohibited from running for the presidency. In Burma, Muslim Rohingyas were unable to attain positions in the civil service, and Muslims and Christians found it difficult to be promoted to upper ranks in the military without converting to Buddhism. In China, it is not illegal for religious believers to hold public office, but the Chinese Communist Party has stated that members who belong to religious organizations are subject to expulsion from the party.

## Targeted Repression

As I argued in chapter 1, politicians in nondemocratic countries must weigh the benefits of repression against its costs. Repression is likely to be most beneficial to leaders when it restricts actual and potential opponents to their rule. So, politicians target repression at the most politically threatening groups, while withholding or failing to impose restrictive policies on groups that help to support the political status quo. Thus, political competition in nondemocratic regimes varies not only at the level of formal state institutions (such as elections for executive or legislative office) but also at the level of civil society. We can better understand how competitive civil society is by examining what portion of it is targeted with state repression.

I analyzed each of the 101 countries in this study to determine the number of groups that were targeted with state-imposed religious regulations. Because religious demographics are often discussed in terms of majority and minority populations, I first compiled a tally of the number of restrictions against each type of religious groups (see appendix B). However, because majority and minority religions can be difficult to identify in some areas, I ultimately assigned each country to a category of religious restrictions based on a more general classification of the number of groups targeted with the harshest repression: all, all but one, some, and none (table 2.1). States that repress *all* religious groups

**Table 2.1 Number of groups targeted with religious repression (2010)**

| All | All but One | Some | None |
|---|---|---|---|
| Algeria | Armenia | Angola | *Albania* |
| *Azerbaijan* | Bangladesh | *Bahrain* | Benin |
| Burma | Belarus | Bosnia-Herzegovina | Botswana |
| *China* | *Georgia* | Chad | Burkina Faso |
| Cuba | *Indonesia* | Congo, Dem. Rep. | Burundi |
| Egypt | Laos | Croatia | *Cambodia* |
| Eritrea | Malaysia | Ethiopia | Cameroon |
| *Iran* | Moldova | *Kyrgyzstan* | Central African Rep. |
| Jordan | Pakistan | Lebanon | Colombia |
| Kazakhstan | Romania | Madagascar | Congo, Rep. |
| Kuwait | *Russia* | Mexico | Côte d'Ivoire |
| Libya | Serbia | Nepal | Ecuador |
| Mauritania | Sri Lanka | Niger | Gabon |
| Morocco | *Turkey* | *Nigeria* | Gambia |
| North Korea | | Rwanda | Ghana |
| Oman | | *Singapore* | Guatemala |
| Qatar | | Thailand | Guinea |
| *Saudi Arabia* | | Uganda | Guinea-Bissau |
| Sudan | | Ukraine | Haiti |
| Syria | | Venezuela | Honduras |
| Tajikistan | | Zimbabwe | Kenya |
| Tunisia | | | Lesotho |
| Turkmenistan | | | Liberia |
| United Arab Emirates | | | Malawi |
| Uzbekistan | | | Mali |
| Vietnam | | | Mongolia |
| Yemen | | | Mozambique |
| | | | Namibia |
| | | | Nicaragua |
| | | | Paraguay |
| | | | *Peru* |
| | | | *Senegal* |
| | | | Sierra Leone |
| | | | South Africa |
| | | | Swaziland |
| | | | Taiwan |

*(continued)*

Table 2.1 (continued)

| All | All but One | Some | None |
|---|---|---|---|
| | | | Tanzania |
| | | | Togo |
| | | | Zambia |

Countries in italics are analyzed as case studies in chapters 3 through 6.

target restrictions against both the majority religion and smaller minority groups. Restrictions against the majority religion often involve control over religious institutions and appointments with the aim of removing religion's independent influence on society. Restrictions against religious minorities are aimed at eliminating the groups from the country. States that repress *all but one* religious group also have high levels of restrictions against minority religions but allow the majority religion(s) to practice largely unhindered. In these countries, politicians recognize that favoring the largest religious groups in society can result in their political support, an important source of legitimacy. States that repress *some* religious groups are selective in the groups they target with restrictions, focusing only on those that pose the most political threat. These are not always the numerically largest groups, however, as their threat potential can lie in their ideological opposition to leading politicians. Some states choose to repress *no* religious groups. Although government regulation of religion still exists in these countries, it is not targeted at particular groups with the aim of neutralizing their oppositional potential.

Even though these classifications take into account significant state repression of religious groups, there is still variation within the categories. For instance, while both Oman and Saudi Arabia are classified as repressing all religions, the degree of repression differs in the two countries. Oman's government is relatively tolerant of most forms of religious practice, allowing both Muslims and non-Muslims to practice their religion in state-sanctioned locations. However, like Saudi Arabia, the Omani government retains control over most mosques and regulates the content of sermons. Unlike Saudi Arabia, Oman does not use its governmental authority to enforce a single variant of Islamic practice. Nevertheless, because both states retain control over majority religious practices and restrict minorities, they are both classified as repressing all religions. These variations exist to some degree in each category of repression, although each category focuses on documenting significant repression of a certain number of religious groups.

Dividing countries according to the number of groups targeted rather than the level of repression paints a clearer picture of how political competition and religious divisions in society determine the variation in repression we find across nondemocratic countries. Figure 2.1 demonstrates this relationship in graphic form. The horizontal axis measures political competitiveness using data from Polity, and the vertical axis is a rough measure of the level of religious divisions in society using data from the Pew Research Center.[8]

As is illustrated in figure 2.1, most of the countries that repress all religious groups have the lowest levels of political competition. Some, such as Saudi Arabia, Qatar, Burma, and China, do not hold popular elections for the highest executive office. Others, such as Azerbaijan and Uzbekistan, do hold elections, but the field of candidates is so restricted that they are farcical. The condition of low political competition gives politicians more power to impose repressive measures against all sorts of groups without fear of retribution at the polls. Among those countries with slightly higher levels of competition—such as Egypt and Yemen—greater religious divisions exist, in terms of both demographics and struggles between secular leaders and religiously based political movements that seek to change the nature of politics. Thus, we find repression targeted at all religious groups, as they are perceived as potentially organizing to challenge the legitimacy of the state and its regime.

States that repress some religious groups are located on either side of the diagonal line on figure 2.1, possessing moderate levels of both political competition and social divisions based on religion. Because most of these states hold elections (though they are not fully free or fair), political leaders cannot afford to alienate all religious groups by imposing harsh restrictions on them for fear of retribution at the polls or political instability. For example, Nigeria has a society characterized by relatively high religious divisions. This results from competition in the religious marketplace between Christians and Muslims and among different sects and denominations within these major religious traditions. Because Nigeria holds multiparty elections and has a highly religious population, political leaders cannot impose harsh restrictions on all religious groups. However, in regions where Christians or Muslims are in the majority, state officials can impose repressive policies on the minority group without fearing retribution or substantial opposition to those policies from the majority. In

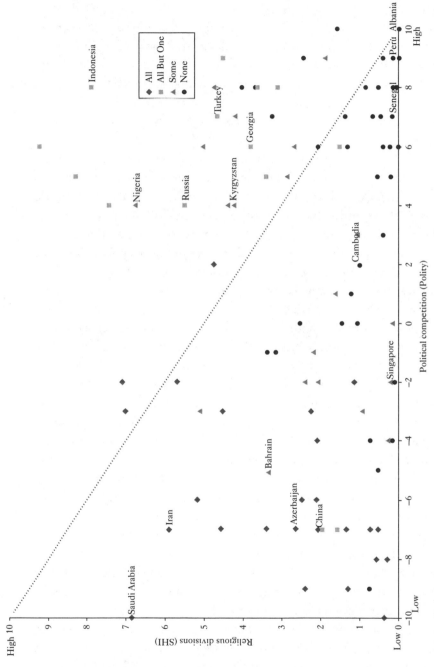

**FIGURE 2.1** Country levels of political competition and religious divisions according to the number of religious groups targeted with repression

*Sources:* Political competition is measured with Polity2 regime scores from Marshall and Jaggers (2011). Religious divisions are measured with the Social Hostilities Index (SHI) from the Pew Research Center (2012b).

fact, such repression may garner additional support from the majority. Thus, states that repress only some religious groups are selective in which groups they target, focusing on those that do not enjoy the sympathies of larger groups or possess the means to launch significant opposition to political leaders.

The states that repress no religious groups tend to have the highest levels of political competition and low levels of religious divisions in society. For instance, Taiwan, which underwent democratic transition in the mid-1990s, has since ranked high on indicators of democracy. Taiwan is religiously homogeneous, and divisions over the political role of religion have not been significant in the country's development. Therefore, few religiously based competitors pose any potential risk to the country's leaders. Even if such opponents did exist, because Taiwan has developed highly competitive formal political institutions in the past two decades, politicians would find it difficult to impose selective repressive policies against their competitors without checks on their power from other branches of government or negative consequences in the electoral arena.

Several countries with less competitive politics do not repress any religious groups. Located toward the bottom left corner of figure 2.1, countries such as Gambia, Cameroon, and the Republic of Congo have less competitive political systems, holding elections that are not fully free or fair and restricting access to executive power. Such a situation makes it possible for ruling politicians to target state policies against political opponents. However, because of low levels of religious divisions in these societies, religious repression is not a beneficial strategy for these political actors to pursue, as it does not strengthen their political position.

A final set of countries targets repression at all but one religious group. They could be considered a subset of countries that repress only some groups but merit separate treatment due to the particular nature of religious divisions in their societies—characteristics the available quantitative measures cannot capture. In these states, including Russia, Georgia, Turkey, and Indonesia, some degree of political competition exists. In fact, states such as Turkey and Indonesia have had relatively free and fair elections in recent years and allowed a larger field of candidates to contest them. Most of these states also have one religion that is a majority of the population and has been closely associated with its national identity. However, all of these states have a legacy of secular or antireligious ideology that continues to be contested within the political arena. Most have had some recent history with communism or a state ideology closely tied to a strict form of secularism that excluded religious influence from politics. Yet because of recent political openings, religious groups have been able to assert greater political influence. Because these religious groups are in the majority, politicians perceive political benefits in showing favoritism to them (and restricting their opponents). The presence of political competition prevents them from controlling the majority religion in the manner of states repressing all religions. They thus make up an intermediate category of repression between states that repress all religions and those that repress some.

Some states on figure 2.1 appear to contradict the patterns I have outlined. This is an artifact of the nature of the quantitative measure used to capture religious divisions in society. The measurement I used counts instances of societal conflict on religious grounds, one component of the definition of a religiously divided society adopted in the present study. However, quantifying other components of the definition, including the guiding ideology of a regime and historical religion-state relations, is more difficult. The absence of these components in the quantitative measure leads to points on the plot that do not cluster with countries in the same category of restrictions. Close examination of these cases reveals why they should be categorized as they are. For example, both Belarus and Laos are classified as repressing all but one religious group, even though they resemble countries that repress all religions in terms of their levels of political competition and religious conflict. Yet examination of how repressive policies are applied in each country reveals that one religious group—the Orthodox Church in Belarus and Buddhists in Laos—is exempted from restrictions on religion and all others are subjected to them in a manner aimed at repressing them. The purpose of the case studies in subsequent chapters is to further explore such cases where the available quantitative data are not as accurate in capturing the actual level of religious divisions in society.

## Case Selection

In the next several chapters, I present studies of a number of states to illustrate how the interaction of political competition and the nature of religious divisions in society results in repression against different numbers of religious groups. Grouping states according to the number (and by implication, types) of religious groups they repress, the case studies use evidence collected from official state agencies, international monitoring organizations, news services, scholarly sources, and personal interviews I conducted between 2005 and 2009 in Georgia and Turkey to show how religion was repressed in a variety of nondemocratic states between 1990 and 2010. The examples identify relevant actors and trace motivations for the enactment of repressive restrictions, carefully examining the roles that the level of political competition and religious divisions play in determining the types of restrictions that exist and their targets.

Within each category, cases were selected to exemplify typical interactions between political and religious interests. Chapter 3 presents four countries repressing all religions: Azerbaijan, China, Iran, and Saudi Arabia. They illustrate two main patterns of religion-state relations that explain the nature of religious repression in countries in this category. Azerbaijan and China represent examples of states espousing ideologies that can be characterized as antireligious. While China continues to follow an atheistic ideology, post-Soviet Azerbaijan has adopted a form of strict secularism that is hostile to religion. Within this category, Burma, Cuba, North Korea, and Vietnam approximate the Chinese model, and the Arab secular nationalist regimes in Algeria, Egypt, Morocco, and Syria and the Central Asian republics come closer to the Azerbaijani model. Iran and Saudi Arabia represent regimes with proreligious ideologies. However, even though these states actively support a single religious sect, they do so with a strict measure of control, resulting in an interdependent relationship between the majority sect and the state. Moreover, religious groups and individuals in these states lack independence over the conduct of their own affairs, which is reflected in restrictions on every aspect of their expression. The Arabian Gulf states also fit this model of religion-state relations.

Chapter 4 presents four case studies—Russia, Georgia, Turkey, and Indonesia—representing two patterns of religion-state relations that occur in countries that repress all but one religion. Russia and Georgia— like the other postcommunist countries in this category—have a history of state-imposed atheism preceded by a history of close relations between the titular Orthodox Christian Church and the pre-Soviet state. These close relations were renewed upon independence and continue to the present day, resulting in state policies that favor the majority religion and impose restrictions on all other groups. Turkey and Indonesia illustrate the second pattern, which has a similar outcome of a majority religion that receives state support (without the same type of restrictive control found in the states that repress all religions) with regulations targeting minority religions. Indonesia and Turkey do not have the same communist past as the other countries in this category, but they do share a strong tradition of secular nationalism that is nevertheless associated with a majority religious tradition. This differs from the type of nationalist regimes ruling many of the Arab states in the Middle East from the previous category. In all of the countries, favoritism toward the majority religion is imposed to give government leaders greater legitimacy and ensure support in elections. Yet all of the countries maintain a secularist orientation to politics and emphasize the independence of political and religious authorities.

Chapter 5 highlights states that repress only some religions. These cases were chosen for several reasons. First, they illustrate how religion-state relations across four different world regions can be similar. Second, they help to highlight similarities and differences within particular regions. Kyrgyzstan and Bahrain are outliers within their regions, as the remainder of the Central Asian and Gulf states discussed in this book fall into the category of states repressing all religions. Nigeria and Singapore are more representative of relations in their neighboring countries. Third, as in the previous chapters, the countries highlighted help to illustrate two main patterns across the countries in this category of states that repress only some religious groups. Bahrain and Singapore are less politically competitive states but also less religiously divided; Nigeria and Kyrgyzstan are politically more competitive but more divided along religious—as well as ethnic—lines, an important consideration for several other countries in this category. This distinguishes them from countries in the other categories and also demonstrates how the interaction of these two variables helps to explain how these states treat religious groups.

Chapter 6 examines four countries—Albania, Senegal, Peru, and Cambodia—that repress no religious groups. With the exception of Cambodia, all the countries have relatively high levels of political competition and low levels of religious divisions. The four countries were chosen either as contrasting cases to those covered in previous chapters or as emblematic of regional religion-state relations (as in Peru). Albania is the only postcommunist country included in this study to not repress any religious groups. Senegal is one of the few Muslim-majority countries with no repression but is similar to many other sub-Saharan African countries in its lack of repressive policies. Unlike other countries in Southeast Asia,

Cambodia does not repress religious groups but does repress other types of groups in civil society. Its relatively lower level of political competition (compared with many other states in this category) helps to explain why the state is able to repress, but its low level of religious divisions explains why the state does not target repression at religious groups. Finally, Peru's pattern of religion-state relations is similar to that of many other states in Latin America, combining higher levels of political competition with lower levels of religious divisions in society.

# 3

# *Regulation as Control*

## STATE REPRESSION OF ALL RELIGIOUS GROUPS

LIKE OTHER POST-SOVIET republics, independent Azerbaijan has faced problems negotiating religion-state relations since the collapse of communism. Purporting to possess a democratic constitution and institutions, the state has actually functioned as a one-party dictatorship since its early years of independence. The government's approach toward religion has been to repress all religious groups, especially Muslims, which it controls through the State Committee for Work with Religious Organizations and a state-approved Caucasian Muslim Board (CMB).

In September 2009, local religious affairs authorities in Gyanja (Azerbaijan's second city) closed the Sunni Juma Mosque days before the end of the holy month of Ramadan.[1] With help from the local police, they confiscated books and sealed the door to the mosque, claiming that the mosque had not registered under the country's 2009 Freedom of Religion Law. The imam of the mosque, Ilham Ibrahimov, claimed that the mosque had been registered under an older law and had filed for reregistration under the new law before the state deadline. The mosque had been in operation for 12 years before authorities shut it down.

The mosque had faced problems before. Its previous imam, Kazim Aliev, had been appointed by the CMB in 1997 but was arrested in 2002 and sentenced in 2003 on charges of organizing an armed uprising (though human rights defenders claim they were "trumped up").[2] Officials claimed that Aliev conspired to establish an Islamic state by gathering young men and attempting to convince one to raid a military unit and seize weapons to use in an uprising. Officials did find weapons in the mosque, although Aliev claims they were planted. He was freed under presidential amnesty in 2006 but not allowed to return to the mosque, as the CMB refused to approve his appointment as an imam. The closure of the Juma mosque in September followed a series of other mosque closures.[3] The government has also imposed an unofficial ban on praying outside of mosques.

Mosque closures are a regular tactic the Azerbaijani government uses to repress independent Muslim groups that refuse to subject themselves to state religious control. Fearing the organizational potential of religious groups, the government maintains strict oversight over all aspects of Muslim religious expression in the country. Groups that resist government regulation are shut down and their buildings closed or demolished. Clerics who refuse to submit themselves to the authority of the state-appointed and co-opted head of the CMB (the mufti) face dismissal and arrest. Non-Muslim minorities are not spared repression, either, although because the country is predominantly Muslim, many of the government's restrictions are focused on regulating and controlling the practice of Islam.

The Azerbaijani government has also imposed repressive restrictions on religious literature. Religion laws require state licensing to sell religious literature; official approval for the production and importation of religious literature, objects, or materials; and censorship of literature by specifying the number of copies of each work that may be printed or imported, checking the contents of bookshops, and following an unpublished list of banned religious literature. Bureaucratic hurdles exist in attempting to obtain licenses to sell religious literature, and failure to comply results in fines. According to a state official in charge of licensing, shops were being denied licenses for legitimate reasons, stating, "Sometimes you even find cases of religious literature on sale in dirty places, and this is regarded as disrespect for religious values and arouses justifiable public dissatisfaction. . . . Preventing such cases is the duty of both the government and every citizen of Azerbaijan."[4] The irony of this statement is not lost on religious believers who have had their mosques closed and torn down, beards forcibly shaved, and headscarves removed by government officials.

Azerbaijan is but one country among the 27 in this study that repress all religious groups. This chapter examines this category of states to understand the conditions under which they are able to repress and their motivations for doing so. Although many governments engage in violent persecution of religion, this study focuses on laws and policies that restrict religious practice and religiously based organizations and therefore repress religion. Almost all of the countries repressing all religious groups display low levels of political competition, averaging –6 (on a scale of –10 to 10) on the Polity regime score in 2010. Because political competition is so restricted in most of the countries in this category, governments are able to impose harsh regulations on religion without checks or challenges to their authority. Government leaders can repress both large and small religious groups without a great fear of losing their positions. Even if religious divisions in society are not high, states in this category have the capacity to repress due to an absence of competitive institutions that can check governmental power. Moreover, political leaders have an incentive to repress both large and small religious groups to ensure that no viable opposition can emerge to challenge the regime's legitimacy.

This chapter examines countries that repress all religions through paired studies of four cases. The repression follows two main patterns. First, Iran and Saudi Arabia are proreligious states that impose a particular interpretation of Islamic law on their citizens. Governments in these countries use religious justifications to punish regime opponents and to restrict the rights and legal protections of religious minorities. State and religion are fused in these two countries, and neither can operate independently. This amounts to religious repression because no aspect of religious expression falls outside of state control. The second pattern is followed by Azerbaijan and China, states following antireligious ideologies aimed at diminishing religion's potential influence on politics and society. Like Iran and Saudi Arabia, these are countries with very little political competition and a history of state suppression of religion. Both countries recognize the danger that independent civil society can pose to the regime's stability and understand that repression can backfire and lead to mobilization. Religious resurgence in both countries heightens regime fears of religiously based opposition, and repression comes in the form of strict state control over religious practice and outlawing of politicized religious groups.

Table 3.1 summarizes the kinds of restrictions on religion found in the countries discussed in this chapter. All four countries impose almost every type of restriction measured in this study on all religious groups, with minor exceptions. First, neither Azerbaijan nor China restricts religious conversions, which is true of the other communist and postcommunist countries in this category as well. These states have followed ideologies predicting and promoting the demise of religion, and we can reasonably

**Table 3.1 Religious restrictions in countries repressing all religions (2010)**

|  | Iran | Saudi Arabia | China | Azerbaijan |
|---|---|---|---|---|
| Religious observance | x | x | x | x |
| Places of worship | x | x | x | x |
| Religious laws | x | x | x | x |
| Conversion | x | x |  |  |
| Proselytizing | x | x | x | x |
| Discriminatory registration/bans | x | x | x | x |
| Clerical appointments |  | x | x | x |
| Religious speech or publications | x | x | x | x |
| Religious education | x | x | x | x |
| Religious political parties |  | x | x | x |
| Religious associations | x | x | x | x |
| Political speech | x | x | x | x |
| Access to political office | x | x | x | x |

expect them not to be concerned with whether individuals are able to change their religious affiliation. Second, Iran does not restrict clerical appointments or religious parties, an artifact of its status as a theocratic regime. The remainder of this chapter examines these four countries in greater detail, explaining how each implements religious repression and why it chooses to target all religious groups.

## *Religious Regimes Repressing All Religions: Iran and Saudi Arabia*
### Iran

The 1979 Iranian Revolution was led by clergy and replaced a repressive monarch with a repressive religious regime. The clergy in Iran are traditionally known to be an independent class of people having resisted temporal rule and basing their legitimacy on religious succession. When Iran adopted Twelver Shiism as the state religion in the sixteenth century during the Safavid dynasty, though, a class of Shiite clergy did not exist.[5] Shiite Arab scholars from Iraq developed a clerical class (*ulama*) with the balance of power tending toward the secular ruler, the shah, and the clergy loyal to the state. The emergence of the Qajar dynasty in the eighteenth century brought the clergy greater power and independence from the state, as well as increasing antagonism toward it. Gradually, the clergy claimed that their religious legitimacy gave them the right to exercise *ijtihad*, or interpretation of law, religious practice, and political acts. Because the Iranian clergy had control over financial resources, such as religious taxes (zakat and *khums*) and endowment lands (waqf), and had historically close relations with the traditional urban merchants, the bazaar classes, and the guilds, they were further able to establish their independence from secular rulers. This financial and political independence, along with the public's willingness to obey the clergy, helped ensure Ayatollah Ruhollah Khomeini's successful revolution in 1979 and his assumption of political power.

Islamic revivalism in Iran was spurred in part by anticlerical policies in the 1920s and 1930s and especially in the 1950s by Shah Muhammad Reza Pahlavi. The Shah initiated a rapid modernization program and increased the power of the state, thus weakening the strength and influence of the clergy and depriving it of its control over some institutions (e.g., education and the judiciary) and finances (endowments). At the same time, members of the traditional class (those not middle-class or wealthy urban dwellers) were alienated by these policies, thus strengthening their attachment to the clergy. The lack of political freedom (the Shah consolidated his dictatorial powers in the 1960s and 1970s), high inflation, economic inequality, perceived wasteful spending by the Shah on arms and personal goods, and the Shah's relationship with Western powers led to dissatisfaction with his policies and greater support from both lower and middle classes for Khomeini. According to Sena Karasipahi (2009), dispossessed Iranians turned to Islam to express their frustration with their condition and to reestablish their dignity. Thus, religious organizations helped to organize and articulate opposition to the Shah's policies and set the stage for his overthrow.

While in exile, Ayatollah Khomeini advocated the idea of the *Vilayet-e Faqih* or jurisprudent leadership, which forwarded the notion that in an Islamic state founded on Islamic laws and principles, only those trained in Islamic law (sharia) are qualified to govern. Under this system, the Supreme Leader (*Vali*) has absolute power based on his knowledge of Islam and piety. Khomeini claimed that in an Islamic regime run by clerics, the government could make any laws it wished to, given that they serve the interests of the regime, which coincide with Islam. This later allowed the Islamic Republic of Iran to create a host of laws that do not seem to stem from sharia (Tamadonfar 2001).[6] Khomeini's ideas were unprecedented. Within the Shia tradition, a *marj'a taqlid* is a senior religious scholar recognized as a source of guidance in following Islamic law among groups of followers. At any time, there may be a number of these learned jurists who provide Shiites guidance in their private lives, and individuals are free to choose a *marj'a* to follow. The establishment of the position of the Supreme Leader challenges this tradition, however, by appointing one cleric as more powerful than others and by fusing religious and political power.

The Shah's overthrow in 1979 was followed by the imposition of Khomeini's version of Islamic law in Iran. The Iranian Constitution was adopted on October 23, 1979. Article 12 establishes the Twelver School of Shiism as the official religion of the country, while granting other Islamic schools "full respect, and their followers are free to perform their religious rites in accordance with their own *fiqh*."[7] Articles 107 to 112 outline the position of the Supreme Leader, whose functions and authority encompass a variety of issues, including defining and executing the general policies of the regime, commanding the armed forces, and appointing and dismissing members of the Guardian Council, the head of the judiciary, and other high offices. The Assembly of Experts, a group of 86 Islamic scholars who are popularly elected, chooses the Supreme Leader.[8] Articles 91 to 99 set up the Guardian Council and delineate its functions and organization. The council's mission is to "safeguard Islamic laws and the Constitution and to verify the compatibility of legislation passed by the Islamic Parliament of Iran with them." It has six Islamic jurists appointed by the Supreme Leader and six lawyers elected by the parliament from among nominees from the head of the judiciary, all of whom serve six-year terms. The Guardian Council must approve all legislation parliament passes to ensure its compatibility with Islam (by the six jurists on the council) and the constitution (by the six lawyers on the council). The Guardian Council also approves all candidates for elected office. Although technically Iran's institutional structure does allow for popular election of some government officials, unelected individuals maintain control over elections by vetting candidates.

### Repression of the Religious Majority

Laws and regulations in Iran result in repression of all religious groups, including the religious majority, Shia Muslims. These affect both regular citizens and clerics. For example, the Islamic Penal Code of 1991 unified a set of provisions that had been used since the 1979 revolution. It was revised in 2009 and approved by the Guardian Council in 2012 (although it was further revised in 2013). The penal code outlines punishments for a variety of offenses in accordance with sharia law and is applied to all Muslims under the assumption that they follow religious law. Although the 2012 version removed stoning as a punishment for adulterers, revisions in 2013 retain stoning to death as a form of punishment for people who engage in adultery or sex outside of marriage.[9] The penal code makes the death penalty mandatory for adultery, incest, being the "passive participant" in a homosexual relationship, being a non-Muslim "active participant" engaged in sodomy with a Muslim, men having sex with their stepmothers, and non-Muslim men having sex with Muslim women (Sanei 2012). Amnesty International has documented at least 77 stonings for adultery between 1985 and 2010.[10] A repressive quality of these sentences is that they have been disproportionately handed out to women and minorities, who suffer from lower literacy rates and are not treated equally before the law. The code also enumerates a number of acts as "crimes against God," including drinking alcohol, insulting the Prophet, and insulting the twelve Shia imams or the Prophet's daughter, which carry fines of lashing, with subsequent convictions leading to the death penalty.

The penal code also contains provisions on "Offenses against the National and International Security of the Country," which give the government broad powers to punish peaceful activities and free expression of dissent. Article 513 of the penal code says that offenses considered to amount to an insult to religion (not specifically defined) can be punished by death or prison terms of between one and five years. Other laws, such as the Press Code, proscribe writings deemed to be against Islam. Article 6 of the Press Code states that those convicted will be "assigned punishments according to Article 698 of the Penal Code," which concerns the intentional creation of "anxiety and unease in the public's mind," "false rumors," or writing about "acts which are not true," even as a quote, and provides for between two months' and two years' imprisonment or up to 74 lashes.[11]

Shia clerics have not escaped repression under Iranian law. Article 18 of the Theologian's Law states that "acts which customarily cause insult to the dignity of Islamic theology (clergy) and the Islamic Revolution are interpreted as an offence for theologians." The Special Clerical Courts were established in 1987 to prosecute clerics for expressing political views deemed controversial by the regime and for engaging in nonreligious activities such as journalism. The Supreme Leader directly oversees the courts, which operate outside the judiciary. Defendants can be represented only by clergymen nominated by the court. Human rights organizations have documented unfair trials against Shia religious leaders held in the Special Clerical Courts, as well as house arrest, incommunicado detention, and torture.[12]

For example, Ayatollah Seyed Hossein Kazemeini Boroujerdi is a cleric who has been targeted by the Special Clerical Courts. Ayatollah Boroujerdi is a senior Shia cleric who rejects the principle of political leadership of the clergy, upon which the Islamic Republic is based, and advocates for the separation of religion and state. He was arrested in October 2006 (along with about 300 of his followers, most of whom were subsequently released) and tried in June 2006. He was initially sentenced to death, but the sentence was overturned and replaced with 11 years in prison. He is reportedly in poor health and being denied medical treatment, and he claims to have been tortured while in detention.[13] Several other clerics and intellectuals have been prosecuted for expressing their disagreement with the structure of the Islamic Republic since the revolution (Baktiari 2012).

Laws in Iran are used to enforce religious orthodoxy among the general public and to keep regime opponents in line. That the clerical establishment is also subject to repression (despite the fact that a cleric has supreme state power) indicates how deeply the regime fears threats to its legitimacy, as criticism from senior clerics is often based on religious premises. The structure of the Iranian state makes such repression easier by using religious authority to legitimize government actions. Moreover, by having codified religiously based regulations into the legal structure of the country, the state can enforce its version of Islamic law within the context of everyday governmental practices.

## Repression of Religious Minorities

The Constitution of the Islamic Republic of Iran also contains provisions related to religious minorities. Article 13 states, "Zoroastrians, Jews, and Christians among Iranians are the only recognized religious minorities and they are free to perform their religious rites and ceremonies within the framework of law and to act in accordance with their own canon in matters of personal law and religious education." Article 14 states that the government and Muslims in Iran must treat non-Muslims according to Islamic norms of justice and fairness, as long as those minorities do not act against Islam or the government. The constitution does not enshrine religious equality, however, notably excluding it from Article 19 that states, "All the people of Iran, regardless of ethnic group or tribe, enjoy equal rights; color, race, language and the like do not bestow any privilege." Article 20 bestows equal protection "in conformity with Islamic criteria," and Article 26 allows the formation of groups, as long as they do not violate Islamic criteria.

With the exception of a few reserved positions in the parliament (*majles*), non-Muslims are not allowed to be elected to a representative body or to hold senior government or military positions, although they are allowed to vote in elections. Article 64 of the constitution assigns one parliamentary representative each to Zoroastrians and Jews, one joint representative for Assyrian and Chaldean Christians, and two representatives for Armenian Christians. Non-Muslims are prohibited from engaging in public religious expression, persuasion, and conversion of Muslims. The Ministry of Islamic Culture and Guidance (*Ershad*) and the Ministry of Intelligence and Security (MOIS) closely monitor minority religious activities, including schools. There are also restrictions on religious publications.

Prohibitions are stricter for minorities not recognized by the constitution, such as Baha'is. These groups do not have the freedom to practice or teach their faith or to hold leadership positions in government or the military. The government of Iran considers the Baha'i faith to be a political sect and its followers to be apostates. The Baha'i religion emerged in the late 1800s in Persia. Prior to the religion's founding, a young merchant named Siyyid 'Ali-Muhammad took the name Bab—meaning "gate" or "door" in Arabic—and proclaimed that a second messenger from God would soon appear to usher in the age of peace and justice promised in Islam, Judaism, Christianity, and other world religions. His revelation was the basis for a separate religion—Babism—upon which Baha'ism was later based. In 1863, Mirza Husein Ali Nuri claimed to be the messenger foretold by Bab and took the name Baha'u'llah. Shortly after this proclamation, he was forced into exile to Constantinople, Adrianople, and finally Akka, in modern-day Israel, where he died in 1892. He appointed as his successor his son, Abdu'l-Baha, who carried on the teachings and established the institutions of the Baha'i faith. Although the Iranian regime considers Baha'ism to be a heterodox form of Islam, the Baha'i emphasize that their religion is distinct and deny being a sect within Islam. Like Muslims, they acknowledge a prophetic succession beginning with Moses and including Jesus Christ and the Prophet Muhammad. However, unlike Muslims, they do not believe that Muhammad was the final prophet, thus leading to charges of heresy by orthodox Muslims.

Currently, Baha'is number around 300,000 to −350,000 in Iran (less than 1 percent of the population) (US Department of State 2012). They experience both repression and persecution, ranging from harassment to imprisonment and death. According to Eliz Sanasarian (2000), of all non-Muslim religious minorities, the persecution of the Baha'is has been the most widespread, systematic, and uninterrupted. After the 1979 revolution, the government seized and destroyed Baha'i properties such as cemeteries, holy places, and administrative centers. During the 1980s, the government organized more than 200 executions of Baha'is, although that level of persecution is no longer present.[14] Numerous state and state-affiliated agencies publish anti-Baha'i articles. As of the end of 2012, more than 80 Baha'is were held in prison in connection with their beliefs.[15] This includes the seven leaders of the Baha'i community who have been detained since spring 2008, accused of "espionage for Israel, insulting religious sanctities, and propaganda against the Islamic Republic," as well as "spreading corruption on earth." In June 2010, they were sentenced to 20-year prison terms, a sentence that was reduced to 10 years in September 2010.

Baha'i community groups are targeted as well. For instance, in 1987, members of the community established the Baha'i Institute for Higher Education to provide education for Baha'i students, who are denied access to universities in Iran. Since then, state authorities have harassed and arrested staff and faculty of the organization. In May 2011, at least seven were sentenced to terms of four to five years for "membership in the deviant Baha'ist sect, with the goal of taking action against the security of the country, in order to further the aims of the deviant sect and those of organizations outside the country."[16] In 2006, a senior political official ordered the expulsion of any identified Baha'i students from 81 universities.

Why would the Iranian government so vehemently repress a religious group that is less than 1 percent of the population? Baha'is have not organized resistance or rebellion against the regime that would justify their repression, although they have engaged in nonviolent protest. Baha'is have used their connections to coreligionists in the diaspora to agitate for greater attention to their repression in Iran, which may be one reason for the government's suspicion of the group. Moreover, because their world headquarters is located in Israel, they have been charged with "espionage on behalf of Zionism," an ideology the Islamic regime strongly opposes. Another objection to the group appears to be religious, as they are regarded as a deviant sect for recognizing a prophet after Muhammad, who is considered by Muslims to be the last prophet, or "seal of the prophets."

Members of other Muslim sects—such as Sunnis and Sufis—are also targeted for repression. Sunni identity tends to overlap with ethnicity (e.g., among the Kurds), making it difficult to distinguish whether they are being targeted for their religion or their ethnicity. Yet as evidence of the religious nature of Sunnis' repression, the government imposes restrictions on building mosques, bans on religious literature and education, and underrepresentation in government. Sufis, particularly those affiliated with the Gonabadi Dervish order (who consider themselves to be Shia Muslims), have been arrested, flogged, and sent into internal exile for their religious affiliation. Sufis have also had their houses of worship and publications confiscated and destroyed.

Iranian Christians number approximately 200,000 to 250,000, less than 0.5 percent of the total Iranian population.[17] They are divided between ethnic and nonethnic Christians. Ethnic Christians include Armenians, Assyrians, and Chaldeans, most of whom belong to their community's traditional Orthodox Church, although some are Catholics or Protestants. These groups have lived in Iran for centuries and do not proselytize. Nevertheless, these groups face government restrictions of religious practice, including prohibition of the use of the Persian language for services, the expectation that they will exclude nonethnic coreligionists from services, surveillance, and limitations on license renewal, church renovations, and property ownership and transfer.

Evangelical Christians face the greatest repression among the Christian communities, especially if they are converts from Islam. Protestant churches have been closed down—especially small, underground house churches—and Persian-language publications restricted. The Ministry of Intelligence imposes many of these limits based on orders from the Ministry of Culture and Islamic Guidance, which oversees religious organizations and churches. By law, the culture ministry must license all recognized minority religious groups to allow them to own or rent buildings, hold services, and establish institutions such as religious schools. But minorities also report a host of other practices that are not codified into law, such as monitoring churches by forcing them to report to the ministry before accepting new members, requiring individuals to carry membership cards and subjecting them to random identity checks outside churches, forcing churches to hold services on Sunday (a work day) rather than Friday (a weekend day), restricting the use of the Persian languages for services, and shutting down churches and confiscating buildings. Reports indicate that starting in 2012, the Revolutionary Guard Intelligence Organization began taking over the task of overseeing churches.[18]

Converts can face the death penalty for apostasy based on Islamic jurisprudence, even though the crime and sentence are not codified in the country's penal code and, to date, only one case of death for apostasy has been documented.[19] For example, Christian convert and Church of Iran evangelical pastor Yousef Naderkhani was arrested in October 2009 after protesting to local education authorities that his child was being forced to read from the Koran at school. Naderkhani was born to Muslim parents and converted to Christianity at age 19. Prior to his arrest, he led a congregation of about 400 adherents in Rasht, a city in northern Iran. In October 2010, he was sentenced to death for apostasy. The Supreme Court ruled in June 2011 that the lower court should reexamine procedural flaws in the case and also noted that the sentence could be overturned if Naderkhani recanted his Christian faith. He refused to do so but was acquitted of apostasy in September 2012, sentenced to only three years' imprisonment on the charge of "propaganda against the regime," and freed for time served. Other members of the Church of Iran have also been imprisoned for propaganda against the regime.

The government targets Protestants for several reasons. Because most conduct their services and publish texts in Persian, and because they proselytize, they are able to convert Muslims. This threatens the regime, which bases its legitimacy on the supremacy of Twelver Shiism. Moreover, the government suspects these groups because of their ties to foreign entities. Many of their ties are religious (for instance, churches belonging to the larger Assemblies of God organization). Evidence of the perceived political threat they pose comes in the crimes with which many of these individuals are charged. While religious crimes bear charges such as "insulting Islam," political crimes are labeled "propaganda against the regime," "acting against national security," and "contact with a foreign enemy" and are prosecuted in Revolutionary Courts. Authorities distinguish evangelicals and house churches from Christianity, which is protected under the country's constitution, claiming them to be a deviant form of Christianity backed by foreign enemies of the Iranian government.

Of course, not only religious minorities and critics of the religious nature of the regime are being targeted by the Iranian government. Political activists, human rights defenders, journalists, bloggers, lawyers, filmmakers, academics, students, and others continue to be repressed by the regime. The regime understands that an independent civil society has the potential to threaten its stability. As explained earlier, even clerics within the ruling establishment who hold opposing viewpoints and citizens who do not wish to follow Islamic strictures as they are interpreted by the state are considered threatening to the regime because state leaders equate pluralism with dissent. And because dissent may signal decreased legitimacy and state power, it must be eliminated.

A focus on the Iranian regime's use of religious repression to target all religious groups and restrain civil society may be more useful for comparing the country with other nondemocratic regimes than currently used measures of regime type. In 2010, Iran had the same Polity regime score as several other countries such as China, Cuba, Kuwait, and Libya. Yet Iran differs in its institutional structure from these countries because it holds elections for president and the national legislature. Even if those elections are not completely free or fair, this institutional difference is significant, given the focus that many political scientists place on elections to explain regime variation. Yet Iran is similar to those countries in its treatment of civil society. The fact that it targets all independent nongovernmental activity may explain how it is able to sustain electoral institutions without fear of the regime being toppled by opposition groups. Therefore, political scientists cannot ignore the importance of restrictions on civil society in understanding and explaining variation across nondemocratic regimes.

## Saudi Arabia

The Kingdom of Saudi Arabia is an Islamic state subscribing to the Hanbali school of jurisprudence. The present state was formed in 1932 out of an alliance between Abd al-Aziz bin Saud, the head of the Al Saud family, and the family of an Islamic preacher, Muhammad ibn Abd al-Wahhab, but goes back to an alliance formed between al-Wahhab and Muhammad ibn Saud in 1744. Because of this, the branch of Islam promoted by and practiced in Saudi Arabia is referred to as Wahhabi, even though many adherents do not use that term. Wahhabi doctrine calls for the reinstatement of exactly the same religious, social, and political customs practiced by the Prophet Muhammad and his followers in the seventh century. Saudi Arabia remains a tribal society, despite attempts by the Al Saud family to centralize authority in the national government. Religious scholars are active in political decision-making in the country, and the Al Saud family gets its legitimacy from religion, particularly in its role as custodian of the holy cities of Mecca and Medina (Nevo 1998).[20] In 1997, Crown Prince Abdullah bin Abd al-Aziz took control of most decision-making after King Fahd bin Abdul Aziz al-Saud suffered a stroke. Abdullah became king in 2005 upon Fahd's death.

The government of Saudi Arabia is a hereditary monarchy, with a few political institutions in place to help the monarch rule the country. The cabinet is comprised of more than 20 members from the royal family, descendants of Muhammad ibn Abd al-Wahhab, and the technocratic class. The king acts as prime minister, and senior members of the royal family head important ministries such as government, defense, internal security, the budget, and oil reserves. Princes and senior technocrats advise the king on almost all major policy decisions. Because these advisory institutions exist, Saudi Arabia is not an absolutist state. According to Anthony Cordesman (2002, 2), "the Saudi monarchy consists more of patriarchal rule by a consensus-driven extended family with large numbers of alliances to other families, than rule by an autocrat who acts upon his personal desires."

The Basic Law of 1992 states that the constitution of Saudi Arabia is the Koran and the Sunna and that the sharia is the source of its laws.[21] The Consultative Council (*Majlis al-Shura*) was created in 1992–1993 and is the country's highest political institution after the royal court and the Council of Ministers. The majlis was created partly in response to criticism from conservative Islamists after the regime allowed US-led troops into the country following the 1991 Gulf War. The purpose of the majlis is to provide advice to the king regarding the kingdom's laws, economic and social development, annual reports, and international laws, treaties, and agreements. It is bound to the sharia and defers to the judiciary on matters of Islamic law. The majlis has 150 members appointed by the king, including 13 part-time, female, nonvoting advisers. Eight committees advise the king on various matters, and committee proceedings are confidential. Saudi observers note that the king uses appointments to the majlis as a way of co-opting critics, especially conservative Salafis and liberals (Dekmejian 1998). Political parties are forbidden, and formal political opposition does not exist inside the country.

King Abdullah has been referred to as a reformer, and he has instituted several changes and innovations during his reign to attempt to moderate extremist elements within the country. For example, in 2007 he replaced the judiciary council, considered to be reactionary, with the Supreme Court and an appeals court. The king appoints members of the courts. In 2008, a Special Higher Commission of judicial experts was tasked with writing laws incorporating all four Sunni schools of jurisprudence, rather than the previous exclusive reliance on Hanbali jurisprudence.[22]

The current relationship between the religious authorities and the state was established under King Faisal in 1971 and represents an increasing institutionalization and legalization of state religion policy. Until 1971, Saudi rulers sought religious justification for their rule from the office of the grand mufti. In 1971, King Faisal created a Council of Senior Religious Scholars (headed by the grand mufti) to serve this role. It has also been tasked with issuing religious justifications (fatwas) for Saudi state policies (Baskan and Wright 2011).

### Repression of the Religious Majority

The Saudi state has several institutions in place to regulate all aspects of religious practice and expression in the country, allowing the state to control and eliminate independent religious activity. The Ministry of Education determines the religious curriculum in schools, and the Ministry of Information manages religious media programming. On August 12, 2010, King Abdullah issued a royal decree banning fatwas from anyone not authorized by the government, in response to fatwas issued by independent clerics using religious media (Teitelbaum 2010). A religious police force, the Committee for the Promotion of Virtue and Prevention of Vice (CPVPV), whose officers are known as *mutawwa'in*, enforces religious laws regarding Islamic dress code, the behavior between men and women, and closure of businesses during prayer time. Its director general is a member of the cabinet.

The Ministry of Islamic Affairs, Pious Endowments, Mission, and Guidance (*Shu'un Islamiyya wal-Awqaf wal-Da'wa wal-Irhshad*, MOIA) is responsible for funding and administering the approximately 75,000 Sunni mosques in the country. The MOIA employs imams and sermon leaders to staff the mosques. It monitors government clerics and removes those deemed to be preaching extremist ideologies. Since 2003, the government has removed 3,500 imams from duty. Mosques are located in cities, private homes, rest stops along highways, in malls, and other locations. Mosques are the only legal public places of worship in the country. Other religious groups are allowed to worship only privately, although violations often occur. Blasphemy against Sunni Islam and apostasy are punishable by death, but long prison sentences and detentions are the more common punishments.

Saudi citizens are assumed to be Muslims; non-Muslims must convert to Islam to become naturalized citizens, and all applicants require certification from a local imam. Government policies apply the state's interpretation of Islamic law, which can be considered repression of citizens who are nominal Muslims but may not wish to live according to Wahhabi strictures. Individual citizens, journalists, and activists who publicly criticize the official interpretation of Islam or are critical of the religious leadership are also subject to government repression. For example, in 2010, the editor of the daily *Al-Watan*, Jamal Khashoggi, was pressured to resign after publishing an opinion piece critical of conservative Islam. In 2003, he had been fired from the same position for criticizing the country's religious police but was reinstated in 2007.[23] The regime also blocks access to thousands of websites considered to be immoral or politically sensitive.

Another manner of repression that targets Sunni Muslims involves accusing individuals of practicing witchcraft or sorcery, both of which are considered to be anti-Islamic. One case involved an Egyptian pharmacist and resident of the northern desert town of Arar, Mustafa Ibrahim. Ibrahim was accused of practicing magic to separate another resident from his wife. According to the Saudi Press Agency, evidence in his home included books on black magic, candles, and herbs. The agency also reported, "He confessed to adultery with a woman and desecrating the Koran by placing it in the bathroom" of the local mosque. He was put to death in Riyadh in 2007.[24]

## Repression of Religious Minorities

Shiites in Saudi Arabia number about 2 million adherents, 10 to 15 percent of the population (US Department of State 2012). Most live and work in the Eastern Province, but there are also communities in Mecca and Medina. In addition to Twelver Shia, there is also a community of Ismaili Shia adherents in Najran, in southwestern Saudi Arabia (on the border with Yemen). Wahhabism considers Shiism to be polytheism (*shirk*), contrary to the creed of the unity of God (*tawhid*), because it associates men and objects with God. Thus, after the founding of the kingdom, Shia religious authority was curtailed, and the community lost its local senior religious authorities (*mujtahids*). Because the Shia minority openly challenged the regime at one point and refused to be co-opted, it has been viewed ever since with hostility and distrust and suffered repression as a result. There were violent disturbances from the minority Shia population in 1979 to 1980 referred to as the uprising (*intifada*) of the Eastern Province, as well as Iranian-sponsored terrorism in the region. In the later 1990s, many Shia groups switched tactics from resistance to demands for equality and recognition of their identity.

Twelver Shiites have been repressed ever since the founding of the modern Saudi kingdom. Several Shia religious practices are currently banned. In 1913, upon taking control over the Eastern Province, Saudi officials banned Ashura processions (marking the martyrdom of Hussein, the grandson of the Prophet Muhammad). In 1993, the Grand Mufti bin Baz declared the Shia Ramadan festival of Qarqi'un a heretical "innovation," leading local authorities to ban such festivities. The government continues to restrict permits to Shia to build or renovate mosques and does not finance construction or maintenance of Shia mosques. In 2009, the government instituted a ban on building Shia mosques. At the same time, it built a large Sunni mosque in predominantly Shia Qatif. The state imposes restrictions on Shia worshipers in Mecca and Medina. Members of the Council of Senior Religious Scholars issue fatwas against them, suggesting that Sunnis avoid greeting or eating with Shiites. The Shia also face discrimination in schools, the justice system, and employment.

Clashes at the Baqi cemetery in Medina in February 2009 and subsequent events demonstrate how Shia Muslims have been treated by the Saudi government. To commemorate the anniversary of the Prophet's death, Shia gathered at the cemetery that is believed to contain the graves of several of the Prophet's wives, many of his companions, and four of his successors. Part of the commemoration includes prayers and rituals that involve such things as picking up bits of sand from around the cemetery. These practices go against Wahhabi teachings that consider veneration of saints and holidays to be a form of idolatry. Religious police filmed pilgrims at these commemorations, causing some pilgrims to clash with the police over the filming of women. Over the next few days, there were protests and violent clashes between police and pilgrims, leading to several arrests. Although King Abdullah later issued an amnesty for those arrested during the clashes, following the events Saudi authorities "effectively attempted to impose a ban on communal Shia prayers" (Wilcke 2009, 22). Authorities closed private prayer buildings and arrested prayer leaders. Such arrests have been ongoing. Between 2001 and 2009, at least 89 Shia in the Eastern Province have been punished with detention for allowing religious recitation in their houses, selling articles used in Shia religious ceremonies, and other worship-related activities.

Shia adherents subjected to repression in Saudi Arabia include the Ismaili subgroup, also known as "Seveners."[25] Ismailis live mostly in Najran, the southernmost province of Saudi Arabia at its border with Yemen and the state's last territorial conquest. Ismailis face discrimination similar to the Shia of the Eastern Province, but they lack an organized opposition outside the country or influential coreligionists in a powerful state like Iran and are fewer in number and more isolated from the world. Ismailis are not allowed to visit their religious leader to receive instruction, and their leader has at various times been detained or placed under house arrest. Prayer leaders have been arrested on charges of sorcery and deviance and sentenced to several years in prison and hundreds of lashes. They are not allowed to print or publish prayer books. They face restrictions in attempting to build or expand mosques. For example, in January 2000, Saudi authorities devised and carried out a detailed plan to close mosques in Najran on the day that they celebrate the feast of Eid al-Fitr (which differs from the date Wahhabis celebrate it because of calendar differences). As the community anticipated the closures, many stayed home, but those who did go to the mosques were arrested (Wilcke 2008).

Christians and Jews also face regular restrictions, including the inability to practice their faith in public. In several instances, private religious ceremonies have been disrupted and worshipers detained and deported. They are not allowed to train clergy in the country, and clergy have a difficult time entering the country to conduct religious services. Non-Muslims are not allowed to proselytize or distribute religious materials. Noncitizens must carry identity cards with a religious designation. Moreover, non-Muslims are discriminated against in the legal system; they receive only 50 percent of the compensation a male Muslim would receive in accidental death or injury compensation (some non-Muslims are entitled to only a sixteenth of a male Muslim's compensation). There are no reports of non-Muslims forcibly converted to Islam, but the Ministry of Islamic Affairs sponsors "Call and Guidance" centers that have the purpose of converting foreigners to Islam. There are reportedly 50 of these in the country with approximately 500 employees. The press covers stories about conversions. Non-Muslim private religious schools are not allowed, although non-Muslims in private schools are not required to study Islam.

The fact that Saudi Arabia allows no real public participation in politics and decision-making helps to explain why religion is one of the many forms of expression that the regime represses. Unlike Iran, Saudi Arabia does not elect government officials, and the king is accountable to only other royals in the al-Saud family. It has both the capacity to repress civil society and an interest in doing so. The reason state policies target religious groups specifically is that the regime depends on Wahhabism for political legitimacy. Moreover, because the religious group upon which the regime bases its power includes vocal clerics and groups that advocate intolerance of other Muslim sects and non-Muslims and a very particular interpretation of Islamic practice, the government is obligated to enforce repressive restrictions on religious minorities.

Although the regime clearly favors a particular Islamic sect, this favoritism is accompanied by strict control over it. As detailed earlier, state agencies are in charge of everything from clerical appointments to mosque construction, which allows the regime to install supporters in important religious positions and to assert its hegemony over religious spaces. The regime controls how religion is practiced, as state agencies and police enforce Islamic law in a manner that punishes any sort of deviation from orthodoxy. The regime also justifies punishing political opponents by relying on strict application of Hanbali law. Thus, in Saudi Arabia—as in other proreligious countries that repress all religious groups—control over religious institutions amounts to religious repression, even of the religious group with which the state is allied and identifies.

## Antireligious Regimes Repressing All Religions: China and Azerbaijan

### China

Mainland China came under the power of the Chinese Communist Party (CCP) and its leader, Mao Zedong, in 1949.[26] Campaigns such as the Great Leap Forward (1958–1961) and the Cultural Revolution (1966–1976) mobilized the masses to encourage social and economic advancement but ended in great numbers of deaths. Deng Xiaoping became China's leader after Mao's death in 1976, during which time he led the country through limited market-based reforms and increased economic growth. The deadly attack on prodemocracy supporters in Beijing's Tiananmen Square in 1989 further cemented the CCP's hard line on political reform, while economic reform continued. In March 2013, Xi Jinping became China's leader, acting simultaneously as general secretary of the Communist Party and its Central Committee, chairman of the Central Military Commission, and president of the People's Republic of China (PRC).

China is ruled centrally by the CCP, with the Politburo making major policy decisions. The National People's Congress (NPC) has 3,000 members elected by subnational congresses. The NPC is a largely symbolic body. It meets for two weeks a year to approve proposed legislation, formally elects the state president, and confirms the premier after the president nominates him. There are elections at the municipal level, but candidate nominations are tightly controlled by the CCP. Opposition groups are suppressed, and freedom of speech, assembly, and association are severely restricted. Official CCP doctrine considers party control over religion to be necessary until religion eventually meets its demise. In the past, this control has taken the form of persecution, but in more recent years, it has involved repression and co-optation.

The current constitution (adopted in 1982) defines the state as "a socialist state under the people's democratic dictatorship." Article 36 of the constitution states that citizens of the PRC enjoy freedom of religious belief and that the state protects "normal" religious activities.[27] The State Council wields executive power in China. The State Administration for Religious Affairs (Guojia Zongjiao Shiwuju, SARA) is an administrative organ of the State Council that monitors religions, supervises patriotic religious associations, crafts national religious regulations, oversees regional religious affairs boards, fights the spread of "cults," and prevents "foreign domination" of religion. Almost all SARA officials are party members and therefore officially atheist. It has offices at the provincial, municipal, district, and sometimes county levels. The Public Security Ministry and its subordinate offices are responsible for enforcing SARA's directives. The Public Security Bureau (PSB) is in charge of law enforcement and therefore is the agency tasked with cracking down on unregistered or illegal religious groups.

The government defines four categories of religious groups: officially sanctioned religions, unregistered groups, cults, and feudal superstitions. Five major religions are recognized nationally: Buddhism, Daoism, Islam, Roman Catholicism, and Protestantism.[28] Among these religions, religious practice is legal only in registered venues, and personnel and religious organizations must also be registered. To register a venue, applicants must demonstrate compliance with 26 sets of central government regulations, as well as local regulations. The process involves a preliminary application requiring documentation, official inspection, establishment of a management body, and endorsement by local government and residence committees, followed by the actual application, which requires further documentation and approvals (Tong 2010). One or more government-controlled patriotic religious associations oversee each sanctioned religion to ensure that it complies with government regulations.[29] These associations closely cooperate with the government and are known to toe the party line. Unregistered groups may be allowed to hold meetings by local government officials, although many are banned and prosecuted. These include Protestant house churches, the underground Catholic Church, Hindus, Jews, Orthodox Christians, Seventh-Day Adventists, Jehovah's Witnesses, and Mormons. When the government deems groups dangerous, they are often labeled "evil cults" and subjected to intense repression. The government frowns on folk religions and feudal superstitions (*fengjian mixin*) but rarely prosecutes them unless they interfere with public order and safety.

State religion policy has undergone several changes in the past decades, as the government experiments with tightening and loosening control over religion through policy mechanisms. In 1982, the party issued Document No. 19, "The Basic Viewpoint on the Religious Question during Our Country's Socialist Period," as a set of guidelines for religious freedom policy in the country (MacInnis 1989). Like previous policies, its stated intention was to pursue the complete disappearance of religion in China, and it reiterated the principle that CCP members could not be religious believers. However, it did state the party's intentions to help religious organizations recover and restore their places of worship, while limiting religious activities. For example, the document advocated returning church property to religious organizations, but local governments failed to comply in many cases. Religious organizations ended up looking to foreign organizations for support, which undermined the party's desire to keep them free from foreign influence and encouraged growth in the religious sector overall.

Alongside the growth in religious adherents and organizations, other incidents in the country—the Tiananmen Square protests and massacre on June 4, 1989; growing restiveness among Muslims in northwest China; the formation of a Chinese Underground Bishops' Conference to oppose the Chinese Catholic Patriotic Association; and the emergence of the Falun Gong movement (Leung 2005)—convinced the party that it needed to tighten control over the religious sector. In response to the growing loss of control over the religious sector, CCP Chairman Jiang Zemin tightened religious policy in the 1990s under the cover of rule of law and the idea that religion needed to accommodate to socialism. New regulations and rules regarding religion were enacted to achieve the aim of subsuming religion under the control of the state. The State Council issued two sets of laws in 1994: Document No. 144 (Regulations from the State Council on Managing Religious Activities) and Document No. 145 (On the State Council's Management of Foreigners Staying in the People's Republic of China) (repealed March 2005) (Spiegel 1997). These laws required that institutions engaging in religious activities be registered with civil authorities, which verify that their activities are in accord with religious regulations and are free from foreign control. Civil authorities also controlled issuing permissions for foreign visitors (i.e., anyone not a Chinese national) to religious organizations. Registration with the government entails submitting to government control over the selection of clergy, financial affairs, building programs, and religious materials and restrictions on educational and social welfare activities. Officials are also authorized to examine church sermons for content.

In 1997, the Information Office of the State Council of the People's Republic of China released the document "Freedom of Religious Belief in China," outlining the various religious freedoms given to citizens of China and their visitors.[30] In the same document, several points were raised that give a great deal of insight into the government's views on religion and religion policy. The most important has to do with the justification for state control over religion as a means of preserving stability and fighting Western imperialism. By painting foreign missionaries, ethnic separatists, and others as villains of socialism and the people's republic, the state made itself look as if it was merely protecting religion by cutting it off from outsiders, rather than repressing it by not allowing groups to function independently.

Yet as China transitioned toward a market economy, relaxation of restrictions on religion followed. After several years of consultation and negotiation among a variety of government parties and the CCP, the Regulations on Religious Affairs (RRA) took effect in March 2005, increasing the autonomy of religious groups and relaxing previous restrictions (Carson 2005). According to the RRA, religious communities are given the same legal treatment as other social organizations, publishers, and social groups. Registration of religious organizations was transferred from

SARA to the Ministry of Civil Affairs, which is charged with registration of all legal organizations.[31] The RRA gives religious communities greater authority in managing their internal affairs, owning and using religious property, engaging in social welfare, and expanding contact with coreligionists outside China. Article 35 of the RRA allows religious personnel to be compensated for performing religious services and allows religious communities to receive funding from domestic and foreign individuals and corporations. Christians are no longer forbidden from worshiping at home, and Protestant and Catholic churches are allowed to perform charitable works such as operating orphanages, homes for the elderly, medical clinics, and kindergartens (although not academic schools).

The RRA removes the requirement to get government approval for conducting religious activities outside registered venues, organizing religious training in venues, appointing the heads of religious venues, setting the number of religious personnel in venues, and controlling religious publications. It also gives back the power (once belonging to local religious affairs bureaus) of religious communities to certify personnel, admit and train students, design curricula, and recruit faculty in religious schools. The RRA also lessens bureaucratic hurdles and processing time for applications from religious communities.

Despite its improvements, the RRA continues to restrict and repress religions in a number of ways: CCP members are still required to declare their atheism, meaning that anyone wishing to serve in government must be outwardly atheistic.[32] Religious bodies are still required to register with the government. To register, groups must have a professional clergy and commit to teach their membership to uphold the CCP, socialism, and patriotism. The government may still refuse registration to any group for any reason without justification. All sites for religious activities must be registered with the government, and those built without prior approval can be banned and torn down by local construction departments. The RRA specifies that the Buddhist patriotic religious associations are to select Buddhist lamas and that the national SARA must preapprove Catholic bishops, thus enforcing state control over the internal affairs of religious groups. Article 12 of the RRA requires that patriotic religious associations vet all religious leaders and religious doctrine. The regulations do not define many key terms, including "normal religious activities," "religious beliefs," "foreign domination," "extremism," and "endangering public security," thus leaving it to the government to provide definitions that suit its purposes on a case-by-case basis.

A year after the promulgation of the RRA, reports indicated that religion policy was still being arbitrarily enforced.[33] Eric Carson (2005, 748) argues that regulations imposed by the RRA "represent continuing strong state supervision of religion, do not protect unsanctioned groups, provide punitive and possibly arbitrary penalties for noncompliance, leave interpretation of important yet vague provisions to bureaucratic discretion, and leave unanswered hosts of questions regarding other religious regulations and implementation issues." On the other hand, Tong (2010, 871) describes the relaxation of control over religious communities and new restrictions on government intervention in religious affairs to be part of a larger process of systemic reforms aimed at achieving limited government. He attributes these reforms to "the demise of Communist ideology, the circumscription of bureaucratic authority, and a move toward less-regulatory government." These changes can also be seen as reflecting movement from a rule-by-law society to a rule-of-law society, as China sets up procedures for religious groups and individuals to appeal administrative decisions, a right not previously granted to citizens.[34] It also set punishments for SARA officials who abuse power or commit crimes in the course of their jobs. However, implementing regulations that were to be devised after adoption of the RRA have yet to be issued.

## Repression of Religious Minorities

Tight controls over the religious sector have not deterred growth in rates of religious adherence. According to data reported by the Pew Research Center, approximately 18 to 30 percent of adult Chinese are religious.[35] Aggregating results from a number of surveys and government sources, they report that Buddhists are the largest religious group, about 11 to 16 percent of the adult population, followed by Christians, who are about 4 percent of the population (although that number may be low because it represents only those individuals affiliated with state-approved religious groups).[36] Protestants outnumber Catholics. Muslims represent about 1 to 1.5 percent of the adult population, and Daoists make up less than 1 percent of the population. If the larger figure of religious adherents is accurate, it translates to approximately 300 million religious adherents. In 2011, the CCP claimed its membership exceeded 80 million.[37] These numbers alone suggest reason for the CCP to fear religious group membership.

China's Roman Catholics have experienced decades of repression revolving primarily around their ability to self-govern. In 1951, the state introduced the Catholic Three-Self Movement to remove the Vatican's influence and in 1957 created the Chinese Catholic Patriotic Association to control the Catholic population. The association recognized the pope's spiritual authority over Chinese Catholics, but it did not give him the right to interfere in the Chinese church, for example, by appointing bishops. After Sino-Vatican negotiations (1987–1999) broke down, a fight began over appointment and consecration of Chinese bishops in January 2000 and the canonization of Chinese saints in October 2001. The Vatican refused to allow the Chinese practice of appointing its own government-sponsored candidates for bishops, only to be approved by the Vatican. In defiance of this policy, on January 6, 2000, China unilaterally appointed five bishops. The fight worsened when on October 1, 2001, the Vatican canonized 102 saints who were martyred in China during the Boxer Rebellion in the nineteenth century.

The underground Catholic Church operates alongside the official Catholic Patriotic Association and has been targeted by the Chinese government with repression. The movement objects to the government's control over clerical appointments and other issues it believes are under the authority of the Vatican. As noted earlier, the Chinese government is highly suspicious of foreign-based movements and has consistently employed regulations prohibiting foreign influence or involvement in domestic religious activities. Human Rights Watch reported on a number of incidents of government repression of underground Catholics in 1996. They share a carefully orchestrated plan of government infiltration and decimation of underground Catholic groups. One example is drawn from a letter sent to the government in June 1996 by Bishop Su Zhimin, the underground Catholic bishop of Baoding diocese in northern Hebei province. In the letter, the bishop details how task forces from the local government used economic sanctions to persuade underground Catholics to renounce their allegiance to the church, affecting almost 4,000 individuals. These sanctions included suspension of retirement benefits, loss of work permits, expulsion from school, dismissal of teachers, and confinement of residents to their villages. People were also required to sign a pledge renouncing their allegiance to the underground church and promising to abide by state religion policy. The authorities also tore down and sealed churches and prayer houses. According to the bishop, in some villages, those who refused to sign the pledge were tortured (Spiegel 1997). According to another source, as of March 2007, 5 bishops and 14 priests from the underground church were in prison, 8 bishops were under house arrest or surveillance, and 2 were in hiding.[38]

The terms "underground church" and "house church" refer to unregistered religious organizations that are subject to state surveillance and monitoring. Their treatment varies from region to region; in some regions, they operate publicly, and in others, they are subject to frequent official crackdowns. Most church growth in recent decades has taken place in rural areas among highly marginalized ethnic minorities (Lee 2007). According to Lauren B. Homer (2010), house churches are not regarded as a political threat to the integrity of the state, as members are recognized as patriotic and loyal to China and have no desire for political autonomy, which is not the case for other religious groups, such as Tibetan Buddhists or Xinjiang Uighur Muslims. Moreover, followers of house churches are found at the highest levels of Chinese society, including CCP members. However, Richard Madsen (2010, 62) argues that while many house churches are innocuous, there are reasons for the CCP to be suspicious, as "a disproportionate number of those 'rights lawyers' and other activists (including imprisoned dissident Liu Xiaobo) who have been pushing for political reforms are also Christians associated with urban house churches." Although the 2005 regulations were intended to implement the rule of law in religion-state relations and contribute to an atmosphere of harmony as opposed to hostility, bureaucratic hurdles remain, and as of 2010, procedures did not exist to make it possible for house churches to be legally recognized outside the framework of the patriotic religious associations. Moreover, registering the large number of house churches estimated to exist in China would prove to be an enormous administrative feat, given the current bureaucratic procedures and apparatus that exist.

A number of new religious movements have arisen in China, incorporating Christian beliefs with Pentecostal practices and native myths and folklore. They attract mostly semiliterate rural dwellers. They are often treated as evil cults by the government and subjected to harsh repression. According to Chinese intellectuals, a "heretical religion" or "evil cult" (*xiejiao*) differs from the Western conception of a cult, which is often defined as a deviant religious organization that has unconventional or untraditional beliefs. The Chinese characterize evil cults as movements characterized by worship of a cult master, secret association, and harm to society. They are understood as "a kind of false religious organization that has serious criminal characteristics" (Zhu 2010, 478).

The religious movement that epitomizes what China considers to be an evil cult is Falun Gong (also called Falun Dafa, "the Practice of the Wheel of Dharma"), which was founded in 1992 by Li Hongzhi. It was originally registered in 1993 as a group of qigong, which is an ancient Chinese deep-breathing exercise system, sometimes combined with meditation, that is claimed to enhance the flow of vital energy through a person's body and promote physical, mental, and spiritual well-being. However, it withdrew from the China Qigong Scientific Research Association in 1996. Membership figures are disputed, but according to Falun Gong, it had more than 70 million followers in China in 1999. The Chinese government estimated 40 million followers at the end of 1998, down to 2 million by 2001 (Spiegel 2002). Practitioners come from all levels of education, occupation, location, and income level. Before the government crackdown, the group also claimed members from the CCP and the People's Liberation Army.

Falun Gong is a spiritual movement that involves ritual exercise performed for the purpose of obtaining mental and spiritual renewal. Its teachings draw from Buddhism, Daoism, Confucianism, and Chinese folklore, as well as Western New Age movements. Beliefs focus on moral behavior and offer members a road to salvation through practice of a righteous way. There are also apocalyptic ideas incorporated into the movement. The exercises are five easy movements that can be performed in a variety of settings. Besides engaging in the physical and spiritual aspects of Falun Gong, members can also become involved in the social aspects of the organization, recruiting members, producing and distributing literature, or joining in protests. While some claim that Falun Gong is not a religious movement, China treats it as such by labeling it an evil cult.

The movement claims to have no organization or hierarchy and no political motives, despite its well-organized and coordinated protests. On April 25, 1999, more than 10,000 followers of Falun Gong gathered in front of the compound in Beijing that houses China's leaders to peacefully protest criticisms of the movement and to demand recognition of Falun Gong as a religion. They arrived in groups and formed orderly columns around two sides of the compound. They were silent, neither holding up banners nor shouting slogans. The size, discipline, and organization of the movement scared the Chinese authorities, who feared it could become a threat to the regime. The government responded in various ways. In June 1999, a Politburo resolution established the Central Leading Group on Dealing with the Falun Gong. On July 22, 1999, the Ministry of Civil Affairs under the State Council issued a decision defining the Institute of the Falun Dafa and the Falun Gong organizations as "illegal organizations" and prohibited all activities organized by Falun Gong, including publications, websites, and thousands of practice sites where members assembled for morning breathing exercises. In August 1999, the General Office of the State Council expanded the ban to include other qigong groups and activities. In October 1999, the 12th Session of the National People's Congress Standing Committee (NPCSC) adopted the Resolution on Banning Heretic Cult Organizations, Preventing and Punishing Evil Cult Activities. This outlawed Falun Gong and other cult organizations and instructed government institutions and agencies to carry out punishments, which included reeducation.[39] In November 1999, the Ministry of Public Security issued regulations banning large public gatherings held near government agencies and other institutions that could threaten national security or otherwise endanger the health and stability of society. In December 2001, the government imposed a ban on using the Internet to organize or coordinate the activities of evil cults (Edelman and Richardson 2003).

The movement's response was defiance. Between 1997 and July 22, 1999, the movement held more than 300 rallies in China, including 18 large and medium-size assemblies (Tong 2002). Over the next several months, thousands protested around Beijing and in Tiananmen Square. They received international attention when police were seen dragging off by their hair peaceful middle-age women who had been meditating in the square.[40] The movement also lobbied Western governments for support and publicized the results of the crackdown in the international media. By late 1999, the authorities had detained more than 20,000 Falun Gong members (Tong 2002, 815). The government's response to those accused of being members varied depending on their category: ordinary practitioners, leading members, and "backbone elements." Ordinary practitioners willing to give up their beliefs were treated as victims and released. Leading members who repented (often in reeducation camps) and provided intelligence to the government were also treated leniently. Although exact numbers of prosecutions are difficult to obtain, most of them appeared to be for organizing assemblies, for involvement in large-scale printing and publication of Falun Gong materials to be distributed in China, or for publicizing abuses overseas (Spiegel 2002). Falun Gong sources document numerous incidents of torture, forced labor, psychiatric incarceration, and death of members in China.[41] The movement's popularity began to decrease after a January 2001 incident in which several practitioners— including a teenage girl—self-immolated in Tiananmen Square. Two people died, including the teen. The Falun Gong denied its involvement in the incident, but Chinese authorities used the events to turn public sentiment against the movement and its leader, Li Hongzhi. According to the Chinese Embassy in the United States, "Facts have demonstrated that Li Hongzhi, the founder of Falun Gong, is in fact an evil figure who, by deceiving, has been seriously disrupting social order and sabotaging the hard-earned social stability of China."[42] By September 2001, the movement had been forced underground.

Why attack Falun Gong and target it as a group to be eradicated? According to Human Rights Watch, when the group was most active in demonstrations, China's leaders were concerned with national stability and feared that economically disaffected Chinese would join the group and threaten the government's power. Since the group itself was already large and had proven to be highly organized (through the April 1999 protests and communication networks), they had the potential to grow large enough to challenge the regime's security apparatus. As a native movement, the group also threatened the claim to ideological supremacy that the Communist Party has in China.

Much of the previous discussion has centered on how the Chinese government represses religion, but despite its official endorsement of atheism, the government does allow religious groups to exist and people to practice individually and in groups. As described earlier, religious practice must occur under the supervision of one of the state patriotic associations, which allows the government to keep close track of religious groups and their activities. The government has also attempted to encourage those types of religious activities that are likely to bring the state economic benefits. For example, religious communities can generate income by operating tourist sites. The Buddhist Shaolin Temple in Henan province generates several million dollars of revenue from tourist admissions, of which it can keep about 25 percent (the rest goes to local and provincial governments). Because the temple brings in so much money and has invested in renovating the surrounding areas, it has received favors in return, such as the removal of villages and shops (resulting in moving more than 20,000 people) to allow for the renovations. The abbot of the temple, Shi Yongxin, has also benefited from the temple's resources; he has been appointed a vice chairman of the Patriotic Buddhist Association and a member of the Henan provincial delegation to the National People's Congress, and he receives a government salary. Yet such cooperation between religious groups and the state can be problematic for other religious groups, as state-sanctioned individuals may work to prevent registration of new groups or support government repression of rival groups.[43]

Like Iran and Saudi Arabia, China targets repressive policies at all independent civil society, including religious groups. Unlike those two countries, the Chinese regime's motivations for repressing religious groups in particular are based on an antireligious ideology. Like other communist regimes in this category (North Korea, Cuba, and Vietnam), the Chinese regime bases itself on ideals that advocate the eventual demise of religion altogether. Yet because the regime recognizes that eliminating religion completely is a long-term goal, it copes with its continuing presence by imposing state control over all religious institutions. Groups that attempt to function independently of the state apparatus are subjected to harsh repression and banned from the country. The regime is especially threatened by groups that have organizations based in foreign countries, such as the Roman Catholic Church, and the actions the state has taken against the Vatican's attempts to govern Catholics in China demonstrate the state's fear of independent religious activity.

## Azerbaijan

Azerbaijan is a post-Soviet republic in the South Caucasus region. Its structure of state regulation of religion is a good example of religious group repression due to general antireligious sentiments. Unlike China, which admits to following an antireligious ideology, Azerbaijan claims to be a secular state that keeps religion and politics separate. However, its view of secularism sees the state as something that must be protected from religion, and the Azerbaijani government attempts to control religious practice to keep it from becoming an independent social force that might threaten the nondemocratic nature of the regime.

Russia colonized the South Caucasus in the early nineteenth century, co-opting Islamic clergy to help control the Muslim population. During the Soviet period, as in other areas, state-enforced atheism severely weakened religious institutions, leaving only cultural practices related to religion intact. A majority-Muslim country (65 percent Shia and 35 percent Sunni), Azerbaijan has small populations of Russian Orthodox, Armenian Apostolics, other Christians, Jews, and nonbelievers (US Department of State 2012). Despite its division between Sunni and Shia Islam—a split that goes back to the sixteenth century—the Muslim population does not emphasize sectarian divisions, although advances in Islamic education in the post-Soviet period have increased knowledge of and identification with sectarian divisions among Azeri youth (Cornell 2006).

Azerbaijan declared its independence from the USSR on August 30, 1991. Ayaz Mutabilov, first secretary of the Azerbaijani Communist Party, became its first president. Elections in June 1992 brought Abulfaz Elchibey of the Azerbaijan Popular Front Party to power as the second president of the country. An armed insurrection deposed Elchibey from power in June 1993, and the National Council conferred presidential powers on Heydar Aliyev, who had been active in Soviet Azerbaijan as first secretary of the Communist Party (1969–1981) and in Soviet politics as a member of the Politburo and the KGB and as USSR deputy prime minister until 1987. After Heydar Aliyev's initial election in 1993, Azerbaijan held three parliamentary elections (1995, 2000, and 2005), three presidential elections (1998, 2003, and 2008), and three referendums (1995, 2002, and 2009).

The country is characterized by a strong presidency, with the parliament dominated by the ruling party, Yeni Azerbaijan (YAP), and the judiciary under the control of the executive. Media freedom is reported to be nonexistent, and journalists are subject to harassment, fabricated charges, and violence from state authorities.[44] Vote fraud, preelection and postelection police violence, and intimidation of opposition supporters and others characterized both the 2003 presidential and 2005 parliamentary elections. Human Rights Watch documented preelection fraud and postelection violence—including beatings and torture of opposition activists—in the 2003 presidential elections that it described as engineered to ensure victory for ailing President Heydar Aliyev's son, Ilham.[45] President Ilham Aliyev was reelected in October 2008 in a flawed election; he subsequently initiated a referendum in February 2009 to amend the constitution and lift the two-term limit on the presidency. Among the tactics used to prevent opposition parties and candidates from gaining strength has been police blocking access to opposition rallies to limit attendance and reducing hours or revoking employment for supporters of opposition parties. With regard to the presidential elections of 2008 and the 2009 referendum, Erik S. Herron (2011, 1579) concludes, "Azerbaijan likely represents a case of uncoordinated interference by officials, in which orders are not explicitly provided through a chain of command but more subtle signals are used to impel officials to deliver the vote adequately." Many political scientists characterize Azerbaijan as an electoral authoritarian regime.

The Constitution of the Republic of Azerbaijan was passed in 1994 and amended in 2002 and 2009.[46] Article 7 declares that the state is a "democratic, legal, secular, unitary republic." Article 18 elaborates that religion is separate from state in the country, that all religions are equal before the law, that the state educational system is secular, and that "spreading and propaganda of religion (religious movements), humiliating people's dignity and contradicting the principles of humanism are prohibited." Article 47 prohibits "propaganda provoking racial, national, religious and social discord and animosity." Article 48 protects freedom of conscience, including the right to possess or not possess religious beliefs, to express them individually or in concert with others, to be free from forced expression of religion, and to spread their beliefs. People are given the right to carry out religious rituals as long as they do not "violate public order and contradict public morals." Article 56 reserves the right to restrict participation in elections by certain kinds of individuals, including military personnel, judges, state employees, and religious officials.

The Law on Freedom of Religious Belief was amended 14 times between 1992 and 2011, with tighter restrictions imposed in each iteration of the law. Changes to the administrative and criminal codes accompanied these revisions, imposing increasingly large fines as well as imprisonment for violation of statutes related to religious exercise. These changes were often prepared in secret and rushed through a parliament dominated by the president's party. They signal an increasing attempt to create legal means to restrict and punish free religious exercise.

The State Committee for Work with Religious Organizations (SCWRO) was created in 2001 and is part of the executive branch. The SCWRO has authority over all religious groups in the country and oversees their registration with the government. The committee has authority over religious publications, including their importation, printing, and distribution. Changes that came into force in May 2009 required all registered religious organizations to reregister with the SCWRO by January 1, 2010, the third time such reregistration was enacted. Other provisions included a ban on refusing to fulfill legal obligations based on religious beliefs; licensing requirements for religious educational institutions; prohibitions against producing, importing, circulating, or selling religious literature without permission from the SCWRO; and conducting religious activities elsewhere than the address where a religious community is registered or conducting activities not specifically listed in the registered community's statute. They also raised fines for offenses from previous levels.[47]

Azerbaijan is known to be a highly corrupt society.[48] Similarly, how religious groups are treated depends greatly on how senior state officials decide to enforce unwritten controls on religion. From the initial registration of religious groups to their daily activities, building practices, and publications, groups that do not have links to senior figures in authority are subject to harassment and threats from police and national security officers.[49] While sometimes these groups and individuals are imprisoned or fined, often they face threats such as job dismissal for failure to comply with the wishes of local authorities. Officials also enforce laws that do not exist. For example, police and local authorities often raided religious communities that chose not to register with state authorities, even though such activities were not illegal according to the law prior to 2009. Local authorities must approve registration applications before they are sent to the SCWRO, allowing these authorities to exercise initial review over unwelcome applications. The SCWRO also deals with registration applications from groups it does not like by pressuring religious groups to withdraw them, ignoring applications, or finding fault with applications, which it returns for frequent corrections or rejects.

## Repression of the Religious Majority

Despite problems regarding registration faced by non-Muslim groups, Muslims actually face the greatest state intrusion into their religious affairs. The government targets groups that are independent and/or considered extremist. All Muslim communities must be part of the state-sanctioned Caucasian Muslim Board (CMB), which has been led by Sheikh-ul-Islam and Grand Mufti Allahshukur Pashazade since 1980.[50] He was declared head of the board for life in 2003. Muslim groups are not allowed to register as entities independent of the CMB. State authorities have had imams they do not like removed, and the SCWRO has gone to great lengths to ensure that regime-friendly imams fill the country's mosques, including issuing a book in 2007 that recommended to imams the topics they should cover in Friday sermons.[51] Since 2009, the CMB is in charge of appointments for all prayer leaders in mosques and restricts the job to citizens of Azerbaijan who have been educated in Azerbaijan. However, original drafts of these amendments required imams to be approved jointly by the CMB and the SCWRO, thus giving control over clerical appointments directly to the state. Faced with protests from the CMB, the wording was changed to give it appointment power, after which it would then notify the SCWRO.[52] Amendments to the Religion Law in

July 2011 instituted a new requirement for Islamic communities to pre-pare reports on their activities to submit to the CMB.

In July 2011, the number of adults needed for registration of a group was raised from 10 to 50. There is no independent appeals process out-lined in the case of official denial of registration, nor is there a time limit given in which officials must decide on registration cases. The European Commission for Democracy through Law (Venice Commission) and the OSCE/ODHIR performed an independent assessment of the Religion Law after the July 2011 amendments were passed.[53] They found the law to contain several restrictions that violated international standards, includ-ing provisions related to the registration, autonomy, and liquidation of religious communities; conscientious objection; proselytism; and the pub-lication and circulation of religious materials. Specifically, the report said that a state could not require religious individuals or groups to become part of a specific religious authority or organization, which the law does by requiring Islamic groups to report to and be subordinated under the CMB.

Mosque closures, like the one described at the opening of this chapter, help to illustrate how Azerbaijani authorities repress Muslim religious practice. The mosque described previously belonged to a Sunni con-gregation (and hence a religious minority), but the state has also taken action against Shiite congregations. For example, on June 30, 2004, police seized the Juma Mosque in Baku's Old City, beating those in atten-dance and damaging property inside. The Shia religious community occupying the thousand-year-old mosque had registered with the Justice Ministry in 1992, but its attempt to reregister in 2001 was denied by the SCWRO because the community refused to subjugate itself to the CMB, a requirement for all Islamic groups.[54] Several community members were detained, but most were released after paying fines.[55] Authorities reput-edly wanted to use the mosque as a carpet museum, as it was during the Soviet period, but the mosque was later given to the CMB, which imposed its own imam, Sukhai Mamedov. Head of the SCWRO Rafik Aliyev claimed that the community was occupying the mosque illegally and that it belonged to the Ministry of Culture as a historical monument.[56] During the same interview, Aliyev claimed that the mosque was pursuing "politi-cal aims" and conducting antigovernment activity, as well as operating without approval from the CMB.[57]

The seizure of the mosque happened to occur after its leaders had openly supported the opposition "Our Azerbaijan" bloc and its candi-date Isa Gambar, head of the Musavat Party, in 2003 elections. Later, community members praying in a private home were detained and had their names recorded by the acting chief of police, despite laws that do not forbid such activities. The official responsible for breaking up the prayer service had various justifications for his actions, including that there were mosques that the community could use, that the home was not a suitable location for religious services because it did not have running water, and that Muslim law required believers to pray in a mosque.[58] The official also claimed that it was his duty to protect the state from the antigovernment ideas and activities of the community's leader. In August 2004, the Supreme Court of Azerbaijan rejected the community's appeal against the eviction order.

The Juma Mosque's problems stem from the government's actions against its leader, Imam Ilgar Ibrahimoglu Allahverdiev. Ibrahimoglu ran the Islam-Ittihad society, known for its charitable work and conferences to promote religious tolerance. The society was stripped of its official registration with the Justice Ministry in 2004. The Justice Ministry also refused to register the Azerbaijani chapter of the International Religious Liberty Association (of which he was secretary-general) and the Devamm religious freedom organization (of which he was the leading coordinator). After being held for several months in detention, in April 2004 Ibrahimoglu was given a five-year suspended sentence for participating in protests against the conduct of presidential elections in 2003. He was tried with eight opposition activists in Baku's "Court for Especially Serious Crimes" and found guilty of participating in mass disorder and resisting the authorities. Ibrahimoglu claimed that he was not participating in the postelection violence, but rather monitoring the elections, and believed that the investigation and charges against him were politically motivated because of his religious and human rights work.[59]

Ilgar Ibrahimoglu is described as a "study in contrasts."[60] He is known by some for his defense of the religious freedom of both Christians and Muslims. The government considers him to be an extremist cleric. Having received his religious education in Iran and human rights advocacy training in Poland, he is seen as a "friend" to human rights advocates but a "dangerous fundamentalist" to the Azerbaijani government. Ibrahimoglu established his reputation as a religious leader by introducing innovations at the Juma Mosque (for which he was appointed imam in 2002), such as abolishing fees for funeral rights. He also was responsible for refusing to register the mosque under the authority of the CMB. Thus, he is perceived as a competitor to the religious establishment, which desires to maintain control over how mosques function in Azerbaijan.

Adherence to Islam has grown in the postindependence period in Azerbaijan, although not at the alarming rates the government uses to justify its repression. The number of mosques grew (595 mosques were constructed or restored between 1989 and 2011), but only about 20 percent of the population could be considered practicing Muslims in 2010, according to data from the SCWRO and public opinion surveys (Yunusov 2012, 22–23). Svante Cornell (2006, 25) attributes the rise in Islamic sentiments in the country to the following factors: "obtaining religious freedom, being able to go to the mosque without fear, and wanting to return to traditional values and roots." Arif Yunusov, an Azerbaijani expert on religion, argues that mosques and Islamism gained legitimacy due to the failures of the secular opposition and the co-opted official Muslim establishment—the CMB—and its leader. Official Islam is closely associated with the ruling regime. Mufti Pashadaze is often quoted making proregime statements, and photos of deceased leader Heydar Aliyev are prominent in mosques. Moreover, the conference hall of the Sheikh-ul-Islam's residence—the Teze Pir Mosque—displays a state banner of Azerbaijan and the ruling Yeni Azerbaijani party. With secular opposition groups unable to challenge the Aliyevs and greater restrictions on free association and expression in the country, "Mosques began functioning as sort of political clubs in the circumstances of de facto ongoing prohibition of rallies and any assemblies of citizens for political and any other reasons. Many of the ordinary adherents of the secular opposition disappointed in western values abandoned and joined or supported Islamists" (Yunusov 2012, 18).

## Repression of Religious Minorities

The Law on Freedom of Religious Belief (described earlier) is also used to repress religious minorities. As of the end of 2008, groups that were denied registration included independent mosques, a number of Baptist communities, Adventists, and a variety of other Protestant churches. Protestant churches that attract ethnic Azeris are under the most suspicion.[61] Because the law does not allow religious objections to fulfilling legal obligations, conscientious objectors to military service, including Jehovah's Witnesses, are imprisoned.

Religious nongovernmental organizations (NGOs) are another target of repression in Azerbaijan. These groups are affiliated with religious organizations but serve nonreligious functions, such as providing charity or advocating for human rights. Groups such as international humanitarian organizations that are founded by religious groups are not allowed to conduct religious activity as part of their work. The Justice Ministry has denied registration to a number of religious NGOs over the past two decades, including the Azerbaijan Center for Religion and Democracy, which analysts believe is targeted because it criticizes official religious structures—such as the CMB—in the country, not because of administrative inconsistencies, as Justice Ministry officials claim.[62]

Like the other postcommunist republics in this category—Kazakhstan, Tajikistan, Turkmenistan, and Uzbekistan—independent Azerbaijan adopted a secular constitution and proclaimed religious freedom after leaving the USSR's atheist federation. Yet in each of these countries, communist-era elites claimed political power, and many of them continue to rule the independent republics to this day. These elites appear to have retained the antireligious ideology they embraced as members of the Communist Party during the Soviet era and continue to rule in a manner that betrays their mistrust of religion as an independent part of civil society. In a manner similar to China, Azerbaijan and other postcommunist republics attempt to control religious institutions and practice to prevent religious groups from challenging the state's legitimacy or organizing opposition to it. As electoral authoritarian regimes, these states hold seriously flawed elections with unsurprising outcomes and manipulate laws to prevent government turnover. They are able to guarantee such outcomes by imposing policies that constrain independent activity. Recognizing that unmonitored nonpolitical organizations hold the potential to become politicized, they target religious activity and expression alongside other forms of civic organization. The states justify repression with charges of extremism. In many instances, what these states interpret as extremism would be characterized as opposition in more politically competitive settings.

## Conclusion

This chapter has examined four states with different political, economic, social, and religious backgrounds. Yet all four states are similar in their repression of all religions. This first set of case studies illustrates what religious repression means. In all of the countries in this category, religious repression takes the form of state control over religious institutions, restriction of religious practice, and discrimination against religious groups. While we often expect repression of minorities and dissenting groups in nondemocratic states, we also expect majorities to be protected or co-opted as regime supporters. Yet in some nondemocratic states, even religious majorities cannot escape state repression. The form that repression takes is control over religion. When states such as Iran and Saudi Arabia mandate that all laws should have a basis in religious doctrine, even if that religion belongs to a majority of the state's adherents, it constitutes religious repression because such a situation places the state in control over the institutions that interpret and enforce religious doctrine, making it impossible for the majority religion to govern itself. Moreover, when states enforce a particular interpretation of religious law, citizens are forced to abide by it by virtue of their religious background or group identity rather than their own conscience. Finally, when states retain the ability to hire and train clerical staff, manage building construction, and even approve sermons, they hinder the ability of groups to function as independent social actors. Religion becomes a tool of the state, ready to be wielded to advance its interests.

The cases in this chapter demonstrate that it is possible for high levels of religious repression to occur at various levels of political competition. That is, they show that even countries that hold elections engage in religious repression aimed at all religious groups. Although Saudi Arabia and China do not elect their executives and legislatures, Iran and Azerbaijan do. This difference in political institutions means that most analysts describe Saudi Arabia and China as "full" or "closed" authoritarian regimes and Iran and Azerbaijan as "competitive" or "electoral" authoritarian regimes. Yet as we have seen in this chapter, the presence or absence of elections does not change how any of these countries views civil society. Political ideologies and historical legacies converge in these cases to create states that seek to completely eliminate all forms of societal and political pluralism. Therefore, these cases point to the treatment of civil society as an important variable in understanding the varieties of nondemocratic rule in the contemporary world.

## 4

# *Repressing Most by Favoring One*

IN 1844, KARL Marx famously declared that religion was the "opium of the people," lulling workers into accepting their temporal fate in exchange for otherworldly rewards and preventing the emancipation of man on earth (Marx [1844] 1978). Inspired by Marx's prognostications of communist revolution, the Bolsheviks, led by Vladimir Lenin, seized power in Russia in 1917 and embarked on a grand initiative to remake society. This included changes to many of Russia's traditional institutions, including the churches. The party nationalized church property, separated the church from the state (by giving only civil marriage legal standing, for example), ended state financial support for religion, and took away education from the church. Priests accused of supporting enemies of the state were executed, and many more were sent to prison camps in Siberia. The League of Militant Atheists was created in 1925 to advance antireligious attitudes, and an aggressive state atheist campaign attacked religion on all fronts.

Upon taking power in the USSR in the mid-1920s, Joseph Stalin increased attacks on religion. A 1929 law forbade religious activities or instruction beyond basic religious services conducted in state-sanctioned religious buildings. Between 1929 and 1939, the government purged almost all religious temples, clergy, and active believers in the country. Stalin continued the repression until the Second World War, when he found himself facing a shortage of soldiers to replace the hundreds of thousands dying on multiple fronts. He sought the help of religious organizations in raising support for the war effort and, in exchange, relaxed restrictions on religion. Once the war was over, Nikita Khrushchev once again tightened the reins on religion, closing and destroying the majority of churches reopened between 1941 and 1957 and arresting and deporting large numbers of clergy and laity. For example, his policies resulted in a reduction in functioning Orthodox churches from more than 20,000 prior to 1960 down to 6,850 by 1972. At the same time, the number of Orthodox priests officially permitted to perform their duties declined from more than 30,000 to 6,180 (Pospielovsky 1988, 135).

Restrictions were again relaxed under Mikhail Gorbachev's policies of transparency and restructuring (*glasnost* and *perestroika*) during the late 1980s. Greater political openness led eventually to the dissolution of the USSR in 1991. Religious movements are given some of the credit for help-ing to organize the mass movements that called for the end of commu-nism. With the end of the atheistic ideology of communism came calls for greater religious freedom under the cover of democracy. Religious open-ings led to the rapid growth of religious believers, with some returning to traditional religions while others joined new religious movements being spread by foreign missionaries. In many cases, this newfound freedom was short-lived, as post-Soviet leaders imposed new restrictions intended to control the religious arena (Sarkissian 2009). Ironically, many of these new restrictions bore striking similarities to Soviet-era regulations.

This chapter examines a set of 14 countries—half of which were part of the Soviet Union or the communist bloc—that repress all religious groups but one. Other countries in this category do not have a communist past but share a legacy of a close association between national identity and a dominant religious group that has historically enjoyed favored status. The chapter presents paired case studies to explain two models of religion-state relations that are found in countries that repress all religious groups but one. First, Russia and Georgia are postcommunist countries in which the government closely allies with a single religious group—the titular Orthodox Church—granting favors to it while imposing restrictions on religious minorities. Other postcommunist countries in this category, including Armenia, Belarus, Moldova, Romania, and Serbia, follow a similar model. Second, Indonesia and Turkey are countries with founding ideologies that are secular but also tied to the idea of a traditional religion forming the basis of national identity. Contemporary religion-state rela-tions in these countries display an acknowledgment of the need to address the demands of the majority religious group in the country. The remain-ing countries in this category—Bangladesh, Laos, Malaysia, Pakistan, and Sri Lanka—follow a similar model of religion-state relations.

Unlike countries that repress all religions, those in this category do not impose restrictions on, or attempt to control, the majority religion. Instead, the majority religion functions mostly independently (with some exceptions in Turkey, which will be discussed in detail later). The majority religion does benefit from government favoritism that is not offered to other religious groups, however. These religious groups have special arrangements with the state giving them autonomy over their own affairs; receive state funding for religious construction, education, and other efforts; have special access to state institutions such as the military; and are exempted from regulations imposed on minority religious groups (table 4.1). These are often offered in exchange for political support of the regime or ruling government and to give the state increased legitimacy.

The countries that repress all but one religion tend to have greater levels of political competition and more religiously divided societies than those that repress all religious groups. The average Polity regime score for countries in this category in 2010 was 4 (on a scale of –10 to 10), compared with an average score of –6 for countries repressing all religions, indicating greater levels of political competition in the present cases. Moreover, most of the states in this category hold elections for executive and legislative positions. This means that these states usually do not possess the capacity or political will to impose harsh repression on all groups, as they need to assemble electoral coalitions to deliver success during periodic and regular elections. The countries in this chapter also tend to have

Table 4.1 **Religious restrictions in countries repressing all but one religion (2010)**

|  | Russia | Georgia | Indonesia | Turkey |
|---|---|---|---|---|
| Religious observance | x | x | x | x |
| Places of worship | x | x | x | x |
| Religious laws | x | x | x | x |
| Conversion |  |  |  |  |
| Proselytizing | x |  | x |  |
| Discriminatory registration/bans | x | x | x | x |
| Clerical appointments |  |  |  | x |
| Religious speech or publications | x |  | x | x |
| Religious education |  |  |  | x |
| Religious political parties |  |  |  | x |
| Religious associations | x |  | x | x |
| Political speech |  | x | x | x |
| Access to political office | x |  | x |  |

higher levels of religious division, with an average score of 4.7 (of a high of 13) on the Pew Research Center's Social Hostilities Index, compared with an average of 3.1 for countries discussed in chapter 3. These divisions reflect historical religion-state relations as well as more contemporary tensions between religious groups resulting from regime transitions and demographic changes.

## Postcommunist Religious Nationalism and Church-State Cooperation
### Russia

Russia is the largest and most populous of the postcommunist states that repress all religions but one. Like other countries in this category, Russia has also had problems in consolidating democracy. The immediate post-Soviet Russian regime has been described as an electoral democracy. However, Vladimir Putin, elected to the presidency in 2000, quickly consolidated power, and Freedom House dropped Russia from its list of electoral democracies in 2003.[1] State repression of religion is part of a larger pattern of state repression of civil society. Repression of nongovernmental organizations and the press has tended to focus on critics of the government. Restrictions on political competition also increased during the administrations of Vladimir Putin and Dmitri Medvedev. For example, a law passed in 2004 made registration of political parties more difficult, making the ruling party, United Russia, even more dominant in the country and weakening the political influence of opponents of the government.[2]

The largest religious group in Russia is the Russian Orthodox Church. About 74 percent of the population is nominally Orthodox, although fewer are thought to be observant. Muslims are the largest minority, approximately 7 percent of the population. The remainder of the population consists of smaller groups, including Buddhists, Catholics, Protestants, and Jews (US Department of State 2012). The Muslim and Buddhist populations are concentrated in specific regions of the country but are also found in large cities like Moscow.

State regulation of religion in Russia has grown increasingly repressive in the post-Soviet period. Before 1997, the legislation On Freedom of Conscience and Religious Organizations, adopted in 1990 by Mikhail Gorbachev, regulated religion. This law granted a great deal of freedom to religious groups to operate and enabled the rapid influx of foreign missionaries and the rise of new religious denominations into the country but threatened the Russian Orthodox Church (ROC), considered the traditional religion of Russia. This led the church to lobby then-President Boris Yeltsin and members of the Duma for legislation that would restrict the growth of new religious groups and grant a privileged position to the ROC. An attempt to revise the legislation in 1993 failed, but by 1995, the ROC was again putting pressure on the reelected Yeltsin and the Duma to accept revisions to the religion law. In 1997, a new law was adopted.[3]

The complicated 1997 Law on Freedom of Conscience and Religious Associations established the individual right to religious freedom but imposed several restrictions on religious groups. The preamble to the law identifies Christianity, Islam, Judaism, and Buddhism as inseparable from the country's history but recognizes the "special contribution" of the ROC to the country. This has given the ROC privileged status with relation to the government.

The law created three categories of recognition for religious associations, each with different legal status and privileges. All religious associations are prohibited from participating in elections, political parties, and movements and from providing aid to political groups. In addition to requiring registration of some religious associations, the 1997 law gives the government the authority to ban religious associations accused of engaging in extremist activity.

The law divides religious associations other than the ROC into groups (gruppy) and organizations (organizatsii). Religious groups have fewer legal rights than religious organizations. Groups are defined as operating without state registration and have the right to worship at premises provided by their own members and to teach existing followers. Groups do not have the right to request military deferment for clergy; create educational institutions or give extracurricular religious instruction to children in state schools; invite foreign citizens for professional purposes or be attached to a foreign religious organization; conduct religious rites in hospitals, prisons, and other institutions; or to produce, acquire, export, import, and distribute religious literature or other forms of media. For a religious group to register and obtain the legal status of an organization, it must prove either 15 years of existence in its locality or affiliation to a central religious organization of the same creed. A central religious organization is made up of at least three local religious organizations. The 15-years rule has sometimes been interpreted to mean 15 years from when the group informs authorities of its existence, not the number of years it has actually existed in a particular locality.[4] Religious associations that do not have legal status are unable to claim historical places of worship confiscated by the Soviets. Some associations choose to remain unregistered on principle or because they want to avoid potential contact with the state bureaucracy. In most cases, inconspicuous religions are able to function without problems as unregistered groups, especially if they have good relations with state institutions. Religions that have had problems include the International Union of Baptist Churches, which adheres to a principle of strict separation of religion and state, thus refusing to register more than 3,000 congregations in Russia.

Despite the federal religion law, the vast size of the Russian Federation and the interests of politicians result in variation in how it is applied. A report from 2003 indicated that religious freedom concerns were dealt with in an "ad hoc manner," with great variation in religious policy depending on the "political agendas and personal loyalties of persons in positions of power." According to the report, the nature of a group's beliefs mattered less than their activities, claiming, "Groups are far more likely to be targeted if they are dynamic and visible, whatever they believe. For the most part, these are evangelical Protestants, but they may also be Catholic or alternative Orthodox communities."[5]

Traditional religious groups—including the ROC and Muslims—have lobbied for stricter restrictions, however. In 2001, religious leaders presented to President Putin the Zhbankov-Ponkin bill that proposed amending the 1997 law to clarify which religions were traditional and to enumerate the privileges they held with the government. It proposed grouping religious associations based on the number of followers, their historical contribution to the country's development, and work "as a creative and unifying spiritual force of the Russian society for the maintenance of peace and stability in the Russian Federation."[6] Eventually, the ROC and the Central Spiritual Department of Muslims leaders dropped the idea of amending the law and suggested adopting a new one that outlined the privileges of traditional religious organizations, to include tax exemption, access to schools and social work, and free access to mass media.[7] Ultimately, neither version of the law was adopted.

The ROC has lobbied for greater restrictions against minority faiths in Russia, but its power to affect state religion policy rests primarily on its historical position as favored church and its role as a legitimating force for the regime. There is evidence of this influence in the speeches and actions of politicians. For example, after his election to the presidency in 2000, Vladimir Putin's statements and actions followed the spirit of the 1997 law, as he focused on distinguishing between those religions that were traditional or native to Russia and those that were foreign—and therefore threatening—to the country. His National Security Concept of 2000 warned of the negative consequences of foreign missionary activity, reflecting the views of some Russians that if people adopted religions based outside Russia, they would also adopt foreign values and allegiances. This led to visa denials and deportations of several religious workers from a variety of religions.[8] These and other actions (described later) demonstrate how the ROC is the favored religion in Russia.

Legislation that is not specific to the religious arena can also result in religious repression. For instance, a 2002 Law on Countering Extremist Activity has been used against media outlets, with reports of the media engaging in self-censorship to avoid targeted prosecution.[9] Yet this law can be used to target religious groups that are accused of inciting religious discord.[10] In 2006, the law was amended to remove the words "in connection with violence or calls for violence" from the definition of extremism, which originally read "incitement to racial, nationalistic, or religious enmity, and also social enmity, in connection with violence or calls for violence." The result is a vague definition of extremism that could be interpreted by the government as justification for prosecuting any faith that contradicts the teachings of the ROC as inciting religious hostility. The extremism law also allows any low-level court to declare literature extremist, which automatically adds it to the Federal List of Extremist Materials and bans it throughout the country. As of the end of 2010, 831 materials were on the list.[11] During a closed session in February 2003, the Supreme Court banned 15 organizations as terrorist, including al-Qaeda and the Taliban. However, it also included Hizb ut-Tahrir, whose status as a terrorist group is debated.

In 2009, the Ministry of Justice set up new expert and scientific advisory boards to judge whether religious groups and materials were extremist and should be prosecuted. The Expert Council for Conducting State Religious-Studies Expert Analysis was met with protests from some religious and human rights organizations, one of which called the council an "inquisition" aimed at all groups other than the ROC (which was the only group to support the council). The council was given powers to investigate the activity, doctrines, leadership decisions, literature, and worship of any religious association and recommend action to the Justice Ministry. The 24 appointees included those who were known to be opposed to certain religious groups, including Alexander Dvorkin, a well-known anticult activist.[12]

In 2006, the Duma passed the Law on Public Associations, commonly referred to as the NGO law.[13] It expanded the discretion of state officials to reject NGO registration, inspect NGOs, and require reporting by NGOs and for the Ministry of Justice to have greater oversight over projects and funding for foreign NGOs. This law allowed government authorities to target controversial, foreign, and oppositional organizations (Schaaf 2009). Medvedev's election as president in March 2008 raised hopes among reformers in Russia that he would remove restrictions on civic organizations instituted during Putin's presidency. These hopes were not met. Beginning in 2008, Prime Minister Putin, government leaders, and state-controlled and state-affiliated media began to question the motivations of foreign-funded NGOs, including accusing them of spying and recruiting terrorists. In 2008, Putin issued a decree reducing from 101 to 12 the number of foreign and international organizations allowed to give tax-free grants in Russia.

There are also ways to repress religion without passing legislation. One is the Soviet practice of the "telephone law," in which a state official phones the director of a state institution (such as a theater or college) and pressures him or her into canceling a lease to a religious minority community. Another method is denying or canceling visas of foreign religious workers. A third method is refusal of permission to build property or refusal to return historical property to religious communities. The state can also impose bureaucratic hurdles. After the Justice Ministry's Federal Regulation Service (FRS) was given greater monitoring powers in 2004, there were more complaints from religious communities about greater state scrutiny and bureaucracy.[14] In July 2008, the FRS was abolished and its powers transferred back to the Justice Ministry proper.

### State Favoritism of the Religious Majority

An example of state favoritism is the ROC's disproportionate share of state subsidies. An NGO devoted to human rights issues, the SOVA Center, reports that the ROC is the main recipient of federal-level subsidies, as well as subsidies at the regional level in most areas. Most subsidies are in the form of real estate.[15] Government authorities have financed the renovation of churches, most frequently those belonging to the ROC. There are also reports of government administrations forcing local businesses to donate money to religious organizations (the ROC). For example, the

SOVA Center reported that in April 2007, "several private Moscow-based internet blogs published letters urging local businessmen to 'make charitable donations to finance the adornment of the Cathedral of Christ the Savior' and then to send copies of the receipts to the district administration. Businesses that failed to pay before the deadline received overdue debt warnings."[16] There have also been reports of government-controlled companies financing the construction of ROC churches. For example, in October 2008, the oil company Rosneft gave 60 million rubles toward the construction of a ROC church in Kursk; the next month, Gorkovskii Railway donated 300 million rubles to renovate a ROC church and parish buildings in Nizhnii Novgorod.[17] The ROC has also been granted property that did not previously belong to it. For instance, in 2010, authorities in Kaliningrad (formerly Germany's East Prussia) gave the ROC at least 16 properties that had been former Lutheran and Catholic churches and cultural and educational institutions that had not belonged to the ROC. Asked by a reporter why it was right that property confiscated during the Soviet period from Catholics and Lutherans was given to the Orthodox, the spokesperson for the Kaliningrad government responded, "You're not Russian, you won't understand."[18]

The ROC's favored status is institutionalized into law. As of 2003, the ROC had negotiated concordat-style agreements with various state institutions that gave the church special access and emphasized Orthodoxy as part of Russian state tradition. These agreements were negotiated in the areas of prisons and police, the armed services, education, health, transport, and foreign affairs.[19] In prisons, the ROC joined an agreement with the Ministry of Internal Affairs to allow clergy to conduct religious talks and church services, and the ROC has also worked with the Federal Security Service (FSB) to build churches next to regional headquarters. The ROC has urged commanders of the armed forces to invite clergy to participate in rituals and celebrations. The ROC has also cooperated with the Education Ministry to teach courses on Orthodox culture and build churches attached to educational institutions. With the Ministry of Railways, the ROC embarked on a joint project to build chapels at each of Moscow's mainline stations and at airports. The projects were all designed to consolidate the position of the ROC as the dominant religious organization of the country and to repel advances made by other religious groups in social life. Thus, the SOVA Center has concluded that the "obvious protection enjoyed by the ROC leads to indirect pressure against any people perceived (or potentially perceived) as the ROC's opponents, not limited to religious minorities."[20] The ROC also has the opportunity to review draft legislation pending before the Duma.[21]

The ROC's favored status is also transmitted through symbolic acts of political theater. For instance, President Putin is often accompanied at political events by hierarchs from the Orthodox Church, and priests are seen sanctifying banks, offices, and even military ships and airplanes. Putin is filmed attending services on religious holidays, and Orthodox services are shown on television. There are Orthodox chapels in public places such as train stations, airports, and police departments. Although Dmitri Medvedev was considered more pro-Orthodox than Putin, since Putin assumed his third term as president in 2012, he has been seen as closer to the ROC. For instance, Archimandrite Tikhon Shevkunov, who presides over the Sretensky Monastery in Moscow, has been described as "Putin's Spiritual Father," although he does not admit to or deny the label. He does admit, however, that Putin saved Russia from "vulgar liberals" who nearly destroyed it in the 1990s.[22] These actions also send signals to regional state officials that the central government allies itself with particular groups, often leading to variation in religious repression across Russia's regions.

The ROC is the main religious group spared from repression and showered with favors, but other traditional groups occasionally enjoy state benefits (although not at the level of the ROC). There are reports of the government allocating money to Islamic organizations, often for the purpose of counteracting support for Islamic groups from foreign governments such as Saudi Arabia and combating extremism. For example, the Presidential Administration reportedly allocated 400 million rubles to Muslim schools and universities in 2007. This sum was doubled in 2008.[23] In 2010, the Presidential Affairs Department issued an executive order giving VIP status to religious officials and delegations at airport border crossings in Moscow, St. Petersburg, and Sochi. In Kalmykia, a traditionally Buddhist republic in the south of Russia, state funds built the largest Buddhist temple in Europe, along with modern housing accommodations for monks. The state also provided assistance to build other temples in the republic, as well as funds for training monks. Yet instances of minority repression, even against groups that sometimes receive favorable treatment, continue.

### State Repression of Religious Minorities

According to the US State Department (2011), the government enforces existing religious regulations selectively, targeting for restrictions nontraditional groups such as the Church of Scientology, Jehovah's Witnesses, the Salvation Army, and several small Protestant denominations. In addition, in recent years, several Muslim groups have been targeted, including most recently Muslims who read the works of Turkish Sufi leader Said Nursi.[24]

Restrictions in Russia do not seem to be focused on religious individuals, but rather on religious associations. They have to do mostly with establishing and using buildings for religious purposes and tend to affect Muslims, Protestants (especially Pentecostals), and new religious movements. Usually, they take the form of arbitrary denial of land rights to construct places of worship. In some instances, government officials attempt to take away existing places of worship. For example, in 2006, local authorities in Tyumen (located in an oil-rich region in Siberia) destroyed a building intended to house a mosque. The building had been a mosque before the 1917 communist revolution, and the local Muslim community had been attempting to reclaim and restore it. Even though local authorities had decided that the building would be given to the community, it was demolished. In 2007, the Russian Council of Muftis published a list of 13 cities in the Moscow region where local authorities refused to allocate land, allow construction, or respond to building requests for mosques.[25] Other groups have also been targeted. In Kaluga (western Russia), Governor Anatoly Artamonov declared that the Word of Life Pentecostal community would be banished from their building, and the mayor of Kaluga handed it over to a Swedish company.

Orthodox churches outside the authority of the ROC-Moscow Patriarchate often experience discrimination and repression. The Russian Orthodox Autonomous Church (ROAC) has also been the target of property seizures. For example, in 2008, a ROAC building in Briansk was given to the ROC-Moscow Patriarchate. The True Orthodox Church—which was formed in 1917 by sections of the Orthodox hierarchy who refused to accept the patriarchate's recognition of the atheist Soviet regime—has faced property seizure, including the loss of a church in the Penza region, reportedly due to pressure from the ROC.[26] In addition, many True Orthodox communities failed to register as religious organizations—in effect, making them house churches—because they did not have the documentation or skills needed to register as separate organizations and could not register as affiliated with the ROC, a centralized religious organization. Others attempting registration faced bureaucratic hurdles.

Discrimination also takes the form of restricting the activities of minority religious groups. For instance, the Federal Drug Control Service (FDCS) has favored the ROC to provide drug rehabilitation facilities, which are often located on the premises of monasteries and actively involve patients in monastery life. At the same time, the head of communications for the FDCS has been quoted as saying that treatment in facilities run by nontraditional religious groups "leads to another kind of dependence—psychological dependence, which is as dangerous as drug dependence, and also damages one's health."[27] Authorities have repeatedly disrupted Protestant churches—sometimes in the middle of services—to impose random inspections and detain individuals for violations that are often found to have no legal basis. Disruption is often targeted at foreign-based groups, which are accused of being used for espionage purposes.

Jehovah's Witnesses are the most targeted of all religious minorities. Local organizations have been banned, publications declared extremist, worship services raided by authorities, children harassed in schools, and followers arrested. In March 2004, a Moscow court stripped the Jehovah's Witnesses of their legal status and prohibited their activity in Moscow. The group was found guilty of forcing families to disintegrate, infringing on the rights of citizens, encouraging suicide or the refusal of medical aid to the critically ill, and inciting citizens to refuse to fulfill their civil obligations established by law. However, in 2010, the European Court of Human Rights ruled that the Moscow court's ban of the Jehovah's Witnesses violated the European Convention on Human Rights and ordered Russia to pay 70,000 euros in damages and costs to the community.[28] Prior to this, in the space of three weeks during the spring of 2009, more than 500 Jehovah's Witnesses communities across Russia were subjected to checks on statutes and documents from prosecutors' offices. Whether these incidents were part of a centralized policy is difficult to determine, however, as no government agency was willing to admit to it. In December 2009, the Russian Supreme Court upheld a regional court decision naming 34 Jehovah's Witnesses publications extremist, which bans the publications nationwide. At the same time, it upheld a ruling that a Jehovah's Witnesses congregation in the town of Taganrog was extremist and thus banned.[29]

Why does the Russian state target small groups such as the Jehovah's Witnesses? One reason may be that the group has a strong organizational base outside the country, which the government cannot control. The group repeatedly calls on the European Court of Human Rights and other external bodies to adjudicate in response to violations by the Russian state. This may have the effect of making members of the group targets of hostility in response, as it indicates an unwillingness of the group to be co-opted by the Russian state on matters of religion-state relations.

There are numerous reports of detaining and harassing individuals related to minority groups. Most recently, laws have been used to repress those who challenge Putin's legitimacy and question the role of the ROC in protecting it. The trial and conviction of three women in the punk band Pussy Riot for staging a protest in Moscow's Cathedral of Christ the Savior is a recent example of how Putin has used the ROC for his own political gain.[30] The band chose the church as their protest venue to call attention to the ROC's support for Putin's reelection in 2012 and to the patriarchy's close relations with government. The three female members of the band were sentenced to prison on charges of hooliganism motivated by religious hatred.

In the mid-2000s, rights-monitoring organizations brought attention to increased abuses in the context of state application of laws related to extremism and terrorism, focused on members of independent Muslim groups located outside the North Caucasus region.[31] On February 14, 2003, the Russian Supreme Court ruled that 15 organizations were terrorist groups (with two additional groups added in July 2006). A Russian Federation Law on Counteracting Terrorism that was adopted in March 2006 defined terrorist activity as "activity which advocates terrorist activity, and which justifies or excuses the necessity of such activity." According to statistics from groups that monitor rights abuses in Russia, between late 2004 and February 2007, 27 people were convicted for extremist activity, including 19 related to Hizb ut-Tahrir.[32]

Under the 2009 National Security Concept of the Russian Federation, the government can pursue groups it suspects of extremist activity and ban them. As of the end of 2011, the government had banned 18 Muslim groups as terrorist organizations. While many of these are clearly violent (e.g., al-Qaeda), others are not (e.g., the Nurcular).[33] Several government entities exist to enforce these regulations. In 2004, a district court in Moscow ruled that a book written by the founder of Wahhabism in the eighteenth century was an extremist text. As a result of this ruling, any reference to this book in public or sharing of the book can be treated as an extremist offense. There have been other bans of Islamic literature on the grounds that it is extremist, even though much of it was mainstream, such as Muhammad Ali al-Hashimi's *The Personality of a Muslim* or the works of Said Nursi. Antiextremist campaigns have also targeted Scientologists. In March 2010, the City Court of Surgut (Khanty-Mansi Autonomous District) banned 28 Scientology titles for being extremist.[34] Even though the case is ongoing, all 28 publications were later added to the federal list of extremist publications.

In Russia, we see religious regulations used as a tool by increasingly authoritarian politicians to preserve the dominant position of the regime-friendly and legitimizing ROC in the country and to suppress group activity by independent and foreign-funded religious organizations. Religious groups are targeted, as are other potential opposition groups and figures in Russia, leading to very limited space for oppositional activity in the country and increasing Putin's control over Russian politics. This is a shift from earlier policy, which was not particularly pro-ROC (Papkova 2007). Yet, perhaps because of growing religious fervor among Orthodox Christians and increasing conservatism and traditionalism among Russians, politicians are beginning to see the benefits of supporting the ROC (Evans and Northmore-Ball 2012).

The nature of religious divisions is an important factor in explaining the pattern of religious repression in Russia. Like the other countries in this category, Russian Orthodoxy has a long tradition of being associated with Russian national identity. Although the Orthodox churches suffered like all other religious groups under communism, they have not emerged as champions of religious freedom since these countries became independent republics. Instead, these churches have viewed initial religious freedoms as detrimental to their own efforts to rebuild their churches and constituencies. Competition from other Christian denominations is viewed as offensive to populations that had been Christian for longer than most of the new groups had been in existence. Therefore, religious competition in these states is an important determinant of the types of religion policy we find, which focuses on protecting the traditional religion(s) and limiting the growth of new ones. Laws specifically target foreign funding for religious groups and limit visas for foreign religious personnel, giving further evidence of the nativist tendencies of these groups.

## Georgia

Like the ROC, the Georgian Orthodox Church (GOC) has been successful in codifying its position in the form of a constitutional agreement and establishing its position as the only religion not suffering from

government repression. This stems from a similar history of close identification with Georgian national identity and persecution during the
Soviet era. Like Russia, Georgia has historically housed multiple ethnic
and religious groups but has always favored the GOC. The country is
small in size and international influence in comparison with its neighbor,
but instances of violence against religious minorities have been greater in
Georgia than in Russia, and progress toward legal recognition of minority
religious groups has been slow.[35]

The GOC is one of the nation's oldest institutions. According to the
2002 census, Georgia's population was more than 84 percent ethnic
Georgian, with most being at least nominal GOC adherents. Azeris are
the largest ethnic minority, at about 7 percent of the population. They,
along with Ajarians and Kists, form the 10 percent of the population that
is nominally Muslim. Next are Armenians at 6 percent of the population,
mostly belonging to the Armenian Apostolic Church. Roman Catholics,
Kurdish Yezidis, Greek Orthodox, and Jews together make up less
than 5 percent of the population, and Protestants, Jehovah's Witnesses,
Pentecostals, and Hare Krishnas less than 1 percent of the population (US
Department of State 2011).

The GOC suffered great losses under the Soviets. In the postindependence period, it attempted to remedy those losses by building new
churches, training clergy, and bringing Orthodoxy back into the daily
lives of the Georgian population. The Georgian Patriarchate had to rely on
contributions from an impoverished population for its survival, making it
more difficult to recruit clergy to work in poor regions.[36] To remedy this,
the state returned church property seized by the Soviets. Furthermore, in
a 2002 constitutional agreement signed by the GOC and the government
(discussed later), the state pledged to compensate the church for losses it
had suffered under Russian imperial and Soviet rule.

The GOC was an important actor in Georgia's independence movement,
participating in mass demonstrations in Tbilisi on April 9, 1989. That night,
hundreds of thousands of Georgians gathered in front of the government
building to express their wish to be independent. Catholicos-Patriarch Ilya
II was present and addressed the people, led them in prayer and song,
and urged nonviolence in the struggle for independence.[37] Soviet troops
attacked and killed 22 Georgians and injured hundreds during these demonstrations. This fueled the nationalist movement.

Zviad  Gamsakhurdia  was  elected  president  upon  independence. A member of the GOC since the 1960s, Gamsakhurdia had

published samizdat protesting corruption of the church hierarchy and the Russification of the church. Gamsakhurdia was arrested in 1977, thus weakening the opposition movements within the Orthodox Church (Peters 1988). Gamsakhurdia and his Round Table coalition eventually won elections in October 1990 in Georgia and formed the first postcommunist government. Gamsakhurdia was elected president with 87 percent of the vote. This government was both nationalistic and pro-Western in orientation and claimed to promote a democratic agenda. However, Gamsakhurdia proved to be more of an autocrat than a democrat. He was a populist who advocated a nationalist agenda and aroused suspicion against the country's national minorities with his rhetoric. Conservative forces within the Orthodox Church hierarchy supported him.

In 1992, Gamsakhurdia was overthrown by a coup led by Eduard Shevardnadze, former foreign minister of the USSR and leader of the Georgian Communist Party. Shevardnadze did implement real reforms in Georgia, including permitting a free and robust media, civil society sector, and opposition parties. Yet at the same time, Georgia was plagued with state weakness, continuing conflicts with the secessionist South Ossetian and Abkhazian regions, and rampant corruption. The parliamentary elections of 1999 and 2003 and the presidential election of 2000 were neither free nor fair. To gain legitimacy and the support of the Orthodox Church, Shevardnadze was baptized as an Orthodox Christian in 1992. At this point, the church was one of the few institutions that people claimed they could trust.

Article 9 of the Constitution of Georgia, adopted in 1995, guarantees freedom of religion but also identifies the GOC as having a special role in Georgia's history.[38] Articles 14, 19, and 38 of the constitution guarantee equality, minority rights, and the rights of freedom of speech, thought, conscience, religion, and belief.[39] In 2001, the government added wording to the constitution that all relations between the government and the GOC would be determined by a constitutional agreement between the two bodies. It also added that the constitutional agreement would have to comply with international law, particularly in human rights and the protection of fundamental freedoms. The Constitutional Agreement between the Georgian government and the GOC was signed in October 2002.[40] It guarantees the immunity of the catholicos-patriarch, exempts clergy from military service, and recognizes the validity of church marriages. It also confers certain benefits on the GOC that are not given to other religious denominations, including chaplaincies in military units and prisons; the right to teach the Orthodox faith in schools; support of the educational institutions of the church;[41] property rights over all Orthodox churches, monasteries, and land, even if buildings are in ruin; tax exemption on religious items, donations, and property; state protection and restoration of church relics and artwork; and state compensation for material losses to the church incurred during the previous two centuries.

In November 2003, Georgia held parliamentary elections, which were expected to be as fraudulent as previous ones. In response to the elections, mass protests were staged, leading to the bloodless Rose Revolution on November 22 and 23. Shevardnadze was forced to resign, and former Minister of Justice Mikheil Saakashvili was elected to the presidency in January 2004, winning 96.2 percent of the vote. While Saakashvili was Western-educated and led a movement promoting greater democracy, he also used nationalist rhetoric to gain support, including use of the medieval Georgian flag (with five red crosses on a white background) as the symbol of his movement. The GOC did not participate in this second revolution, however, supporting Shevardnadze and advising people not to take to the streets.[42] After the Rose Revolution, the Saakashvili government was faced with a problem of building up state capacity to build infrastructure, fight corruption, deal with breakaway regions and the problem of state sovereignty, and develop the economy. To do so, it centralized power, which had the result of undermining democratic progress in the country (Mitchell 2009). In January 2004, Saakashvili introduced constitutional reforms that increased the president's power and reduced the influence of the parliament. Media independence and freedom declined. Defense spending increased dramatically, as did nationalist rhetoric about territorial integrity (Cheterian 2009). The brief (and lost) war with Russia over South Ossetia in August 2008 can be seen as a culmination of this state-building process.

### State Favoritism of the Religious Majority

After Mikheil Saakashvili's rise to the presidency in 2003, the GOC dropped its opposition to the revolution and gave its support to the new government. In return, the administration cooperated closely with the church, invited the patriarch to take part in all government ceremonies, and publicly declared its close connection with the church. At the opening of a new cathedral in Tbilisi in 2004, President Saakashvili praised Catholicos-Patriarch Ilya II for his service to the Georgian nation (Jibladze 2004). Although Saakashvili's government was more Western-oriented than previous administrations and claimed to represent a movement toward greater democracy in the country, it forged strong connections with the GOC, often at the expense of other religious groups. Many agreed that the situation of religious minorities had improved since the Rose Revolution, but even those in the more democratic factions of parliament called for a limitation on the activities of religious minorities, including Chairman of Parliament Zurab Zhvania, who suggested in 2000 that Georgians adopt laws similar to neighboring Armenia that restrict the activities of minority groups. Some argued that the Saakashvili administration was afraid of the GOC and claimed that the church could use its power over the population to destabilize the country.[43]

While the Georgian government utilized national symbols to bolster its legitimacy, the GOC allied itself with more conservative nationalist groups within the country to push its agenda and protest the opening of the marketplace to new religious movements. It also distanced itself from other Christian churches. For example, in 1997, the GOC decided, in an emergency meeting of the church's synod, to withdraw its membership from the World Council of Churches (WCC) and the Conference of European Churches. The GOC claimed that the international ecumenical body did not take into account Orthodox interests regarding church authority and organization and disagreed with attitudes toward female ordination and homosexuality.[44] In the fall of 2003, the Catholic Church was set to sign a protocol with the government protecting the local Catholic community, but public opposition from the patriarch and large anti-Catholic protests caused the government to abandon the agreement.[45]

The GOC wields great public influence in Georgia. Although the GOC provides symbolic support for the government in the form of its presence at official functions and through speeches and sermons supporting the president, it does not hesitate to voice its public opposition to elements within the administration that do not provide unconditional support for the church. It justifies such support as necessary for upholding the strength and unity of the Georgian nation. How it has been able to gain its strength is under question. According to an official representative of the patriarchate, it is because Georgians are highly spiritual.[46] According to those more critical of the church, it is a result of support from Russia, corruption, and infiltration of the church hierarchy with radical fundamentalists.[47]

These fundamentalists have been responsible for leading the call for restrictions on minority religious freedom and in persecuting minorities.

The most extreme example was the series of attacks against religious minorities led by defrocked Orthodox priest Basil Mkalavishvili and the Jvari (Cross) group led by Paata Bluashvili in Rustavi.[48] From 1999 to 2002, there were hundreds of attacks, with group members destroying property, blocking religious services, and physically attacking Jehovah's Witnesses, Pentecostals, and other religious minorities with wooden and iron clubs and crosses.[49] The patriarchate denied involvement in or support for the attacks, although individual priests and some politicians were vocal supporters. Because the attacks were not perpetrated by the state, technically they do not constitute state repression of religion. Yet, extensive delays in apprehending and punishing the perpetrators of these crimes and police refusal to protect minorities may be considered state favoritism toward the GOC and implicate the state in the actions of groups connected to it.

Criticism of the GOC is often met with an official response from the patriarchate. In late 2005, Ombudsman Sozar Subari presented a report to parliament finding the constitutional agreement between the government and the Orthodox Church to violate principles of equality by privileging the Orthodox Church and the agreement between the Ministry of Education and the church to violate the principle of the separation of church and state.[50] The church criticized the report, calling the ombudsman anti-Orthodox and rejection of the Constitutional Agreement "equal to rejection of national interests."[51] Parliamentarians from both the ruling National Movement Party and opposition parties also condemned the ombudsman, walking out of the session in which he presented the report and subsequently calling him anti-Georgian and anti-Orthodox. At the same time they accused him of being critical of the Orthodox Church, parliamentarians called him soft on human rights, apparently not equating religious freedom and equality with human rights protection.

Overall, the relationship between the GOC and Saakashvili's administration appeared to be a pragmatic one; the government provided subsidies to the church, and the patriarch, in turn, supported the government in the wake of protests. For instance, the GOC was the only religious group to have a line item in the government budget, receiving $13.75 million in 2012. Yet over the years, the church began to turn against the government as it appeared to be more pro-Western than the church desired. As evidence of the distancing of the GOC from the Saakashvili administration, the church—while remaining officially neutral—appeared to back his rival Bidzina Ivanishvili in the 2012 parliamentary elections. Among other things, members of the hierarchy expressed optimism that the change in government would result in improved relations with Russia.[52]

## State Repression of Minority Religions

After Saakashvili's government came to power, thoughts were mixed on whether the plight of religious minorities improved, especially considering that difficulties remained in constructing new churches (due to pressure on local authorities from Orthodox priests), and the lack of a religion law meant that the GOC remained privileged. According to one non-Orthodox priest, "When Orthodox priests are behind a decision, the government won't intervene."[53] The agreement between the GOC and the state gave the GOC monopoly over the title "Orthodox" and the GOC veto power over all places of worship built in the country, including those of other faiths. Religious groups continued to report problems building churches, despite government claims that no policies prevented them from doing so. Those that built churches reported constructing small, unobtrusive places of worship disguised as private homes, with no signage to call attention to their groups.[54]

The lack of a religion law combined with the official agreement between the GOC and the state in 2002 led to a situation in which the GOC was the only officially recognized religious group in the country and thus enjoyed rights that were denied to other groups. For example, without regulations regarding religious property, it was very difficult for groups to own property or build churches. Sometimes building permits depended on the approval of the GOC, which was rarely granted.[55] Yet despite the lack of a religion law, the legal system allowed believers to be punished for violating Article 199 of the Code of Administrative Offenses. A carryover from the Soviet administrative code, it punished those who refused to register their congregations and who organized religious work with young people and was used by the police to threaten a Pentecostal pastor who was using his home for religious services without permission.[56]

Yet Saakashvili's government did initially seem to be interested in increasing rights for religious minorities. In December 2004, parliament adopted a new tax code granting some tax exemptions to religious organizations. In April 2005, President Saakashvili signed amendments to the civil code allowing religious communities to register as unions or foundations, putting them on equal footing with secular nonprofit groups. A union is based on membership (a minimum of five members is required); a foundation involves one or more founders establishing a fund for furtherance of a certain cause for the benefit of the particular group or the general public. In both cases, registration is a function of the Ministry of Justice (MOJ), which must grant or deny registration within 15 days of application; a refusal may be appealed in court. However, the changes would not allow groups to register as public religious organizations, leading to protests from several religious groups. As of the end of 2010, there were approximately 20 religious organizations registered.

Previously, religious groups were required to register as public entities (thus regulated by the state), but there was no mechanism in the law to do this, even though there was a fine for not registering. Unregistered groups could not legally rent or construct buildings or import literature. To get around this, members of religious groups bought property or imported religious literature as private citizens. The new law did not make any provisions for transferring ownership of such property to the newly registered religious groups, therefore preventing many religious minorities from registering. Furthermore, many groups, particularly those existing in Georgia for several centuries, such as the Armenian Apostolic Church (AAC) and the Catholic Church, objected to their status as private organizations, pointing out that if the GOC could be considered a public organization, then they should have similar legal status.[57]

More recent policies have improved the position of religious minorities. In 2011, an amendment to the civil code granted five minority religious groups acknowledged as having "historical ties to Georgia" (the AAC, the Roman Catholic Church, the Evangelical Baptist Church, and the Muslim and Jewish communities) the status of "legal entities of public law." The GOC called on President Saakashvili to veto the amendment and released a statement after it was signed into law warning that the law "contradicted the interests of both the Georgian Church and the state" and that its "negative consequences will become apparent very soon."[58] By the end of 2012, the government had registered 14 groups as legal entities under public law, indicating an improvement in the fortunes of religious minorities.

As in Russia, Jehovah's Witnesses are subjected to some of the harshest repression among religious minorities in Georgia. In 2009, Jehovah's Witnesses claimed 35 incidents of harassment. Despite having reported all of the incidents to government authorities, individuals were charged in only two of the cases. The complaints included harassment when Jehovah's Witnesses members tried to talk with others about their beliefs; physical damage to meeting places, especially kingdom halls under construction, and to cars associated with the buildings; and physical violence. In addition, crosses were painted on the ends of kingdom halls and other buildings, as was other graffiti. The Jehovah's Witnesses also report that since 2004 they have not been able to rent facilities in Tbilisi to host large religious gatherings.

Historical religious divisions in Georgia are important for explaining its pattern of repression. Most of the religious minorities in Georgia are also ethnic minorities who have been living in the area for centuries. They include Armenian Apostolics and Catholics, Assyrian Catholics, Russian and Greek Orthodox, Jews, and Azeri Muslims. At the same time, newer religious movements (including Baptists and Pentecostals practicing in the country since the nineteenth and early twentieth centuries and other groups starting in the early 1990s) contain members of all ethnic groups, including Georgians, Armenians, and Russians. The more traditional groups consider their claims to legal protection more valid than those of the newer religious organizations, thus leading to a situation in which even the ethnic religious minorities are often opposed to other religious minorities. This creates difficulties in mobilizing minorities to protest against the privileged position of the GOC or to lobby for greater religious freedom.

For example, the AAC has been present in Georgia for centuries. Before receiving status as a public organization in 2011, the AAC argued that, by virtue of being a traditional church itself, it should be able to enter into a concordat type of agreement with the Georgian government, similar to that of the GOC. The Armenian Church claimed, however, that other religious minorities, particularly new Protestant movements, should not be given the same rights as traditional minorities. Property restitution continues to be the most important issue for the AAC in Georgia. Five churches in Tbilisi and one in Akhaltsikhe (an ethnic Armenian enclave in southern Georgia) remained jointly disputed by the GOC and AAC in 2012, along with at least 30 other churches throughout Georgia. One of the churches in Tbilisi was the Surb Nshan church, which collapsed from disrepair in 2009. The church was reportedly constructed in 1356 but was closed during the Soviet era and used as a warehouse. The church did not reopen after the country's independence, when title to the property passed to the Ministry of Culture. A joint government-GOC commission created to monitor property disputes included no minority representation, and according to Roman Catholic and AAC officials, the government was often unwilling to resolve disputes "for fear of offending GOC constituents."[59]

In summary, competitive elections in Georgia, especially after the Rose Revolution, created a clear need for politicians to court the GOC, one of the strongest social groups in society. Imposing restrictions on religious minorities in exchange for church support is unlikely to harm politicians seeking office because minorities are small and not politically mobilized. In that minorities themselves are divided among those that consider themselves to be traditional—therefore meriting separate treatment—and those that are more recent additions to the country's religious landscape, they pose no threat to politicians that support restrictions against them. Instead, politicians who win office seek alliances with the GOC for continued support and the legitimacy that comes from being associated with one of the most trusted institutions and important symbols of national identity in the country.

## *Secular Nationalism and Religious Cooperation*
### Indonesia

Indonesia is one of the few majority-Muslim countries in the world that has had some success with democracy. Yet prior to democratic transition in 1999, the country experienced decades of authoritarianism after independence from Dutch colonial rule. Considered an electoral democracy since 1999, Indonesia still suffers from incomplete protection of civil liberties, official corruption, and religious violence—including acts perpetrated by the military, police, and government officials.[60] Outright religious repression has eased since the transition to democracy, but it is not possible to argue that Indonesians enjoy complete religious freedom. State regulations require all citizens to be adherents of a religion, impose Islamic law in some regions and in particular areas of life, and target specific religious minorities.

Indonesia is ethnically and religiously diverse. Ethnically, Indonesians belong to hundreds of native linguistic and ethnic groups and several immigrant communities, including ethnic Chinese and Arabs. Religiously, Muslims constitute a large majority (80 percent, mostly Sunni), followed by Christians, Hindus, Buddhists, Confucians, and other smaller religions. Indonesian Islam is also diverse, and Islamic organizations represent the different viewpoints. Anthropologist Clifford Geertz (1960) described the main division between Muslims as between the *abangan*, characterized as practicing a syncretist form of Islam incorporating indigenous animism and Hinduism, and *santri*—pious or orthodox

Muslims. Another way of describing Muslim cleavages is to distinguish between traditionalists and modernists. Traditionalists follow the Shaf'i school of legal interpretation and rely on legal scholars (*ulama*) for their knowledge and interpretation of Islam. The most prominent traditionalist organization is The Awakening of Scholars and Teachers (Nahdlatul Ulama, NU). Modernists believe in direct interpretation of religious texts by believers and do not have as great a respect for the ulama. The largest modernist organization is *Muhammadiyah*. Muslims are further divided among liberals and conservatives. Although liberals tend to allow more open readings of the Koran and accept non-Muslims as equal members of Indonesian society, conservatives tend to be more literalist Koran readers and distrust non-Muslims. Conservatives tend to be modernists and support establishing Indonesia as an Islamist state. There are also smaller Muslim sects in the country, including Shiites and Ahmadis, which have their own organizations and viewpoints.

Independent Indonesia has seen four regimes: parliamentary democracy (1950–1957), authoritarian "Guided Democracy" under Sukarno (1959–1965), the authoritarian "New Order" under Suharto (1966–1998), and presidential democracy (1999 to the present). The founding father of independent Indonesia, Sukarno, introduced the term *pancasila* in 1945, which became the founding ideology of the state. Pancasila encompasses five pillars: belief in one God, humanism, national unity, democracy, and social justice. Sukarno introduced the concept to deflect the demands of some Muslim leaders to make Islam the foundation of the new state. Later, under Suharto, all political parties and social and religious organizations were forced to adopt Pancasila as their ideology. The government engaged in an indoctrination program to promote Pancasila, offering courses for civil servants, teachers, lecturers, university students, and others (Hamayotsu 2002).

Suharto's regime was not interested in promoting religion, instead supporting a pluralist or modernist form of Islam and a secular-nationalist view of Indonesian national identity. However, under his rule the society increasingly Islamicized, and Suharto was forced to seek support from the Muslim population. Initially organized as the political arm of the military, the ruling Golkar Party was transformed gradually under Suharto into a more civilian organization with greater attention to including Muslim candidates and projecting an Islamic image to win elections (Suryadinata 1997). The New Order regime promoted Muslim social and cultural development with infrastructural support in fields such as education and social welfare, including subsidizing mosque construction. The regime's lack of control over Islamic NGOs allowed a diverse array of religious groups to flourish during this time, leading to a phenomenon Robert Hefner (2000) refers to as "civil Islam."

Yet the Suharto regime's response to Islamic revival in the 1980s was repressive. In 1985, the Law on Mass Organizations required all organizations to accept Pancasila as their sole basis, forcing Muslim organizations to give up Islam as their foundational principle. The regime used the Indonesian Ulama Council (Majelis Ulama Indonesia, MUI) to control Islamic activism and established the Union of Mosque Youth (Ikatan Remaja Masjid, IRM) to control political activism in Islamic youth organizations. It supported an Islamic Renewal movement (Pembaruan) that emphasized the separation of Islam from politics. Islamic preachers criticized the New Order, and student-led demonstrations contributed to what would become the prodemocracy Reformasi movement.

An economic crisis that sparked massive antiregime protests led to Suharto's resignation on May 21, 1998. Vice President Bacharuddin Jusuf Habibe assumed the presidency and ushered in a period of political transition. The previous unitary system was decentralized, and free parliamentary elections were held in June 1999, with the president to be elected by the new parliament in October 1999. Religious affairs were left under the control of the central government.

During the 1999 elections, the MUI released three recommendations (*tausiyahs*) that can be read as advocating for Muslims to vote for Islamist parties (Gillespie 2007). However, Islamist parties did not fare well in this election (garnering about 16 percent of the vote during the primaries). During the 2004 elections, the MUI was not as open in its pronouncements, but the Islamist parties did better, winning about 21 percent of the vote. The MUI's Fatwa No. 7 in 2005 declared it forbidden (*haram*) for the Islamic community to follow the notions of pluralism, secularism, and religious liberalism. The NU responded by criticizing the MUI and defending plurality (and the philosophy of Pancasila) and the secular state; Muhammadiyah was divided on it between liberal, radical-puritan, and pragmatic-political camps.

In August 1945, seven words that made it obligatory for Muslims to follow Islamic law were removed from the Preamble to the Indonesian Constitution. After Suharto's departure in 1998 and during the period of constitutional reform from 1999 to 2002, Muslim groups and some political parties proposed reintroducing Islamic law into the constitution.

Both NU and Muhammadiyah opposed it. The constitution was amended in 2000 to add human rights provisions. Article 28E guarantees individuals the right to choose and practice the religion of their choice. Article 28I specifically guarantees freedom of religion and freedom from discrimination. Prior to these changes, the relevant sections on religion decreed that the state should be based on the belief in the "One and Only God." There are six recognized religions in Indonesia: Islam, Protestantism, Catholicism, Buddhism, Hinduism, and Confucianism. All citizens must profess adherence to a religion.

### State Favoritism of the Religious Majority

Suharto's resignation in 1998 and the start of democratic transition was the beginning of a shift away from a secular order that sought to keep religion out of politics and toward greater state favoritism of the Sunni Muslim majority in an effort to increase its legitimacy and gain the support of the largest and most organized religious group in society. Two examples illustrate how the state has regulated religion to favor the majority. First, the state allowed the Aceh region to adopt sharia law. Second, the state passed local and national-level laws inspired by sharia (and backed by the largest Muslim organizations) to appease more conservative Muslims and allow religious minorities to be repressed.

Since 1999, the autonomous region of Aceh is the only part of Indonesia that has the right to apply sharia law. The region is unique in that it is the most devout area of the country and is commonly considered to be the place where Islam first entered Southeast Asia. The decision to implement sharia in the region was partly an attempt to bring peace after decades of fighting between the government and the Free Aceh Movement (Gerakan Aceh Merdeka, GAM). The government and military saw this as a way to compete with GAM and establish legitimacy in the region, where GAM had been leading an insurgency since 1976.[61]

A series of laws govern how sharia is implemented in Aceh. Law 44 gave the local government authority to set policies on religious life, customs, education, and the ulama's role. The Office for Syariat Islam (Dinas Syariat Islam) was created in 2001 as a new religious bureaucracy tasked with drafting new regulations (*qanuns*) to implement Islamic law, overseeing personnel training, ensuring the orderly functioning of places of worship, providing guidance on matters of Islamic law, and supervising adherence to it. Law No. 18/2001 allowed the creation of sharia courts with jurisdiction over both family/private issues and criminal cases. In March

2003, the Supreme Court ruled that sharia courts in Aceh could adjudicate sharia violations and impose punishments. The first three offenses to
become part of sharia regulations were alcohol consumption, gambling,
and illicit relations (*khalwat*). With the exception of gambling, none of
these offenses are prohibited in the rest of Indonesia. Religious scholars were enlisted to determine punishments, which were taken from the
Koran, as well as from observations of how punishments were enacted in
other countries. In 2005, they decided to impose the penalty of 40 lashes
(via caning) for alcohol consumption, between 6 and 12 lashes for gambling (with a fine given to gambling establishments), and between 3 and
9 lashes and/or a fine for couples guilty of illicit relations. Another law in
Aceh requires all Muslims to wear Islamic attire. For men, this covers the
area of the body from knee to navel. For women, this means covering the
entire body with the exception of the hands, feet, and face. The covering
must be opaque and cannot reveal the shape of the body.

The Vice and Virtue Patrol (Wilayatul Hisbah, WH) was set up in
2004 as an institution separate from the police to monitor compliance
with Islamic law. Because the decree setting up the institution had vague
and overly general qualifications to become a WH member, the resulting
force ended up poorly disciplined and supervised and therefore highly
unpopular. As a result of a number of incidents sparking complaints
from the population, the requirements were raised to include graduation
from an Islamic law faculty, a regular law faculty, or at least seven years of
Islamic boarding school (*pesantren*) education; the ability to recite a specified number of Koranic verses and write in Arabic script; and meeting
the requirements to be an imam. But the WH is not alone in implementing sharia, as communities are encouraged to participate in enforcing the
*qanuns* by reporting offenders to the authorities.

Human Rights Watch reports that most often the lower classes are targeted with claims of breaking rules, not wealthier or well-connected people, presumably because the authorities worry about offending those who
can get them into trouble. The authorities do not seem to be motivated
by money (although there are some reports of asking for bribes), but they
do collect fines. They also report villages taking matters into their own
hands so they can benefit from fines rather than the WH. Local police
and the WH seldom prosecute those who engage in community-inflicted
violence against alleged perpetrators.[62]

There are sharia-inspired laws implemented in other localities around
the country. Between 2001 and 2007, Muslim activists and political

parties in 53 of the country's 470 districts and municipalities passed sharia-influenced bylaws mandating the mastery of basic religious skills or duties for Muslim citizens (Hefner 2012). In 1965, a presidential instruction inserted into the Indonesian Criminal Code Article 156(A) what is commonly referred to as the "blasphemy law." This makes it a crime to misuse or disgrace one of the six officially recognized religions. Since 2003, more than 150 people have been detained and dozens sentenced under the law.[63] Most have been convicted of insulting Islam, and many of them identify as Muslim. However, most of the convicted are leaders and followers of minority religious groups or Muslim sects that are considered to be deviant or unorthodox, such as the Ahmadiya. In April 2010, the Constitutional Court ruled that the blasphemy law was valid after an NGO lodged an application for judicial review based on the claim that it was contrary to religious freedom. Supporters of upholding the law included Indonesia's two main Islamic organizations, NU and Muhammadiyah, and the MUI.

An example of the blasphemy law being put into practice comes from April 1991, when Arswendo Atmowiloto, a newspaper editor in Jakarta, was sentenced to five years in prison on charges of insulting a religion. These charges stemmed from his decision to publish the results of a poll conducted in September 1990 by the Christian-owned weekly *Monitor* asking people to list their most admired individuals. The Prophet Muhammad came in eleventh (after President Suharto, a number of politicians, a pop singer, Saddam Hussein, and the newspaper editor himself). Even though the editor apologized for printing the poll, protesters tried to storm the newspaper's offices, claiming that the story was offensive to Islam, and a number of protests were held in other parts of the country. The government's reaction to the affair has been attributed in part to political motivations, as it occurred close to national parliamentary elections and an upcoming presidential election in which Suharto was expected to have opposition for the first time. By prosecuting Atmowiloto, the government was signaling its support for the politically active Muslim population.[64] This includes pressure from the government-funded MUI, which took a conservative turn in the post–New Order era (Gillespie 2007). The International Crisis Group argues that under the Yudhoyono government (2004–2014), the MUI took on a more influential policy-making role, with some of its fatwas used as the basis for law enforcement by the attorney general's office and other ministries. It also noted that the MUI's influence stemmed from the president's need to maintain the coalition of

Islamic parties that helped him get elected in 2004 to be reelected in the 2009 elections.[65]

## State Repression of Religious Minorities

Indonesia is often cited as a model of religious pluralism and a good example of how a majority-Muslim country can be tolerant of other religions. Yet despite a level of official toleration of religious minorities, radical Islamic groups continue to perpetrate violence with impunity. There is evidence that the violence has actually increased in the post–New Order period. During the New Order, more than 450 places of worship were vandalized and destroyed by radical Islamic groups. Since 1998, the number of church attacks totaled 156 under President Habibe (1998–1999), 232 under President Abdurrahman Wahid (1999–2001), 92 under President Megawati Sukarnoputri (2001–2004), and 100 in President Susilo Bambang Yudhoyono's first term (2004–2009). These numbers do not include attacks on other minorities' places of worship. Therefore, there were more places of worship destroyed during the first 10 years of democratization than during the 30 years of the New Order regime (Crouch 2010, 406).

Aside from the government's failure to protect minority religions from attack, there is evidence that local enforcement of national-level regulations has led to repression. Decentralization of control over permits to construct places of worship, implemented with the Joint Regulation on Places of Worship in 2006, has resulted in local officials' denial of permits to religious minorities. This appears to be done to serve political purposes, as it helps them to appease Islamic constituencies (Crouch 2010). In early 2014, Aceh passed a revised version of the criminal code that applies sharia law to non-Muslims. This occurred prior to elections, when local legislators had an interest in presenting themselves as more pious Muslims than those in the rest of the country.[66]

One of the more repressed of the religious minorities is the Muslim sect Ahmadiyah, which the government claims has about 200,000 adherents in Indonesia. The Ahmadiya are an Islamic reformist movement that recognize Mirza Ghulam Ahmad as a prophet, a teaching that goes against Islamic teachings that Muhammad was the last prophet of God. In 2008, the government issued a joint ministerial decree that banned proselytizing by the Ahmadiya community and at the same time made vigilantism against the group illegal. Ahmadi Muslims are not prohibited from worshiping in their community, but proselytizing carries a maximum five-year prison sentence for blasphemy. Mosque closures and acts of violence did not cease after the decree was issued, and the government failed to prosecute perpetrators.[67]

In sum, Indonesia represses all religions but one, the Sunni Muslim majority. Favoritism of the majority is illustrated by government submission to pressure from hard-line Islamists (some from the semigovernmental MUI) to enforce sharia law (as in Aceh) or to enforce restrictions aimed at religious minorities. Repression of minorities is exacerbated by the government's failure to punish perpetrators of violence. Once democratic transition brought greater political competition to Indonesia, politicians seeking victory at the polls had to establish coalitions of supporters. As religious civil society was already well established in the country, Islamist groups were able to trade support in the polls for beneficial state policies, including regulations in accordance with Islamic law that had the effect of repressing minority religious expression and practice. Because minorities do not have the same level of organization and influence, they are unable to counter majority pressure on the government to support laws that disproportionately favor Sunni Muslims.

## Turkey

Turkey's model of religion-state relations up until the past decade could be characterized as repressing all religions. Its strict application of secularism brought religion under the control of the state and prevented religiously oriented groups in civil society from becoming involved in public affairs. Yet the election of an Islamic-inspired political party to power in 2002 changed the landscape of religious regulation in Turkey. In the name of greater democratization, the governing party has advocated for policies to increase religious freedom in the country. However, the regulations that the party has adopted and supported most fervently have disproportionately favored the party's Sunni Muslim base. Muslim and non-Muslim minorities continue to be subjected to state restrictions under a party that has advocated greater democracy for the majority but failed to advocate for pluralism and greater openness for those who do not share its identity.

The precursor to the modern Republic of Turkey was the Ottoman Empire, a vast territory controlled by a sultan and incorporating a variety of ethnic and religious groups. The state was ruled according to Islamic law but used the *millet* system to rule over non-Muslim minorities. Each group was organized into communities that could self-govern to a certain degree under the leadership of their religious rulers. Islamic affairs were run by the Shaykh al-Islam (later the Office of the Mufti of Istanbul) on behalf, and under the authority, of the state (Erdem 2008). The Shaykh al-Islam and clergy had amassed great wealth and political power by the eighteenth century, sometimes threatening the authority of the sultan, who relied on the religious sector for legitimacy and assistance in keeping peace over the empire.

The founder of the modern Turkish Republic, Mustafa Kemal Atatürk, abolished the caliphate in 1924 and enacted measures aimed at modernizing Turkish society. His ideology—referred to as Kemalism—promoted secularism, nationalism, economic development, and Westernization. His secularist policies included changing the Arabic script to Latin, purging the language of words from Arabic and Persian, discouraging traditional attire, and secularizing the education system. Turkish secularism (laiklik) takes as its model the French laïcité, a model of strict religion-state separation. Established in 1924, the Directorate of Religious Affairs (Diyanet İşleri Başkanliği, DRA) regulates Sunni Islam and reports to the prime minister. Its functions are to administer mosques, appoint and remove religious personnel, and produce religious knowledge.[68]

The Kemalist state discouraged the development of autonomous groups outside of state control as potential threats to its modernization program and level of political control. This affected not only religious organizations but all of civil society. One-party rule continued after Atatürk's death in 1938 until 1950, when Atatürk's party, the Republican People's Party (Cumhuriyet Halk Partisi, CHP), lost its parliamentary majority to the Democratic Party (DP), headed by Adnan Menderes. The DP drew some previously marginalized groups—including Kurds and religious individuals from the country's periphery—into politics. They considered religion a necessary part of Turkish society, helping to create social cohesion. Menderes's policies were seen as dangerous by Kemalists and prompted the first military coup in 1960. The military turned power back to civilians in 1961 but only after instituting reforms to strengthen its own role, including creating the National Security Council (MGK), which had the power to judge whether the government's policies were in line with the basic tenets of Kemalism, including secularism.

The new constitution (1961) also expanded associational freedom, allowing the proliferation of nongovernmental groups, including religious organizations. This created conditions that allowed Islamist parties to arise. Necmettin Erbakan founded the National View (Milli Görüş) movement in the 1970s to challenge the country's secular establishment. His first party was the National Order Party (MNP), founded in 1970 but shut down in 1971 after a military intervention. He then founded the National Salvation Party (Milli Selamet Partisi, MSP) in 1972. The party won third place in the 1973 election and formed a coalition government with the CHP. After the coalition collapsed, the MSP joined the National Front governments headed by Suleyman Demirel in 1975 and 1977. Civil violence in the 1970s led the military to intervene in 1980 to restore order and to use the strategy of strengthening the role of Islam to combat communism and leftist groups. This is referred to as the Turkish-Islamic Synthesis, a process of fusing Islamic symbols with nationalism intended to reduce the influence of both radical leftist ideologies and Islamic ideas from outside Turkey, including radicalism from Iran (Toprak 1990). The MSP was closed after the 1980 military coup, and Erbakan was banned from political activities for 10 years. The party reemerged in 1983, calling itself the Welfare Party (Refah Partisi, RP).

The 1982 Constitution established a strong president and semistrong parliament and was strictly secularist.[69] Article 2 states, "The Republic of Turkey is a democratic, secular and social state governed by the rule of law." Article 10 guarantees equality, and article 24 guarantees freedom of conscience, religious belief, and conviction and the free practice of religion as long as these do not violate Article 14, which states, "None of the rights and freedoms embodied in the Constitution shall be exercised with the aim of violating the indivisible integrity of the state with its territory and nation, and endangering the existence of the democratic and secular order of the Turkish Republic based upon human rights." Article 68 of the 1982 Constitution declares that political parties cannot violate the principles of the secular republic. The Political Parties Act of April 22, 1983, restricted parties in terms of organization and ties with youth, women's, and local groups and set a 10 percent vote threshold for parties to win seats in parliament. The Constitutional Court has dissolved political parties 18 times since 1980 (Kogacioglu 2004).

In the 1980s, Prime Minister Turgut Özal oversaw economic and political reforms that strengthened Islamic groups, including helping to create a new middle class referred to as the Anatolian bourgeoisie that had strong ties to Islam. Özal's policies gave greater freedom to Muslim groups and brotherhoods, which allowed them to finance private schools, universities, and media outlets. He had close connections to the Nakşibendi Sufi brotherhood, giving them high positions in the party and government, thus allowing more Islamists into the bureaucracy and civil service positions (Ayata 1996). Özal became president in 1989.

In the general elections of 1994, Erbakan's newly formed Welfare Party won 19 percent of the vote (up from 9.9 percent in 1991) and 28 of 75 mayorships in the local elections. By 1995, the Welfare Party had gained strength by focusing on social issues through an extensive grassroots network and formed a coalition with the True Path Party, placing Erbakan in the position of prime minister. Rather than intervening directly in the face of Islamists in power in government, in 1997 the National Security Council issued a list of recommendations to curb antisecular activity, referred to as the February 28 Process. When Erbakan refused to follow the recommendations, the military forced him to resign in June 1997 in what is often called a silent or postmodern coup. In January 1998, the Welfare Party was closed down and Erbakan banned from politics for five years. The next iteration of Islamist party was the Virtue Party (Fazilet Partisi, FP), which was shut down by the Constitutional Court in 2001. The Islamist movement then split into traditionalists, who formed the Felicity Party (Saadet Partisi, SP), and the Justice and Development Party (Adalet ve Kalkınma Partisi, AKP), led by Recep Tayyip Erdoğan, the mayor of Istanbul, and his close associate, Abdullah Gül. The AKP refers to itself as following an ideology of conservative democracy and denies that it is an Islamist party. It has ruled as a majority government since 2002. It won 34 percent of the vote in the 2002 elections, 46.6 percent in 2007, and almost 50 percent in 2011, relying on the support of those who would have previously voted for center-right and Islamist parties. Upon winning the 2002 elections, Erdoğan declared economic stability and European Union (EU) membership as his top priorities. Yet secularists and others wary of Islamism remain unconvinced that the AKP does not want to pursue an Islamist agenda. As evidence, they point to such things as the AKP government's attempt to criminalize adultery in 2004 (which they were ultimately forced to withdraw) and the increased appointment of religiously trained personnel to civil service positions.

Turkey received EU candidate status in the 1999 Helsinki Council Summit and subsequently adopted several constitutional reform packages that led to the start of accession negotiations with the EU in 2005. In 2001, Turkey adopted 34 constitutional amendments that created openings for greater rights and liberties, democratic control of the military, and liberal market reforms. A 2002 reform package of constitutional amendments included lifting the death penalty, allowing radio and television broadcasting in Kurdish, and greater freedom for non-Muslim religious minorities. It also reformed the Law on Foundations to allow foundations to buy and sell property. Remaining bureaucratic hurdles to minority property rights were resolved with a 2003 reform package. Despite these reforms, analysts of Turkish policy note, "Turkey's response to the demands for improving non-Muslim minority rights does not go beyond, in a sense, a glossing of minority rights on paper" (Toktas and Aras 2009–2010, 711).

In 2011, the Constitutional Reconciliation Commission (AUK) was tasked with writing a new constitution for the Republic of Turkey (which had not yet been ratified as of the end of 2013). Some of the issues at question with regard to religion were the status of the DRA; compulsory school religion classes; the obligatory recording of religious identity on national identity cards; the accommodation of manifestations of religion, in particular the headscarf in public schools and government offices; and the lack of adequate legal status for religious communities.[70]

### State Favoritism of the Religious Majority

Turkey is 99 percent Muslim, with small populations of Christians, Jews, and other religious communities. The majority of Turks are Sunni Muslims, although there is also a significant Alevi minority (about 20 percent of the population) that practices a form of Shia Islam (US Department of State 2012). Among Muslims, Sufi orders (*tarikats*) have been influential throughout Turkish history. Sufi orders are important religious and social networks, but they were outlawed under Atatürk in 1925 and forced to operate underground. Law 677 (1925) bans places of worship other than mosques, including shrines, dervish lodges, and Sufi gathering places. Article 174 of the 1982 Constitution forbids declaring this law unconstitutional, as it is one of the reform laws adopted before the constitution that aims to "raise Turkish society above the level of contemporary civilization and to safeguard the secular character of the Republic." This enshrines the privileged status of Sunni Islam in the country.

Yet Sufi orders remain active and influential in Turkey. Two traditional orders are the Nakşibendi and Kadiri brotherhoods. Many prominent political and business leaders have ties to Sufi orders, and Islamist parties such as the MNP and MSP were established with support from the Nakşibendi order. Connections with the order remain in today's AKP. Another is the Fethullah Gülen movement, which is active in Turkey and around the world.[71] It is a web of organizations, including schools, business and financial institutions, and media organizations that promote Gülen's vision of Islam as a basis for building social capital. It identifies with a mission of service to humans, the country, and the world (*hizmet*). Islamic foundations (*vakıfs*) are also important religious actors, providing social welfare services where the state has been insufficient.

The DRA does not recognize divisions in Islam, as its authority is over the Hanafi school of Sunni Islam and therefore does not acknowledge the existence of Alevis or other Islamic sects. Moreover, groups like the Baha'is cannot record their faith on identity cards because the DRA considers it a sect, not a religion.[72] Other religions—such as Christianity and Judaism—are self-governing but subject to Turkish laws and regulations. The DRA is financed through taxes, as well as through the DRA Foundation, which supports the DRA's work both financially and substantively (Turan 2008). It supervises religious scholars (muftis) who give legal opinions on matters such as the use of the headscarf. There is a mufti in each of Turkey's 81 provinces and 900 districts. Provincial muftis are nominated by the prime minister and approved by the president; the president of the DRA appoints district muftis. All imams and muftis are state employees who are educated at faculties of theology or the state religious education institutions that offer a mix of secular and religious instruction (Imam-Hatip).[73] Within each province, muftis and imams meet monthly to discuss and prepare Friday sermons, although imams are allowed to prepare their own sermons as long as the Provincial Commission of Sermons approves them (Er 2008). The Higher Board of Religious Affairs within the DRA is comprised of religious scholars who issue "answers on religious questions" (*fetwas*) (Öcal 2008). The DRA also selects and trains imams to serve Turkish Muslim communities in other countries. The president of the DRA is nominated by the prime minister and approved by the president. Between 2002 and 2011, the number of DRA employees increased from 74,000 to 117,541, and its budget is larger than that of some government ministries.

The AKP has succeeded in relaxing some of the tighter restrictions on religious expression since it took power in 2002. However, these relaxations of restrictions have disproportionately benefited Sunni Muslims, their electoral base. An example can be seen in what is commonly referred to as the headscarf controversy. According to Turkish law, women are not allowed to wear the headscarf at public universities or official spaces, such as government offices. In 1984, the Council of Higher Education allowed female university students to cover their hair in a modern form of headscarf, arguing that this was in line with the council's requirement of "modern clothing" in universities. In 1989, the Turkish Constitutional Court ruled this was unconstitutional because it contrasted with Turkey's constitutional entrenchment of modernity and constituted discrimination against students of other religious backgrounds. The case reached the European Court of Human Rights, which in 1993 dismissed an appeal filed by a Turkish student who was ineligible to receive her degree without submitting a photo of herself with her head uncovered. In 2002, the European Court of Human Rights affirmed rulings by the Turkish Supreme Military Council that allowed the military to dismiss soldiers who belonged to Islamic sects and had wives who wore headscarves.

The AKP government argues that people should be allowed to express their Islamic identities in public, while secularists argue that the presence of the headscarf in public spaces constitutes an attack on the secular state and is a symbol of the Islamization of Turkey, especially when worn not as a traditional scarf around the head, but as the more politically tinged *tesettür*.[74] In February 2008, parliament passed constitutional amendments that would create a framework allowing the ban on headscarves in universities to be lifted. The head of the Higher Education Council (YÖK) responded by instructing universities to start admitting students wearing headscarves. However, not all universities complied with the order.

### State Repression of Religious Minorities

The lack of official recognition of diversity within Islam is a form of state repression of religious minorities. Although official figures are not available, Alevis are estimated to be about 20 percent of the Turkish population. Alevism is a belief system related to Shia Islam incorporating elements of Shamanism, Bekstashi Sufism, and Zoroastrianism. It differs from orthodox Sunni Islam in that it does not observe sharia law, fasting during Ramadan, mosque attendance, daily prayer, female veiling, or pilgrimage to Mecca. Alevis meet in houses of worship (*cemevi*) and have unique religious institutions, such as religious leaders known as elders (*dede*). Alevi meeting houses are not recognized as houses of worship by the DRA and therefore are not state funded, although the DRA has been known to build mosques in Alevi villages, which one analyst claims appear "to be part of pressure politics exerted by the state to implant Sunnite belief in this section of society" (Gozaydin 2008, 224). Most Alevis are ethnic Turks, but there are also Arab and Kurdish Alevis in Turkey. Alevis have tended to support the secular republic and secularist parties. Traditionally, they were associated with leftist politics. There are Alevi groups that are more religious and closer to Shia Islam, but they are only a small minority of mainstream Alevism.

In recent years, despite some greater recognition and freedom given to Alevi religious practice, formal institutional restrictions remain. Religious Alevis themselves are internally divided into groups that emphasize calls for incorporation of Alevi Islam into the DRA versus those who consider Alevism to be a religion in its own right that should have autonomy over its own religious affairs, like that given to other recognized minorities (Dressler 2008). According to the head of the DRA since 2003, Ali Bardakoğlu, "We cannot accept attempt[s]. . . to portray Alevism as a separate religion. Alevism is a cultural system and a sect within Islam."[75] The fact that there is diversity within Islam is also neglected by Turkish scholars. For instance, in an article "Minority Rights in Turkey," Ilhan Yildiz (an academic but also an educational expert for the DRA) considers only non-Muslims to be minority religions, repeating more than once that 99 percent of Turkish citizens are Muslims (Yildiz 2007).[76]

After the 2007 elections, the AKP embarked on a policy referred to as the Alevi opening (*Alevi açılımı*) process, an effort to deal with the Alevis' identity-based issues with symbolic gestures and speeches that for the first time recognized the Alevis as a separate identity group (Köse 2010). The right-wing National Action Party (Milliyetçi Hareket Partisi, MHP) also announced an Alevi policy, with the stated platform of allocating money to their meeting houses, providing Alevis with representation in the DRA, opening government-funded Alevi research centers and institutes, publicly broadcasting shows on Alevis on official state television, and teaching Alevi culture and beliefs in religion classes. Few of these reforms have been implemented.

Turkey's present policy toward non-Muslim minorities is based on and reflects classifications set out in the Treaty of Lausanne (1923), which divided portions of the Ottoman Empire after World War I and established Turkish independence. The treaty recognized non-Muslims as minority groups and guaranteed them full freedom of religion. The Turkish government interpreted this to include only Armenians, Greeks, and Jews. It also gave them other privileges not granted to other non-Muslims, such as the right to use their own language and to open church-owned private schools. These schools currently operate under the supervision of the Ministry of Education. Only minorities are allowed to attend the schools, and the curriculum includes Greek Orthodox, Armenian Apostolic, and

Jewish instruction. The principals are Turkish Muslims paid by the government, and the minorities pay for all other expenditures themselves.

While the status of these three minorities is often referred to as "privileged," due to their special protection under the Lausanne Treaty, they are subject to a number of restrictions that curtail their autonomy. First, only Turkish nationals are eligible to act as clergy, creating problems for communities that have small populations and lack clerical training facilities within the country. For example, the Greek Orthodox community's Halki Theological Seminary was closed in 1971 when the Turkish government nationalized all private institutions of higher education. Despite some hopes that the AKP government would allow the reopening of the seminary, it remained closed in 2014. Second, unlike Sunni Muslims, religious leaders of the minority communities do not receive income from the state. Third, state business pertaining to these minorities is the purview of the Ministry of Interior. Minorities must receive permission for all activities, although this has been difficult for groups to obtain, and they have no means of appealing decisions (Yildiz 2007).

Besides the non-Muslim minorities recognized by the Lausanne Treaty, minorities fall into two other groups. The first are groups that were present in Turkey at the time of the treaty but were not recognized, including Arab and Syrian Orthodox groups. One of the biggest challenges for these groups has been training clergy and religious teachers. They are not allowed to operate their own schools because they are not recognized minorities. They are allowed to use their property only for strictly religious purposes, not education or fundraising. The second group of unrecognized minorities arose in Turkey after the treaty was signed, including Protestant groups and others such as the Jehovah's Witnesses. These groups are not allowed to establish churches, schools, or other institutions.

Turkey since 2002 can be considered a country that represses all religions but one, the Sunni Muslim majority. The ruling AKP has used existing state regulations on religion to support its devout religious base. Moreover, the party used the opportunity afforded by its obligations to meet EU accession standards to increase the religious expression rights of Sunni Muslims. This has meant an overall increase in religious freedom protections in the country, which is a positive development for Turkey's efforts at democratization. However, because such openings have been confined to the majority, religious minorities continue to be subjected to repressive policies that prevent them from being recognized, owning property, and governing their internal affairs without state intrusion. This strategy has helped the AKP retain political power for more than a decade. Yet its failure to live up to promises of greater freedom for all groups may hinder its electoral success in the future and curtail Turkey's democratic gains.

## Conclusion

This chapter has examined four states that are similar in their repression of all religious groups but one. Compared with the states in the previous chapter, the present examples impose similar types of repressive policies on religious groups but focus them on minorities. Often, this is done to gain the support of the religious majority, which is more politically organized than minority groups. Moreover, support from religious groups grants states that have undergone recent regime change—a characteristic of almost all of the countries in this category—an important source of legitimacy.

Because most of the countries in this category have more political competition than those in the previous chapter, they do not have the capacity or political will to impose harsh repression on all groups in civil society; they need such groups to support them during elections. Belarus and Laos are the two exceptions, as both retain strongly authoritarian regimes. Yet like the other countries in this category, both countries retain a strong national identity that is associated with the traditional majority religion of the country and rely on its support for legitimacy.

Unlike the countries discussed in chapter 3 that repress all religions, those discussed in this chapter single out a group from which they withhold repression. In most cases, these groups also enjoy state favoritism above and beyond the de facto favoritism that comes from being the only group not repressed. This is different from the state control that comes from being officially affiliated with the state that we find in the previous chapter. In the present set of countries, the state sees the majority religion as a valuable and loyal partner that offers political legitimacy and therefore gives it relative freedom to govern itself without state interference.

The cases in this chapter demonstrate how some nondemocratic states view civil society as a partner to state power rather than as an independent realm in which societal pluralism can manifest itself. By granting one group benefits, the state is able to co-opt civil society and prevent the growth of an independent arena in which different interests can be expressed. By repressing the ability of groups to express and govern themselves free from state interference, nondemocratic governments can thwart the growth of potential opposition groups that may challenge their continued rule. We are more likely to see this in places where one religious group has historically dominated society, especially when that group has strong ties to the country's national identity.

# The Need to Choose

## SELECTIVE STATE REPRESSION OF RELIGIOUS GROUPS

IN EARLY 2014, Nigeria's President Goodluck Jonathan signed into law the Same-Sex Marriage Prohibition Act. The law bans same-sex marriage and punishes it with 14 years in prison. It also imposes a penalty of 10 years in prison for anyone who enables or witnesses a same-sex union or who participates in, or even supports, gay clubs and organizations.[1] The bill had been debated in the National Assembly for several years before its final passage but reflected similar antihomosexual legislation already in existence at the state level.

Nigeria's high level of conservative religiosity helps to explain why such a measure might have popular support in the country. Since 2001, 12 northern states have adopted sharia law for criminal and civil matters, and Nigerian Pentecostal Christians—one of the fastest growing denominations in the country—largely support the idea that politicians should take steps to make their country a Christian nation (Pew Research Center 2006). In the predominantly Muslim north, laws against homosexuality had existed as part of Islamic law but had not been applied with any vigor. The signing of the national law "redoubled the zeal against gay people," with authorities using religious motivations to actively pursue arrests and punishment of homosexuals in the region.[2]

Despite the ongoing struggle with religiously based violence in Nigeria, federal law has not traditionally focused on restricting religious groups. Instead, a combination of locally enforced sharia law in the northern states, failure by the central government to protect victims and prosecute enforcers of violence, and the use of religion as a political tool by entrepreneurial politicians results in a situation in which no one religious group is targeted by the central government but different groups are repressed around the country on the basis of religion. These conflicts stem from interreligious competition, ethnic tensions, and disputes over resources.

As religious groups have grown stronger in the face of weak state capacity and continuing clientelism in politics, the country has witnessed increasing state-imposed regulations related to religion. Antihomosexuality laws do not restrict the activities of religious groups per se, but they do impose religiously inspired laws onto the entire populace, which violates norms of citizen equality, restricts the freedom of the dissenting and nonreligious, and imposes a particular version of religious orthodoxy on the entire population. The rise in these laws can be attributed to political leaders recognizing the need to court strong religious leaders in the face of decreasing legitimacy due to corruption, declining economies, and growing health and environmental problems. Although such laws might help to unite Christian and Muslim groups that have been engaged in conflict since Nigerian independence, they do it at the expense of the protection of broader civil rights and pluralism.[3]

Nigeria and the 20 other countries in the category of countries that repress some religions do not practice the kind of repression discussed in chapter 3, among countries that repress all religions. There, not only do repressive state policies target all religious groups (whether they are large or small, majorities or minorities) but also they span a large range of policies, from repressing the free conduct of religious worship to banning political speech and organization into parties by religious leaders and their groups. The countries examined in chapter 4 similarly impose a host of repressive measures on all religious groups but one, usually the religion considered to be traditional in the society. Religious minorities in those countries do not enjoy the types of benefits given to the majority religion(s)—funding for religious buildings and clergy, the ability to teach religion in public schools, and other favorable policies.

Countries in the category of repressing *some* religions are the most widely varied of the four categories this book addresses. In some countries (e.g., Bahrain, Kyrgyzstan, and Zimbabwe), the government enforces restrictions only against those groups that are politically active and critical of the state. In other countries, religious policy is seen as a vital tool in maintaining societal peace. In Nigeria and Singapore, for example, the government encourages religious activity yet restricts actions deemed to provoke conflict in societies that are multireligious and multiethnic.

Interactions between ethnic and religious identities are significant in explaining the character of religious repression in several of the countries in this category (including Bosnia, Croatia, Kyrgyzstan, Niger, Rwanda, and Uganda). In those countries with a history of conflict and regionally concentrated religious and ethnic groups (including Bosnia, Lebanon, and Nigeria), religious repression tends to be enforced by local actors who overzealously apply national policies or who enforce local rules targeted at minorities in the region. As in the other categories, these states also repress very small, marginal groups that would not seem to be threatening to any stable government. The justifications given for these bans can be either religious or political. For instance, Kyrgyzstan has banned the Ahmadiya Muslim Community for being "a threat to traditional Islam," and Singapore has banned the Jehovah's Witnesses for refusing to serve in the military and salute the flag.

This chapter presents case studies of four countries that repress only some religious groups: Kyrgyzstan, Bahrain, Nigeria, and Singapore. States in this category tend to have higher levels of political competition than those that repress all or all but one religion (scoring an average of 2 on the Polity regime scale in 2010). Yet political competition varies across the four countries discussed in this chapter, with Kyrgyzstan and Nigeria holding relatively competitive elections in 2010, while Bahrain and Singapore had more closed political arenas. These divergent cases were chosen to illustrate how religious divisions in society interact with a country's political situation to create the conditions for selective repression of religious groups. Singapore's less competitive political system allows government leaders to target politicized religious groups with restrictions, even though its lower level of religious divisions in society—compared with other countries in this category—might predict less religious repression. Kyrgyzstan's political upheavals created openings for political leaders to impose increasingly harsh restrictions aimed at religious groups perceived as challenging the incumbent government. In Bahrain, a constitutional monarchy led by members of the religious minority, repression is targeted at members of the Shia majority who challenge the legitimacy of the ruling family. Finally, in Nigeria, low state capacity leads to a situation in which politicians must cater to the demands of strong and organized religious groups calling for restrictions on competing religions and the imposition of religiously based laws in a formally secular state. Table 5.1 summarizes the types of restrictions found in each country.

Table 5.1 Religious restrictions in countries repressing some religions (2010)

| | Kyrgyzstan | Bahrain | Nigeria | Singapore |
|---|---|---|---|---|
| Religious observance | x | | | x |
| Places of worship | | x | x | |
| Religious laws | x | | x | x |
| Conversion | | x | | |
| Proselytizing | x | | x | |
| Discriminatory registration/ bans | x | x | | x |
| Clerical appointments | | x | | |
| Religious speech or publications | x | x | x | x |
| Religious education | x | | | |
| Religious political parties | x | | x | |
| Religious associations | x | | | x |
| Political speech | | x | | |
| Access to political office | x | | | |

## Kyrgyzstan

Kyrgyzstan's post-Soviet experience has been tumultuous, character-ized by a period of high hopes for democracy, followed by autocratic rule, revolution, and authoritarian reentrenchment. Despite some initial suc-cess with constitutional reform and more competitive elections after a regime change in 2010, the country remains nondemocratic. Religious freedom has suffered a similar fate, waxing and waning alongside the level of political competition in the country. Kyrgyzstan's combination of political upheavals and religious demographics places it in the category of repressing some religious groups. Politicians and administrative officials have targeted religious groups as potential political opponents capable of destabilizing the regime. They have been especially focused on prevent-ing foreign-sponsored and independent Islamic groups from legally oper-ating in the country. Given the lack of significant religious reform and increasing repression since regime change in 2010, Kyrgyzstan faces the prospect of joining its Central Asian neighbors in the category of repress-ing all religious groups in the future.

During the first few years of post-Soviet rule by President Askar Akaev (1990–2005), Kyrgyzstan was described to be an "island of democracy" in Central Asia (Anderson 1999). However, the regime grew increasingly authoritarian in the mid-1990s, with government repressing opposition groups and the independent media and failing in economic growth. This culminated in the Tulip Revolution in 2005, which ousted Akaev and brought Kurmanbek Bakiyev to power. Despite hopes of renewed democracy in the country, Bakiyev's regime proved to be even more authoritarian than the previous one, and Bakiyev was violently overthrown in 2010, replaced by Roza Otunbayeva as interim president and a renewed commitment to democratic reform among the country's elite. Elections in 2011 brought President Almazbek Atambaev to power. Kyrgyzstan's democracy ratings improved between 2010 and 2011 largely because of the competitiveness of the elections and the adoption of a new constitution in 2010 designed to diminish the power of the presidency and establish a more competitive parliamentary system.[4] Nevertheless, Kyrgyzstan remained in the category of nondemocratic regimes at the end of 2013 because of its tenuous history with democratization and inability to impose real political reform.

Kyrgyzstan is more religiously and ethnically diverse than most of the other Central Asian states (which repress all religions). The country is approximately 75 percent Muslim, most of whom are Sunni (there are about 1,000 Shia). Russian Orthodox adherents are about 7 percent of the population. The remainder of the population that is religious (less than 5 percent) includes Protestant Christians (such as Baptists, Lutherans, Pentecostals, Presbyterians, and Seventh-Day Adventists), Jehovah's Witnesses, Roman Catholics, Jews, Buddhists, and Baha'is. Ethnically, the population is approximately 70 percent Kyrgyz, 15 percent Uzbek, and 8 percent Russian, with a number of smaller ethnic groups including Dungans and Uighurs (US Department of State 2011). Ethnic Uzbeks are concentrated in the southern part of the country, especially in the Ferghana Valley region. The country's ethnic heterogeneity is significant, as it has contributed to conflict and suspicion of movements based outside the country, especially from neighboring Uzbekistan.

Religious groups operated generally freely under the first Kyrgyz president, Askar Akayev, despite a 1996 decree requiring all religious groups to register. Religion was regulated under the 1991 Law on the Freedom of Religion and Religious Organizations, amended in 1997. When President Bakiyev took power in 2005, both registered and unregistered religious groups were able to function relatively freely, including the often-persecuted Jehovah's Witnesses. Problems included female pupils

being unable to wear the hijab in some parts of the country and unpros-
ecuted attacks against Christian groups trying to preach to Muslims in
southern Kyrgyzstan. A survey on religious freedom in 2004 reported
that Kyrgyzstan had no discriminatory laws on religion, including no
provision for compulsory registration of religious groups.[5] Groups perceived to be potentially politically threatening were subject to repression,
however. For example, the government actively pursued members of the
Islamist political party Hizb ut-Tahrir and in the meantime targeted individuals known for being religiously devout. Moreover, the Pentecostal
Church of Jesus Christ, claiming a membership of around 10,000, was
banned from registering in several places, and its churches were closed
or threatened with massive tax bills. Church members claimed the cause
was that authorities feared the group for being large and well organized
and that it had been successful in converting ethnic Kyrgyz Muslims.

The Law on Freedom of Religion and Religious Organizations
(Religion Law), passed and signed in 2008, continued to govern religious
affairs in Kyrgyzstan as of late 2013, despite the existence of a new constitution (2010) that required revision of the Religion Law. New laws related
to religion were being developed and discussed in parliament in 2013,
although implementation was slow. The 2008 law requires all religious
groups to apply for approval of registration from the State Commission
for Religious Affairs (SCRA). Registration does not grant tax exemption
to religious organizations. The number of members required for registration was raised from 10 to 200 adult citizens. Registrants were required to
be adult Kyrgyz citizens providing, in person, information including their
addresses, job titles, and passport numbers to elected local administrations (*keneshes*).[6] Groups could be rejected for not complying with the law
or for being considered a threat to national security, social stability, interethnic and interdenominational harmony, public order, health, or morality. Groups whose charters needed to be amended to meet the strictures
of the new law were required to reregister.

If approved by the SCRA, religious organizations must register with
the Ministry of Justice to obtain status as a legal entity, which gives
groups the right to own property, open bank accounts, and enter into contracts. One of the ways the Religion Law prevented religious groups from
registering was by requiring a certificate confirming the physical location of the religious organization from the State Agency for Architecture
and Buildings. Lawyers representing religious groups attempting to register claimed that the SCRA and the State Agency for Architecture and

Buildings were working together to make registration more difficult by introducing additional requirements for registration, such as the need to be a certain distance away from school buildings and mosques and to provide certificates from other agencies, such as utilities providers.[7] The Religion Law banned children from being active in religious organizations and banned religious organizations from educational institutions other than religious schools that were officially registered with the state. The law also banned proselytizing and restricted the importation and distribution of religious media. Since independence, the constitution has prohibited political parties that are based on religion and forbids religious organizations from pursuing political goals.

The 2008 Religion Law was passed while President Bakiyev faced increasing public dissatisfaction with widespread corruption and failed economic and political reform. He was driven to centralize his power in the face of decreasing legitimacy and public support. During the period before the July 2009 election, Bakiyev adopted laws limiting freedom of speech and assembly, replaced heads of security structures and administrative offices with family members, and used the judicial system to prosecute the political opposition. His Ak Zhol political bloc controlled a majority of seats in parliament, obtained during uncompetitive and largely falsified elections in late 2007. At this point, political legitimacy was so low in the country that 50 leaders from opposition parties formed an alternative shadow parliament in early 2008. The shadow parliament included former members of parliament, heads of opposition parties, former government officials, and NGO leaders.[8] It attempted to compete with the ruling party in local elections in 2008 but failed to garner victories in severely flawed elections.

The Religion Law was passed during this period of crisis and entered into force in January 2009, at which time authorities commenced cracking down on religious organizations, despite the fact that regulations to enact the new law were still being resolved by a government commission. Religious communities such as Jehovah's Witnesses and Protestants reported being contacted by government officials to check documentation and having received warnings not to share their faith with others and distribute religious literature, all elements of the new law that remained to be resolved by the government commission.[9] The new law also banned unregistered religious activity, prompting officials to order such groups to halt their activities, although they had been able to meet in the past. Asked what would happen to religious communities who had fewer than

200 members and were ineligible to register, Kumar Dushenbayev of the SCRA responded, "Why should religious communities such as the Presbyterians try to open a branch in every corner of the country? Why can't they come together in one place, where they would not have a problem gathering 200 people?"[10] As of the beginning of 2012, the SCRA had given state registration to 138 organizations: 135 state-backed Muslim and 3 Russian Orthodox organizations. Hundreds of religious communities, including mosques and some Protestant churches, had not had registration applications approved by authorities.[11]

As of 2011, the SCRA considered the following associations to be "destructive and totalitarian" sects: the Unification Church of Sun Myong Moon (Moonies), the International Society for Krishna Consciousness, the Church of Jesus Christ of Latter-Day Saints (Mormons), the Sri Chinmoy Church, Dolmar Channong, Falun Gong, followers of Sri Aurobindo Ghose, the White Brotherhood, and Satanists. The associations regarded as terrorist and extremist were the East-Turkistan Islamic party (also known as the Islamic movement of East Turkistan), the Organization of East Turkistan Liberation, the Islamic party of Turkestan, Hizb ut-Tahrir, al-Qaeda and the Taliban movement, the People's Congress of Kurdistan, and Jaamat al-jihad.[12]

As is common across the Central Asian states, Muslim religious life in Kyrgyzstan is regulated by a state-backed but formally independent Spiritual Administration of Muslims, or muftiate, which is the highest Islamic body in the country. The muftiate oversees all Islamic institutions, including schools, mosques, and Islamic organizations. It also has the authority to ban publications. Allegations of corruption in the muftiate are rampant and extend to the appointment and security of its leaders.[13] In May 2011, the muftiate was given complete oversight over the hajj, which was previously overseen by the SCRA. This did not seem to stop allegations of corruption surrounding the pilgrimage, however, as there were still multiple complaints about individuals being forced to pay bribes to secure a slot.[14]

Despite legal restrictions, non-Muslim religious groups that refrain from attempting to convert ethnic Kyrgyz and Uzbek Muslims operate with relatively few problems in Kyrgyzstan. Local officials and inhabitants have targeted groups that they believe attempt to convert Muslims, however. For example, in southern Kyrgyzstan in 2006, a Baptist preacher was beaten in his home by a mob of about 80 Muslims, who also burned his religious literature. Reportedly, three police officers who were watching the actions did nothing to intervene. The SCRA officers questioned about the event maintained that Protestant missionaries provoke violence by their presence in Muslim areas and by trying to convert Muslims. Similar events and threats against Protestants have been reported throughout southern Kyrgyzstan, with fewer reports from other parts of the country. Protestants reported being told by SCRA officials to halt their activities and being threatened with registration revocation.[15]

Yet Kyrgyz religion policy is focused primarily on preventing the rise of political Islam, a force that may threaten the secular parties and leaders that have ruled the country since independence. For example, the government attempts to control signs of Islamism in educational institutions. The government closed unregistered religious schools (*madrasahs*) but opened the first official regional Islamic school in the southern city of Batken in 2009 in an attempt to standardize the schools with government-approved curricula and teachers.[16] The muftiate and the government also keep track of students studying in Islamic colleges in Egypt and Iran and require permission for missionaries to travel through the region and preach. While there is no law banning the hijab in schools, it is common practice that female students are not allowed to wear headscarves.[17] In 2003, there were reports that regional administrators in southern Kyrgyzstan (where there are large populations of religiously observant Uzbeks) had held a conference that issued a decision to "wage a widescale war on religious extremism, making use of teachers and imams."[18] As a result, there were reports of teachers in schools punishing students who observed Islamic rituals, such as daily prayers and wearing the hijab.[19] This pressure reportedly continued in 2006, when teachers were said to be targeting daughters of Hizb ut-Tahrir members who were wearing the hijab to school, despite there being no laws banning it.[20] Regional officials also seemed to have control over religious structures. In 2003, a local official from a district of Jalalabad in southern Kyrgyzstan destroyed six mosques, claiming they were built on state-owned land. The official also claimed the need to monitor the behavior of imams.[21]

Thus, the main focus of government repression has been Muslim groups it asserts to be threats to the country's stability and security. The Kyrgyz government and the muftiate have aimed to eliminate independent Islamic groups (those not under the control of the muftiate) by labeling them religious extremists. These are active in the southern regions of the country—which are also home to most of the country's Uzbek minority. Groups such as Hizb ut-Tahrir and the Islamic Movement of Uzbekistan

(IMU) have been lumped together under the label of Wahhabism and accused of recruiting members in the region. In fact, Kyrgyzstan did not declare Hizb ut-Tahrir illegal until 2003 and only at Uzbekistan's urging (Radnitz 2010). Regulations against religious literature and foreign aid for religious groups appear to target these types of groups. For instance, the law "On Combating Extremist Activity" was adopted in August 2005. It defined one form of extremism as asserting the "exclusivity, superiority, or inferiority of citizens on the basis of their attitude to religion or their social, racial, national, religious, or linguistic group."[22]

Kathleen Collins (2002, 2003, 2007) has studied the success of groups like Hizb ut-Tahrir in the region and described the level of perceived threat from these groups by the region's autocratic leaders, despite their avowed nonviolent platform. She notes that Hizb ut-Tahrir has not been as successful in Kyrgyzstan as it has in neighboring Uzbekistan, partly because of its focus on targeting the Uzbek government. This suggests the Kyrgyz government has exaggerated the level of threat posed by the group to justify its restrictions against independent Muslim groups more generally. In fact, the number of criminal cases against alleged members of Islamic extremist groups such as Hizb ut-Tahrir increased to 30 in 2011, up from 10 cases in 2010.[23]

Although a state can justifiably pursue groups that are violent or extremist, Kyrgyzstan has also targeted with repression groups not known for extremism. For instance, Ahmadiya Muslims were denied reregistration under the 2009 law under claims that the group is a "dangerous movement and against traditional Islam."[24] In 2011, Kyrgyz officials from the SCRA again refused to reregister the Ahmadiya Muslim community, which has about 1,000 members in the country.[25] An official from the SCRA claimed that the muftiate recommended suspending the group because of "threats to religious security."[26] These threats were left unspecified.

Kyrgyzstan is categorized as repressing some religious groups because it targets independent and foreign-based religions as potential political opponents. Fearing outside interference in corrupt political and economic practices that have benefited autocratic leaders and their family and clan members, ruling politicians have imposed restrictions on all types of activities that contribute to free speech and association and allow expression of opposition viewpoints. Religious repression can also be attributed to ongoing ethnic tensions in the country. The current international boundary of Kyrgyzstan (and neighboring Central Asian states) was drawn by Soviet administrators and does not correspond to existing ethnic and clan divisions in the region. The Ferghana Valley, the most fertile area in Central Asia in terms of both vegetation and religious fervor, is divided among Kyrgyzstan, Uzbekistan, and Tajikistan. In Kyrgyzstan, residents of the Ferghana Valley are mostly of Uzbek ethnic background, sparking suspicion and repression from the Kyrgyz government, which fears the region is a bastion of extremist activity, fed by radical groups from neighboring Uzbekistan.

Tensions rose after Bakiyev's ouster in April 2010, when the interim government appealed to Uzbeks for support, which led to calls for greater political power from Uzbek leaders. Weeks of increasing tensions culminated in interethnic violence in June 2010 in southern Kyrgyzstan, where, over four days, 400 people were killed and close to 2,000 houses were destroyed. The majority of victims were ethnic Uzbeks, though ethnic Uzbeks also constituted the majority of those arrested for participating in the violence.[27] Ethnic Uzbeks have been traditionally underrepresented in politics, but they have been prominent in the private sector as small businessmen. A commission appointed by President Otunbayeva published a report in 2011 concluding that leaders of the Uzbek community and the clan of President Bakiyev had provoked the conflict. A later report published by a commission headed by an OSCE parliament member concluded that some of the attacks against Uzbeks constituted crimes against humanity. The government claimed the report was biased in favor of ethnic Uzbeks.

Thus, the association of Uzbek identity with Islamic extremism, along with a distrust of Uzbeks due to their economic position, has made them a convenient target for government (and societal) repression. However, because Uzbeks share an Islamic affiliation with the majority Kyrgyz, religious restrictions affect most Muslim practice. Restrictions that specifically focus on extremism attempt to target specific groups, yet the stricter rules set in place by the 2008 Religion Law have resulted in a more restricted religious environment overall. This has been amplified by the political turmoil of recent years, making enforcing restrictions more arbitrary and attempts at reform difficult to achieve.

The passage of the Religion Law in 2008 can be seen as one of the tools Bakiyev hoped to wield as a more effective way of repressing potential political opposition in the form of religious groups. Despite significant constitutional reforms under Otunbayeva's interim presidency and the adoption of a new constitution in 2010, the law had not been struck down or amended as of the end of 2013. Its continued use can also be seen as a way for the current regime to maintain stability in the southern regions where ethnic Uzbeks are concentrated and were opposed to Bakiyev's policies that seemed to target Uzbeks. Without significant political reforms allowing participation by opposition forces, it is unlikely that religious repression will be reduced in Kyrgyzstan.

## *Bahrain*

Bahrain is another example of how changes in leadership can alter a state's religion policy and determine which groups it targets. In the 1990s, Bahrain's religion policy clearly favored the Sunni minority over its Shia majority and repressed religiously based expressions of political opposition, but a change of leadership in 1999 ushered in a period of reform that decreased pressure on Shia Muslims. However, as the country began to experience political unrest and protests calling for political reform in 2011—inspired partly by similar protests in other Arab countries—repression of the Shia majority resumed.

Bahrain has a population of about 1.25 million, 46 percent of whom are citizens. Of the citizens, 99 percent are Muslim, the majority Shia, and 1 percent are Jews, Christians, Hindus, and Baha'is (US Department of State 2011). Bahrain was under British control until it gained independence in 1971. The monarchy is Sunni Muslim. Shiites are barred from most positions in the military and security services. They also complain of having access to fewer educational and employment opportunities. In 1993, the Consultative Council was established, which formed the basis for more significant reforms in 2001.

Sheikh Hamad bin Isa al-Khalifa took power in Bahrain in 1999 after his father's death. As emir, Hamad introduced many reforms. First, he set up a National Charter Committee (NCC) of 45 members in 2000 to examine and approve the National Charter put to referendum in February 2001. The charter included references to transparency, accountability, justice, equality between the sexes and among ethnic/religious groups, equal opportunity, respect for human rights, an independent judiciary, and a new two-chamber parliamentary system (Ehteshami 2003). After the referendum, the emir abolished state security laws and the state security court, which had been used to suppress opposition, and replaced it with a new committee to oversee the implementation of the charter. He also announced that as of February 2002, the country would be known as the Kingdom of Bahrain, to establish it as a constitutional monarchy. Constitutional changes also allowed women to participate in local and national elections and established a constitutional court and an independent audit bureau.

According to the 2002 Constitution, the official state religion is Islam, and sharia is a principal source of legislation (Article 2). It declares the equality of citizens and bans discrimination based on religion (Article 18). According to Article 22, "Freedom of conscience is absolute. The State guarantees the inviolability of worship, and the freedom to perform religious rites and hold religious parades and meetings in accordance with the customs observed in the country." According to Article 23, "Everyone has the right to express his opinion and publish it by word of mouth, in writing or otherwise under the rules and conditions laid down by law, provided that the fundamental beliefs of Islamic doctrine are not infringed, the unity of the people is not prejudiced, and discord or sectarianism is not aroused."[28] These provisions are very similar to those laid out in the previous (1973) constitution.

The Bahraini government monitors all official Sunni and Shia Islamic institutions, including mosques, community centers (ma'tams), charitable foundations (waqfs), and the separate Sunni and Shia religious courts. The government must approve construction of places of worship, and the king has sole legal authority to allocate public land for religious buildings. The High Council for Islamic Affairs reviews and approves clerical appointments for both Sunni and Shia communities. It also oversees citizens studying religion abroad. Every religious group is required to obtain a permit from the Ministry of Justice and Islamic Affairs (MOJIA) to operate, and holding religious meetings without a permit is illegal. Public religious events are permitted, but they are closely monitored by police, as is access to Internet sites considered to be antiregime or anti-Islamic.

A number of changes in the application of religion policy occurred after the transfer of power to Hamad. The government was not known for tolerating political dissent in the past, and until the early 2000s, the government clearly favored the Sunni Muslim minority, especially in government appointments. Shia Muslims expressed frustration with their generally lower level of social and economic status compared with Sunni Muslims and fewer opportunities for economic and professional advancement. Until February 14, 2001, the government held in detention hundreds of Shiites, including religious leaders, for offenses involving national security. In 1999 and 2000, the government released or pardoned more than 700 Shia political prisoners, detainees, and exiles. In February 2001, Hamad pardoned and released all remaining political prisoners and religious leaders. The government also suspended its policy of closing mosques that allowed political demonstrations on their premises or that allowed religious leaders to deliver political sermons. Also in 2001, the government registered new religious NGOs, including some with legal authority to conduct political activities.

The government lifted other constraints on religious political expression as well. In the 2002 municipal council elections, candidates associated with religious political groups campaigned and won 40 of the 50 contested seats. In the 2002 legislative election, candidates associated with religious groups won more than half of the Council of Representatives' 40 seats. In both elections, candidates from religious political groups conducted their campaigns without any interference from the government.

Between 1999 and 2010, government repression against Shia Muslims declined as Hamad instituted promised political reforms. During this period, the Shia opposition won 40 percent of the vote in a general election in 2006, and a Shia Muslim, Jawad bin Salem al-Oraied, was named as a deputy prime minister. However, beginning in 2010, the government arrested hundreds of Shia for holding political demonstrations and engaging in street violence, mostly in Shia areas. The riots were sparked by Shiite perception of unequal treatment. Of those arrested, 25 were tried on allegations of conspiring against the government, ties to terrorism, and spreading false information. According to the US State Department (2011), "Some rioting and other illegal activity was actively encouraged by political extremists," although no specific groups are named in the reports.

Parliamentary elections were held in October 2010. Before the elections, the government began to enforce restrictions on using places of worship for political campaigning and arrested Shia clerics accused of inciting violence. Inspired by the Arab Spring protests in Tunisia and Egypt, a period of sustained unrest began in February 2011, with mass protests calling for political reform and some sectarian violence. Security forces killed several protesters in the government response. The government declared martial law in March and censored Shia clerical sermons, arrested Shia clerics and laypeople, and demolished more than 50 Shia religious structures in a blatant show of politically motivated religious repression. Although the government conceded that it had used excessive force against prodemocracy protesters, in February 2012 the police once again cracked down on protesters commemorating the anniversary of the previous year's mass demonstrations. Sporadic antigovernment protests continued throughout 2013.

Despite variable government repression of the majority Shia Muslim population, non-Muslims in Bahrain are generally free to practice their religions and are subjected to few or no repressive policies. Non-Muslim religious groups must register with the Ministry of Social Development (MOSD) to operate. As of 2012, 19 non-Muslim groups were registered, including Christian churches and a Hindu temple. The Baha'i community did not seek registration. Nevertheless, they were able to maintain a cemetery and community center and were granted land for a future temple. This is unlike policy in many other Muslim-majority states, where Baha'is are banned and public practice of the religion severely restricted. Non-Muslims are allowed to maintain places of worship, display symbols, and worship in private without government interference. Christian publications are sold openly in bookstores. The government discourages proselytization by non-Muslims and conversion away from Islam, but neither is prohibited by law.

As of 2009, the Jewish community in Bahrain numbered a mere 36 members, mostly older adults who are descendants of merchants from Iraq and Iran. In 1948, there were about 600 Jews in Bahrain, and a single synagogue still exists, although it does not bear any Jewish symbols and is not in use. There is still a small cemetery in Manama. King Hamad has made open efforts to show tolerance of Bahrain's Jewish community by appointing a Jewish woman, Houda Ezra Ebrahim Nonoo, as ambassador to the United States in 2008 and appointing Jewish business leaders to the Shura Council.[29]

A Catholic church was built in 1939 and a meeting hall in 1958. The church was expanded in 1990. There are approximately 100,000 Catholics in the country, most of them Indians and Filipinos. A second church is shared with the Anglican community.[30] Other Christian groups include Orthodox Christians, Protestants, Pentecostals, Seventh-Day Adventists, and several churches from South India. In May 2002, unknown individuals vandalized and damaged graves in the Christian cemetery in Manama. The Ministry of Finance funded repairs to the cemetery.[31]

In many ways, Bahrain is a very clear-cut case of a regime repressing only those religious groups it finds politically threatening. Like other Muslim-majority countries that retain strong state control over Muslim religious practice, the Bahraini government retains authority over most elements of religion, including religious buildings, charitable institutions, clerics, and the pilgrimage. Yet unlike those countries that repress all religions, Bahrain does not impose many restrictions on its non-Muslim communities. Similarly, it refrains from repressing its Baha'i minority, despite the fact that many orthodox Muslims consider the group to hold heretical views. This may be due to the more secure position of the al-Khalifa regime, which until recently ruled absolutely but did not rely heavily on Islam for regime legitimacy, as they were members of the religious minority. The shift to constitutional monarchy in 2002 established some oversight and greater political participation by individuals outside the royal family, including members of the Shia majority. However, when such participation began to threaten the stability of the ruling family, it once again imposed strict repressive measures against those groups capable of posing a serious political threat. As it called on assistance from Sunni allies such as Saudi Arabia to help suppress political protests and violence, it risked further inflaming sectarian tensions and calling into question the regime's legitimacy.

## Nigeria

Nigeria differs from Kyrgyzstan and Bahrain in that the central government is not as closely involved in regulating and repressing religion, in part because of the federal system that is intended to devolve power to individual states. This has led to variation in the types of restrictions on religion imposed around the country. At the same time, because Nigeria practices a weak form of federalism, the central government has retained a great amount of authority with respect to internal security and distributing resources. In both of these areas, government activities have resulted in the politicization of religion, inconsistent and ineffective protection of religious rights, and ongoing religious violence. Nigeria can therefore be thought of as a country where the government does not actively repress many groups, but the lack of state capacity leads to a situation in which some groups are repressed by virtue of not being protected as they should be by the government or because they are used as pawns by politicians seeking to gain office and access to valuable resources. These actions, in turn, contribute to ongoing religious violence around the country, which the government is incapable of controlling.

Ethnicity has always been a fault line in Nigeria, but religion has attracted greater attention since the beginning of the 1990s. Simeon

Ilesanmi (1995) notes that the relationship between religion and state in Nigeria is best described by the "hegemonic state thesis." Ilesanmi argues that because all loyalty must be channeled through the state, buffer institutions have not formed in society. Thus, by wanting to assert its power in all realms—including religion—state elites undermine the country's pluralistic institutions and thus subject the country to religious conflict. Others agree with the assessment that the state has used religion to its advantage. According to Elaigwu and Galadima (2003, 128), "It would appear that there is a convenient matrimony between religion and politics, where religion legitimizes politics and vice versa, the resultant conflicts are usually more severe and intractable over time." By using religion as a political tool, politicians have exacerbated religious tensions, highlighted religious divisions, and failed to protect citizens' rights.

Nigeria is Africa's most populous country. Religious divisions follow the approximate array of Muslims in the north, Christians in the east, and mixed populations in the southwest. Clerics and merchants from North and West Africa and the Arab world introduced Islam to northern Nigeria mostly peacefully between the eleventh and seventeenth centuries. There was a second phase of conversions at the beginning of the nineteenth century by the Sokoto Caliphate, an Islamic revivalist movement. The caliphate was an ethnic Fulani empire of autonomous emirates with a caliph based in Sokoto who acted as both political leader and spiritual guide. It was one of West Africa's largest states before British colonial rulers defeated it in 1903, although the caliph remained the spiritual leader of Muslims in the region.[32] Emirs were allowed to retain both political and religious authority. British indirect rule retained Islamic law in the north but limited it to civil matters. It did, however, protect core Muslim areas from Christian migration and missionaries to preserve the north's Islamic identity and avoid tensions between different groups.

Portuguese traders introduced Christianity to Nigeria in the fifteenth century. It did not begin to flourish until the mid-nineteenth century, when freed slaves returned to the region and began to spread Christianity among their tribes. These missions were especially successful in Yorubaland, although native-led missions opened up in all areas of Nigeria, especially in the middle belt and plateau regions (Sodiq 2009). Some argue that the Anglican Church was the unofficial state church during British colonial rule (Olupona 1990). During colonial rule, a Muslim theocratic elite remained in power in the north, but Westernized educated Christians in the south were the ones with access to political office.

Today, Nigeria is both ethnically and religiously diverse. Current estimates put the Muslim population (predominantly Sunni) at 50 percent, Christians at 40 percent, and those exclusively practicing indigenous religions at 10 percent (US Department of State 2012). Many Muslims and Christians also practice indigenous religions. The north of the country is predominantly Muslim and is dominated by the Hausa and Fulani ethnic groups, who are also a plurality in the large cities of the southwest. There are significant numbers of Christians in the urban centers of the north and in the middle belt, particularly in Kaduna and Jos. The east is predominantly Igbo and Christian, with some Igbo also practicing an indigenous religion. The Yoruba, who live in the southwest, practice Islam, Christianity, and traditional African religions.

Nigeria's Muslims are approximately 95 percent Sunni (of the Maliki school of jurisprudence) and belong to the Qadiriyya and Tijaniyya Sufi orders, which are represented by a number of organizations, including the Jama'atu Nasril Islam (JNI), the Nigerian Supreme Council for Islamic Affairs (NSCIA), and the Supreme Council for Sharia in Nigeria.[33] Nigeria was admitted as a full member of the Organisation of Islamic Cooperation (OIC) in 1986, following a secret application by President Ibrahim Babaginda, who had not consulted the Armed Forces Ruling Council (AFRC). Also in 1986, the president announced the establishment of a National Advisory Council on Religious Affairs to regulate the activities of religious organizations and promote interfaith dialogue. There are also several Islamic revivalist movements in Nigeria. The anti-Sufi Izala movement, which became strong in the 1980s, favors Islamic government. After the death of its charismatic leader in 1992, it can no longer be considered a structured movement.[34] Other revivalist movements include the Muslim Students Society of Nigeria and the Muslim Brotherhood. Radical groups include the Maitatsine, the Nigerian Taliban, and Boko Haram ("Western Education Is Forbidden").

Nigeria was a British colony from 1900 until independence in 1960. It was composed of Muslim feudal states in the north and Christian and indigenous kingdoms in the south and east, with about 250 ethnic groups speaking different languages and having different religions. Nigeria's ongoing experiment with federalism began under colonial rule as the region prepared for independence. The 1954 Lyttleton Constitution established the Northern, Western, and Eastern regions with internal policy and administrative autonomy. According to David Laitin (1986), the politicization of religion was more pronounced in the northern states than in the south (i.e., Yorubaland), where ancestral city and tribe were more politically salient because British colonial policy reestablished defunct kings as a way to implement the policy of indirect rule. By giving ancestral city kings power and legitimacy over particular tribal areas, they were able to control and manage conflict in Yorubaland and defuse potential Muslim-Christian tensions. This pattern persisted in the postindependence period.

At independence, Nigeria adopted a federal constitution that outlined three regions defined by predominant ethnic group: Hausa and Fulani in the north, Yoruba in the southwest, and Igbo in the southeast. Together, these groups make up about 60 percent of the population. Under the Independence Constitution of 1960 and the Republican Constitution of 1963, the three regions had considerable powers, some of which they shared with the federal government, such as judicial and police power. Yet this federation proved untenable because of the size imbalance of the regions—the proportionately large northern region was seen as dominating the federal government and giving preference to the Hausa. The first republic of Nigeria lasted from 1960 to 1966. In January 1966, Christian Igbo military officers staged a coup; in July, a group of mostly Hausa army officers staged a countercoup. A massacre of Igbo residents in the north followed. In 1967, the head of the eastern region declared the independent Republic of Biafra, and civil war ensued. The blockade of Biafra by Nigerian forces resulted in widespread civilian hunger and starvation. In 1970, the region was reunited with the rest of Nigeria. The final death toll was 1 million civilians and countless more refugees.

Under successive military regimes following the civil war, rulers centralized power. At the same time, they expanded the number of states (from 12 in 1967 to 19 in 1976, 21 in 1987, 30 in 1991, and 36 in 1996) as a way of diluting regional power. By cutting revenue to the states, they weakened the units, and by breaking up larger ethnic groups, they prevented them from joining together to challenge the regime. During military rule, northerners were dominant in politics and the military, and many southerners and minority groups perceive this domination to have continued since the end of military rule in 1999 (with a brief period of unstable civilian rule from 1979 to 1983 called the Second Republic).[35] Under military rule, the economy shifted from one based on agriculture to heavy dependence on oil, and poverty levels rose, especially in the north. The military government also intervened in religious affairs. For instance, following religious rioting in Kaduna state in 1987, the government issued the Religious Societies Temporary Prohibition Decree, which suspended all religious organizations and religious broadcasting and prohibited the formation of new religious associations in institutions of higher education for one year (Olupona 1990). The return to formal democracy led to greater dispersion of rule and also a greater role for religion in politics.

General Sani Abacha declared himself president in 1994, ruling over an extremely repressive and corrupt regime until his death in 1998. Major General Abdulsalami Abubakar was sworn in as the country's head of state, and he subsequently led the democratic transition that resulted in the People's Democratic Party's (PDP) candidate Olusegun Obasanjo's election as president in 1999. The return to civilian rule was accompanied by a new constitution, which remains in force today. Like previous constitutions, it is seen as centralizing power in a way contrary to the principle of federalism. It gives ultimate power to the central government in resource control and revenue allocation (e.g., state ownership of all oil and gas in the country), sparking numerous conflicts over oil revenues.[36] An attempt to reform the constitution in 2005 failed.

Obasanjo was reelected president in 2003, serving until 2007. He had previously served as head of state under military rule from 1975 to 1979 and participated in an aborted coup, after which he was imprisoned until 1998. While in prison, he became a born-again Christian. Obasanjo ruled over a one-party state. In 2007, Umaru Musa Yar'adua, a Muslim from the north and a PDP member, was elected president in elections marred by irregularities and violence, calling the legitimacy of his regime into question.[37] Illness prevented him from exercising much power. Upon his death in 2010, another Christian, Goodluck Jonathan, was declared president. Before the 2011 elections, Jonathan visited the Pentecostal Redeemer's Christian Church of God, where the pastor prayed openly for his election. Other church leaders also openly campaigned for Jonathan, arguing that a Christian president was needed to counter the long domination of Muslims in Nigerian politics. Election results confirmed the Christian-Muslim split in the country, as Jonathan won the Christian-dominated areas in the south and Christian areas in the north–middle belt region, while the Muslim candidate, Muhammad Buhari, won all 12 northern states. Widespread allegations of vote rigging accompanied the election, and postelection violence set off by Kaduna youth spread to other parts of the north, resulting in hundreds of deaths and the destruction of churches, mosques, and houses (Onapajo 2012).

The Nigerian constitution does not allow state and local governments to adopt an official religion, but does allow them to use sharia or other customary law courts. Nigeria currently relies on three legal traditions for its laws: customary law, Islamic law, and English (common) law (Oba 2011). Under British rule, states were allowed to apply Islamic law with respect to civil matters such as family law, although not with respect to criminal law. Since 2001, 12 northern states—Bauchi, Borno, Gombe, Jigawa, Kaduna, Kano, Katsina, Kebbi, Niger, Sokoto, Yobe, and Zamfara—have adopted Islamic law for both civil and criminal matters. However, the extent of its application varies by state; some allow common and traditional law to be applied as well, and others have not adopted all aspects of Islamic law, such as punishment for apostasy. Non-Muslims in these states are not required to submit to sharia jurisdiction. All 12 states with sharia law have a Ministry for Religious Affairs, which has the authority to license panels for imams and preachers, register religious groups, and plan for new mosques and churches. Northern Nigeria also has a separate penal code from the rest of the country. The constitution permits proselytizing, but several states have banned or limited outdoor mass proselytizing for security reasons.

State governors have autonomy in decision-making but receive a majority of their material resources from the federal government. The federal and state governments are involved in religious affairs. They regulate mandatory religious instruction in state schools, church and mosque construction and financing, and financing pilgrimages to Mecca and Jerusalem. The Corporate Affairs Commission (CAC) registers Christian and Muslim groups seeking to build new churches or mosques. Each group is required to name a board of trustees, place a notice of the group's intent to organize in three nationwide newspapers, and send trustee information to the CAC. Groups can proceed if no objections are raised to their plans.

The Prohibition of Certain Associations Act of 2002 bans associations or quasi-military groups formed for the purposes of furthering the interests of a group, which can include political, religious, ethnic, tribal, cultural, or other social interests. Until 2005, the government had legal authority to ban gatherings whose political, ethnic, or religious content might lead to unrest. However, in June 2005, the Abuja High Court struck down the provision that gave the government this power. Several state governments continued to ban public processions and rallies on the grounds of preventing violence and protecting public safety. The constitution designates all police as federal. The federal government assigns police to states, but they are under the authority of the federal police inspector general. Thus, there is little police loyalty to the populations they serve.

In October 1999, the governor of the northern Zamfara state, Ahmed Sani, signed laws establishing new lower sharia courts and changing the jurisdiction of the sharia court of appeal. In January 2000, he signed the sharia penal code. These established lower sharia courts that had jurisdiction over civil and criminal sharia offenses and established a State Council of Ulama. The Grand Khadi of the Sharia Court of Appeal was given control over sharia courts. Crimes were classified according to sharia categories of *hudud, qisas,* and *ta'zir.*[38] According to the BBC, "Governor [Ahmed] Sani has even said that only men with beards will be awarded government contracts" (Ludwig 2008, 610). Yet non-Muslims were not to be affected by the laws, as nonsharia courts were retained to deal with crimes involving non-Muslims. A few non-Muslims, however, did choose to be tried by sharia courts, as they were seen to be faster. A report by Human Rights Watch did not find a campaign to enforce sharia upon non-Muslims.[39] Christians did complain about discrimination as a result of the laws (Ludwig 2008).

Other states in the north soon followed suit, although the actual implementation of sharia law varied across the states. For instance, in Zamfara and a few other states, the state organizes alms (*zakat*) collection. Other states, such as Kaduna and Gombe, established parallel Christian organizations to allow those groups to have ties to state government. Kaduna is described as having the most lax application of sharia, given that half of the state's population is Christian and the region is divided into sharia-compliant and non-sharia-compliant areas. Because nothing prohibits residents from crossing over into another area, Muslims can easily engage in sharia-prohibited behavior, such as drinking alcohol or hiring prostitutes, without consequence. In other states with sharia law, Islamic law enforcement (*hisbah*) organizations monitor sharia law observance and report breaches to police. In some states, these groups receive funds from state governments. In most places, they act as a moral police force, encouraging the use of sharia methods to keep conflicts out of the police and court systems.

In 2001, Zamfara passed a law titled the "Certain Consequential Reforms (socioeconomic, moral, religious, and cultural) Law" prohibiting "indecent dressing in public" and "indecent hair cuts," as well as association in public of members of the opposite sex. The law also set specific dates for fasting, which caused problems with a local Muslim minority group that had different requirements for when fasting begins. Several members of the group were arrested, jailed, and fined, while others were dispersed with tear gas for praying on a different date than that set by the government.

Sharia courts in most states function similarly. Each state has lower sharia courts where cases are heard first. Upper sharia courts in each state have appellate jurisdiction and can hear appeals from lower courts. Each state also has a sharia court of appeal that hears appeals from cases tried in the upper sharia courts. Further appeals go to the Federal Court of Appeal and ultimately the Supreme Court. There is no specialized sharia court of appeal at the federal level, and federal justices are often not well versed in sharia. Sharia court judges often consult legal scholars (*ulama*) for advice on specific sentences, especially if they lack thorough training. State governors—who have the power to authorize or commute sentences of death or amputation—also often rely on ulama for advice on cases. This role for the ulama is not governed by any specific regulatory framework, making it subject to corruption. Capital cases in nonsharia courts require legal representation for defendants, but sharia courts do not. Several sharia death penalty cases were tried without legal representation in the court of first instance, although they were allowed at the appeal stage. State authorities have been reluctant to carry out death sentences handed down by sharia courts. Human Rights Watch has documented multiple cases of police torture, lack of legal representation, abuse of power by police and prosecution officials, sentencing of children to amputation, floggings, and other rights abuses performed in the context of sharia courts.[40]

Initially, there was significant public support for sharia criminal courts in the north because of widespread frustration with increasing crime, corruption, and the inadequacy of state law enforcement. Moreover, it was seen as a reaffirmation of Muslim religious identity in a context of tensions between Muslims and Christians. This support has waned over the years, for several reasons. First, sharia legislation was in many cases rushed through in an incomplete manner, leaving many issues unresolved. Judges from the former area courts accustomed to hearing personal status law cases were assigned to hear criminal cases with little or no training, leading to many errors and inconsistencies in judgments. Second, the public was not taught about the new legal system, and thus people were not aware of their rights or procedures under the new policies. Third, while many people welcomed the new *hisbah* forces tasked with enforcing sharia observance, over time, abuses by these forces in carrying out their tasks turned people against them. Moreover, many were disappointed that implementation of sharia was focused on punishment, rather than on fulfilling the social and economic responsibilities laid down by the law. Support for sharia law was also seen as a political tool used by candidates in elections in the north, as well as in the election campaign of Muhammidu Buhari, the main opposition candidate against Obasanjo in the 2003 presidential election.

Some of the opposition to sharia law comes from the fact that, in practice, it is unequally applied more often toward poor people and women (Elaigwu and Galadima 2003). It could also be argued that it discriminates against Muslims, who are not allowed to choose whether to be tried in sharia or nonsharia courts. Critics of the application of Islamic law point to a number of problems it has created in the northern states. Among these are discrimination against non-Muslims who are not allowed to sell alcohol or gamble in public, prohibitions against Christians building churches, state funding for imam salaries for which Christians are not eligible, transportation problems for Christian women who are not allowed to ride with men or on buses reserved for women wearing the hijab, and the exclusion of women from public positions (Sodiq 2009).

There is debate around sharia law's constitutionality. Opponents argue that the constitution prohibits the establishment of a state religion (section 10). Proponents argue that section 38 of the constitution, which guarantees freedom of religion, allows sharia law to be implemented, for to be a good Muslim, one has to live in an Islamic order, which requires sharia law. Others support it on practical grounds, as Islamic criminal law is seen as helping to curb corruption and crime through its harsh punishments. Moreover, sharia courts are often seen to be more transparent and more expedient than secular courts. Yet many argue that the punishments imposed by Islamic law, such as stoning, caning, and amputation, are cruel and inhumane, treatment prohibited both by the federal constitution (section 34) and international law (including Article 16 of the 1984 UN Convention against Torture and Other Cruel, Inhuman or Degrading Treatment or Punishment).

There is debate within the Muslim community about sharia law in the northern states as well. Some argue that the imposition of punishment is discriminatory against the poor and has allowed politicians to become personally wealthy, a state of affairs contradictory to the aims of sharia law itself (Okpanachi 2011). There is also quite a bit of variation in its implementation. For example, the role of the government in implementing sharia law is strong in Kebbi State, while in Kaduna State,

Muslim civil society organizations are more active in implementing it. In Kebbi State, the government created and funded a State Department of Religious Affairs (which included a Hisbah Committee, Preaching Board, and Zakat and Sadaqat Board) to deal with matters related to Muslims. In Kaduna State, the government established a Bureau for Religious Affairs with separate branches for Muslims and Christians that work together to resolve common problems. It appears that these sharia areas are worse for Muslims than for non-Muslims. Human Rights Watch Report has several instances of individuals being arrested, detained, or subjected to other types of abuses for expressing views against sharia. In many cases, however, people self-censor.

Another set of state regulations that has become associated with religious conflicts relates to laws on indigeneity. In addition to ethnic identity, the Nigerian state also recognizes the difference between indigenes, whose lineage can be traced to a particular region, and settlers, who are not native to a region. Thus, citizenship in a state is separate from Nigerian citizenship and is tied to one's status as an indigene or settler, not residency. These categories have led to discrimination at the state level, where lacking a certificate of indigeneity from local officials and district heads deprives individuals of meaningful citizenship and thus access to employment in federal institutions, admission to universities, and access to schools, health care, and jobs, as well as participation in local politics. Indigeneity is thus a way for those in power to exclude potential competitors. The Indigeneity Clause in the 1999 Constitution (section 147) declares that the president must appoint at least one cabinet minister from each state, who is in turn an indigene of that state.

An example of how indigeneity laws overlap religion-state issues comes from Plateau State. The middle belt region (where Plateau State is located) was historically majority Christian, although it was increasingly subject to settlement by Muslims. Ethnicity and religion often overlap in the state, but not always. The Berom, Anaguta, and Afizere (BAA) are the main indigenous ethnic groups, and the Hausa-Fulani are a major settler group. Tensions between the groups also have a religious element. Indigenes tend to be Christians, and settlers tend to be Muslims, even though some of them have been living in the area for several generations. The BAA argue that the Hausa-Fulani settlers have a hidden agenda to Islamize the middle belt.[41] Government positions have tended to be dominated by Christians in recent years, leading to resentment among some Muslims. But Christians have complained that Muslims dominate or monopolize economic activities in some areas. Disputes between the groups have been around political positions, land use, and other economic issues, although starting in the early 2000s, these issues began to take on religious overtones.

Ongoing violence in the middle belt stems from indigene-settler conflicts, even though it is often attributed to religion. Violence in Jos (the administrative capital of Plateau State) in 2008 surrounded the results of a local council election that was thought to be rigged in favor of an indigene candidate. The violence erupted before the electoral results were announced, and there was evidence of large-scale preparation on the part of Hausa-Fulani. Groups targeted churches and Christian houses, and retaliatory attacks by Christians targeted Muslim houses and businesses. In the end, more than 200 people died in the attacks, with an additional 130 killed in alleged extrajudicial killings by soldiers.[42] Another outbreak of violence in January 2010 resulted in an additional 500 deaths. Involvement of the Islamic extremist group Boko Haram in the Jos violence was reported in 2011 and 2012. Yet analysts in the region argue that religion is used to mask disputes over citizenship and access to communal resources.[43]

How the state manages and distributes resources is an important part of understanding the nature of conflicts in Nigeria. Nigeria is an oil-exporting nation, with oil accounting for approximately 95 percent of state revenue. Fitting into the model of the "resource curse," oil wealth has contributed to the corruption of the country's political and economic systems (Ross 2001). Political power holders are able to use their control over oil resources to provide patronage to their political allies or to buy off dissenters. The seeming endless supply of oil revenue also encourages fiscal irresponsibility, leading to increased foreign debt and less reliance on tax revenues for government income. Because oil has dominated the Nigerian economy, private enterprise has suffered, meaning that the state has had to play a large role in subsidizing projects and inducing development. The inability of the state to provide for welfare and security has driven many Nigerians to depend on religious organizations to articulate their demands, provide protection, offer arenas for professional advancement, and connect them to international networks. This, in turn, has led to conflict as these groups compete with each other for adherents and influence.

The imposition of sharia law in the 12 northern states and the religious conflict between Muslims and Christians in the middle belt of the country illustrate ways that politicians have manipulated religion to serve their own needs, to the detriment of Nigeria's citizens and its societal peace. Rather than imposing a host of repressive measures against all religious groups, both national and state-level politicians manipulate religion policy and control its enforcement in ways that exacerbate existing tensions and create greater religious ferment. This, in turn, allows them to gain electoral support by promising to protect coreligionists, to favor them in the allocation of scarce resources, or to pass laws that reflect their religious teachings. Moreover, security forces at the federal level have failed to defuse religious conflicts and instead have further inflamed them by using indiscriminate force targeted at members of particular religious groups, regardless of whether they have been guilty of crimes. Therefore, by failing to adequately manage conflict in a country where religion is an important part of many people's lives, politicians in Nigeria have selectively targeted some religious groups in pursuing their own political and economic interests.

## Singapore

Like Nigeria, Singapore is a state that crafts its religion policy in response to the issues that arise from governing a heterogeneous population. There are significant differences between these countries as well. First, Nigeria has seen a greater amount of actual conflict over religion than Singapore in the period of independence. Thus, while preserving religious harmony is a stated goal of both governments, in Singapore it is a proactive strategy, and in Nigeria it is reactive. Second, politicians in Singapore do not use religion for political gain in the same way that politicians do in Nigeria. This has partly to do with the difference in state power and capacity in the two countries: Singapore is a small country with a strong central government; Nigeria is a large and populous country with a federal system that the central government attempts to control but often fails to manage effectively. Therefore, the government of Singapore has been more effective in managing religion policy and preventing violent conflict within its borders than the Nigerian government. This means that when the government of Singapore represses religious groups, it is because of a deliberate policy to target specific groups, rather than because of a failure to protect them, as is often the case in Nigeria.

The Southeast Asian island city-state of Singapore gained independence from Great Britain in 1959. Since then, the People's Action Party

(PAP) has won every election. Lee Kuan Yew was prime minister from independence to 1990. In 1993, Ong Teng Cheong became the country's first directly elected president, but in 1999, S. R. Nathan was declared president without election after being the only candidate eligible to run (he was reelected in 2005). In 2004, the eldest son of Lee Kuan Yew, Lee Hsien Loong, became prime minister (without an election) and remains in the position to this day. In 2011, Tony Tan was elected president. The country is well known for its prosperity and is often referred to as one of Asia's economic tigers.

Religion and ethnicity often overlap in Singapore, especially among non-Christians. According to statistics from 2012, 74.1 percent of the population is ethnic Chinese, 13.4 percent ethnic Malay, 9.2 percent ethnic Indian, and 3.3 percent other (US Department of State 2012). The ethnic Chinese are Buddhist (54 percent), Daoist (11 percent), and Christian (16.5 percent). Ethnic Malays are almost all Muslim. Ethnic Indians are Hindu (55 percent), Muslim (25 percent), and Christian (12 percent).

The Constitution of the Republic of Singapore dates from September 1963. It has been amended multiple times, most recently in April 2010.[44] The constitution guarantees the individual right to profess, practice, and propagate religion. Unlike neighboring Malaysia, Singapore refrained from adopting a state religion and instead has followed a policy of secularism. Religious groups are given the right to manage their own affairs, establish and maintain institutions, and acquire and own property. Religious groups are also given the right to establish educational institutions. The constitution recognizes the special position of the Malay minority as indigenous to Singapore and guarantees their protection. With regard to the Muslim religion, article 153 states: "The Legislature shall by law make provision for regulating Muslim religious affairs and for constituting a Council to advise the President in matters relating to the Muslim religion."

The state is actively involved in regulating religious affairs. Its justification for this level of involvement is to maintain ethnic and religious harmony in a multicultural environment. There are regulations on the use of commercial space for religious activities and religious organizations that apply to all groups. The regulations impose limits on the amount of space that can be used by groups, and religious activities are permitted only twice weekly. The Societies Act requires registration of all groups of 10 or more persons, including religious groups.[45] Registration confers legal identity, allowing owning property, conducting financial transactions, and holding public meetings. Acting as a member of or attending a meeting of an unlawful society is punishable by a fine, imprisonment, or both.

The Maintenance of Religious Harmony Act of 1990 (revised in 2001) gives the government the power to prevent religious group leaders and members from carrying out political activities, creating "ill will" between groups, carrying out subversive activities, and inciting "disaffection" against the government.[46] The Presidential Council on Religious Harmony reports to the minister of home affairs. The council has the authority to recommend the issuance of restraining orders against individuals who have been accused of causing problems among religious groups, engaging in aggressive and "insensitive" proselytizing, or mixing religion and politics. As of 2008, no restraining orders had been issued, although scholars have argued that this does not mean that the executive has not used its authority under the act to issue warnings to keep religious leaders in line and religion out of politics (Tey 2008).

The government does not allow religious instruction in public schools, but it is allowed in private schools. In 1982, the government changed educational policy to require every student in the third year of secondary school to enter a two-year program on religious knowledge. However, in 1989, the government ended the program, replacing it with a civics and moral education program. The program was part of a larger project to revitalize and increase the popularity of Confucianism and to reethnicize the Chinese population of the country for the purpose of reinforcing traditionalist values and achieving strong economic development (Tamney 1992).

The government does not explicitly favor a particular religious group, but it does not tolerate religious groups that become politically active. In the 1970s and 1980s, for example, the government prosecuted Catholic, Muslim, Sikh, and Hindu groups and individuals for being too political (Kuah 1998). It has also prosecuted Protestant groups for proselytizing, claiming it upsets religious harmony. Government officials have made statements about the threat to social cohesion caused by mixing religion and politics and by religious intolerance. For instance, the minister for home affairs was quoted by the US State Department (2011) as saying, "We cannot have unbridled freedom of religion, at the expense of nation-building and social cohesion, or to such an extent that it foments divisiveness among our people."

The Islamic Religious Council of Singapore (Majlis Ulama Islam Singapura, MUIS), set up under the Administration of Muslim Law Act (1966), is a semiofficial agency that advises the government on the concerns of Muslims and has some regulatory functions over religious matters. The president appoints members to three-year terms. It drafts the weekly sermon (approved by the government) used in mosques. The council also oversees a mosque building fund financed by voluntary payroll deductions. The Administration of Muslim Law Act gives Muslims the option to have family affairs governed by sharia law. It also establishes a Fatwa Committee, chaired by the mufti, that issues legal opinions (fatwa).

There is historical precedent for the existence of separate institutions for Muslims in Singapore. During colonial rule, the British officially recognized Muslim personal law with the Mahomedan Marriage Ordinance of 1880. The Mohammedan Advisory Board was established in 1915 to advise the colonial authorities on matters related to Muslim religion and customs. In 1946, it was replaced by the Muslim Advisory Board, which was instrumental in promoting legislation for the administration of Islamic law. The Muslim Ordinance of 1957 established the Shariah Court (SYC) to deal with Muslim family law (Rahman 2009).

Malay Muslims lag behind ethnic Chinese and Indians in education and income levels, a fact acknowledged and addressed by the government. Despite governmental sensitivity to Muslim concerns, the headscarf (*tudong*) has been controversial. Since the early 1990s, increasing numbers of parents of public school students had been requesting permission for their daughters to wear headscarves. In January 2002, four young primary school students were suspended for wearing the headscarf in violation of uniform requirements.[47] Following this, the MUIS issued a public statement that Islam did not require young girls to cover their heads, while a nongovernmental Islamic scholars and teachers organization countered with a statement arguing that modest covering was compulsory for women (Kadir 2010). An opposition leader who criticized the government's ban on wearing the headscarf in public schools was convicted of violating the Public Entertainment and Meetings Act, which restricts discussing sensitive religious or ethnic issues in public. His conviction barred him from seeking public office for five years.

In June 2003, the government adopted the Declaration on Religious Harmony following a period of heightened sensitivity to Muslim concerns (e.g., the *tudong* debate), along with increased radicalization among some Muslims, as evidenced by the discovery of a bomb planted in December 2001 by Jemaah Islamiah, a group with links to al-Qaeda. The declaration affirms the importance of religious harmony for peace and prosperity in the country and pledges the state's commitment to promoting societal cohesion, respecting freedom of religion, fostering interreligious communication, and ensuring that religion is not used to create conflict in the country.[48] The declaration is not legally binding, although it does represent consensus on the part of political and religious actors on the need to foster religious harmony, moderation, and toleration in the country (Li-Ann 2004). It echoes previous statements by President Lee Kuan Yew about the nature of Confucian culture and its responsibility for maintaining the stability and prosperity of Singapore.[49] In this sense, religion is viewed as a traditional force that can be harnessed to aid the state in managing its citizens.

The government claims to be sensitive to ethnic and religious concerns, but it also recognizes religion's potential to be a political force. The government deregistered and banned the Jehovah's Witnesses in 1972 because its members refuse to perform obligatory military service, salute the flag, and pledge allegiance to the state. The government also banned publications by the group's two publishing arms, the International Bible Students Association and the Watch Tower Bible and Tract Society, and possession of such materials makes one subject to a fine and jail time. In 1996, the Court of Appeals upheld the right of Jehovah's Witnesses to practice and propagate their religious belief. However, because they are deregistered, meetings are considered illegal; they are able to meet in private homes. The government deregistered the Unification Church in 1982. It prohibits importation of publications by the Unification Church, the Church of Scientology, the Children of God (also known as the Family of Love, the Family, and Family International), and the Church of Satan, and possession of such publications is punishable by a fine and imprisonment.

Like other states in Southeast Asia, Singapore's government selectively represses religious groups according to their level of perceived threat to the regime. Despite some religious heterogeneity, societal divisions based on religion have been low, as ethnicity and religion tend to overlap, and groups have not made strong attempts at religious conversion. Therefore, in Singapore, selective repression of some religious groups results from the interaction of low political competition in a country governed consistently by a single party since 1959 with a desire by those in power to demonstrate their strong control over society by repressing independent groups that may arise to challenge the ongoing regime. Although religious repression is not a consistent policy as in other similarly repressive regimes, Singaporean officials do use state policy on religion to target religious groups that challenge the political order. Thus, the state punishes groups accused of fomenting religious discord and those, such as the Jehovah's Witnesses, that challenge political norms. These policies are motivated by the regime's need to maintain a stable society capable of continued economic prosperity, which allows the regime to justify its repression of independent political groups and civil society.

## *Conclusion*

This chapter has examined four states from different parts of the world that similarly target only some groups for religious repression. In Kyrgyzstan and Bahrain, repression is targeted at the religious majority; in Nigeria, it is targeted at those who are a minority in particular regions of the country. Singapore targets only politicized religious groups or those that are perceived to threaten societal harmony. Despite these differences in targets, what all four countries (and others in this category) share is relative religious freedom for those groups that avoid the ire of politicians by staying out of politics.

As this book has argued, the interaction of levels of political competition and the nature of religious divisions in society can explain why countries display similar patterns of religious repression. Even though they vary somewhat in terms of how much political competition they allow, each case discussed in this chapter contains a religiously (and in some cases ethnically) heterogeneous society and some history of struggles over political power based on these societal divisions. In Kyrgyzstan, secular politicians battle both Islamist-inspired political movements and prosperous Uzbek ethnic minorities (and sometimes groups that overlap in those qualities) for control over a postcommunist republic split by inherited ethnic divisions and clan-based infighting. In Bahrain, the Sunni minority monarchy continues to rule over an increasingly mobilized Shia majority demanding greater representation and access to the political system. In Nigeria, strategic politicians manipulate religious divisions and sentiments to gain support from coreligionists, to whom they promise protection and a larger share of scarce resources. In Singapore, the government washes over ethnic and religious heterogeneity by reference to an imagined shared set of Asian values that masks the repressive efforts the state enacts to impose harmony on the population.

At the heart of policies targeting religious groups is a need to control independent civil society. While they vary in their levels of political competition, all of the regimes similarly lack a commitment to pluralism despite significant societal heterogeneity. By selectively imposing restrictions on religion, politicians in these countries can restrict the diversity of civil society and prevent the growth of groups that might challenge the political status quo. Unlike states that repress all but one group, many of the ruling governments in this category do not ally with a single religious majority to obtain their support. And unlike states that repress all religious groups, most of the political leaders in these countries still must rely on some sort of election to gain and retain political power and therefore cannot impose blanket repressive policies without facing recrimination at the polls. Even in the absence of meaningful elections (as in Bahrain and Singapore), the need to project an image of political and societal harmony trumps the government's absolute repressive tendencies and moderates them to be more selective in their application. In the end, religious groups that remain private and inwardly focused are able to function relatively freely, and those that seek involvement in public affairs are rewarded with restrictions aimed at silencing dissent.

# 6

## *Paradoxical or Rational?*

### RELIGIOUS FREEDOM IN NONDEMOCRATIC STATES

IS IT PARADOXICAL for nondemocratic states not to repress religious groups? This chapter addresses this question by examining a set of 39 states in which no religious groups are subjected to harsh government restrictions on their ability to associate or express themselves. In this set of countries, the religious majority did not receive special favors from the government, nor did the government seek to control it. Religious minorities existed and were not restricted in their activities. The few regulations that did exist were enforced with little discrimination and were intended to ensure the peaceful conduct of religious activities in the country (see table 6.1). This chapter argues that in countries that continue to experience nondemocratic rule, the lack of perceived political threat from religious groups explains why leaders refrain from attempting to repress them. The countries closely examined in this chapter are Albania, Cambodia, Senegal, and Peru.

The countries that did not repress any religious groups in 2010 had higher levels of political competition than those in the other categories of repression, scoring an average of 4 on Polity's regime scale (which ranges from −10 to 10).[1] Yet the range of political competitiveness across these countries was still quite wide. While there were several countries that had been successful in implementing democratic institutions and qualified as electoral democracies as of 2010 (e.g., Taiwan and Senegal), others fell on the less competitive end of the regime spectrum (e.g., Cambodia and Swaziland). Therefore, more political competition did not automatically translate to less religious repression—a phenomenon observed across all of the countries in this study.

Table 6.1 Religious restrictions in countries repressing no religions (2010)

|  | Albania | Cambodia | Senegal | Peru |
|---|---|---|---|---|
| Religious observance |  |  |  |  |
| Places of worship |  |  |  |  |
| Religious laws |  |  |  |  |
| Conversion |  |  |  |  |
| Proselytizing |  | x |  |  |
| Discriminatory registration/bans |  |  |  | x |
| Clerical appointments |  |  |  |  |
| Religious speech or publications |  | x |  |  |
| Religious education |  |  |  |  |
| Religious political parties |  |  | x |  |
| Religious associations |  |  |  |  |
| Political speech |  |  |  |  |
| Access to political office |  |  |  |  |

A feature many of the countries in this category did share was lower levels of religious division in their societies. In countries such as Albania and Cambodia, a history of extremely harsh persecution of religion under previous regimes made it impossible for current governments to enforce such repression for fear of being associated with the past. Some of the countries—such as Albania—had populations that were not highly religious. In these cases, repressing religion was not an effective strategy for politicians attempting to gain or retain office, as religious groups were not politically mobilized. In other places—such as Senegal and many of the other sub-Saharan countries in this category—popular religiosity was much higher. Yet politicians did not repress religious groups either because they relied on religious organizations for political support or because other sorts of divisions—such as ethnicity—were more politically salient. In some of the countries in this category—such as Peru—changing religious demographics and political openings shifted religion-state relations from favoring one group to expanding benefits for all religions. Such examples point to the dynamic nature of religion-state relations and the importance of understanding how both political and religious factors can affect them.

The chapter begins with case studies of Albania, Cambodia, Senegal, and Peru to illustrate how the level of political competition and the nature of present and historical religious divisions interact to lead to a particularly interesting situation of nondemocratic states that have high levels of religious freedom. It concludes with a discussion of the similarities across the 39 countries in this category that help to explain why they choose to refrain from repressing religious groups.

## *Albania*

Albania is the only postcommunist country examined in this book that did not repress religious groups as of 2010. That represents a dramatic turnaround from the communist era, when the regime severely repressed religion. How was Albania able to overcome its communist legacy of religion-state relations? Why does the current government refrain from imposing restrictions that target religious groups specifically or favor one group over others? The role that religion plays in Albanian society, its particular religious demographics, and its unique experiences under communist rule (as compared with other communist bloc states in Central and Eastern Europe) explain why Albania, though not a fully democratic regime, nevertheless does largely refrain from religious repression.

Albania is a religiously diverse society. According to the 2011 census, Sunni Muslims were nearly 57 percent of the population, Roman Catholics 10 percent, Orthodox Christians (the Autocephalous Orthodox Church of Albania) nearly 7 percent, and Bektashi (a form of Shia Sufism) 2 percent (although the percentage of people sympathizing with the order is thought to be much greater) (US Department of State 2012). Other groups present include Baha'is, Jehovah's Witnesses, and the Church of Jesus Christ of Latter-Day Saints (Mormons).[2] Surveys suggest that religion does not play a strong role in Albanian daily life. According to the 2002 World Values Survey (the most recent one conducted in Albania), 23 percent of respondents report never attending religious services, and only 24 percent report attending services once a week or more often.[3]

Article 10 of the 1998 Constitution declares that there is no official religion in Albania and that the state is "neutral in questions of belief and conscience."[4] It states that relations between the state and religious communities are to be regulated based on agreements between the groups and the Council of Ministers, to be ratified by parliament, and that religious communities are juridical persons. Article 24 guarantees freedom of conscience and religion, including the right to choose and change religion and to express it individually and collectively. Article 9 of the Constitution outlaws religious political parties only if they are based on "totalitarian methods, which incite and support racial, religious, regional or ethnic hatred, which use violence to take power or influence state policies, as well as those with a secret character."

The Law on Associations allows religious groups to register as nonprofit organizations and to be recognized as juridical persons, giving them the ability to hold bank accounts and own property. Religious communities do not have tax-exempt status, however. Religious groups are not required to register or be licensed. The State Committee on Cults, founded in 1999, regulates relations between the state and religious groups. In 2010, the committee reported that more than 230 religious groups, organizations, foundations, and educational institutions were operating in the country. Religion is not taught in public schools, but private religious schools are allowed. The State Committee on Cults is authorized to approve their curricula.

As in other postcommunist countries, property restitution claims remained an unresolved issue in Albania. In July 2004, the parliament approved a law on the restitution and compensation of properties that the communist regime had confiscated from religious communities. The law gave religious communities the same rights as private individuals in such matters, although it limited property restitution to 150 acres. The government also announced its intention to remove bureaucratic hurdles that had hindered the return of properties and to establish a fund for monetary compensation.

In October 2008, the government signed bilateral agreements with the Orthodox, Muslim, and Bektashi communities, in line with Article 10 of the Constitution. These agreements gave the communities official recognition, prioritized property restitution (through the State Agency for the Restitution and Compensation of Property), and tax exemption. The Albanian Evangelical Alliance (VUSH) signed an agreement with the government in November 2010. A law on the financing of religious communities was passed in June 2009 that gave them government financial support and subsidized clergy salaries. In February 2010, a new antidiscrimination law was passed, creating the Office of the Commissioner for Protection from Discrimination.

Religious minorities in Albania are also free from state repression. The Catholic Church was severely persecuted under communist rule, but postcommunist Albania attempted to normalize relations by granting citizenship to Mother Teresa of Calcutta (born in Skopje in 1910). In 1993, Pope John Paul II ordained two archbishops and two bishops and in 1994 ordained the first Albanian cardinal. Jehovah's Witnesses, who have experienced high levels of repression in other postcommunist countries, have operated with relative freedom. Despite some issues with media coverage of the Jehovah's Witnesses giving false accounts of youth members committing suicide, the government worked with the group to quell the rumors. The Jehovah's Witnesses have not reported any other hindrances to carrying out their programs in Albania. Even Baha'is, who are often subjected to repression in traditionally Muslim countries, operate freely in the country.

The fact that the Albanian government chooses to repress no religious groups can be explained by three factors: a legacy of harsh religious persecution under communism, demographic patterns, and the character of religious practice in the country. First, because of harsh repression under the previous communist regime, current Albanian leaders have attempted to distance themselves from association with the past by adopting more tolerant policies on religion. Upon independence from the Ottoman Empire in 1912, Albania was declared secular, and freedom of religion was guaranteed. Sunni Muslims, Orthodox Christians, Catholics, and the Bektashi community were represented in the High Council of the Regency. In 1939, Albania was invaded by Fascist Italy, and the Communist Party of Albania was established in 1941. During World War II, Enver Hoxha commanded the Communist Party's National Liberation Movement that defeated the Italian and German occupation armies in 1944. The communists then established a provisional government with Hoxha as prime minister.

The first constitution of the Hoxha government (1946) guaranteed religious freedom to Albanian citizens, declared the church separate from the state, forbade the use of religion for political purposes, and banned political organizations based on religion. It was soon replaced with laws restricting freedom of religion, which reached a climax in 1967, when the state was declared atheist (Ramet 1988). Article 37 of the 1976 Constitution declared, "The state recognizes no religion whatever and supports atheist propaganda for the purpose of inculcating the scientific materialist world outlook in people." Article 55 stated, "The creation of any type of organization of a fascist, anti-democratic, religious, and anti-socialist character is prohibited. Fascist, anti-democratic, religious, war-mongering, and anti-socialist activities and propaganda, as well as the incitement of national and racial hatred are prohibited."[5]

The campaign against religion was particularly harsh under communism, with all remaining religious buildings destroyed, clergy dismissed or killed, and the state engaging in an active propaganda campaign against religion (Trix 1994). Under the Hoxha regime, 2,169 mosques, churches, monasteries, and other religious institutions were closed (Gjuraj 2000). Clergy were subjected to show trials, sentenced to death, and, in some cases, simply killed by the regime. Ramiz Alia succeeded Enver Hoxha upon his death in 1985. Alia introduced gradual reforms in the country, which eventually led to the collapse of the one-party state and regime transition. A provisional constitution was adopted in April 1991. In March 1992, the anticommunist Democratic Party won in the country's first multiparty elections, Alia resigned, and Sali Berisha's party took control. Berisha served as president from 1992 to 1997 and has been prime minister since 2005. Postcommunist Albania has made significant progress toward increasing political competition; Freedom House still classified the country as "partly free" in its 2013 report, despite describing it as an electoral democracy (Freedom House 2013). Corruption, media bias, and political pressure on the courts contribute to continued problems with democratic consolidation. Yet the government generally respects religious freedom. Hoping to distance themselves from association with the prior regime, postcommunist leaders have not used religious repression as a strategy to punish regime opponents or prevent the formation of political opposition.

Second, the pattern and history of religious divisions in Albania also help to explain why it does not repress religion today. Albania is a traditionally multireligious society, with Catholicism practiced mostly in the north, Orthodoxy mostly in the south, Sunni Islam in the central and eastern regions, and Bektashism in the south. Religion in Albania is often described as syncretistic; it is not uncommon for people to adhere to more than one religion at a time, and religious practice is not particularly orthodox. According to one analyst, "Belonging to a religion means belonging to a social group. Although the individual may share group prejudices towards other religious groups, the essential group values are defined by a system of kinship and alliance, of solidarity and hostility, of status and social position. . . as being common to all Albanians" (Doja 2006, 88). Others have argued that kinship ties trump religion as the primary marker of identity in Albania, thus leading to intermarriage and limited religious conflict (Young 1999). Therefore, there are few divisions for politicians to exploit for political purposes.

Other issues related to religious demography and historical relations may also explain the lack of religious repression today. Historically, there has been little conversion between Islam, Catholicism, and Eastern Orthodoxy. These groups seldom proselytize each other's adherents, and traditional religious identities are generally respected. Moreover, new religious groups—either Islamic or Christian—have not grown at rapid rates over the past decades since transition away from communism. Traditional groups have not had to fear strong competition for adherents from other traditional religions or from groups new to the country. Not fearing religious competition, religious groups do not pressure politicians to impose restrictions. Related to the first point, harsh repression during the communist period may also have fostered religious harmony by leading the traditional religious groups to develop an extraordinary ecumenism that persists to this day and results in little religious competition or strife in the country (Gjuraj 2000).

Third, culturalist theorists argue that the character of religion as it is practiced in Albania is not likely to provoke conflict between groups. Bektashi Islam, which has a long history in the country, differs from orthodox Sunni Islam in important ways. Bektashis are a Sufi order arriving in Albania from the Ottoman Empire in the seventeenth century that became more deeply rooted in the nineteenth century. Bektashi doctrines have been described as having both Islamic and non-Islamic elements, with "beliefs and customs originating in Christianity and antique religions as well as ancient Turkic elements" (Doja 2006, 85). It is often described as a more tolerant form of Islam. Although official figures do not show Bekstashi adherence to be high, Bektashism has been associated with Albanian nationalism and national identity since the early nineteenth century.

More orthodox forms of Islam are practiced in the country, as Sunnis are the majority of Muslim adherents in Albania. In the early 1990s, funding for mosque construction came from Muslim countries such as Saudi Arabia and Kuwait. There have also been Islamist political movements. Motherland is a Muslim party calling for religious education, a ministry of religion, and status for clergy.[6] In 2004, it was denied registration on the basis of inaccurate member lists. The Union of Imams is an independent organization that represents Muslim theologians. In 2011, it issued an open letter protesting a proposed bill that would ban wearing headscarves in public schools.[7] Unlike other countries, however, Albania does not have a government-sponsored or affiliated Muslim organization that oversees mosques, clerics, and schools. Thus, the government does not control the practice of the largest religion in the country or grant it benefits that it withholds from religious minorities.

Albania's relatively competitive electoral arena and low levels of religious division explain why it refrains from repressing any religious groups. Despite having failed to consolidate democracy, the country has made progress in opening up political competition to a larger number of groups since its transition from communism. Generally open competition makes it more difficult for incumbent political leaders to impose repressive policies on particular social groups without facing opposition from other parts of government or voters at the polls. Politicians fail to impose repressive religion policies because religious divisions have historically been low in the country. Thus, there are few conflicts politicians could exploit to obtain greater support or repressive policies needed to prevent religiously based opposition from arising. Yet if religious divisions increase or democratic gains are reversed, we may find politicians using religion as a tool in their arsenal of manipulation in the future.

## *Cambodia*

Despite being located in a different world region, Cambodia shares some features with Albania. Both countries have had experience with communism, though Cambodia's continues to the present day. Both countries also have similarly low levels of religious conflict. Unlike Albania, however, the current Cambodian regime does not afford opportunities for political competition. In fact, Cambodia has among the lowest levels of political competition in the category of countries that repress no religious groups. Despite this major difference, the countries share a harsh legacy of religious repression from the previous regime, making the strategy an unwise one to pursue for a current regime that wishes to distance itself from the past. Therefore, although Albania and Cambodia have significantly different political institutions and levels of political competition, neither imposes repressive policies on religious groups.

A communist government—led by the Vietnamese-installed Cambodian People's Party (CPP) and Prime Minister Hun Sen—has governed Cambodia since 1979. When elections have been held, they have been characterized by fraud, political intimidation, and violence. Cambodia's head of state is King Norodom Sihanouk. Although the monarchy is respected as a symbol of national unity, the king has very little political power. The opposition Sam Rainsy Party has garnered seats in the National Assembly, but its namesake has suffered intimidation and been exiled from the country.

In addition to intimidation of political opponents and voters at the polls, the government represses the media both through legal means and by violence against journalists. Political activists are subject to arrest and police violence for protesting against government policies. Civil society organizations that focus on human rights issues are also subject to government harassment, although groups that provide social services are allowed to practice relatively unhindered (Freedom House 2013). Thus, the state seeks to repress politicized civil society, especially if it is mobilized against the ruling regime.

Despite strong government repression of civil society, religious groups operate relatively freely in the country. Cambodia is approximately 96 percent Buddhist, and ethnicity and religion are closely connected. Ethnic Cham Muslims make up less than 3 percent of the population and are concentrated in specific regions of the country. The remaining less than 2 percent of the population is Baha'i, Jewish, Cao Dai (ethnic Vietnamese), or Christian (US Department of State 2012).

Buddhism is the state religion in Cambodia, and the government provides some support for Buddhist institutions. Moreover, Buddhist religious instruction is the only type allowed in public schools; non-Buddhists may provide instruction in private schools. Yet like other religious groups, Buddhist organizations must apply to the Ministry of Cults and Religions for approval to construct places of worship and conduct religious activities. There is no penalty for not registering, and there are no reports of churches or mosques being denied permission to construct new facilities. Places of worship may not be used for political purposes.

In its initial years in power, the CPP limited the restoration of Buddhism in the country. However, recognizing the need to establish greater legitimacy and gain popular support, the government removed remaining restrictions on ordination of monks and temple restoration. Political leaders also began to display public piety and attend rites at Buddhist shrines. In 1991, the government declared Buddhism the state religion and officially allied itself with the Buddhist monastic community (sangha).[8] In return, traditionalist monks have offered their support to the CPP and spoken out against critics of the regime (Harris 2001). However, other groups of monks are either critical of the government or choose to remain apolitical.

Despite some favoritism granted to Buddhists, the government fails to repress minority religions (a condition required to categorize a country as repressing all religions but one). Religious minorities are relatively small and associated with ethnic groups that have not been politically active or agitated for group-based rights. Despite concerns about Islamic terrorism related to the Cham Muslim community in recent years, the government has taken no action against the group. In 2003, the Directive on Controlling External Religions prohibited public proselytizing, although enforcement was limited to banning door-to-door proselytizing during lunch hours.

The legacy of the genocidal Khmer Rouge regime (1975–1978) under Pol Pot is important for understanding contemporary religion-state relations in Cambodia. That regime left approximately 2 million of the country's 7 million inhabitants dead. Cambodian Buddhism suffered heavily under the regime, with an estimated five of every eight monks executed and many temples destroyed (Keyes 1990). The ideology of the regime was radically antireligious, and it sought to erase Buddhism as a fundamental source of Khmer identity and replace it with a new Kampuchean one.

Despite being a communist party, the CPP did not pursue an antireligious policy upon assuming power in 1979. In fact, one of the first actions of the new government was to restore Buddhism, allowing exiled monks to return and new ones to be ordained. This was mainly due to the party's need to establish native political legitimacy, as it had been put into power with Vietnamese backing. Moreover, because religious persecution was so strongly associated with the violence of the Khmer Rouge regime, the CPP could not legitimately attack religion once it came into power and expect to receive popular support.

The political and religious legacy of Cambodia explains the absence of religious repression in this strongly authoritarian country. Despite the ability of the government to impose repression—as evidenced by its repression of opposition parties, the media, and civic organizations—it chooses to allow Buddhist and other religious communities to operate relatively freely. This choice can be explained by the violent legacy of the Khmer Rouge regime and its association with extreme persecution of Buddhism, one of the most important institutions in Cambodian society (alongside the monarchy). Given the CPP's need to establish popular legitimacy in the face of a continuing monarchist presence in the country, the party and government chose to tolerate rather than repress religion.

# Senegal

Like Albania, the sub-Saharan state of Senegal has a majority-Muslim population with a tradition of active Sufi brotherhoods. Like Cambodia, Senegal has one religious group that is a large majority, which ruling politicians have courted for support and legitimacy. Like Albania but unlike Cambodia, Senegal has a recent history of competitive elections. Senegal's higher level of political competition, combined with the fact that religious divisions have been historically low in society, explains why it belongs in the category of states that repress no religious groups.

Islam is practiced by about 94 percent of the Senegalese population. Most Muslims belong to Sufi brotherhoods. At independence in 1960, 50 percent of Muslims belonged to the Tijaniyya brotherhood and 40 percent to the Murides (Clark 1999). Christians constitute about 4 percent of the population, and approximately 2 percent practice indigenous religions exclusively or have no religion (US Department of State 2012). Senegal is characterized by a high degree of religiosity plus a high degree of tolerance of religion. Alfred Stepan (2012, 380) characterizes Senegalese society as practicing a pattern of secularism he calls "rituals of respect," defined as "recurrent, public, and reciprocal political practices" through which groups and the state interact and develop mutual tolerance. The country does house non-Sufi Islamic reformist groups that challenge the kind of Islam practiced by Sufis and argue for a greater role for Islam in society and the imposition of Islamic law in the country. One important group is the Society of the Servants of the Merciful (Jama'at 'Ibad ar-Rahman, JIR), founded in 1978. Yet they have not grown strong enough to challenge the dominance of the Sufi brotherhoods.

The constitution of Senegal (2001) defines the country as secular and guarantees the equality of all citizens regardless of religion. Article 4 forbids parties from identifying themselves with a race, ethnicity, sex, religion, sect, language, or region. Despite this, parties such as Serigne Modou Kara Mbacké's Party for Truth have been religious in nature. Article 24 guarantees freedom of conscience, belief, and religious practice and the independence of religious organizations.[9] Religious or secular associations must register with the Ministry of the Interior to attain legal status. Registration allows associations to own property, establish bank accounts, receive donations, and acquire tax exemption. Registration is generally granted to groups. The government directly funds religious groups for maintaining places of worship and schools and for special events, without discriminating among groups. The government also encourages (by providing free airplane tickets) and helps to organize pilgrimages to Mecca for Muslims and to the Vatican for Catholics.

Prior to 2002, religious education was prohibited in public schools and permitted in private ones. In October 2002, the government passed a law allowing two hours of optional religious education in the public school curriculum in an attempt to increase school enrollment. It could be Islamic or Christian, according to student demand. The government also began to operate Islamic schools. Demand for these is high, with enrollment up to 60,000 as of 2012. Public demands for additional schools continue.

The state and religious groups have worked together on legislation. For example, in 1999, the government passed a law banning female genital mutilation (FGM) and enlisted the help of religious groups such as the National Association of Imams in Senegal to support the ban with religious arguments and to train imams on how to speak about it (Stepan 2012). A unified family code was passed in 1972 under President Léopold Senghor. At the time it was passed, religious leaders opposed it because it abolished the French colonial policy of applying French or Islamic law, depending on the status of the individual. The debate was reopened after the 2000 elections, and in 2002, the Islamic Committee for the Reform of the Senegalese Family Code (Comité Islamique pour la reforme du Code de la Famille au Sénégal, CIRCOFS) launched a campaign to adopt an alternative Islamic Personal Code (Code du Statut Personnel Islamique) that would apply sharia law to Muslims. Muslims are allowed to choose either the family code or Islamic law to adjudicate family conflicts on issues such as marriage and inheritances.

Senegal has a long history of religion-state cooperation. Under French colonial rule, the administration worked to contain Muslim leaders who rebelled in the name of their religion. However, colonial rulers did cooperate with brotherhoods, permitting them to recruit members, organize pilgrimages, and establish religious schools. As long as the religious leaders (marabouts) stayed out of politics and taught their followers to cooperate with the secular state, colonial administrators did not interfere in religious matters. This policy continued in the immediate postindependence period.

Senegal became independent in 1960. Léopold Sédar Senghor (a Catholic) was elected president in 1960. Under his rule, Senegal developed into a de facto single-party state, although some opposition parties were permitted and regular elections were held. In 1981, Senghor stepped down in favor of his chosen successor, Abdou Diouf. During Diouf's rule, presidential term limits were abolished, and election regulations became more restrictive. The March 2000 presidential election was the first change of power after 40 years of Socialist Party (PS) rule and 20 years of President Abdou Diouf. Abdoulaye Wade of the Senegalese Democratic Party (PDS) won a seven-year term. Wade was reelected to a new five-year term in February 2007 with nearly 56 percent of the vote. In 2010, Wade reversed the constitutional provision that limits presidential terms to two, allowing him to run in the 2012 elections. However, in the end, Macky Sall of the Alliance for the Republic party won the election, and Wade conceded.

Postindependence politicians used their connections to Sufi brotherhoods for political support and to mobilize constituents (Ellis and Ter Haar 2004). In return, the government rewarded religious leaders with official patronage, including material resources (Cruse O'Brien 2003). For example, President Senghor actively sought the support of the Murides. During a constitutional crisis in 1962, Muride and Tijaniyya leaders supported Senghor against his main rival, Mamadu Dia. In exchange for support from the government—including the declaration of towns as independent religious centers—religious leaders defended Senghor against protesters and urged the public to vote for Senghor in successive elections.

Senghor's successor, Abdou Diouf, was a Tijaniyya and received strong support from the brotherhood, which was politically influential. Government contracts favored the brotherhoods, especially the Murides, who were the largest investors in the country. At the same time, the government stayed out of internal religious matters. Religious leaders supported PS candidates and instructed their followers to turn out and vote for the PS (Clark 1999). However, by the late 1980s and into the 1990s, the religious leadership was declining to give political advice to followers, as leaders were too close to the government to challenge it, and their fate was tied with that of the government (Cruse O'Brien 2003).

More recent leaders have used religion to gain popular legitimacy. President Wade successfully used Muride support to his advantage. For example, in the 2002 local elections, the Muride caliph, Serigne Saliou Mbacké, was on the PDS candidate list, though his name was withdrawn after protests. Before the 2007 presidential election, the caliph of Touba appeared on national television saying that reelecting Wade would help the completion of the modernization of the city's infrastructure. The president's son, Karim Wade, also has a great deal of influence and uses religion to further his goals by publicly handing out tickets for pilgrimage to Mecca or giving gifts to mosques.

Although the Senegalese state's treatment of the two major Sufi brotherhoods may resemble favoritism, religious minorities do not suffer as a result (which is the pattern followed by states that repress all but one religion). Political leaders have made a point of reaching out to religious minorities, despite their relatively small numbers. For example, in early 2004, anonymous threats were made against some Catholic clergy, and the government quickly denounced the threats and confirmed that it would protect the clergy. In 2008, after protests that not enough Christians were in high political positions, President Wade appointed a second Catholic to his cabinet.

Senegal's history of low religious division and more recent increases in political competition help to explain why the state fails to repress any religious groups. Because religious identities are strong and religious groups have always been active members of civil society, successive governments have viewed them as a means to gaining political support rather than potentially problematic groups to be repressed. The larger Sufi brotherhoods have benefited the most from government courtship, but religious minorities have not suffered. This could be because the brotherhoods did not consider minorities to be threatening and therefore did not lobby the government to impose restrictions on them. Political leaders have also not considered religious repression—even of small minorities—to be necessary because there has been very little religious conflict in the country. Thus, religious civil society continues to be seen as a potential supportive actor in the country's politics, rather than an impediment that needs to be controlled through restrictive state policies.

## Peru

Peru has experienced periods of military and presidential dictatorship, but since 2001, it has held generally free and fair elections and is considered one of the world's electoral democracies. Traditionally, the Roman Catholic Church enjoyed a privileged position in society, receiving preferential treatment in areas such as education, taxation, and immigration of religious workers, as well as state funding for clerical salaries. However, in recent years, new regulations have given tax exemption and other benefits to non-Catholic groups, reducing the church's monopoly on state benefits. These changes have come about both as a result of political openings and because of the growth of evangelical Protestant groups (at the expense of the Catholic Church). As the country has become more religiously diverse, restrictions on all religions have decreased.

The 2007 census reported 81 percent of the population was Roman Catholic, 13 percent Protestant (mainly evangelical), and 3 percent other, including Seventh-Day Adventists, Mormons, Jehovah's Witnesses, Israelites of the New Universal Pact Baptists, Assemblies of God, Jews, Baha'is, Hare Krishnas, and Muslims (US Department of State 2012). There are also some who adhere to both Christian and pre-Columbian indigenous beliefs.

After achieving independence from Spain, the Peruvian Republic was created in 1821 and alternately ruled by civilian and military regimes. The 1823 Constitution established the Roman Catholic Church and prohibited the public exercise of other religions, as did subsequent constitutions in the nineteenth century (Garcia-Montufar and Coco 1999). However, the twentieth century brought increases in religious freedom. In 1915, Congress passed the Law of Freedom of Worship, abolishing the total protection of the Catholic Church and the prohibition of other religions. Article 23 of the 1920 Constitution protected freedom of conscience of the individual. The 1933 Constitution added freedom of belief for the individual (Article 59) and religious liberty for groups (Article 232). It also declared that relations between the state and the Catholic Church should be governed by agreements of the executive power and approved by Congress.

Civilian governments have ruled the country since 1980. In the 1979 Constitution, all individuals and groups were granted the right to freedom of conscience and religion. The constitution also abolished persecution due to ideas or beliefs and guaranteed public exercise of all religions, as long as they did not offend public morality or alter the public order (Article 2). The state could, for the first time, collaborate with non-Catholic groups (Article 86). This version still favored Catholics in education and recognized the Catholic Church as an important element in the historic, cultural, and moral foundation of Peru.

Traditionally a strong institution in the country, the Catholic Church did not play an important role in the country's democratic transition in the 1980s, as a conservative turn in the church's hierarchy changed its focus from political and social issues to moral ones. Prior to this period, the Peruvian Catholic Church had been among the most progressive in Latin America, as one of the most influential theorists of liberation theology, Gustavo Gutierrez, was from Peru. Some priests, nuns, and lay activists were politically active at the local level, but church leadership had little impact at the national level (Fleet and Smith 1997). In the meantime, Protestant denominations began to grow in the country. Over 20 years, the Protestant population grew from about 2 percent to approximately 12.5 percent, though the National Evangelical Council (CONEP) estimated that evangelicals were about 15 percent of the population. At the end of 2009, 115 non-Catholic religious groups were registered with the state (US Department of State 2011).

Alberto Fujimori's government, taking power in July 1990, included several evangelicals, even though he himself was a practicing Catholic. One of his two vice presidents was Baptist minister and lawyer Carlos Garcia, former president of CONEP. In addition, 53 evangelicals ran on Fujimori's Change 90 party ticket for seats in the Senate and House of Deputies, and about a dozen won.[10] While Fujimori had help from evangelicals during his campaign, the Catholic Church supported Mario Vargas Llosa, who described himself as agnostic. During the election, the Catholic hierarchy criticized evangelicals and blamed their rise on priest shortages in the country.[11]

On April 5, 1992, President Fujimori took control of government in a self-coup (*autogulpe*), declaring a state of emergency, dissolving Congress and the judiciary, and ruling by decree. He argued that such actions were necessary because of the dire economic situation and the Shining Path guerrilla insurgency.[12] A new constitution was approved in a state-controlled referendum in 1993. It featured a stronger presidency and a unicameral legislature. In 1996, Congress passed a law allowing Fujimori to run for a third term, despite the constitution's two-term limit. In 2000, amid emerging evidence of corrupt election practices, Fujimori fled to Japan and resigned as president. In 2007, he was detained and extradited from Chile, and in 2009, he was sentenced to 25 years in prison for overseeing death-squad killings and kidnappings. The most recent elections in 2011 were deemed generally free and fair (Freedom House 2013).

The current constitution of Peru guarantees the rights of individuals and groups to liberty of conscience and religion; protection from persecution for ideas, beliefs, and opinions; and the free exercise of religion as long as it does not offend public morality or alter the public order (Article

2). It declares that religious education should not violate liberty of conscience and that parents must be able to choose schools for their children according to their religious beliefs (Articles 13 and 14). It also declares that covenants of collaboration may be established between the state and confessions (to be administered by the Department of Justice) (Article 50). However, the Catholic Church is still the only religion named in the constitution.

The International Agreement between the Holy See and the Republic of Peru (aka Concordat) of July 1980 governs relations between the state and the Catholic Church. It gives the church independence from the state and freedom to govern its internal matters without state interference. The church is given rights as a judicially recognized legal entity under public law, allowing it to purchase goods and get foreign assistance. Some church officials, including bishops, receive state-funded personal allowances. The church receives tax exemptions for rents, imported donated goods and funds, and other contributions. The agreement gives the Catholic Church liberty to establish private educational institutions at all levels and to teach Catholic religion in public schools, with the bishop having the right to assign teachers. The church has the right to have chaplains in the military, police force, state-run medical centers, and penitentiaries and is authorized to perform religious marriages that carry civil validity. It also has the authority to establish private cemeteries.

As political competition has increased in Peru, so have the rights of religious minorities, while state favoritism toward the Catholic Church has declined. Non-Catholic religions have the status of civil associations and entities of private law. They have the right to establish private educational institutions, medical centers, and cemeteries. In 2003, the Register for Non-Catholic Religious Faiths was created, allowing non-Catholic religious denominations to register with the Ministry of Justice and setting out the procedures for doing so. Although it did not grant legal status to religious organizations (that is still done by forming a civil association), it did allow the government to process the approvals needed to import donations without paying taxes on them. Registration is not mandatory. To register, groups are required to have a presence in Peru for seven years. An executive order in February 2003 gave non-Catholic groups permission to receive donations as religious entities and thus receive the same tax exemptions as the Catholic Church. These are processed through the Office of Interfaith Affairs within the Ministry of Justice.

An interfaith working group of non-Catholic religious groups advocated for a law to promote further religious freedom and equality, and in 2009, a draft law was formulated. The Religious Freedom Law, passed in 2010, recognizes the individual right to freedom and gives registered non-Catholic religious groups many of the same tax benefits that were previously reserved for the Catholic Church. However, it also reaffirms the 1980 Concordat, which gives the Catholic Church preferential treatment in education, taxation, immigration of religious workers, and other areas. Regulations implementing the 2010 law in 2011 required non-Catholic religious groups to reregister with the Ministry of Justice to get tax exemptions and form legal entities that had the right to own property, operate schools, and solicit donations.

Despite being subject to some regulations that the Catholic Church avoids, religious minorities in Peru are not repressed by state policies. Moreover, the favored position previously granted to the Catholic Church has declined in recent years. Increasing Protestant conversion has changed the religious landscape in Peru but has not led to hostilities between Protestants and Catholics, and the groups collaborate on the issue of human rights. Instead, increased political competition has allowed Protestant groups to demand greater religious rights and obliged the government to grant them. Thus, the state refrains from repressing any religious groups in the country, as such repression does not serve the interests of politicians hoping to win votes from organized religious groups in a more competitive political atmosphere.

## Conclusion

This chapter has examined four countries that fail to repress religious groups despite being current or recent nondemocracies. In Albania and Cambodia, extreme abuse of religion by past regimes has made religious repression an unpopular and untenable political strategy for current regimes. In Senegal, politicians must court historically strong Sufi brotherhoods for support, but the generally amicable relations between the majority Muslim population and religious minorities have resulted in little minority discrimination. In Peru, as religious demographics changed to lessen the hegemonic position of the Roman Catholic Church, religious minorities have enjoyed greater religious freedom; they are a larger portion of the population and, consequently, the electorate.

Aside from these four case studies, two important patterns emerge across the 39 countries that were nondemocratic at some point between

1990 and 2010 but did not repress any religious groups as of the end of that period. First, while the average Polity regime score for this set of countries was higher than the scores for countries repressing either all or some religions, more than half still qualify as anocracies or autocracies, according to Polity's system of classifying regimes. Therefore, political competition still varied across the countries in this category and did not improve enough by 2010 to explain why none repress religious groups. Many of the less politically competitive countries lacked significant religious divisions, thus explaining why even autocratic politicians would not find it politically expedient to repress religious groups. This is best illustrated by the observation that most (27) of these countries that repressed no religious groups were located in sub-Saharan Africa, a region that has traditionally experienced societal divisions centered on ethnicity rather than religion. Moreover, low state capacity may explain why some of the least politically competitive of the African countries (e.g., Cameroon, Republic of Congo, and Swaziland) failed to repress religious groups despite the political ability to do so, given the lack of viable opposition.

Second, a good portion of the remaining countries repressing no religious groups (7 of 12) are former Spanish colonies in Latin America with a history of close relations between the state and the majority Roman Catholic Church. However, many of these countries have had recent success with increasing levels of political competition (only Ecuador and Haiti were classified as anocracies by Polity in 2010). These political openings have been accompanied by relaxation of restrictions against minority religions. Even though the Catholic Church may still benefit from state favoritism in some of these countries, it is not at the expense of religious minorities, as was seen in those countries repressing all but one religious group (chapter 4).

Examining countries that repress no religious groups helps to illustrate the role that the treatment of civil society plays in determining the character of nondemocratic regimes. Leaving aside the states that qualified as democracies—if perhaps imperfect ones—in 2010, those that continued to lack competitiveness in the electoral arena did not refrain from targeting independent groups in society with repressive restrictions. As was illustrated in the case of Cambodia, leaders of nondemocratic regimes did repress organized and potential opposition groups. Thus, the nondemocratic regimes in this category of countries did not refrain from targeting civil society completely. However, they did not target religious civil society with repression because, in most cases, religious divisions were not strong enough to mitigate the potential backlash that can accompany excessive use of repression. Nondemocratic leaders did not stand to benefit from repressing any religious groups in these societies because doing so would not have gained them support from competing groups or helped to increase their own legitimacy. Thus, their actions were not paradoxical, but rather completely rational, given the costs that would come from repressing groups not deemed to be threatening to the political order or to other religious groups in society.

# 7

# *Conclusion*

## WHY RELIGIOUS REPRESSION MATTERS

RELIGIOUS REPRESSION IS a useful tool that nondemocratic leaders have at their disposal to control political opposition. Through discussion of specific types of religious regulations in a number of countries around the world, this book has demonstrated how nondemocratic regimes implement religious restrictions, explaining the variation in their numbers and targets by examining the competition between religious and political interests. This final chapter summarizes the findings of this study and discusses its implications for the future of the study of regimes in political science. Finally, it explores the consequences that close examination of religious repression and civil society can have on foreign policy.

Comparing 101 nondemocratic countries from around the globe during the 1990 to 2010 period, this book makes two contributions to the study of religion and politics. First, by focusing on the full range of nondemocratic regimes—from autocracies such as Saudi Arabia to hybrid regimes like Nigeria—it demonstrates that higher degrees of political competition do not necessarily result in greater religious freedom. Instead, it argues that a consideration of how religious divisions in society interact with the strategic interests of politicians in different types of institutional settings explains when, why, and how politicians will decide to impose repressive restrictions on religious groups. Therefore, it combines a rational choice-based framework with a focus on societal structures to explain the great variation we see in levels and types of religious repression in a range of nondemocratic regimes.

Second, this book advances the study of regimes in political science by taking a holistic view of the important role that competition plays throughout the various parts of public life. It does this by measuring differences in nondemocratic regimes according to how they interact with religious groups, an important part of civil society. While prior studies of nondemocratic systems tend to focus on competition in formal procedures such as elections, this book turns to the nature of civil society to understand how competition can be constrained in countries that are not fully consolidated democracies. Recognizing that almost all regime types must account for the existence of an associational realm outside of formal state structures, it turns the focus to the number of these groups that states target with repression to understand how nondemocratic regimes vary. Rather than categorizing states as closed or electoral authoritarian, or partial or electoral democracies, it compares states according to whether they repress all, all but one, some, or no religious groups to understand differences and commonalities among nondemocratic regimes across world regions.

## The Legalization of Religious Repression

Chapter 2 presented an overview of religious repression, a concept distinct from religious persecution. While prior scholarship has focused on explaining why states persecute—that is, imprison, torture, or kill their citizens for religious (and other) reasons—fewer scholars have investigated other types of activities that states take against their citizens on religious grounds. In this book, I turn the attention to religious repression, defined as lower intensity forms of state coercion, such as banning religious groups, imposing restrictions that make religious practice difficult, forcing citizens to abide by particular religious laws, and restricting what religious leaders are allowed to say in public. Because these types of restrictions tend to operate under the cover of the rule of law, they are often overlooked in studies of religion and politics in favor of higher intensity forms of religious persecution.

In an age when democracy is considered to be a highly legitimate form of rule, even the most brutal dictators feel the need to pay lip service to it by hiding repressive policies under the cover of legalism. Therefore, in nondemocratic countries, religious groups are increasingly targeted through laws, policies, and government enactments rather than through violent persecution. Although repression is largely absent in consolidated democracies, politicians across the full range of nondemocratic regimes rely on restrictive regulations related to religion to suppress potential opposition and maintain their hold on political power. Therefore, religion policy becomes one of the tools leaders in nondemocratic states can use to manipulate the political arena to their benefit.

I have analyzed available quantitative and qualitative data to demonstrate how political competition and societal structures interact to explain the nature of religious repression across a range of countries. Using readily available measures of regime competitiveness and a dataset I compiled on types of religious regulations, chapter 1 presented evidence of a negative relationship between political competition and religious repression; that is, as regimes become more politically competitive, they impose fewer restrictive regulations on religion. Yet, as I argued in that chapter, the relationship is not perfect, and there are still many states with low levels of political competition that choose not to impose a large number of restrictions on religion, while some nondemocratic regimes with relatively higher levels of political competition impose a large variety of restrictive regulations on religion. Therefore, merely examining the number of restrictions imposed on religious groups is not enough to understand the varieties of religious repression. Instead, I introduced the idea of the structure of religious divisions in society as an important explanatory factor in understanding when and why political leaders will engage in religious repression. These religious divisions include conflicts over the role that religion should play in the state and politics and the competition between religious groups for adherents, legitimacy, or influence.

In chapter 2, I tested the main argument of the book using data from the Pew Research Center that measures the level of social hostilities based on religion. Approximating the concept of a religiously divided society, comparing the data on social hostilities to a commonly used measure of regime competitiveness helped to illustrate how states array themselves according to the number of religious groups they choose to target with repressive policies. I demonstrated that states with very low political competition that are religiously divided tend to repress all religious groups, while those with higher levels of political competition but less religiously divided societies repress none. States in the middle of the political competition and religious division scales repress some religious groups. Finally, a subset of states that have higher religious divisions but more competitive political systems target repression at all but one religious group.

In chapters 3 through 6, I subjected these findings to closer analysis using brief case studies of 16 countries—four in each category of religious repression. Using evidence from official state agencies, international monitoring organizations, news services, scholarly sources, and personal interviews, these chapters presented a series of case studies that identified relevant actors and traced motivations for imposing repressive restrictions on religion. Within each category, cases were selected that exemplified typical interactions between religious and political interests. I traced how the level of political competition and religious divisions in society determined the types of restrictions that were imposed and their targets. Comparing states according to how many religious groups they repress thus helps to uncover the motivations for repression, which this book argues tend to be political, rather than theological.

The four case study chapters uncovered a number of patterns of religion-state interaction that help to explain why thinking of religion as part of civil society contributes to scholarly understandings of nondemocratic regimes. Chapter 3—which examined countries repressing all religions—showed how regimes coming from opposing antireligious and proreligious ideological positions similarly target all independent groups in society as a way of preventing potential political opposition from arising to challenge the legitimacy of the regime. Moving to states that repress all but one religious group, chapter 4 demonstrated how four different countries similarly chose to court one historically strong and important religious group at the expense of all others to build state strength and legitimacy based on national unity. Yet this comes at the expense of pluralism, further inhibiting democratic development. Chapter 5 examined states that target only some religious groups with repression as a way of negotiating more complicated societal divisions that may or may not overlap religious divisions. The examples of Kyrgyzstan, Bahrain, Nigeria, and Singapore illustrated how regimes in the middle range of political competitiveness must be more selective in their repression of religious groups to obtain winning political coalitions and maintain regime stability in countries that are societally plural but perhaps not ready to accept pluralism in the political realm. Chapter 6 examined the seemingly paradoxical situation of nondemocratic countries that repress no religious groups, demonstrating the quite rational calculations that politicians in these situations make in deciding not to target religious civil society with repressive policies.

## *Social Science and the Study of Religion*

This book has drawn attention to the importance of understanding historical and contemporary religious divisions as motivating factors for state-imposed religious repression. It has also argued for a more general focus on state targeting of civil society as a means of restricting political competition and extending nondemocratic rule. The recently expanding scholarship on authoritarianism has explored the ways that dictators manipulate parties and electoral rules to their advantage. Expanding on this attention to manipulating democratic rules to enhance authoritarian durability, this book has argued for paying attention to the legalization of restrictions on civil society as a method of nondemocratic governance. Moreover, by extending the study of authoritarianism to capture the full range of nondemocratic regimes, it has demonstrated how increasing or relaxing restrictions on civil society influences the degree of political competition in society and, therefore, regime type.

This book does not examine religious repression in democratic states. This is not to imply that it does not exist. In fact, in recent years there have been increasing examples of democratic states instituting restrictions on religious expression that mimic those discussed in this book. It is thus a mistake to conclude that religious repression is part and parcel of nondemocratic rule or that democracy implies religious freedom. By moving away from simple categorizations that classify countries as either democracies or dictatorships toward a more nuanced analysis of the interaction of formal institutions and societal structures, this book has drawn attention to the complexities inherent in the study of regimes. The focus on religion illustrates how these interactions occur around the world. Yet such an approach could also be used to investigate how states target the media, ethnic groups, and other aspects of civil society that together determine the wider field of political competition in a country.

Considering religious repression in nondemocratic states raises the issue of how to define democracy. Many current political scientists continue to rely on minimal definitions that focus on whether and how elections are conducted. Yet these fail to note that in addition to holding regular elections, democratic countries must also protect the rights of their citizens to organize into political groupings to contest elections and to express their viewpoints and pursue their interests in the public arena to influence policymaking. This requires state protection of a host of civil liberties, including the right to hold and express religious beliefs, individually and in groups. Even though some religious groups do not involve themselves with politics, many do deal with issues that are related to politics or to activities that the state is involved in regulating. To deny individuals and groups the opportunity to express their preferences in the political arena amounts to withholding one of the basic rights given to democratic citizens.

This argument is not meant to advocate close relations between religious groups and the state or to argue against secularism as a political philosophy. In fact, many versions of secularism acknowledge the important role that religion plays in daily life. Therefore, a state can be secular and respect the religious preferences of its citizenry at the same time. This means that the state is not allowed to interfere in the internal governance and conduct of religious groups. It also means that religious groups are not allowed to interfere in state governance outside democratic institutions or to demand preferential treatment at the expense of the rights of others. To elaborate, the argument of this book confirms Dahl's (1971) contention that in democratic states, unelected religious leaders should not have the authority to make political decisions. However, that prohibition does not mean that religious individuals and groups should not be able to organize like any other interest group to present their views to politicians and try to convince the public to support their policy preferences—which constitutes another form of political competition. I do not single out religious groups for preferential treatment above other social groups, but I do argue that they should be treated like other groups in civil society.

Despite the importance of defining and understanding democratic concepts of religious freedom, this book has focused on religious repression in nondemocratic countries. One reason is that the scholarship on religion and politics thus far has been predominantly focused on democracies, explaining democratic forms of religion-state relations and how religious freedom is a vital component of democratic societies. Yet this book has demonstrated that religious freedom varies significantly across the range of nondemocratic regimes as well. Moreover, it is not just the level of restrictions on religion that vary but also the number of its targets; that is, some states target specific groups with regulations, others impose blanket restrictions, and still others do not repress at all. A second reason for focusing on the varieties of religious repression in nondemocratic regimes is, as explained earlier, that repression often is framed in democratic terms, using the rule of law as justification for restricting the rights of individuals in less democratic settings.

There are many potential avenues for further research in this field. Future work might examine the application of specific types of restrictive policies on religion more closely to assess their effects on pluralism and the ability of groups with different viewpoints to express their ideas in the public sphere. For instance, states currently impose different types of restrictions on religious groups that attempt to convert others, a practice referred to as proselytization. These restrictions range from making all proselytizing illegal, or allowing proselytizing only by members of the majority religion to minorities, to limiting visas to foreign missionaries. The types of restriction imposed on proselytizing can illuminate the intended targets of the restrictions and how state officials hope to shape the public sphere. Such close analyses can also be used to study specific types of restrictions on religious education, registration laws, and laws on blasphemy and other types of religious speech.

A second research agenda might look more closely at the institutional mechanisms through which religious restrictions are applied, to connect religion policy to other types of institutional manipulation practiced by leaders of nondemocratic states. A particularly fruitful potential avenue for such research involves the courts. While policies are often drafted and ratified by executive or legislative branches of governments, the judiciary is the arena in which challenges to state policy are raised and debated. In nondemocratic states, judiciaries often lack independence or transparency. Yet tracing how the courts handle such challenges may uncover the various means that nondemocratic leaders use to ensure compliance by national courts and ensure results favorable to the government in power. Moreover, increasing international integration brings challenges to domestic legislation into international courts to test adherence to international human rights law. Tracing linkages to international and regional organizations may uncover the influence of such foreign actors on domestic politics in nondemocratic countries.

Expanding the study of civil society past religion, the approach taken in this book could be applied to studying state policies related to other types of organizations that are formally independent of the state. Media outlets, corporations, labor unions, and NGOs are all subject to state regulations on their organization and activities. While prior research has examined regulation of these different aspects of nonstate organization, researchers might examine state policies with a focus on the number and types of targets to develop a more holistic picture of the ways that nondemocratic governments attempt to shape and mold civil society to their benefit. Such research can also be tied back to the issue of religion, however, because religious associations involve themselves in publishing and broadcasting, profit-making enterprises, charity work, and other types of nonspiritual activities. Therefore, future research might trace how regulations of these sectors comparatively affect religious and nonreligious organizations with a view to better understanding religion-state relations.

Finally, while the present study focuses on nonviolent forms of religious repression in contrast to prior studies that emphasize violent religious persecution, space remains for closer examination of the linkages between the two phenomena. Brian Grim and Roger Finke's (2011) study of religious persecution analyzes cross-national data to show how governments that impose more legal restrictions on religion tend to engage in more religious persecution. Future research could trace pathways through which specific types of laws and policies result in state or societal violence toward religious groups. This can be done both quantitatively and qualitatively. Further quantitative analysis would require the compilation of a dataset that codes the full range of regulation, restriction, and persecution that both governments and societal actors impose. Qualitative analysis would help to uncover the causal pathways through which a specific type of regulation on religion turns into a violent attack on it.

## A Note on Repression in Muslim-Majority Countries

Although many of the examples of repressive countries cited in this book have involved countries with majority-Muslim populations, I do not argue that something inherent in Islam makes religious repression a foregone outcome. In fact, the book presents several examples of states with majority-Muslim populations (such as Albania and Senegal) that do not engage in religious repression. Moreover, repression is not the exclusive strategy of governments ruled by individuals claiming to be motivated by Islamic law; it is also wielded by rulers espousing strictly secularist ideologies, as in China and Azerbaijan.

Why, then, is religious repression so high across Muslim-majority countries? Forty-one of the 101 countries in this book have majority-Muslim populations. In previous work, I have demonstrated an empirical relationship between levels of religious repression in majority-Muslim countries and low levels of democracy in them (Sarkissian 2012). These correlations can be explained by looking at the importance of religious divisions in many Muslim-majority countries, where religion presents both a basis on which governments can gain legitimacy and an ideology around which opposition groups can organize. Moreover, governments use religious justifications for imposing restrictions on particular groups to gain political support from others.

Other scholars have pointed to qualities inherent in some religions that allow them to be used for political ends. Monica Duffy Toft, Daniel Philpott, and Timothy Shah (2011) introduce the concept of political theology as the set of ideas a religious tradition holds about political authority and justice. It is undeniable that aspects of Islamic political theology acknowledge, and even emphasize, the interaction of politics and religion. Yet this is not to say that Islamic teachings require an integration of state institutions. In fact, Islam, like other religions, is "multivocal," with a variety of interpretations (Stepan 2001). The Islamic tradition—like others—includes ideas political leaders and activists can use to justify a close relationship between religion and politics. This can work to the advantage (or disadvantage) of both rulers and members of the opposition. For rulers, it can serve two functions. First, it can help them justify maintaining state control over religious institutions. This book has presented examples of states controlling clerical appointments, mosque construction and finance, pilgrimages, and even the content of sermons. States justify doing so on the basis of their responsibility to uphold a particular version of Islam in the face of sectarian differences. Second, rulers ally themselves with a particular interpretation of Islam—often, but not always, that of the majority of the population—to benefit from the legitimacy that close cooperation with religious leaders (who often have the confidence of populations) brings. At the same time, this allows rulers to justify repression of nonallied Islamic groups, as well as non-Muslim minorities or heterodox sects.

For opposition groups, Islam also offers an inspiration to organize and fight oppression, especially from authoritarian leaders. These groups use two common arguments to oppose governments. First, groups may argue that current leaders are not upholding the proper Islamic principles and thus need to be overthrown. This may be on the basis of specific practices or because they subscribe to a different branch, school, or sect of Islam. Second, opposition groups may argue that leaders devoted to secular ideologies need to be overthrown and replaced with those who will rule according to Islamic law. Both are religious justifications. Yet both involve competition over who is authorized to rule politically. When opposition groups pose enough of a threat to incumbent rulers, they can be subjected to repression (and sometimes persecution). Sometimes, however, these groups can convince governments to repress other groups in exchange for political support.

For example, chapter 4 included the case of Indonesia, one of the more politically competitive countries included in this book, as an example of a country that represses all but one religious group. Despite a tradition of religious tolerance and secularism, post-Suharto Indonesian governments have imposed harsh restrictions on the Ahmadiya Muslim community, a minority Muslim sect. Although Indonesia's mainstream politicians and Islamic associations have traditionally advocated religious coexistence, pressure from highly religious and extremist groups has led political leaders to support bans on Ahmadiya Muslim practice to gain political support in elections. Thus, despite the seeming desire of Indonesian politicians to respect religious freedom—especially since transition in 1999—some have been led to impose repressive measures because of political considerations, not theological ones.

## Policy Implications

The importance of religion in contemporary politics is impossible to ignore. The events of September 11, 2001, in the United States and subsequent attacks in other countries turned the attention of foreign policy analysts and practitioners to international religious terrorism. Aside from security concerns, all governments have an interest in understanding religious regimes and political movements, as they currently rule over a number of states in the Middle East, North Africa, and Asia and continue to contest politics in countries where they have not yet won power. Even in states founded on secular principles, politicized religious movements are challenging the nature of religion-state relations and questioning the exclusion of religiously motivated actors and interests from public debates about the future of their societies.

Alongside concerns about the potentially violent interaction of religion and politics, international organizations such as the United Nations, national governments, and NGOs pay great attention to democracy promotion as an aspect of foreign policy. This book's discussion of the varieties of religious repression that nondemocratic states use to maintain their hold on power raises a number of policy implications. Attention to the varieties of religious repression can be integrated into foreign policy in at least three ways. First, democracy-promotion programs can emphasize religious freedom as an aspect of good governance. Second, policymakers and NGOs can develop a better understanding of important societal (including religious) divisions in the countries in which they work and use that knowledge to tailor democracy-promotion activities to specific settings and incorporate religious actors in implementing them. Third, those who develop foreign policy can pay closer attention to the types of religious repression highlighted in this book as an indicator of the potential for more violent religious persecution and conflict in the future.

Democracy promotion cannot mean only encouraging the free and fair conduct of elections in countries undergoing political transition. I have argued that a focus on electoral institutions does not accomplish enough in understanding the quality of governance in a society. For elections to meaningfully represent the preferences of citizens, they must be conducted in a competitive and participatory manner. These qualities are developed long before citizens go to the polls, when they express their viewpoints in public forums and organize with others to advance their interests. This book's focus on exploring the varieties of religious repression has attempted to draw attention to the importance of understanding how legal regulations imposed on religious expression and practice can result in stifling political opposition at the level of civil society.

American democracy promoters can incorporate a focus on religious freedom into their activities by using tools already available from the US government. The Office of International Religious Freedom within the Department of State was established by an act of Congress in 1998 to "monitor religious persecution and discrimination worldwide, recommend and implement policies in respective regions or countries, and develop programs to promote religious freedom."[1] The office publishes the *Annual Report on International Religious Freedom* that describes the status of religious freedom in every country around the world. The report provides details on religious demographics, the legal framework surrounding religion, and government and societal violations of religious freedom. Moreover, numerous NGOs and academics track religious legislation and religious freedom abuses around the world. Using these sources, democracy promoters can incorporate an understanding of the role that state policies play in restricting religious groups' access to public debates and the political arena. They can also do more to peg democracy assistance to progress on improving religious freedom as an aspect of larger civil liberties promotion programs.

This book has highlighted the importance of examining the nature of religious divisions in society to understand the varieties of religious repression practiced in nondemocratic regimes. Government restrictions on religion are often targeted at specific groups because their size, composition, or ideas threaten incumbent politicians or groups that support them. Understanding the intended targets of regulations can help democracy promoters better tailor their activities to specific settings. For instance, organizers of interreligious dialogue can use their knowledge of religious divisions to include the appropriate parties in efforts to promote greater understanding between religious groups. Religious civil society organizations can be used to disseminate democracy-promotion activities to their constituents, increasing the range of recipients of such efforts. Religious groups pressuring the government to impose repressive restrictions on other groups or on nonreligious individuals can be identified to isolate sources of pressure on politicians to engage in religious repression.

Finally, prior scholarship has demonstrated a relationship between government restrictions on religion and violent religious persecution (Grim and Finke 2011), as well as national security (Inboden 2012). This book has focused on uncovering the targets of those restrictions by examining the many varieties restrictions take around the world. The foreign policy community can pay closer attention to the varieties of religious repression as a way of anticipating the potential for more serious persecution of religious groups and conflict within and between states over religion.

For example, the Uighur Muslim community in the western province of Xinjiang in China has experienced state repression of its ethnic and religious identity through restrictions on fasting during Ramadan, religious education for children, and Uighur-language education. The effects of this repression appear to have reached a breaking point in recent years. Riots, attacks against security personnel, and violence against Chinese citizens can be seen as a result of years of state repression and lack of recognition of the Uighurs' rights to religious and ethnic expression in particular and societal pluralism in general. These incidents include a March 2014 knife attack by government-termed "Xinjiang Extremists" in a railway station in Kunming, killing 29 people and injuring 140. Closer attention to legal repression of this minority group (and others in China) might help to focus attention on the importance of accepting pluralism as a means of discouraging radicalism and promoting peace.

Religion has become increasingly central to politics within and among countries over the past several decades. To understand the implications of more active and politicized religiosity, as well as of seemingly benign state religion policies, requires understanding these complexities and contextual nuances. To ignore these complexities may lead to misguided foreign policy and ineffective efforts at promoting democratic reforms in an increasingly diverse and shrinking world. In the end, however, paying attention to religion serves not only American interests but those of all people, whether they are religious or not.

# Measuring Regimes and Religious Divisions in Societies

States included in this study were nondemocratic at any point between 1990 and 2010. They include countries that range from the most entrenched dictatorships (e.g., Saudi Arabia) to hybrid regimes that combine elements of both democracy and authoritarianism (e.g., Russia). Some of the included countries were nondemocratic for the entire 20-year period; others experienced transition to or from democracy during the period. I consulted four commonly used data sources (Cheibub, Gandhi, and Vreeman 2009; Freedom House 2013; Geddes, Wright, and Franz 2012; Marshall and Jaggers 2011) to select the states. The sources are in agreement on dates of authoritarian rule for 39 of the countries.

José Antonio Cheibub, Jennifer Gandhi, and James Vreeland (hereafter CGV) developed a dichotomous variable that measures the presence or absence of democracy, based on whether governmental offices are filled by means of contested elections. Barbara Geddes, Joseph Wright, and Erica Franz (hereafter GWF) coded autocratic regimes exclusively, dividing them into a number of subtypes, an extension of data from Geddes's previous work (Geddes 2003). The two sources agree on which states had authoritarian regimes for many of the countries. Exceptions include disagreements on dates of authoritarianism. Moreover, GWF code the following countries as authoritarian for a number of years during which CGV code them as democratic: Armenia, Guatemala, Mongolia, Nicaragua, Paraguay, Sri Lanka, and Venezuela. CGV code Ecuador as authoritarian in 2000 and 2001, and GWF code it as authoritarian those years. GWF exclude Bahrain, Qatar, Bosnia-Herzegovina, and Lebanon from their coding. Finally, both sources code Colombia, Croatia, Honduras, Moldova, Romania, Turkey, and Ukraine as democratic during the entire 1990–2010 period.

Freedom House and Polity are two additional sources for regime scores. Andreas Schedler and Larry Diamond use Freedom House scores to classify countries into a range of categories, with an average Freedom House political rights and civil liberties score of 4 (of 7) as the cutoff between electoral democracy and electoral authoritarianism in most cases (Diamond 2002; Schedler 2002, 2006). Philip Roessler and Marc Morje Howard (2009) use a combination of Freedom House and Polity scores to classify regimes, with countries scoring 5 or lower on the combined Polity index classified as authoritarian. Taking into account these sources, the seven countries excluded by CGV and GWF for having democratic regimes can be included among the nondemocratic countries examined in this study. Afghanistan, Iraq, and Somalia are not included because of missing data on regime type due to warfare or state failure during the period under study.

The Polity dataset was consulted for data on authoritarian regime characteristics and to measure differences in levels of competitiveness across the 101 states in this study. The Revised Combined Polity Score (POLITY2) ranges from −10 (hereditary monarchy) to +10 (consolidated democracy) and measures the institutionalized authority patterns characterizing each state. It combines separate scores on institutionalized democracy and institutionalized autocracy, taking into account the competitiveness and openness of executive recruitment, constraints on the chief executive, and the regulation and competitiveness of participation (Marshall and Jaggers 2011). The authors of the dataset recommend the following conversions for regime scores to categories: "autocracies" (−10 to −6), "anocracies" (−5 to +5), and "democracies" (+6 to +10). Three special values (−66, −77, −88) code countries that are administered by transitional governments, countries where central authority has collapsed or lost control over a majority of its territory, and countries where foreign authorities maintain local authority. These countries are included in the category of anocracies.

The Pew Research Center's Forum on Religion and Public Life compiled a Social Hostilities Index (SHI) to measure the level of social hostilities involving religion around the world. The SHI combines a number of questions measuring the behavior of societal (not state) actors, including the existence and level of crimes, malicious acts, and violence motivated by religious hatred or bias; violence between groups; and attempts by religious groups and individuals to enforce religious norms. Their report, "Rising Tide of Restrictions on Religion," lists SHI scores for 197 countries for the years 2007, 2009, and 2010 (Pew Research Center 2012b). Scores range from 0 to 10. I use an average of scores for the three years in my analyses. The Pew Forum suggests the following score conversions for categories of social hostilities: low (0–1.4), moderate (1.5–3.5), high (3.6–7.1), and very high (7.2–10). I use the SHI score as an approximate quantitative measure of the level of religious division in a society. Table A.1 presents POLITY2 scores for 2010 and average SHI scores for each country included in the study.

### Table A.1 Regime and religious divisions scores for 101 countries

| Country | Polity2 (2010) | Average SHI |
|---|---|---|
| Albania | 9 | 0.1 |
| Algeria | 2 | 4.8 |
| Angola | −2 | 2.4 |
| Armenia | 5 | 3.4 |
| Azerbaijan | −7 | 2.6 |
| Bahrain | −5 | 3.3 |
| Bangladesh | 5 | 8.3 |
| Belarus | −7 | 2.0 |
| Benin | 7 | 0.1 |
| Bosnia-Herzegovina | −66 | 2.7 |
| Botswana | 8 | 0.0 |
| Burkina Faso | 0 | 1.4 |
| Burma | −6 | 5.2 |
| Burundi | 6 | 1.3 |
| Cambodia | 2 | 1.0 |
| Cameroon | −4 | 0.7 |
| Central African Republic | −1 | 3.4 |
| Chad | −2 | 2.1 |
| China | −7 | 2.1 |
| Colombia | 7 | 3.2 |
| Congo, Democratic Republic | 5 | 2.9 |
| Congo, Republic | −4 | 0.2 |
| Côte d'Ivoire | 0 | 2.5 |
| Croatia | 9 | 1.9 |
| Cuba | −7 | 0.7 |
| Ecuador | 5 | 0.2 |
| Egypt | −3 | 7.0 |
| Eritrea | −7 | 0.5 |
| Ethiopia | −3 | 5.1 |
| Gabon | 3 | 0.4 |
| Gambia | −5 | 0.5 |
| Georgia | 6 | 3.8 |
| Ghana | 8 | 3.7 |
| Guatemala | 8 | 0.8 |
| Guinea | 1 | 1.2 |
| Guinea-Bissau | 6 | 0.4 |
| Haiti | 0 | 1.1 |
| Honduras | 7 | 0.5 |
| Indonesia | 8 | 7.9 |
| Iran | −7 | 5.9 |
| Jordan | −3 | 4.5 |
| Kazakhstan | −6 | 2.1 |
| Kenya | 8 | 4.0 |

*(continued)*

Table A.1 (continued)

| Country | Polity2 (2010) | Average SHI |
|---|---|---|
| Kuwait | −7 | 1.3 |
| Kyrgyzstan | 4 | 4.4 |
| Laos | −7 | 1.6 |
| Lebanon | 7 | 4.2 |
| Lesotho | 8 | 0.1 |
| Liberia | 6 | 2.0 |
| Libya | −7 | 2.0 |
| Madagascar | 0 | 0.2 |
| Malawi | 6 | 0.2 |
| Malaysia | 6 | 1.5 |
| Mali | 7 | 0.7 |
| Mauritania | −2 | 1.1 |
| Mexico | 8 | 4.7 |
| Moldova | 8 | 3.6 |
| Mongolia | 10 | 1.6 |
| Morocco | −6 | 2.5 |
| Mozambique | 5 | 0.5 |
| Namibia | 6 | 0.0 |
| Nepal | 6 | 5.0 |
| Nicaragua | 9 | 0.4 |
| Niger | 3 | 1.0 |
| Nigeria | 4 | 6.7 |
| North Korea | −10 | n/a |
| Oman | −8 | 0.3 |
| Pakistan | 6 | 9.2 |
| Paraguay | 8 | 0.5 |
| Peru | 9 | 0.0 |
| Qatar | −10 | 0.4 |
| Romania | 9 | 4.5 |
| Russia | 4 | 5.5 |
| Rwanda | −4 | 0.3 |
| Saudi Arabia | −10 | 6.9 |
| Senegal | 7 | 0.2 |
| Serbia | 8 | 3.1 |
| Sierra Leone | 7 | 0.5 |
| Singapore | −2 | 0.2 |
| South Africa | 9 | 2.4 |
| Sri Lanka | 4 | 7.4 |
| Sudan | −2 | 5.7 |
| Swaziland | −9 | 0.8 |
| Syria | −7 | 4.6 |
| Taiwan | 10 | 0.0 |
| Tajikistan | −3 | 2.2 |
| Tanzania | −1 | 3.2 |
| Thailand | 4 | 4.2 |
| Togo | −2 | 0.1 |

| Country | Polity2 (2010) | Average SHI |
|---|---|---|
| Tunisia | −4 | 2.1 |
| Turkey | 7 | 4.7 |
| Turkmenistan | −9 | 1.3 |
| Uganda | −1 | 2.2 |
| Ukraine | 6 | 2.7 |
| United Arab Emirates | −8 | 0.6 |
| Uzbekistan | −9 | 2.4 |
| Venezuela | −3 | 0.9 |
| Vietnam | −7 | 3.4 |
| Yemen | −2 | 7.1 |
| Zambia | 7 | 1.4 |
| Zimbabwe | 1 | 1.6 |

*Sources*: Marshall and Jaggers (2011) and Pew Research Center (2012b).

# Categorizing Religious Repression

In this appendix, I explain how I code types of religious restrictions to create the index of religious repression and the categorization of number of targets of repression used in this book. I rely on a number of sources. Two comprehensive quantitative datasets provide the information for the bulk of my coding: the International Religious Freedom (IRF) dataset compiled by Brian Grim and Roger Finke (2006) and the Religion and State (RAS) dataset compiled by Jonathan Fox (2011). Both are available from the Association of Religion Data Archives (www.thearda.com). In addition to these datasets (which code restrictions only up to 2008), I rely on a number of reports from governments, international human rights organizations, the media, and other sources. Sources for specific restrictions are cited in the text.

Originally conceptualized by Brian Grim and Roger Finke, the International Religious Freedom Dataset (IRF) codes reports prepared by the US State Department. In accordance with the International Religious Freedom Act (IRFA) of 1998, the Office of International Religious Freedom within the State Department prepares annual reports on the status of religious freedom in countries around the world. The US embassies prepare drafts of reports based on information from government and nongovernment sources in country and send them to the Office of International Religious Freedom, which revises and publishes the reports online (US Department of State 2011). The IRF dataset quantitatively codes the individual country reports into composite indices that measure government restriction of religion, social restriction of religion, and government favoritism of religion for 197 countries and territories. Data are available for the years 2001, 2003, 2005, and 2008.

Jonathan Fox has created the most comprehensive resource on state religion policy with his Religion and State Dataset (RAS) (Fox 2011). Fox measures four aspects of government involvement in religion for 177 countries between 1990 and

2008: the official relationship between religion and the state, government support for and legislation of religion, government restriction of the majority religion, and discrimination against religious minorities (Fox 2008, 47–55). Each category measures multiple types of policy, and restrictions are coded individually according to their intensity. The RAS dataset also includes more detailed distinctions between support and restriction of religion than the IRF dataset. For instance, the RAS dataset measures multiple forms of government legislation of religious precepts as examples of government support for religion, because government enforces religious law or customs using the force of its coercive apparatus. The dataset also codes the existence of certain types of institutions—such as government religious bureaus or government-issued identity cards containing religious information—as separate types of state religion policy.

As detailed in chapter 2, I consider state-imposed restrictions on the following aspects of religion:

1. Individual or group observance of religious services, festivals, or holidays in public or private
2. Places of worship
3. Observation of religious laws
4. Conversion
5. Proselytizing
6. Formation of religious communities
7. Clerical appointments
8. Religious speech
9. Private religious education
10. Religious political parties
11. Nongovernmental associations affiliated with religious groups
12. Political activities and/or speech of religious leaders or individuals
13. Access to political office based on religious identity or position

In addition to counting whether states impose significant or large-scale restrictions on these activities (include banning the activity), I also note whether each of the restrictions is imposed against the religious majority, minorities, or both.

This categorization of religious restrictions is a departure from the RAS dataset. First, it is less comprehensive, aiming to describe general patterns of restrictions rather than capturing every possible type of restriction imposed. Second, it does not consider all kinds of state enforcement of religious laws (which fall under the RAS dataset "religious legislation" variables) as constituting religious repression (see Fox 2008). Therefore, the present study focuses primarily on two categories of restrictions the RAS dataset codes: religious discrimination against minority religions and regulation of and restrictions on the majority religion or all religions. As these data are current to 2008, I use other sources to update the data to 2010.

Table B.1 lists the total number of state-imposed restrictions, the number of restrictions imposed against the religious majority, and the number of restrictions imposed against religious minorities. Higher numbers correspond to higher levels of state repression against religious groups. Tables in chapters 3, 4, 5, and 6 list the specific types of restrictions found in each of the countries I isolate for closer study.

Table B.1 Number of state-imposed restrictions by type of religious group (2010)

| Country | Total | Majority | Minority |
|---------|-------|----------|----------|
| Albania | 0 | 0 | 0 |
| Algeria | 10 | 8 | 9 |
| Angola | 2 | 0 | 2 |
| Armenia | 8 | 1 | 8 |
| Azerbaijan | 12 | 11 | 10 |
| Bahrain | 6 | 6 | 6 |
| Bangladesh | 3 | 3 | 1 |
| Belarus | 11 | 6 | 11 |
| Benin | 1 | 1 | 1 |
| Bosnia-Herzegovina | 4 | 1 | 3 |
| Botswana | 0 | 0 | 0 |
| Burkina Faso | 1 | 1 | 1 |
| Burma | 10 | 7 | 9 |
| Burundi | 1 | 1 | 1 |
| Cambodia | 2 | 1 | 2 |
| Cameroon | 0 | 0 | 0 |
| Central African Republic | 2 | 1 | 2 |
| Chad | 7 | 5 | 5 |
| China | 12 | 11 | 12 |
| Colombia | 1 | 1 | 0 |
| Congo, Democratic Republic | 2 | 0 | 2 |
| Congo, Republic | 1 | 1 | 1 |
| Côte d'Ivoire | 2 | 1 | 2 |
| Croatia | 2 | 0 | 2 |
| Cuba | 11 | 10 | 11 |
| Ecuador | 1 | 0 | 1 |
| Egypt | 11 | 10 | 10 |
| Eritrea | 12 | 9 | 12 |
| Ethiopia | 6 | 2 | 6 |

*(continued)*

*Appendix B*

Table B.1(continued)

| Country | Total | Majority | Minority |
|---|---|---|---|
| Gabon | 0 | 0 | 0 |
| Gambia | 1 | 1 | 1 |
| Georgia | 5 | 2 | 5 |
| Ghana | 1 | 1 | 1 |
| Guatemala | 2 | 1 | 2 |
| Guinea | 1 | 1 | 1 |
| Guinea-Bissau | 1 | 1 | 1 |
| Haiti | 1 | 1 | 0 |
| Honduras | 2 | 1 | 2 |
| Indonesia | 9 | 8 | 9 |
| Iran | 11 | 5 | 11 |
| Jordan | 11 | 7 | 10 |
| Kazakhstan | 9 | 7 | 8 |
| Kenya | 2 | 1 | 2 |
| Kuwait | 11 | 7 | 8 |
| Kyrgyzstan | 9 | 9 | 7 |
| Laos | 8 | 4 | 7 |
| Lebanon | 6 | 2 | 5 |
| Lesotho | 1 | 0 | 1 |
| Liberia | 2 | 2 | 2 |
| Libya | 8 | 6 | 6 |
| Madagascar | 3 | 1 | 3 |
| Malawi | 1 | 0 | 1 |
| Malaysia | 12 | 7 | 10 |
| Mali | 2 | 2 | 1 |
| Mauritania | 9 | 4 | 7 |
| Mexico | 6 | 5 | 5 |
| Moldova | 6 | 2 | 5 |
| Mongolia | 3 | 1 | 3 |
| Morocco | 12 | 8 | 10 |
| Mozambique | 3 | 3 | 3 |
| Namibia | 0 | 0 | 0 |
| Nepal | 6 | 4 | 5 |
| Nicaragua | 3 | 2 | 3 |
| Niger | 7 | 7 | 4 |
| Nigeria | 5 | 2 | 5 |
| North Korea | 11 | 10 | 11 |
| Oman | 7 | 4 | 6 |

| Country | Total | Majority | Minority |
| --- | --- | --- | --- |
| Pakistan | 9 | 7 | 9 |
| Paraguay | 1 | 1 | 1 |
| Peru | 1 | 0 | 1 |
| Qatar | 10 | 6 | 8 |
| Romania | 6 | 2 | 5 |
| Russia | 8 | 2 | 8 |
| Rwanda | 4 | 3 | 4 |
| Saudi Arabia | 13 | 9 | 13 |
| Senegal | 1 | 1 | 1 |
| Serbia | 4 | 1 | 4 |
| Sierra Leone | 1 | 1 | 1 |
| Singapore | 5 | 1 | 5 |
| South Africa | 0 | 0 | 0 |
| Sri Lanka | 3 | 0 | 3 |
| Sudan | 8 | 5 | 6 |
| Swaziland | 1 | 0 | 1 |
| Syria | 12 | 9 | 9 |
| Taiwan | 0 | 0 | 0 |
| Tajikistan | 10 | 10 | 4 |
| Tanzania | 3 | 2 | 3 |
| Thailand | 5 | 3 | 4 |
| Togo | 3 | 3 | 3 |
| Tunisia | 12 | 8 | 10 |
| Turkey | 10 | 8 | 9 |
| Turkmenistan | 10 | 7 | 9 |
| Uganda | 2 | 1 | 2 |
| Ukraine | 4 | 2 | 4 |
| United Arab Emirates | 7 | 5 | 6 |
| Uzbekistan | 11 | 10 | 10 |
| Venezuela | 4 | 2 | 4 |
| Vietnam | 12 | 10 | 12 |
| Yemen | 10 | 5 | 9 |
| Zambia | 1 | 0 | 1 |
| Zimbabwe | 3 | 1 | 3 |

# *Notes*

CHAPTER 1

1. The category of nondemocratic regimes includes authoritarian and semiauthoritarian (or hybrid) regimes, as well as partial or electoral democracies. These are states that lack fully free and fair elections and that do not have fully open and institutionalized political participation. Leaders of nondemocratic states may include elected presidents, military rulers, civilian dictators, and monarchs.

2. Calculated using the dataset "International Religious Freedom Data, 2008." *Association of Religion Data Archives*: www.thearda.com/Archive/Files/ Descriptions/IRF2008.asp.

3. A Pew Research Center study shows that 84 percent of the global population in 2010 was religiously affiliated. Among those who were unaffiliated, belief in God or a higher power was shared by 7 percent of Chinese unaffiliated adults, 30 percent of French unaffiliated adults, and 68 percent of unaffiliated US adults; 7 percent of unaffiliated adults in France and 27 percent of those in the United States said they attend religious services at least once a year (Pew Research Center 2012a, 24).

4. Although in many countries people do combine adherence to Islam or Christianity with traditional beliefs, it is rare to find individuals who identify as bireligious (e.g., Jewish-Muslim), for instance.

5. In 2008, Turkey received a Polity score of 7 (10 indicating most democratic), and two widely used data sources ranked the country "democratic" (Cheibub, Gandhi, and Vreeland 2009; Geddes, Wright, and Frantz 2012).

6. The Religion and State Dataset, founded and compiled by Jonathan Fox, is available at www.religionandstate.org.

7. More recent scholarship on secularization theory includes Bruce (1999) and Norris and Inglehart (2004).

8. Svolik argues that, moreover, authoritarian politics also has a greater potential for violence, further distinguishing it from democratic politics.

9. Even rational choice theorists have admitted that ideas cannot be completely discounted in understanding the motivations of political actors. See Gill (2008, 57–59). A study focusing on the actions of religious actors rather than the state in determining religion-state outcomes argues that religious actors will be more likely to promote democracy when they are institutionally independent from the state and when they have a democratic "political theology." The political theology of religious groups is the set of ideas that religions hold about political authority and justice and determines whether they will be engaged in politics. Thus, these authors focus on ideology as an important part of religion-state relations, a perspective that theorists from the rational choice tradition reject (Toft, Philpott, and Shah 2011).

10. The study begins at 1990 for two reasons. Staffan Lindberg (2009) notes that 1989 marked a "watershed" in terms of the empirical landscape for studies of regime breakdown and transition, as after the fall of the Berlin Wall on November 12, political changes occurred in no fewer than 92 countries in the former Eastern bloc, Africa, and Asia. Thus, by 1990 we have the beginning of a large amount of data for countries undergoing transition. Second, data on religious restrictions before 1990 are difficult to obtain. The Religion and State (RAS) dataset begins its coding in 1990, the earliest point at which we have quantitative data on religious policy (www.religionandstate.org). However, the case studies do consider policy from earlier periods, as many current restrictions are based on circumstances and events occurring before 1990.

CHAPTER 2

1. Article 18 of the International Covenant on Civil and Politics Rights states the following: "1. Everyone shall have the right to freedom of thought, conscience and religion. This right shall include freedom to have or to adopt a religion or belief of his choice, and freedom, either individually or in community with others and in public or private, to manifest his religion or belief in worship, observance, practice and teaching. 2. No one shall be subject to coercion which would impair his freedom to have or to adopt a religion or belief of his choice. 3. Freedom to manifest one's religion or beliefs may be subject only to such limitations as are prescribed by law and are necessary to protect public safety, order, health, or morals or the fundamental rights and freedoms of others. 4. The States Parties to the present Covenant undertake to have respect for the liberty of parents and, when applicable, legal guardians to ensure the religious and moral education of their children in conformity with their own convictions." http://www.ohchr.org/en/professionalinterest/pages/ccpr.aspx.

2. The US State Department's *International Religious Freedom Report* (2001–2012) is used as a general source for information on religious demographics and government policies in this and subsequent chapters (www.state.gov/j/drl/rls/irf/index.htm). Any regulations or policies not separately cited are obtained from this source throughout this and subsequent chapters.

3. Author's interview with pastor in Seventh-Day Adventist organization, Yerevan, Armenia, October 12, 2005. The pastor noted that appeals to the State Ombudsman's Office and various human rights organizations had not resulted in any changes to the policies.

4. Nicholas Birch, "Turkey: Headscarved Graduate Students Lead Libertarian Movement." *EurasiaNet*, March 12, 2008. www.eurasianet.org/departments/insight/articles/eav031208.shtml.

5. Felix Corley, "Armenia: Jailings of Conscientious Objectors Resume." *Forum 18 News Service*, September 20, 2012. www.forum18.org/Archive.php?article_id=1745.

6. Felix Corley, "Turkmenistan: Another Conscientious Objector Prisoner of Conscience." *Forum 18 News Service*, August 17, 2012. www.forum18.org/Archive.php?article_id=1733.

7. John Kinahan, "OSCE Region: OSCE Commitments on Freedom of Religion or Belief." *Forum 18 News Service*, September 22, 2009. www.forum18.org/Archive.php?article_id=1351.

8. Chapter 1 and appendices A and B give details on these measurements.

CHAPTER 3

1. Azerbaijan is a majority-Muslim country, split between Shiites (65 percent) and Sunnis (35 percent).

2. Felix Corley, "Azerbaijan: Mosque Unable to Invite Back Freed Imam." *Forum 18 News Service*, March 10, 2006. www.forum18.org/archive.php?article_id=741.

3. Felix Corley, "Azerbaijan: Mosque Closed Four Days before Ramadan Ends." *Forum 18 News Service*, September 18, 2009. www.forum18.org/archive.php?article_id=1350.

4. Felix Corley, "Azerbaijan: 'Sword of Damocles' Hangs over Religious Booksellers." *Forum 18 News Service*, April 12, 2011. www.forum18.org/archive.php?article_id=1561.

5. Twelver Shiism recognizes only the family of the Prophet as legitimate successors to Muhammad's role as leader of the Muslim community. Since the occultation of the Twelfth Imam, Muhammad al-Mahdi, in 874, only those who can claim to rule on behalf of the Hidden Imam have legitimacy. The Imam is thus the legitimate successor to the Prophet, playing a role in legal, administrative, and military matters, as well as being considered the interpreter of the Koran and Islamic law and the leader of the Muslim community.

6. Tamadonfar engages in a detailed analysis of the sources of Islamic law in this article, as well as tracing the principles the Iranian regime has used to justify its laws.

7. Constitution of the Islamic Republic of Iran, 1979 (last amended 1989). www.parliran.ir/index.aspx?fkeyid=&siteid=84&pageid=320.

8. Ayatollah Khomeini was the first supreme leader of Iran. Upon Khomeini's death in 1989, Ali Khamenei (president of Iran from 1981 to 1989) was appointed to the position of supreme leader, despite issues related to his clerical rank (Behrooz 1996).

9. Human Rights Watch, "Iran: Proposed Penal Code Retains Stoning." June 3, 2013. www.hrw.org/news/2013/06/03/iran-proposed-penal-code-retains-stoning.

10. Amnesty International, "Iran: Executions by Stoning." December 23, 2010. www.amnesty.org/en/library/asset/MDE13/095/2010/en/968814e1-f48e-43ea-bee3-462d153fb5af/mde130952010en.pdf.

11. Amnesty International, "Iran: A Legal System That Fails to Protect Freedom of Expression and Association." December 2001. www.amnesty.org/en/library/info/MDE13/045/2001.

12. Amnesty International, "Iran: Shia Religious Leaders as Victims of Human Rights Violations." June 3, 1997. amnesty.org/en/library/asset/MDE13/024/1997/en/1c972ca2-ea77-11dd-b05d-65164b228191/mde130241997en.html.

13. Amnesty International, "Iran: Further Information on Arbitrary Arrest: Fear for Safety: Possible Prisoner of Conscience: Medical Concern: Torture and Ill-Treatment: Ayatollah Sayed Hossein Kazemeyni Boroujerdi." May 19, 2009. www.amnesty.org/en/library/asset/MDE13/047/2009/en/dd427800-5b55-476a-abac-dc7ee0a0461f/mde130472009en.html.

14. Minorities at Risk Project, "Assessment for Baha'is in Iran." www.cidcm.umd.edu/mar/assessment.asp?groupId=63003.

15. Amnesty International, "'We Are Ordered to Crush You': Expanding Repression of Dissent in Iran." February 2012. www.amnesty.org/en/library/asset/MDE13/002/2012/en/2b228705-dfba-4408-a04b-8ab887988881/mde130022012en.pdf.

16. Ibid.

17. Minority Rights Group International, "World Directory of Minorities and Indigenous Peoples." April 2009. www.minorityrights.org/5109/iran/christians.html.

18. International Campaign for Human Rights in Iran, "The Cost of Faith: Persecution of Christian Protestants and Converts in Iran." 2013. www.iranhumanrights.org/2013/01/cost_of_faith/.

19. Pastor Hossein Soodmand was executed for apostasy in 1990.

20. The king's official title is "Custodian of the Two Holy Mosques."

21. Kingdom of Saudi Arabia Ministry of Foreign Affairs, "Saudi Government," www.mofa.gov.sa/sites/mofaen/servicesandinformation/aboutKingDom/ SaudiGovernment/Pages/BasicSystemOfGovernance35297.aspx.

22. Freedom House, *Freedom in the World 2011*. www.freedomhouse.org.

23. Ibid.

24. Reuters, "Saudi Executes Egyptian for Practising 'Witchcraft.'" *ABC News*, November 3, 2007. www.abc.net.au/news/2007-11-03/saudi-executes-egyptian-for-practising-witchcraft/714652.

25. The majority of the world's Shia Muslims are Twelvers, who believe in 12 divinely ordained leaders or Imams and recognize Muhammad ibn Hasan al-Mahdi as the Twelfth Imam, who is currently alive and in occultation, to return at the end of time. Sevener Muslims believe in a different line of succession than the Twelvers and consider Isma'il ibn Jafar to be the true Seventh Imam; there are several Ismaili subgroupings. Fiver or Zaidi Shia recognize a different fifth Imam. Most are concentrated in Yemen, although some live in the western provinces of Saudi Arabia.

26. This section deals with religious repression in mainland China (including Tibet) but does not include Hong Kong.

27. "Constitution of the People's Republic of China," translated on the People's Daily Online website, http://english.people.com.cn/constitution/constitution.html.

28. In addition to these five, the Russian Orthodox Church is recognized in Heilongjiang Province.

29. These are the Buddhist Association of China, Daoist Association of China, Chinese Catholic Patriotic Association, Chinese Catholic Bishops' Conference, Chinese Catholic Religious Affairs Committee, Three-Self Patriotic Movement Committee of the Protestant Churches in China (TSPM), China Christian Council (CCC), and Chinese Islamic Association. The Chinese Catholic Bishops' Conference is in charge of approving the selection and ordination of bishops. The Chinese Catholic Patriotic Association is a mass organization of laity and clergy that is charged with helping the Catholic Church implement the three-self policy. The China Christian Council (CCC) is directly involved in internal pastoral affairs, and the Three-Self Patriotic Movement (TSPM) handles relations between individual Protestant churches and the Chinese government.

30. Information Office of the State Council of the PRC, "White Paper: Freedom of Religious Belief in China." Beijing: Religion and Law Consortium. October 1997. www.religlaw.org/common/document.view.php?docId=793.

31. The 1998 Regulations for Registration and Management of Social Organizations require registrants to have 50 or more members, a fixed location, staff with qualifications, and lawful assets. They require complete documentation of financial and identity records, permissions, and documents. Religious groups must obtain approval from a professional leading unit (SARA) and allow only

one social organization of a particular type in any given administrative area. This makes it difficult for independent organizations (such as Protestant house churches) to qualify for registration.

32. However, there does exist the phenomenon of "religious communists," party members who claim to be atheists even though they are religious. The idea behind this concept is that religion is a private matter, so it is becoming increasingly acceptable for Communist Party members to be privately religious. See Magda Hornemann, "China: 'Religious Communists' and Religious Freedom." *Forum 18 News Service*, February 13, 2007. www.forum18. org/Archive.php?article_id=910.

33. Hans Petersen, "China: Despite New Regulations, Religious Policy Still under Strain." *Forum 18 News Service*, March 8, 2006. www.forum18.org/Archive. php?article_id=740.

34. "Rule by law" refers to a political system in which power holders use laws and law enforcement to maintain stability, regulate society, protect the interests of the ruling class, and strengthen and enforce the government's authority. It is often found in authoritarian systems. "Rule of law" is practiced in democratic societies, where procedures exist for making and implementing laws that all persons must follow. These laws and procedures restrict individual citizens, but they also restrict lawmakers and law enforcement, who are not above the law.

35. Brian J. Grim, "Religion in China on the Eve of the 2008 Beijing Olympics." *Pew Forum on Religion and Public Life*. May 1, 2008. www. pewforum.org/Importance-of-Religion/Religion-in-China-on-the-Eve-of-the-2008-Beijing-Olympics.aspx.

36. As China is officially atheist, there is no one religion that can be considered the majority faith in the country. Therefore, all religious groups can be thought of as minorities and are subject to government-imposed repression.

37. "China Communist Party 'Exceeds 80 Million Members.'" *BBC News*, June 24, 2011. www.bbc.co.uk/news/world-asia-pacific-13901509.

38. Figures are from the Cardinal Kung Foundation, based in the United States, and reported in Magda Hornemann, "China: China's Catholics, the Holy See and Religious Freedom." *Forum 18 News Service*, April 12, 2007. www.forum18. org/Archive.php?article_id=942.

39. Other banned organizations included Lingling Jiao, Mentu Hui, Chongsheng Pai, Dongfang Shandian, Yilya Jiao, Guo Gong, Cibei Gong, Zhong Gong, and Xiang Gong.

40. Danny Gittings, "Falun Gong Defies Police to Protest; Followers of Banned Spiritual Movement Stream into Capital for Campaign of Civil Disobedience in Tiananmen Square." *Guardian*, October 30, 1999.

41. See www.faluninfo.net, a website focused on reporting on Falun Gong in China, for stories claiming instances of abuse at the hands of Chinese government authorities. This website also claims that the Chinese government

has been engaged in illegal organ harvesting of individuals arrested for being Falun Gong practitioners.

42. Embassy of the People's Republic of China in the United States of America, "True Face of Li Hongzhi," www.china-embassy.org/eng/zt/ppflg/t36564. htm.

43. Magda Hornemann, "China: The Economics of Religious Freedom." *Forum 18 News Service*, August 16, 2006. www.forum18.org/Archive.php?article_id=831.

44. Human Rights Watch, "Beaten, Blacklisted, and Behind Bars: The Vanishing Space for Freedom of Expression in Azerbaijan." October 2010. www.hrw.org/reports/2010/10/26/beaten-blacklisted-and-behind-bars.

45. Human Rights Watch, "Crushing Dissent: Repression, Violence and Azerbaijan's Elections." January 2004. www.hrw.org/reports/2004/01/22/crushing-dissent-0.

46. Constitution of the Republic of Azerbaijan (amended up to 2009), www.unhcr.org/refworld/docid/4d4828112.html.

47. Felix Corley, "Azerbaijan: Repressive New Religion Law and New Punishments Enter into Force." *Forum18 News Service*, June 3, 2009. www.forum18.org/Archive.php?article_id=1305.

48. In 2010, Azerbaijan was given a score of 2.4 (where 0 is highly corrupt and 10 is very clean) and ranked 134th of 178 countries in terms of its relative level of corruption (higher rankings signify greater corruption). Transparency International's Corruption Perception Index ranks countries based on how corrupt their public sector is perceived to be. It is a composite index, drawing on corruption-related data from expert and business surveys carried out by a variety of independent institutions. See www.transparency.org.

49. Felix Corley, "Azerbaijan: Religious Freedom Survey, September 2008." *Forum 18 News Service*, September 24, 2008. www.forum18.org/Archive.php?article_id=1192.

50. Analysts often describe Pashazade as a government ally who does not contradict its actions or decisions (Cornell 2006, 63). This sentiment was conveyed to me personally in interviews with Islamic leaders in Tbilisi, Georgia (who are also under the authority of the Caucasian Muslim Board), in November 2005.

51. Felix Corley, "Azerbaijan: Religious Freedom Survey, September 2008." *Forum 18 News Service*, September 24, 2008. www.forum18.org/Archive.php?article_id=1192.

52. Felix Corley, "Azerbaijan: 'The Government Doesn't Want to Give Up Control over Religion.'" *Forum 18 News Service*, July 22, 2009. www.forum18.org/Archive.php?article_id=1330.

53. European Commission for Democracy through Law (Venice Commission), "Joint Opinion on the Law on Freedom of Religious Belief of the Republic of Azerbaijan." October 15, 2012. www.legislationline.org/countries/country/43.

54. Felix Corley, "Azerbaijan: Muslims Ordered out of Mosque Authorities Want as Carpet Museum." *Forum 18 News Service*, January 19, 2004. www.forum18. org/Archive.php?article_id=231.

55. Felix Corley, "Azerbaijan: Twenty Seven Juma Mosque Members Detained, Many Fined, Four Beaten." *Forum 18 News Service*, July 7, 2004. www.forum18. org/Archive.php?article_id=357.

56. Having served in this position since 2001, he was removed in June 2006.

57. Felix Corley, "Azerbaijan: Judges Not Police to Expel Muslims from Mosque?" *Forum 18 News Service*, February 2, 2004. www.forum18.org/Archive. php?article_id=241.

58. Felix Corley, "Azerbaijan: Muslims Can't Pray at Home, Says Police Chief." *Forum 18 News Service*, August 2, 2004. www.forum18.org/Archive. php?article_id=382.

59. Felix Corley, "Azerbaijan: 'Half-Free' Imam to Challenge Suspended Jail Sentence." *Forum 18 News Service*, April 5, 2004. www.forum18.org/Archive. php?article_id=294.

60. Thomas Goltz, "Closure of Mosque Does Not Auger Well for Azerbaijani Freedoms." *EurasiaNet*, May 26, 2004. www.eurasianet.org/departments/ civilsociety/articles/eav052704.shtml.

61. Felix Corley, "Azerbaijan: Religious Freedom Survey, September 2008." *Forum 18 News Service*, September 24, 2008. www.forum18.org/Archive. php?article_id=1192.

62. Felix Corley, "Azerbaijan: Religious NGOs Still Banned from Registering." *Forum 18 News Service*, June 27, 2005. www.forum18.org/Archive. php?article_id=594.

### CHAPTER 4

1. Freedom House, "Russia." www.freedomhouse.org/country/russia.

2. Robert W. Orttung, "Nations in Transit 2011: Russia." www.freedomhouse. org/sites/default/files/inline_images/NIT-2011-Russia.pdf.

3. Many scholars have documented these developments. For a concise summary, see Gill (2008). In a book on relations between the ROC and the Russian state, Irina Papkova (2011) explains that the passage of the 1997 law was due to three circumstances. First, there was societal demand for restrictive legislation because of the increasing growth of new religious movements. Second, she argues that the Duma was opposed to religious freedom, perhaps as a way of opposing Yeltsin. Third, the state wanted to regain control over the religious sector after the 1990 law had abolished the Council for Religious Affairs.

4. Geraldine Fagan, "Russia: Unregistered Religious Groups." *Forum 18 News Service*, April 14, 2005. www.forum18.org/Archive.php?article_id=543.

5. Ibid.

6. Alexander Verkhovsky, "Religious Xenophobia: Within Religious Orders and between Religious Orders." *SOVA Center for Information and Analysis*, April 28, 2003. www.sova-center.ru/en/religion/publications/2003/04/d358/.

7. There is a difference between defining groups as traditional religions versus traditional organizations. "Traditional organizations" allows religious associations such as the ROC to argue against the rights of competing Orthodox churches such as the Russian Orthodox Autonomous Church and the Old Believers. It also allows the Central Spiritual Department of Muslims to argue against the rights of other Muslim associations, such as the Mufti's Council.

8. Geraldine Fagan, "Russia: Religious Freedom Survey." *Forum 18 News Service*, July 29, 2003. www.forum18.org/Archive.php?article_id=116.

9. Orttung, *Nations in Transit 2011: Russia.* www.freedomhouse.org/sites/default/files/inline_images/NIT-2011-Russia.pdf.

10. Four clauses in the 2002 law define extremist activity in a specifically religious context: incitement of religious hatred, committing a crime motivated by religious hatred, obstruction of the lawful activity of religious associations accompanied by violence or the threat of violence, and propaganda of the exclusivity, superiority, or inferiority of citizens according to their attitude toward religion or religious affiliation. See Geraldine Fagan, "Russia: How the Battle with 'Religious Extremism' Began." *Forum 18 News Service*, April 27 2009. www.forum18.org/Archive.php?article_id=1287.

11. Russian Federation Ministry of Justice, "Federal List of Extremist Materials" (in Russian). http://minjust.ru/ru/extremist-materials?search=&page=4.

12. Geraldine Fagan, "Russia: Widespread Protests at New 'Inquisition.'" *Forum 18 News Service*, June 2, 2009. www.forum18.org/Archive.php?article_id=1303.

13. The full name of the law is the Federal Law on Introducing Amendments to Certain Legislative Acts of the Russian Federation No. 18-FZ, 2006, amending the law on Closed Administrative Territorial Formations No 3297-1, 1992; Law on Public Associations No. 82-FZ, 1995; Law on Non-Commercial Organizations No. 7-FZ, 1996; and article 61 of the Russian Federation Civil Code. It is referred to for simplicity's sake as the NGO law.

14. Geraldine Fagan, "Russia: Religious Freedom Survey, April 2007." *Forum 18 News Service*, April 26, 2007. www.forum18.org/Archive.php?article_id=947.

15. Alexander Verkhovsky and Olga Sibireva, "Problems Relating to Freedom of Conscience in Russia in 2006." *SOVA Center for Information and Analysis*, April 17, 2006. www.sova-center.ru/en/religion/publications/2007/04/d10651/.

16. Alexander Verkhovsky and Olga Sibireva, "Restrictions and Challenges in 2007 on Freedom of Conscience in Russia." *SOVA Center for Information and Analysis*, March 27, 2008. www.sova-center.ru/en/religion/publications/2008/03/d12955/.

17. Alexander Verkhovsky and Olga Sibireva, "Restrictions and Challenges in 2008 on Freedom of Conscience in Russia." *SOVA Center for Information and Analysis*, April 10, 2009. www.sova-center.ru/en/religion/publications/2009/04/d15726/.

18. Felix Corley, "Russia: Orthodox Can Get Catholic and Lutheran Churches—but Catholics and Lutherans Can't." *Forum 18 News Service*, December 14, 2010. www.forum18.org/Archive.php?article_id=1521.

19. Geraldine Fagan, "Russia: Orthodox Becoming First among Equals." *Forum 18 News Service*, May 27, 2003. www.forum18.org/Archive.php?article_id=64.

20. Alexander Verkhovsky and Olga Sibireva, "Restrictions and Challenges Related to Freedom of Conscience in Russia in 2009." *SOVA Center for Information and Analysis*, April 26, 2010. www.sova-center.ru/en/religion/publications/2010/04/d18593/.

21. US Department of State, "Russia." *International Religious Freedom Report 2011*. www.state.gov/j/drl/rls/irf/religiousfreedom/index.htm?dlid=192855.

22. Sophia Kishkovsky, "Russians See Orthodox Church and State Come Closer." *New York Times*, October 31, 2012.

23. Alexander Verkhovsky and Olga Sibireva, "Restrictions and Challenges in 2008 on Freedom of Conscience in Russia." *SOVA Center for Information and Analysis*, April 10, 2009. www.sova-center.ru/en/religion/publications/2009/04/d15726/.

24. A number of reports from the Forum 18 News Service since 2009 document the government's targeting of readers of Said Nursi. See www.forum18.org.

25. Alexander Verkhovsky and Olga Sibireva, "Restrictions and Challenges in 2007 on Freedom of Conscience in Russia." *SOVA Center for Information and Analysis*, March 27, 2008. www.sova-center.ru/en/religion/publications/2008/03/d12955/.

26. Olga Sibireva and Alexander Verkhovsky, "Freedom of Conscience in Russia in 2010: Restrictions and Challenges." *SOVA Center for Information and Analysis*, April 21, 2011. www.sova-center.ru/en/religion/publications/2011/04/d21460/.

27. Alexander Verkhovsky and Olga Sibireva, "Problems Relating to Freedom of Conscience in Russia in 2006." *SOVA Center for Information and Analysis*, April 17, 2006. www.sova-center.ru/en/religion/publications/2007/04/d10651/.

28. *Jehovah's Witnesses of Moscow v. Russia*, Application no. 302/02, Council of Europe: European Court of Human Rights, 10 June 2010. www.refworld.org/docid/4c2090002.html.

29. Geraldine Fagan and Felix Corley, "Russia: 34 Jehovah's Witness Publications and One Congregation Banned." *Forum 18 News Service*, December 8, 2009. www.forum18.org/Archive.php?article_id=1385.

30. Sophia Kishkovsky and David M. Herszenhorn, "Punk Band's Moscow Trial Offers Platform for Orthodox Protesters." *New York Times*, August 8, 2012.

31. Alexander Verkhovsky and Olga Sibireva, "Problems Relating to Freedom of Conscience in Russia in 2006." *SOVA Center for Information and Analysis*, April 17, 2006. www.sova-center.ru/en/religion/publications/2007/04/d10651/.

32. Alexander Verkhovsky and Olga Sibireva, "Problems Relating to Freedom of Conscience in Russia in 2006." *SOVA Center for Information and Analysis*, April 17, 2006. www.sova-center.ru/en/religion/publications/2007/04/d10651/.

33. The Nurcular, or followers of Turkish theologian Said Nursi, were banned as an extremist organization in April 2008.

34. Alexander Verkhovsky, "Inappropriate Enforcement of Anti-Extremist Legislation in Russia in a First Half of 2010." *SOVA Center for Information and Analysis*, October 1, 2010. www.sova-center.ru/en/religion/publications/2010/10/d19880/.

35. This case study excludes examination of religious repression in Abkhazia and South Ossetia, two autonomous regions not under the control of the Georgian government.

36. According to the press secretary for the Georgian Orthodox Patriarchate, each priest depended on donations from his parish to pay his salary. Interview in Tbilisi, Georgia, November 9, 2005.

37. Ilya II was elected patriarch in 1977 and remains in the position in 2014.

38. The Constitution of Georgia, adopted August 24, 1995, and last amended December 27, 2006. www.parliament.ge/files/68_1944_951190_CONSTIT_27_12.06.pdf.

39. A new constitution was adopted in October 2010 that would take effect after the presidential elections in 2013. This changed the system from a presidential one to a mixed system, putting executive power in the hands of the prime minister.

40. I am grateful to Levan Abashidze, of the Georgian Parliamentary Research Services and the CIPDD, for giving me the English translation of this agreement when it was not available. It can now be accessed on the website of the Patriarchate of Georgia, www.patriarchate.ge/_en/?action=eklesia-saxelmcifo.

41. The type of support given to these educational institutions is not specified, leaving open the question of whether the state is funding religious schools.

42. Interview with Beka Mindiashvili, head of the Department of Equality and Justice, Ombudsman's Office of Georgia, Tbilisi, November 14, 2005.

43. Interview with Archpriest Basil Kobakhidze, Georgian Orthodox Church, Tbilisi, Georgia, November 14, 2005.

44. "An Orthodox Church Leaves the WCC." *The Christian Century* 114, no. 18 (June 4–July 11, 1997): 554–555.

45. Giorgi Sepashvili, "Brethren in Christ, Divided: Orthodoxy and Catholicism Clash in Georgia." *Civil Georgia*, September 29, 2003. www.civil.ge/eng/article.php?id=5019.

46. Interview with Father David Sharashenidze, November 9, 2005.

47. Interviews with several religious leaders, experts on religion, and leaders of nongovernmental organizations in Tbilisi, Georgia, November 2005.

48. Basil Mkalavishvili was defrocked by the Georgian Orthodox Patriarchate in 1996 and is currently under the jurisdiction of the Old Calendarist Metropolitan Cyprian of Oropos and Fili in Greece.

49. Many of these attacks are documented in the *International Religious Freedom Report* published by the US State Department from 1999 to 2002. www.state.gov/j/drl/rls/irf/index.htm.

50. "Ombudsman Criticized for Stance on Church, Being 'Too Soft.'" *Civil Georgia*, December 23, 2005. www.civil.ge/eng/article.php?id=11410.

51. "Georgian Orthodox Church Slams Ombudsman." *Civil Georgia*, December 25, 2005. www.civil.ge/eng/article.php?id=11414.

52. Ellen Barry, "Church's Muscle Aided Win of President's Rivals in Georgia." *New York Times*, October 14, 2012.

53. Felix Corley, "Georgia: Religious Freedom Survey, August 2004." *Forum 18 News Service*. August 23, 2004. www.forum18.org/archive.php?article_id=400.

54. Felix Corley, "Georgia: 'Orchestrated Reaction' against Religious Minorities' Buildings." *Forum 18 News Service*, October 26, 2006. www.forum18.org/Archive.php?article_id=861.

55. Felix Corley, "Georgia: Why Can't Minority Faiths Build Places of Worship?" *Forum 18 News Service*, November 14, 2003. www.forum18.org/Archive.php?article_id=184.

56. Felix Corley, "Georgia: 'We Want Legal Status!' Say Minority Faiths." *Forum 18 News Service*, November 17, 2003. www.forum18.org/Archive.php?article_id=185.

57. Interviews with representatives of religious organizations in Tbilisi, Georgia, November 2005.

58. "Armenian Church Hails Georgia's Religious Minorities Law." *Radio Free Europe/Radio Liberty*, July 8, 2011. www.rferl.org/content/armenian_apostolic_church_georgia_orthodox_church/24259999.html.

59. US Department of State, *International Religious Freedom Report for 2012*. www.state.gov/j/drl/rls/irf/religiousfreedom/index.htm?year=2012&dlid=208316.

60. Freedom House, *Freedom in the World 2012*. www.freedomhouse.org/report/freedom-world/2012/indonesia.

61. International Crisis Group, "Islamic Law and Criminal Justice in Aceh." July 31, 2006. www.crisisgroup.org/~/media/Files/asia/south-east-asia/indonesia/117_islamic_law_and_criminal_justice_in_aceh.pdf.

62. Christen Broecker, "Policing Morality: Abuses in the Application of Sharia in Aceh, Indonesia." Human Rights Watch, December 2010. hrw.org/reports/2010/12/01/policing-morality-0.

63. US Commission on International Religious Freedom, "Factsheet Indonesia." October 2013. www.uscirf.gov/sites/default/files/resources/Indonesia%20Factsheet%20%20OCTOBER%20%202013%20finalrev.pdf.

64. Human Rights Watch, "Indonesia's Salman Rushdie." April 10, 1991. www.hrw.org/reports/1991/04/10/indonesias-salman-rushdie.

65. International Crisis Group, "Indonesia: Implications of the Ahmadiyah Decree." Crisis Group Asia Briefing, July 7, 2008. www.crisisgroup.org/en/regions/asia/south-east-asia/indonesia/B078-indonesia-implications-of-the-ahmadiyah-decree.aspx.

66. "Indonesia's Aceh Province: Laying Down God's Law." *The Economist*, February 15, 2014.
67. US Commission on International Religious Freedom, "Factsheet Indonesia." October 2013. www.uscirf.gov/sites/default/files/resources/Indonesia%20 Factsheet%20%20OCTOBER%20%202013%20finalrev.pdf.
68. All mosques in Turkey must be operated and administered by the DRA. Those that are built by nongovernmental actors must be transferred to the DRA within three months of their completion (Er 2008).
69. Republic of Turkey Ministry of Foreign Affairs. "Constitution of the Republic of Turkey." 1982. http://global.tbmm.gov.tr/docs/constitution_en.pdf.
70. Mine Yildirim, "Turkey: The New Constitution Drafting Process and Freedom of Religion or Belief." *Forum 18 News Service*, November 30, 2011. www. forum18.org/Archive.php?article_id=1641.
71. Gülen's teachings rely heavily on those of Said Nursi (1876–1960), a Turkish theologian whose *Risale-i Nur Külliyatı* is an commentary on the Koran. The Nur movement (followers are called Nurcu) went on to be the basis of a number of Islamist political parties, including those founded by Necmettin Erbakan.
72. Mine Yildirim, "Turkey: The Diyanet—the Elephant in Turkey's Religious Freedom Room?" *Forum 18 News Service*, May 4, 2011. www.forum18.org/ Archive.php?article_id=1567.
73. Imam Hatip schools are public vocational secondary schools established in the 1950s that prepare students in Islamic subjects, preferably with the goal of being employed as prayer leaders (imams) or religious teachers upon graduation. Approximately 40 percent of the curriculum at these schools is on religious subjects. The Ministry of Religious Affairs and the Ministry of National Education regulate Imam Hatip schools. The schools are popular among conservative and religious families. As the number of graduates exceeds the state's religious personnel needs, many graduates instead attend university or find jobs in nonreligious sectors. They have been controversial in recent years because the AKP government has been placing their graduates into government positions, which opponents of the party claim is their way of introducing a greater role for religion in the government.
74. The *tesettür* is a conservative Muslim veil consisting of a long overcoat worn with a headscarf that covers the hair, neck and shoulders. It carries political connotations for secularists, as it is perceived as an insult to Kemalism and a threat to the secular state.
75. Quoted in Canada: Immigration and Refugee Board of Canada, *Turkey: The Situation of Alevis (January 2002–April 2005)*, April 14, 2005, TUR43493.E. www.refworld.org/docid/42df61b311.html.
76. The Shia Caferi community has also argued that they are not allowed to open their own mosques and that the DRA appoints Sunni imams to the mosques

they use. See Mine Yildirim, "Turkey: The Right to Have Places of Worship – a Trapped Right." *Forum 18 News Service*, March 2, 2011. www.forum18.org/Archive.php?article_id=1549.

CHAPTER 5

1. United Nations High Commissioner for Human Rights, "UN Human Rights Chief Denounces New Anti-Homosexuality Law in Nigeria." January 14, 2014. www.ohchr.org/FR/NewsEvents/Pages/DisplayNews.aspx?NewsID=14169&LangID=E.
2. Adam Nossiter, "Nigeria Tries to 'Sanitize' Itself of Gays." *New York Times*, February 8, 2014.
3. Jonah Fisher, "Nigerian Leaders Unite against Same-Sex Marriages." *BBC News*, December 5, 2011.
4. Freedom House, "Kyrgyzstan." www.freedomhouse.org/country/kyrgyzstan.
5. Igor Rotar, "Kyrgyzstan: Religious Freedom Survey, January 2004." *Forum 18 News Service*, January 7, 2004. www.forum18.org/Archive.php?article_id=222.
6. Mushfig Bayram, "Kyrgyzstan: Restrictive Religion Law Passes Parliament Unanimously." *Forum 18 News Service*, November 6, 2008. www.forum18.org/Archive.php?article_id=1215.
7. Mushfig Bayram, "Kyrgyzstan: Property Obstacles Used to Stop Registrations." *Forum 18 News Service*, August 21, 2009. www.forum18.org/Archive.php?article_id=1338.
8. Erica Marat, "Nations in Transit: Kyrgyzstan." *Freedom House*, 2009. www.freedomhouse.org/report/nations-transit/2009/kyrgyzstan.
9. Mushfig Bayram, "Kyrgyzstan: Crackdown Follows New Religion Law. *Forum 18 News Service*, May 28, 2009. www.forum18.org/Archive.php?article_id=1302.
10. Mushfig Bayram, "Kyrgyzstan: 'Don't Meet for Worship.'" *Forum 18 News Service*, August 13, 2009. www.forum18.org/Archive.php?article_id=1336.
11. Mushfig Bayram, "Kyrgyzstan: 'We Have Not Been Able to Pray and Worship Together.'" *Forum 18 News Service*, January 18, 2012. www.forum18.org/Archive.php?article_id=1657.
12. Dmitry Kabak and Almaz Esengeldiev, *Freedom of Religion and Belief in the Kyrgyz Republic: Overview of the Legislation and Practice.* Bishkek: Open Viewpoint Public Foundation, 2011. www.osce.org/bishkek/93786.
13. Tolkunbek Turdubaev, "Kyrgyzstan: Row over Mufti Change." *Institute for War and Peace Reporting*, February 21, 2005. iwpr.net/report-news/kyrgyzstan-row-over-mufti-change.
14. "Kyrgyzstan: Hajj Questions Highlight Opaque Nature of Muftiate." *EurasiaNet*, January 14, 2013. www.eurasianet.org/node/66400.
15. Igor Rotar, "Kyrgyzstan: Mob Goes Unpunished as Intolerance of Religious Freedom Rises." *Forum 18 News Service*, September 27, 2006. www.forum18.org/Archive.php?article_id=846.

16. "First Official Regional Madrasah Opens in Southern Kyrgyzstan." *Radio Free Europe/Radio Liberty*, September 7, 2009. www.rferl.org/articleprintview/1816657.html.

17. "Kyrgyz Protesters Demand Hijab Be Allowed in Schools." *Radio Free Europe/ Radio Liberty*, September 19, 2011. www.rferl.org/articleprintview/24333454. html.

18. Igor Rotar and Mushfig Bayram, "Kyrgyzstan: No Prayers in School, Muslim Children Told." *Forum 18 News Service*, May 12, 2003. www.forum18.org/Archive.php?article_id=51.

19. Igor Rotar, "Kyrgyzstan: Islamic Headscarves Arouse School Director's Anger." *Forum 18 News Service*, May 12, 2003. www.forum18.org/Archive.php?article_id=52.

20. Igor Rotar, "Kyrgyzstan: Pressure against Schoolgirls Wearing Hijabs." *Forum 18 News Service*, April 11, 2006. www.forum18.org/Archive.php?article_id=757.

21. Igor Rotar, "Kyrgyzstan: Official Begins Destruction of Six Rural Mosques." *Forum 18 News Service*, October 21, 2003. www.forum18.org/Archive.php?article_id=167.

22. Igor Rotar, "Kyrgyzstan: Wide-Ranging Extremism Law Not Seen as Threat." *Forum 18 News Service*, October 19, 2005. www.forum18.org/Archive.php?article_id=673.

23. "Large Increase in Number of Kyrgyz Religious Extremism Prosecutions." *Radio Free Europe/Radio Liberty*, October 18, 2011. www.rferl.org/articleprintview/24363441.html.

24. Mushfig Bayram, "Kyrgyzstan: 'I Received It from Heaven.'" *Forum 18 News Service*, December 21, 2011, www.forum18.org/Archive.php?article_id=1650.

25. The Ahmadiya Muslim community is a reformist movement that was founded in the nineteenth century in India by Mirza Gulam Ahmad Kadiani, whom Ahmadis consider to be the promised Messiah and Mahdi. It is regarded by many Muslims to be non-Islamic, although members consider themselves to be Muslims. It is not commonly known for espousing extremist or violent views.

26. "Kyrgyz Officials Reject Muslim Sect." *Radio Free Europe/Radio Liberty*. December 30, 2011. www.rferl.org/articleprintview/24438562.html.

27. Ole Solvang, "Distorted Justice: Kyrgyzstan's Flawed Investigations and Trials on the 2010 Violence." *Human Rights Watch*, June 2011. www.hrw.org/reports/2011/06/08/distorted-justice-0.

28. The Constitution of the Kingdom of Bahrain, February 14, 2002. www.servat.unibe.ch/icl/ba00000_.html.

29. Michael Slackman, "In a Landscape of Tension, Bahrain Embraces Its Jews. All 36 of Them." *New York Times*, April 6, 2009.

30. "The Catholic Church in Bahrain." *Apostolic Vicariate of Northern Arabia*. www.avona.org/bahrain/bahrain_about.htm#.UYU77ZW6664.

31. Willy Fautre, "Christians in Bahrain." *Human Rights without Frontiers International,* February 2012. www.hrwf.net/publications/research-papers/christians-in-bahrain-2012.

32. Tensions did exist, however, among Muslim groups in the north. One axis revolved around the Qadiriyya and Tijaniyya Sufi brotherhoods. The Sokoto ruling aristocracy was mostly Qadiriyya and aligned with the colonial rulers, while leaders in other areas were mostly Tijaniyya and anti-Western and anti-colonial. Both groups were perceived as powerful, and political parties competed for their allegiance in 1951.

33. Christians have their own umbrella organization, the Christian Association of Nigeria (CAN), founded in 1976.

34. International Crisis Group, "Northern Nigeria: Background to Conflict." *Crisis Group Africa Report,* December 20, 2010. www.crisisgroup.org/en/regions/africa/west-africa/nigeria/168-northern-nigeria-background-to-conflict.aspx.

35. The 1979 Constitution included recognition of sharia courts within the federal system.

36. International Crisis Group, "Nigeria's Faltering Federal Experiment." *Africa Report,* October 25, 2006. www.crisisgroup.org/en/regions/africa/west-africa/nigeria/119-nigerias-faltering-federal-experiment.aspx.

37. International Crisis Group, "Nigeria: Failed Elections, Failing State?" *Africa Report,* May 30, 2007. www.crisisgroup.org/en/regions/africa/west-africa/nigeria/126-nigeria-failed-elections-failing-state.aspx.

38. *Hudud* crimes include theft, robbery, illicit sex, and alcohol consumption. *Qisas* are crimes involving bodily injury or loss of life. *Ta'zir* crimes are ones committed against public peace.

39. Carina Tertsakian, "'Political Shari'a?' Human Rights and Islamic Law in Northern Nigeria." *Human Rights Watch,* September 2004. www.hrw.org/reports/2004/nigeria0904/nigeria0904.pdf.

40. Ibid.

41. International Crisis Group, "Curbing Violence in Nigeria (I): The Jos Crisis." *Africa Report,* December 17, 2012. www.crisisgroup.org/en/publication-type/media-releases/2012/africa/curbing-violence-in-nigeria-the-jos-crisis.aspx.

42. Ibid.

43. International Crisis Group, "Nigeria's Faltering Federal Experiment." *Africa Report,* October 25, 2006. www.crisisgroup.org/en/regions/africa/west-africa/nigeria/119-nigerias-faltering-federal-experiment.aspx.

44. "Constitution of the Republic of Singapore," August 9, 1965. *Singapore Statutes Online.* http://statutes.agc.gov.sg.

45. "Societies Act," 1966 (revised 1985). *Singapore Statutes Online.* http://statutes.agc.gov.sg.

46. "Maintenance of Religious Harmony Act," 1990 (revised 2001). *Singapore Statutes Online.* http://statutes.agc.gov.sg.

47. Seth Mydans, "By Barring Religious Garb, Singapore School Dress Code Alienates Muslims." *New York Times*, March 2, 2002.

48. "Declaration of Religious Harmony." *Inter-religious Organization (Singapore)*. "Religious Harmony-Walking the Line." *Nanyang Technological University Student Affairs Office*. www.ntu.edu.sg/SAO/Pages/ReligiousHarmony.aspx.

49. Fareed Zakaria, "A Conversation with Lee Kuan Yew." *Foreign Affairs*. March 1, 1994. www.foreignaffairs.com/articles/49691/fareed-zakaria/a-conversation-with-lee-kuan-yew.

CHAPTER 6

1. In 2010, countries repressing all religious groups had an average Polity2 score of −6. Countries repressing all but one religion had an average score of 4. Countries repressing some religious groups had an average score of 2. See appendix A for details on individual countries.

2. Twenty percent of respondents declined to answer the optional census question about religious affiliation.

3. Online data analysis from the 2002 World Values Survey conducted in Albania. www.worldvaluessurvey.org/WVSDocumentationWV4.jsp.

4. Constitution of the Republic of Albania, October 21, 1998. www.ipls.org/services/kusht/contents.html.

5. The Constitution of the People's Republic of Albania, December 28, 1976. http://bjoerna.dk/dokumentation/Albanian-Constitution-1976.htm.

6. "Albanian Court Rejects Recognition of Muslim Motherland Party." *BBC Monitoring European*, April 6, 2004.

7. "Albanian Imams Write Open Letter against Ban on Headscarves in Schools." *BBC Monitoring European*, January 10, 2011.

8. Around the same time, the CPP also divorced itself from doctrinaire communism and embraced capitalism.

9. Constitution de la République du Sénégal, January 2001. www.gouv.sn/-Constitution-du-Senegal-.html (in French).

10. John Maust, "Evangelical Politics, Peruvian Style." *Christianity Today*, July 16, 1990, 41.

11. James Brooks, "Religious Rift Joins Politics in Peru Race." *New York Times*, April 29, 1990.

12. Shining Path (Sendero Luminoso) was established in the 1960s by Abimael Guzman as a regional section of the Maoist Communist Party of Peru but became independent in 1970s. It was not a popular movement; its members were mostly university students, with some peasants and workers among the ranks. Funding for the group came from cocaine mafias. The group's violence was directed at the poor, police, and elected officials. It was able to get supporters because of young people's resentment of military rule. The group went

underground in 1980, when the country returned to democracy after military rule. Between 1980 and 1992, more than 25,000 Peruvians were killed in the war between Shining Path and the government (Klaiber 1998).

CHAPTER 7

1. US Department of State website, www.state.gov/j/drl/irf/index.htm.

# Bibliography

Acemoglu, Daron, and James A. Robinson. 2001. "Inefficient Redistribution." *American Political Science Review* no. 95 (3):649–661.

Amnesty International. 2012. *Choice and Prejudice: Discrimination against Muslims in Europe.* London: Amnesty International.

Anderson, John. 1999. "Religion, State, and Society in the New Kyrgyzstan." *Journal of Church and State* no. 41 (1):99–116.

Ayata, Sencer. 1996. "Patronage, Party, and State: The Politicization of Islam in Turkey." *The Middle East Journal* no. 50 (1):40–56.

Baktiari, Bahman. 2012. "The Islamic Republic of Iran: Shari'a Politics and the Transformation of Islamic Law." *The Review of Faith & International Affairs* no. 10 (4):35–44.

Baskan, Birol, and Steven Wright. 2011. "Seeds of Change: Comparing State-Religion Relations in Qatar and Saudi Arabia." *Arab Studies Quarterly* no. 33 (2):96–111.

Behrooz, Maziar. 1996. "The Islamic State and the Crisis of Marja'iyat in Iran." *Comparative Studies of South Asia, Africa and the Middle East* no. 16 (2):93–100.

Berger, Peter L. 1967. *The Sacred Canopy.* New York: Anchor.

Blaydes, Lisa. 2010. *Elections and Distributive Politics in Mubarak's Egypt.* New York: Cambridge University Press.

Brownlee, Jason. 2007. *Authoritarianism in an Age of Democratization.* New York: Cambridge University Press.

Bruce, Steve. 1999. *Choice and Religion: A Critique of Rational Choice Theory.* Oxford: Oxford University Press.

Brumberg, Daniel. 2002. "The Trap of Liberalized Autocracy." *Journal of Democracy* no. 13 (4):56–68.

Carson, Eric R. 2005. "China's New Regulations on Religion: A Small Step, Not a Great Leap, Forward." *Brigham Young University Law Review* no. 2005 (3):747–797.

Casanova, Jose. 2001. "Civil Society and Religion: Retrospective Reflections on Catholicism and Prospective Reflections on Islam." *Social Research* no. 68 (4):1041–1080.

Chandra, Kanchan. 2004. *Why Ethnic Parties Succeed: Patronage and Head Counts in India.* Cambridge: Cambridge University Press.

Cheibub, José Antonio, Jennifer Gandhi, and James Raymond Vreeland. 2009. "Democracy and Dictatorship Revisited." *Public Choice* no. 143 (1–2):67–101.

Cheterian, Vicken. 2009. "The August 2008 War in Georgia: From Ethnic Conflict to Border Wars." *Central Asian Survey* no. 28 (2):155–170.

Clark, Andrew F. 1999. "Imperialism, Independence, and Islam in Senegal and Mali." *Africa Today* no. 46 (3–4):149–167.

Collins, Kathleen. 2002. "Clans, Pacts and Politics in Central Asia." *Journal of Democracy* no. 13 (3):137–152.

———. 2003. "The Political Role of Clans in Central Asia." *Comparative Politics* no. 35 (2):171–190.

———. 2007. "Ideas, Networks, and Islamist Movements: Evidence from Central Asia and the Caucasus." *World Politics* no. 60 (1):64–96.

Cordesman, Anthony H. 2002. *"Saudi Arabia Enters the 21st Century: Politics and Internal Stability."* Washington, D.C.: Center for Strategic and International Studies.

Cornell, Svante E. 2006. The Politicization of Islam in Azerbaijan. In *Silk Road Paper*. Washington, D.C.: Central Asia–Caucasus Institute/Silk Road Studies Program.

Crouch, Melissa. 2010. "Implementing the Regulation on Places of Worship in Indonesia: New Problems, Local Politics and Court Action." *Asian Studies Review* no. 34 (4):403–419.

Cruse O'Brien, Donal B. 2003. *Symbolic Confrontations: Muslims Imagining the State in Africa.* London: Hurst.

Dahl, Robert A. 1971. *Polyarchy.* New Haven: Yale University Press.

Davenport, Christian, and David A. Armstrong II. 2004. "Democracy and the Violation of Human Rights: A Statistical Analysis from 1976 to 1996." *American Journal of Political Science* no. 48 (3):538–554.

Dekmejian, R. Hrair. 1998. "Saudi Arabia's Consultative Council." *Middle East Journal* no. 52 (2):204–218.

Demerath, N. J., and Karen S. Straight. 1997. "Religion, Politics, and the State: Cross-Cultural Observations." *Cross Currents* no. 47 (1):43–58.

Diamond, Larry. 2002. "Thinking about Hybrid Regimes." *Journal of Democracy* no. 13 (2):21–35.

Dobson, William J. 2012. *The Dictator's Learning Curve: Inside the Global Battle for Democracy.* New York: Anchor Books.

Doja, Albert. 2006. "A Political History of Bektashism in Albania." *Totalitarian Movements and Political Religions* no. 7 (1):83–107.

Dressler, Markus. 2008. "Religio-Secular Metamorphoses: The Re-Making of Turkish Alevism." *Journal of the American Academy of Religion* no. 76 (2):280–311.

Edelman, Bryan, and James T. Richardson. 2003. "Falun Gong and the Law: Development of Legal Social Control in China." *Nova Religio* no. 6 (2):312–331.

Ehteshami, Anoushiravan. 2003. "Reform from Above: The Politics of Participation in the Oil Monarchies." *International Affairs* no. 79 (1):53–75.

Elaigwu, J. Isawa, and Habu Galadima. 2003. "The Shadow of Sharia over Nigerian Federalism." *Publius* no. 33 (3):123–144.

Ellis, Stephen, and Gerrie Ter Haar. 2004. *Worlds of Power: Religious Thought at Political Practice in Africa*. New York: Oxford University Press.

Engh, Mary Jane. 2007. *In the Name of Heaven: 3000 Years of Religious Persecution*. Amherst, N.Y.: Prometheus Books.

Er, Izzet. 2008. "Religious Services of the PRA." *The Muslim World* no. 98 (2–3):271–281.

Erdem, Gazi. 2008. "Religious Services in Turkey: From the Office of Şeyhülislam to the *Diyanet*." *The Muslim World* no. 98 (2–3):199–215.

Evans, Geoffrey, and Ksenia Northmore-Ball. 2012. "The Limits of Secularization? The Resurgence of Orthodoxy in Post-Soviet Russia." *Journal for the Scientific Study of Religion* no. 51 (4):795–808.

Fetzer, Joel S., and J. Christopher Soper. 2005. *Muslims and the State in Britain, France, and Germany*. New York: Cambridge University Press.

Fish, M. Steven. 2002. "Islam and Authoritarianism." *World Politics* no. 55 (1):4–37.

Fleet, Michael, and Brian H. Smith. 1997. *The Catholic Church and Democracy in Chile and Peru*. Notre Dame, Ind.: University of Notre Dame Press.

Fox, Jonathan. 2008. *A World Survey of Religion and the State*. Cambridge: Cambridge University Press.

———. 2011. "Building Composite Measures of Religion and State." *Interdisciplinary Journal of Research on Religion* no. 7:1–39.

Fox, Jonathan, and Deborah Flores. 2009. "Religions, Constitutions, and the State: A Cross-National Study." *Journal of Politics* no. 71 (4):1499–1513.

Freedom House. 2013. *Freedom in the World 2013: Democratic Breakthrough in the Balance*. www.freedomhouse.org/report/freedom-world/freedom-world-2013.

Furman, Uriah. 2000. "Minorities in Contemporary Islamist Discourse." *Middle Eastern Studies* no. 36 (4):1–20.

Gandhi, Jennifer, and Adam Przeworski. 2007. "Authoritarian Institutions and the Survival of Autocrats." *Comparative Political Studies* no. 40 (11):1279–1301.

Garcia-Montufar, Guillermo, and Elvira Martinez Coco. 1999. "Antecedents, Perspectives, and Projections of a Legal Project about Religious Liberty in Peru." *Brigham Young University Law Review* no. 1999 (2):503–529.

Geddes, Barbara. 2003. *Paradigms and Sandcastles: Theory Building and Research Design in Comparative Politics*. Ann Arbor: University of Michigan Press.

Geddes, Barbara, Joseph Wright, and Erica Frantz. 2012. "New Data on Autocratic Breakdown and Regime Transitions." http://dictators.la.psu.edu.

Geertz, Clifford. 1960. *The Religion of Java*. New York: Free Press.

Gill, Anthony. 1998. *Rendering unto Caesar: The Catholic Church and the State in Latin America*. Chicago: University of Chicago Press.

————. 2008. *The Political Origins of Religious Liberty.* New York: Cambridge University Press.

Gill, Anthony, and Arang Keshavarzian. 1999. "State Building and Religious Resources: An Institutional Theory of Church-State Relations in Iran and Mexico." *Politics and Society* no. 27 (3):431–465.

Gillespie, Piers. 2007. "Current Issues in Indonesian Islam: Analysing the 2005 Council of Indonesian Ulama Fatwa No. 7 Opposing Pluralism, Liberalism and Secularism." *Journal of Islamic Studies* no. 18 (2):202–240.

Gjuraj, Tonin. 2000. "A Stable Ecumenical Model? How Religion Might Become a Political Issue in Albania." *East European Quarterly* no. 34 (1):21–49.

Gozaydin, Istar B. 2008. "*Diyanet* and Politics." *The Muslim World* no. 98 (2–3):216–227.

Grim, Brian J., and Roger Finke. 2006. "International Religion Indexes: Government Regulation, Government Favoritism, and Social Regulation of Religion." *Interdisciplinary Journal of Research on Religion* no. 2 (1):1–40.

————. 2011. *The Price of Freedom Denied: Religious Persecution and Conflict in the Twenty-First Century.* New York: Cambridge University Press.

Grzymala-Busse, Anna. 2012. "Why Comparative Politics Should Take Religion (More) Seriously." *Annual Review of Political Science* no. 15 (1):421–442.

Hadenius, Axel, and Jan Teorell. 2005. "Assessing Alternative Indices of Democracy." In *Committee on Concepts and Methods Working Paper Series.* Mexico City: CIDE.

Hamayotsu, Kikue. 2002. "Islam and Nation Building in Southeast Asia: Malaysia and Indonesia in Comparative Perspective." *Pacific Affairs* no. 75 (3):353–375.

Harris, Ian. 2001. "Buddhist Sangha Groupings in Cambodia." *Buddhist Studies Review* no. 18 (1):73–106.

Hefner, Robert W. 2000. *Civil Islam: Muslims and Democratization in Indonesia.* Princeton, N.J.: Princeton University Press.

————. 2001. "Public Islam and the Problem of Democratization." *Sociology of Religion* no. 62 (4):491–514.

————. 2012. "Shari'a Politics and Indonesian Democracy." *The Review of Faith & International Affairs* no. 10 (4):61–69.

Herron, Erik S. 2011. "Measuring Dissent in Electoral Authoritarian Societies: Lessons from Azerbaijan's 2008 Presidential Election and 2009 Referendum." *Comparative Political Studies* no. 44 (11):1557–1583.

Homer, Lauren B. 2010. "Registration of Chinese Protestant House Churches under China's 2005 Regulation on Religious Affairs: Resolving the Implementation Impasse." *Journal of Church and State* no. 52 (1):50–73.

Huntington, Samuel P. 1991. *The Third Wave: Democratization in the Late Twentieth Century.* Norman: University of Oklahoma Press.

————.1996. *The Clash of Civilizations and the Remaking of World Order.* New York: Simon and Schuster.

Ilesanmi, Simeon O. 1995. "Recent Theories of Religion and Politics in Nigeria." *Journal of Church and State* no. 37:309–327.

Inboden, William. 2012. "Religious Freedom and National Security." *Policy Review* no. 175 (October–November):55–68.

Jibladze, Kakha. 2004. "Defending the Faith? Religion and Politics in Georgia." *Central Asia–Caucasus Analyst* no. 5 (23):12–13.

Kadir, Suzaina. 2010. "Uniquely Singapore: The Management of Islam in a Small Island Republic." *Islam and Civilisational Renewal* no. 2 (1):156–176.

Karasipahi, Sena. 2009. "Comparing Islamic Resurgence Movements in Turkey and Iran." *Middle East Journal* no. 63 (1):87–107.

Karatnycky, Adrian. 2002. "Muslim Countries and the Democracy Gap." *Journal of Democracy* no. 13 (1):99–112.

Kedourie, Elie. 1992. *Democracy and Arab Political Culture.* Washington, D.C.: The Washington Institute for Near East Policy.

Keith, Linda Camp. 2002. "Constitutional Provisions for Individual Human Rights (1977–1996): Are They More Than Mere 'Window Dressing'?" *Political Research Quarterly* no. 55 (1):111–143.

Keyes, Charles. 1990. Buddhism and Cultural Revolution in Cambodia. *Cultural Survival Quarterly,* July 31, 1990, 60.

Klaiber, Jeffrey. 1998. *The Church, Dictatorships, and Democracy in Latin America.* Maryknoll, N.Y.: Orbis Books.

Kogacioglu, Dicle. 2004. "Progress, Unity, and Democracy: Dissolving Political Parties in Turkey." *Law & Society Review* no. 38 (3):433–461.

Köse, Talha. 2010. "The AKP and the 'Alevi Opening': Understanding the Dynamics of Rapprochement." *Insight Turkey* no. 12 (2):143–164.

Kuah, Khun Eng. 1998. "Maintaining Ethno-Religious Harmony in Singapore." *Journal of Contemporary Asia* no. 28 (1):103–121.

Laitin, David. 1986. *Hegemony and Culture: Politics and Religious Change among the Yoruba.* Chicago: University of Chicago Press.

Langlaude, Sylvie. 2010. "The Rights of Religious Associations to External Relations: A Comparative Study of the OSCE and the Council of Europe." *Human Rights Quarterly* no. 32:502–529.

Lee, Joseph Tse-Hei. 2007. "Christianity in Contemporary China: An Update." *Journal of Church and State* no. 49 (2):277–304.

Lerner, Hanna. 2013. "Permissive Constitutions, Democracy, and Religious Freedom in India, Indonesia, Israel, and Turkey." *World Politics* no. 65 (4):609–655.

Leung, Beatrice. 2005. "China's Religious Freedom Policy: The Art of Managing Religious Activity." *The China Quarterly* no. 184 (894):894–913.

Levitsky, Steven, and Lucan A. Way. 2010. *Competitive Authoritarianism: Hybrid Regimes after the Cold War.* New York: Cambridge University Press.

Lewis, Bernard. 1996. "Islam and Liberal Democracy: A Historical Overview." *Journal of Democracy* no. 7 (2):52–63.

Li-Ann, Thio. 2004. "Constitutional 'Soft' Law and the Management of Religious Liberty and Order: The 2003 Declaration on Religious Harmony." *Singapore Journal of Legal Studies* no. 2004 (2):414–443.

Lindberg, Staffan I. 2009. *Democratization by Elections: A New Mode of Transition.* Baltimore, Md.: Johns Hopkins University Press.

Linz, Juan J., and Alfred Stepan. 1996. *Problems of Democratic Transition and Consolidation: Southern Europe, South America, and Post-Communist Europe.* Baltimore, Md.: Johns Hopkins University Press.

Lipset, Seymour Martin. 1963. *Political Man: The Social Bases of Politics.* New York: Anchor.

Ludwig, Frieder. 2008. "Christian-Muslim Relations in Northern Nigeria since the Introduction of Shariah in 1999." *Journal of the American Academy of Religion* no. 76 (3):602–637.

Lust-Okar, Ellen. 2005. *Structuring Conflict in the Arab World: Incumbents, Opponents, and Institutions.* New York: Cambridge University Press.

MacInnis, Donald E. 1989. *Religion in China Today: Policy and Practice.* Maryknoll, N.Y.: Orbis.

Madsen, Richard. 2010. "The Upsurge of Religion in China." *Journal of Democracy* no. 21 (4):58–71.

Magaloni, Beatriz. 2006. *Voting for Autocracy: Hegemonic Party Survival and Its Demise in Mexico.* New York: Cambridge University Press.

Marshall, Monty G., and Keith Jaggers. 2011. *Polity IV Project: Political Regime Characteristics and Transitions, 1800–2010.* Version p4v2010. College Park, Md.: Center for Systemic Peace, University of Maryland. www.systemicpeace. org/polity/polity4.htm.

Marx, Karl. 1978. "Contribution to the Critique of Hegel's *Philosophy of Right.*" In *The Marx-Engels Reader,* edited by Joshua A. Tucker, 53–65. New York: W. W. Norton.

Mazie, Steven V. 2004. "Rethinking Religious Establishment and Liberal Democracy: Lessons from Israel." *Brandywine Review of Faith and International Affairs* no. 2 (2):3–12.

McKenzie, Brian D. 2004. "Religious Social Networks, Indirect Mobilization, and African-American Political Participation." *Political Research Quarterly* no. 57 (4):621–632.

Midlarsky, Manus I. 1998. "Democracy and Islam: Implications for Civilizational Conflict and the Democratic Peace." *International Studies Quarterly* no. 42 (3):458–511.

Mitchell, Lincoln A. 2009. "Compromising Democracy: State Building in Saakashvili's Georgia." *Central Asian Survey* no. 28 (2):171–183.

Monsma, Stephen V., and J. Christopher Soper. 1997. *The Challenge of Pluralism: Church and State in Five Democracies.* Lanham, Md.: Rowman & Littlefield.

Nevo, Joseph. 1998. "Religion and National Identity in Saudi Arabia." *Middle Eastern Studies* no. 34 (3):34–53.

Norris, Pippa, and Ronald Inglehart. 2004. *Sacred and Secular: Religion and Politics Worldwide*. New York: Cambridge University Press.

Oba, Abdulmumini A. 2011. "Religious and Customary Laws in Nigeria." *Emory International Law Review* no. 25 (2):881–895.

Öcal, Samil. 2008. "From "the *Fetwa*" to "Religious Questions": Main Characteristics of *Fetwas* of the *Diyanet*." *The Muslim World* no. 98 (2–3):324–334.

Okpanachi, Eyene. 2011. "Between Conflict and Compromise: Lessons on Sharia and Pluralism from Nigeria's Kaduna and Kebbi States." *Emory International Law Review* no. 25 (2):897–919.

Olupona, Jacob. 1990. "Religion, Law and Order: State Regulation of Religious Affairs." *Social Compass* no. 37 (1):127–135.

Onapajo, Hakeem. 2012. "Politics for God: Religion, Politics, and Conflict in Democratic Nigeria." *The Journal of Pan African Studies* no. 4 (9):42–66.

Özler, Ş. İlgü, and Ani Sarkissian. 2011. "Stalemate and Stagnation in Turkish Democratization: The Role of Civil Society and Political Parties." *Journal of Civil Society* no. 7 (4):363–384.

Papkova, Irina. 2007. "The Russian Orthodox Church and Political Party Platforms." *Journal of Church and State* no. 49 (1):117–134.

———.2011. *The Orthodox Church and Russian Politics*. New York: Oxford University Press.

Peters, C. J. 1988. "The Georgian Orthodox Church." In *Eastern Christianity and Politics in the Twentieth Century*, edited by Pedro Ramet, 286–308. Durham, N.C.: Duke University Press.

Pew Research Center. 2006. *Spirit and Power: A 10-Country Survey of Pentecostals*. Washington, D.C.: Pew Forum on Religion & Public Life.

———. 2012a. *The Global Religious Landscape: A Report on the Size and Distribution of the World's Major Religious Groups as of 2010*. Washington, D.C.: Pew Forum on Religion & Public Life.

———. 2012b. *Rising Tide of Restrictions on Religion*. Washington, D.C.: Pew Forum on Religion & Public Life.

Poe, Steven C., and C. Neal Tate. 1994. "Repression of Human Rights to Personal Integrity in the 1980s: A Global Analysis." *American Political Science Review* no. 88 (4):853–872.

Posner, Daniel N. 2005. *Institutions and Ethnic Politics in Africa*. New York: Cambridge University Press.

Pospielovsky, Dimitry V. 1988. *Soviet Antireligious Campaigns and Persecutions*. 3 vols. Vol. 2: *A History of Soviet Atheism in Theory and Practice, and the Believer*. New York: St. Martin's Press.

Radnitz, Scott. 2010. *Weapons of the Wealthy: Predatory Regimes and Elite-Led Protests in Central Asia*. Ithaca, N.Y.: Cornell University Press.

Radu, Michael. 1998. "The Burden of Eastern Orthodoxy." *Orbis* no. 42 (2):283–300.

Rahman, Noor Aisha Abdul. 2009. "Muslim Personal Law within the Singapore Legal System: History, Prospects and Challenges." *Journal of Muslim Minority Affairs* no. 29 (1):109–126.

Ramadan, Tariq. 2010. "Islam Is a European Religion." *New Perspectives Quarterly* no. 27 (2):52–53.

Ramet, Pedro. 1988. "The Albanian Orthodox Church." In *Eastern Christianity and Politics in the Twentieth Century*, edited by Pedro Ramet, 149–159. Durham, N.C.: Duke University Press.

Regan, Patrick M., and Errol A. Henderson. 2002. "Democracy, Threats and Political Repression in Developing Countries: Are Democracies Internally Less Violent?" *Third World Quarterly* no. 23 (1):119–136.

Roessler, Philip G., and Marc Morje Howard. 2009. "Post–Cold War Political Regimes: When Do Elections Matter?" In *Democratization by Elections: A New Mode of Transitions*, edited by Staffan I. Lindberg, 101–127. Baltimore, Md.: Johns Hopkins University Press.

Ross, Michael L. 2001. "Does Oil Hinder Democracy?" *World Politics* no. 53 (3):325–361.

Sanasarian, Eliz. 2000. *Religious Minorities in Iran*. New York: Cambridge University Press.

Sanei, Faraz. 2012. *Codifying Repression: An Assessment of Iran's New Penal Code*. Washington, D.C.: Human Rights Watch.

Sarkissian, Ani. 2009. "Religious Reestablishment in Post-Communist Polities." *Journal of Church and State* no. 51 (3):472–501.

———. 2012. "Religious Regulation and the Muslim Democracy Gap." *Politics and Religion* no. 5 (3):501–527.

Sarkissian, Ani, Jonathan Fox, and Yasemin Akbaba. 2011. "Culture vs. Rational Choice: Assessing the Causes of Religious Discrimination in Muslim States." *Nationalism and Ethnic Politics* no. 17 (4):423–446.

Schaaf, Matthew. 2009. *An Uncivil Approach to Civil Society: Continuing State Curbs on Independent NGOs and Activist in Russia*. New York: Human Rights Watch.

Schedler, Andreas. 2002. "The Menu of Manipulation." *Journal of Democracy* no. 13 (2):36–50.

———.2006. "The Logic of Electoral Authoritarianism." In *Electoral Authoritarianism: The Dynamics of Unfree Competition*, edited by Andreas Schedler, 1–23. Boulder, Colo.: Lynne Rienner.

———. 2010. "Authoritarianism's Last Line of Defense." *Journal of Democracy* no. 21 (1):69–80.

Shah, Timothy S. 2012. *Religious Freedom: Why Now? Defending an Embattled Human Right*. Princeton, N.J.: Witherspoon Institute.

Slater, Dan. 2003. "Iron Cage in an Iron Fist: Authoritarian Institutions and the Personalization of Power in Malaysia." *Comparative Politics* no. 36 (1):81–101.

Sodiq, Yushau. 2009. "Can Muslims and Christians Live Together Peacefully in Nigeria?" *The Muslim World* no. 99:646–688.

Spiegel, Mickey. 1997. *China: State Control of Religion*. New York: Human Rights Watch.

———.2002. *Dangerous Meditation: China's Campaign against Falungong*. New York: Human Rights Watch.

Stahnke, Tad. 1999. "Proselytism and the Freedom to Change Religion in International Human Rights Law." *Brigham Young University Law Review* no. 251 (1):251–350.

Stark, Rodney, and Roger Finke. 2000. *Acts of Faith: Explaining the Human Side of Religion*. Berkeley: University of California Press.

Stepan, Alfred. 2000. "Religion, Democracy, and the 'Twin Tolerations.'" *Journal of Democracy* no. 11 (4):37–57.

———. 2001. *Arguing Comparative Politics*. Oxford: Oxford University Press.

———. 2012. "Rituals of Respect: Sufis and Secularists in Senegal in Comparative Perspective." *Comparative Politics* no. 44 (4):379–401.

Suryadinata, Leo. 1997. "Golkar of Indonesia: Recent Developments." *Contemporary Southeast Asia* no. 19 (2):190–204.

Svolik, Milan W. 2012. *The Politics of Authoritarian Rule*. New York: Cambridge University Press.

Tamadonfar, Mehran. 2001. "Islam, Law, and Political Control in Contemporary Iran." *Journal for the Scientific Study of Religion* no. 40 (2):205–219.

Tamney, Joseph B. 1992. "Conservative Government and Support for the Religious Institution in Singapore: An Uneasy Alliance." *Sociological Analysis* no. 53 (2):201–217.

Teitelbaum, Joshua. 2010. The Struggle over Religious Edicts in Saudi Arabia. In *BESA Center Perspectives Paper No. 119*. Ramat Gan, Israel: The Begin-Sadat Center for Strategic Studies.

Tey, Tsun Hang. 2008. "Excluding Religion from Politics and Enforcing Religious Harmony—Singapore-Style." *Singapore Journal of Legal Studies* no. 2008:118–142.

Toft, Monica Duffy, Daniel Philpott, and Timothy S. Shah. 2011. *God's Century: Resurgent Religion and Global Politics*. New York: W. W. Norton.

Toktas, Sule, and Bulent Aras. 2009–2010. "The EU and Minority Rights in Turkey." *Political Science Quarterly* no. 124 (4):697–720.

Tong, James W. 2002. "Anatomy of Regime Repression in China: Timing, Enforcement Institutions, and Target Selection in Banning the Falungong, July 1999." *Asian Survey* no. 42 (6):795–820.

———. 2010. "The New Religious Policy in China: Catching Up with Systemic Reforms." *Asian Survey* no. 50 (5):859–887.

Toprak, Binnaz. 1990. "Religion as a State Ideology in a Secular Setting: The Turkish-Islamic Synthesis." In *Aspects of Religion in Secular Turkey*, edited by

Malcolm Wagstaff, 10–15. Durham, NC: University of Durham, Center for Middle Eastern and Islamic Studies, Occasional Paper Series No. 40.

Trix, Frances. 1994. "The Resurfacing of Islam in Albania." *East European Quarterly* no. 28 (4):533 (17).

Turan, Omer. 2008. "The Turkish *Diyanet* Foundation." *The Muslim World* no. 98 (2–3):370–384.

US Department of State. 2011. *July–December 2010 International Religious Freedom Report.* Washington, D.C.: Bureau of Democracy, Human Rights, and Labor. www.state.gov/j/drl/rls/irf/2010_5/index.htm.

————.2012. *International Religious Freedom Report for 2012.* Washington, D.C.: Bureau of Democracy, Human Rights, and Labor. www.state.gov/j/drl/rls/irf/religiousfreedom/index.htm#wrapper.

Verba, Sidney, Kay Lehman Scholzman, and Henry Brady. 1995. *Voice and Equality: Civic Volunteerism in American Politics.* Cambridge, Mass.: Harvard University Press.

Warner, R. Stephen. 1993. "Work in Progress toward a New Paradigm for the Sociological Study of Religion in the United States." *The American Journal of Sociology* no. 98 (5):1044–1093.

Wilcke, Christoph. 2008. *The Ismailis of Najran: Second-Class Saudi Citizens.* New York: Human Rights Watch.

————. 2009. *Denied Dignity: Systemic Discrimination and Hostility toward Saudi Shia Citizens.* New York: Human Rights Watch.

Wintrobe, Ronald.1998. *The Political Economy of Dictatorship.* Cambridge: Cambridge University Press.

Yang, Fenggang. 2006. "The Red, Black, and Gray Markets of Religion in China." *The Sociological Quarterly* no. 47 (1):93–122.

Yildiz, Ilhan. 2007. "Minority Rights in Turkey." *Brigham Young University Law Review* no. 3 (2007):791–812.

Young, Antonia. 1999. "Religion and Society in Present-Day Albania." *Journal of Contemporary Religion* no. 14 (1):5–16.

Yousif, Ahmad. 2000. "Islam, Minorities, and Religious Freedom: A Challenge to Modern Theory of Pluralism." *Journal of Muslim Minority Affairs* no. 20 (1):29–41.

Yunusov, Arif. 2012. *Islamic Palette of Azerbaijan.* Baku: Adiloglu.

Zakaria, Fareed. 1997. "The Rise of Illiberal Democracy." *Foreign Affairs* no. 76 (6):22–43.

Zhu, Guobin. 2010. "Prosecuting 'Evil Cults': A Critical Examination of Law Regarding Freedom of Religious Belief in Mainland China." *Human Rights Quarterly* no. 32 (3):471–501.

# Index

# The Devil's SECRET NAME

by

## Jim Morris

**Daring Books**
Canton • Ohio

Published by Daring Books
P.O. Box 20050, Canton, Ohio 44701

Printed in the United States of America.

**Library of Congress Cataloging-in-Publication Data**

Morris, Jim, 1937-
    The devil's secret name / by Jim Morris.
      p.    cm.
    ISBN 0-938936-82-4
    1. National liberation movements--History--20th century.
2. Military history, Modern--20th century.  3. Morris, Jim, 1937-
. 4. Soldiers of fortune--United States--Biography.  I. Title.
D842.M65  1989                         89-1079
322.4'2--dc19                                CIP

*To Kathryn*

*Who Brings Magic To My Life*

# Table of Contents

RENAULT: What are you doing in Casablanca?
RICK: I came for the waters.
RENAULT: There are no waters in Casablanca. We're in the middle of a desert.
RICK: I was misinformed.

—Casablanca

# Acknowledgments

There are many people to thank for their help on this book: my wife Kathy, who wrote the first draft of the story of her experiences in Cambodia, Tom Reisinger, who graciously told me his story of that experience, and, of course, the prince of darkness himself, RKB, "god-king of the killer elite."

Great thanks are also due to Dennis and Patrice Bartow of Daring Books, Maggie Lichota of DELL, whose contribution cannot be overestimated, and the entire DELL editorial staff, whose support, encouragement, and tolerance was so helpful, and Paul H. Williams, for his fine hand with the English language.

Others who helped are too numerous to mention, except for the Committee for State Security of the Union of Soviet Socialist Republics, without whose active meddling in the affairs of the world, there would have been no story.

# 1

# Flame Of The Forest

In the spring of 1973 I heard that my old interpreter from Vietnam, Kpa Doh, had become a major in the Cambodian army, and was at Ft. Benning, Georgia, taking the Infantry Officer's Advanced Course. I went to see him. He told me it was his intention to return to Vietnam after the war, to wage revolution against the Vietnamese on behalf of his people, the Montagnards of the Central Highlands.

"How you think I should do this?" he asked.

Kpa Doh had been chief interpreter for my camp on the first and best of three tours with Special Forces, the Green Berets, in Vietnam. Civilian life had not been especially kind to me, or I to it, and ever since leaving Vietnam I had dreamed of going back.

"That's kind of a tough question on short notice, Kpa Doh," I said. "Let me do an area study and some planning. I'll come over this summer and tell you what I think."

What I wanted to do was evaluate his plan in light of Mao Zedong's teachings on the War of National Liberation, to see whether he had a chance.

I had two college degrees, but the most intellectually demanding study I ever undertook was the Special Forces Officer's Course at Ft. Bragg, and what we learned was Mao. He had devised a model for revolution that was brilliant, practical and comprehensive. You could lay his theory over the American Revolution of 1776, for instance, and it fit perfectly. It's a template for any revolution, communist or not.

At Ft. Bragg we had been shown *Viva, Zapata* as a training film. Again, so we could watch Mao's principles worked out in detail. They were all there.

The basic tenets of Mao's model for revolutionary warfare are easy to remember because they are organized in three sets of threes.

There are three *sine qua nons* of revolutionary warfare. In all of recorded history no revolution, barring the occasional *coup d'etat,* has succeeded without them, and I know of none that failed in which all three were present.

The first is support of a significant percentage of the population. A majority is not necessary. Fifteen percent will do it. Of the majority, it is only necessary that they be indifferent. It is also necessary that the guerrillas have secure areas from which to operate. A handy border to duck over, which government troops are forbidden to cross, is best, but an impenetrable swamp or mountain vastness will do in a pinch. The third necessary ingredient is help from a foreign government, which can provide arms, ammunition, medical supplies, money. Perhaps the most invaluable thing the outside source provides is legitimacy. Without it the guerrillas have the feeling that they are only bandits in an evil place.

The revolutionaries themselves also fall into three distinct groups. First are the guerrillas, then the underground of spies and saboteurs in towns and cities, and then the auxiliaries, the aforementioned fifteen percent who provide active support.

Revolutions then proceed in three stages. The first is political organization. Second comes guerrilla warfare, smallstage raids and ambushes up to battalion-size. Only in the third stage, when the guerrillas graduate into a regular, conventional army, do they attempt to take and hold territory. By then government troops are usually in rout, and territory falls easily into guerrilla hands.

According to Mao, Kpa Doh didn't have a chance.

I left in May to check out the situation in Vietnam first, then go on to Phnom Penh.

It was limbo time in Vietnam. The American combat units had gone home; all that was left was a kind of caretaker advisory effort. There was also an international commission to control the "truce," and next to no fighting. This was the time of the "decent interval," Kissinger's term for that face-saving period after the U.S. withdrawal, before the inevitable fall.

My aircraft arrived at Ton Son Nhut at one in the morning, an hour after curfew. When the bus let me off at the Continental Palace Hotel, it was closed and barred. There was a bell for the night porter, but I didn't know that and couldn't see it in the dark. Saigon was not a good place to be roaming around after curfew.

Fortunately, the Continental had an open terrace. I mounted the two steps from the sidewalk, took off my hat and sat down on one of their wicker chairs, and put my feet up on a small table.

Five years, and I was back in the country that had mutilated my body and reduced by half the number of living people I call, "friend."

In the park across the street, a propaganda banner whipped by the wind popped loose on one end and flapped frantically. Occasionally a crumpled newspaper skittered across the square. The scene was lit by the kind of ghastly yellow streetlight which makes everything look like a colorized Dracula movie.

Every ghost I knew marched through me that night, from the *yang*, the spirits of the mountains, to the company of my dead friends. It wasn't frightening—sort of cozy, in a grim way. It was always Halloween in Vietnam.

At five a.m. a ferocious siren sounded for a full minute. Soon after that the petulant sputter of a single Honda 90 rattled hollowly between the silent buildings. Two ladies bobbed by in black pajamas and conical hats, carrying long balance poles, with baskets suspended by ropes on either end.

A jeep containing four "white mice," Vietnamese national policemen in white uniforms, careened around a corner and ran over a cat.

A tallish porter from the Continental, about a hundred years old, in a dirty white uniform three sizes too large, came out with a three-foot-long broom, and a dust pan on a three-foot-wire handle. He gave me not so much as a glance with his expressionless eyes. He began to sweep the terrace with a desultory shuffle.

A small boy came up and offered to sell me a three-day-old *Stars and Stripes* for thirty cents. A nine-year-old girl with one arm held a basket containing garlands of white blossoms to my nose and insisted,

"You buy frower!"

The traffic in the street continued to build: Hondas, cyclos, jeeps, more Hondas, blue-and-yellow thirty-year-old Renault taxis, International Control Commission-Saigon jeeps, ARVN military vehicles, all roaring by at thirty miles an hour, with no discernible muffling, all emitting a vile, noxious, blue smoke which fogged the air by six o'clock.

Represented on paper, comic-book fashion, the resulting RO-A-A-A-A-R-R-R-R!!!, *screeeeeeech*, HONK! and SLAM! of red-and-black cartoon letters would overlay each other in a blur that would fill the entire page.

The crowd in front of me had grown, too. There was a guy on crutches, with one leg missing, wanting to sell lacquerware, a healthy fellow with used books who had been there the first time I stayed at the Continental ten years before, a lady selling incense made by kids at the Buddhist orphanage, several beggars, mostly with missing limbs and/or napalm scars. In the early Sixties the beggars had been just as numerous, but suffered from leprosy, yaws, and malnutrition.

I could no longer see the street. These people were six inches from my face, tugging and gesticulating wildly, crying for relief. Since there was no possibility of alleviating one one-thousandth of the human misery displayed before me, I rose, towering over the crowd, and shouldered my rucksack.

"HEY! WHERE YOU GO?" shouted a cyclo boy. Several taxi drivers and a guy on a Honda 90 also yelled, "HEY! WHERE YOU GO?" From all corners of the square, young honeys in hip huggers, sheer blouses without bras, but with hungry, hostile smiles, began walking briskly in my direction. I surged through the mob of clutching, crying people. "Ride!" "*Eat!*" "FUCK!" "*BUY!!*" "*YOU WANT CHANGE MONEY???*"

Get me out of here!


Pleiku: flat, red dust everywhere, churning under two-and-a-half ton truck wheels, big, bluegrey skies stretching off to the mountains in the distance.

Along the roads into town were Montagnards, men in black, red-bordered loincloths wrapped around their waists, pulled up tight between their buttocks, with a flap in front. The women wore shimmery, black, tubular skirts; some had been put in blouses by missionaries, but they didn't take them very seriously, and if a button popped and a breast showed nobody seemed to care, or even notice.

From a leisurely French mountain town, with one family of Vietnamese, fifteen years before; Pleiku had grown into a quagmire and a pesthole. Plywood, packing crate shacks lined every road, filled with Vietnamese people who had come from God-knows-where, for God-knows-what reason. Some had been forcibly resettled by the government, and there was also a large community of pimps, whores, bartenders, and other parasites who had come to live off the U.S. Army, and were now reduced to slim pickings from the ARVN and the ICCS.

I went looking for Sprague's house.

"The Ahmy! I hate the fuckin' Ahmy!" Sprague spat out the words at me, staring in distaste at my G.I. rucksack and cammie jacket. He grinned the hard, twisty smile of a retired, Special Forces master sergeant with no quit in him.

In truth, he didn't look very military for a retired master sergeant. His silver-grey hair slopped down over his collar and curled out over his ears. He came from the part of Boston where they have not yet discovered the letter, "r," and twenty years of southern army posts had yet to put it into his diction.

His living room in the USAID compound was filled with Montagnard memorabilia: crossbows, arrows, carvings, woven cloth, mostly in red and black, because those were the only dyes Montagnards knew how to make.

On his wall was a brass plaque that read, *"Special Forces has done so much for so long with so little that now we are expected to do everything with nothing forever."*

Indeed, about the only things Sprague found in my favor when I first arrived were that I, too, had worn a green beret and we shared a taste for rock 'n' roll.

He had a huge reel-to-reel tape deck, playing the Blue Ridge

Rangers, all of whom were John Fogerty, formerly of Creedence Clear-water Revival, overdubbed on every instrument. On top of the tape deck was a color photo of three young people, two boys and a girl, the boys bearded and long-haired, the girl with dark, straight hair, parted in the middle in the style of the day. They were Ed's three older kids, in college in the States. His wife and the younger kids lived in Taipei, where he could see them sometimes.

My first impression of Sprague was that he was a crotchety old fart, and I couldn't figure what he was doing here, since most of his contemporaries had returned home to drink beer and reminisce.

But the answer was simple enough; he had a bad case of what the French call *Le Jeune Mal*. He was a Far East addict, with a serious Montagnard fixation.

Ed was excited because his son, Mark, a former one-hitch Special Forces medic, but not a Vietnam veteran, was arriving the next day, after which we would go to Cheo Reo, and then to an outlying Jarai Montagnard village for the week-end.

Because the road simply stopped at the river, the Vietnamese seldom went to that village. Sprague stopped his Bronco and we all got out: Sprague, me, Mark—Sprague's Jesus-haired son, H'yak, Sprague's lovely, brown-eyed Montagnard maid, and Ksor Bem, an eighteen-year-old who was a cousin in Sprague's adopted Montagnard family. Bem was a thin, lively little dude in a newsboy cap, tank top, purple flare jeans, and two-tone purple saddle-shoes.

It took us a few minutes to unload our stuff, take off our shoes and boots, and roll up our pants legs. The river was wide and flat, and we had brought a lot of stuff: food for the family, bedrolls, and so on. The water was warm and bright, deep enough to get our pants wet, rolled up or not.

On the other side we walked on a winding path of hot sand that burned our feet, making me skip and look for grassy patches. As we came up the path the Yards came out to look at us. They had seen Sprague many times before, of course, and H'yak and Bem, but Mark Sprague and I were new and unusual. Before the U.S. Army pulled out they had become used to G.I.'s but neither Mark nor I had seen a barber or a razor in a long time.

It was a very clean village, no trash piles or other debris, just row after row of large longhouses, up on stilts thick as telephone poles. The houses were about thirty feet across in front and maybe a hundred feet long, six feet off the ground on their poles. Entire extended families lived in the houses; cousins, aunts, uncles, everybody. A few men wore loincloths, but most had on western pants or cut-offs. We moved through the village, past cows, chickens, and sad, draggy, prehistoric-looking grey pigs that snuffled in the mud under the longhouses.

*"Hiam droi jian muon!"* people greeted us as we passed.

*"Hiam muon!"* we replied, with a quick nod of the head.

We scampered up the notched log that served as stairs on the longhouse. As we entered, the first thing to hit my eye was a poster of the rock group, Canned Heat. Times had changed.

There was a large crowd of people waiting for us. Sprague made as many introductions as he could as we trooped inside.

The walls were soft rattan, but the rattan floors of former years had been replaced by planks, and most of the longhouses were roofed with USAID tin. Easier to build, of course, but in no way an improvement in looks or comfort.

Sprague wasted no time breaking out his portable cassette player. "Got a new Jawge Hahison heah!" he said. At the sound of that magic name forty people clustered around to hear, "All Things Must Pass."

Soon Sprague turned down the music and some men approached with a big jug of rice wine, reeds and glasses.

Sprague took me aside and explained that Mark was to be initiated into the family with the rice wine ceremony. "It don't mean nothing when they don't do you," he said to me. "They're accepting Mark because he's my son."

I nodded. I knew the custom well. I'd already been given four bracelets, but they hadn't been sent home with my stuff after my last wound. I had lost them all.

The old Spirit Man came in and took off Mark's right hiking boot, placing his foot on a Montagnard ax blade, which looked something like a metal boomerang. He put some cotton between his toes, siphoned rice wine through the reed and liberally doused Mark's foot with it.

Throughout the ritual the Spirit Man kept up his chant, calling on the *yang* of the mountains, and the *yang* of the forests, to bless Mark.

They put the bracelet on Mark's arm.

After the ceremony Nyot, the drummer from Ayunapa, an all-Montagnard rock 'n' roll band that Sprague sponsored, got out his acoustic guitar and sang Jarai Cheo Reo folk songs. Their weird, eccentric rhythm, played on gongs instead of a guitar, had haunted my dreams for nine years. Even now I cannot summon that sound consciously; it is too alien. But in the dark hours just before dawn, the jungle, the heat, and that rhythm chase themselves through my dreams.

"This is a new one," Sprague said of a song just completed. "It's the story of a Montagnard soldier and his girl. She sings, 'The helicopters came and took my man away. He's been gone for such a long time. Oh, helicopters, please bring my man back to me.'"

The next morning we got up, eager for a swim and a bath. The river was only a short distance away, but half the kids in the village, and all Sprague's friends and family came along. The boys capered and chattered, making faces at us all the way; the little girls were demure, eyes shining.

I kept my cut-offs on and waded into the river, soap in hand. Pretty soon we were all in the water, laughing, lathering ourselves until we were covered with foam, and then diving underwater, letting the current carry us a little distance downstream.

A boy, about nine, came up and splashed water on me. I grinned and surged through the water after him, running, laughing....

Memories and a heavy sadness rolled over me. Nine years before, same river, same jungle, ten miles north. My patrol came across three Bahnar Montagnard boys, in their teens, clearing a field by the river. We surrounded them on three sides, river on the fourth side, wide as a football field. Who would try to escape across it?

The boys would. They did. We only wanted to question them. I surged after them, over the bank and into the river, weighed down by my rifle, ammo, canteen, surging through the water that splashed before me in sunbright shimmers, same as now. Yelling at my Jarai troops not to shoot, and yelling at the boys to stop. But my two

Americans fired warning shots over their heads. The Jarai didn't understand the difference between warning shots and aimed fire. They had been fighting the Bahnar with crossbows for nine hundred years. They opened up, full-auto, shooting to kill.

Maybe the fact that I was there saved two of them. The Jarai had to fire high to avoid hitting me. One of the boys was hit, bright red blood cascaded down his back. We put a bandage on his wound and tried to raise a chopper on the radio. But we couldn't, so we stood there and watched him die.

And that's in my dreams with the gongs in the mornings.


I caught the kid, threw him up on my shoulder, and strode back through the water to the deepest part, spun around enough times to make him dizzy, and threw him into the water. He came up and splashed me again, now joined by three of his buddies.

I gave up, sank to the bottom, and floated out of range.

After the swim we returned to the longhouse. Sprague put on Creedence and, as if by magic, the jugs appeared again.


The history of mankind has been, among other things, a search for the highest expression of the human spirit. Several hundred years ago, the Yards discovered how to distill alcohol and quit worrying about it.

Bem and some of the other young men laughed and pointed at me. "King Kong!" Bem said. "They call you King Kong, like from movie, 'cause you so big. 'Specially when you carry little boy."

I laughed. Sprague changed the tape and Nyot hung a nine-inch loop of quarter-inch brass welding rod on my right wrist, a Montagnard bracelet. It felt great.

A little later, bladder full, I lurched up. Absolutely smashed, I wandered down the notched log, stepped around a couple of pigs, passed two bare-chested ladies with baskets slung over their backs, crooked pipes in their mouths, and found a convenient bush to step behind.

Coming back I stopped. Rock 'n' roll music poured out of the longhouse, and I was drunk and happy, but I wanted to be alone for a few minutes. A big tree stood in front of the longhouse, a big, gnarled Flame of the Forest, with lurid blossoms in the upper reaches. It was beautiful, and it had a low fork that I could get my foot into.

It was an easy climb. I stopped when I was even with the door of the longhouse, looked in for a moment, than went on up twenty more feet. Bem came out and said, "Hey, King Kong! You climb tree?"

"Yeah!"

"You no 'fraid?"

I laughed out loud. "Are you crazy? I used to be a fucking paratrooper." I charged on up, bare toes hunting for stubs and limbs, higher and higher in the Flame of the Forest.

# 2

# The Peach-Colored Lotus

In Phnom Penh that summer the press corps gathered every evening at a little outdoor cafe in front of the Ministry of Information. We sat under another spreading Flame of the Forest tree, its huge branches gnarled and beautiful, dropping fire-colored blossoms over the thirty-odd journalists.

The war in Vietnam was quiescent, but in Cambodia it was hot. The Khmer Rouge were slowly tightening their stranglehold on Phnom Penh, and the Cambodian army fought back in its languid way, sure that the Americans would bail them out in the end.

The ministry posted a single, double-spaced typewritten page daily, a summary of the day's military activities, in French. Every day someone would get up and amble over to see whether it contained anything newsworthy. It never did.

At the table were Malcolm Browne, the distinguished Far East correspondent of the New York *Times*, and Dieter Ludwig, a cameraman for German television who wore a Rolling Stones T-shirt and blond hair to his waist. The others represented all politics, fashions and lifestyles between. I had secured credentials from *Rolling Stone* as a cover, and they were legitimate, but I had my other reasons for being there. I was meeting Kpa Doh when he returned from the field.

Al Rockoff, a gnomelike free-lance photographer, crinkly hair tied back in a ponytail, sat cross-legged, rolling the tobacco out of a Juan Bastos cigarette, refilling it with something more to his liking from a film can.

I introduced myself to Malcolm Browne and told him I had enjoyed his book, *The New Face of War*; that I had been in Special Forces and shared many of his conclusions.

We were interrupted by an overwhelmingly healthy young man seated across the table, who broke in to announce that he, too, had been in Special Forces. He looked like Superman, except for blue jeans, a sly smile, and a predatory glint in his eye. He has since become immensely respectable and does not wish his name used in this book, so I will call him by the nickname he subsequently acquired, Captain America.

We shook hands and felt each other out in conversation. He had been an ROTC lieutenant, and had only been out of the army for six weeks. "Right after graduation, I went to Kathmandu. That way, when I went on active duty the government had to pay my travel from Nepal to Fort Bragg and back."

While either going to or coming from Kathmandu, Captain America had hitchhiked, at the height of the war and in civilian clothes, all over Vietnam. G.I.'s had greeted him with shouts of, "What the fuck are you doing here?"

It is not often one meets a madman of these proportions. I invited him to join Rockoff, the photographer, Haney Howell, the CBS correspondent, and me, for dinner.

Later that evening I stepped outside of Haney's apartment at the Hotel Royale to bum a light from the security guard in the parking lot. He stood beside a peach-colored Lotus owned by a Cambodian film director. It seemed an odd sort of status symbol in a country where you couldn't drive more than fifteen kilometers in any direction without a military escort.

The ground rumbled under my feet. Bomb run somewhere out in the countryside. It felt and sounded exactly like the New York City subway system from street level, bombs falling out of the night sky, twenty-five miles away.

Next morning Rockoff asked Captain America and me if we'd like to go out to the Battle of Ang Snoul. I agreed; Captain America was eager.

For the Cambodian Army the war consisted of trying to keep the roads open to the cities they did control; Phnom Penh, Kompol Som, Battambang.

We walked to the market and got a ride on the back of a three-wheel Lambretta minibus.

The sounds of battle were audible a long way out. Our driver wouldn't go any further than a mile from Ang Snoul, so we got out and walked along the blacktop highway, listening to the rat-a-tat WHOOM!!! soundtrack get louder. We walked into the town which had been rocketed by the Khmer Rouge and looted by the Cambodians; there were no civilians.

Television doesn't convey that noise, nor do motion pictures. These were tremendous shock waves, from 106MM recoilless rifles and mortars that leave your ears ringing, shake the ground under your feet and hit your stomach with palpable tremors of air.

I hadn't heard those sounds for five years, not since the NVA mortared a field hospital while I was on the operating table. We came upon Haney and his crew— Joe Yue, who was putting on his camera brace, and Sophan, who fiddled with the knobs on the sound equipment.

Christine Spengler, the French photographer, fresh and pretty in a red-and-white checked top and Levi bellbottoms, photographed some Cambodian G.I.s playing cards in front of a gutted store. They looked up and grinned gold-studded smiles for the camera.

Al announced he was going forward to get some shots of the fighting. Once past the town, the layout of the battle became clear. The Khmer Rouge had the road from about a mile out of Ang Snoul, and apparently controlled the woodline on the other side of the paddies that lay just outside the town. The Cambodes were drawn up in a long line, pretty much out in the open, about a hundred and fifty yards from the woodline. A frontal assault had broken down and they were all down behind some paddy dikes, not moving.

Way off to our right, cannonlike 106MM recoilless rifles mounted on armored personnel carriers, slammed away at the woodline.

"I'm going out to those 106s," Captain America announced, strolling across the paddies toward the battle.

"I'm going forward for some shots of the infantry," Al said. I stuck with Al; he was the guy who knew the territory.

Both of them had fought in paddies before; I had not. I had fought in jungle-covered mountains, the brush sometimes so thick you couldn't see somebody three feet away. This was a whole different game, flat, with no cover. If you walked, you did it in full view of an enemy a hundred and fifty yards away.

Al walked boldly down the road, although the firing now came from our right *rear*. He strode across paddy dikes out toward the troops, who lay flat on their bellies behind the dikes, which only gave about a foot of cover. They looked at us as though we were insane, a position with which I was in total agreement.

"Hey, man!" I called to Al.

He turned around and said, "Just keep on the dikes and you won't get your feet wet."

"I wasn't thinking about that. Those fuckers can see us."

He explained that firing broke out sporadically at different parts of the line and you could walk around when they weren't firing in your sector. When they did fire at you, the thing to do was to get down.

"What about snipers?"

He shrugged. Apparently his regard for Cambodian marksmanship was low.

We settled in by a big tree in the middle of the field and Al started taking pictures of the Cambodians.

*Psnap! Psnap!* Two bullets passed about six inches from my head.

"Hit it!" I yelled. I was flat on my face behind a paddy dike, with no recollection of having moved at all.

After a while the firing drifted off again. Captain America strolled over. He'd borrowed an M-79 grenade launcher from one of the Cambodes. He and Al got into a contest to see who could come closest to a little house that had somehow remained standing to our left front. It took them six grenades to totally destroy it.

Brigadier General Les Kossem's villa sprawled behind a low wall, just off Monivong, one of the main streets of Phnom Penh. As Kpa Doh and I entered, the guards lounging in the courtyard, wearing a variety of knives, grenades and automatic weapons, mostly AK-47s, came to attention and saluted. In the courtyard there was also a jeep-mounted recoilless rifle, a couple of .30 caliber machineguns, a 60 millimeter mortar, and a number of the general's sleek, happy children playing.

General Les Kossem advanced through the door, slender, tall for an Asian, maybe 5'11", looking about twenty-seven except for the deep lines around his eyes and mouth. He wore a blue baseball cap, sky blue jumpsuit, and a forty-five in a shoulder holster. His smile was boyish, friendly and eager.

His people, the Cham, were coastal fishermen from central Vietnam. They are Moslem, and his father had come to Cambodia as a political refugee.

I had first read about Les Kossem in 1968, in a top secret CIA report on FULRO—*Fronte Unife de Lutte des Races Opprimees*: Unified Fighting Front of the Oppressed Races. FULRO had been conceived as a revolutionary organization of ethnic Vietnamese nationals both in Vietnam and in exile. They were Camodians, Cham, and Montagnards; peoples who had been subjugated by the Vietnamese.

The general's house was a meeting place for cabinet ministers, university professors, and high-ranking army officers, all from families originally from South Vietnam. They sat around on the verandah in their white shirts and ties, sweating freely, fanning themselves and plotting revolution against the Vietnamese.

While there, we drank copiously of a bottled orange drink called, Howdy Cola, poured into huge, iced glasses. They talked slowly and reasonably, citing historical precedent, unreeling this pipe dream which had no consonance whatever with political or military reality.

FULRO, and more specifically Kpa Doh's Montagnards, lacked two of Mao's essentials for a successful revolution; they had no serious backers among the superpowers, and no support among the Vietnamese people. Being ethnically dissimilar to the Vietnamese, they could not blend into the general population. Also, the Vietnamese outnumbered them fifteen to one. They had no chance within the present equation.

I told Kpa Doh if he tried to go back and lead a revolt he would fail, and he would get a lot of people killed.

He shrugged. "I must still try."

Okay, what were the Vietnamese's weak points? The main one was that, whatever Vietnamese were in power, they would be heavily dependent on U.S. aid for survival. Aid was controlled by Congress, and Congress was influenced by public opinion. Maybe the outside support could be obtained.

In small ways I'd been able to affect that before; good PR had kept the Pentagon from disbanding the Green Berets, and I'd been part of that, and I'd done PR for the defense fund on the Green Beret Murder Case. Nixon had freed the seven defendants because of adverse public opinion.

The story of their release had come over the wire while I was being interviewed about the case by Mike Wallace for *60 Minutes*. We had gotten a lot of publicity in that situation, and it had done the trick. Maybe we could use the press to pressure the South Vietnamese into granting Montagnard autonomy.

Toward that end I convinced Haney to do a story on one of the Montagnard battalions which had come over the border with Kpa Doh. This battalion had been the Strike Force at a Special Forces camp called, Buon Sar Pa. During the Montagnard revolt of October 1964, they had machine-gunned their Vietnamese commanders and dumped the bodies down a three-hole shitter. That had made it awkward for them to stay in Vietnam when the revolt failed, and there was work available for trained soldiers in Cambodia.

The plan was for me and Captain America to stay in the field with them for a couple of weeks after the TV crew went home, to function as free-lance advisors. Then I'd go home and write it up for *Rolling Stone*.

The day before we were scheduled to go out to the battalion, Kpa Doh and I were walking along a residential street in Phnom Penh. "You know, Kpa Doh," I said, "I never have been convinced that Cowboy was dead. During Tet I manned a mortar with a sergeant who said he got away on a bicycle." I was referring to another of our Montagnard interpreters, Philippe Drouin, a.k.a., "The Cowboy." Phil had been my best Montagnard friend, and my patrol buddy. He was the only Asian I'd go with on patrol without taking another American along.

By the time I returned for my third tour, Cowboy had become a colonel in FULRO, but his arrogance and high-handedness had created problems for him within the organization. Finally, he killed a Vietnamese Special Forces sergeant in a barroom fight and the Darlac Province chief was after him. He didn't have enough friends in the organization to save him, and, according to the CIA, had been killed by other FULRO factions seeking an accommodation with the Vietnamese.

"Oh, he is dead, for sure," said Kpa Doh. "Man who kill him live two block from here. You want to go see?"

I shook my head. I had no desire to meet my best friend's executioner. I wondered what Kpa Doh's position in that fracas had been. Then I shook it off. It was an intramural squabble, no business of mine.

"Okay, let's go!" the Cambodian colonel snapped crisply. I strode out through his front office, and stopped on the second floor balcony, overlooking the security detail.

The security detail was definitely professional. The men were neither overexcited nor oblivious to the fact that we were heading out through country where ambush was not only possible, but likely. They stood, smoking calmly, weapons draped casually across their bodies. They wore crisply tailored fatigues and old green berets mashed down over their brown, flat noses.

Most of them wore U.S. parachute wings from their days in the Mike Force in Vietnam, and Thai wings over their right pockets, earned when they trained with the Thais after joining the Cambodian Army.

Kpa Doh's wife, Miss Mlo, came out of the house on the other side of the headquarters building. She scooped up her littlest son and took him inside the house, where the oldest couldn't beat on him for a while.

I smiled. She was one of the prettiest women I have ever known; slender, graceful, with huge eyes, and long, glossy, black hair. She didn't look old enough to be the mother of three wispy roughnecks—or the son who had died while Kpa Doh was in the States. He had told me about it the night he invited me to Cambodia. "When I get letter...I cry," he had said.

I remembered the night the first one had been born, almost ten years before. Kpa Doh was on patrol, and Miss Mlo panicked. She wanted him home. He was twenty klicks into VC territory, and I had to tell her to forget it. I was still maybe not her favorite person.

I stood in the steamy heat on the balcony for a long time while the soldiers below became more and more impatient. Apparently what the colonel meant when he said, "Okay, let's go!" was, okay, let's begin to get ready to think about it. The cockiest of the soldiers took off his armored vest and began to run through a series of karate forms, punching the air, kicking a jeep tire.

"I tell you, Morris, I never see army like this before," Kpa Doh said as he came up beside me. "Supply officer no want give gas for operation. Now we have hard time to go because he want to sell gas. He want to give money to girl downtown. My men know the girl he have." His voice grated harshly, the result of a round he'd taken through the vocal chords in 1965 or '66.

Before he got caught up in the war, he had sung professionally, propaganda songs on the radio for the Diem regime. He had detested Diem, but it was a gig, and nobody took the songs seriously. That was where he met his wife; they sang duets.

He pointed out a fat Cambodian in fatigue pants and an undershirt, poking avariciously around the vehicles, a cigarette dangling from his lips.

In Cambodia, everybody was on the take. Every worthless officer debutante in the Cambodian Army tooled around Phnom Penh on government gas in a jazzed-up jeep with glossy, olive drab paint and white sidewalls. Except Kpa Doh; he drove a beat-up old civilian jeep, passed on to him by an American friend in the USAID program. Kpa Doh bought his own gas, usually heavily laced with water, in one liter bottles from street vendors.

"Why don't you just shoot the son of a bitch?" I inquired.

He gave me a reproachful look. "He is my colonel's cousin."

"Okay, kidnap the girl and sell her back to him for the gas."

He looked interested.

"If I were you, Kpa Doh," I said, "I'd be picking myself an escape route. This little country isn't going to make it."

I only said it once. I wish I'd said it a hundred times.

The colonel must have persuaded his cousin, because we finally got started, three army trucks and the TV crew's grey Peugeot, toward the river.

The Tonle Sap River was wide, brown and flat; the shore cluttered with sputtering Hondas, throbbing military vehicles and pushcart vendors selling square coconut popsicles on bamboo sticks to the throngs waiting for the ferry.

Drifting across the river on the ferry, we passed what was left of a beautiful steel and concrete bridge. The North Vietnamese had blown it, dropping three spans out of the middle. Twisted steel shot off the end of the bridge into space. It had been built with U.S. money and the North Vietnamese were willing to sacrifice 86 out of a 120-man unit to destroy it.

It had been a long time since I'd been out with an M-16. We were okay as long as there were civilians going up and down the road; generally, civilians do not wander through the killzone of an ambush. But the civilians soon petered out and we were out there by ourselves with nothing on either side but rice paddies. Low jungle started one or two hundred meters back from the road. Occasionally, we passed a farmer working a water buffalo; sometimes houses, up on stilts, built open to catch the breeze.

"Isn't this beautiful country, Morris?" Kpa Doh asked.

"Yeah, beautiful for ambushes." I muttered, chewing nervously on a toothpick. I jacked a round into the chamber, selector on safe, my finger on the switch.

About five minutes after I armed my rifle, the others did, too. They knew the country, so I hadn't missed it by much.

We crossed a little river and entered into a fair-sized village. We pulled into a schoolyard, ringed by wire and trenches. The battalion's mission was the defense of an administrative district, and they had inherited the school as their headquarters from the previous battalion.

Brigade headquarters had been informed a TV crew was coming, and every staff officer for a hundred miles, including the crooked supply officer, came out to pose for American television.

They crowded in front of the camera, guns holstered low, glancing at the camera from the corners of their eyes.

Haney led me aside and said, "Sorry, Ace, but we've been shooting without film for half an hour. We can't get anything with these shitheads in the way."

"Yeah," I muttered. "I can see that."

He slapped me on the shoulder. "But I know Kpa Doh now, and if this outfit ever gets in some heavy action, I'll hurry down and shoot that. We can use the action as a carrier for the Montagnard story."

You take what you can get. I thanked him.

Before they left, Joe Yue asked me and Captain America if we wanted to go back to town. There were rumors that the battalion was to be assaulted that night.

We both laughed and shook our heads. This was the best dug-in defensive position we'd seen in Cambodia, and there weren't enough Khmer Rouge in the province to overrun it.

Haney and his crew jumped in their air-conditioned Peugeot and headed back to Phnom Penh with our escort, and our rifles: mine and Captain America's. We were to draw others from the battalion.

As soon as the TV crew left, we went inside headquarters and borrowed a couple of rifles and some ammunition. That was when the holes in their defenses started to appear. They could only give us four magazines apiece. In a serious firefight that would last maybe ten minutes. Then we'd be lying in the dirt, in the dark, trying to load magazines by the intermittent light of drifting flares, frantic to get the weapon back in operation before the next rush.

They were short of magazines because the supply officer who hadn't wanted to provide gas to come out here had sold them. The only possible buyer was the enemy.

I was beginning to understand how this war worked. The Khmer Rouge didn't get supplies down the Ho Chi Minh trail. It was much easier and cheaper for the Chinese to send them money to buy stuff from the Cambodians. The U.S. supplied both sides and the Khmer Rouge let the Cambodes hold the cities while they consolidated their hold on the countryside.

When we made the rounds of the defensive perimeter with Y Bun Sur Paul, the battalion commander, that night, Captain America pointed out a number of minor flaws...poor fields of fire, things like that. He had never worked as an advisor, and he baldly explained the deficiencies to Y Bun, which is not the best way to advise. You almost have to apologize for suggesting you might know something your counterpart doesn't. Then you carefully explain that although you have learned far more from him than you could possibly teach, there is this one little item he might find helpful.

Y Bun pointed out some cows, grazing inside the outer perimeter wire.

"If we get hit tonight, we'll have steak for breakfast," I said.

"The Cambodes I was with in Vietnam used to eat VC liver," said Captain America.

"You ever try it?" I asked.

"Sure."

"Cooked or raw?"

"Cooked, of course," he snapped.

After a supper of rice, an indecipherable goulash, and Howdy Cola without ice, Captain America and I sat on the verandah of the headquarters, enjoying the sunset and the evening breeze.

As he started the daily entry in his spiral notebook, he asked me if I'd seen anything abnormal in Phnom Penh.

"In all honesty, Captain, the most abnormal thing I saw in Phnom Penh was you."

"Well, fuck you!"

"No, really. I never met a cannibal before."

He looked at me, amazed. "You mean to say if everybody around you was eating VC liver, you wouldn't do it?"

I shuddered. "Absolutely not."

He shook his head.

Y Bun and Kpa Doh came up to tell us, as tactfully as possible, that we would have to return to Phnom Penh the next day. Y Bun said that if we got waxed, and there was a diplomatic flap over it, he would be in serious trouble. He also said the local people hated Americans so much, because of the bombing, that our presence was threatening the rapport he was trying to build with the people of the district.

The Cambodian battalion which had preceded them had lost no opportunity to alienate the population. He figured that eighty-five percent of the locals were with the Khmer Rouge. During the short time he'd been here he'd been winning them back by being nice and having his soldiers be polite and helpful.

All this was part of the Civil Affairs/Psychological Operations program I'd laid out for him when I first visited the battalion a month before. I was pleased that he'd listened, and that my advice was working.

But I should have realized that after ten years of war they didn't need a junior Jesus to tell them how to run raids and ambushes in their own jungle. We had already done that job.

I felt like Kid Shileen, the old drunken gunfighter in the movie *Cat Ballou*.

Captain America thought I was nuts. To him this was an excursion, an outing, not a serious mission. We were on an *adventure*, in *Cambodia*, for chrissakes, and what did I want anyway?

Our only hope for a little action would be if the Khmer Rouge hit the camp that night. Captain America went to sleep out on the perimeter.

I lay down in the headquarters with my boots on and my rifle beside me.

Couldn't sleep, though. After a while I got up and went outside to listen to the troopers and their wives talking in their coughing language, laughing in the cool evening air, scented with tropical blossoms and woodsmoke. Their kids were asleep by then. The soldiers kept their families dug in behind the perimeter.

I had missed those sounds and smells.

Around four-thirty in the morning, Captain America saw something poking around the perimeter and squeezed off a burst. Scared the hell out of the whole camp, but nobody fired back.

The next afternoon we went back to Phnom Penh. I got ready to leave the next day. Maybe I could get these people some good publicity back home. If I could get the rest of America to see them like I saw them, we could get backing for their revolution, or at least pressure the Vietnamese for fair treatment.

Before he said good-bye, Kpa Doh asked me if I would forward a letter to John Wayne. In 1966, while doing research for *The Green Berets*, Wayne had lived for two weeks with the Pleiku Mike Force, which Kpa Doh had commanded. He wore the Montagnard bracelet Kpa Doh gave him until he died.

Kpa Doh was angling for an assignment to the Command and Staff College at Ft. Leavenworth. If he got it he would need a dress uniform, and he couldn't afford one. His letter asked John Wayne for two hundred dollars to buy a dress uniform.

Captain America urged me to stay, said we could go out with Cambodian units and do some fighting. I said no. In my opinion, the Cambodians were going to lose, and deserved to lose. I'd been shot four times in Vietnam. I might risk it again for the Montagnards, but if they didn't need me, I sure wouldn't do it for fun.

John Wayne's secretary wrote me later that he had sent Kpa Doh the two hundred dollars, but Kpa Doh never got to go to Ft. Leavenworth. Rockoff said that his unit was one of the last to break up when the Khmer Rouge took the country. He changed to civvies and took his family to the French Embassy. They were among the roughly two hundred Cambodians ejected from the embassy in the final days, led away, presumably for execution by the Khmer Rouge.


My plan to publicize the Montagnards failed. I couldn't even sell my story to *Rolling Stone*. When their editor read it he realized that, in essence, they had financed a mercenary for the Lon Nol government. Hardly in keeping with their editorial policy, and not something they wished to publicize.

By 1973 the American public was so tired of Vietnam they didn't want to hear anything more about it.

# 3

# Fayetteville, Arkansas

June 1981, the last day of my last semester. I had finished teaching three classes of bonehead English, and completed the coursework for an MFA in Creative Writing. In the preceding week I had taken three finals, and given three, and I was done. I dropped my tabulated, signed gradebook on the stack of identical books on Dr. Van Scyoc's unoccupied desk, and checked my box for the last time. I felt that sudden let-down which comes from a release of tension when you're still wired.

Leaving the building, I walked down the hill from the English department. The campus thronged with young, attractive, and, at that moment, very worried students. The air was clear and clean, and the trees green.

I was in love, and living with the woman I loved, in a nice house on a tree-shaded street in a pretty town. Other than the fact that I had no money and no prospects of money, it was just about the best time in my life. But it would soon be over, and I had nothing lined up to replace it. I had applied for teaching jobs, but had no acceptances yet.

I walked into our empty house—Kathy was taking her finals too— threw my books on the sofa, and went to the kitchen for a beer, Coors. Not then sold in Arkansas, it was a status item, especially imported by pick-up truck from Oklahoma. It was only noon, but I was dead beat from lack of sleep and release from nervous tension caused by taking all the courses I'd put off for three years in one semester, while simultaneously teaching three sections.

The next day I planned to take off with a backpack for four days alone in the Ozarks. Then I'd have a full summer to read for comps.

But first I was going to finish this beer and take a nap.

I kicked my sneakers off and propped my feet up on the coffee table. I put my lips to the can, and the phone rang. I let it ring three times while I took a long swallow. Then, languidly, I reached out and snatched up the receiver. "Hello!"

"Morris? This is Jim Graves at *Soldier of Fortune*. Can you go to Beirut for us?"

I sat up, electrified, my feet slapping the floor. "Sure. No problem. When?"

His voice cracked over the line. "Thursday. Fly to Boulder tomorrow. We'll brief you and give you some things for the Phalangists. Here, I'm going to put Venter on the line."

"Hello, Jim. Hello!" A middle-class British accent on the line, strong baritone voice. I didn't know Venter, but I'd read some of his stuff, solid new journalism about the wars in Rhodesia and South Africa. His photos were excellent, and he'd had to stick his neck out a long way to get them. "I'm just back from Beirut for *Eagle*," he said, referring to *SOF's* principal competition within the genre. "It's a great story. The Phalangists—nobody knows anything about them, and they're really very good. Got in a hell of a punch-up...rockets and machine guns on the rooftops. My guide went for more ammo and fell seven stories down an elevator shaft. Jesus! He was a great kid. Engineering student. I can't stay to brief you, but I'll write you a long letter. Cheerio, Mate!"

I sat for a long moment, stunned. My life hadn't taken such a sudden unexpected turn since 1962, when I'd gone to the Pentagon to see about getting out of the army and come away assigned to a three-year tour in the 1st Special Forces Group on Okinawa. Just as I had on that occasion, I started to laugh, a rolling, belly-flexing guffaw that didn't stop for three minutes.

My relationship with Bob Brown, the founder, publisher, and editor-in-chief of *Soldier of Fortune*, went back to '76, just before the magazine started. I had read in the paper that some guy out in Boulder,

Colorado, was starting a trade journal for mercenaries.

That struck me as about the squirreliest idea I'd ever heard, but I had an entire cardboard box full of unsold stuff I'd written about the war, and about my later trip to Vietnam and Cambodia. In 1976, unless your work was subtitled, *mea culpa*, all you had to say to a publisher was "Vietnam" and a steel curtain descended in front of you.

So I called Brown, who, as it turned out, had commanded a Special Forces "A" Detachment in Vietnam, just as I had.

"Great!" he bellowed over the phone when I told him about my writing. "I'm going to an Army Reserve summer camp in Illinois next week. I'll drive down and look at your stuff." Sure, why not? It was only five hundred miles out of his way.

Brown drove up in an old dun-colored two door, covered with road dust and crammed with luggage and uniforms. He pulled into the parking lot in front of my apartment and exploded out of the car, barefoot, wearing cut-offs and an old J.C. Penney sport shirt. He grabbed my hand, a broad-shouldered guy with thinning sandy hair, long torso, and short, pale, hairy legs; talking a blue streak, cackling insanely during the pauses, snarling outrageous war stories from Vietnam, from Rhodesia, from some strange coup attempt in Haiti. Colonel Brown.

At dinner, the lady I was with was nonplussed when Brown ate his salad with his hands.

The bond between Special Forces people is a little hard to explain to someone who has never experienced it, but it's closer than friendship and closer than most family. Brown and I had so many overlapping experiences that as soon as we met, I felt I had known him all my life. If it weren't for that, and the fact that my work habits as a writer were not yet professional, I would not have done what I did, which was to give him my cardboard box full of Vietnam stories.

He didn't have to ask; I was desperate to be read. I had no carbons.

He took the box to Boulder and lost it. It disappeared into the maw, the Fibber McGee's closet, of his so-called filing system—apparently forever.

Over the next three years I made four trips to Boulder and turned the *SOF* office upside down each time. No stories. Mary Lou Jones, Brown's associate editor, searched between times as well. No stories.

By that time I was in print again and no longer desperate for publication. And I was a little put-off by the rabid tone of Brown's magazine, the mad-dog ferocity of the ads. Brown knew what would sell; his style was your basic snake-eater animal act, on display in bars at low dives worldwide. Personally I prefer a more low-key approach. I try not to talk about heroics for fear someone will ask me to do some. I decided to chalk the loss of my stories up to experience and forget it. But I still loved the guy, and went to see him every time I was in Boulder.

Three years after I gave Brown my box of stories, and long after my G.I. Bill had run out, I entered the graduate program in creative writing at the University of Arkansas. Being a teaching assistant was a way to make a few bucks while I wrote, and, who knows, I might learn something. As it turned out, I learned a great deal; the program was hard, but very good.

Like most graduate students, I didn't have much money, so I was delighted, if puzzled, a year or so later, to receive a postcard from a guy at *SOF* I had never heard of, saying my story had been accepted, and they would be sending me a check for $250.00. I called to find out what story. I hadn't sent them anything since Brown lost my cardboard box.

His new managing editor, Bob Poos, had gone through their entire inventory and found my stuff.

Before I finished at Arkansas, they bought two-thirds of my cardboard box. It has never been a mistake to trust Brown, but sometimes it looked like one for a long time.

Poos, a former Marine drill instructor, former AP reporter in Vietnam, molded Brown's combination wild-west show and G.I. Joe comic book into a professional, slick-looking magazine. In addition to what was in the cardboard box, I did a couple of long pieces about genuine heroes I'd known in Vietnam, but I'd never thought about going overseas for them. Couldn't have even if I'd wanted to; I was teaching and taking courses.

But I had a window of opportunity here, and this was my first chance to do something really exciting in eight years. The thought of passing it up never crossed my mind.

I had the summer free except for my reading, and I could take my Cliffs Notes along and study in Beirut.

At this writing it is eight years later, and I still have seven books to read for my comps.

Two days later, walking back from the *SOF* offices to Brown's house, I found an eagle feather in my path. If you believe in omens, you couldn't ask for better.

# 4

# Our Man In Beirut

I sort of expected my Lebanese contact on Cyprus to be like Sidney Greenstreet or Peter Lorre, wearing a panama hat. What I got was a collegiate-looking kid in a new Corvette, who grabbed my hand, shook it, and said in perfectly accented American English, "Hi, my name's Masoud."

Masoud gunned the 'vette through the narrow, twisting streets of Limassol. People, small cars, and motorcyclists flew from our path and flowed back around the 'vette. We pulled up in front of a pleasant restaurant with a verandah overlooking the city.

We ate seafood on the verandah. Over a plate of shrimp, a salad and a bottle of excellent white wine, Masoud told his story. He had been a junior, majoring in electrical engineering at Oklahoma State when the war with the Syrians got hot in '78.

He returned to Lebanon to find himself in charge of a squad of what the papers call the Christian Phalangist Militia. He told me about it in grammatically correct, but eccentric, English. The eccentricity was that even though he had six months of combat experience, he didn't know any military terminology, at least not in my language.

"One night one of my boys woke me up; I looked out through a chink in the wall and saw about six thousand enemy. So I called the boys with the mortars and had them fire right on us. We were in very strong houses, and they were in the open, so that drove them away."

We swapped war stories for a while until he finally said, "You know, the things they do to our people, after a while they drive you crazy. So once, when we captured a Syrian, I tied him to the back of my jeep and drove him all over town, on cobblestones, down alleys. When I got through there was no more left of him than this." He held up a plate of shrimp shells and sauce.

"It gives me the creeps to think about it now," he said. "It scares me to think I could ever have been like that. When I go home I ask the boys not even to tell me their stories. They are fanatics."

That night I got the shakes. I thought back on my briefing from Jim Graves, the new managing editor at *SOF*. "Look, Jim," I had demanded, "every combat situation is different. Before I go in, I like to know what I can do and not do, where I can go and not go. And most important, who are the good guys and who are the bad guys?"

Graves looked up from his desk and shot me an evil grin. "Well, Jimbo," he said, "that's what we're sending you over there to find out!"

Maybe I shouldn't write about fear; maybe I should play it stoic and close to the chest, but I think it needs to be talked about. Everybody goes through it. This fear is as much a necessary part of preparation for combat as is cleaning your weapon.

I wasn't mad at anybody in Lebanon. So the deal I made with myself was that I would take it a step at a time, and reserve the right to back off anywhere along the line. I would not, for instance, go into combat against a well-armed, well-trained, determined enemy, with a bunch of clowns.

That was the intellectual part. Physically, I got alternating chills in the gut and a lethargy that made me want to stay in my nice warm bed. What was needed now was for my body to accustom itself to the fact that the decision had been made. Once that happened, the transformation began, a transformation as complete as man into werewolf. I am convinced that it is a sustained, low-level release of adrenalin that keeps you alert and ready for combat.

All the tension I had accumulated since 1973 in Cambodia disappeared. A lower-back pain that had plagued me for three years vanished instantly.

It was an old, sweet feeling, one I had missed, and the closer I got to combat the sweeter it would be. That's the *Devil's secret name*, that feeling that suckers you into *the game.*

The next day Masoud arranged for my passage to Jounieh, a Christian-controlled port twenty miles north of Beirut. Boat travel was necessary because I had no visa, and because the airport was in West Beirut, under the control of the enemy.

Once we were underway I ordered a beer at the bar. One of the other passengers, a chubby Lebanese in one of those shiny, brightly-colored shirts, the kind favored by Vegas dealers and low-level mafiosi, approached me in true Peter Lorre style, and identified himself as an agent of...Christ! I didn't even know what these people called themselves.

I had been told they were trying to shake the "Phalangist" tag. The word comes from Phalanx, a Greek word meaning a military formation. The Christian Phalangist parties were political organizations formed for the purpose of organizing a militia to defend their homes, shops, and towns, when the central government was too weak and indecisive to do so. Unfortunately, the name, "falange", is also associated with Franco's fascist party in Spain, not a good tag from a public-relations standpoint.

At any rate, I was sitting at the bar, sipping a Heineken and chatting with the ship's heavily-muscled West Indian steward, when this sharp-nosed bureaucrat, scowling, sweating heavily, his belly jiggling against a shirt designed for a man with no waist at all, approached with my passport in his hand. "You have no visa!" he announced.

I nodded. "True. There is a man in Jounieh who is supposed to pick me up."

"His name!"

I gave him the name.

Just saying the name had an effect similar to that of racking back the bolt of an automatic weapon. The whole tone of the conversation changed. "Well, if you know Joe, then you won't have any trouble."

I grinned. I wanted to see if I could make him sweat again. "Oh, I don't know him. My Cyprus contact is supposed to have called him that I was coming."

The beads of sweat popped right back out on his brow. "I will radio ahead and see if it is okay. You may have to go back to Cyprus."

I shrugged. "I get paid the same, either way."

Not true. Brown would have my guts for garters if I went this far and didn't get a story. But I wasn't too worried; a high-handed air and a few names work wonders in these ceiling-fan countries. That's how I thought of Lebanon then: Vietnam with sand.

The only ocean-going vessels I had been on before were submarines. So that night I borrowed a blanket and slept on a foam pad on the flying bridge, under the stars. At night, on the sea, the stars are almost as bright as they are on the desert. I finally fell asleep with my glasses still on.

The next morning we were scheduled to arrive in Jounieh at 8:30, so I bounded down the ladder at first light, eager for coffee and breakfast.

The revolutionary bureaucrat came up to me at the bar, which also served as a lunch counter. "They didn't know you were coming and they can't find Joe." Not good news, but I still wasn't worried. A couple of phone calls should fix it. I gave him some numbers from my notebook.

When we had eaten breakfast I went to the bow to watch slick blue water run under the boat, and a grey line of mountains appear on the horizon. The first Lebanese boat I saw in the water was an ancient fishing sailboat which looked like the Flying Dutchman, reinforcing all my prejudices. But the second was a low, sleek outboard, pulling a skier.

*Oh, Lord,* I thought. *They told me this was going to be different, but this is different from the different I had in mind.*

The ten or eleven Lebanese men on the bow began singing a folksong, a rhythmic Middle Eastern chant, and one began beating his right fist into his left palm, muttering along with the music: "Syrians—kill fuckin' Syrians."

Shortly after that, a motor launch with two open rows of hard-backed wooden benches came out to our ship. Standing up in the boat was another overweight official in a slick shirt. He carried a handy-talkie in one hand and wore a snub-nosed revolver on his right hip. As soon as the launch pulled alongside, two highly bronzed young men in obscene Mediterranean bathing suits came aboard and began transferring our baggage.

But the thing that held my attention was the shore in front of us, crowded with swimmers; its little amusement park going full blast— complete with two gaily-colored ferris wheels, a merry-go-round and some bumper cars.

The guy with the pistol on his hip and the bureaucrat from the boat engaged in animated conversation over my passport. A moment later my sweaty friend from the boat came back to where I sat and whispered in my ear, "As soon as we dock, take your bag and go across the street. Stand by the BMW."

The guys in the nasty swimsuits lobbed a couple of lines onto the dock as we coasted in. I grabbed my black B-4 bag which, with its 20 pounds of Second Chance armored vest, three sniper manuals, and sixteen copies of *SOF*, immediately threw my lower back out of alignment. I lurched onto the Lebanese shore.

It's easy to forget, but there is a legal government there. Its representative stood on the dock in rumpled khakis, with some sort of off-the-wall black epaulets on his shirt. My two accomplices, both of whom seemed much more in charge than the official representative, chatted with him while I heaved past as inconspicuously as a tall man with a red beard carrying a hundred-pound suitcase can.

I got across the street okay and stood admiring the palms and the handsome people on the beach. But I didn't see a BMW anywhere.

Just as the official from the ship approached me, an old blue Plymouth sedan, with two red lights exactly like the ones on American cop cars, drove up. "Get in that car," said my sweaty friend. I was not eager to do it.

Two young guys got out. They wore green fatigues and black berets, and carried folding-stock AKs slung over their shoulders. These lads were not part of any mariachi band. They handled their weapons with the familiarity with which most people handle their wallets. One of them opened the trunk for my suitcase and camera bag.

The other shot me a quizzical look. He didn't know whether he was picking up a prisoner or a VIP. I didn't either, but I nodded imperiously toward the door handle. He popped it open and I entered like an ambassador.

We drove through a nice seaport and resort town, with signs advertising seafood, scuba gear and discos, in French, English, and Arabic;

the big movies were *L'Histoire d'O* and *The Wild Geese*. After a drive of about three miles, the car turned into a walled compound with a small guardhouse at the entrance. Inside were civilian villas, surrounded by spiny tropical vegetation and flowers. The guard at the gate, a listless lad of seventeen or so, appeared to have his attention focused on something else, probably his radio, from which top 40 music poured. If necessary, he'd be a snap to disarm and get past. But then what?

We went inside the first building. I had been informed that this was a militia without rank, but, rank or no rank, one sweep of the eyes sorted out the chief clerk, sergeant major, and adjutant, and tabbed this as an MP outfit, since the adjutant, a small, bespectacled, finicky-looking man, had handcuffs on his belt.

I was pleased they were on his belt instead of my wrists. These people didn't know me, and had reason to be nervous. If they decided they didn't like me, or my magazine, I was in a world of hurt. Even if by some feat of *James Bondismo* I bashed and battered my way out of this compound, I'd be conspicuous, ignorant, and illegal.

I sat for a long time behind a desk across from the adjutant, nervous and sleepy from my night on the bridge of the ship. Then the guard who had driven me here approached and loomed over me, concentrating, looking for words in English, "Woood yooo lihk zome coffee?"

After I'd drunk my coffee, I was ushered into another office to meet Joe. He welcomed me and we had a pleasant chat. He had gone to college in the States and for a time had been a police reporter in Miami. He called the Lebanese Forces G-5 to tell them I was coming. In the American staff system, G-5 handles propaganda, and the public relations is a separate function under G-1, Administration. But the Lebanese saw no reason for such an arbitrary distinction; G-5 handled all information functions.


No guard this time, only the same driver who had driven me from the harbor, smiling and friendly. Before we reached our destination, my driver wrote his name and phone number in my notebook so we could go out and hell around a bit before I left Lebanon.

Back in Jounieh, I had begun to wonder whether the war in Lebanon was a joke or a comic-opera game. As we came into East Beirut all such misconceptions were dispelled. The closer we got to the center of town the greater the destruction: apartment houses with great shell-hole gouges, and collapsed buildings. But the streets were filled with European and American cars, some of them also pockmarked with shrapnel holes, and the sidewalks were thronged with people dressed no differently from those in Little Rock, Arkansas.

What really amazed me was that everywhere I looked there were construction cranes and new high-rise buildings going up. Some buildings under construction were already pockmarked with shell holes, and others bore patched holes, but they just went right on slapping them up. I thought, these people must be either the ballsiest in the world, or the smartest, or the craziest, or all of the above. Although I was to learn a great deal about Lebanon and the Lebanese in the coming weeks, nothing contradicted this initial impression.

My driver turned off a main boulevard and shot up a long hill, into an area of narrow two-lane streets fronted by high-rise apartments with balconies. The construction looked like something you'd see in Miami, Florida, but the doorways were barricaded with 55-gallon drums filled with dirt and topped with sandbags, and the street was full of young men wearing fatigues and carrying slung weapons, mostly AKs, but a few M-16s.

Very few of these people wore caps with their fatigues, but a semi-military haircut was in style, short, but no crewcuts, no sidewalls. I saw no rank or unit insignia of any kind. These troops looked pretty sharp, but casual about it; no spitshines. Their uniforms fit well, and that lost, hangdog look often found in Third World military units was totally absent.

We stopped in front of an apartment building. My driver led me around the barricade and up the steps to a second floor apartment. A plant hung just inside the door. Across the room was a conversational grouping of plush furniture, seating a three-man French TV crew, in animated conversation with a tall, skinny, bearded Lebanese wearing a crewcut. He wore a genuine Vietnam-issue Special Forces tiger suit and a .45 in a spring-clip shoulder holster. He had on the last pair of WWII wrap-around combat boots I ever saw or expect to see.

All of these guys looked up when I came in, then went back to their conversation. I set my bag down and looked around.

In the dining room, several young men in fatigues sat at a large table, poring over newspapers, magazines and photos. Working with them was a truly stunning girl, model-thin, with long strawberry blonde hair. She wore tight, faded jeans, sneakers and a white top. She appeared tired, strained.

The guy in the tiger suit got up. He and my driver exchanged a few words in Arabic. He turned to me with an expression of weary exasperation. We shook hands. "My name is Samir," he said.

My driver said good-bye, reminded me to come see him in Jounieh, and left. Samir gestured toward the couch and we sat down across from the TV crew. By way of a conversation opener, I asked him where he had gotten his tiger suit.

"A friend in your Special Forces got me six pairs," he said. "This is the last."

A kid whom I took to be an American student walked in the door I had just entered. He walked with a slouching saunter and wore Addidas sneakers and beat-up grey cords. He had the scraggly beard and long hair I associated with college students. But over his Izod shirt he wore an old French army cammie bush jacket.

*Hey, kid,* I thought, *that thing can get you killed here.*

He went into the dining room, leaned on the table where the young people in fatigues worked and began jiving in French with the exquisite young woman. She looked up and they smiled at each other.

From what sounded like two blocks over, I heard a burst of AK fire, followed by another farther away and then a muffled *crump...crump.*

I looked up, startled. "We are two hundred meters from the front," Samir said. His accent was English public school, overlaid with the musical, rolling Lebanese lilt. Wearily he lifted his wrist, pulled a green and black tennis sweatband away from the face of his watch, and said, "Would you like to go to lunch?"

If he wasn't worried about being two hundred meters from the front, then I saw no reason why I should be. "Sure."

We got up and sauntered out of the apartment. "Do you like

Lebanese food?"

I nodded. It seemed an appropriate thing to do; I had never eaten any.

Outside, a kid in jeans expertly steered a skateboard down the slope of the street and around the rubble. Around the corner another bunch of kids played soccer.

Our restaurant consisted of two rickety tables set outdoors behind a sandbagged wall. The kebab was done on an open grill made from a 55-gallon drum, halved lengthwise. But what a lunch: the best tabouleh, homus, kebab, fresh fruit and Arak, a clear liquor that turns milky white when mixed with water. It tastes like licorice, but watch it!

"This country is sure different from what I expected."

He smiled. "You expected a desert."

I nodded.

While we ate I watched Sam closely, trying to take his measure. I liked what I saw. He was wary at first, but when he saw I had no preconceived notions, he warmed up quickly. I never saw a man slide into and out of a thousand-yard stare as quickly as Sam did. He had the spaced-out mystical-militant quality of an El Greco monk trapped by the Inquisition. The feeling I had about Sam was that somehow he had been burned clean.

Lebanon's form of combat had its compensations, like this lunch, and the high incidence of truly lovely women; but when it got hot, it was very, very hot, and none of the parties was a signatory of the Geneva convention. Sam had lived through seven years of this stuff. I could only guess at his weariness.

Once when I saw him slide into that long-gone stare I asked him what he would have done if this war hadn't interrupted his life. He replied, "Oh, I'd have found one someplace."

I asked him about the atrocities Masoud had described on Cyprus.

"Yes," he replied. "The Palestinians excel at that sort of thing. But our boys decided if those were the rules, we would play, too. They backed away pretty fast."

Raised in Cairo, Sam had spent a year and a half in an Egyptian Commando unit as an 18 and 19-year-old kid. He was under no illusions about the general quality of Egyptian forces, but claimed his unit had been exceptional. The quality of their desert training, specifically, had been excellent.

He told one story about this Egyptian training. "There was a group of us sitting cross-legged around our instructor on the grenade range. He pulled the pin on a Russian grenade and threw it in my lap. "Get rid of it," he said. I knew it was either a dud, or had a long fuse, so I threw it back at him and said, 'Get rid of it yourself.' It had a long fuse, but it wasn't a dud. He left me alone after that."

He was quite frank about the fact that he had gone into G-5 work because his nerves were shot. "It's quite amusing, really," he said. "I get shot at twice as much as before, because I'm always taking journalists to where the action is. Before, I stayed in my unit, and only fought sporadically."

As we talked, we found that we had read an amazing number of the same books. I asked if he had read *The Centurions* and The *Praetorians*, by Jean Larteguy, two Special Forces' favorites. He had not only read them, he had read all of Larteguy, and met him when he came to Lebanon.

At the end of lunch my situation was very different from what it had been at the beginning. For the first time since 1968, when I left the 5th Special Forces Group in Vietnam, I felt completely at home with my environment, at ease and happy. These were my kind of folks.

Walking back across the street to the press bureau, we passed the American college kid we had seen earlier, unloading the French TV crew from a white VW bug, into which they and their equipment had been jammed. The kid had an AK slung over his shoulder. *Hmmmmmm,* I thought, *things are not always what they appear.*

When we got back upstairs and flopped down on the couch, Sam said, "Well what can we do for you?"

"I've got a bulletproof vest and a sniper manual from Venter to deliver to a guy named Rocky in a place called Sodeco, and another couple of manuals for a guy named Tony in Hadath. Let's get rid of the bloody vest first. Then we'll play it by ear."

He went to check with Lebanese Forces command to see if it was okay if I went to Sodeco, wherever that was. I had visions of a tiny village near Beirut that we would have to tiptoe over the mountains at night to get to. I still had a firmly fixed idea of Vietnam in the desert, with these guys playing a role sort of like the Hoa Hao, a militant Buddhist sect in the Delta. I unzipped my bag and dragged out the vest.

The college boy with the AK and the French TV crew came clattering up the stairs.

Sam came back and said, "Okay, you're supposed to spend the night in Sodeco; Rick will take you."

"Who's Rick?"

He indicated the college boy.

"Who's that gorgeous French creature?"

"That's Christine. She's Rick's friend. May I see the vest?"

I handed it to him. Rick left the Frenchmen, who sat down with their beers, and came to examine the vest. He was distant and none too cordial. He looked tired. He and Sam spoke to each other in bursts of rapid-fire French, too fast and complicated for me to follow. But after they spoke, Rick was open and friendly.

The vest had two tiers of alloy plates in front and back that slid into OD-nylon pockets. Second Chance makes heavier ones, with more armor, to cover the crotch, but that was a lot more weight than I'd wanted to carry. In any case, the heavier vests would not have covered the area under the arms. They had been made primarily for police work, just as the Army and Marine flak vests were made for indirect-fire weapons. Sam and Rick wanted something that would cover you both ways.

"You ready?" Rick inquired.

I looked around the apartment, considering that once again I had gotten myself into a situation where I was racing off to get shot at with people I didn't know. "Just like that, huh?"

"Unless you've got something else to do here."

I made a transatlantic call to *SOF*, to tell Graves I was there, was okay, and was going out.

"What's it like?" he asked.

"So far it's been a Humphrey Bogart movie."

"Well, don't get yourself killed just to get a story."

"I won't." I hung up the phone. "Okay," I muttered. "Let's go." I picked up my camera bag.

"Don't take that!" Rick commanded.

"That's just my camera bag."

"I know, but our people cross over into West Beirut all the time;

some of us work over there. We have relatives over there. We can't afford to have our faces shown. We can't let our positions be revealed either."

Great, I thought. No photos. Brown's going to love that. Rick was telling me rule number one for this war, and once more I was thinking when I should have been listening, an omission I was to regret later. Just as rule number one for Vietnam had been never set a pattern, rule number one for Lebanon was never let them know who you, personally, are. Because, if you do, they will definitely send someone to do a number on you.

But all I could think about was the bloody photos—in the end, they gave me more photos than I could ever use.

We went back downstairs and got in Rick's beat-up old VW bug. He eased it past the quiet block of apartments, and the pinball arcade, and accelerated at the end of the block. But the instant we hit a major traffic artery, two blocks down, he floored it and we roared through empty, shattered streets. We blasted through a red light, entering a major intersection at about 85 kph. "Stop at that light and you'll draw mortar fire almost every time," he muttered, and gave me a piratical grin, taking quick glances down the six intersection streets to see whether he might be run over by an oncoming tank.

He twisted down three or four more streets, slewed sideways into the entrance of a parking garage, and parked correctly between two white lines.

"Is that a stock VW engine in there?" I asked, when I caught my breath.

Rick grinned wryly as he opened the car door. "Not exactly," he said. "Okay, this is it."

No midnight infiltration over the mountains. Sodeco was a neighborhood in Beirut, like Flatbush is a neighborhood in Brooklyn.

A handsome, well-built young man with curly brown hair and an engaging smile walked toward us. He wore a pair of fatigue pants and an OD t-shirt. He looked to be about 20 or 21, and carried himself with an unself-conscious air of command.

"This is Rocky, the Sodeco commander," Rick said. We shook hands and I passed him the manuals and his bulletproof vest. Rocky and Rick grinned greetings. They were obviously friends.

"See you in the morning," Rick said. He jumped in the bug and screeched backward up the ramp, through a blue haze of exhaust; he went so fast that if I'd blinked, I'd have missed it. A squeal come from upstairs as he speed-shifted into low and roared off down the street.

Rocky took me on a walking tour of his section of town. A couple of his boys went along with us. One of them had a pistol on his hip, but nobody carried a rifle. The buildings in the neighborhood were all concrete, closed in, and shot straight up for many stories. Holes, pockmarks and rubble were everywhere. We walked easily until we approached a little open area in front of a church. "Stay on the right here," Rocky said. "On the left side of the street a sniper can hit you."

I remembered downtown Nha Trang during Tet, where a foot either way made the difference.

Rocky wanted to show me the church. It was shot all to hell. But I was interested in why they weren't armed, and were unconcerned, if this was such a hot area.

"Venter told me you had a hell of a fight when he was here," I said.

"Yeah," Rocky replied. "Up on the roofs. His guide got on the elevator on the twelfth floor. Unfortunately the elevator was in the basement. It shook Al up pretty badly..."

On the roofs there were no ground assaults, but nowhere to hide except behind a few sandbags.

We went on back downstairs to the parking garage. "You want a beer?" Rocky asked. This was a front-line position and I had to settle for a Lowenbrau, but it was ice-cold.

There were also a couple of nice-looking girls downstairs, one in heels and a purple pair of those ugly, baggy pants which were in fashion then. She held her cigarette at an affected angle, and had a toy poodle on a leash. The other girl wore jeans and a t-shirt. The one with the poodle looked French; the other was dark enough to be Lebanese.

From the way they were jiving the young men, I began to understand that here, a first-rate resistance fighter got all the best girls. I smiled. I had finally come to a place where people had their priorities right.

Just at that point, Rick came screaming back down the ramp in his bug and screeched to a stop beside me. "I came to pick you up.

Headquarters wants you back at G-5." He hadn't shut off his engine and the garage was filling up with noxious fumes. I didn't like this. I was all jazzed up for a fire fight and...ah, well, no point in arguing. Rick wasn't a decision maker.

"Maybe next time," I said to Rocky, and got in the VW.

We backed up the ramp and screamed once more through the blasted streets., "Why did they pull me out?" I asked.

"I don't know," he said. "I'll try to find out when we get back."

"Are you Lebanese?" I asked. "When I first saw you I thought you were an American college student."

He laughed. "I'm almost 30. I was born here, but my father is American. I went to college in the States. I have a B.A. and an M.A. in political science from Berkeley."

"Berkeley?" I grinned.

"Yeah, I used to have hair halfway down my back and a ring in my ear, to blend in, you know. But I always spent my summers training and fighting here. There was only one guy I was really tight with at Berkeley, and he was a Marine colonel back for an advanced degree."

We pulled in at the G-5 apartment house, skipped around the sandbags and went upstairs.

Sam looked up from the couch where he sat chatting with a Swedish TV crew. "Hello," he said, "How was the trip?"

"Not very satisfactory," I grumbled. "Look, if I'm going to get a story for a combat magazine, I have to see some combat. I'm no good to anybody dead, but the more action I see and get away to write about, the better story for all of us."

"We'll see what we can do," Sam said wearily.

A moment later Rick came back. "That was it," he said. "They expect a heavy attack on Sodeco, and they don't want you caught in it."

When working entirely at the sufferance of somebody else's army it is best not to throw a tantrum. "I'm not the reporter from *Women's Wear Daily*," I snapped. "Next time gimme an AK and let me stay."

They both grinned. "We buy our own," Rick said. "I doubt anybody is going to want to give you his and do without."

Rick and Sam went out on the balcony. I followed them. We sat down in wicker chairs and propped our feet up on the rail. Christine came out and joined us. She leaned easily against the balcony and threw her long hair back to let the breeze air her neck.

"You don't get paid, you buy your own guns, your own ammo, your own uniforms, and there's no rank in your army?"

"That's right," Sam said.

"I don't see how you can fight a war that way."

Rick grinned. "We can do it because our fighters are very good."

"What happens if you want to leave?"

Rick shrugged. "I've been working straight through for a month, being with the reporters during the day, and doing some other little things at night. Next week I'm going to take a couple of days off and go to the beach."

I shook my head. "How do you know who's in charge?"

"Well," said Sam, "we don't have rank, but we have job titles. When the war is hot, everybody takes orders. When it's not, we talk it over. When it dies down for a while, we go back to our regular jobs."

"Rick," I asked, "why don't you wear a uniform?"

He grinned his old grin. "Our G-5 asks me the same question all the time," he said. "I don't like them. Besides, you see those boots?" He nodded toward Sam's combat boots. "Those are boondockers." He wiggled his sneakers at me. "These are better for city fighting. I have a friend who fights in flip-flops. He's not any good in boots." He shrugged.

What was his headquarters to do? They couldn't bust him; he had no rank. They couldn't fine him; he didn't get paid. They couldn't fire him; he was too valuable.

After a while Rick said, "Look, we've got to leave. You're welcome to crash here tonight. Anything you like in the fridge is yours."

I sat on the balcony for a long time watching the sun go down and the streets clear.

Some of the guys from the G-5 section sat inside, sipping beer or coffee, watching a *Charlie's Angels* segment on a 24-inch color TV with subtitles in French and Arabic. Completely oblivious to the automatic weapons fire in the street outside, they stared fascinated as those three adorable kumquats battled imaginary bad guys with .32 caliber automatics.

I heard no indirect fire, but lots of AK and M16 bursts from a few blocks west, toward Sodeco.

# 5

# Three Sisters From Hadath

Sodeco wasn't hit that first night, so it hadn't really mattered where I slept. But I still had two sniper's manuals to deliver, so the following day Rick drove me to Hadath, a suburb of Beirut. There is no real break between the two; Hadath is an old town that the city has grown beyond.

As usual Rick drove at top speed, and took a route that went all the way around Robin Hood's barn. Sometimes he sneaked slowly down narrow streets, driving carefully to avoid hitting anyone, then turned a corner, already accelerating, bursting across a street with a clear line of sight to Palestinian-controlled territory before a sniper could squeeze off a round.

"The Palestinians tried a probe on Hadath the day before you arrived. There's a small Lebanese army platoon in position there, between the Palestinians and our guys, but they were outnumbered and had to withdraw. Then our boys counterattacked and drove the Palestinians off."

We coasted down a long hill, between narrow, close-set buildings, burst through one turn, rounded another, and pulled up across the street from an imposing building, which looked like a police station, but with the usual arrangement of sandbags outside.

"Nothing to worry about," Rick said. "But it's best to cross this street rather quickly."

"Sniper?"

He nodded.

The space in which the sniper had a clear shot was only about six feet wide, in the middle of the street. We hopped across it and went into the building, the Hadath headquarters of the Kataebe Party, now given over to the Lebanese Forces.

A couple of lads in fatigue pants, T-shirts and flip-flops, and a dark and animated girl with big eyes and blue jeans, sat in wooden chairs in the shade of the building, talking, smoking cigarettes and drinking Turkish coffee. They were four feet from the sniper zone, totally unconcerned.

Rick asked a question, and when they replied, turned to me and said, "Tony's in a meeting. He was due back an hour ago." I had been informed that the commander in Hadath was "Sheik Tony," but other than the name, I knew next to nothing about him.

Rick had to get back to the bureau, so he turned me over to a hard-looking kid in a black T-shirt. His name was Rais, as near as I could make it out, and he offered to take me on a tour of the front.

The front was all streets, alleys and buildings. These buildings were old, constructed of solid masonry. Turning them into fortifications hadn't been much of a trick, but getting to and from them was a tortuous job. To avoid being shot at, we crouched low, leaped ditches and dodged down alleys. We arrived at a small chink in the masonry wall of an almost totally destroyed building, through which I could see the Syrians' sandbagged emplacements in a half-completed building across a 200-meter wasteland of rubble.

We went through a half-dozen of these outposts, until he was satisfied that I had the idea.

Rais was in Lebanese Forces, but he had spent a year in the Lebanese Army and was on friendly terms with the platoon between them and the Palestinians, so he took me to their Command Post. A dozen-or-so Lebanese soldiers stood around outside a house, drinking coffee. They seemed like nice boys, but handled themselves more like high school kids than soldiers.

The difference between them and their Lebanese Forces' counterparts was amazing. The army kids were younger and less sure of themselves than the militia. There were Christians and Moslems in the platoon, and although they seemed to get along well, it was obvious they did so by not talking about certain things.

The uniforms of both groups were almost identical, except that the army guys wore helmets or helmet liners. They carried their rifles like someone had handed them these things fifteen minutes before, and they were looking for a place to put them. By contrast, the Lebanese Forces militia usually went bareheaded, carried their weapons with the familiarity bred of good training and long, continuous use, and, to a man, wore gold crucifixes on chains around their necks, usually with another medallion, a small, gold map of Lebanon.

As one of the soldiers brought me a cup of Turkish coffee, their platoon leader drove up in his jeep. Rais introduced us, and I took my coffee and followed him down into his CP, which was in a shelled-out basement apartment.

He gestured me into the seat of honor, an easy chair, half-torn apart by shrapnel. I balanced my coffee on my knee.

The lieutenant sat down facing me on a couch that was as ripped apart as my chair, and a G.I. brought him his own cup. The furniture was arranged so as to face a black-and-white portable TV, sitting on top of two ammo crates. The sound was turned way down, and the picture was awful, but through the snow I could make out Henry Winkler as Fonzi, as Ron Howard stood by with a stupid grin on his face.

"Pretty nice," I said. "Is there one for the enlisted men?" I was just kidding. The line was the caption to one of Bill Mauldin's WWII Willie and Joe cartoons. The lieutenant assured me, however, that the lounge was for the entire platoon.

The lieutenant was sharp enough. His closest U.S. equivalent would be a Sigma Chi who had gone through ROTC. He was about 28 years old, in excellent physical condition, and he seemed intelligent and knowledgeable. However, he had a six-block front to cover with nineteen men, which was not a possible mission. Bunched up, as they were, they could be flanked. Spread out they could be easily penetrated.

In theory, both his platoon and the Syrians were here to keep peace between the Palestinians and Lebanese Forces. But, in fact, the Syrians were sending shells and rockets into Christian areas on a daily basis, and were perfectly happy to let the Palestinians try a probe whenever they felt like it.

With nineteen men, spread that thin, all the lieutenant and his men could do was zing a couple of bursts at the attacking Palestinians and then get the hell out of their way. But the firing alerted the Christians, so they always drove the Palestinians back. There were more than 500 armed and trained members of Lebanese Forces in the town—more than enough to chew up anyone the Palestinians could squeeze through the alleys and across the rubble.

The lieutenant was Christian, as were most of his men, but there was very little love lost between the Moslem members of his platoon and the Palestinians. He was more than happy to be the early warning system for the defenders of Hadath.

But that wasn't what the lieutenant wanted to talk about. He wanted to talk about the Infantry Officers' Advanced Course at Fort Benning. He wanted to get there the next year. I assured him that he would do well, as I had no doubt he would. He would also probably profit from an association with officers from several different countries. But I doubted that the advanced course itself had much to teach that was applicable to his present situation.

It was way past time for Tony to return, so Rais and I went back to the Kataebe headquarters.

We went the usual circuitous route; a cautious walk down a trench, a quick sprint down an alley, camera case thudding against my groin.

I decided the next time I went to Lebanon, or any other war, for that matter, I was going to take a BAR belt for my camera stuff. If possible, I'd also take a few extra bucks and buy an AK on the way in and sell it on the way out.

Correspondents say you can shoot pictures before and after a firefight, but not during, so I might as well go ahead and get me some boom-boom time.

When we arrived at the Kataebe headquarters, a different set of kids was taking a break in the shade. But just as we arrived, a new Audi screeched to a halt across the street. It snuggled against the curb, so that its near side was a good eighteen inches away from the sniper zone. Three doors sprang open, and three young men got out and stepped briskly across the street. Two were in uniform, but the big guy who had been in the right front seat wore a blue warm-up suit, and had a .45 tucked under his left armpit. "Hi! I'm Tony," he said, and stuck out his hand for a shake.

I had been told the commander in Hadath was, "Sheik Tony," but I had no frame of reference for a sheik in a warm-up suit who looked like Buddy Holly, except for about twenty extra pounds of solid muscle. He grinned disarmingly and blinked through thick, black-framed glasses, then led us into the headquarters with a long-legged, confident stride.

We went down a long corridor and a dark hallway, into a fair-sized room, lit by a naked light bulb. Mounted on a wall, on a standard sheet of four-by-eight plywood, was his situation map, which showed every house and alley in Hadath, with Syrian, Palestinian, Lebanese Army, and Lebanese Forces positions marked in different colored crayons; weapons positions, sniper positions, and observation posts were marked with different colored pins.

It was not a military map; it seemed the sort of map the city water department would have. Had I not toured those positions it would not have made much sense. Tony pointed out what, at first, looked like a major street. When it was identified I realized it was a tiny alley down which Rais and I had scuttled like crabs, sometimes walking, sometimes ducking, sometimes sprinting.

"This is my apartment," Tony said bitterly. Small wonder he was bitter. It was marked as a Palestinian sniper position.

Tony introduced me to the two men with him. The short, compact one, Max, was his artillery commander. The stocky, good-natured guy was chief of his mortar section. His name, he said, was, Bob. They invited me to tour their artillery positions, and to join them for dinner afterward.

Outside we quick-stepped across the street. Bob put the Audi in gear, gunned around the corner before the sniper could take aim, and then started driving normally—that is, like a maniac.

Tony wanted to drop by his dispensary before we went to the artillery positions. In addition to being commander, he was a fifth-year medical student, and he took a personal interest in treatment. "I still have two years to go on my medical studies," Tony said. "I should have finished by now, but the war..." He shrugged.

The dispensary was run by two attractive young nurses in civilian clothes. One wore jeans, a T-shirt and platform shoes, her hair hanging down to the middle of her back, the other was in a fashionable summer frock. Despite looking like a pair of disco queens, they were all business.

There were eight or ten wounded or ill people waiting in the anteroom. The treatment room was well-equipped with examination tables and instruments, but there was little medicine on the shelves, and all the expendable items seemed to have been expended. "What are you short of?" I inquired.

"Everything," Tony said. "All that you see here is outdated."

After another short race through the streets, we pulled into a parking garage. Among the cars there was also a motor pool for a commando platoon down there. Two or three young guys in fatigue pants and black commando T-shirts bent over an engine under the open hood of a Land Rover pick-up, with a 106mm recoilless rifle mounted in back. There were two or three jeep-mounted 106s, and a jeep-mounted .50 caliber machine gun drawn up in the same line. The vehicles were all clean, and freshly painted olive green, but their bodies were dented all to hell.

The three guys under the hood and the two or three others hanging around were all laughing and jiving. As usual, the guys with the most difficult, most dangerous duty had the highest morale.

Max, Bob and Tony led me down a long, narrow tunnel, which had been chopped out of the raw concrete; electric wire and naked bulbs hung from the ceiling. We emerged from it into another room, freshly made from thick concrete. That wet concrete smell still hung in the air. Maps, charts and plotting instruments lay on plywood tables, slanted like drawing boards, leaning against the wall to the right.

"Ah! Your FDC."

"What is FDC?" Max inquired.

"Fire direction center."

"Yes, this is my fire direction center."

I talked about his gear for a few more minutes. It soon became clear that neither Max nor Bob knew much about artillery, at least not the way they teach it at Fort Sill. Not that they didn't know what they were doing, or that their stuff wasn't set-up efficiently. It just didn't look like what I was used to. And none of their terminology was like anything I had heard before. "Where did you guys get your training?"

"We didn't," Bob said grinning. "We captured the guns and figured out from there."

"Jesus, how did you do that?"

Max shrugged. "I'm an architect and Bob's an accountant. The math wasn't that hard."

"You worked out your own firing tables?"

Bob nodded. "Yes, we can usually hit a target after two shots. We have to be very careful. We all have friends and relatives on the other side. We don't want to hurt anybody but the Syrians."

I thought about the rubble upstairs. "It doesn't seem as though they're that cautious."

Bob sneered in contempt. "They open the gun and look down the barrel. If they can't see the building in front of them they start firing over here. They keep it up until we hit their positions. We have to be quick and accurate."

"Two rounds?"

"Right! Two rounds."

We went down another long tunnel, and emerged into what amounted to a large, vacant lot, with sandbagged emplacements for their mortars. These were among the best-made mortar positions I have ever seen, neatly and cleanly dug, and sandbagged so carefully that nothing but a direct hit would have much effect on them.

Their pride and joy was a huge, newly-captured Soviet 160mm mortar. They were in the process of constructing a pit for it when I saw it. Its tube was longer than that of a 105mm howitzer, and the baseplate was wider across than I am tall.

After that we went to dinner. The original plan was to treat me to some Lebanese food, but the restaurant they wanted to go to was closed, so we wound back down the mountains, raced through streets and stopped at a couple of check points, laughing and talking about the war, politics, girls, everything.

During the course of the conversation, Max said the thing that stuck most in my mind during the entire time I was in Lebanon. I don't remember how it came up, but it fit smoothly into the flow of conversation. It had to do with why his people had risen, almost to a man, to fight with rage and intelligence against clearly impossible odds. "I think we fight," said Max, "for the human dignity."

We had our dinner on the veranda of a pizzeria. Tony reached over and took his .45 back from Bob, who had been holding it for him while he drove. He put it in his lap and carefully looked over the four or five people eating on the verandah. It was wonderfully cool out there, and the lights of the city shone all around us. "What?" I asked, nodding toward the pistol.

"We might get a bomb or a grenade," Tony said. "It's not very likely, but you never know." It all seemed so quiet and normal out here.

As we talked, Max mentioned that he worked in West Beirut. Every morning he got up, put on his suit and tie, picked up his briefcase, and drove into enemy territory, to the office of his architectural firm. Then, at night, he drove back, put on his fatigues, and went down to the FDC.

"I don't tell them I am a fighter," he said. "If anybody talks about the war, I just act as though I am afraid."

"I'm sure the Syrians didn't plan on anything like this uprising," I said to Max. "I wonder what the Syrians think about you guys?"

Max deals with the enemy in his business on a daily basis. To do so, he has to see them as people. But he misunderstood my question and started explaining the Syrians' rationale for being in Lebanon.

Tony would have none of it. The bastards had invaded his country, delayed his career, usurped his apartment, and God knows what else. He totally lost it, screaming in Arabic, raging and waving his arms.

What impressed me most about this incident was the way Max handled it. Despite being a kid in bop glasses and a jogging suit, Tony was his commander, with responsibility equal to that of a lieutenant colonel in the U.S. Army. In every army with which I am familiar, if the main man put on a display like that, all his flunkies would fall immediately into line, tug at their forelocks, and exclaim, "Yassa, massa! You sho' right. Them bassar ain't got no rationale."

Max did nothing of the sort. He patiently sat and waited for Tony to sputter to a halt, then went right back into his explanation.

Actually, Tony was right. The bastards' rationale was totally false. But I was impressed by the fact that Max could fight them effectively and still see them as people.

I slept in Tony's Tactical Operations Center that night. The next day he had to rush off and do something important, and none of the guys I had met the day before seemed to be around. I was actually quite pleased with the chance to be alone to collect my thoughts. I found a chair out in front of the headquarters, propped my feet up on a couple of sandbags and spaced out, watching flowers and palms rustle in the breeze in the back yard of a pockmarked villa across the street. I went over everything that had happened since Cyprus, sorting out what was usable and what was not, how to tell it, and in what order.

Several times young men stopped and exchanged a few words. A kid named, Jamil, stopped. He was going out to drive around in a van to collect foodstuffs for Lebanese Forces from merchants and households. It seemed to me that he had been carefully selected for this job, since he was about as engaging and non-threatening as it is possible for a man to be; a skinny, doofus kid, with a grin that never left his face. He wore jeans and a checked sport shirt. The only military things about him were his baseball-style fatigue cap and the old, long-barreled .38 in the waistband of his jeans.

All the kids who were trying to improve their English chatted with me; Jamil was no exception. "Last year I spent six months in San Francisco," he said. "I meet many heppies. You know heppies?"

A while later, a pleasant-looking kid, a boy of about seventeen, came lurching up the steps. His left leg was stiff all the way down, and his left arm was braced from the shoulder out, at a 45 degree angle from his body, and bent at a 45 degree angle from his elbow. When he saw me he gave a big, delighted smile, and said, "Bonjour!"

"Hi!" I replied.

"You speak English?"

I shrugged. "Je parle Francais un peu, pas tres bien."

"I woood prefer English," he said. "I am learning."

He was a B-10-rocket gunner who had been wounded in a shoot-out with the Syrians.

"Tony was a B-10 gunner at Tall Zaatar," I said, something I had learned the night before.

The kid's smile widened. "He is my brother. Not my real brother, but he teached me the B-10. Three days I stay at his apartment. He teach me everything about the B-10."

I had never before heard a trooper say of his battalion commander, "He is my brother."

After the B-10 gunner had gone, I sat there for another hour or so, until a remarkably beautiful young lady tapped me on the shoulder. "Are you sad?" she asked.

I suppose a man starting into space with a blank look on his face looks neither happy nor busy, although in truth, I was both.

The girl was just plain beautiful; big dark eyes, olive skin, aquiline nose, glossy dark hair; she was just a kid, maybe eighteen or nineteen, with the careful smile and manner of a "nice girl."

"I'm fine," I replied.

Clearly she didn't believe me. "Come inside for coffee," she said.

We went inside the communications center of the headquarters. One entire wall was filled with ranked row upon row of two-way radios, some military, some commercial. A girl wearing fatigues sat and muttered Arabic into a microphone. A speaker sputtered back at her. Her sad look had nothing to do with a long shift in the communications center. I never found out what caused it, but in Lebanon the possibilities were endless.

There were three more women in the room. One, also in fatigues, lay dead asleep on a small bed against the wall opposite the console, her boots neatly lined up beside the bed, OD socks still on her feet.

The other two were girls about the age of my new friend, wearing civilian clothes; jeans and pants. They and my friend were all pretty, and obviously sisters.

For the next three hours they entertained me to make sure I was not blue and lonely, not moping around in front of the headquarters. They told me jokes; they fed me coffee and a great lunch. Since their English wasn't much better than my French, we spent a lot of time groping for the right words. Sometimes it took all four of us to put together a sentence for one of us, all of us laughing at the fluffs we made.

Although they were sisters, the girls were very different. Farrah, the oldest, was a beauty queen, with a great body, and long, wavy hair that framed her face and fell below her shoulders. She wore a carefully chosen, fashionable top, pretty little sandals that offered her feet no support whatsoever and showed off her painted toenails.

When we got to the inevitable part where I whipped out my wallet and showed the pictures around, she studied Kathy's picture long and hard. "Nott badd," she said at last, clinically.

Gina, the girl who had brought me in from outside, had the most beautiful face, but she was obviously not interested in her looks. She planned to be a journalist, and showed me an article she had written, printed by one of the Kataebe magazines. I couldn't get much out of it, since it was in Arabic. I encouraged her though, and offered to send her some texts from the University of Arkansas bookstore when I got home.

I did so with reservations, because I liked her. All the newspaper people I have known in the States are burnt and bitter by 35, from too much coffee, booze, cigarettes, dinner from cardboard cartons, and marriages that don't work because of the above. Still, some people are suited to such work, and Gina didn't look like a potential housewife to me.

The youngest girl, Lida, interested me most. The whole time I was there she was smiling and laughing, but it was the sort of laugh you'd expect from your teen-age point man, terribly one-pointed, and a little crazy. She wore jeans, a none-too-fresh yellow T-shirt, and combat boots.

Later when I mentioned the three sisters to one of the guys, he said, "Oh, Lida. She's a fighter." He did not mean only that she had a lot of moxie. He meant that when the Palestinians came to town, she grabbed her AK and went into the line with the guys. Most women are not good for heavy work, and sometimes their presence creates havoc in the ranks, but there were plenty of them who could not be faulted for guts; Lida was one of those.

Several young men came through the communication center while I was there, and it was interesting to see how they and the girls handled each other. There was a lot of kidding, but it was all pointedly nonsexual. They treated the girls like comrades, who happened to be made of Dresden china.

Later I mentioned this to a lady in a fairly high staff position at Lebanese Forces headquarters. "Yes," she said, "the boys act like brothers...and like boys." From this I deduce that there is some hanky, but very little panky, unless the boy is dead serious. Every one of these girls has about forty big brothers to hammer into a bloody pulp anybody who does her wrong.

The girls were careful to make sure of my religious convictions. "Do you believe in Jesus?"

"Yes."

"Mary?"

"Yeah, sure."

"Do you like Lech Walesa?"

They took me on a walking tour of Hadath. One of the funniest and scariest things I have ever seen was Farrah, running through a sniper zone in those damned sandals.

They showed me the main street of Hadath, gutted and boarded up, their uncle's restaurant, gutted and boarded up, their parent's pharmacy, gutted and boarded up. "They want us to go to the mountains with them, but we want to help the fighters."

They showed me their church, a beautiful, modern structure, as modern as the one in Sodeco, and as badly shot up. They showed me the refugee families living in the church basement.

I wanted a shot of Farrah and one of the guys walking down the street, from the back, no faces. People are not much interested in rubble; they are interested in people. I wanted a human interest shot. Her eyes grew huge, and she flatly refused. I couldn't really blame her. If she were recognized crossing into West Beirut, she would be subject to arrest, interrogation, torture, rape and murder; not necessarily in that order, and, except for the first and last, not necessarily just once.

When Tony returned that afternoon, he and I went back over to his mortar emplacements, so I could take a few pictures of the way they were dug in. One of his artillerymen came out while I was shooting and went into a panic for fear I would give their position away. Tony assured him all would be well.

It was mid-afternoon by then, and Tony still hadn't had lunch. He drove to a small *patisserie* and we went inside. We each had a strawberry tart and a glass of milk. I remembered Asian LRRP rations with the Mike Force, and the famous ham-and-lima-bean popsicle from frozen Chosen. These tarts had an incredible, light flaky crust, and were surmounted by red, luscious strawberries that burst in your mouth like ecstasy bombs. The milk was so cold it crackled in your throat.

"I still can't get over this."

Tony shrugged. He had never tasted C-rations. "You have to eat," he said.

Tony was the biggest hero in Hadath. He practically had to browbeat the proprietor into taking money for the food.

We went back outside. Three teen-agers came walking slowly down the street. They walked slowly to give one of them, the girl, a break. She was pretty, almost as pretty as Farrah, but she walked with a bad limp, and wore an obvious above-the-knee prosthesis. The Syrians had blown her leg off.

I've seen a lot of dead men, and made a few, but none of them affected me like the sight of that pretty girl, who would never dance again, whose body would always hurt, who would never get to run for the Lebanese equivalent of homecoming queen.

Later that afternoon Sam came to take me back to the G-5 bureau. On the way I told him something I had in mind. "It sounds like a good idea to me," he said, "but I didn't expect it from a magazine."

"Well," I said, "you'd kind of have to know the magazine. It started out as a trade journal for mercenaries, but it's grown to be the unofficial magazine of the Combat-Arms Old-Boy Network, world-wide. Obviously you guys should be in it."

He and I sprinted up the stairs. I called Tim Leifield at Paladin Press and ordered $1,500 worth of demo and ranger manuals. Then I called Brown at *SOF.*

I had my spiel rehearsed. What I was going to suggest was going to cost him a fair amount of money. But, well, you have to know Brown.

"Robert, these are the good guys, and I think they have a chance to win." I was about to mention our larger duty to mankind, when he cut in. "Great! How can we help?"

"Well, I wouldn't want you to send a Military Training Team. Heaven forfend the thought. But I have a friend who is much better qualified to make a survey of Lebanese Forces technical innovations than I am. And, who knows, they might pick a few points up from him. He's the best small-unit leader I ever met. His leg's kind of gimped, but his brain works great."

"Who is he?"

"Name's Larry Dring. He's going to learn as much as he teaches. He's no journalist, but he's a great storyteller. We'll debrief him when he gets back, and get another good story out of it."

"Roger that!"

That was all it took. We talked for a minute more, and I hung up the phone.

Something had clicked in me. For a lot of years I had been like half a puzzle, looking for the other piece. I took the phone out of the bedroom, where I had gone for quiet, back out into the outer office, where eight or ten people were working, howling into telephones, poring over newspapers.

# 6

# A Night On The Town

One of the first things Sam did when I moved into the G-5 head-quarters was to show me a special phone. "On this phone," he said, "you can call anywhere in the world and talk as long as you want. It took me a while to get used to this idea, but finally, after I asked him several times, he said again, "Yes, really, any time you want, for as long as you want."

The guys in the G-5 section were in the habit of working very late, and they also did odd combat jobs, defending their neighborhoods, and Rick had hinted that they were running an effective psy-war operation against the Syrians, Palestinians and Mourabitoun, in West Beirut, and elsewhere. Usually they slept until eight or nine in the morning.

I got in the habit of getting up around seven and fixing myself a cup of coffee. Then I took the phone out on the balcony and called Kathy in Fayetteville. With the time difference, I'd catch her at midnight the night before. The air was still cool, so I'd sit there with my coffee and watch the sky shade in over the buildings, and listen to the first firefights of the morning.

Ordinarily we'd talk until the first of the G-5 guys got up. I'd give her a summary of the preceding day's events and assure her that I was still in one piece. She had signed up for two summer dance classes, and had broken a bone in her foot the week before I left. She needed some classes to graduate, so she was dancing in pain every day. I wanted reassurance that she wasn't killing herself. Finally, she would ring off to get some sleep before her eight o'clock class.

One morning Sam came out on the balcony with his first cup of hot, sweet, Turkish coffee, just as I started on my third. "How is Kathy?" he asked.

"I don't think she ought to be dancing on that foot," I said. "She's a smart girl, but she's got more guts than sense."

"Is she Lebanese?" He was kidding. He knew she was mostly Irish and English, and about an eighth Cherokee.

"No, but she might as well be."

We shot the breeze in a desultory way for a while. When we went back inside he said, "I want to show you something." In an inner office room he shook out the contents of a maroon cotton bag. Inside was a grab-bag collection of passports, driver's licenses, and other ID's from various Arab countries, Leftist countries, Muslim countries, from southern Africa, from Asia, from I.R.A. provos—an international bazaar of anti-Western types. "All of these are from people we have captured in combat," he said. "This is our 'Civil War.' Webster's defines civil war as one between citizens of the same country. Very seldom do we fight Lebanese, Muslims or not. Our war is with the Palestinians, whom we gave refuge, and who have taken over large parts of our country, and with the Syrians, who view Lebanon as a rebel province, and with these people." He shuffled the mound of documents. "I asked one of these people why he was here. He said, 'To fight the Zionists.' Do I look like a Zionist?"


That afternoon Fouad carefully nosed the Land Rover around a herd of goats. They ran bleating to get out of his way. The herdsmen scarcely looked up as we passed. Even in this Christian area of the Sannine mountains, the herdsmen wore the Lebanese hillbilly costume; burnoose, a white shirt and black trousers, tight at the calf, but baggier than any other trousers I have ever seen.

Below us the road twisted downward. Around us, mountains dived steeply, flattened into a wide valley far below, and climbed sharply back up through row on row of gray-rock mountains, sparsely vegetated, beautiful, climbing into snow-capped peaks.

Fouad, a Lebanese Forces nurse, Claude du Plessis, and I had left

Beirut early that morning. We had been driving for more than two hours. Fouad, the Lebanese Forces Information Officer, is a man about my size, six-two, weighing 190 to 195 pounds. His powerful shoulders were a trifle stooped from hours over the books; he was a lawyer in civilian life, with both Lebanese and French degrees. The Lebanese nurse sat quietly. She wore fatigues, boots and a bush hat and held her aid bag in her lap.

Next to her was Claude, photographer for a French news service, who had even less English than I had French. We had shared a room for several days, but I barely knew him, since we couldn't talk to one another. He was taller than I and about twenty pounds lighter. He wore his frizzy brown hair almost shoulder length and smoked Gitanes incessantly. Around the bureau he wore strange-looking French-made cowboy boots, but he had put on combat boots for this job, and wore jeans, a black T-shirt, and an old safari jacket with the sleeves cut off, pockets jammed with film.

After another half-hour's drive, we came to a stop in a little shaded grove of trees, under which a couple of tents and some poncho lean-tos had been set up. Three or four Lebanese Forces fighters sat around, cleaning weapons, smoking, drinking coffee. We got out of the car. Fouad spoke to one of the fighters, who disappeared into the tent. He came out a second or so later, bringing with him the first bum I had seen in Lebanon: a small, bleary-eyed man with a three-day stubble, his face slick with sweat. He wore a dirty white T-shirt, and his left arm was missing from two inches below the elbow.

"This is Michel," Fouad said. "He is commander of this outpost." Michel looked sullenly at me, then extended his hand. We shook. My right hand is brittle and wasted because the arm is missing two nerves and an artery, a wound from an RPD automatic rifle. The hand looks okay, if you don't look too close, but a lot of meat has withered off it. The last time I broke it, it wasn't set properly and the bones meet at a jagged angle.

Michel's right hand, however, was incredibly strong, since he had to do everything with it. He grabbed my hand in a bone-crushing grip.

I tried to keep a straight face and ignore the pain. He noticed that my hand didn't feel right and dropped it.

He spoke briefly to Fouad, in French, and disappeared into the tent.

"He apologizes for his appearance," said Fouad. "He was out all night on an operation."

I started to ask for a description of the operation but restrained myself. Michel was obviously a soldier to the core; if he had been out all night and slept all morning, he hadn't told the tale yet, and it would come rolling out of him in due course, probably sooner than later.

Michel popped back out of the tent, wearing his fatigue shirt. He expertly flipped a patrol harness over his shoulders. It was put together from Russian gear, and the ammo pouches were smaller than ours. His M-16 had an extra-long sling, which he draped around his neck, so the weapon hung about where Elvis used to wear his guitar.

We got back in the Land Rover. Michel took the nurse's place, and the vehicle headed into the mountains. It was all barren rock up there, with not a sign of cover. Fouad drove, keeping the mountain between us and the Syrian positions on the next ridge line over. The Land Rover rumbled and lurched over the rocks. Michel directed him to pull into a concealed position between two fingers of bare rock, and we got out and started humping. I was glad I lived in the Ozarks as we pounded up the steep trail, but even so, I was breathing like a bellows to keep up.

At last we came to a shallow depression in the rock, just big enough to hold a small tent. A squad of troops was living in it. Three or four of them sat around outside. "The men who were with me last night are sleeping inside," Michel said in English. He had a very heavy French accent.

"What was that operation?"

"We mine the Syrian positions."

"What?"

"It is maybe one and one-half kilometers to the Syrian positions, but it takes three hours to walk there. Then we go to the road maybe fifty meters from their positions and plant the bouncing-betty mines in the road."

"How many men did you take with you?"

"Six, but for the last fifty meters to plant the mines, only me and one other."

Michel led us further up the mountain to an observation post at the very peak. "Stay close to the rock here," he said as we went up. "They shoot the rocket every time they see anyone move." I hugged the rock, snuggled right up to it.

At the peak we four squeezed ourselves into a tiny perch behind a rock that gave us three feet of cover. Except for Michel we were all big men, and Claude and I both had big camera bags as well.

"You must take off your glasses," Michel said to me. "They will shoot at the glare."

"These are prescription shades," I insisted. "If I take them off, I can't see at all."

He favored me with a look that is cultivated, but seldom achieved by all the world's drill instructors.

"Got any tape?" I inquired. "I can cut about 90 percent of the glare by taping the outer edges."

Without a word he took his canteen out and made a tiny mud puddle at my feet. I daubed mud on the outer edges of my glasses. Not as good as tape, but it ought to help.

While I was doing this, Claude shot pictures with his long lens. Then I looked over the top of the rock, moving slowly. Over the next ridge line I could see a dirt road S-curving along the ridge, but I couldn't see any tracked vehicles or personnel.

For a moment I wished the Syrians would shell. I wanted some action for my story. Then I felt guilty. These kids got shelled almost every day. I didn't want one of them killed or wounded just so I could write about it.

I snapped a couple of shots, but there really wasn't anything to shoot, and I didn't have a telephoto lens, even if there had been. After that, we crept back down to the tent. Some of the guys who had been out with Michel on his raid the night before were awake.

They sat on top of this barren rock for a week at a time, getting shelled almost every day, and still they were laughing and joking. I really liked those kids.

I had worn fatigues, and they wanted to know whether I was an Israeli. To a man they fervently wished for an Israeli intervention.

One of them, a slender, good-looking young man, came up and said, "Hi!"

"Hello!"

"You ever been to Dallas?"

"Sure," I replied, in amazement. His English was almost as good as Rick's. "How do you know Dallas?"

"I worked there for two years. I was a flight instructor."

I grinned. "How'd you like it?"

"Great!" he grinned back. "I like the pushover." He put the accent on the second syllable.

I laughed and shook my head. "So why are you here?"

He shrugged. "My country is at war."

That must have been some decision. A young man can have a good time in Dallas, Texas.

"So why are you here on this rock?"

He shrugged. "We have no airplanes."

Nobody made him do this. He had left one of the good-time centers of the world, and paid his own way back to risk his life, to squat on this barren rock.

I decided to see exactly how far this went. "What'll you do after this is over, stay in Lebanon or go back to Dallas?"

He shrugged. "I'll probably have to go back to Dallas. There aren't enough flying students in Lebanon."

"What's your name?"

"Roger."

That's the only name in the Lebanon chapters I haven't changed, but since, in my short time in Lebanon I met five Rogers, it's not much of a risk. So, to all the girls in Dallas, Roger says, "hello."

Fouad, Michel and Claude were ready to go back down the mountain, so I said good-by to Roger. We walked with a good interval between each of us, pausing at Michel's CP to drop him off and share a cup of coffee with the folks there.

Then we wound down the mountain, and the traffic and the civilian population picked up. Fouad got on the CB radio mounted under the dash, probably telling them that we were coming in. I'm not sure because he spoke in Arabic. But a few English words had come into general use in Lebanon, and I was able to pick them out.

There were some significant differences in American and Lebanese radio procedure: Instead of "Roger," he said, "Okay," and instead of "Out," he said, "Bye-bye."

When I mentioned this to him later, he said, "Well, we must still laugh."

I thought I had seen some driving in Lebanon before, but Fouad was the prince of kamikazes. Once we reached the Jounieh-Beirut Highway, traveling an entire city block without four near-collisions counted as a breathing space. He used the horn and he had a siren. He also had a complete inventory of hand gestures for any other driver who got in his way. I was only familiar with one of them, but none seemed complimentary.

Travel on the shoulder of the road, where there was one, was routine. Once, when traffic on our side of the road jammed up, he unhesitatingly jumped the center island and ran three blocks in the left-hand lane, traveling at sixty miles an hour and shaking his fist at oncoming drivers if they didn't get out of the way fast enough to suit him.

"Listen," I said, as laconically as I could manage under the circumstances, "if you're looking for work after the war, I can probably get you a job driving in Burt Reynolds' movies."

He smiled, hit the siren and accelerated into a space two feet narrower than the Land Rover.

Because of the Palestinians' tendency to take their war with them wherever they go, Rick advised me to do my article under an assumed name, and not to do the interview Fouad had set up for me with the Lebanese Forces paper.

We were talking about it out on the balcony, over a Coke. "I don't see how it can cause a problem," I said. "They're not going to use my name in the interview. It's just that Fouad thinks a pat on the back from a former Green Beret major would be good for morale."

"I don't like it," Rick said. "I just don't like it."

Sam said nothing, but he looked glum.

The young lady who conducted the interview was very polite, as was her interpreter, a young man. We sat at Fouad's antique dining table in his apartment across the street from the press bureau. It was a beautiful apartment, except for a couple of shrapnel cracks in the smoked glass mirror on the wall by the coffee table and some rents in the sofa from the same source.

The first thing the interviewers asked about was the quality of their troops, which I couldn't praise highly enough.

Then they asked me whether I thought they could win, and if so, how?

I responded that, like them, I was a Christian, and that I believed both in prayer and miracles. And on a more practical level, I knew of no historical case of an army with true spirit losing a defensive war to one that lacked it.

Last, they asked me why I was involved in their cause on a personal level.

"Well," I replied, "I once had a friend, a very close friend. He and I fought together, off and on, for ten years. When the United States pulled out of Cambodia, he was a major in the Cambodian army. I have reliable information that he and his wife and three little boys were executed in the street out in front of the French embassy. I guess I've just seen enough of that stuff."

There was another reason I took this action, which, for a journalist trained to be "objective", seems unprofessional. Before I went to Lebanon, I didn't know anything about the war there. But as a veteran, it had been my habit to read everything that appeared in the papers about combat anywhere. I couldn't make any sense out of what I read about Lebanon.

As it happened, the entire Beirut press corps lived in the Commodore Hotel, located in West Beirut. The hotel was Palestinian owned, and that part of the city was under the control of the Syrians. Almost the entire Mideast was covered from there. While I was in Lebanon, the Israelis bombed the nuclear reactor in Iraq, and things were hopping in Iran, but it was relatively quiet in Beirut itself.

For the entire time I was in Lebanon, I lived in the Lebanese Forces Press Bureau. I did not see another American in that time, much less another American reporter. Sure, they were busy, but for twelve days they didn't cover one side of the war they were in the middle of. On the 2nd of August of that year, the Denver *Post* printed a story by Michael Kennedy of the Los Angeles *Times*. He wrote, "Syrian soldiers peer into each passing car as it passes. Often the Syrians ask for passports and want to know where the passengers are going. 'I told them, we are going to the port,' the driver said. 'You do not tell them you are going to the other (Christian) side.'"

Well, if you couldn't tell them you were going to the other side, what do you suppose would have happened to any reporter who told the true story of what was happening and tried to maintain his residence in the Commodore? People disappeared over there all the time, and at that time seven of them had been journalists. A guy from ABC was killed just after I left. Nobody knew why; he was just dead.

What do you suppose would happen to anybody who wrote that the Syrian so-called, "Arab Deterrent Force", was sanctioned by the Arab League to conquer Lebanon in order to hold down Lebanese fighting the Palestinian "state within a state," thereby freeing Palestinians to fight the Israelis?

You couldn't really blame the reporters. Most of them were locked into their assignments for a number of years. Many had established themselves as Middle East "experts." They'd all be out of business if they couldn't go into or even pass through an Arab country without fear of assassination. So nobody covered the Christian side, and nobody covered the story of why they couldn't cover the Christian side. There was no possibility of objective journalism in Lebanon. The only honest thing to do was announce your bias and drive on. That was what I was doing.

We had lunch after the interviewers had gone. In the kitchen, Celeste, Fouad's lady, a wonderfully sweet, zaftig young woman, had supervised their Ceylonese maid's cooking. The results were perfection.

"This is delicious," I said, over the main dish, a light fluffy meat. It was like nothing I'd ever eaten before. "What is it?"

"Lamb's brains," Fouad said, rolling both the l's and the r's.

Amazing. I ate them with relish.

After lunch he asked me whether I'd like to see some training. I was feeling a little heavy, but I was eager to see Lebanese Forces' techniques. Dreading the ride and the sun, I got up and reached for my camera bag.

"Where are you going?"

"Training."

"Let's watch it on television," he said. "It's easier that way."

We went into the living room, and he slipped a cassette into his video cassette recorder. Celeste brought us coffee and we watched training for an hour.

Their training aid for street fighting interested me most. They had filled stacks of old tires with dirt and made a corridor out of them, representing a street, alley, or hallway, with openings for doors. Squads of ten were sent down the passageway, a squadleader and three 3-man fire teams. The fire teams leapfrogged down the hallway, while the squad leader covered their back and directed traffic. As a team approached a door, one man lobbed a grenade in; then, with the fireteam leader covering their backs, and watching their squad leader, two men entered the door, one fanning a burst sweeping left, and the other right. They were as smooth as a well-drilled basketball team.

It was Claude's last evening in Lebanon and Sam and Rick asked me to join them and Christine in giving him a rousing send-off.

Since both Rick's and Sam's apartments were right on the Green Line, they and Christine had rented another place a few miles from the center of the city. We were to meet there for drinks before dinner. It was about six-thirty when Sam drove Claude and me to the apartment. Rick and Christine were just getting out of the shower when we arrived. Rick greeted us at the door, wearing old grey cords, his hair still slicked back and wet. Christine ran down the hall to the bedroom in an old terry robe, toweling her hair as she went.

"Fix yourselves a drink," Rick said. "We'll be out in a minute."

I spotted a cassette player and a box of tapes on top of a huge white drawing board with a matching artist's lamp clamped to it, beside the bar. Going over Rick's albums I discovered we had about a seventy-percent overlap in musical taste. I put Jackson Browne's *Running on Empty* on the player, with *Workingman's Dead* in reserve.

Sam, meanwhile, was fixing our drinks. We had all asked for Arak. I took mine and mellowed down onto a stack of big cushions behind a low coffee table.

Rick was dressed and out in a few minutes; Christine took a while longer. While we waited, Sam showed Claude and me his new AK. It was a Czech model, and some parts of the receiver were aluminum. He told me the stock was a laminated plywood that had been test-boiled at 4,000 degrees without coming apart.

"Do you want to see those pictures?" Rick asked. I had forgotten what pictures he meant. "The little girls?"

"Yes."

Christine came in, smashing in a white silk suit and open-collared shirt. She had been hiding great legs under her jeans. She wore heels held on by tiny little straps.

"They're pretty rough," he said.

I held out my hand.

He handed me a flimsy 8 1/2 x 11 envelope. I slid the 8 x 10 glossies out of it.

"I'm sorry," Christine said, choosing her English words carefully. She had already seen them, and knew what I was feeling. Two little girls, about six and seven, had been caught in a rocket attack. In death their expressions were sweet, as though they were sleeping, but their tiny bodies were ripped and torn in a dozen places. The six-year-old's foot lay beside her body.

"Nobody will print them," Rick said.

"Brown will," I replied. Rick promised me copies, but he never brought them, and I never pressed it. On the one hand, we both wanted every civilized person in the world to have his nose rubbed in the reality of Lebanon. On the other, none of us wanted death junkies drooling over those photos. Let the little girls have their peace.

Rick took the photos back. Sam had put his new AK up and was seated by the window, a drink tilted at a 45 degree angle in his hand, long gone in his thousand yard stare. I watched him for a long time. He did not move. For perhaps the tenth time in the week I'd been there, it struck me that this man had stayed too long at the fair. If he didn't get a chance to go off and get his head straight pretty soon, he was going to zone out in the middle of a firefight, and that would be it for old Sam.

Rick caught my look and winked. He knew what the deal was with Sam; that was why he kept him laughing. It seemed to be one of his major goals, to make Sam laugh everyday, reading over his shoulder, jiving in a fake Mexican accent, "I keel for money, Sahm, but you my fran'; I keel you for notheeng."

You had to be there.

We strolled into the restaurant they had chosen for Claude's farewell party. We contrasted unfavorably with the other patrons. The men wore suits, the expertly coifed women—exquisite designer clothes. Christine was the only one of us who looked like she belonged there.

Claude looked like a French Hell's Angel, Rick's pants were ripped about half an inch in the crotch, and a handy-talkie crackled in his right hip-pocket. He had shaved off the scruffy beard, however, and looked like the young Turk in the Camel ad. After a week in the same clothes, a khaki safari suit I had picked up at Harrod's in London on the way over, was growing a trifle funky. But Sam looked great, obsessively neat, huge eyes, beard and crewcut. He wore sandals, tailored khaki pants and a loose black shirt with a mandarin collar. He was very quiet, and could have been anything from a mad monk to a tong killer.

We elected to eat outdoors, where chairs and tables had been set up under red canopies, high on a hilltop overlooking the bay. We could see the lights of the city climbing toward the mountaintops.

The view was breathtaking, the crowd around us sophisticated, and the meal one of the best I have ever eaten.

The conversation was U-shaped. Claude and Christine spoke little English. I speak little French. Rick and Sam had to relay any conversation between the three of us. It was embarrassing. Even our waiter spoke perfect French, English and Arabic.

Claude told a great story about two Legion officers in North Africa who made a bet that they would finish their dinner on the verandah of their club, even though a firefight was raging across it. While each was brave enough to sit through it while they ate, neither was anxious to linger over coffee and a cigarette, and it was only with the greatest of difficulty that the waiter could be coaxed into pouring more wine. They both won the bet, but neither ordered dessert.

Rick asked me what I thought the Americans would do if we were confronted with the same situation as the Lebanese. I replied that we were much alike, and I thought we would do about the same.

One of the things I had noticed was that the cream of Lebanese Forces, including Rick, Fouad, and Christine, came from the same socio-economic stratum of Lebanon which, in America, had furnished most of the opposition to the Vietnam War. I don't think that these folks are any better or braver than their American equivalents; they just face harsher circumstances.

It was fairly late when we finished dinner, and Sam had an early call, so he went on home. But Rick said he had something that Claude and I must see. We drove back down the mountain and into the city. We drove past all the neighborhoods I was familiar with, and closer to the sound of AK fire. Finally we parked about one street over from a firefight. Claude and I both had a difficult time unfolding out of the back of Rick's VW.

Christine was already far enough ahead of us that her white suit was disappearing into the gloom. *"Allez, Messieurs!"* she called. Claude and I finally got out, popped the joints in our knees, restored the circulation in our feet and followed.

With Christine in the lead, she and Rick turned the corner toward the firefight. Claude and I exchanged glances. I was certain that Rick would never expose Christine to unnecessary danger, but they had just turned a corner down a street where bullets were actually flying.

We turned the corner. The street bent slightly. As long as we stayed within eighteen inches of the building wall we were okay, but rounds were snapping past our ears in the street. It was sort of like driving in the right-hand lane on a crowded two-lane highway. As long as you don't stray over the line you're okay, but death lies a few inches to the left.

Rick reached in his pocket and produced a set of keys, fiddling with the lock before opening a door in the wall we were pressed up against. We all crowded through, and he locked it from inside. The smell was musty and I could vaguely tell we were in a large room, but what the...Rick flipped on the light. At first my view was blocked by a large hanging plant. I stepped around it. To my left a long bar ran the length of the room. Straight ahead were a couch and two chairs facing each other over an Oriental rug and a coffee table. To the right was a dance floor, surrounded by similar conversational groupings of furniture, not standard night-club furniture, but furniture lovingly selected. In one place the coffee table was an ancient, hand-carved marvel, worth many thousands in the States; in another the coffee table was an old GI foot locker. The hanging plants were everywhere. The ceiling was an ancient stone arrangement of arches. It looked like what you'd expect to find in the cellar of a monastery. A direct hit upstairs wouldn't even make it quiver.

Rick grinned, obviously delighted. "It's my nightclub," he said. "It's called the Living Room. It's where we used to come to get away from the war, but now the back door opens onto the line." It was interesting to know that the back door opened onto Palestinian positions, and that anyone attempting to leave that way would be instantly gunned down. Especially since we'd had to skulk down the alley with rounds snapping past our ear to get in the front.

Rick zipped around us and turned on more lights. "What'll it be, ladies and gents?" he laughed. "On the house." We gave him our orders and he got busy behind the bar.

He and Christine spoke to each other in French for a moment and laughed. Then Christine, Claude and I took our drinks and sat down, facing one another across a coffee table. I sank into the comfortable chair with a big grin on my face.

Christine actually understood quite a bit of English, but was not used to speaking it. She sat for a long moment, rehearsing the question in her mind, then turned to me and smiled warmly. "Do you like your life?"

"Yes, very much," I replied.

"You are happee man?"

"Yes."

"Gude." She sank back into the couch and drank.

Rick, meanwhile, had been fiddling around with the sound system. I heard the opening strains of a familiar piece of music that I couldn't quite place. Then I recognized it, the music from the movie musical *All That Jazz*. Just as I recognized it, I heard the *crump-crump* of incoming mortars somewhere upstairs. It was very faint, but with that ceiling it could have just as easily been a direct hit on the building we were in. I really don't think anybody else noticed it. Christine turned to me, smiled and spoke.

Her voice is high, flute-like, and when she speaks French it is difficult to remember it is a regular language, designed for communication, and not simply music. The harsh Saxon syllables of English do not give the same effect, but her accent was still charming. Just as the mortars slammed in upstairs, she grinned and spoke the line that serves as a signature and recurring theme for *All That Jazz*: "It's showtime, folks!"

It was about four in the morning when Rick brought Claude and me home. Nazih, the bleary-eyed young man who opened the door, looked at me in amazement. "You are going to the range with Fouad at five-thirty," he said. Ah, well, under no circumstances would I have wanted to miss the party at Rick's club, and this wouldn't be the first day of training I had gutted after a night without sleep. I went to shower and change.

As we rode out of town in Fouad's carryall, a few joggers loped through the blasted early morning streets. It had been more than a week since I had run, and I was feeling my chest start to slide down to my belly. I decided to get back into it. I was beginning to be able to find my way around, and I trusted myself to run a couple of miles without fear of turning a corner into a Palestinian position.

The ride to the range passed in a blur. On the way I told Fouad that I was eager to fire the AK. Over the few days I had known Fouad, he had mentioned a long list of mostly Soviet weapons used by both sides in this war—the Soviets supplied the Leftists through Syria, as they did in most Communist insurgencies, and the Rightists bought them from the enemy. I had to confess that, although I had been shot at by most of them, I had never fired them.

"Sometimes it seems as though you have never fired a weapon in your life," he said.

I laughed. "I was an advisor in Vietnam. My weapons were flattery and blackmail."

The range was in the mountains on the way to Michel's position. When we arrived the other car was already there. In it were Michel, who had rotated his platoon back in for a week's rest, Nazih, who was the G-5 treasurer, and Toufik, another young man in the office. Toufik looked like a young Omar Sharif, and played the role to the hilt, smoking his cigarettes in an ivory holder. He was deadly serious, however, when there was a job to be done.

Fouad had brought his own FAL, and an M2 carbine for me. There was a decal of the Virgin Mary on the stock of my weapon.

Michel and Toufik both had M16s. Michel had switched to the 16 after he lost half of his left arm at Tall Zaatar. To fire, he laid the plastic guard that covered the barrel over the stub of his elbow. He was deadly accurate.

Toufik professed to genuinely like the M16, although few others did. Sam had said, "If you think the M16 is prone to jam in the jungle, wait until you get some sand in it." Nazih had a brand new AK he had bought, and also a P38 pistol.

The range at first appeared to be an improvisation; in fact, it didn't look like a range at all, but merely a place guys could go to plink a few rounds. I suspect that was how it had started; then it was gradually modified as training required. None of the modifications involved anything like a conventional target, either bull's-eye or silhouette. We stood on a small raised area, a natural platform that looked across a small valley. Some hills formed a natural backstop about 500 meters to our front. Between us and the hills, at 200 meters, a zigzag trench had been dug for defensive problems; at 100 meters were three little hillocks, maybe two dump-truck loads of rock and gravel each. Fouad looked around, found a Coke can, took it and put it on top of one of them. When he came back, we began to fire.

I didn't know if my weapon was zeroed or not, so I started firing aimed shots into the dirt bank. The dirt seemed to be flying pretty much where I was aiming, but I fired six rounds just to make sure. Then I shifted my attention to the Coke can and popped it off the berm on the second round.

"Who hit it?" Michel asked.

"Morris." Toufik said.

Michel looked at me in obvious annoyance. "We were firing like this," he said, jamming the weapon into his hip. "It was a game."

They were all firing either from the hip, or with the buttplate jammed right into the solar plexus, just below the belt buckle. "Oops, sorry!"

They set another can up, and we went back to firing from the hip, to no discernible effect.

I had a run with Nazih's new AK. He had no sling, so I fired it from the hip. It was a great weapon, accurate and easy to handle.

I had not fired a weapon of any sort in about three years, but I upheld the honor of *Soldier of Fortune* and the United States. Only

Fouad and Michel outshot me, and then it was close.

"Here, try it with this," Fouad said, and handed me his FAL. I packed it into my hip to fire a three-round burst into the dirt bank, just to see where it might hit.

"Try it this way," Fouad said. His FAL had an extra-long sling. He draped it around my neck. I started to switch the right side of the strap over my shoulder, but he stopped me.

"Here," he said, and jammed the buttplate into my groin. "Let the sling support the weight of the weapon. Just use your left hand to keep it from rising. Don't look at the weapon; look at what you want to hit. Shift your point of aim by shifting your body, not the weapon."

"Okay," I shrugged, and squeezed off a three-round burst. I failed to observe the bullet's strike due to extreme pain, and decided to move the buttplate a couple of inches higher.

The technique was deadly effective. Whatever I was looking at exploded into flying rocks and gravel when I squeezed the trigger. It was as fast, and three times as effective, as firing from the hip, and critical seconds faster than firing a well-aimed shot. For hitting a man out to a hundred meters on full auto, it was deadly.

I was feeling a bit smug about my shooting when Fouad asked us to cease firing for a moment. As soon as we did he took off running in a zigzag diagonal across the front of those hillocks we were shooting at. Going at a dead run, he crossed their front from about 50 meters out. His first round was about six inches out, but after that he put a three-round burst from the FAL into an area about 18 inches square in the center of mass of each of those little hillocks, firing from the hip. It was the most impressive display of combat shooting I have ever seen.

After we quit firing, the others went back to Beirut, but Fouad wanted to show me something up in the mountains, so off we went.

On the way I asked him where he had learned to shoot like that. He said he had learned at the Lebanese Forces Commando Course, so I started asking questions and comparing that course with the U.S. Ranger School. They are quite different. Much of the Ranger course is designed to put pressure on the student to see how he will stand up under the stress of combat. No one went to the LF Commando Course until he had at least a year of combat.

I mentioned that in the U.S. Army one of the most prized awards is the Combat Infantryman's Badge. Fouad laughed. "I think that in Lebanon everybody would have ten of these medals."

The Ranger School also emphasizes land navigation in all types of terrain, and being able to subsist for days on few rations, while moving in the swamps, or the mountains of Georgia. The Lebanese Commando is operating in his own back yard. His six-week course is all physical training, tactical problems, and range-firing on all types of weapons, under simulated combat conditions.

Fouad pulled the Land Rover into a line of military vehicles parked in front of what appeared to be, and in fact was, a ski lodge. "There is a commando company here," he said, "and some support troops. Would you like to talk to some of the boys?"

Of course, and we went inside. He checked in with the executive officer of the company, an old friend of his. Actually, he kicked him out of bed. Since it was eleven in the morning I assumed he had been up all night on an exercise of some sort.

We stepped out on the balcony outside of his room and, immediately, I was surrounded by grinning teenagers in fatigues. The one who spoke the best English was an 18-year-old squad leader who had been fighting for three years. He said he was trying to finish high school so he could study electrical engineering in the States.

I asked him how long he had known the boys in his squad, and he seemed puzzled. Finally I found out he had known them all his life; they were the kids he grew up with. He was their leader now because he had been their leader in kindergarten.

Another kid, a tall, smiling boy, wanted to show me his rocket-propelled grenade launcher. On the side of its receiver it had been stamped: "Made by Fateh." Fateh is the largest group in the PLO, Yasser Arafat's group.

"How did you get that?" I demanded.

He shrugged and grinned. "Killed two Palestinians."

Fouad took me to lunch with the command group of the company. The company commander was new, recently promoted from second-in-command of another company. He was a short man with a mustache, built like a fireplug, whose arm muscles stretched the sleeves of his T-shirt. Lunch was informal, in the commander's room, with guys sitting in chairs and on the bed.

There was none of the joking and laughing I'd seen with the kids upstairs. All conversation was in Arabic, so I didn't know what was discussed, but their voices were low and the silences long. Although one or two men were moving in the room more or less continuously, bringing messages or scooping up homuz with pita, I never heard a step or a shuffle. This was the most silent group of men I'd ever met. A black T-shirt was part of their uniform, frequently imprinted with their blood type in red over the heart. One wore an exact copy of *Soldier of Fortune's* Rhodesian Army T-shirt, except the logo on this one read, "Be a man among men. Join the Kataebe Army." I tried to get one, but found they had been made in '76 and were prized possessions of those who had them.

On the way back, when we entered the city, we saw a pall of smoke rising from the center island of the boulevard we were on. "Hmmm," said Fouad, "it looks as though there has been some shelling." He hit the ramp to switch to another traffic artery. There was a long string of cars going the other way. "It is very hot," he said. "Everybody is going to the beach."

The day after he came out of the mountains, which was the day after Claude went back to France, Michel moved into the room with me. "I must get my rest," he said. There was a steady traffic of beautiful women there to see Michel during the day, and most nights I had the room to myself.

Once I got up early for my run, and there was a knock at the door. I opened it and there stood the most beautiful girl I saw in Lebanon. *"Ou est Michel?"* she demanded. She had the face of an angel, and a stunning body. I sighed and went to wake Michel up. They were both gone when I got back from my run.

But he was there a lot during the day. He stayed at the press bureau even though he had an apartment with a live-in girlfriend in town. Maybe that was the problem; the live-in didn't like the nights out.

I had already stayed longer than intended, but I wanted to be in Lebanon when Larry arrived, to brief him. Michel and Larry were already talking over the phone. Michel wanted him to bring some ammo pouches for the "M-seize." He was always fiddling with his gear, trying different placements of ammo pouches, knives. He rigged a hook on his left shoulder harness so he could throw grenades with one hand. He wanted M16 pouches primarily for the grenade retainer snaps on the side. His Russian pouches didn't have them, so he had to carry another pouch or two, just for grenades. He also wanted 30-round magazines.

Once he got his gear tricked out in a new way, he tried it on and jumped up and down to make sure it didn't rattle. If it did, he took it off, fiddled with it some more and tried it again.

Michel was a great fighter, and although I had sworn never again to go straphanging, I figured he was one guy you could go into the gulf with. You might buy it, but if you did, it wouldn't be because somebody screwed up and left you hanging.

I really wanted to go on a raid. I've been on night ambushes, heliborne assaults, search and destroys, blind stupid charges, blocking actions, encirclements, recons, recons in force, and even a sort of ricky-tick combat jump. But I have always considered the commando raid to be the ultimate military operation. Go in quick, make your snatch or blow your objective, shoot the hell out of everything and everybody, and get the fuck out.

I knew I had passed some sort of test on the range that day, but it was one they had almost hoped I would fail.

"Well, Jim, I cannot go whenever I want. I must go when they order."

I knew that. I knew it probably wouldn't happen. But for a day or so there I actually had myself convinced it might. I got myself psyched all the way up to that very pure adrenalin high. I could almost feel that green paint on my face. Once more I was looking down that long red tunnel, free and at peace.

"Jim, you should know," he said. "If you are wounded in the assault, I cannot carry you out, and I cannot let you be captured. I cannot even let them find your body. We do not want them to think you are *le mercenaire*. I must destroy you."

"How are you going to do that? One hundred and ninety-five pounds of dead caucasian is difficult to disintegrate instantaneously."

He shook his head. "No, no, no, no."

"Oh, come on, Michel. I'm a big boy. How can you do that?"

He really didn't want to tell me, but I insisted. He looked at the floor, sort of guiltily. "I would put a *grenade* in your mouth."

I must confess that gave me pause.

"It is very dangerous," he said. "You shoot well, but you do not know the terrain, you would not know well your equipment."

There it was. I was a danger not only to myself, but to his patrol, and to the mission. The last thing in the world he needed was an unknown factor.

The real problem, for me, was that, while I had the right to risk my own life, I didn't feel I had the right to increase the risk to the patrol. My own best military judgment was that I should back off. "Besides, I would waste a *grenade*," he said.

I laughed. "Well, Jesus Christ," I shot back. "Will you let me go if I pay for the grenade?"

We finally agreed on a compromise, in which I'd go with his fire-support team, and I'd watch the action, if any, from beside a machine gun on an overlooking hill. If it was a mine-planting expedition there'd probably be nothing to see. Finally, I had three days before my boat left. Not enough time to prepare, even if he got a warning order. Maybe next time I'd have time to go through the commando course, and things would be different.

No action. There had been an Arab foreign ministers' conference going on over in West Beirut, almost from the day I arrived. "I don't like it, Jim. It's too quiet, too quiet." Michel stood on the balcony, beating on his thigh with his fist. I had seen everything there was to see and interviewed nearly everybody in Lebanese Forces who spoke English. Still there was no action. All I was doing was waiting for Larry Dring to arrive, or my boat, whichever came first.

Then came that familiar high, shrieking whistle. I hadn't heard that sound since March 1986, but I wasn't the last guy to hit the deck, in this case the checkered tile under the dining room table. It went over us and killed two women and a man a mile further east. It was in the papers the next morning.

That evening I was alone in the apartment when Youssef, a young man in the political section, ran frantically into the apartment, and stared wildly about the room.

"What's up?" I demanded, bounding from my chair, thinking, *action at last!*

"*Starsky and Hutch*," he cried, and bolted for the TV.

# 7

# The Birthday Party

We drove north through Jounieh and along some beautiful Mediterranean coastline, through another town or two, and then into one I had a hard time believing was real. A row of buildings lined the road, but what buildings! If they hadn't been lined up in regular rows, I'd have thought they were caves. They appeared to have been made of brick daubed with mud, centuries before. "Jesus!" I exclaimed.

"This is Byblos," Sam explained. "It's the oldest continuously inhabited town on Earth. The alphabet was invented here, writing as we know it. As in Bible and bibliography...Byblos."

I nodded, awed. "The oldest building in Oklahoma, where I grew up, is about a hundred years old." Then I remembered Sequoyah's cabin, a log cabin in eastern Oklahoma, carefully preserved as part of a state park. In that cabin Sequoyah, whom the whites had called George Guess, had devised the Cherokee syllabary, an 87-character alphabet which was so clear and logical that a person who spoke the language could go from total illiteracy to complete literacy in two weeks. I thought of Sequoyah's gentle face, the eyes burning with intelligence, long-stemmed pipe in his mouth, loose Cherokee turban on his head, in my seventh-grade history book, and later the original oil painting in the rotunda of the state capitol.

For an instant, even though I don't know the Cherokee language, and have not a drop of Indian blood, I felt like a connecting link between those long-ago scholars in Byblos and their spiritual kinsman in the old part of the New World. I had, after all, come here to find something to write about.

Sam turned left, off the highway and around a large outcropping of rock. Down past a winding road was a typical Mediterranean resort restaurant, called Byblos-sur-Mer. The sea crashed over rocks on the other side of the parking lot.

Several cars were drawn up by a dock, and families were unloading picnic boxes, ice chests, styrofoam chests, straw picnic baskets. The women were dressed in bikinis, dresses, jeans. The men wore LF uniforms, jeans, or those unbelievably gross European bathing suits. The men also carried a spectrum of light armament, M-16's, AK's and a variety of pistols. A guy in one of those bathing suits bent over to pick up an ice chest; the outline of the .45 tucked into the waistband of his bathing suit, barrel nestling between the cheeks of his buttocks, was thrust into startling relief. One of the shoelaces on his Adidas sneakers had come loose and was dragging through the dirt in the parking lot.

Sam, who was in uniform, turned me over to a boatload of people, about a family and a half, and went away to do things concerning security. I helped them load the boat, which was long and narrow, sort of like a pirogue, driven by a small outboard motor. One of the bathing suit guys started the engine and we headed out into the Med, spray crashing over the bow. Out at sea the sun was setting and a pastel orange glow lay atop the dark green of the horizon. The boat crashed through the waves for quite some distance, to a small rocky island. I don't know how far it was from shore, but it was further than an RPG could fire. The party would be undisturbed.


I spent a couple of minutes helping unload the boat, but after that I was no help at all. The folks I was with knew what was to be done, but none of them spoke English, and it was more trouble than it was worth to tell me what to do by gesture. I watched for a while, and then wandered over to the sunset side of the island and gazed at all the subtle colors streaming across the sky; cerise, mauve, chartreuse, orangy-pinks, and deep blazing reds that hinted of blood. I sat on a jagged chunk of black rock and watched that Wurlitzer of a sunset, thinking about the sunsets west of Norman, Oklahoma, where it's flat, and there aren't many clouds, and the air is full of dust for the light to reflect from. It's the best show in town.

In all my travels I had never encountered another so vivid until now, but here the air was full of salt spray, not dust. At home the sunsets were more violent, more dramatic. This was peaceful, a musical comedy of a sunset.

This was the first time in about three weeks that I'd had a chance to feel totally alone, to sit down and let my thoughts unravel. I couldn't understand how people as decent as my Lebanese friends could have gotten themselves into the vicious war they were in. Sure, they were a little on the short-fused side, but certainly not without provocation. One thing I knew for certain; these folks were in no moral or intellectual way inferior to Americans. Beirut was very different from Oklahoma City, where I grew up, but no more so than Miami, Florida. In fact, in those pre-Mariel days, aside from language, Beirut and Miami were very much alike, same white buildings and tropical vegetation, a similar European-Mediterranean ethnic mix. The major differences were that Miami lacked a Syrian army of occupation and an unrestricted flow of Soviet arms across the border.

Strange thoughts for a Mediterranean sunset. And what about me? I should be going home soon, but I really wanted to wait until Larry arrived. I wondered about my reawakened thirst for combat. It wasn't blood lust or anything like that. It was just that desire to take chances as far as you could. It was as Stirling Moss had said about auto racing; 'you could live ten years on a Sunday afternoon.' When I got to Lebanon I felt like I was waking up after a long sleep, but now I didn't just want to be awake. I wanted to rock 'n' roll.

But I missed Kathy very much, and I knew if I got back into all this, I'd lose her; and for that matter, at 44, I wasn't in good enough shape to live through much combat—too slow, not enough endurance.

But the memory of the rising surge of pure energy that comes when you go into an ambush or a hot LZ drew me as nothing else does. I wondered whether I could squeeze in one more, and if so, would I be satisfied with one?

I got up and wandered back to the party. It was dark, but a fire was roaring, racks of shish kebab had been laid out, along with more great Lebanese food than three times the number of people there could possibly eat.

Fouad and Celeste were there, and Michel. Rick was not, but I had no idea why. Fouad loaded me a plate and a glass of arak, and we chatted. I felt no sense of my own foreigness. There was laughter; there was singing. It was great.

Fouad pointed out his brother Teddy, whose birthday it was. Teddy was a shock. I had been told a few things about him. I knew he was Fouad's younger brother, that he had fought at the Battle for the Holiday Inn in 1976 and been wounded badly enough to retire from combat, and he had become a scuba instructor in Jounieh. But none of that prepared me for Teddy. This guy was *messed up.*

Fouad pointed him out, but I never got a chance to meet him that night, because he was always in the center of an admiring group of friends and relatives. The guy was a legend, but he had paid for it. He looked like he'd taken an RPG on his left foot. On land he moved awkwardly on a specially constructed leather boot that partially compensated for his mangled leg and foot. He leaned heavily on a cane. But I could see he'd have no trouble moving underwater, with flippers. One of his eyes was larger than the other, as though a plastic surgeon had been able to repair the flesh, but not the muscle.

*By God,* I thought, *if my leg was screwed up like that I'd have it whacked off below the knee and replaced with a prosthesis.*

These thoughts were interrupted by a burst of middle-eastern music from a portable tape player, accompanied by a skinny teen-age kid with a silly grin and fast hands, bopping with great virtuosity on a small drum with a fluted body. By then I was on my third arak and believed the young lady who came out to dance to be the most beautiful I had ever seen.

Remove from your mind any Egyptian belly-dancer stereotype. Such a performance is perhaps a branch of the same tree as this one, in the sense that, say, Jackson Browne and KISS are branches off the same tree, but this was, after all, a family picnic. The girl wore a boutique terry jumpsuit, reminiscent of the belly-dancer's costume only because the pants were full and gathered at the ankle. Aside from the lack of come-hither looks, the moves seemed fairly standard, but hip-shaking or no, this performance was not intended for sexual excitement. It was just for fun. She was shortly joined by a stocky young man in a CAT baseball cap and a Michigan State football jersey. After a while the girl dropped out and was replaced by a matronly lady in her mid-fifties who could really sling it around.

I found myself leaning back and watching the moon, thinking about Kat, how much I missed her, and how much she would have loved this party. I had seen a lot of the world that she hadn't, and this little bit of it I'd have loved to have shared with her, as she had shared her backstage world with me.

Michel came over and asked me whether I'd ride home with his girl, since he had found another one he wanted to check out.

I had too many more araks. I'm not much of a boozer, but arak tastes like licorice, and I hadn't learned to take it seriously. I slipped and fell down climbing into the boat on the way to Byblos-sur-Mer. I have a vague memory of the ride home. I think Sam was driving, but I'm not sure. Michel's girl was in the back seat, but her mood had turned somber.

It was a great evening, but I have one regret. On my one trip to the town where writing was invented, all I can claim to have done was get drunk and fall down in a boat.

A couple of nights later Teddy came up to the apartment to see Fouad. He leaned heavily on his cane and walked with a horrible limp on his blasted, misshapen leg. The one eye that was round and staring gave a contemptuous and angry cast to his face. Or perhaps he was just contemptuous and angry, either toward life itself or toward the circumstances in which he found himself. I left my reading and looked in on the two brothers, talking in Fouad's office. "Teddy, could I talk with you a bit before you leave, about the Battle for the Holiday Inn, for my article?"

He looked back at me balefully and nodded assent.

The television station had gone off for the night when he and Fouad finished their conversation, and so we had that corner of the living room to talk in. He clumped in on his cane, sat across from me, and cocked his head. "Well?"

I grinned. "I've stayed in Holiday Inns all over the southwest United

States—Texas, Oklahoma, Arkansas. The idea of a battle in one seems ludicrous. My idea of a battle is hosing down a jungle trail from ten feet away."

He didn't return my smile, but his voice was soft and pleasant. He seemed to regard my comment as a serious one, and he replied seriously. "This one was very strategically placed; three major hotels in a row, on the Green Line, on commanding terrain. One could observe practically the entire city. The hotels were the Holiday Inn, the St. Georges, and the...ah...Phoenicia."

"It's very hard for me to visualize a battle like that. In my life I've only fought one day in a city, and that was in a neighborhood of one and two-story houses, during the Tet Offensive of 1968."

"It was very difficult," he said. "I had twenty-four men to defend a 1700 meter front."

That seemed as though it might be minimally possible with commanding terrain, clear fields of fire, good weapons, and an inexhaustible supply of ammunition, but in the end the ammo supply proved exhaustible.

At one point I touched on the issue of atrocities. I wanted very much for my friends to be the good guys. I, and the Americans I have fought beside in the past, have been scrupulous in the matter of handling prisoners.

"With only twenty-four men," he said, "I wanted them to be as afraid of us as I could make them."

I had no reply to that. I was very conscious of the fact that the torture killing of prisoners is pretty much *de rigeur* throughout the Third World, and that the Palestinians had a particularly unsavory record in that regard.

"Why don't you have that leg cut off and get a prosthesis?" I asked. "You could probably get around a lot better."

"Many times they want to take it," he replied. "At my first operation on Cyprus they wanted to take it, but I always say no. I do not believe in...it is not a good idea to sacrifice a part of your body when maybe a way to fix it can be found."

I smiled. "Maybe so. In the water I expect you're as good as anybody."

He smiled back. "I like to think I am better."

For all his ferocious appearance Teddy spoke very gently and calmly about these things. I got no sense that he was a man who had never wanted to fight or kill, but that he had been confronted with a situation where there was no choice, and had responded with a cold, intelligent rage. In any case, that part of it was over for him now.

# 8

# Bye-Bye Beirut

I took my accustomed sunrise seat on the balcony and dialed the thirteen digits it took to reach my home in Fayetteville. Two rings.

"Hello!"

"Hi, darlin', what's happ'nin'?"

"Well, I've scheduled a wedding on the 27th of June. Think you can make it?"

That was about two weeks past when I'd said I'd be home, but I'd stayed, hopefully, to go on an operation with Michel. Also, I'd wanted to be there to brief Larry when he arrived. But it had become obvious Michel wasn't going out for a couple of weeks, and I couldn't just sit around doing nothing in the meanwhile. And it wasn't actually necessary that I be here when Larry arrived. Mostly I just wanted to show off.

"Sure," I said, "I'll be there, but what changed your mind?" I had been asking her to marry me about twice a week for the preceding two years.

Her husky Southern voice crackled over the phone, "I was talkin' to your mother, and I suddenly realized that if you buy the farm on one of these deals I won't be anything but your ex-girl friend."

I guffawed. "Okay, I'll be there." I was delighted, no matter what her reasons. Later, she admitted this had been the only way she could think of to get me home.

The morning I was to leave I woke up to realize that I'd better do something about finding a ring. I asked Michel, and he said there were excellent jewelry bargains in Beirut. The gold cost the same, but the workmanship, although excellent, was dirt cheap. "Sounds good," I said. "Let's go!"

He took me to what had been an exclusive shop in a corner location, near the Green Line. There was a lot of black velvet on display, but their stock was way down. I knew exactly what she wanted, however, and they had it, a thin gold circle with a spiral of gold around it; beautiful, delicate, and stylish.

Michel took me back to the apartment that had been my home for three weeks which seemed like a hundred. I was still concerned about the Palestinians. That interview had made it fairly easy to pin down approximately when I'd be leaving. I wanted a weapon, but I couldn't carry one through Cypriot customs. But on a bookshelf in the apartment there was a cedar cone roughly the size and shape of an old WWII pineapple hand grenade.

Not a bad souvenir of Lebanon, that. I figured I'd carry it off the boat and out of the customs shed. If there was someone waiting for me on Cyprus, the sight of it might give them enough pause for me to get away. There was really only a slight chance they'd be after me, but enough of one that Rick was concerned. Rick hadn't lived through five years of this shit by being a fool.

I said my good-byes and Sam drove me to Jounieh, to the boat. He laid his Czech AK in the seat between us and set off, grimfaced, in Rick's old VW. He looked more and more depressed as we headed north. "What the hell's the matter with you?" I asked. "You look like you could eat a bowl of nails!"

"I don't like to go to Jounieh," he snapped. "I almost hate those people. We're dying every day in Beirut, and they face almost no danger at all. All they care about the war is to make money from it."

I nodded, but what I was thinking was, how can you expect the Americans half a world away to come to your rescue when you can't get the full support of your countrymen twenty miles up the road? But I didn't say it. It would only have made him angry. Instead I took my last Montagnard bracelet off my arm. Once I'd had many of them, but now I had only one. It was just six inches of quarter-inch brass welding rod, with some notches carved on it, bent into a bracelet that turned your wrist green. But it was my most prized possession. It was my badge of membership in another tribe I had loved in another time and place. Another bunch of good folks my government had sold down the river.

"Here!" I said. "This is my good luck. You need it worse than I do."

He slipped it on his wrist and said, "Thanks." His manner was offhand. He lived in a world where these are the things one does.


On the boat back to Cyprus I fell in with a couple of young Lebanese Christians. Roger, the stocky one with the broad grin, was just going to Cyprus for a holiday, catch a few rays on the beach, and hit the discos at night. John, an Errol Flynn look-a-like, had a job as a civil engineer in Saudi Arabia. Since both John and Roger were part-time Lebanese Forces militiamen it was quite possible that John had been shot at by weapons furnished by his employers. "They don't care that you're a Christian?" I asked.

He shrugged. "They want engineers."

As we chatted, Roger put a tape in his small stereo deck. It was middle-eastern music, but with a solid back beat, middle-eastern music by someone who was also a Beatles fan. It was terrific, the best new stuff I had heard in years.

"This is Marceil Kalife," Roger said. "He is a communist, but his music is good. We all listen."

We listened to Kalife and they told tremendous stories of being teen-agers in the militia, making impromptu raids on Palestinian positions after a few too many beers on a Saturday night.

John teased Roger about the trouble a young man could get into on Cyprus. "One time in the Cosmos Disco on Cyprus I meet a girl. She is very beautiful, with long, long hair, and a shape...ahh, that shape." He flashed a grin that was pure malevolent Captain Blood. "I ask her out and she say meet her outside so I follow and bump into this guy.

"He say, 'Filthy Arab!'" The Flynn grin was replaced by a grimace of total, focused berserker rage, even now, at the memory. "So I *grab* him, and I *slam* him against the wall, and I say, 'Don't call me, *Arab*! I kill you, you son of a bitch! We follow JEESUSS!'"

The next day I left the boat with my bags in one hand and my cedar cone in the other.

# 9

# Where'd He Get
# That Buddha?

The wedding was beautiful, the bride was lovely, and the reception afterward was the best party I ever attended. The guest list was a strange mix, though. Kathy had her friends from the drama school, and I had mine from the English department, and we both knew some combat vets with lots of stamps in their passports.

My best man was Paul H. Williams, a former Marine artillery forward observer from Vietnam, and a fellow writing student. He looks like Edgar Allen Poe and writes grim Faulknerian tales about Indians and mixed bloods in Oklahoma. Kathy's bridesmaid was Terry Brustar, her dance instructor. I had known Terry for over a year, and only seen her in a leotard, jean skirt, hair knotted into a bun. For the wedding she looked great, dress clothes, her hair done in electric brillo.

Our ushers were Peder Lund, an ex-Special Forces captain who looks like a killer koala, publisher of my book, *War Story*, and Marty Jordan. Marty is a stocky, blond half-Choctaw who made staff sergeant in one three-year hitch, which included two Vietnam tours. In his ruffled shirt and dinner jacket, he was one of the most frightening-looking persons I had ever seen.

Kat had lectured Lund and Martin on decorum, and they were trying hard. The first guest to seat in the chapel was a young lady, one of my students. "Are you a friend of the bride or the groom?" Lund inquired correctly.

"I guess it really doesn't matter," she replied.

Our photographer, Jim Adair, another former SF man, and an old skydiving buddy, leaned over a pew and said, "Then find your own goddam seat."

My heart flopped over when Kathy came up the aisle of the chapel. She wore a simple white gown (she says it was "ecru", but it looked white to me) with a modified empire line, her design, and a white gardenia over the right ear, on her shoulder-length dark hair. She is slender and frail-looking, with delicate features and huge dark eyes, and she moves with a gliding grace. But she has Tom's sense of humor and Huck's sense of adventure and none of Becky about her at all.

Music was provided by a friend named Abby, who played, at an appropriate tempo, Willy Nelson's "Whisky River," on the autoharp. It sounded just right if you didn't remember the lyrics.

The ceremony was held up for a moment while I pondered my answer to the question, "Wilt thou have this woman..." but I allowed as how I would, and we adjourned to Paul's two-story Victorian for the aforementioned best party ever.

Kathy had pulled out all the stops. Champagne flowed from fountains. There were hors d'oeuvres, and Tequila Sunrises. Larry Dring and the guys from Beirut had sent a gorgeous bouquet of roses.

After the party got rolling my friend David, from the writing program, decided the air was too close, left the party, and was later arrested for crawling against a red light.

The next day we packed a U-Haul and headed for Boulder. Like most of my classmates, I had no viable teaching offers, but Brown wanted me to work for *Soldier of Fortune*.


After Larry got back from Beirut, he came to visit and tell his story for the magazine. He had seen pretty much the same things I had, but, being more technically qualified, he was able to give the Lebanese Forces instruction in vehicle maintenance and advanced demolitions. In return they taught him their anti-tank tactics, and gave him a lot of Russian weapons they had captured, weapons that nobody in U.S.

intelligence had bothered to come over and collect.

He and Michel had become fast friends, as I expected they would. They were both super-soldiers, and Larry couldn't talk about Michel without grinning. Once, in a three-quarter-ton truck, Michel had driven them over the side of what appeared to be a cliff, but turned out to be an eighty degree incline, which they slid down in a shower of rocks and dirt.

Larry also laughed about the poor, hash-addled Syrian trooper whom they had captured when he wandered into their camp one night, carefully explaining that they couldn't capture him because he was invisible.

"Do they sell bras in this town?" he asked as we drove through the streets of Boulder, eyeing beautiful U. of Colorado girls in cut-offs and halter tops or T-shirts, riding bicycles.

"Yeah," I said. "They're a prescription item."

Larry loved the hot tub place, because the water was great for his leg. The first day of Tet '68 an NVA trooper had shot six inches out of his left femoral artery. Larry cut him in half with a burst from his M-16, but the damage was done. It always hurt, always. I can still remember him floating on his back under the stars in a hot tub, singing Civil War songs at the top of his lungs, to the extreme consternation of the freaks in the next room, who were trying to smoke a little pot and get into the Moody Blues.

One night we went to a party at Haney Howell's, my CBS buddy from Cambodia, in Denver. Larry was in a suit of Palestinian cammies he had gotten from Fouad. We had taken an AK and an M-16 into the Rockies, which looked just like the mountains in Lebanon, to get some shots of the LF firing techniques.

Having been on his leg all day, Larry was gobbling prescription codeine like popcorn; he was loquacious and charming and brilliant. He fell into conversation with Sandy Sells, wife of George Sells, then-anchorman on a Denver TV station. "I had this company of Cambodes and we were having a drink, me coke, them beer, one night in the cantina after an operation. This one troopie had a Buddha medallion he claimed had been blessed by an extra-powerful *bonze*, and nothing could kill him. Just to prove his point he held his hand over the end of his carbine and pulled the trigger.

"Nothing.

"All the other guys looked at him and marveled. He got so cocky he stuck the barrel in his mouth and pulled the trigger. Blew the back of his head clean off.

"All the other guys were standing around, scratching their heads and saying, 'Where'd he get that Buddha?'" Larry grinned.

# 10

# Waiting In Bangkok

We found a house in the Capitol Hill section of Denver, a kind of liberal-intellectual-artsy neighborhood, and Kathy found work in the costume shop at the Bonfils Theater.

Over the next nine months I did a series on Lebanon and covered several other stories in the U.S., mostly to do with the POW situation.

Kathy wasn't eager for me to go back overseas, but nine months later, when Brown asked me to go to Thailand, I jumped at the chance. It would be a pleasure to get back to Southeast Asia. Maybe I could even make contact with FULRO and find out what the deal was with the Montagnards. There were plenty of other stories in Thailand as well.

"Goddamn it!" I muttered. "This is driving me batshit." I took five steps away from Coyne's hotel window, turned and took five steps back. I looked down on what appeared to be a modern city growing out of the jungle. Actually, the tropical trees were neatly planted in rows around palatial villas, but from the tenth and topmost floor of the Nana Hotel you couldn't see the houses, so you saw this jungle, studded with apartments, hotels, Buddhist temples, the spire of the Dusit Thani building, cement factories. From Coyne's room you could not see Sukhumvit.

"*You're* driving *me* batshit," said Coyne. "You're wired way too high for this. Nothing moves fast in this country."

"We've been here ten days," I said; snarled actually, "and I've already spent more time in Bangkok than I did in Saigon in three tours in Vietnam. I didn't come for a good time. I was having a good time in Boulder."

When we first got there, Coyne said, "This is better than Saigon." Truly this was more like Saigon than Saigon had been. But before Bangkok, I had hated Saigon worse than any place I had ever been in my life.

This was, in fact, the first time I'd ever been in Southeast Asia that I was in any particular hurry to get home. Kathy needed me; I had work stacked up to the rafters, and while I was glad to be here, I was desperate to get on with it. I was supposed to be back in Boulder by the end of the month, and nothing was happening.

"I just don't like cities," I muttered. I would not have much cared for this lurid scene, even when I was young and unattached. In Vietnam I had sought the green leafy places, and the occasional firefight, which was what I had hoped to recapture here, but it wasn't happening.

I had liked that life better than anything that went before, and most of what came after. I wanted another piece of it.

Coyne and I both had four or five stories we were working on, the work for which consisted of pestering people on the telephone, and waiting for their reply. Thailand is a *manana* country; if you pushed these people hard enough, they could simply blow you off—no connection, no story.

But Thailand is an important story, simply because it had not gone down the tubes as expected. The Domino Theory racked up South Vietnam, Laos, Cambodia and stopped at Thailand, then jumped three oceans and started again in Africa, the Middle East, and Central America. Why the Thais were succeeding was important, but nobody was covering it.

The local papers were full of great combat stuff, but nobody outside of Thailand picked it up. It was a very difficult story to cover, unless you had an interpreter or spoke Thai, because the Royal Thai Army didn't seem to have any Public Information set-up; we were dealing with colonels and generals, because they had been lieutenants and captains when the Americans were here, and were the only soldiers around who spoke English.

They were very nice and hospitable, but they were running several wars simultaneously—three separate insurgencies and periodic fighting against the opium armies from Burma. Further, they had to keep tabs on the Laotian and Cambodian resistances. If there were any great demand from the international press to cover these wars, they would have come up with some public affairs' officers to handle the influx, but there was no such demand, no demand for success stories.

This merely confirmed my suspicion that the regular press only publishes stories reinforcing the world view of the intelligentsia, which seems only natural since the intelligentsia does most of the world's writing and reading. But that world view screens out a large amount of significant information.

Coyne had been here before and knew the deal. He liked the bush well enough, but he was single, had a girlfriend, and was perfectly content to sit poolside, waiting for a telephone call to confirm an appointment. Of our two attitudes mine might seem more commendable, but his worked and mine didn't.

"What the hell is Brown doing in Chile?" I demanded.

Coyne gave me a helpless look and a wry smile. "Hey," he shrugged, "you know Brown."

Yes, I know Brown; a man crazy enough to think he could make a success of a trade journal for mercenaries is capable of anything. But this was a bit much, even for Brown. Originally, he was going to come with us, but was delayed by an illness in his family. He decided to send us on ahead. Three days later we called the office; his family situation was okay, and he had gone to Washington.

We figured he had gone to see his intelligence cronies about some new development in the POW/MIA issue. That was okay; that was the main thing we were here for.

A week later we called again. Brown had gone to Chile.

Chile?

If you could just write Brown off as a screwball, it would make things easier. But Brown is not a screwball: he's a wizard. A wizard is somebody who does totally irrational things that work even though they make no sense. I didn't doubt that there was a good reason for his going to Chile, but I felt like a lion in a closet. No matter what we started, once Brown arrived we'd be faced with a whole new set of priorities.

"I'm going to get ready for dinner," I snapped.

"Yeah," said Coyne, wistfully, "take it easy."

He was, I am sure, looking forward to another evening of my conversation.

Leaving his hotel, I ignored the eight drivers who leapt up and yelled, "Taxi!" I went to the street and bellowed, "Tuk-tuk!" Immediately a Honda motorcycle with a passenger chassis, a sort of motorized rickshaw, sputtered to a halt at my feet, "Windsor Hotel, twenty baht." A regular taxi would want forty for the same ride. Coyne had taught me about tuk-tuks. I climbed in and propped a Tony Lama up on the railing between me and the driver. The tuk-tuk sputtered off.

Emission controls are unknown in Thailand. A blue mist of monoxide hung over Sukhumvit, a major traffic artery, like a smoke snake, its bloodstream the honking, snarling traffic. I blocked off my nose, breathing as shallowly as possible through my teeth.

At the hotel I bathed and was just changing into a khaki safari suit, every correspondent's first purchase in Bangkok, when a naked general charged into my room.

Brigadier General Hiney Aderholt, USAF (Ret.) is self-described as "one of those rough old sonsabitches." He was our only high school dropout general. When I first met him at the Stapleton Airport in Denver I wondered how this crude bastard ever got past lieutenant colonel. He talked tough and butchered the English language like a construction boss, but in the days we traveled with him he switched effortlessly from good-old-boy camaraderie to diplomatic polish to brilliantly reasoned analysis, as required. I saw him blister the ears off a deputy assistant cabinet secretary, and heard him charm the socks off a nun, over the telephone. "Crude bastard" was but one of his many personas.

When I first met him I spelled his name, "Heine", and thought he had German ancestry. Later I learned Hiney was a childhood nickname that stuck, earned when he was three years old because his ass was always hanging out.

He was in Thailand, representing a POW-family group from Tampa called the Forget-Me-Nots, to pick up the remains of a fighter pilot who had crashed in Laos. The deal had been set up by a retired Air Force colonel named Donovan, who had lost his son in Laos. "Donovan's spent more on POW/MIA's out of his own pocket than the whole goddam United States government," Hiney said. "I figured with my connections I could save him a few bucks."

"Goddammit!" said General Aderholt, standing in the connecting door of our rooms, G.I. glasses down on his nose, a newspaper in his hand. "Have you seen this?"

He referred, I hoped, to the newspaper. Normally Hiney wears a towel, as a sarong, Thai style, in his hotel room, but it tends to come loose when he lies down to read.

"What, Sir?" I inquired.

He referred to Hill 508 at Surat Thani, where the Thais were waging a marginally successful battle to take an entrenched Communist Party of Thailand guerrilla base. The Thais fight like they do everything else, cleverly. They fight to minimize casualties, and who can blame them for that? There's no end of tour and rotation home in the Royal Thai Army.

"Here, read this!" he concluded, and padded back into his room.

I sighed and looked around the room. Hiney had chosen this hotel before the rest of us arrived. Coyne had come late, through Hong Kong, and checked immediately into the Nana, where he had a top floor room, an FM radio, and a great view. Probably the reason most military decor is so drab is that the other generals have taste like Hiney's, which runs to Early Dayroom. Also, he is convinced that the best thing which could happen to the younger generation is to live through the Depression, like he did, and I believe he chose our rooms in an attempt to replicate that experience.

Downstairs in the lobby, going out, I passed an old American who had obviously been in the Orient for a long time. He looked like something that had been sculpted out of mashed potatoes and left out in the sun a long time ago. I repressed a shudder. *Got to get out of this place,* I thought. I remembered the line at the beginning of *Apocalypse Now.* "Every day Charlie stayed in the jungle he got stronger, and every day I stayed in this hotel room I got weaker."

We ran into Coyne's girlfriend, Som Kit, coming out of the elevator as we started down. She had a paper bag of street-stand food in her arms. "Where you go?" she said to Coyne.

Back in Boulder, Coyne was a kind of easygoing, happy-go-lucky jazzbo, but when he speaks bargirl English he goes squat and growls out monosyllables like Sessue Hayakawa, always with a bit of a smile playing around the corners of his mouth. "We go Oriental for drink. You want come?"

She thought a second, then shook her head. "My sister come later. We go movie." When Kit thinks, you can see the synapses connect behind her eyes. When she sits down and puts her feet in the chair, her rail-thin body folds up like a carpenter's rule. She is very bright and more than once saved us a lot of trouble by correctly identifying some person we had to deal with as a phony.

"Why he laugh?" she demanded, looking at me.

"He make fun of way we do," said Coyne.

She aimed a desultory kick at my kneecap, gave us from her sack two ears of roasted corn on popsicle sticks, and went off down the hall.


The Oriental Hotel in Bangkok has been voted the world's best hotel by the International Bankers Association, or some such organization, and is a high-class joint, indeed. You can't just arrive there in a tuk-tuk. We rented a white, air-conditioned taxi.

Dismounting at the Oriental, we left our corncobs neatly wrapped in Kleenex in the back seat of the taxi, and walked through the plush, spacious lobby. At the Oriental it is virtually impossible to light your own cigarette, because they employ too many uniformed flunkies.

We walked out back to the verandah, where a cool breeze blew across the muddy expanse of the Chao Phrya River, which reflected a lurid Asian sunset behind the slums on the other side, two hundred yards away.

"All that construction we passed, the freeway, all new since I was here last summer," said Coyne.

"Another significant difference between Thailand and Vietnam," I replied. "In Vietnam nothing was made out of anything but bamboo and sheet tin from the time the French left until the Americans arrived. Things move at their own pace here, but they do move."

Four *farang* women, who looked sort of frizzy and heavy after seeing only Thai women for a couple of weeks, sat at the next table. A couple of them were nice-looking, although it seemed strange to hear the assertive cadences of American women's conversation. Their laughter was throaty and confident.

"Ah, Jim," said Coyne, sweeping them with a glance, "I want them all."

"Yeah," I said. "Right now! I know the feeling."

Coyne ordered a German white wine with a five-syllable name, mostly consonants. "The last time I was here," he said as we sipped our wine and the last cerise line of the sun faded from the horizon and barge lights drifted by like squadrons of fireflies in formation, "this depressed Japanese businessman chose that moment to take a high dive out his window on the eighth floor. They were having a wedding reception below..champagne, seven-tier cake. Somebody took a picture just before he hit. There were all these people laughing and talking, raising their glasses in a toast, and these blurred feet, just at the top of the frame. It was a very surreal picture."

The breeze ruffled the hair over the ears of the American women at the next table.

"They go in big for omens in this country," I said. "That's not a good start for the marriage."

"The hotel management thought the Japanese had jumped from the seventh floor and broke the door open with an axe on a guy from the *Times* who was boffing a hooker. 'Thank God you're alive,' they exclaimed. 'Get the fuck out of here,' he screamed; it was a tremendous hassle."

After finishing our drinks we left the Oriental. Out front, ignoring the pleas of white-uniformed flunkies, wearing matching topis, that we hire another air-conditioned limo, we strolled to the street and rented a tuk-tuk.

"Tiger's?" Coyne inquired. "I got a Jones for Tiger's beans." Tiger serves a bowl of homemade beans and ham that is the best cheap meal in Bangkok.

Later Coyne and I steered a meandering path down Pat Pong, winging between the outstretched palms, fruit carts, good-looking shills offering some combination of drink, haircut, massage, steambath and/or blowjob. I stepped around a dead dog, keeled over in its own vomit.

Coyne pushed open the door of the Grand Prix Disco Bar and walked into the dark and the noise.

Behind the circular bar, on a raised platform, ringed by circus lights, three young ladies in sequined bikinis ground away, with varying degrees of skill and enthusiasm, to Bob Seger's *Nine Tonight.*

We wound our way around the bar to the back where the big screen TV was showing *The Towering Inferno* for the handful of people who listened to the soundtrack from headsets at the bar.

Back in the corner was a smaller bar, presided over by Rick Menard, an ex-GI who had come to Bangkok on R&R, liked it, and had come back to stay. He looked and talked like a younger Phil Foster, a Brooklyn comedian of the Fifties.

Facing him was the man I was looking for, Alan Dawson, a columnist for the *Bangkok Post.* A Canadian by birth, Dawson made the mistake of dropping out of school in the U.S. and got drafted. If ever there was a guy with good reason to skip to Canada it was he; instead he went to Vietnam and stayed on as a reporter after his enlistment. He even stayed for six months after the fall of Saigon, which he chronicled in his book, *55 Days.* In the dim light at the little bar, with his cadaverous cheeks and lank hair, Dawson wore the bemused and wary expression of a vampire, who, unable to get back to his coffin, had chosen to ride out the daylight hours at a Bugs Bunny Film Festival.

The reason I wanted to see Dawson was that he had been contacted by FULRO, the Montagnard underground in Vietnam, to see whether he wanted to make a run into the Central Highlands. He had declined on the grounds that he would have to go through Khmer Rouge territory. Dawson will not voluntarily stay in the same room with a Khmer Rouge.

If there was any way possible, I wanted to make that trip.

"Hi, Honee!" A small brown girl in a sequined bikini, with a tight, shapely brown body, stood under my armpit. A slender arm went around my neck, and a fine brown hand ran up the inseam of my trousers. "How long you stay Bangkok?"

"Excuse me, ma'am, but your hand is on my wazoo."

"You work Saudi?"

"I'm here on business," I insisted.

She looked puzzled for a while longer while I talked to Dawson; then she went away.

Dawson shook his head. "No possibility of a trip," he said. "Too much activity on the border."

"Are they in town?" I asked.

"I'll call you," he said.

I looked for Coyne. He was in animated conversation with an American couple at the other end of the bar. As I approached them I realized he was talking only to the blonde, while her husband stared transfixed at the Go-Go girls. Coyne leaned forward intently. "Sure, you can get away for a couple days," he said. "We'll go to Penang; we'll have a great time."

She looked as though she were considering it.


Tuesday morning I woke with a chill and sat bolt upright in bed. It dawned on me that all this grab-assing around was lulling me into a false sense of security. One phone call and I could be on an airplane, and in an hour or two I would be in another world, a world of jungled mountains and armed, angry people. I rolled out of bed and checked my gear, checked the wrist strap on my camera. For the hundredth time I cursed my civilian status, cursed the fact that when I went into one of these deals, I had to borrow whatever weapons and ammo they gave me, if any.

In '73, before I was doing this for *SOF*, the Cambodes had given me an M-16 and four, count 'em four, 20-round magazines. That was all they had apiece, and there was no reason why I was so special that I should have more. What I really wanted was a Galil SAR, which is basically an Israeli-made AK that shoots M-16 ammo. Rare indeed is the customs official who will let you through with one.

My next chore was three laps around Lumpini Park, which is about a mile and a half per lap. Even at seven in the morning I was soaked with sweat after five steps. But it was fun to lap the park and see the Chinese ladies practicing their Tai Chi Chuan, and Thais practicing some kind of weird sword fighting—little ladies and gentlemen whirling across the grass, flashing their chromed scimitars—and other runners.

One was a slender, muscular Thai lady in great shape. Every time I went around, she passed going twice as fast the other way. I tabbed her for a marathoner, which I later learned she was. After that came the fitness center and an hour or so of pumping chromed iron.

The life of a writer is primarily sedentary, and if I wanted to keep humping the hills with teen-age troops, I had to work out. The older you get the quicker you get out of shape, and the longer it takes to get back in.

After my workout I shared the sauna with a sweaty, towel-wrapped Brit, and another sweaty, towel-wrapped American.

"How's old Gordon?" the Brit asked the American.

"Son of a bitch's still taking 'em on two at a time every day. He gets one with a tight pussy, and one that gives good head and takes 'em both upstairs. Sixty-five years old. The son of a bitch is amazing." I knew Gordon; he was an Australian who had forsaken booze because of a heart condition, and had become addicted to sex instead. He was in great shape and very dapper in white shorts and knee socks and a white shirt.

Back at the hotel I worked on my notes for a while, and then went down to breakfast. No point calling anybody before nine-thirty. Some would consider it rude even to try. I went back upstairs, made five telephone calls and struck out five times. Seventeen minutes. I never got through a day's work so fast in my life.

I looked through the window and sighed, then checked my other set of gear, trunks, towel, lotion, flip-flops.

At the conclusion of tanning activities that afternoon, I returned to find a note to the effect that Lt. Gen. Tenchai Sirisumphan, the originator of Thai Special Forces, had agreed to give me an interview that Friday, two days away. Thank God. It wasn't an action story, but General Tenchai had one of the greatest names in counterinsurgency; an interview with him was a real coup.

As soon as I got to my room the phone rang. It was Coyne. His friend, General Piechtr, had cleared us to go to Surat Thani, down south in the peninsula where the Royal Thai Army was battling guerrillas of the Communist Party of Malaysia. Great!

Now we were lined up for two good stories, only I didn't want to leave for Surat Thani until after the interview, which was still three days away.

Blam! Blam! Two knocks on the door. When I opened it, Colonel George Goetzke, Chief of the Army section of JUSMAG Thai, turned his shoulders sideways to enter the room. Goetzke was a huge man, blond, with a crewcut and GI glasses. He wore jungle fatigues, with both U.S. and Thai Master parachutist wings. To avoid frightening normal people, Goetzke had cultivated a pleasant expression and a soft, soothing tone of voice. "You and Coyne are making the Mitrapab jump Saturday," he said. "You'll fly into Haad-Yai on a Thai C-130 Friday."

Friday, that was my interview. Jesus! But I really wanted to make that jump. Not only was it a good story, but we'd be awarded Thai wings, the most gorgeous military decoration known to man. I had coveted a pair for twenty years.

Col. Goetzke went to the map of Thailand taped to my wall. Haad-Yai was way down south on the peninsula, in Muslim country, almost in Malaysia. Insurgent country. I'd have to try to postpone with General Tenchai.

"You want to join us for a drink downstairs?" Goetzke asked.

"Yessir, I've got to make a couple of phone calls first."

The "us" he wanted me to join was the U.S. Special Forces Advisory detachment from Korea, here for the jump; the crew of their U.S. C-130; and Col. George Marechek, now operations officer of the Green Beret headquarters at Fort Bragg, former commander of U.S. Special Forces, Thailand, when there was such a thing. Indeed I would be delighted, be crazy not to.

I got General Tenchai on the phone. He understood. Certainly we could do it later. When? Oh, week after next, maybe the week after that.

I called Coyne and told him about the jump. "We've got two days before we go to Haad-yai. You want to go to Surat Thani tomorrow so we can get it in before the jump?"

He actually laughed.


The next morning at eleven we were at the pool. No sense rushing things. Over on the other side of the pool, on a chaise on the grass, a young American groped the tawny thing in the wet bikini beside him. The several couples around them paid not the slightest attention. Directly across from us a German hausfrau, who strongly resembled a boiled Alex Karras, also in a bikini, doused herself with lotion. She had a great-looking redheaded daughter, also boiled, and unfortunately, what appeared to be a son-in-law as well.

From our right I caught a snatch of conversation from two men, one a businessman in a size 44 swimsuit, the other a rough type in a safari outfit.

"As I see it," said the businessman, "he has two choices. He can either be silent or be silenced. This must be made clear to him."

Sunlight shimmered as the blue water of the pool dappled and rippled, making instant little troughs and valleys, forming and vanishing in an ever-changing, never-repeating pattern. It was marvelously soothing.

# *11*

# Buddha On The Drop Zone

Our first clue that all was not wonderful came when somebody said, "Helmet," and I realized neither Coyne nor I had one. We were in a hotel coffee shop in Haadyai (or Haad-Yai, Hadyai, Hatyai or Haatyai, Thailand, depending on which sign you read). The restaurant had been done in a Moorish motif, appropriate since Hatyai was Muslim country. Under an awning in a white Moorish arcade, parachutists sat around us in a strange assortment of gear: fatigue uniforms, okay diver suits, coveralls, jogging outfits.

Coyne and I wore the tiger-striped camouflage fatigues that were sometimes our work clothes. Since we were going to be jumping MC 1-1s, a military parachute, out of a Royal Thai Air Force C-123, we had, in our own minds, classified this as a troop jump, and the helmet as something we should be issued.

Coyne was deep in breakfast-table conversation.

I immediately sprang up and went to the next table, "Anybody got an extra helmet?" Col. Goetzke, a bull with a crewcut looked up.

He was a skydiver with 1,600 jumps. Beside him sat Major Mark Smith, cocky little wiseass commander of the Special Forces advisory detachment in Korea. Smith had the distinguished Service Cross, and had been a POW for 364 days. He boasted of being the only field-grade high school dropout in the U.S. Army.

Another jumper was a young, olive-complexioned guy with coal-black hair. He wore a bright red camouflage suit, which would fit into no known background on this planet. Next to him sat a beautiful, very blonde, very pregnant lady in blue jeans. The guy in the Martian cammies immediately reached down into his kit bag and pulled out a gleaming white Bell helmet. "Just happen to have one here."

"When you go jumping it's customary to bring a helmet," Goetzke muttered, his eyes over a coffee cup inspecting me for signs of mental incompetence.

"Where'd ya get the red cammies?" I asked my benefactor, hoping to make somebody else look dumber than I did.

He grinned. "Maid washed 'em in Clorox," he said.

I thanked him for the helmet and went back to our table, where Coyne was deep in conversation with two men; Jack Phillips, a retired Special Forces lieutenant colonel who had spent his last six years in the Army in Thailand, learned to speak and write Thai fluently, and stayed on as an oil company exec., and Jack's friend, later identified as Dr. Sivavudh Devahastin Ayudha, advisor to the deputy prime minister for economics. His Ph.D. is from Claremont College in Orange County, California.

"This first time you make jump?" Coyne asked him, speaking slowly and carefully.

"Yes," said Dr. Sivavudh, "it's something I've wanted to do for a long time, but I only recently made the decision to proceed."

"You better get yourself a helmet," I said to Coyne, as I sat down.

He gave me a look of annoyance, since I had procured only one and kept it for myself.

"There's bound to be one on the flight line," he said, and went back to his conversation.

This part of Thailand is on the southern peninsula, which had not one but two insurgencies going at the same time, one from the Communist Party of Thailand, theoretically backed by the Chinese, although the Chinese had largely pulled the plug on them, and the other from PULO (Pattani United Liberation Organization), a Muslim separatist group, mainly trained and supplied by Libya.

For that reason the jump we were making was in every sense operational. It was part of a joint Thai-U.S. Civic Action project to build a school at Tambon Pang La, Sadao District, Songkhla Province, the 230th such school financed by the Mitrapab (Friendship) Educational

Foundation in the 21 years of its existence, all paid for by selling tickets to jumps like this one.

What made the program significant was that it was a valuable tool for national stability; what made this jump possibly significant was that it was the first to be made from U.S. aircraft since the United States pulled out six years before. Maybe it signified closer military cooperation between the U.S. and Thailand; maybe it only meant that Mark Smith, his team, and the Air Force flightcrew had wrangled a free trip to Thailand, a Hollywood jump, and ten days *per diem* from the U.S. government.

Mitrapab began in 1961 on a field training exercise near a village called Ban Yang. During a sudden tropical downpour, Lt. Col. Prathip and his counterpart, a Capt. Carver, took shelter in a nearby one-room schoolhouse. To their surprise there was just about as much rain inside as outside. It was a mystery to both of them how any learning could take place there during the rainy season.

They decided to get a bunch of their jump buddies together, put on a demonstration, and charge admission. They hoped to raise enough money for a new schoolhouse.

There's not much to do in a Thai village on a Sunday afternoon. The night before, some villagers had walked a block and half to watch me eat noodles in a restaurant; what would they give to see a whole flock of Thai and *farang* paratroopers falling through the air under clouds of bright nylon?

At the Haadyai Airport, Coyne and I went our separate ways, I to shoot pictures of pre-jump activities, he to scrounge a helmet, which after much cursing and not a little apprehension, he did.

It's natural to be scared on a jump, and paratroopers have a number of rituals to minimize that. But they have to be done right. Nothing builds confidence less than getting the MACO (marshaling area control officer) briefing in a foreign language. Even so, the Thai major who served as MACO had an excellent chart of the DZ (drop zone); it wasn't that hard to follow, the symbols and numbers were the same as ours, even if the alphabet wasn't.

Col. Goetzke came up and said, "Coyne just told me he's never jumped a steerable before. Tell him how it works, will you, so he won't land in Malaysia."

"Okay, Sir," I said. No problem there, a steerable is the easiest thing in the world to operate.

"Face into the wind and hold at 150 feet no matter what," he shouted over his shoulder as he walked away.

Oh, yeah, I forgot.

Stateside, as a safety factor, the army requires paratroopers to take a day of refresher training before a jump if they've been off airborne status for as little as six months. This was Coyne's first jump in sixteen years. If I had realized that, I'd have had him doing PLF's (parachute landing falls) off the dresser in his hotel room. It wouldn't have hurt me to do a few either. I hadn't jumped in two years.

Glen Gamble, a former U.S. Army captain, vice president of the Mitrapab Foundation, had organized this jump. He was geared out with a jumpsuit but walking with a limp.

"You gonna jump on that?"

"Yeah, it's twisted a little. The ankle's wrapped so tight it won't bend, that's all."

I didn't say anything. It was his ankle, his ass for that matter.

If you haven't jumped in a long time you forget too many things. Before chuting up I put my notebook and pen in my left breast pocket, which turned out to be a mistake.

Finally everything was ready; everybody chuted up, rigger checked, standing around hunkered over, bound up tight in seventy-five pounds of parachutes, in loose formation, watching the airplane sit on the runway, showing no sign of going anywhere. I sighed, about to do this thing that had been the greatest joy of my young life. This was about the hundredth time I had done this exact same thing, in almost exactly the same way.

Mark Smith, bound in his heavy gear, waddled up from behind and slapped me on the shoulder. "What are you thinking?" he asked.

"I'd like to do something for the first time again," I said. "It's been about twenty years since I did anything this much fun for the first time."

The loadmaster waved us aboard for the 50-klick flight to Tambon Pang La.

Five minutes after we took off, seated in red nylon bench seats along the side of the aircraft, Goetzke stood and took the jumpmaster position by the tailgate. He lifted his arm and blew across the face of his watch, then held up three fingers, the sign for a three-knot wind.

On the first pass, Mark Smith was to jump with the Thai flag, while a Thai colonel jumped with an American flag from the other aircraft, a U.S. C-130. From a journalistic standpoint, either Coyne or I should have been on the ground to photograph this moment, but screw it, we were both paratroopers long before we became journalists. Neither of us would pass up this jump for a couple of lousy photographs.

Smith stood crouched in the door for a long time, his static line whipping in the windstream, and then the green light flashed. Presto, he disappeared.

The first stick of jumpers was made up primarily of petite lady parachute riggers from the Royal Thai Army, in cute gold and black jumpsuits and oversize white helmets. They were the only demure parachutists I have ever seen. Then it was our turn.

As we stood hanging onto our static lines like New Yorkers on the rush-hour subway, I was surprised that I had none of the usual pre-jump flutters, no frantic gulping for air, no butterflies in the stomach. That *really* frightened me. This was a Hollywood jump, no rifle, no pack, no 120 pounds of gear in a griswold bag, and it was from a skydiver's altitude, 3,000 feet, as opposed to the 1,000 from which paratroopers drop, which meant that in the event of a malfunction we'd have a generous thirty seconds to repair the damage, instead of nine, but there is no such thing as a casual parachute jump.

When it goes it goes like a freight train. Quickly, one by one, the jumpers ahead disappeared as their static lines went taut from the anchor line cable to the door. Then I had both hands in the door, one toe over the edge, hundred and thirty-knot wind in my face, a glimpse of blue sky, wispy clouds, a rice paddy in the lower third of my vision. Go!

Up and out, feet together, hands on the reserve, but my elbows weren't in right and the prop blast turned me face to earth as I felt the tug at my back that pulled my trash out. It billowed and inflated, stopping me rather abruptly in midair.

No sweat, maybe one twist in the lines. I kicked it out as the sound of the airplane droned away and I was left alone in a clear blue sky.

Then I heard Coyne's eerie cackle as the olive-drab hemisphere of his chute drifted under my feet. Below I could see paddies, some kind of off-the-wall industrial plant, not a sign of a DZ.

Swinging under my olive-green canopy, turned blazing lime by the sun behind it, I pulled the toggle on my right riser, turned right, swinging out, and ran with the wind. There it was, maybe two-fifths of a mile ahead, 2,500 feet below, a great scar of earth with a canopied reviewing stand, right center on a rectangle about the size of six football fields, little dots of people all over it, coming toward me with a velocity more appropriate to a balloon race than a jump.

I looked for grenade smoke on the ground to mark the wind direction, but instead there was a smoking brush fire. The smoke was flat to the ground and streaming. This was no three-knot wind; more like thirty. I turned and held, even though I was still at 1,200 to 1,500 feet. This rig should have about a 10-knot forward speed, and I was still going backwards at a good clip. Even so, from where I had turned I should come in pretty close to the skydiver's target.

Time to take some pix. Only, whenever I took my hands off the toggles to shoot my wrist-mounted camera, the wind turned me around to run with it. All my shots were only half-aimed, and I was blown way off course and way over the target, over halfway to the far edge of the DZ.

Fuck photography! I turned and held, still moving like I had driven a motorcycle off a second-floor ramp, backwards. I cursed every ounce of the eight pounds of Singha Beer and restaurant food I had put on since Boulder, knowing from previous unhappy landings that it could make the difference between an okay fall and hitting two sides of a garbage compactor. I got my feet and knees together and my toes involuntarily curled upward. I held, caught one glimpse of the earth racing in a streaming blur backwards beneath my feet, then locked my eyes fixedly on the horizon while my entire reproductive apparatus withdrew into the perineum cavity, for I did not want what I knew was coming.

SLAM! I felt something snap in my chest. It felt like I'd been speared; intense pain spread from a point near the heart. Compared to that the bashing my thigh and back took as I completed my PLF—a maneuver sort of like turning oneself into one rocker of a rocking chair, bent over, feet and knees together, elbows in to the sides, hands on the chest pack reserve parachute—was as nothing. Good training pays off again. I tried to move around and encountered no difficulty. But the pain in my heart was incredible. I got to my feet and pulled the quick release on my bellyband. Seven Thai kids already grabbed and collapsed my chute. They and I took it off.

I withdrew the notebook and pen from my breast pocket. I had been stabbed; what snapped was the spine of my notebook. If I could still breathe this easily no ribs were broken, but I had bruised them badly.

A 10-year-old girl in a scout uniform came up and extended a tray filled with cold glasses of ice water, easily the nicest thing which has ever happened to me on a drop zone.

"Thanks!" I grinned like an idiot to excuse my inability to exchange pleasantries.

Airborne pride made me take my kit bag, filled with seventy-five pounds of main and reserve parachute, from the Thai kids, and lug it to the turn-in point myself.

"Congratulations!" Mark Smith yelled at me as we came in. "You're one of six people who hit the DZ."

"Where's Coyne?"

He pointed. Mekong Jimmy stood two hundred feet away, in front of the reviewing stand, shooting photos, laughing. "I did a perfect PLF right in front of the reviewing stand," he said.

Were I a more generous-spirited man, this news would have pleased me, but it did not.

Glen Gamble turned too low and augered in. He broke an arm and his pelvis. The next day they put him on the airplane on a stretcher, moving very carefully. At every abrupt movement he clenched his teeth and his body tensed, but he said nothing. He did not look happy.

One of the Thais broke his pelvis also.

Dr. Sivavudh landed in the trees a long way from the DZ, but he was okay. He came in grinning, talking real fast about his next jump, about maybe getting into freefall. We all smiled, remembering our own first ones.

As we came off the DZ, we were led under the saffron canopy over the reviewing stand, before an ancient, wizened, saffron-robed and shaven-headed Buddhist monk. His look was enigmatic, but amusement and compassion were in his eyes. As I knelt before him, he placed a medal of the Buddha around my neck, hanging from a saffron ribbon.

# 12

# Khao Kor

Being in Thailand gave me an opportunity to work with Thai Special Forces, something I had wanted to do for a long time. An assignment to the U.S. 46th Special Forces Company, which had advised Thai Special Forces before the American pullout, had been one of the most coveted in the Green Berets, one that I never achieved.

Thailand was especially fascinating to me because it was so close to Vietnam. The nature of the threat was similar, and yet the Thais had survived and the Vietnamese had not. I wanted to lay Mao's principles, and my own experiences and conclusions, over the Thai situation and see how it varied from the Vietnamese experience.

Toward that end I asked Colonel Rut Komalvanich at the Royal Thai Special Warfare Center to set it up for me to visit an active Special Forces Group. He was happy to oblige and sent me to the Fourth Group at Pitsanulok.

The country on either side of the car looked like the Central Highlands of Vietnam. Exactly like the Highlands. Green hills stretched off into green mountains in the distance. Fields close to the road were cut short for dry rice farming, and on the other side of the fields stood ranked rows of thatch-roofed houses on stilts. Occasional clumps of stooped brown people in tribal dress, baskets on their backs or handmade hoes on their shoulders, shuffled along the side of the road. They grinned blasted betelnut smiles as we drove past.

Eighteen years before, such a scene would have been an everyday thing. But this was Thailand in the '80s, not Vietnam in the '60s. The road ahead was a curving ribbon of new blacktop, and our vehicle a pale green '78 Valiant with the Beatles' *Good Day Sunshine* blasting from the radio.

An RTA motor pool sticker on the dashboard and a locked and loaded CAR-15 that leaned against the bench seat between me and the driver, Colonel Udom Ketprom, were other reminders of the old life. We were on our way to visit one of his "A" detachments, deep in what had recently been terrorist country, a place called Khao Kor.

Udom, slender and wiry, with a tough but good-humored face, idly bopping the steering wheel with the heel of his hand to the beat of Ringo's drums, wasn't dressed like a colonel. He wore matched faded denim pants and shirt, slick white loafers and a golf hat. I had been amazed when he came out dressed like that this morning. "Not good wear camouflage if draw fire," he replied sensibly when I asked him about it.

When the U.S. pulled its large advisory force out of Thailand in 1976, at the Thais' request, it was widely believed that Thailand would be the next domino to fall, after Laos and Cambodia. This never happened.

Thai Special Forces has basically the same mission as ours: to organize, train and direct indigenous forces in the conduct of guerrilla operations, with a secondary mission of organizing counterguerrilla operations. Their public success has been in the latter. They are quite willing to express gratitude for the help of the U.S. Special Forces in getting started, but their success has equaled, and in many cases, surpassed ours.

They may have run guerrilla missions in Laos and Cambodia, but if so, they don't admit it.

By now it should have occurred to our deep thinkers in the Pentagon that those of our client states who have succeeded against the "War of National Liberation" strategy have, at some point, had to do so on their own. Many examples come to mind; Guatemala, Venezuela, Bolivia, but the most striking is Thailand, which squelched not one, but three insurgencies simultaneously. They used principles learned from the now-departed Americans, animated by a peculiar genius of their own.

The day before, reviewing a graduation parade for a company of black-uniformed paramilitary rangers who had been trained by his group, the Fourth, he invited me to join him on the reviewing stand, with a three-star general, and the inevitable saffron-robed Buddhist monk.

In Thailand, where our advisors had pulled out in 1976, the people who knew the Americans best are now colonels and generals. If you turn up as an ex-GI and correspondent for a U.S. military magazine, you find yourself hanging out with important people.

This means you get the VIP tour, which has its good points and bad points. You see things it would be very hard to see otherwise, and you usually have the situation explained by the most savvy person around. On the other hand, nobody wants you to get shot at on a VIP tour. It's difficult to explain to a man who's giving you the best he's got that your real job is to sleep in the rain like a dog and try as hard as possible to shoot and get shot at.

The new rangers looked very sharp as they goose-stepped past the reviewing stand. The Thais have had German as well as American military training, and they have learned a type of precision that we never attempted to teach in Vietnam.

Later we went over to his little "O" Club for a beer. He was delighted by a visit from a former American Special Forces person. We knew a couple of people in common, including Larry Dring, who had done a tour there.

As a young lieutenant, almost twenty years before, Udom had been executive officer of a joint U.S.-Thai "A" Detachment. His best memory of that experience was a night HALO jump. Twelve of them, six Americans and six Thais, had spun off the tailgate of a C-130 at 30,000 feet, at night, on oxygen, and fallen at 125 miles per hour for two minutes, straight down into the darkness. Then they deployed their parachutes. This is a way to get in under radar.

Another reason Udom was glad to see me was that he had been working twelve-hour days for more than two weeks straight, and protocol demanded that he knock-off and show me the sights.

When we got to town he took me to the temple of the Golden Buddha of Pitsanulok. Almost a thousand years old, this Buddha was the premier attraction of the town. The ancient temple lacked the juke box look of Thailand's newer *wats*. The reverence of the common people kneeling before the Buddha, the incense, the great gold Buddha itself, gazing with transcendent compassion out over the open interior of the temple, filled me with deep respect.

This Buddha was a most potent defense against Communism; people need it to give their lives meaning, and the Communists don't have anything like it.

Udom invited me to his favorite restaurant for a few beers and some dinner. We drove across a bridge and down along the river. Across the wide, flat expanse of red-brown water was a fair-sized town of maybe 100,000 to 150,000. A few modern buildings shot up out of the jungle maze of Thailand, but most of the city was unpainted grey wooden houses on stilts. The city was clean, people appeared well-fed, and a big smile was the most common expression.

He braked to a stop along the river and we walked down a long wooden gangway to a little, flaking-green wooden houseboat restaurant bobbing at the edge of the water. In my memory it has a rusty Coca-Cola sign on its side, but maybe that was the one in Louisiana.

We bounced down the gangway and across the swaying deck, taking seats on folding chairs, beside the water. The river was wide and beautiful, lined with palms and banana trees on either side. A few small boats plied the river, narrow and graceful with upturned bows and sterns, piled high with wicker baskets of fish or fruit. The boatmen stood and poled, their faces shielded by conical straw hats. A goodly breeze blew across the river.

The waiter brought us two huge bottles of Kloster beer and a tray of tiny green peppers. I have been known to munch hot peppers like popcorn, peppers so hot that other Americans can't smell them without crying. People have tried to ambush me with hot peppers from Mexico to Lebanon. It's my one macho trick.

"Hot, very hot," said Udom.

I smiled condescendingly and popped a couple of them into my mouth.

Pain, very intense pain, raced along the blood vessels on the underside of my tongue. Tears sprang to my eyes and the lingering traces of a sinus condition disappeared instantly; the top of my head felt as though a stake had been driven through it. I immediately chuga-lugged half a quart of beer.

Udom carefully controlled his smile.

I finished that beer and half another before I could talk again.

I asked him how long he had been in the army, and he said twenty years. I asked him how long he had been in Special Forces and he said twenty years. Score one for the Thais. The U.S. Army had con-sistently refused to make SF an officer's career field. I asked how long he had been in Pitsanulok and he said he was born there. Score another one for the Thais. They seemed to have learned not only from our successes, but from our mistakes as well.

Just as Mao's model for revolutionary warfare is organized in three sets of threes, counterinsurgents also use a three-pronged strategy; military operations to combat the enemy, civic action, as it is called—the use of army assets to build roads, dig wells, treat illnesses, and other actions to win the support of the people—and a public-relations campaign to spread the word that this is going on. Obviously being a hometown boy is a big help in such an effort.

There was no way a Green Beret could have arranged to be born in Pleiku, but it was powerfully discouraging to spend months building up that rapport without which it is impossible to operate effectively with paramilitary troops, or to build a good intelligence net among the local tribes, only to be pulled out on the eve of major success because of the army's personnel rotation policy.

This dedicated man sat at ease in his favorite restaurant, but his lines were out everywhere. He knew the people; he knew the coun-try, and he knew his stuff. For the Communist terrorists to try muscling in on his territory was like a cat trying to scratch its way inside a bowling ball.

The restaurant owner, a high school classmate of Udom's, brought our food. He was a laughing man, wiry and strong. He introduced himself as Sam Long.

Our dinner was hot seafood soup. I dug my spoon in, and out came a little squid, tentacles dangling four inches down from the spoon. Its beady little dead eyes stared past. I mashed the tentacles off on the side of the bowl and swallowed him. He was delicious, but very

hot. It required several more beers to get through the meal. The pleasant afternoon turned into a long crazy night.


We were halfway to Khao Kor the next morning before my brain
engaged.

Khao Kor had been a Communist Party of Thailand guerrilla base
area, a region of thickly-jungled mountains, very difficult to probe.
General Pichitr (pronounced peach-it) Kullivanijaya had elected not
to probe it. He dozed it off. He lashed logs around the Cat operators
for protection and ran operations up to battalion-size around them.
"A year from now we'll be putting up hotels and schools," one of
his officers had said. Now it was a year later and we were going back
for the victory celebration.

Colonel Udom's Fourth Group had provided reconnaissance
elements for the initial operation. Some of his "A" Detachments were
now deployed in a role very similar to the Strategic Hamlet program
in Vietnam, developing hilltribe villages and dry rice farming on mountains that had hidden hundreds of guerrillas. Many of those guerrillas
were still hidden in the mountains around, and they seriously didn't
want those villages to succeed.

When we arrived at the Khao Kor headquarters there were no hotels
in evidence yet, but there was a terrific-looking school, which had
been let out for the occasion.

There was a raw frontier quality about the place. The headquarters
building was sheet tin and there was an awful lot of red dirt and earth-
moving equipment. Two green and white agriculture department Bell
Jetrangers were tied down across the road below.

Udom had to go immediately into the headquarters for a briefing
conducted in Thai; I elected to nose around outside. There were a
few TV crews and print reporters from the Thai press there for the
occasion.

Udom wasn't the only one in jeans, but a lot of it wasn't jean cut.
I saw one denim business suit. I was at a loss to understand it, and
there was no one to explain to it me.

Another chopper came in, an army Huey, and out jumped General
Pichitr in a denim safari suit, and Jim Coyne in a khaki safari suit

similar to my own.

I shook hands with General Pete, his West Point nickname, and he disappeared into the briefing.

Coyne and I strolled down the raw, red road, past the earth-moving equipment. "How come everybody's in jeans around here?" I asked.

"This operation was run by a joint command that is strictly a Thai innovation," he replied. "CPMU 1617, Civil-Police-Military Unit. Everybody was under General Pete, the Ag department, the Border Police, everybody. He thought the people in the headquarters ought to have the same uniform, and he hit on the idea of putting everybody in jeans."

I grinned. "He unifies his command and at the same time makes his staff identify with the people."

Coyne lit a cigarette and took a deep overhand drag. "Pichitr is an authentic military genius. When I was up here last year the German military attache was along and we were up on this mountain, looking down on this whole brilliant operation, which was like nothing anybody else had ever done. This goddam German was simply overcome with admiration. He grabbed Pichitr and hugged him and exclaimed, 'You...you're another Hitler!'

"Then he gave me a kind of sheepish look and said, 'You know what I mean.'"

"Did you know what he meant?"

"No!"

After the ceremonies and congratulations were over, and the last helicopter had taken off, Udom took me out to visit one of his "A" detachments. Split into four sites, each on a mountaintop, all within sight of at least one other, each separate site detachment had one company of paramilitary rangers, and each company provided security for a large hilltribe village. We toured a couple of these. The villages were much like Montagnard villages in Vietnam, with the houses off the ground on poles, except that they were single-family dwellings, and instead of thatch they were roofed with sheet tin.

We paused to visit with one family sitting on the porch of their house. In Vietnamese Montagnard villages, Vietnamese officers had not been welcome. The people clammed up and averted their eyes. The man of this family, strongly-muscled and obviously delighted to see the Thai team sergeant who was taking me and Udom around, grinned around his crooked pipe. His wife held up a fat healthy baby for us to tickle and cluck over.

The houses were laid out in neat rows and the rice fields around were beginning to show a crop.

We left that site and headed for the one under direct control of the "A" detachment commander.

Udom pointed out the tallest mountain in the area as we drove. "Khao Kor," he said, "mean Grandfather Mountain. I lose twenty men on Khao Kor. Recon." His face was stoic, but I looked deep in his eyes and saw that he was prey to the worst occupational hazard of the combat infantry, grief.

The new two-lane blacktop highway ran right up to the villages, tangible evidence to the villagers of their government's concern. It caused me to flash back almost twenty years to the South Vietnamese officer in our province who defected to the VC rather than do Civic Action among the "filthy Montagnards," to the district chiefs who had kept their areas in a constant state of turmoil, because every time a family was relocated it was allocated 1000 piastres in USAID money (about $10.00) and the district chief was pocketing 800 of it.

The Thais aren't like that. They are very smart people, they have guts to spare, and they love their country.

The road to the last camp stopped at the bottom of the hill. We left our car and walked to the camp. When we reached the crest we turned and looked back at the hills, and the village we had come from, the black ribbon of road leading to it, and a small local security patrol that crossed an open area at the foot of the hill.

Further up the hill was a wonderfully laid-out mini-A camp, with an excellent defensive perimeter and neat thatch-roofed rattan buildings. The camp was immaculate. The young CO reported in jeans and a white T-shirt. He was Captain Sootom Sriklon, about 5'10", maybe 180 pounds, a big man for a Thai.

He took us on a brief tour of the camp, and I asked, if possible, to accompany his troops on a local security patrol.

They readily agreed, but it didn't turn out exactly as I expected.

I can imagine what the sergeant's instructions to the patrol were when he got the men in the hootch. "All right, men, this is for a big-time international magazine, so wear your best uniform. I want everything to go perfectly. That's the Group Commander out there, so whatever you do, don't fuck up! And act natural."

He had a squad fallen out five minutes after I made my request. They looked good. The sergeant was sharp, calm and serious. The point man looked a trifle addled, but they all do. There were a couple of kids among them, one looked very earnest and watched the older guys to see whether he was doing it right. The other kid was a cocky little shit, the kind who makes a champion warrior, if he lives long enough. He let the corner of his mouth smirk when I took his picture, looking hard over his weapon.

We moved into the woods on a short patrol. There was no noise and no grabass. The troops kept their interval and watched the patrol leader's hand and arm signals. Each one had an assigned area to watch and kept alert. When the leader held up his hand everybody stopped without bunching up. When he pushed his hand down they went into a low squat, their weapons ready. They were supposed to be paramilitary troops, but they moved very professionally.

The one thing that sticks in my mind the most about that trip was a casual remark by the "A" detachment commander. "Well, Captain," I said, "you've built yourself a pretty nice little empire here."

The young captain gave me a reproachful look. "Is not for me," he said. "Is for the people."

# *13*

# Average Days

In Thailand, with the jungle and Vietnam so close, I began dreaming about my days in Special Forces; not the bad days, not days when I had done something especially brave and/or stupid, the days on which I got shot. I had already come to terms with those memories in dreams, and they didn't haunt me anymore.

There were a couple of other recurring dreams I'd been dreaming for years. In the first I was in an alley in Saigon, in the present day, with the city under the NVA I was in an alley, unarmed, in a tiger suit, with my caucasian face, running and hiding. In the other recurring dream, I was sitting next to a bunch of Yards camped in the jungle. They wore rags, and carried old weapons. They were eating a meager dinner, and they were thin and grim. I knew they were FULRO, and I knew they were still fighting the Vietnamese, but I wasn't armed and they couldn't see me. I was like a ghost.

I wondered whether there was anything to astral projection. I was sure I wasn't the only guy dreaming that dream, and I wondered whether they could feel that we were still with them, that we were now the *yang* of the forest, lying in our beds in the States with our souls still roaming the jungle.

But here in Bangkok I was dreaming about average days, the ones that stuck in memory as everyday life. It was some life.

Once, after I got out of the Army, I visited my friend Tom Kiernan, who had done two tours with the Forces and one with MACV as an advisor. We were spending an evening with some of his law school classmates, shooting the breeze, telling a few stories.

One of his classmates mentioned that Tom had two Silver Stars. I hadn't known that, so he must have earned them with MACV. "How in the hell did you get two Silver Stars?" I asked. The only guy I knew with two Silver Stars was Larry Dring, and the stories of what he had done to earn them made my hair stand on end. But criteria for those medals vary from unit to unit.

"You remember what an average day was like in Special Forces?" Tom replied.

"Yeah, sure."

"We had two days like that."

I dreamed of average days.


In early 1964, in the northern part of Phu Bon province, the VC weren't active within a day's march of our camp, and we made no contact the first day. We made camp beside a stream, close to a Bahnar Montagnard corn field and banana grove, and slept all night under a creaking bamboo tree. The next morning we were up and off early.

Our Jarai Montagnards shuffled noisily through large dry leaves, called Elephant Ears, which lay under the trees. I halted the company and told Kpa Doh, our interpreter, to have them quit kicking the leaves. This was very early in the war and most of our equipment was WWII stuff. A couple of months later we got the first M-79s and AR-15s, issued on an experimental basis.

But even then we were the most heavily-armed force in these woods, eighty-five Yards with M-1 carbines, one hand-held sixty-millimeter mortar, and four Americans with M-2 automatic carbines.

That early in the war the most we could expect to encounter was a squad of VC-controlled Bahnar Montagnards with maybe one automatic weapon between them. But they'd be gunning for the Americans. We were obvious targets, and there was a price on our heads. It was only about twenty-five bucks, but that was big money in the Central Highlands. The Special Forces "A" teams were losing about eight percent a year killed in action at that point.

Our Yards expected to frighten the VC away by making a lot of noise. I didn't want to frighten them; I wanted to kill them.

It took three more halts to get them to quit shuffling through the leaves, but finally they moved silently.

We were in unusually open terrain for Vietnam. We were able to keep on the trails, with flank security in sight, and still make good time.

Since we had no fixed objective, but were just out looking for a fight, and since, if we found one it was likely to be us getting ambushed, we had devised a combat formation that consisted of three parallel columns, each platoon with three files of one squad each, abreast, about twenty meters apart. If they ambushed us from close to the trail, we already had a squad behind them. If they ambushed from further back, we could lay down a base of fire and flank them easily. For that terrain, and with those troops, it was a great formation.

We found one bare footprint and spent the rest of the morning running down that trail, finally coming into a valley surrounded on three sides by low, forested mountains. A pretty little stream came down through a cut in the hills to the right.

I spread the company out in a skirmish line and we went through the valley looking for the owner of that bare footprint. We found a small Bahnar village clustered under tall trees. They had individual family houses instead of the multiple-family longhouses of our Jarai. But, like Jarai houses, they were up on log-size stilts, with the same rattan porches in front, and a notched log leaned against the porch for stairs. Some of their fires were still warm. The villagers had gotten out just ahead of us.

It seemed very likely that they'd send somebody to tell armed VC we were in the area.

Dappled light through the trees made a pleasant, shady place of the village.

I walked over to the nearest house and pulled a handful of thatch out of the roof, then dug around in my pocket for a lighter. I set fire to one end of the clump and shoved it into the roof. "Burn it!" I said, thinking wryly that this was probably the first touch of civilization these people had ever seen.

The concept of operations we were using was to bring the Bahnar into lightly fortified villages along the main highway, and train them to defend themselves against the VC, thus denying access to their food to North Vietnamese passing through the province to become replacements in VC units further south. This concept didn't work, because the Bahnar weren't going to leave their hills no matter what anybody did. But we didn't have a better plan then, although later we did, so we stuck to the old one.

Armies are not precision instruments, and every time they go to work innocent people get hurt.

It was easy to understand why the Bahnar didn't want to leave these hills. Their houses had been built with care, each strip of bamboo split by hand, each of their wicker baskets painstakingly woven by their women, each water gourd grown and fashioned carefully into a dipper.

With the last of the burning clump of thatch I lit a Parliament, and, with the filter a cool quarter-inch away, watched flame and smoke billow around the fourteen houses in that village.

"Sir, sir," Nay Re, the company commander, called. "We find buffalo, many buffalo." We moved quickly through the woods to an open clearing where the buffalo were boxed in on three sides by low hills. We closed the box on the other side.

They were large peaceful-looking beasts, their enormous grey-black bodies topped by a hump, the weight of their flattopped, backcurving horns keeping their heads low. This herd most likely was the entire wealth of this village. With these gone and their crops destroyed, maybe, theoretically, they'd be desperate enough to pay attention to our psyops messages and leave this backcountry for the strategic hamlets. I had to believe that, but even then it didn't feel right.

I stood with a blade of grass stuck in a corner of my mouth, reached up and cocked back my hat to let the breeze cool my forehead and pushed my shades back up on my nose. Slowly my three Americans arranged themselves beside me and the Yards spread out until we formed a solid wall of armed men. I put my carbine on single shot and carefully took aim at the head of an old cow.

I squeezed off a round and a small red dot appeared in the center of her forehead. She stood there and looked at me stupidly, as though she had been bitten by a mosquito.

The rest of us opened up on the herd. There didn't appear to be any effect. Then they started lowing a little and walking around in circles. We moved in closer.

I put the switch on full auto and moved in on the old cow I had shot first. She looked at me quizzically as I fired a six-round burst into her neck and shoulders. She dropped to her knees and went, "MOOOOOOOO!" blood streaming from a half-dozen holes in her huge slab of a body. I fired another three-round burst into her and something in there must have broken because a great gush of blood came out of the holes in her chest. She rolled over on her side and lay there panting, trying to get some air into her lungs, only they wouldn't hold it anymore. I put a round into her brain and she lay back dead before her head hit the ground.

Now the buffalo were milling faster, lowing louder. One calf tried to run out of the box. I picked her off in mid-stride, went over and fired another round into her brain. Then I changed magazines.

It took about half an hour to kill them all. It was hot work in the sun.

I took a long cool pull from my canteen and lit another cigarette. I allowed the Yards thirty minutes to cut off what meat they wanted from the buffalo. Minutes later they ran by with great red hunks in their hands.

More meat was slung on poles or tied to the backs of their packs where it hung dripping down the canvas and sometimes onto the tigerstriped seats of their pants.

Then we spread out again in a skirmish line and combed the entire valley. All we found was an almost dry creek bank with many foot-prints running down it, and wicker baskets where the Bahnar had dropped them.

"It looks like they went up that creek," I said. "We'll run that out and see what we find."

I moved the company a little way up the creek and stopped in the shade. It was going to be a long climb. The Americans came up and we sat there on the boulders in the middle of the creek, smoking and refilling our canteens. The creek bed was fifteen or twenty feet wide, all grey, worn rocks. Now, in the dry season, the stream only flowed in a foot-wide trickle, and there were many small stagnant pools trapped in little depressions in the rock. All around were abandoned wicker baskets and gourds that the Bahnar had left behind, crushed and broken on the ground. Nay Re, the company commander, and Kpa Doh, the interpreter, came up and I offered them each a cigarette.

There was one small wicker basket left behind that contained a litter of puppies. Their eyes were barely opened and they tumbled over each other in the basket, small bundles of soft flesh and hair.

"I hope the momma dog comes back," Augie DeLucia, our medic said. "They sure are cute." Augie was a short, blond, good-hearted farm boy, an E-6, and about my age, twenty-five.

"She probably will," I said.

Nay Re saw us pointing and talking about the puppies so he reached in the basket and picked one up. He looked at it for a moment as it squirmed in his hand, then dashed it against the rocks, smiling good naturedly.

Maybe it was our fault. He'd just helped us kill fifty or sixty animals, but I didn't think of that. To me the difference was self-evident.

"You son of a bitch," I said.

DeLucia became so angry that John Watson, our weapons man, reached out and took his carbine away from him. John was nineteen, a rangy E-5. He looked like a classic frontiersman.

"Now you've broken its back," said George Stogdill, our intel sergeant. "Go on and kill him. But leave the rest of the litter alone," he said.

"Tell Nay Re," I snapped, "that Americans do not kill for fun. Only for food and for enemies."

I was never able to work effectively with Nay Re after that. I couldn't help hating him, maybe because of the killing I'd done myself that day. He knew I disliked him, though he probably never figured out why.

When the break was over we started off again, climbing steadily upward. The grade steepened until finally we were climbing straight up, a hundred feet or more, over dried waterfalls. Craning my neck upward I could see the first platoon stretched out above, clinging to bare rock. And far below, partially obscured by trees, Augie skipped from rock to rock, his rucksack bouncing on his back, carbine gripped in his right hand as he grabbed for rocks with his left. I had to sling my carbine to climb over an outcropping, and for a moment my feet dangled over a sheer, forty-foot drop as I hauled myself over the next shelf.

It took two and a half hours for us to climb to the top. We could see thirty kilometers or more across the valley below. Through binoculars I could make out our forward operational base, a small camp that we had left two days before. Beyond that, six or seven klicks further, the Song Ba snaked its way down toward Cheo Reo. The valley was crisscrossed with Bahnar rice fields.

We went down the reverse slope of the hill and that night made camp beside another stream.

We spent all the next morning moving east up a gradual slope. We had almost crossed the line into Plciku province and were halfway out of chow anyway, so I gave the order to start looping back toward the FOB. It was either cross that mountain or go back down the same valley we came up, and there was no point in that. Anytime you go back the same way you came you run the risk of ambush.

But going down the steep reverse slope of the mountain after a lunch of cold rice balls and C-ration cookies was not the easy job that walking up the gentle forward slope had been. It was a nearly straight drop down.

The three columns moved parallel to each other, reaching, grabbing for handholds, gradually gathering momentum until we were falling down the hill a foot or two at a time. I swung from tree to tree, feet constantly slipping out from under me, reaching for trees seen from the corner of my eye, sometimes pulling a hand back just in time to avoid grabbing a gray trunk covered with three-inch thorns.

It was a mad scramble to the bottom and when we got there we lay on the ground, except for the security detail, heads cradled on our rucksacks; we panted and smoked and gulped some of our water and smoked some more until finally I just couldn't put it off any longer.

"Okay, saddle up. Let's get out of here."

It was easy walking on the valley floor, and the center of the column couldn't move fast because the flanks guiding on us were slowed by brush. Strolling was pleasant and my mind started to wander. We were on the way home and still hadn't made contact, and I was eager for action.

Behind me Kpa Doh whispered, "Sir! Sir!" and I looked in the direction he was pointing. At first I didn't see anything. Then I walked quietly over to the right flank security squad and peered through the trees. Another village lay open in the sunshine. It appeared deserted. I gave the first and third platoons thirty minutes to move around in an encirclement. While they were getting into position, the second platoon spread into a skirmish line. When the half hour was up we moved into the village.

Ksor Yul, leader of the first platoon, had been a corporal under the French. He watched me curiously out of the corner of his eye. We were still sizing each other up. I liked him very much. His moves were sure and skillful, and his gaze was steady. He was fair to his troops, but allowed them little slack.

The village was empty.

I slung my carbine, propped one foot up on a paddy dike and lit a cigarette. Then I mopped my face with my patrol cap and slapped it back on my head soaked with salty sweat. Waving Re and Kpa Doh over, I dropped my rucksack. The minute my ruck hit the ground the Yards shrugged out of theirs and started hacking down sugar cane with their knives, but the ones on the outer edges still faced outward with their weapons ready.

Kpa Doh and Re hacked off stalks of sugarcane on their way over to where I stood. Kpa Doh got two and gave me one.

"Thanks," I said.

I unsnapped the kaybar knife from my harness suspenders and slowly peeled the outer skin from the cane stalk. "You think Bahnar work in fields now?" I asked.

"Yes, I think maybe so," Kpa Doh replied.

"Maybe they know we here," I said. "But if we burn house they know for sure."

Kpa Doh nodded and told Re what I had said. Re nodded.

"I think maybe we no burn house, then might make contact. Better no burn house, kill VC."

They conferred in their harsh tribal language. "Re think that good idea," Kpa Doh said.

While they nodded again I bit down on the tip of the sugarcane; sweet juice ran down my throat and coarse, tough fibers caught between my teeth.

I glanced at my watch. "Okay, let's form up and get back on the trail. We got a long way to go before dark."

It took too long to get the company squared away. Our formation had gotten scattered in the encirclement. Finally we got back on the trail and marched down the valley toward the creek. It was smooth, easy walking and I had started to enjoy the scenery when a burst of automatic-weapons fire snapped my head around.

I knelt, carbine chattering sixty rounds into the foliage across the river as fast as I could change magazines. It was stupid to waste the ammo, but if we were going to have a firefight I wanted my share. A hard charge of adrenalin blew me straight into another plane of existence, where everything is serene and stands out sharp and brilliant.

They were firing from our left, from maybe thirty meters away. We didn't seem to have taken casualties, so I stood up and gave the hand and arm signal for skirmishers. Down the line with the first platoon, I saw John Watson stand up at my signal and give the same command to his troops. The whole company was standing now, as far as I could see. We spread out in one long, thin, straight line.

I shouted, "LET'S GO!" and started moving forward. All up and down the line the Americans moved forward, tall, lonely targets ten meters ahead of their troops. We were all firing, but in my heightened state I couldn't hear. I could see little puffs and the high shiny arc of ejected shells, crystalline in their exactness.

Ksor Yul came up beside me, "Punjis," he said and pointed at the sharpened bamboo stakes hidden in the grass, angled to about fourteen inches, shitsoaked and ready to infect. "Fuck a bunch of punjis," I muttered and promptly took one through the toe of my boot. I couldn't feel it and kicked it away. It went flying off in the grass. "COME ON! COME ON! LET'S GO! LET'S GO!"

Yul looked at me happily and said, *"Oui, mon captaine."* I knew then that I had passed his test. It was a good feeling, for he was an old soldier and I was a very young one.

*"Un groupe traverson la fleuve,"* I said to Yul and motioned that I wanted one squad to cross the creek and swing back toward the center. We came to very tall grass and thick brush and couldn't see where we were moving. Our forward movement started to bog down. "All right," I yelled, "LET'S ROLL!" and gave the move out hand-and-arm signal.

"Captaine," Yul said, *"le mortier, le mortier."*

"Huh?" I said. "Oh yeah, you want to mortar in there. Okay, good idea. Go ahead. *OUI! OUI!"*

The mortarman came up, unwrapped the red scarf from his neck and used it as a potholder on the tube of his little 60mm mortar, firing hand-held and getting good accuracy. The mortar is an indirect fire weapon that lobs a shell in a high arc, good for getting to men in holes and behind cover. Crump............BLAM! Crump..........BLAM! Crump.............BLAM! White puffs of smoke drifted out of the bush across the river.

Before we could get up to get the attack moving again, Augie DeLucia, our medic, and George Stogdill, the intelligence sergeant, ran up panting, their faces smudged and dirty. "They bugged out," George said. "We found a little firing platform on the other side of the creek. It had maybe two or three guys with a submachinegun and a couple of carbines." I hadn't realized that either of them had gone across with the squad I'd sent. Later I found that they had crossed even before I gave the order.

"Any stiffs?" I asked.

"Maybe so," DeLucia said. "There was some blood on the platform. We got one old man took a round through the arm; we gotta get him back. And maybe eight or ten guys with punji wounds. They'll infect fast."

"Yeah, I know," I said. "Got one myself."

"Let me see it."

"Look at that old boy with the wounded arm first. This isn't anything."

He told me to take off my boot while he looked at the old fellow with the arm wound. I watched. It wasn't a bad wound; he was just grazed on the upper arm. But he was almost fifty years old, far too old to be on a combat patrol. We would have to weed these old guys out and put them to work around the camp.

My punji wound was a small puncture between my left big toe and the one next to it. My boot had taken all the damage. Augie put some merthiolate on it, and a bandaid.

"That's a Purple Heart for you, Sir," he said.

"For that? I've cut myself worse on the edge of a piece of paper."

"The regulation doesn't say how bad. It just says wounds resulting from enemy action."

I didn't argue; I wanted a medal badly. I was afraid the war would soon be over and I'd never get a chance for another one. No matter, I would earn the next three in spades, after the NVA arrived.

Some of the Montagnards with punji wounds did not get off so easily. It took another half hour to bandage them all, and then three of them required help to walk fast enough to keep up.

In the morning when I remembered this dream that had really happened, it occurred to me that I was now about the same age as the old guys I'd wanted to get out of the field and put in administrative jobs. I pushed this thought aside.

# 14

# At The Hot L Chaing Rai

I had been told we'd only be in Thailand for three weeks, and more time than that passed before Brown arrived. Finally he got there, after having been diverted to an air show in Chile. While there he'd concocted a scheme to bomb the main Russian air base in Kabul, Afghanistan, from ultra-light airplanes. None of us even pretended to take him seriously.

Three weeks after his arrival, during which time we accomplished little or nothing, and appeared to be no closer to finishing, I told him flatly that Kathy and I had been married less than a year, and either she came over or I went home. Then I made a serious pitch to bring her over. Why not? She's a terrific administrator, great hostess, good photographer, pretty good writer, and has great charm in social situations, something the rest of us were lacking. He bought it.

When she arrived two weeks later, his welcoming present was a weekend in the Hyatt in Chaing Mai, the northernmost city in Thailand, a beautiful place. But while we were there he also wanted us to buzz on up to Chaing Rai, further north, and make contact with Khun Sa, the so-called "Opium Warlord" and his Shan United Army, to arrange for *SOF* to go into Burma. I figured for Kat it would be a good introduction to our "method"—if that is indeed the term—of operation.

At sunset, three *samlors*, the Thai version of the bicycle-rickshaw, carrying Kat, Chan, and me arrived at our tiny, hidden-away hotel in Chaing Rai, the northernmost city in Thailand large enough to have a hotel. The people we didn't want to know we were there would, theoretically, be staying at the luxurious Wiang Inn on the other side of town.

Dr. Seuss, who had set up the meet, was a stickler for keeping a low profile, so he had chosen this out-of-the-way place. Dr. Seuss was a former CIA spook who had been cashiered for excessive drinking. Now he was off the sauce totally, and worked for Brown very professionally.

But I don't think he ever appreciated the difference between a magazine and an intelligence agency. As a magazine, we couldn't just dazzle each other with bullshit, graphs and charts, endless intelligence reports that never led anywhere. We had to tell stories to sell the magazine and pay for all this. I think Dr. Seuss thought we were a rogue detachment of the CIA, with a weird cover.

The low profile was part of the reason Kat was along. Two men, one a farang, and the other looking like an account executive for a Chinese ad agency, would draw unwholesome attention. "If they're not here to buy dope, jewels, or women, what the hell are they here for?"

But if the redheaded joker is seen to follow a foxy farang lady from jewelry store to jewelry store, then all the Chinese has to do is sit at his favorite cafe, glance at his watch, order a drink, and all is explained.

The diamond-shaped muscles of my samlor driver's calves relaxed to a halt. I dismounted awkwardly from the springy rickshaw seat behind his bicycle saddle and escorted Kathy into the lobby, while Chan fumbled for the fare.

Four orientals sat reading papers in the tiny lobby. "That's Mr. Loy," Chan muttered from behind, as we picked up our bags and headed toward the stairs. "I think they are already here." I muttered a curse, and checked my watch. It was seven o'clock. The deal was that they would show up any time after eight. We had come back this early specifically to avoid this encounter. But it did reveal that they were even more antsy about this than we were.

"Well, so much for your plan not to let them know I'm here," Kat said. I had expected we would be settled into our room when they arrived in town, from whatever torturous route they had followed from Burma. Their mission was theoretically friendly, but they were known to be hard boys, and our liaison was built on a transitory mutual interest; we had no history of friendship or trust. This was the first contact between the *SOF* staff and agents of Khun Sa.

I had wanted to bring Kat on this trip. She'd arrived in Thailand only two days before, after a seven-week separation, and this jaunt into hill tribe country was the best chance I would ever get to show someone I loved why I kept going back to Vietnam. But I didn't want her involved with these people in any way.

The way I had it figured, the opium-growing Shan tribesmen had much to gain and nothing to lose from cooperating with *SOF*, and much to lose and nothing to gain from assassinating a reporter. But I did not want to test this theory on Kathy.

The idea was that Brown, Coyne, Reisinger and I were going into bandit country to interview Khun Sa; Brown and me for the magazine, Coyne to do video. This was the meeting to set up that trip.

Khun Sa's version of the story was that his organization, the Shan United Army, was a legitimate revolutionary movement, at war with the socialist government of Burma, and that their relationship to the opium trade was roughly analogous to that of the North Carolina National Guard to the tobacco industry. They wanted to use *SOF* as a vehicle to sell this version to world opinion, and also wanted to get a message to the CIA and the DEA that they'd be delighted to get out of the drug business if they could come up with another way to finance their operation.

Of course, there was no chance that Bob Brown's magazine would endorse dope runners.

And the U.S. government, I was quite sure, would not bankroll a revolution against a non-Communist government in Southeast Asia, even if by so doing they could take 60% of the Golden Triangle out of opium production, especially since organized crime could cover the shortfall with purchases from a half dozen other places. Even if, by some magic, Khun Sa could be induced to stack arms, no junkie would miss a fix.

I hoped we could get in, cover the story, and get out before they figured that out.

Kathy and I went upstairs, into our room, locked the door, and flopped down on the twin beds. Kathy returned to her *Newsweek* and I to a bloody fat file on Khun Sa.

I figured Chan would come get me in about a half hour, but that half hour crawled by, then another, then another.

Clouds outside closed off the sun even before it went down, and there were long ripping peals of thunder. Lightning flashed in the mountains. One moment it was dry and still, and then there was rain, as though one enormous bucket was being continuously dashed on the town. Air came into the room, cold, muggy and sodden; heavy enough to make the ricepaper Far East edition of *Newsweek* swell and wrinkle.

Our lights flickered and went out. There was an enormous crash, which was never explained and a peal of hysterical farang laughter from down the hall. It sounded like a lady passenger from the tourist bus, booked here by a greedy and sadistic travel agent in Bangkok.

"I guess that's it for the hill tribes fair," Kat said, lifting her head from her magazine. We had thought we might go see some Yao handicrafts after the meeting.

"At this rate there wouldn't have been enough time anyway." I suppressed a smile at the thought of those poor tourists who had traveled for three hours by bus from Chaing Mai, only to spend the night in the muggy darkness of these spartan quarters, then to ride the same bus back the next day.

We lay on one of the two narrow single beds in the room, talking for a long time, catching up on what had happened to our friends and families after I had left the States.

We talked for more than an hour after the lights went out, and never did mention our friends down the hall. Then there was a knock at our door and I jumped like I'd been stuck with a cattle prod.

Opening the door a crack, I saw Chan's scholarly face, gone all weird over a white flickering candle. "They are ready," he said.

I followed him to the end of the hall, one room down from ours and across. He knocked and the door opened. The tallest Chinese I have ever seen, his face made fierce in the candlelight by a Fu

Manchu mustache, looked out. He bowed us in.

Then the lights came back on and it was all changed. There was an untouched basket of green grapes and bananas on the table. They stood and looked at me with a trace of desperation in their manner. There was no threat there.

But they were known killers. I examined their eyes to see what kind of killers they were. The guy on the left was a short man, in his forties, in businessman's slacks, a starched, ironed white shirt, and flip-flops. His smile was genuinely warm and friendly, but there was a hardness in his eyes. This man would not kill unless he had to, but if necessary he would do it as efficiently and unemotionally as he would change the oil in his car.

The one in the middle was the galoot with the Fu Manchu. He was about my height, six-two, maybe 165 pounds. He grinned delightedly, and he was no killer at all. He handled himself like a man who's been in a couple of firefights and done all right, but who really likes the girls and the cafes. He was not a man to be dismissed lightly, however. He would do what was necessary.

Understand, if we went in, we would be completely at these people's mercy for at least four days. I was not giving them the once-over-lightly. Nor was I dealing from limited experience.

The one on the right was an old man in a thin, white, collarless Chinese shirt and grey slacks. He wore the hightopped crewcut I associate with the NVA. He had the face of a man who believed in nothing and would do anything, but he was old and tired.

They were introduced to me as Mr. Lee, Mr. Young, and Mr. Lee. We all shook hands and sat down.

The Mr. Lee on the left, looking very sincere under his straight, swept-back hair, smiled a warm smile and began speaking in a language full of quiet "sch" sounds. Mr. Young translated. "We are very happy that you have taken an interest in our movement. Much has been written about us, but no one has come to see what they are writing about."

I smiled. "To be honest," I said, "I must tell you that our magazine takes a generally favorable view of revolutionary movements against socialist governments, but an unfavorable view of the drug trade. You must expect me to ask hard questions."

Conversation through an interpreter is always difficult, and many shades of meaning are lost in the process. Mr. Young pondered my statement for a moment before translating for the two Mr. Lee's. The elderly gentleman soaked it all in with no sign of response. The younger Mr. Lee pondered the translation of my statement for a moment, then composed a diplomatic reply, which I feel sure, Mr. Young further diluted in translation.

"We are glad that you support revolutions against socialist governments. Nobody wants the name of a drug trafficker, but we cannot let the Burmese conquer our homeland."

I nodded. "We know from our study of revolution that no resistance movement in history has succeeded without outside help. We know that no government has offered to help you; your only source of aid has been the opium trade. But most Americans have never heard of the Shan states. All they know is that their families are subject to attack by junkies needing money for dope. What can I tell such a person?"

This was buzzed back and forth for a while, but no satisfactory answer was found.

"Your missus is with you?" he replied, tactfully changing the subject, and almost causing me to jump six inches off the chair.

I hesitated, but they had seen her, and the worst thing I could do at this point was get caught in a lie. "Yes."

"Will she be coming to Burma with you?"

I laughed. "No. I think she likes the city too much for that."

There were smiles all around. Nobody wanted the extra work that having a western woman in the jungle trails.

"Do you think you might like to try a country girl while you are there?"

I laughed again. "No," I said, "but my friends will have to speak for themselves. I will probably have two other people with me, Colonel Brown, our publisher, and Jim Coyne to do television." I handed them Polaroid shots of the three of us. Brown had asked me to get a shot of our SUA contact in case for some reason I didn't come back up with them, but I didn't want to throw them into a fit of worry and doubt about security, so I didn't bring it up.

"Colonel Brown looks much younger than he did on the cover of your magazine," Mr. Young said in English. We had sent two copies of different issues, and as we talked I began to realize that in Mr. Young we had created an instant hard-core *SOF* fan. Before the meeting was over he was pushing hard for a complimentary subscription.

I laughed at his remark about Brown. That cover photo with the Lao resistance was shot after an all-day straight-up-the-mountain climb to their camp. Brown was dead tired and it showed; he looked like a man coming out of the anesthetic after a lobotomy.

"I want to interview your leader," I said, "but there are always leaders. As soon as one is gone another takes his place. You can tell much more about a movement by talking to average soldiers."

"It would take a long time to do that."

I smiled. "Just a few; I don't have to talk to them all."

The younger Mr. Lee spoke earnestly for quite a spell. Mr. Young looked slightly pained as he translated. "This is very hard to arrange. We are all in Burma now. We are on a war footing; we have to change our location constantly. We must have horses for you, and soldiers to guard the route. If we arrange all this you must promise to come."

We had been forced to cancel a previous trip to visit these folks because the Lao resistance was supposed to be bringing two American POWs over the border, and we had made arrangements to be there when they did it. Brown had figured that there was maybe one chance in three that it would happen, but after working on that story for two years we couldn't afford to take the chance that it wouldn't. Of course the POWs didn't come, and we missed our first chance to interview Khun Sa. I explained that we couldn't just wait for them. We had to be free to cover other events.

We finally hammered out a deal whereby they would give us two weeks notice before they were ready, and we would give them 48 hours notice that we were coming. As I said, they wanted this story.

Toward the end of the conversation, Mr. Young asked me what I knew about their movement. I replied that I had read everything printed about it in the past six months.

"Trash," said Mr. Young without hesitation. "All trash."

My experience with Vietnam, the war in Lebanon, and other stories in which I had been an observer/participant, had given me no reason to reject that claim out of hand.

"We had some reporters come to see us two or three years ago," said the younger Mr. Lee, "but when they left they wrote stories like the others. They called our leader an Opium Warlord. We are hoping that a soldier magazine will tell the truth."

I nodded. "We are soldiers of truth," I said. "I promise to report what I see as fully and accurately as possible.

"But you must understand that to change someone's mind you have to start where they are. I might start my story with a lead like, 'I am not an Opium Warlord, says Khun Sa.'"

"It would be better if you said, 'I am a revolutionary, says Khun Sa,'" said the younger Mr. Lee with a smile. I find it difficult to dislike a quick-witted, humorous man.

There was no use trying to explain to them that no journalist is going to relinquish his "Opium Warlord" story, the term itself is too colorful. If Khun Sa were not an "Opium Warlord," no one outside Burma or Thailand would have heard of him, and I wouldn't be doing the story. There were three other Shan revolutionary armies, but none so colorful. They get no publicity.

The Nationalist Chinese 93rd Division, which went south into Burma in 1949, when the communists took over China, and muscled into the opium business, occasionally gets a mention, but its circumstances are weird enough to make a good story. The hill tribes of Burma—Shan, Karen, Kachin, Lahu, Wa, all of whom fought with the American OSS or with the Brits—are in revolt because the Burmese have reneged on the terms under which the tribes joined Burma in the first place, treating the tribes like conquered people. But these conflicts are ignored.

The Karen had a charismatic leader named Bo Mya, who looked like a mahogany Jackie Gleason in British-style fatigues and a green beret, but no one had heard of him in the West—not without a spiffy tag like "Opium Warlord." Khun Sa has as much chance of shaking that description as Ringo Starr has of becoming something other than a "former Beatle."

"We live in a world of misunderstanding," said the humorous Mr. Lee. "I came to speak the truth about our movement, and my wife thinks I have come to Thailand to see the girls."

We all had another good laugh at that.

There was no question that these guys considered themselves the aggrieved party in their dispute with the Thais. "When the Thai Border Police raid our headquarters at Hin Taek," said Mr. Young, with a kind of innocent, injured outrage, "they loot, they smash things, they urinate in the kitchens." I tried to look sympathetic, but it was obvious that he knew nothing about young troops, psyched-up and mean for battle.

The essential business of the meeting taken care of, we relaxed, munched a few grapes and shot the breeze. "Well," said Mr. Lee, "now that you've seen we're not junkies, what do you think?"

"You seem like pretty good guys to me," I said.

"We want to tell the CIA and the DEA that we are ready to get out of the drug business. Is there any way you can help us; can you get the message to them?"

I shrugged. "I know they read the magazine, but I don't know them. I have no way to know how they'll react."

We talked for an hour or so. I was comfortable in their company, and looked forward to the trip.

The next morning, when we awoke, Kin said, "Black coffee. I can't move before I have black coffee."

I was responsible for this situation. At home I liked to get up early, make a pot of coffee, read the paper over a cup, then write for a while, or run three or four miles. Then she got up and we drank coffee and shot the breeze until noon, then I worked from lunch until between ten p.m. and four a.m., depending on deadlines. Neither of us suffered much jet lag coming over. The world just adjusted itself to our schedule.

I picked up the phone and a voice said, *"Sawadee, krap,"* and went off in a long string of Thai.

"Room service," I said. "ROOM SERVICE!"

"Ah, you want restaurant?"

"Yes, restaurant please."

A moment later I got a young lady who spoke no English at all. I bellowed, "Black coffee!" and our room number several times, and hoped for the best.

Kat lay in bed, waiting for her caffeine injection while I went into the bathroom to brush my teeth and shave my neck.

"How'd it go last night?" she called.

"Pretty good," I replied. "I really like those guys. They'd kill you in a minute if it suited their purposes, but shit, everybody I know is like that. This one guy, Mr. Lee, is really funny. You know what he said..."

"These are the people who killed the DEA agent's wife?" she asked, a slightly shocked tone in her voice.

"That's what it says in the papers," I said sheepishly.

If this were a novel, this chapter would build from this atmosphere of intrigue into a stunning denouement during which Brown, Coyne, and I go into Khun Sa's camp with a homing device cunningly concealed in our gear. We would bring the Royal Thai Border Police in on a raid that ends the dope trade forever, and we kill Khun Sa and his henchmen in a thrilling shoot-out.

What actually happened was that the Border Police got on Khun Sa's ass and he had to cancel because he was running. We never went to Burma, and we never met him.

Fortunately, we shortly got another chance to get in with a guerrilla army, one more important to the U.S. strategic defense posture.

# 15

# Public Relations
# In Cambodia

The Khmer People's National Liberation Front, led by remnants of the old Lon Nol government, was waging guerrilla warfare against the Vietnamese-backed Heng Samrin regime and against our old enemies, the Vietnamese. We wanted to do a story on that for the magazine, and if possible get in some combat against the Vietnamese ourselves.

The original idea was for the four of us, Brown, Tom Reisinger, a former Special Forces medic who was our business manager, Jim Coyne, and me to go into Cambodia, essentially the same way Brown and Company had gone into Laos the year before, armed, sneaking through the jungle in cammies.

But the Cambodian situation was entirely different from Laos. Thailand is shielded from invasion through Laos by rugged mountains and the broad, flat expanse of the Mekong River. But where the highway crosses into Cambodia, near Aranyapathet, the terrain is flat, and during the dry season it turns hard. This is tank country, and a perfect invasion route for the Vietnamese. So the Thais had built a mile-wide swath of tank traps, moats, heavily-armed patrols, guards, and searchlights on the Cambodian border.

It is theoretically possible to crawl across this barrier in the dark, but highly dangerous. It seemed like there should be a better way to get into Cambodia.

As it turned out, there were two better ways, both with problems. One was simply to apply to the Thai government and go in as journalists. Son Sann, president of the KPNLF (Khmer People's National Liberation Front) had announced tentative plans for a press conference, but he could hold it only if the Thais allowed journalists to cross their border.

The purpose of the press conference was to discuss plans for a proposed coalition of the three Khmer anti-Vietnamese resistance movements.

On January 7, 1979, the Chinese-sponsored government of the Khmer Rouge had been toppled by the Vietnamese, who installed their puppet Heng Samrin regime. As refugees, the Khmer Rouge fled west to the Thai border, already dotted with the camps of refugees who had fled from the Khmer Rouge.

Cambodia was occupied by Vietnamese troops who were and are draining the country of food, raw materials, manufactured goods and national treasures.

In the liberated zones of Cambodia, three main resistance factions had established themselves. The Khmer Rouge was led by a committee, formerly chaired by Pol Pot. Because of his international reputation as the man who committed genocide on his own people, he had been replaced by Khieu Samphan, but they were both still members of the same committee. The KR was by far the strongest rebel group, with 25,000 troops, and the richest, since they received plentiful aid from China.

The Sihanoukian National Army (Moulinaka), led by Prince Norodom Sihanouk, had a force with a reported strength varying from 800 to 5,000 troops. Their real strength was Sihanouk's international reputation; this was also their greatest drawback. Sihanouk was by no means universally admired.

The Khmer People's National Liberation Front, led by Son Sann had, at the time of our visit, a reported military strength of 3,000 to 9,000, depending on whether you listened to critics or supporters. The KPNLF's main strength was its free-world ideology and its growing ability to spread that ideology into the interior of Cambodia.

Its main problem was to feed the growing population of 115,000 refugees in the civilian camps, through sometimes cantankerous aid organizations, and to equip its military by scrounging whatever it could from wherever it could.

The political leader, Son Sann, a seventy-one year old economist and former minister under Lon Nol, was tagged early on as the most important anti-Communist leader. Living in exile in France until 1979, Son Sann, in spite of poor health, had returned to the Cambodian jungle.

The KPNLF's military leader, General Dien Del, 50, a brigadier under Lon Nol, had the reputation of being one of the few honest generals in that army. He had risen rapidly and been given command of the 2nd Division in the early '70s.

Of the three things necessary to fight a revolutionary war—secure areas from which to operate, outside support, and support of a significant portion of the indigenous population—the KPNLF and the Khmer Rouge each lacked one major factor.

The Khmer Rouge had alienated half the population of Cambodia by murdering the other half. Since the Vietnamese and their quisling flunkies, the Heng Samrin regime, were almost as bad as the Khmer Rouge, almost every Cambodian with a choice in the matter rallied to Son Sann's KPNLF. However, without an outside source of resupply, the KPNLF could not arm and train new fighters very quickly.

The Thais allowed humanitarian aid, but they were not about to provoke the Vietnamese by providing arms, ammunition or the radios that are indispensable to modern warfare, not without the concurrence of their allies in the Association of Southeast Asian Nations (ASEAN). The United States was forbidden by law to provide such aid.

Many Thais were embarrassed by their failure to help the KPNLF, and as usual when you're embarrassed the temptation was to blame the other guy. One of their complaints about the KPNLF was that it didn't fight much.

But without radios, much less ammunition, it would be suicidal to initiate conventional operations against the Vietnamese.

The KPNLF (Khmer Seraika in Cambodian), at least according to the theory of revolutionary warfare I learned at Fort Bragg, was doing exactly what it ought to be doing, which was sending armed propaganda teams into the countryside to broaden its base of support. Ho Chi Minh kept his cadres in this stage for twelve years before he launched so much as a platoon-size raid.

There was pressure on Son Sann's general, Dien Del, to go out and kick ass. But the pressure came from people who denied him the means to do so. Dien Del wisely used his main force units to defend KPNLF settlements.

Meanwhile the Chinese were pouring in military aid to the Khmer Rouge. But the Khmer Rouge had no popular support whatever. They had an army and they had slaves. Many of the slaves were children as young as eight, delighted to escape a life sentence of hard labor by joining the army at age fourteen.

It was an army of what my friend, Alan Dawson, called "teen-age robots," an army which was, among other things, almost totally illiterate. In fact, literacy outside the party appeared to be an offense punishable by death under the Khmer Rouge.

The Khmer Rouge had an army at least twice as large as that of the KPNLF, since they could arm anybody they could shanghai. They seemed to have a policy of not letting their soldiers live long enough to think up any embarrassing questions.

Khmer Rouge defectors were one of the KPNLF's largest sources of arms, ammo and recruits.

ASEAN had promised a measure of aid if the KPNLF would form a coalition with the Khmer Rouge, uniting the popular support with the outside aid. Also included would be good old Prince Sihanouk, who had a deft hand with the press, even though he had changed his political stance as often as Fleetwood Mac has changed guitar players.

But there was resistance to the coalition within the KPNLF. Mme. Suon Caset, their press officer, for instance, was against it. Her reason was that the Khmer Rouge had tortured her husband to death. He had been director general of the agriculture department under Lon Nol. Before the Khmer Rouge took over, she grabbed her children and left for Paris. He didn't want her to leave. "They won't harm us," he said. "I am no politician; I am a technician. We can work together for the Khmer people."

He had misjudged them.

For what it's worth, neither Reisinger nor I was in favor of the coalition either. We both had legitimate bitches against the Khmer Rouge. Mine was that I thought they had executed my Montagnard friend, Kpa Doh, along with his wife and three little boys, in front of the French embassy the day they took over Phnom Penh.

In Reisinger's case, a company of Cambodians from the Loch Ninh Strike Force, which his team advised, had been transferred to the Cambodian Army after the Americans pulled out. They were presumed to have been killed in the final days of their war with the Khmer Rouge. One of the main things he wanted to do was to see whether he could find any survivors.

Neither of us felt it would be wise for Son Sann to form a coalition with the Cambodian Reds.

Those urging that course of action insisted that this was no time to be sentimental; this was a time for hard-headed pragmatism.

It seemed to me that a hard-headed pragmatist would consider that every Communist revolution since the Indochina War, whether Soviet—or Chinese—backed, has begun by forming a broad coalition against a repressive oligarchy in a third-world country, then, when the time was ripe, the Communists co-opted and/or murdered outright the effective leaders of the other factions. This is not an optional extra. It is a standard feature of the "War of National Liberation."

The Cambodians have an example within their own experience of this tactic. Sihanouk was in coalition with the Khmer Rouge until they took over. He barely escaped with his life, and he lost four members of this family to them. He plays footsie with them now, but he has taken care to get on the good side of the Chinese first. Whatever one can say about Sihanouk, he is the most accomplished skater in Asia.

The ASEAN policy was to deny Son Sann supplies until he agreed to a coalition with the Khmer Rouge, but he required guarantees of his own movement's survival.

Even if the Thais allowed Son Sann to go ahead with his plans for a press conference, there was a strong possibility that *SOF* would be denied permission to attend. Many Thai officials were convinced that *SOF* was a U.S. intelligence operation, using the magazine as a cover.

The fact that we ran agent nets from our apartments, through Dr. Seuss and Chan, did nothing to dissuade them. The only people in Thailand who knew for sure we weren't spies were the real U.S.

intelligence organizations.

Mme. Suon had another idea. It was for a couple of us to volunteer as relief workers with some of the international agencies working with Cambodian refugees. The Thais let a lot of these people across every day.

Coyne and I immediately volunteered and were immediately turned down. Mme. Suon explained, "Both of your pictures have appeared in the magazine. You would never be cleared. They know who you are. Tom and Kathy are the only ones who could get through."

I sighed.

# 16

# Kat's Cambodia Story

While I was fighting the war in Vietnam, Kat was demonstrating against it. She had been with me and the *SOF* crew long enough to have serious doubts about the rightness of her stance during the Sixties. This expedition offered a first-hand look at the results of the student demonstrators' handiwork. Maybe that's why she was so eager to go.

When I first got out of the Army I came to know and like the student demonstrators at the University of Oklahoma. I told them that if all I knew about the war was what they knew I'd be against it too.

"I'm willing to accept that you guys are decent people acting from decent motives, if you're willing to give me the benefit of the same doubt; then, at least maybe, we can establish a dialogue."

But I'd always secretly wanted to rub their noses in it a bit. I lost more friends in Vietnam and Cambodia than I had remaining. I believed Kpa Doh and his family had been executed by the Khmer Rouge. Once, in Vietnam, I helped load a truck full of bodies of the wives and children of men I had fought with, killed in an ambush, thirty-four in all. Other friends had died in re-education camps after our government abandoned them to the NVA.

None of this had made me a happy man or an easy one to live with. No matter how close Kat and I grew, I often wandered into jungles in my mind where she could not follow. I felt that in pulling out of Vietnam, we had betrayed friends who had risked their lives for ours.

For that, and perhaps for other reasons, from the time I left Vietnam until I met her, I was indifferent to life. She was not my only reason for living, but she was the only reason I liked it.

I kissed her good-bye in the parking lot of our apartment complex in Bangkok. She was excited to be setting off on her adventure with T.R. and Mme. Suon. I grinned to see her adrenalin up like that, even higher than it was on an opening night. I told her to be careful, and I told her I'd pray for her, and I told her not to take chances.

She told me not to worry. Their van pulled out of the parking lot, and I waved as it disappeared around a corner.

You fool, I thought. You have put her in range of Vietnamese mortars.

On the drive to Aranyapathet she flaked out in the back of the Nissan van, trying to keep the afternoon sun off. The steamy green countryside rolled by. Every once in a while a pair of Thai feet appeared from under a bush. Everything alive was trying to avoid the afternoon sun.

Kat was apprehensive. She and Tom were with two people they didn't know very much about: Mme. Suon Caset, the slender, charming, and irascible KPNLF press liaison officer, who had served as Princess Monique's secretary under the old regime, and the driver. They had to trust them to get in and out in one piece. The driver, who had yet to say a word, looked like Oddjob, the oriental hitman in the James Bond movie.

They drove along a two-lane blacktop that was in much better repair than many in Arkansas or Louisiana. Farms and farmhouses zoomed by. The only difference between Thailand and home was that the houses were on stilts and the people plowed with water buffalo instead of John Deere tractors.

Temples gleamed white, blue, and gold in the sunset. She wondered whether Vietnam, Cambodia, and Laos were like this before the wars. They pulled into a Shell station for gas. The station offered a free blow-up beach ball with a 90 baht purchase.

The next day they drove across Cambodia via a rickety bridge, switching immediately from the left to the right-hand side of the road.

The Thai road system had been set up by the British; Cambodia was a former French colony. They made their way to Shrok Srang village, a collection of low bamboo huts, laid out with miitary precision and kept carefully clean. There they toured the military training camp and interviewed Son Sann.

Over the next three days they watched this elderly, wispy gentleman move among his men. He appeared to inspire respect bordering on reverence.

Over tea, in an open-sided bamboo hut, he said of the proposed coalition, "If I am to go into the tiger's cage, I must be given full power to do so, because to do otherwise would deceive our friends, the ASEAN countries, but most of all it would deceive the Cambodian people."

The men of the military camp were the same as GI's all over the world. They stared at Kat boldly and flashed big grins, or cast sidelong glances and smiled sheepishly.

The civilian camps got rice from international aid agencies once a week. The people there didn't stare at foreigners the way people in rural Thailand do; foreigners were frequently seen here—relief workers, nurses, doctors. The children rushed to a camera, delighted to have their pictures taken.

Nearly every household in these villages had a two-year-old toddler. Under Pol Pot, marriages had been forbidden unless arranged by the government, and couples were allowed only one night a week together. Lovers caught together were executed. Everywhere Tom and Kat went, mothers proudly held their healthy, beautiful babies up for inspection.

Each woman and female child above the height of 3'5" was given 2.7 pounds of rice and 10½ ounces of fish per week. Each woman was allotted enough food to feed three members of her family, including herself. But none of this was supposed to go to combatants; i.e., the husbands and fathers. The women were faced with a serious dilemma every day: which children do I feed, or does my husband need the nourishment today?

Five kilometers away from the Vietnamese, so highly did they value their culture, the KPNLF had built an Arts Center for teaching classical Cambodian dance, complete with elaborate costumes, to talented children.

The next day Tom and Kat visited Rithisen, a refugee camp that had just joined the KPNLF in July 1980. Older men and women stared at their air conditioned bus, with eyes that had seen too much pain. Some had allowed it to break their spirit. There were black-market goods there, which had not seemed to be the case in other camps, but only in small quantities—soap, candy, gum, soda, bicycle parts, and ratchet wrenches.

Several people had motorcycles or bicycles. There was an affluence in Rithisen that didn't exist in the other camps. Funny, she'd suddenly tagged as "affluent" the owner of a half-dozen bottles of Fanta Orange, a couples of boxes of soap flakes, and a bicycle.

The new buildings and huts put up since the camp joined the KPNLF had the same appearance of cleanliness and efficiency as Shrok Srang. The older parts of the camps had bottles, cans, and undefinable pieces of litter scattered about.

She asked to see the military camp first, and apparently took them by surprise. The deputy commander had just finished Sunday lunch with his family. Tom and Kat were served tea and chatted politely as though they had just dropped in to have a Sunday afternoon gossip with an old friend. As discreetly as possible, the deputy commander dispatched a young man in fatigues, an AK slung over his shoulder, on a yellow Yamaha enduro, to warn the troops of the VIPs' impending visit.

Presently he screeched up in a shower of fine red grit, and after a five minute conference, the deputy commander climbed on the back of the bike and motioned for them to follow in the van.

Along the road to the camp men emerged from their huts, buttoning camouflaged shirts, slinging rifles, and buckling on ammo pouches. They had interrupted lunch. Kat saw men melting into the bushes on side trails to beat them to the camp.

These men defended themselves from the Khmer Rouge, their ostensible allies, who were camped a few kilometers away. The Rithisen camp also had a problem with the Vietnamese; at night they slipped people in to poison the wells. Every time a well was poisoned, a family died. Samples of water were taken and the well sealed. The samples were turned over to local intelligence agencies, and the International Committee of the Red Cross sent people to look at the bodies. Neither organization had responded to requests for results of the analyses.

At the entrance to the military camp a sharp-looking honor guard had been turned out. Weapons were spotless, as they had been the day before. The area needed to be picked up, but the soldiers wore clean uniforms. They took obvious pride in their organization.

The last day Kat spent in Cambodia, things were tense. The Thais had denied journalists entrance to Ampil military camp for the scheduled press conference with Son Sann, diverting them to another camp instead.

Dr. Guffar, a high-level officer of the KPNLF, who had formerly taught poli sci at the University of Michigan, was furiously typing when they arrived at headquarters. Dr. Guffar and the people around him appeared to be evaluating the new proposal for coalition and formulating their plans. Kathy asked him about the chances of the coalition being formed. Wryly he replied, "We are determined to form a coalition."

"On what terms?"

"On terms acceptable to all three parties; on terms acceptable to the Cambodian people."

They departed for Nong Chon, their third and last camp. They were to go on a patrol to the front lines. They had also been to the front the previous two days, but by the time they had arrived the sun was so hot that neither side moved. The Vietnamese made their attacks in the morning.

A motley assortment of press had managed to get passes to this camp. But since there would be no conference, the press corps opted for a three-hour stroll in the merciless sun. Mme. Suon told them they would walk twelve kilometers to a Vietnamese camp the KPNLF had recently taken. They were assigned a platoon from Battalion 219. Kat hated being with the other correspondents. Unlike the catlike and all-but-invisible Cambodian soldiers, they stomped through the jungle like the city people they were.

Thirty minutes out she started having chills from sweat drying on her skin. She was neither trained for this nor in shape for it. Artillery thundered in the distance; gunshots sounded from the right.

She turned around to discover that their driver had followed. He wanted to see where they were going. The Cambodians had to send two men back with him anyway, and she decided to accompany them.

She felt bad about leaving. She knew she'd be razzed unmercifully when she got back, but thought she might become a burden if they got into serious combat. I had told her many times that the only weapon a correspondent has is the ability to back off if things don't feel right.

She came back through the jungle with one soldier. The fat driver had quickly fallen behind with the other men bringing up the rear. The quiet of the trek was broken only by the sound of sneakers crunching on sand, an artillery barrage, and gunshots.

Back in the camp she sat watching people work in the offices. It was the same as administrative work anywhere. A secretary brought file folders full of papers and gave them to Colonel Chea Chhut, the commander of the camp. He sat reading, asking questions, and signing something every once in a while. Several men, obviously part of the heirarchy, sat around a rough lumber table with a green oilcloth cover. Occasionally the commander asked a question or dispatched somebody with papers.

One of the soldiers sitting at the table of officials pulled out a grenade. "Buy Vietnam," he said, gesturing with the grenade. It had been bought from the enemy; most of the soldiers were carrying them.

Later they took a break and she sat with them in their open, thatched restaurant, listening to gunfire in the distance. It started to pick up, becoming louder and more frequent. There were dark clouds in the sky and a strong wind came up. At first she thought the rumbling in the distance was thunder. Unfortunately there was no one there who spoke English, except, of course, for the phrase, "I do not speak English."

There was one Cambodian soldier who spoke Thai. The driver, with a lot of effort, translated questions and answers for her.

The phone buzzed. "Hello!" came over the line. Commander Chea listened for a few minutes, muttered a few works, turned to the men, who, a minute before, had been concerned only with city sanitation and whether to dig a well near the front entrance.

They quickly scattered. Commander Chea disappeared into his

house. Men who had been lounging in the shade in sarongs suddenly reappeared in camouflage uniforms, complete with yellow kerchiefs tied in perfect square knots. Men and boys she had thought were just hanging around, slapped loaded magazines into the receivers of their weapons.

A platoon leader came double-timing from the village, yelling two indecipherable words. Men fell in behind him from the huts and alleyways. The leader stopped and yelled two new words. The men dressed right and covered down.

Commander Chea emerged from the hut in full camouflage uniform, boots gleaming and pants bloused perfectly over their tops. He carried a short, carved riding crop that he used to punctuate his sentences.

The men were briefed by a captain. A beat-up blue Toyota truck pulled up in the yard and the twenty or so men started trying to wedge their equipment and bodies on board. A few minutes before, she had been jiving with these guys, trying to trade her bush hat for one of their yellow scarves. Not one would trade a thread of his uniform for her hat or for anything else. As they pulled out she saw the faces of the young boys, some with fear in their eyes, or maybe a reflection of her fear for them.

She smiled and gave them the thumbs up; a few managed a smile and one returned the gesture.

She asked the location of Tom and Mme. Suon. The driver inquired and came back with a confused answer. He also informed her that two hundred Vietnamese were attacking three kilometers away.

*My God,* she thought, *two hundred Vietnamese!* She asked him to verify the information; he asked again and came back with the same information. She told him to move the van closer to the restaurant, and to load all their gear.

He argued that the van would get too hot in the sun. She surprised herself when she turned around and in a low, commanding voice said, "Do it! Now!"

The driver scurried away.

She was determined to stand in that restaurant until Tom came back or the Vietnamese rolled over them, whichever came first. But she saw nothing wrong with having the van two seconds away.

Soon a man in a green and black print shirt came in and sat down behind the head table. Here was a man who was in charge, and he spoke excellent English. She waited for him to consult with another man carrying maps covered with plastic. She asked him about Tom. He said, "Oh, they're on their way in. They engaged ten to fifteen Vietnamese and are very tired. We're sending motorcycles out to pick them up because they had to circle way around to get out."

"Ten to fifteen!" she exclaimed. "The driver told me two hundred."

Their laughter was broken by the arrival of a kid with a rucksack. He placed it on the table and snapped to, then unloaded the contents onto the table; a blood-splattered helmet, two plastic water bottles, a hammock, and a mosquito net. The man in the green and black shirt, Colonel Bory Chhut, said that this stuff had just been taken by a patrol. The helmet was the only thing that wouldn't be recycled for field use.

Relieved to know her friends were safe, she sat down and visited with the colonel. He, like Colonel Chea Chhut, had been a successful insurance man in Orange County, California. They had left their safe jobs and lives in the States when called back to fight for their country. Both men told her they had men who served under them in Lon Nol's army, living in the States, who would come when called.

In the meantime the men in the States were waiting for the time when rice, boots, and arms became available, working and sending what money they could.

Two motorcycles roared up and deposited their exhausted loads. Two journalists staggered in, gesturing for something to drink. After downing a glass of warm Fanta Orange, one Japanese reporter told her about his walk in the woods.

The patrol had gone six kilometers with no contact; they decided to push on. A couple more strap-hangers, including this reporter, had to be left back because of their light-colored, highly-visible clothing. Four men were left to guard them and bring them out. The journalist told her they had been sitting on a bare hilltop. "The four men are around me, guarding me. Then *Boom! Boom!* and then *dat-a-dat-a-dat!* They pushed me in the bunker." He wiped his face. "Very exciting, very exciting!"

By this time another load of journalists had been deposited. Still no Tom. Finally two more bikes appeared in the distance. At last,

Tom. Special Forces, first in the field and last out. She quickly checked him over for signs of blood, then took a picture of his filthy, tired, but smiling face.

As they drove out of the camp, they passed a boy in a wheelchair, wearing a fatigue cap. His legs had been blown off about twelve inches above the knee.

A toddler playing in the dirt looked up at the air-conditioned van cruising by and mouthed the word, "Okay."

# 17

# Tom's Story

Even though T.R. and Kat were together for much of their trip into Cambodia, Kathy was seeing things for the first time, and she noticed small details that Tom took for granted. Conversely, as a former SF trooper he was looking for militarily significant details that she was unaware of. Perception of this shared experience was very different for each of them.

The first thing Reisinger did on their trip was start searching for his missing Cambodians. He had made many friends on patrol with that company. They had shared cigarettes and rice, coffee and tea. The lack of a common language had been no barrier to friendship. They weren't supposed to talk on patrol anyway.

Tom had kept in touch with his Cambodians for a couple of years after leaving Vietnam, but after the Americans pulled out, it was almost impossible to get mail through. In 1970 most of the Cambodians in Special Forces camps were pulled out and sent to Cambodia. They formed the 7th Division of the Cambodian Army and had a reputation as the best fighters in that war.

The Company from Loch Ninh fought as part of the 47th Infantry Brigade. Kim Long, who had commanded the company in Vietnam, was Brigade Commander.

They fought in the final defense of Phnom Penh, and Reisinger later heard that Kim Long had led them in a last minute punchout through the attacking forces. He lost track of them completely after that.

There was not much chance that many of them had made it, but maybe a few had, and the logical place to look for them was with the KPNLF.

The first place they visited was Camp Ampil, the military head-quarters, a part of the Shrok Srang refugee camp, a huge city of bam-boo houses, laid out like barracks on a dusty plain.

The troops at Camp Ampil were a very different kind of Cambo-dian from the troops he had led at Loch Ninh. For all that the Loch Ninh Cambodes had been super field soldiers, they had cultivated a scruffy image, even in camp.

Compared to them, the KPNLF kids looked like an ROTC drill team. The KPNLF troops were perfectly turned out in brand-clean cammies, their weapons spotless, and they could fall in, fall out and present arms like clockwork. These skills are not as highly prized today as they were in, say, the War of 1812.

Still they were obviously well-trained, within the limits of what Reisinger saw them do.

It became clear that what Tom and Kat were seeing was a canned demonstration. The KPNLF leadership was well aware of the precariousness of their own situation, and good press was essential to their very survival. They weren't about to let our people nose around at will.

It was that way for the first couple of days of the trip. Even so they were only five klicks from Vietnamese combat units. There was always firing in the distance.

We knew two Americans in Thailand who might legitimately be considered experts on revolutionary warfare. Both had visited the KPNLF camps. One was a senior U.S. Army officer with Special Forces and Vietnam experience. The other was Dawson.

The colonel liked the KPNLF people, and wished them well, but he didn't think their officers had done their homework. "They haven't read their Mao," he said. "They haven't read their Giap. They'll in-troduce you to their armored cavalry expert. They're living in Never-Never Land."

Maybe he was right. On the other hand, maybe they showed him their dog and pony show, and he saw through that, but did not perceive the reality behind it. Dawson claimed that they were sending out armed propaganda teams, and that their conventional troops were to defend their safe areas and cover the evacuation of those hundreds of thousands of civilians, should the Viets launch an attack.

Shrok Srang had been overrun and rebuilt once, and Nong Chon twice, so there was plenty of defending to be done.

The picture that emerged during Tom's and Kat's visit was halfway between those two versions. The Khmer admitted to a propaganda school, but Reisinger didn't get a look at the curriculum.

He learned, however, that they were graduating six hundred people every three months. He didn't know where they were going, but they weren't hanging around Shrok Srang. They had an advanced course that graduated one hundred every three months. Even our doubting colonel admitted that somebody, and he didn't know who, was waging effective guerrilla warfare in the interior. We thought it might be those cadres.

Reisinger and Kat didn't meet the armored cavalry expert, or if they did he had learned to keep quiet about it. Several officers asked *SOF*'s help in getting guerrilla warfare manuals, and said they were seeking Special Forces training from friendly Asian countries.

There was a military academy at Camp Ampil, with about two hundred and fifty students, both cadets and company-grade officers. They also had a basic training camp and an NCO academy.

Except for courtesy titles for officers who served in the Lon Nol army, they had no rank; they used job titles.

After two days of inquiries, Tom was finally introduced to a survivor of the 47th Brigade, but he wasn't from Loch Ninh. He told Reisinger that the remnants of the 47th had fought their way into eastern Cambodia. There they were trapped by a superior force and annihilated. This man had gotten away, but he didn't know anyone else who had.

Later that day Tom and Kat linked up with some other journalists— an NBC-TV crew, a man from the London *Times*, and a stringer for UPI. The correspondent with the NBC crew was Neil Davis, a huge blond Aussie who had been a legend in the Saigon press corps for courage and journalistic professionalism.

They were given an escort of what was described as a half company of the 219th battalion, about fifty troops, and set out to film a recently captured Vietnamese camp.

Reisinger observed the troops carefully. They worked very smoothly together, kept a good interval between men, and looked alert. There was no kidding around. There was a squad on each flank and a small point element. The journalists accompanied the command group, behind the first squad of the main body. They set off on a small trail through fairly open, flat terrain.

After a while Kat felt faint, and went back with the driver. Further on they found the remnants of a few huts, a bloody poncho, and a few empty tin cans with Russian writing on them. The TV crew had not shot a single foot of film, nor did they rise to this bait.

The KPNLF were no fools. They knew that if their movement was to survive it must have outside support, and to get that they must have publicity. It was decided to go another four klicks and attack a Vietnamese battalion outpost, so the TV crew would have something to film.

Despite the showbiz aspect of this operation, it was carried out in a smooth and professional manner. Its purpose was neither to take territory nor to kill the enemy, although if that happened it would be fine. This was a propaganda mission.

Finally they came upon a small Vietnamese outpost. Our guys lobbed in a few B-40 rockets and fired a few bursts. The other guys responded with B-40s and mortars. It lasted only about a minute, long enough to look like a furious battle on television.

Reisinger was impressed by the fact that there was no bitching and no clowning. The lowest private seemed to understand that this was necessary. It was a business situation.

# 18

# General Khanh's Coup

The days passed in false starts. Stories were developed, and then pre-empted by other stories that never happened. My frustration mounted. Tom and Kat had their moment, but nothing brought us intrepid correspondents closer to the field, or to guerrillas, or to the adrenalin rushes of old. I continued dreaming of Vietnam and my glory days. Maybe because of the false starts, I dreamed of General Khanh's coup in early 1964 and the events it had set in motion at our forward operational base in northern Phu Bon province, another adventure in frustration.

"Why no patrol?" Cowboy demanded when he came into the shack, sweeping off his cowboy-rolled bush hat and wrap-around shades. He and Ksor Yul, now in command of the company at the FOB, who had been a corporal under the French, came in and seated themselves on some C-Rats boxes.

"They had another coup in Saigon," I replied. Their expressions remained unchanged. Clearly they saw no connection between our war and events in Saigon. "Anyhow, the big headquarters in the sky doesn't want us to run any more patrols. I guess until they find out if the U.S. is for or against the new regime."

Cowboy told Yul what I said, and they both shrugged. "Okay."

"We'll run local security patrols until this is over. Maybe we can scare up one of these snipers firing into the camp." I picked up my map and turned it over to the white side, drawing diagrams with a grease pencil.

"We use all three of Yul's platoons and run three local patrols a day. One platoon will run a close circle, about one kilometer out from the camp. One will go north and check out that long ridge line over-looking the FOB, about two kilometers out. The other can loop around south three or four kilometers.

"I want the one that goes along the ridge line," I said. I'd been wanting to check it out for some time. "Augie can take the close one and Hank will go with the one south. You all got any ideas?"

They didn't. I had not yet learned the trick of asking for sugges-tions before giving our plan. They would never offer a change for fear of hurting our feelings.

The next morning Cowboy, Yul, and I set out with the first pla-toon. We splashed across the little creek running just north of the camp, and entered the woods on the other side, cutting down a trail which led to the western end of the ridge line. Golden light filtered through the canopy of trees, turning them to a translucent, shimmer-ing green. The trees were tall and stately. For Vietnam this was open terrain.

It took the better part of two hours to gain the top of the ridge line, all hard climbing. It was flat and grassy up there, pockmarked with 81mm shell holes from rounds fired by the FOB to discourage observation.

We took a break, and the Yards flaked out under the trees. I lit a cigarette, and Cowboy, Yul, and I took a look around. A walk of the perimeter of the flattop we were on revealed that it was not a part of the main ridge line, something a study of the old French map had not indicated. That early in the war our maps were English-language copies of old French maps, one over 100,000, compared to the stan-dard U.S. map ratio of one over 25,000, and grossly inaccurate. At our in-country briefing I had seen a wall map on which a river jumped ten kilometers going from one map-sheet to the next.

The main ridge line hooked south so that the hook faced our FOB. It was joined to the main ridge line by a small saddle. We were stand-ing on the end of the hook. You couldn't tell from the map that this wonderful little observation post was up here, and as far as I knew, the team we replaced had never patrolled the ridge line. Like us, they tried to go as far out as they could before they ran out of chow.

Our local security patrols were usually squad size and didn't come out this far.

"Man!" I said pointing back the way we had come. "Look at that." We were looking right down into the FOB. I got out my binoculars. Through them, the camp looked twenty meters away, but standing in a curiously flat depth-of-field. I looked down at the back side of the commo shack. Ken Miller, our comm chief, came out, walked over to a lister bag hanging from a tree limb and filled his canteen.

He turned and walked back to the commo shack, barechested as usual, a slender, well-made, middle-age man with the face of a presidential candidate. I could make out his homemade rosary, a knotted cord, one knot for each bead, with a crucifix on the end. His lips moved as he spoke to someone, and for a second I wondered why I couldn't hear him.

I handed the binoculars to Cowboy. "You can pick out the mortar positions, the commo shack, the Americans' shack. You could just sit up here and pinpoint your targets." He passed the binoculars on to Yul. Their looks were grave.

We formed the company up again and started down off the edge of the hill, into the saddle that led back to the main ridgeline. The way was steep, grassy and slick and stubbled with gray rock.

The climb up the hill was arduous; I could feel the strain all the way down the backs of my legs. I grabbed at rocks, tree trunks and clumps of grass, anything to haul myself up that bloody hill.

Just as I was about to reach the military crest of the hill, one of the squad leaders went by me like a rocket, to be the first man to arrive at the top. A moment later I arrived beside him, breathing hard. Bubbling out of the rocks was a pure steam of clear water. Not a big one, but enough; a clear, steady stream, and around it in the mud and dirt were the marks of tire-soled sandals. I called down, "Hey, Cowboy! Yul! Come here!" A moment later they hauled up beside me, "What, Sir?"

"Look at this."

*"Un Croupe! Securite!"* Yul called, and the lead squad went the

rest of the way to the top. We followed them up and found the tracks and cold campfires of at least one company of VC. The fires were one day old.

Later I questioned Cowboy closely about the squad leader who had passed me going up the hill. We normally assumed that up to fifteen percent of our strike force was made up of VC infiltrators, and I thought maybe one of them had just given himself away. Cowboy assured me that he had known him for years, that he was just a very straight, ballsy guy. I still didn't trust him, though. He must have had some idea what was on that hill.

I turned on the radio and put the handset to my ear. "Bolen Alpha, this is Bolen Handy. Bolen Alpha, this is Handy, over."

Ken came up, and I told him what we had found.

"Roger, Handy. Kildare reports spotting estimated VC squad in vicinity Bravo Quebec 249580." Kildare was Augie DeLucia, our senior medic.

"Roger that, Alpha," I said. "I figure that's part of the company that passed through here. I think they split up into small groups when they left."

"Roger, I agree. Alpha out."

"You know what, Sir?" Cowboy said.

"What?"

"VC always have spy in camp. They know you plan to leave for patrol with only small force to guard FOB. They have company here for attack. Plan to hurt us, get weapons, kill Americans."

"You're probably right," I said. I turned and faced in the general direction of Saigon and muttered, "And thank you, Major General Nguyen Khanh." It was Khanh's coup, after all, that had saved the FOB.

We hadn't come equipped for an overnight stay, and the ridge line proved too long to cover in one day, so we returned to the FOB. The next day we set out to come back up the ridge line from the other end. Since the VC company might have moved only a kilometer or so down the ridgeline and holed up again, I took two platoons with me.

It was a long, hot, dry walk. I stuck with the company headquarters. Hank Johnson, our junior weapons man, and Augie each took a platoon. All we found on top of the ridgeline were rocks and trees. We sat down on the rocks, in the shade of the trees and ate lunch.

I twisted my ankle on the way down, which may have saved our lives, because I couldn't walk fast.

As long as we were on fairly level, fairly open terrain, it was fine. We held a good formation. Flank security was good, and the three parallel columns cut through the brush ready for action. Then we hit some thick brush and a small stream, and in less than thirty seconds my command changed from a disciplined force, moving as fast as terrain would allow, to sixty separate guys trying to get home as quickly as possible.

"Hold it," I said to Yul in a calm, reasonable, friendly voice. He looked at me, then looked helplessly at his troops. All Jarai like to be liked, and he didn't want to make a scene.

"Halt the company," I said again. Yul looked around at his men and held up his hand, but they were too far gone now, heading for home.

"ALL RIGHT, GODDAMIT!" I bellowed, "ALLA YOU SON-SABITCHES STOP!"

They stopped.

"Now," I said to Yul, "get your company back in a secure march formation and we will go. But only as fast as we can maintain march discipline. Got it?"

He nodded his head.

We moved out again slowly. But soon the pace picked up again and the formation started to fall apart. I halted them again and ranted some more. Then I moved up right behind the point man so I could control his pace. We moved out.

I kept about ten meters behind the point. If he went too fast, I told him to slow down. Five minutes after we moved out he turned and came screaming back toward me, yelling something that sounded like, "Say ton mean! Say ton mean!"

Finally I understood, *"C'est un mine!"* It is a mine. I grabbed him by the wrist and said, "Okay, babe, calm down!" He tried to jerk loose and run off again, but I held fast and said, "Show me the mine. I want to see it."

Yul, Hank, and Augie came up. I made them stay back twenty meters, and together the point man and I went up to look at the mine. I expected something like one of the U.S. Army's little hockey puck antipersonnel mines, so at first I didn't see the fine nylon string stretched across the narrow trail we were on.

It was connected to a cast-iron grenade, shaped like a tin can, but with the edges serrated into squares like the U.S. World War II hand grenade. Apparently the idea was for us to trip over the wire and set off the grenade. The top was stoppered with a bamboo cork, sealed in wax. From this a string loop was tied to the trip cord. It would have taken me and the point man both out if he hadn't seen it. I told the point to get back, and DeLucia to come in a little closer.

"Augie," I said, "keep the company back. I'm going to try to disarm this thing."

I traced the string to the other side and gingerly, slowly, knelt and pulled out the peg that held the other side of the string. Then I went back over and examined the grenade again. It was fixed in place by a stake hammered to an iron ring protruding from its bottom. I took out my knife and started digging around the stake.

"Don't pull it out, Sir," Augie said. "Sometimes they put another one underneath that goes off when you try to disarm that one."

"Good point. See if you can rustle up about thirty feet of suspension line off somebody."

He had line in his pack so I tied one end to the stake. Then I ran back over a small fold in the ground that furnished protection if we lay down flat and motioned for everybody to get down.

"Okay, pull the line," I said. Augie pulled it slowly at first, then hard. Nothing happened. "The line is fouled somewhere," he said.

"Okay! Let the slack out." He did, and he and I went out and unfouled all the kinks and places where the line had caught on rocks and twigs.

"Okay, one more time." We both took hold of the line this time and tugged all the slack out. Then slowly, very slowly, the line budged, and budged some more, and then sprang free. We lay there and waited a moment, panting a little. Nothing happened.

"Okay," I yelled. "Everybody stay down." I got up and tiptoed over to the grenade. It lay in the dirt, the stake still through the ring, with little clods still clinging to it.

I explained to Yul in bastard French that I was going to carry the grenade in and wanted everybody to stay at least thirty meters from me. It didn't require much explaining. They gave me lots of room.

The big question in my mind was whether it had an instantaneous fuse, or whether I had a couple of seconds to get rid of it if I tripped or something caught on the loop.

It took about two hours to get back to the FOB, and by that time it was an hour after dark. Ken was kind of mad when we got in.

*"Sir,"* he said, giving it that particular inflection only an old NCO can. In some fashion it changes the meaning of the word to "you stupid bastard." "If you can't get back before dark, the *least* you can do is call in on the PRC-10."

"Tried," I said. "Couldn't make contact."

"Too bad," he said, "Then I could have told you about this." He handed me another message. It read, "MAKE NO ATTEMPT TO DISARM VC MINES OR BOOBY TRAPS. TOO MANY CASUALTIES FROM THIS PRACTICE. BLOW ALL IN PLACE." Later I found that this message was the result of some poor guy having done exactly what I did about two days before, and blown himself all over the map.

Augie took the grenade down to our main camp in the truck the next day. He and the Old Man and Slattery, our senior demo man, took some pictures of it for a tech intel report and then took it out past the perimeter and blew it. It had an instantaneous fuse.


I awoke lathered in adrenalin and ready for action, only to realize I was in a king size bed with Kat, under an air conditioner.

# *19*

# Blood Moon Over Bangkok

Our air-conditioned bedroom was huge. As usual I awoke early and pulled on a pair of athletic shorts and a T-shirt.

Working for *SOF* you accumulate a certain number of macho T-shirts without trying. This Special Operations Association T-shirt was at least fairly discreet, sporting only a small crest on the left breast, a bereted skull on a red shield, blood dripping from its mouth.

I looked at Kathy's slender, sleeping form in the bed.

She had a fair number of those T-shirts herself. Once, traveling cross-country alone at night, she gassed up our black Firebird in Dalhart, Texas. She wore jeans, boots, and a tight "AIRBORNE: Death from Above" T-shirt, which sports a skull superimposed on parachute wings.

An outlaw motorcycle gang pulled in just as she was hanging up the hose. They looked at her with a strange shock of recognition, and gave her the thumbs up as she roared off into the night.

The sauna serving as Bangkok's air hit me as I left the bedroom. Brown thrashed on the floor, already out doing his exercises. He has a long waist and lower back problems. Once his back went out at a major gun show, and he was carried out in a wheelchair.

But an old girl friend had shown him some exercises that kept him limber. She had wisely not told him they were yoga. Brown did stretching exercises, had quit drinking except for an occasional white wine, and ran three miles a day. He lived like a new-age guru, and for his age, 51, was in fantastic shape.

I dropped down and pumped off thirty-one pushups, rolled over and started the half-sit-ups Brown had shown me—as hard on the gut but easier on the lower back. Brown did a hundred every day. I was up to sixty-five. I got up and did some stretchers for our run.

Bangkok is not laid out in blocks. Major streets have narrow half-mile alleys off them, called *sois*. Homes front on the *sois*. Brown and I ran up and down the soi beside our apartment building for three miles. Then we stretched again.

After breakfast, Kathy and I joined Hiney on the balcony for coffee. Something he said had got me to thinking, and I wanted to pursue it. I led the conversation to his experiences in Laos. He had said that he loved the little people but could barely tolerate the big people. Once a Lao general had told him, "You Americans are creating monsters that we will have to deal with after this is over." He was referring to those people the U.S. had insisted be promoted on merit rather than family connections. Perhaps if they'd made a few more monsters those generals wouldn't be in exile now.

Hiney said the best fighter pilot he had ever seen was a Hmong tribesman they had trained to fly T-28s. "Flew four or five missions a day, and crewed his own airplane," he said.

I took a sip of coffee. "Whatever happened to him?"

"Fifth mission of the day. He was tired; he'd been flying for years. After that he couldn't go back to the village, and there was no place else for him to go. He flew that T-28 right into a Vietnamese anti-aircraft gun that was shooting at one of our fighters."

I tried to get him back to the sociological implications of guerrilla warfare. At one point he had ventured the opinion that one of the reasons Thailand had not been the next domino was that the American presence had created an active middle class. There had been a way for poor people who were sharp to make money without overthrowing the government. After the Americans left, the new middle class had found ways to sustain itself.

Kathy and I both sucked in our breath and sat up straight as See, our Wa tribesman houseboy, came around the outside ledge of the building, sweeping the ledge. The Wa are a hilltribe, reputed to be headhunters, who live their lives on narrow mountain trails. The ledge was only a foot wide and had no corner. For a moment, as he came around the edge of the building, he was suspended over the courtyard and the pool below. He grinned as he passed us and swept on. He was just showing off.

We went back inside. Coyne was reading the first draft of my Mittrapab jump story. "No getting around it," he said ruefully. "You are good."

I smiled with no attempt at modesty. Coyne is the most naturally talented storyteller I know. I always told him, "Jimmy, any story you tell me, and don't get into print in sixty days, is mine." He thought I was kidding.

We went back into our bedroom. Our dirty clothes from the night before were gone. See would have them washed, ironed, and back in the closet by one o'clock.

A half hour later Brown walked in unannounced. Bad timing again. "Uh....." he said, and closed the door behind him.

"Be out in a few minutes," I bellowed.

What he wanted was for me and Hiney to go over to Hiney's old headquarters that afternoon. Hiney had completed his POW business, at least for the time being. He had secured the remains of one American airman, and was going home. I already knew Colonel Goetzke, Hiney's replacement, but this would give me a chance to get in solid with what was left of the American advisory effort, under the best possible circumstances.

On our way back Hiney got into a conversation with our driver about his recent six-month stint as a laborer in Saudi Arabia. "Six month, no fucking," the driver said. "Very bad. I never do again."

"Do ye drink the blood?" Hiney asked.

"Say what?" I interrupted. Hiney explained that vendors came to Lumpini Park in the morning and sold cobra blood. They hang a live cobra upside down, slit its throat, and you drink the blood as it dies. "Makes ya horny," he summed up. I think he meant virile.

When we got back to the penthouse, I told Brown about the cobra blood and he got all excited. He wanted the four of us, Brown, Coyne, T.R., and me, to go down to Lumpini Park the first thing in the morning and drink it. "C'mon," he insisted. "We can put our picture in the magazine. It'll be real macho."

"Not me," said Coyne.

"Bob," I said, "it's not macho to do something you don't want to do, just to prove to somebody else you've got the guts to do it."

He raved on for a while, but finally saw we were adamant. "You could do it by yourself," Coyne suggested. He would shoot it, and I could write it up for the magazine. But Brown didn't want to do it by himself.


After lunch Dr. Seuss showed up with his girlfriend. He brought her because their Thai hotel room was too spartan to leave her there, and he could not throw her into the city. Dr. Seuss lived up country.

Dr. Seuss, chunky and fifty, had worked for the Agency but had been fired for drinking on duty. He had the booze under control now. The girl was seventeen, but she looked fourteen, a Thai Brooke Shields, but with the brains of a gnat and an inexhaustible supply of chewing gum and Siamese movie magazines. It seemed to me that his pedophilia carried within it the seeds of its own punishment.

Kathy detested him, even before she met the girl. She said she didn't trust any man who carried a purse. For myself, nothing I ever did with the man came to any good.

Brown, T.R., Dr. Seuss, Colonel Boon Lert and I sat around the conference table, which was also our dining room table, and plotted revolution against the Vietnamese, the regional sport of Southeast Asia.

After we had finished our scheming for the day, it was time for Kathy's exercises, which she took in the pool.

We hit the highly chlorinated water in our fairly good-sized pool about six or six-thirty. She did twelve lengths a night. Usually so did I. I floated on my back and watched the soot from Sukhumvit drift down onto the water.

"Fuckin' pollution!" I muttered.

Kathy splashed water on me. "What's the matter with you? You don't like the pollution; you don't like Bangkok; you don't like anything."

"Yeah, well, I'm really cranked," I replied.

"You've been acting like an asshole," she said. "What's your problem?"

I stood on the bottom of the pool and leaned against the rope that separated the deep and shallow ends. "My problem," I said, "is that this is my last chance to relive the greatest adventure of my life, and it's so close, but it's not happening."

"It's like you're not happy unless you're trying to kill somebody or somebody's trying to kill you," she snapped.

I shrugged. I guess it did look like that, but there was more to this than simple adrenalin addiction. Even to Kathy I couldn't seem to explain that I had found more than war in Vietnam; I had found peace. I missed the solitude and the jungle. I didn't want to kill anybody, and I sure didn't want to die. I just wanted a couple of weeks of bush time.

She splashed water full in my face. "This is a good place," she said. "Lighten up."

I splashed her back and dived for her. "Don't tickle me," she shrieked. "Jim! Don't *tickle* me!"

After dinner we dressed to meet Dawson, my Bangkok *Post* buddy, and Tuk, his Thai girlfriend. Kathy had bought a gold lamé spacesuit, not the NASA kind, but the skin-hugging Buck Rogers kind, and a pair of shoes that were two thin gold straps on four-inch heels, so we were going dancing.

The disco was extravagantly lurid, but the Thai preference for bubblegum music drove us into the street after an hour.

The four of us pub-crawled Pat Pong. We hit Rick Menard's Grand Prix, which featured a videotaped movie at the back bar, with earphones for those who would rather listen to the movie. The music was played by a Thai D.J. in a booth at the front. Rick's dancers were not the best on Pat Pong, but my favorite worked there, a tough-looking tawny woman with hair to her ass and thigh-high purple boots.

We ricocheted across the street to the King's Castle, and waded into the press of the crowd: squareheaded Americans, foxy young Thai girls, and a few American or European women. Some of the Thai girls wore street clothes, but most, dancers who worked there, wore high-heeled shoes, pastel bikinis, and red plastic buttons with numbers on them.

For most of these girls this life was their only way out of the paddy. For some, life was a party that went on too long; for others, it was just a gig, and for some lucky ones, a steppingstone to something better.

Up on the stage one of the more beautiful girls thrashed listlessly to Steve Miller's "Livin' in the U.S.A." while picking her nose.

In Thailand a homosexual transvestite is called a katoy. The eyes of the one who hangs out at the King's Castle lit up when he saw Kat's jumpsuit. I knew this particular, avid little creature from the night when, successfully dressed as a girl, he had tried to pick up Coyne.

He was dressed like a tough street chick, in a tight black skirt and a newsboy cap. Big-eyed, he squeezed up to Kathy, and his mouth formed a silent "Oooooh!" He reached out and caressed the shiny smooth fabric on her shoulder, turned his limpid eyes to me, and murmured, "Beautiful madame; madame sexee!"

After one drink we went on to the Superstar. This club had the best sound system in Thailand and the most beautiful girls. Many of them could actually dance. It was the most tastefully flashy of all the clubs; the girls were more raucous and more daringly suggestive in their dancing.

Once Dawson and Tuk went with Kat to the Superstar while I was on a story with Coyne. They tablehopped, and for a while she was alone at the table. One of the girls, seeing she had no date, invited Kat to share noodles with all the girls after the club closed. We both thought that was pretty decent.

The music thudded and slammed and lifted us along to our table; we ordered our drinks and sat back to enjoy the tableau.

There weren't many Americans living in Bangkok, aside from tourists, but almost to a man they were Vietnam veterans. The room was suddenly filled with the *whop-whop* of helicopters right down on us, and for a moment we all felt that exact degree of apprehension you get going into a hot LZ. Then the sound segued into the Doors, and we realized the D.J. had once again ambushed us with the music from "Apocalypse Now."

After the bar closed we said goodnight to Dawson and Tuk and grabbed a tuk-tuk. It roared off into the night, up Silom Road, through the traffic circle at Lumpini Park, and along Embassy Row. The night

Bangkok air, jungle smells through motor exhaust, poured over us. I propped my boot on the frame of the tuk-tuk and leaned back. The moon over Bangkok was the color of dried blood. It's the pollution.

# 20

# Brown Blasts Balloon

From the balcony of our penthouse, traffic noises from Sukhumvit were frequently so loud, even on the eighth floor, that all conversation had to be conducted at a bellow. When agitated, Coyne screamed, "I'M READY TO JUMP THE FUCKING BALLOON!"

Coyne and I had first learned about the balloon on the Mittrapab jump when a couple of guys from Mark Smith's SF advisory team-Korea showed up wearing weird wings such as we'd never seen. "They're Thai balloon jumpers wings," Mark had said, chuted up, one foot propped on the tailgate of an RTAF C-123.

"They have a barrage balloon on a thousand-foot cable. They winch it down; six jumpers climb in the gondola and hook up. They run it back up to about eight hundred feet and go out on individual tap-outs. Jump school trainees make their first two jumps from it."

"How was it?"

He shrugged. "There's no wind blast. You just float out of the gondola. It takes a six thousand count to open, which scares the shit out of you, and by the time you open you're at five hundred feet. I've got more than three hundred and fifty jumps, and this was the worst."

Coyne and I had the same thought simultaneously. *Brown!* Brown has to jump the balloon.

As soon as Brown got to Thailand I called Colonel Rut Komolvanich, Operations Officer of the Thai Special Warfare Center. Col. Rut would do anything he could for the Special Forces old-boy network. He put us on the manifest for the following Wednesday.

But that jump was pre-empted by the first of our long-range strategy sessions.

When we canceled that first drop, Brown decided we'd do the jump last thing before we closed out in Thailand, so as not to take a chance of missing a combat patrol because of a broken leg.

We used up two months skulking in alleys, holding secret meetings over sputtering candles in hotel rooms cooled by ceiling fans, making anxious, coded telephone calls. We accumulated enough secret information to get a military intelligence detachment an increase in budget and personnel; but, aside from Tom and Kat's jaunt to Cambodia, none of it was anything we could print in the magazine without getting people killed.

With each new disappointment Coyne yelled, "I'M READY TO JUMP THE FUCKING BALLOON!" This became the *leitmotif* of our expedition.

Brown became morose. He spent hours locked in his room with a book on commando operations. I took him aside and gave him a little lecture on how it's always darkest just before the dawn.

"Don't worry about it," he said. "I'm not going over the rail." I was not cheered; he was the only one who had mentioned suicide. Brown abandoned his commando book and moved to the living room, where he sprawled across the arms of an easy chair in his sprung jockey shorts, chewing his mustache and staring at his feet. Finally things got so bad he went four days without even screaming, "You're fired, Asshole!" at Coyne. Something had to be done.

"I'M READY TO JUMP THE FUCKING BALLOON!" Coyne bellowed in frustration.

I called Col. Rut.

"Sure," he said. "Come tomorrow. In the morning we jump the balloon, and in afternoon you can jump C-130 if you want."

"Good, we'll do them both," I replied.

The next morning I rented an air-conditioned taxi to take Brown, Coyne, T.R., Kat, and me to Lop Buri and back. Coyne decided to take his video camera, a large, heavy, professional model. Kat had been a news and sports photographer in Little Rock, so she shot the stills. We had six people, including the driver, and a lot of gear, in the car. It was a squeeze.

"Should have got two cars," Coyne muttered.

"You fuckhead," I sneered. "You got an air-conditioned limo. You used to ride out to jump in a two-and-a-half-ton truck."

"I was nineteen," Coyne muttered. "I didn't know nothing."

There was a consensus that Coyne had been spoiled by his association with the motion picture business.

"I'm hungry," said T.R. Although he ate very little, Reisinger seldom stopped. "Could we stop for breakfast?"

"No sweat," I said. "We'll stop at the next Dairy Queen." T.R.'s stomach rejected everything but basic Cheeseburger-in-Paradise American cuisine. I often wondered how he'd made it in Vietnam, but he had.

For miles, Thailand shot by outside: flame trees, houses on stilts, entire families on small motorcycles. I said nothing, lost in my pre-jump funk.

Skydivers wonder why paratroopers feel fear, but skydivers pack their own chutes and open at three grand. Paratroopers jump rigs packed in a speed shop, by somebody else, which open at a thousand feet.

Further, the military reserve parachute has no pilot chute. A rip-cord must be pulled, and then the canopy must be grasped and shaken out like a sheet, and this must be done with the wind. If it is done against the wind, the reserve will be sucked into the main canopy, in which case the jumper has two malfunctions to correct in what's left of his nine seconds. This requires a cool head and an enormous jolt of adrenalin. The adrenalin starts on the ground; the cool head is something you have to put together for yourself.

The paratrooper's sky is filled with other paratroopers, and frequently with falling objects as well—rifles, rucksacks, jeeps, 105 millimeter howitzers. Small wonder paratroopers tend to be tightly wired.

Brown was very quiet on the drive. He was fifty-one and had a bad back. Coyne and I had set up this jump as a joke, to test his macho image. A major factor in the success of his magazine is that Brown puts his ass on the line two or three times a year, on camera. I got a quick mental image of him being taken out of the S.H.O.T. Show in a wheelchair when his back went out.

I don't know whether he was afraid or not, but he was damn serious.


At Lop Buri, Colonel Rut placed us under the guidance of a suave and intelligent young staff captain, Kitti Patummas, only recently returned from the States, where he had attended the Ranger and Special Forces Officers' courses. His English was better than Coyne's. With a confident saunter, he led us into the balloon hanger, where it bulked and bobbed against the ceiling like a fat, friendly fish on a dozen lines.

A tightly-muscled, very short Thai sergeant, with a young, tough face and excellent English, gave us gondola training. He taught the difference between a balloon exit and an aircraft exit. "You just step out of balloon. If you jump up and out, like on airplane, you might hit cable," he said, referring to the quarter-inch steel cables that suspend the gondola from the balloon.

A two-and-a-half-ton truck with an enormous winch on the back towed the British-made balloon out, while we did refresher parachute landing falls from a wooden platform into sawdust. We jumped off from about six feet, practicing the various landing positions; front, left-front, right-front, left and right rear. I did them fairly well, but hit a lot harder than when I went through jump school in 1962. Twenty years later and thirty-five pounds heavier, what the hell was I doing here?

But I loved it—the ritual of procedure, the comradeship of shared risk, the risk itself, and the adrenalin jolt that went with it. I shared that with Brown, which is why he never held our joke against us, or even recognized it as such.


We drove to the drop zone where the balloon was parked, etched low against a pale blue, cloudless sky. A huge Thai word was painted on the side, but since the Thai alphabet is a derivation of Sanskrit, I could neither read nor pronounce it. Alongside was parked a two-and-a-half-ton truck loaded with parachutes. As a stick of six Thai jumpers boarded the gondola and was winched into the sky, Coyne strapped into his video rig, and Kat started shooting stills. The balloon's cable drooped in the direction of the wind.

I could see the value of the balloon as a training device. It was much cheaper than flying students on their first two jumps, and provided an excellent vantage point from which to grade them on canopy work and PLF's, but was absolutely useless for practicing door exits.

It took only a couple of minutes to winch the balloon to altitude. Very shortly the jumpers dropped out, one by one. Unlike a C-130 jump, where the speed of the aircraft snaps their chutes open before jumpers have fallen four feet below the flightpath, these jumpers were almost halfway to the ground before their chutes fully extended, billowed and inflated. By then Brown, T.R., Coyne, and I were chuted up, ready to board the balloon, which was quickly winched back down. Single file, we waddled around to the front of the gondola and boarded.

The jumpmaster moved us into position and hooked our static lines to a cable above us. We stood there for a moment, looking at each other in our bulbous helmets and parachute gear. The gondola swung free and the ground dropped away. Then it was so quiet and the breeze so pleasant that I couldn't believe it was dangerous. Our jumpmaster or "dispatcher," as he was called, said they had never had a malfunction.

Our dispatcher was the same tough young sergeant who had given us refresher training. He wore Thai, U.S., and British jump wings. "How often you jump balloon?" I inquired.

"Almost every day," he said. "It's my balloon."

As we rose, the horizon extended further and further, until it became a haze blending sky and ground, miles away. The sky grew enormous, and the people and cars below shrank, but never so much that they became dots, or even toys. It was like looking down from the fifth floor of a building, only there was no building. Then we stopped, and swayed. The cables creaked, and the wind hummed faintly around them.

The dispatcher nodded and dropped the safety bar from the entrance to the gondola. He gestured Brown into the door. As soon as Brown had a good door position, the dispatcher tapped him on the ass.

Brown yelled when he went over the edge. He claims it was a battle cry, but it sounded like terror to me.

Then it was my turn. I wheeled into the door and assumed a standard door position. The DZ was way down there, almost like a sand table.

"Ready!" said the dispatcher. I came to something like attention, grasped my reserve at the sides and took one step forward, like a little tin soldier.

It wasn't like skydiving, where you don't feel weightless until you get away from the aircraft. There was a feeling of instant buoyancy, like the Moonwalk or Big Slide, only longer and better. My legs sort of floated up so that I was sitting midair in an L position, then I felt the first soft tug at my back, then three more; my trash streamed out and ever-so-slowly billowed and inflated.

I reached for the right toggle, even as I checked my canopy. The plan was to hold against the wind and save myself a long walk to the turn-in point. It worked pretty well. For a while it looked like I was dropping straight down on one of the two trees on the DZ, but I drifted away without correction. Then the ground got close and I locked my eyes on the horizon and got my feet and knees together.

Crump! No sweat, good one. I was up and running to collapse the chute, but two little boys who were hanging around the DZ beat me to it.

Meanwhile, in the air, Coyne could not find his toggles. He still swears he jumped an unsteerable T-10. He got his feet and knees together and crashed in for a right front fall, moving at about ten knots, hitting his left heel and twisting his ankle. No more jumps that day. All the better for him to tape the C-130 jump.

A little over an hour later, engines roared and we were airborne. Brown, T.R. and I sat on the incline of a closed tailgate on a C-130, staring out at a sea of eager young faces. We were jumping with a class of junior cadets at the Royal Thai Military Academy, for whom this was the fourth of five qualifying jumps.

Smaller and lighter than Americans, the Thais put about a hundred jumpers on a C-130 that would hold sixty Americans, but to do it they leave the seats up and everybody sits cross-legged on the floor.

I was the first man in the right door, then T.R. right behind me. Brown was first in the left. I love being first man, and what I love most is that moment the door is opened, the wind grabs you, and paddies below go by, close below.

The light went green. The jumpmaster didn't tap me out. Once, over Okinawa, a navigator's sleeve triggered the green light by accident, and if the jumpmaster hadn't grabbed my harness I would have led an entire stick into the East China Sea. I took a quick peek. The third man was going out the left door.

Bye-bye.

Out and open, I grabbed my right toggle and pulled, turning into a surprise; the entire stick from the right door was drifting right toward me. The cadets were jumping T-10's. They had no directional capability, and the forward thrust of my directional chute drove me into them. Too late to turn. I held into the wind as a ragged, but solid line of olive-green parachutes headed my way.

I drifted into the glistening green dome of a canopy. It billowed as I bounded across, sinking further and further into it, finally breaking into air on the other side before either canopy collapsed, wondering what the kid below thought when he saw the imprint of my size twelves sprint across.

Brown and I landed well, but T.R. sat flat on his ass and did mischief to his spine. Nothing serious, several days of twinges and awkward motions, plus a football-size bruise on his hip. I think it is no coincidence that the two old farts who ran every day got away clean, while our two young *bon vivants* were mangled.

"Well, we finally did something," said Brown as he came striding in, wearing a big, evil grin, still in his helmet, parachute kit bag slung across his back.

He was in an expansive mood at our very late dinner in the apartment over Sukhumvit that night. "This is good fuckin' shit," he said through a mouthful of spaghetti.

I laughed. "The Bob Brown equivalent of 'My compliments to the chef?'"

Brown gave me an injured look. "Well, it is good shit." He called out to the kitchen to See, our Wa cook, "See! Hey, See!"

See padded barefoot in from the kitchen, wearing a concerned frown. He wore warm-up pants and an *SOF* T-shirt. Brown grasped his arm, grinning. "Good shit!" he bellowed. "Good fuckin' shit!"

See went back to the kitchen beaming, walking like a pouter pigeon.

Brown belched mightily and wiped his mouth with the hair on his arm. "Well, guess I'll hit the rack," he said. He slid back from the table and walked to his room. Covered with wiry brown hair, in his sprung jockey shorts, Brown had a helluva build, incredible for a man his age. He looked like what a papatrooper ought to look like.

"Ah, sweet mystery of life, at last I've found you," he sang as he padded away, flip-flops flapping on the floor, arms waving wildly to the meter of his croak. He began to yodel as the door closed behind him.

# 21

# The Laotian Resistance

Brown and Coyne took off for Afghanistan with the video camera, looking for a little more action before we closed out. This was my last chance to really do something here; I wanted to get into Laos.

"You do not understand our customs," said Chan, the intelligence agent. "You must spend money to gain face, so you will be respected." He looked at me earnestly over the dining room table in the penthouse. Across the table with Chan was Colonel Boon Lert, allegedly a big wheel in the Lao Resistance. All we had was Dr. Seuss's word for that.

Actually, I do believe he was fairly important. He carried himself like a Lao colonel, was a man of simple dignity with an active, if limited, intellect. We had seen pictures of him with a column of troops moving through the jungles in Chinese-style uniforms and with Chinese weapons. The Chinese will support anybody they consider likely to stick a thorn in the side of the Vietnamese. Chan was also intelligent and likeable.

He looked at me astonished as I pounded the table and snarled at him. "Look," I bellowed, "I have just about had it with this bullshit. I wanta go into Laos with the resistance. You say they're willing to take me. Great! They say they don't have weapons. They have to rent them from the Thais. Fuck that!

"They want money. Okay, I understand that. Fine, but no money up front. They get the weapons, we go in, they get the money. It's that simple." We had spent almost four months putting up front-money for things that never happened. Enough already.

"But we must have some money first," Chan said earnestly. "Otherwise they will think you are not men of importance."

I smiled broadly, and said nothing. Chan gave me a look like a puppy that didn't know why it had been whipped, and Colonel Boon Lert sat hunched over, cowed.

"You know, I understand your customs a lot better than you understand ours. One of our customs is that anybody who lets himself get ripped off repeatedly is an idiot. We have a word for such a person. It is 'sucker.' If they want to take me in, fine. We've backed Dr. Seuss and Boon Lert to the tune of many thousands of dollars.

"Now you wanta talk about face. What do you think it's gonna do to my face to go back to Boulder and tell them that my wife got into Cambodia, and I couldn't get into Laos, or anywhere else? So I lose face if I give you money up front and this thing falls apart, and I lose face if I don't go in.

"So you guys get me in if you're so fuckin' hot. Get me in or so help me, I'll do everything I can to insure that Brown shuts down your entire operation. No more bucks from the looney magazine."

Two days later T.R. and I were on our way to Nakon Phanom to prepare to go into Laos. Kathy stayed in Bangkok, manned the phone, and worked on some reports for Brown.


Contemplate this scenario: two Americans come to town in a rented car, which drops them at the hotel and leaves. They check in with a smattering of Thai and a great deal of gesticulation. The astute observer, one who had seen both American military and civilians, would take these two for Vietnam vets by age and demeanor. A true connoisseur of walks and mannerisms would not have much difficulty placing them under a pair of green berets.

So these two check in and don't do anything. They don't phone anybody, except for two calls to Bangkok. They don't see anybody.

Oddly enough, nobody seemed to pay it much mind. I would assume the cops kept tabs on us, but they did it discreetly.

It was about two-thirty in the afternoon when we got there. We were supposed to be contacted at six. So we dropped our gear and went for a walk.

We had driven straight in from Bangkok and hadn't eaten, so we set out to explore the town. We'd been there once before, with Hiney, but he had been commander at the now-closed U.S. airbase, knew the town, and just took over. We had followed him around and not learned the town.

Most of NKP was along the river. The town stretched for about three-quarters of a mile, maybe three blocks deep, along the Mekong. There was a hotel at one end of town and a semi-fancy restaurant at the other.

We left the hotel and walked to the restaurant, passing row after row of flat, fake-front stores on the way, open front food and hardware stores jammed with goods, and several bell, bangle, and Buddha shops for religious artifacts. The Thais not only worship Buddha, they love him. They give a lot to their religion, and have every appearance of getting a lot back.

We passed a group of young men at an intersection, teen-agers taking a break, playing a game with what appeared to be a soccer ball woven from bamboo plaits.

The game they played was simple in concept but difficult in execution. The idea was for a bunch of guys to stand in a circle and keep the ball in the air with their feet. In Lumpini Park I have seen rings of young men who were wizards with their feet, but these lads were just fair. Two of them were playing in flip-flops, and when one of those boys saw Tom and me coming, his foot connected at an angle and the ball spun off into the street, sending him chasing after it.

Several of the old buildings were of concrete construction, like a rough stucco, usually painted a dirty pastel, with the old signs from when GIs were here; Bar Butterfly, O.K. Corral. We finally came to the restaurant and went inside. We sat at a rickety table on red vinyl seats in the back, by the river. It stretched wide, flat, and placid, to Laos, about three-quarters of a mile away: a broad, calm river the color of red mud.

The waiter, in white shirt and tie, brought us some dusty menus with an English translation, and we selected a hot seafood and rice concoction, but we didn't do as well as when Hiney was with us.

A concrete sidewalk, with a stone wall on the river side, extended north of the town for quite a distance. After dinner we walked along the Mekong, talking about this story, about Vietnam, about working for Brown, walking further than we actually had time to walk. We had to get back to the hotel for our scheduled contact.

There was alleged to be a guerrilla encampment about fifteen kilometers north of town. Colonel Boon Lert was supposed to be making arrangements for us to go into Laos with them.

Tom placed the call. He understood Boon Lert's accent over the phone better than I did. He sat on the bed, surrounded by field gear: packs, poncho, patrol harness, his M-5 aid kit, and field chow, mostly beanie weenies.

By now maids in the hotel had undoubtedly conveyed a complete inventory of this stuff to the local gendarmes.

"They haven't been able to set anything up," Tom said. "The Thais have called some kind of moratorium on guerrilla operations. Some kind of big meeting is going on."

"Wonderful," I said. "Only they told us before we left that it already *was* set up. All we had to do was wait until they picked us up."

"Well, I guess we'll just have to wait a little longer," he said. He put a Meat Loaf tape into his cassette deck and started waiting.

I went back to my room and fretted. Then I went to sleep.

We spent the next two days prowling the town and the banks of the Mekong, hovering over the phone, listening to the same tap dance from Bangkok.

By breakfast the third day I was snarling, "Fuck this! Either they come through today or we go back to Bangkok, and I have a little chat with Chan and the Colonel."

Suddenly there was an ungodly series of internal combustions out in the parking lot. It sounded like a two-stroke firefight. Then it ceased. An Ichabod Crane-like young man, about twenty-four, sauntered self-assured into the lobby. A mop of curly-red hair tumbled all over his head. He spied us, turned, and walked to our table, sat down, crossed his legs and smiled as though we were long lost fraternity brothers.

"Hi, I'm R-r-roger W-warner." He held out his hand. We shook and introduced ourselves. "Do either of you know where I might get my motorcycle repaired?"

We couldn't read Thai, but we could read the word "Honda," so we knew where that shop was. We told him, and he joined us for breakfast.

Roger told us his story over breakfast. He was a free-lance journalist, here to do a story on the refugees. Roger was a Yale graduate. He had been a rewrite man for *Time* for a year after graduation, and then taken what little money he could scrape together and headed for the Orient with a camera and a portable typewriter. His objective was to sell enough stuff so he didn't have to use his return ticket. So far he had made it nine months, which impressed me. Freelancing is a tough gig.

Roger was six-four, 170 lbs., broad at the shoulders, narrow at the hips, twenty-four years old, good-looking, a graduate of one of the three best universities in the U.S., and off on the adventure of his life. I envied him. Like Captain America in Cambodia, he could take his adventure as it came. I felt compelled to tie my adventure to something that was long gone.

He seemed to have that bland assurance taught in Ivy League schools that pretty much anything he did would be okay. I had known his type in the army, and they had not done well. They tended to wander, oozing charm and ad hoc analyses, into situations that would either get you shot by the other side or arrested by your own.

But Roger was not in the army and could wander anywhere he wanted. People would usually decide he was amiable enough, and give him whatever he asked for.

I have long used the down-home Okie version of the same technique, which works in the army, but not on the State Department.

"What brings you gentlemen to this unlikely place?" he inquired.

I saw no reason not to tell him.

He smiled. "I speak a little Lao," he said, and held up a Lao dictionary to prove it. "How about joining forces. I could cover it for another magazine. We can hire a tuk-tuk and cruise the villages along the river until we find one that's affiliated with the resistance."

I shrugged. "Might as well. It beats sitting here on our duffs, waiting for something to happen."

We put Roger's bike in the shop, and that afternoon he and I took a long walk upriver, while T.R. went to see *The Jazz Singer* at the local moviehouse. Roger had great free-lance stories to tell. Somehow he had managed to get the Heng Samrin government to let him into Ankhor Wat, which had been closed for years, to Khmer and foreigners alike.

Finally, Roger and I walked the paddy dikes across a rice field past a small boy prodding a water buffalo, who eyed us curiously as we passed. We walked around the village and found a sheltered spot by the river, stripped and went swimming.

By nine-thirty the next morning, thanks to Roger's dictionary, we were in a small resistance village, and my spirits soared. We were going to get in without Chan, without Boon Lert, without Dr. Seuss. The village was hidden in a grove of trees by the road, on the side away from the river. It was a small village, maybe fifty people, a collection of bamboo, rattan, and thatch shacks. There were families, but all the men were of military age.

With the aid of his dictionary, Roger was in painstaking conversation with a tall Lao in cut-offs.

"Ask them if there are any sick people I can treat?" Tom said. His M-5 kit was slung from his shoulder.

As soon as Roger had dragged this message out of his dictionary the man he spoke to led us into his hut, where his own baby lay dying.

Swiftly and efficiently Tom opened his kit and went to work. The problem, as it turned out, was that the boy's mother was also sick; her milk was killing the child. Tom also ministered to the mother, and that afternoon we brought a six-week supply of infant formula to the village. Through Roger, Tom delivered a half-hour lecture on field sanitation. That's how long it took to say, "Always boil water," with the aid of the dictionary. But for the time being, at least, he had saved the child, and possibly the mother as well. We were in with the people of the village.

They seemed a simple, happy people, just as my Montagnards had been, and I felt an open warmth and friendship coming from them, such as I had not felt in many years.

That afternoon though, when we came back with the infant formula, the headman of the village told us we would have to deal with someone higher up in the hierarchy.

I had just assumed they would take us over that night, and we would hook up with the people they fought with on the other side of the Mekong. When was anything ever so simple in Southeast Asia?

The next day we rented a truck to take us to one of the large refugee camps nearby, to pick up the man who was supposed to make it all happen, a "major" in the Lao Resistance. After a long, anxious wait at the gate, closely scrutinized by Thai guards, our man showed. He was tall for a Lao, and slim, and wore neatly pressed slacks, sandals, and a white shirt. Like our guide, he was smiling; but unlike the headman, whose smile was open, friendly and ingenuous, this man's smile was the phony smirk of a used car salesman. But he did speak excellent English, and we talked some in the truck.

He had a military bearing, but not the look of someone who had seen much combat. I guessed correctly that he had been an administrative officer, a first lieutenant in the *Force Armee du Royoume* of Laos.

I didn't find this news particularly reassuring. I never fought in Laos, but I did serve for a time with the Allied Officer Liaison Office at Ft. Benning, where we ministered to the needs of foreign students at the Infantry School. I had been highly impressed by some of those officers, and appalled by others. The ones who had appalled me the most were the Laotians and the Iranians. For arrogance, ignorance, and inefficiency they were unrivaled, although later I was to find out their like throughout the so-called "upper classes" of the Third World.

With a surprisingly warm and hospitable manner, he explained that it would take another day to arrange for weapons for us to take across. The Thai government tolerated the Lao Resistance, but they would not allow the Lao to bring weapons into Thai territory. This seemed reasonable enough, since they didn't want to give the Vietnamese an excuse to invade. Then he asked us to a party in the village that night. All the while we were driving from the refugee camp into NKP.

By the time we reached town he had sprung the happy news that while the Lao were giving the party for us, *SOF* was paying for it. He made it seem so reasonable. As hosts with honored guests, etiquette demanded that they throw a party, but these people were poor and had nothing, so we must buy the stuff for it. Noblesse Oblige! It was as slick a con as I had ever seen, and, low as the stakes were, and as much as we stood to gain, I decided to let it run on to see how far it would go. We bought a few cases of beer, a couple of bottles of Mekong Whiskey, a couple of 100 kilo bags of rice, enough actually to last the village for about six weeks, and some odd groceries. It came to about a hundred and twenty bucks.

That night Roger, T.R. and I sat cross-legged around a fire in the village with lukewarm beers in our hands, the village men seated around us. The women served a thick soup in battered tin bowls, rice in the same, corn on the cob, and later, papaya.

Until sunset, the sky was clear and blue and the forest crowded our little clearing of bamboo huts. The men wore only pants or cutoffs; the women wore sarongs, stained from being washed in muddy water, some wore tops, and some did not. Some of the women wore turbans, and some smoked green cheroots. It was a moment of peace such as I had not known since Vietnam.

As it got dark they built a huge fire. It blazed in the dark and sparks flew off into the night. The air was light and fragrant, clear and sweet. It was to city air as champagne is to sludge. For a moment I felt...did I actually feel it or only remember as it dopplered away? For an instant I was back in the mountains, a natural man.


The next evening T.R. and I went out to the village dressed normally, but carrying our field gear in kit bags. Once there, we suited up. Normally I don't wear socks on a combat patrol. What they do to your feet after walking across a river is not nice. But the only boots I'd been able to get on short notice were too wide and I had no choice but to wear two pair.

I had also thoughtfully put a taped hacksaw blade in one boot and a woodsaw blade in the other, in case of capture. I had no illusions about the quality of the troops we were going in with. I wore a regular Vietnam-style tiger suit, bush hat, and standard load bearing equipment, ammo pouches, two canteens, field dressing bandage, knife, compass secured to the harness by three feet of parachute suspension line—and no weapon. Weapons were on the other side of the Mekong.

Roger wore jeans and a dark shirt. He was guided by standard journalistic ethics and had no plans to carry a weapon. Besides, he'd never fired an automatic weapon before, and this was not the place or time to learn. The troops wore motley camo.

At dark we set out. The troops took up a good interval and moved silently, and very swiftly. I wasn't having any trouble keeping up, but my glasses were bifocals, and my feet were lost in a fog below. The ground was irregular, giving me a mild case of the stumbles. Nothing I couldn't handle, but I hated feeling awkward in the field. And I knew we wouldn't be out long enough to get over it. It takes about two weeks to get used to the field, and about six to get good at it.

But the air was clear, and it felt good to be out in the night. We crossed the highway and entered the dry paddy on the other side. The troops lengthened their stride and it was a bitch to keep up with them. I focused my total attention on the task, and stayed that way until we entered the jungle by the river. Then everything slowed down and the air became dank and ripe.

Slowly we groped our way down to the river's edge, where the boats were, and took up a defensive position while we waited for the light on the other side that would signal us to come over. We spread out and sat down. I found my insect repellent and gave myself another good coat. They buzzed around my face all night, but I got only two or three bites. In that situation you can't smoke, and you can't talk. You can't move around. You just sit and wait for word to move out.

I sat in the dark and felt the power of the river. This was life. No cities, no hustle, just the power of the river and the clean air, the moon, and clear bright stars. I had not expected that moment, but I would have come to Thailand for it alone.

Good thing, because the light on the other side of the river never shined.


The Laotian resistance major looked up at me with big sorrowful eyes, unable to believe that we and our traveler's cheques were actually leaving. He would have to go back to the refugee camp. Word was that the Thais were still cracking down on the resistance. There was no action on the border.

"We can go across without guns," he said desperately. "You can see the other side."

And what? Take pictures of village life; take a picture of a Russian-made truck on the highway? "Look, Major," I snapped. "You don't get it; we're a gun magazine. No guns, no story."

We finally agreed to his bringing some young leaders of the resistance over to the hotel that afternoon, to tell us their stories of derring-do from the other side.

When we got back to the hotel T.R. said, "Boy, am I glad you decided not to go over tonight. Those guys don't have it."

"That motherfucker," I said of the major. "I'm tempted to start a fund to buy salt for the Vietnamese, so they can turn Laos into a desert."

That afternoon the major brought over three or four of the young Lao resistance leaders. They were real guys, and you only had to look at them to know they dealt with death on a daily basis. They were young and dark, not light-skinned like the upper-class Lao, and their eyes blazed. Three days before they had raided a Soviet information center in Savanaket, on motorcycles; cheap little trail bikes. Five guys had ridden into town on bikes, thrown a grenade apiece into the center, fired up a magazine apiece and zoomed back out of town.

They sat in our hotel room, quiet and stolid, telling their story when the phone rang. I picked it up and heard Brown's conspiratorial snicker. I quickly filled him in on what had happened.

"Never mind that," he snapped. "We're through here. Coyne and I got in with the Afghan rebels. We attacked a Russian A-camp. There were about twelve of them holed up with maybe four hundred Afghan troops. We laid out on the next hillside and pasted them all day with mortars and a 12.7 anti-aircraft machinegun. Killed two Russians and God knows how many Afghans."

"You rotten bastard!" I screamed. "You beat me again!"

Again the snicker. "So how about you and Kat going to Israel for a couple of weeks on your way to Beirut?"

# 22

# Aloha, Vietnam

The night before Kat and I left for Israel I dreamed of my first leave-taking from Vietnam and of a jump I'd made when, as I'd told Mark Smith on the Mittrapab jump, everything was for the first time.

Four of us, Special Forces officers, squeezed under the porch of the Ops Shack to get out of the rain.

I had just brought my last patrol back into our camp, four klicks north of Cheo Reo, after having taken Walt Swain, a good friend and executive officer of our replacement detachment, on his orientation patrol. We had killed three VC and captured a Walther PPK pistol that I confiscated as my personal war trophy. We had sprung the ambush at two-thirty in the afternoon, less than eight klicks from a Vietnamese district headquarters. Even Captain Charley Judge, Walt's CO, was impressed, not something that happened often. Judge turned the Walther over and over in his hands. Swain told the story of how it happened.

"So you didn't put out flank guards?" the Old Man, Captain Crews McCulloch, said.

"Nope," Swain replied. "Just got on the trail and barreled on through."

The Old Man looked a little embarrassed. "We usually keep off the trails and put out flankers," he said.

I started to explain that it was a fairly safe area—our intelligence had put the VC crossing the ambush site at a certain time—and that I had wanted Swain's first patrol to be a success, so they'd stay with our concept of operations.

I'd made my decision based on the best facts available and had been right. I didn't need to apologize to anybody. "I'm going to get cleaned up," I said, moving off into the rain, toward the wash house.

I was proud of that operation. We had spent our first four months wandering around in the woods trolling for ambushes. But by then the Old Man had evolved a concept of operations that got us in solid with the tribespeople, one that didn't involve shooting buffalo or burning villages, and from that I had been able to set up a superb intel net. For the past two months we had been going on short patrols, setting up on the trails, waiting for an appointment that Victor Charlie didn't know he had.

We knew that place cold. The Old Man could stand anywhere in Phu Bon province and call out a four digit coordinate without reference to a map. We had the highest kill score in II Corps, and we had got two-thirds of it in the past sixty days. Never in my life had I been any place that I wanted to leave less.

My stomach cramped badly. I'd been operating with a constant bellyache for more than two months, losing a steady five pounds a month to amoebic dysentery for six months.

That night at supper the Old Man said there wasn't time for any more patrols. "The operational fund has to be taken into finance at Nha Trang by an officer. Judge and I have to inventory weapons tomorrow, so you're elected."

I wasn't happy about it because there was still one patrol planned. But that night I packed an AWOL bag and shined up a pair of jungle boots. The following morning I caught the II Corps courier aircraft, a Caribou, at the airstrip.

It was still the dry season in Nha Trang and the sky was a hard, pale blue from the mountains to the sea. The air was lemon yellow and the sun baked my bones. I was covered with a fine film of sweat as soon as I jumped off the Caribou. It felt good. The passengers stood with their baggage beside a long row of new, whitewashed concrete hangers, the hard concrete of the runway stretching off in the distance.

I went inside one of the hangers, blinking to adjust to the light, my body turning suddenly cool as I passed into the shade. The 7th Aerial Port Squadron's passenger desk was an upright, homemade counter painted a glossy gray. It was manned by a young Airman 2nd class in fatigues and a blue baseball cap.

"How do I get to the new Special Forces Headquarters?" I asked. I hadn't been to Nha Trang since we came in country.

"It's way across on the other side of the runway, Sir," he said. "Just a minute and I'll call over and get you a ride."

I took the manila folder with the ops fund in it inside the door marked FINANCE. A fat Spec 5 behind a big steel desk took it, turned and handed it to a pretty Vietnamese girl, who put it at the bottom of a pile of paper on her desk. "Where's the transient officer's quarters?" I asked the Specialist.

"All the way down the street and to your left, Sir," he said.

I grunted thanks and went back through the door, out into the hard yellow sunshine. I looked around, always feeling uneasy in Nha Trang. Mountains loom over the town, within easy mortar range.

I walked down the street and turned left where a row of barracks stretched off to the right. Like the rest of the buildings, they were gleaming white one-story structures with pitched roofs and lots of windows to let in the air. A walkway ran in front of the barracks, and across from the barracks was another row of bigger buildings, three of them. The sound of splashing water indicated they were latrines. In front of each barracks was a small teal and gold metal sign hanging from an inverted L-shaped bracket. The sign in front of the first barracks said, BRODT BARRACKS, and there was another over the door that said, "Transit Officers Quarters." It should have read, "transient," but who was I to bitch?

Every barracks was named after a Special Forces man killed in Vietnam. Too many had been friends of mine.

The last time I saw Jim Brodt, he and I and a guy named Morgan Jones sat in the bar of the Ft. Buckner Officers Club on Okinawa. Morgan and I made up rowdy songs, and Brodt bought beer to keep us fueled.

A kid named Neil McIver was killed in the same action as Brodt. His building was down the street. He and Mike Iten, our junior commo man, had gone through basic, jump school, and training group together. Mike was in Vietnam on his first tour when they were killed. He and McIver used to talk in Morse code back and forth in the evening. Then McIver quit sending. Mike didn't find out why for a couple of weeks. His team sergeant got him drunk, told him, then sent him to Dalat for three days. Mike and McIver were both eighteen at the time.

We were free enough for that sort of kindness in those days.

It seemed almost indecent to be sleeping in Jim Brodt's memorial. I went inside and threw my gear on the first empty bunk. In back was a Dutch door with the top part open and a sign that said, "Transient Personal, Check in Here." There was a fat, gray-haired "leg" sergeant back there, reading a true adventure magazine.

"I sign in here?"

"Yes, Sir, and check your sidearm."

I signed his register and slipped my scrounged USMC shoulder holster over my head. "Anywhere around here to get a drink?"

"Prayboy Crub's down at the end of the barracks row, Sir," he said.

"Is it open?"

"Noon to midnight, Sir."

I went back into the sunshine. The white rows of buildings closed in around me, and for a moment my eyes started flicking from shadow to shadow. Then I realized what I was doing and walked with my eyes fixed straight ahead, to the end of the row.

It was dark inside the Playboy Club after the brightness outside. The club was in a regular barracks building, long and narrow, but there were rows of chrome and leatherette couches on the left, with round, black formica-topped coffee tables. The bar ran almost the entire length of the right side, and the mirror behind it ran the length of the bar. It was two o'clock in the afternoon. The bar was three-quarters empty. Mostly the customers were transients like me, with bleak faces and very wide eyes. Their shoulders slumped and they seemed to cluster on the couches, with their backs to a wall. Over in one corner was a bunch of young PFCs and Spec 4's.

They were very clean and eager and talked loudly. Most likely off-duty commo men and truck drivers. Next to them was a glowing, multicolored Seeburg juke box. At the other end of the room were two pinball machines.

I went over to the bar and sat down, staring at the rows of canned cashews, Polish sausages, and my own face in the mirror. It looked ten years older than it had six months before. The barmaid came over. She was almost thirty, and had aged fast too, become stringy and hard-faced. She wore black capri pants and a purple blouse. But she had beautiful long, straight black hair, drawn into a ponytail, flipped over her shoulder, and spilling down the front of her blouse in a shimmering cascade. "Gimme a San Miguel and a bag of Fritos, Angel," I said.

I took my beer and went over to the juke box. There were three good songs on it, loud and rhythmic enough to preclude rational thought. I put in a dollar's worth of quarters and played them four times apiece: *Twist and Shout* by the Beatles, *Deep Purple*, by Nino Tempo and April Stevens, and *Green Onions* by Booker T. and the M.G.'s.

The hard-driving rhythm drew me out of myself, and I stood, letting the beat drive me along. I killed my beer and went back for another.

Then I took the beer and the Fritos and sank into one of the deep chairs along the wall. I flipped my feet up on the low coffee table and let a long gurgle of beer slide down my throat.

I sat there until my twelve records played through, then broke a five, put in another dollar and played them again, four more times apiece. I did it fast, before anybody else could have a chance to make a selection, but somebody had slipped in a dime and Sinatra sang, *All the Way.*

I got another beer and some pork skins. I ate a lot of junk food that afternoon, missed lunch, and drank through suppertime.

Some guys I knew came in. I grunted enough greeting to acknowledge their presence without inviting conversation.

My belly felt kind of crumby and my head was hot and it seemed a good idea to roll the cold beer bottle over my forehead. As soon as the beer was gone I got up, thinking I might go downtown.

But then I felt very sick and walked quickly out the door and across the space to the latrine building. It was dark and stars shone down between the buildings. Then there was the brightly lighted latrine with a row of stalls on the left and porcelain sinks on the right, each with its little square of mirror. I bolted for one of the stalls.

I got my pants down just in time. My bowels emptied in great racking spasms. I sat on the stool and rocked back and forth, trying to hold my stomach down. Then I grabbed the chain on the French-style crapper and, holding my trouser tops in my hands, whirled and watched the last of the stool swirl down the drain, as I threw my guts up in a sour green and yellow gusher, just finishing in time to sit back down again. This time it was all liquid.

I alternated like that for half an hour, until finally there was nothing left. Then I buckled up and went back to the Playboy Club, the closest place where there was help.

I barely got the door open, and stood there in the doorway, looking into the dim interior at all the green butts on barstools. *Green Onions* was still playing, and I couldn't have cared less.

Two young sergeants I had known on Okinawa came up. One of them said, "Sir, you all right?"

"No," I said.

One of them clamped a hand over my forehead. "You better believe it," he said. They half-dragged, half-carried me to a jeep, got my AWOL bag and weapon from the BOQ and drove me to the 8th Field Hospital on the other side of the airstrip. The ride was a dark blur.

A white-coated medic gave me a card to fill out and stuck a thermometer in my mouth. "Hundred and five," he said when he took it out.

For three days I lay in a bed in the hospital, between crisp, clean sheets, floating free in a bright white swirling cloud of feverish hallucinations.

It got cold, so cold I shivered for a long time, floating in the cloud. Then it turned warm again, and I became conscious and ate a clean meal off a clean tray, with salad.

"What have I got, Doc?"

"Gastroenteritis."

"What's that?"

"It's a badly upset stomach condition, characterized by diarrhea, vomiting, and a high fever."

I slept, twelve, fourteen, sixteen hours a day. Three days later I woke up. I grabbed a medic and said, "Man, I gotta get out of here. My team leaves Vietnam day after tomorrow, and I got stuff scattered all over that camp."

"You sure you feel well enough to go?"

"Sure, sure. I feel great. See!" I swung down out of the bed and walked about four steps, briskly, with my head held high. Then I stopped and grabbed a bedpost so I wouldn't fall down.

"Okay," he said. "Get your gear and check out."

As soon as I could get dressed and clear the hospital, I lurched weakly into the street, AWOL bag in hand, and thumbed a ride on a passing three-quarter.

The driver let me off at the little building beside the warehouses: the Transportation Movement Control office.

I pushed through the screen door and leaned on the counter. My stomach still had a few butterflies, but by and large, I felt okay. There was a sleek, efficient-looking Airman 1st class with a boogie haircut, ducktails on the sides and crewcut on top, and a clipboard, working behind the desk. Two pilots sat in back, drinking coffee, their feet up on desks. They wore flight suits and S&W .38s in cowboy rigs. They both had survival knives and good boots. One wore a U.S. army blocked fatigue cap and the other a camouflage duck hunting cap. They looked tired, but real solid. I didn't trust anybody in Vietnam who didn't look tired. They were Air Commandos.

"You got anything going to Cheo Reo this afternoon?" I asked.

"Yes, Sir," the Airman 1st said. "Leaves at 1200 hours."

"Okay," I replied. "Book me on it. Name's Morris."

As soon as I got my name on the manifest I went back up to Special Forces headquarters and picked up our clearance for the ops fund and my pistol, got some lunch, and came back down to the TMC.

"Sorry, Sir," the airman said as I came through the door. "That aircraft is a scrub. The right wheel is flat."

It was already too late to catch the courier, and even if I could, it only went to Pleiku today, then back to Cheo Reo tomorrow. By that route I'd be lucky to get back before the team left. "You got anything else going that way?"

"No, Sir, not until day after tomorrow."

"Aw," I said, "I have to get there. You got anything going over it?"

"Yes, Sir. There's an air drop at Plei Ta Nangle this afternoon. But it won't land at Cheo Reo."

"Have you got a weather check?" I asked. "What's the ground winds?"

"Eight to ten knots, Sir," he said, checking the chart behind him.

"Okay, what time's the aircraft take off?"

"Fourteen-hundred, Sir."

"Book me on it." I went to the Special Forces supply office next door. There was another clerk behind a desk there, an Army guy.

"Who do I see to draw a backpack, reserve, and kit bag? And preferably a helmet," I asked him.

"Chief McKee, Sir," he said. "He's the rigger officer."

"Where's he at?"

He pointed toward the back of the office, on the other side of a partition. I went back there and found an earnest gentleman in his forties, laboriously pouring over some paperwork. He had a shaved fringe of hair around a gleaming bald head, and his face looked far older than his years.

"Chief McKee?" I said.

"Yes, Sir." He stood up, and I saw he wore master parachutist wings and rigger wings. He was well-built, actually in a lot better shape than I was, a highly conscientious man.

I explained the situation to him and asked for a T-10 parachute assembly.

"Sir," he said. "I don't approve of jumping in on these unprepared DZs. That's a very unsafe practice. I highly recommend against that."

From his standpoint, of course, the chief was absolutely right. But that didn't help solve my problem.

"Approve of it or not," I said, "will you give me the rig?"

"No, Sir," he said. "I won't."

"The hell with it. You must work for somebody around here that can authorize it. Where's he at?"

"Major Kollat is the S-4, Sir. His office is in the front."

I walked back up to the front of the Supply office and through the door marked, Supply Officer.

He was seated behind his desk. The desk had a nameplate on it that said Zoltan F. Kollat, Major, United States Army. He was a very muscular man with brown curly hair. He had been physical training instructor for my class at the Special Forces Officer's Course at Ft. Bragg, and with his shirt off, from behind, if he wiggled a finger, his entire back looked like a flag waving. He sat at his desk, staring off into space. Perhaps he was practicing his glower.

"Major Kollat," I said.

He reached up and scratched his nose, almost splitting his sleeve up around his bicep. "What?" he replied.

"You mind if I borrow a T 10 assembly? I want to jump into my camp this afternoon."

"Naw, I don't care."

"Thanks." I got out of his office fast, before he could change his mind. Avoiding Chief McKee, I went to the warehouse and drew the rig and a helmet. Then I went back to the TMC.

There was still an hour to wait, so I got a cup of coffee and sat down with it. They had some old magazines for the flight crews to read. I picked up a dog-eared *Argosy*.

At one forty-five the Airman 1st class came back and said, "About time to load up, Sir."

"Thanks." I slipped my shoulder holster over my head and picked up the heavy kit bag with the two parachutes in it, and my AWOL bag with the other hand.

"You want some help with that, Sir?"

"Nope."

The crew squatted over their map under the wing of their C-47. Over by the door a fork lift put cargo pallets up on the conveyer inside the aircraft. Up inside, two door-bundle kickers tied on G-13 cargo chutes. Directing the whole operation was Chief McKee.

"Major Kollat loaned me a rig," I said.

"All right," he replied, but he didn't look very happy about it. An old jumper, he must have seen a lot of guys bent out of shape on better drop zones than the Cheo Reo airstrip. I sat down my kit bag and went over under the wing to talk to the crew. "Going to Cheo Reo?" I asked.

The pilot looked up. "Can't land there," he said. "Not on the flight plan."

"Just go over the airstrip at about twelve hundred," I said. "I'm going to jump."

"Okay, fine."

I squatted down over the map and showed him the approach I wanted. He suggested a better one and I agreed to it. "Look," I said, "if you got one of these little message-dropping jazzers, why don't you come down over Buon Beng and I'll lob it in and have somebody meet me at the airstrip. I don't relish walking all the way out to camp."

"Sure," he said. He reached into his flight suit and came out with an iridescent red streamer, about fifteen feet long, with a small weighted pocket for messages in one end.

The pilot got up and looked questioningly at his aircraft. "All right," he said. "Let's see if this sucker'll fly."

He went back to climb up the ladder. Chief McKee's men had already stowed my chute in the back.

The flight took about two hours, which gave me plenty of time to write out, "Have somebody meet me with the ambulance at the airstrip. Will jump about a half hour from now. —Morris."

Then I went up to the door and looked out. This pilot was flying a lot lower than the one who'd taken my team in. That was because the weather had been better then. No clouds. We followed the flat, looping river, Song Ba, all the way up from the coast. The country was as beautiful as ever. The green seemed to shimmer in the rainy season, and the flat square paddies were filled with water that gave off a sheen, like a thousand mirrors laid out on the ground, stubbled by uniform sprigs of rice. I watched the shadow of the airplane flying off to the left and the reflection of it just below. The three of them: the real one in the sky, the shadow on the ground, and the reflection in the stagnant water, flew in perfect formation until we came to the mountains. The reflection disappeared and the shadow broke apart on irregular country.

Down below was the district headquarters on Highway 14, and I could see the big trail that ran a hundred feet from where we had ambushed the VC company commander and his two buddies four days before. A little to the west was the spot where Bill Foody, our junior medic, got hit in the leg. It was saddening to look down and see the ground we had made our own with so much effort, only to have our tour end just as we had achieved a real mastery of the area.

Our past was written all over the land below. And the future was written in the past, if you could see it.

I could see some of it. We knew the Montagnard revolt of September 1964 was coming, had reported that intelligence to higher headquarters, and not been believed.

The first bundle blocked the door and I couldn't lean out, so I ducked back inside and went up to talk to the crew chief.

"Drop down over Buon Beng," I howled over the engines, "and I'll lob out the message. Then I'll jump on the way back from Plei Ta Nangle."

"Rodge," he said. He turned and spoke into his microphone, nodding to the pilot. Then he turned back to me.

"We're ten minutes out from Cheo Reo now," he bellowed. "We'll be dropping down in about five."

I nodded and went back to the door, working my way around the door bundles and the conveyer belt all the way back. The wind caught my face again as I got to the door. It seemed only a moment later that the aircraft started dropping. I knelt and took the message streamer from the front of my shirt, peering around the bundle. The ground below rose swiftly, and we started passing over the road complex around Cheo Reo. I could have reached out and touched the treetops underneath.

I leaned out as far as I could and made out the great oval of dozed trees around the camp, thatched-roofed buildings, and the shiny tin roofs of the supply building, commo shack, and dispensary up ahead and closing fast. Then the dozed trees were underneath, scattered helter-skelter with great dried clumps of dirt clinging to their snarled roots. We passed over the trenches, like parallel brown mole burrows, and a water buffalo ran over a pig to get out from under the shadow of the wing. We couldn't have been over forty feet off the ground.

I thought, I better get rid of this, and threw the message streamer out the door as hard as I could. It immediately disappeared from sight. I wondered where it landed. The aircraft ascended.

Fifteen minutes later we were circling Plei Ta Nangle, the great triangle of the camp laid out on a plateau. We circled once. Then the first bundle got jammed in the door and we took it around again. The aircraft flew about a hundred and fifty feet over the DZ, high enough to give the cargo chutes time to open, low enough that they wouldn't drift far. We had plenty of time, plenty of fuel, and a small DZ, so the pilot made one pass per bundle. Mr. McKee and his two riggers hooked up the static lines and manhandled the bundles into the door. As the aircraft made its approach, the two kickers tipped the bundle out so it was just balanced on the edge of the door. They had to lean back hard to hold it in. Mr. McKee leaned around and stuck his head out the door to judge the exact moment they passed over the panel. Then he looked back and yelled, "GO!" and the door was suddenly empty, the static line dragging back and down, taut and hard. Then the two kickers dragged the static line back in and dumped it in the back.

Figuring the time to get back to Cheo Reo, I decided to chute up. I went aft and opened my kit bag, reached down and pulled out the rig.

I ran the leg straps through the handle of my AWOL bag so I wouldn't have to carry that. By the time the last bundle was out, I was ready for some help with the reserve. Chief McKee cinched it up for me and made a thorough rigger check. The helmet was a little loose, but it was too late to worry about that. I wrapped my glasses in my beret and shoved them down the front of my shirt. Mr. McKee went around and behind me to check the backpack and then he handed the static line over my left shoulder.

My adrenalin was up and I was ready to go. I started waddling back to the door. When I got about six feet away I stopped and hooked up the static line, inserting the safety wire through the snap link.

Then I moved into the door. Below were the trails and jungles we had run over for this too-short time. We passed over the village where Ksor Ay, our oldest platoon leader, who had fought for the French before us, whose front teeth were filed and whose earlobes were pierced and stretched into big loops in the old Jarai manner, would be assassinated when he went home on leave wearing a uniform. We passed over the spot where Nay Re, our psychotic company commander, was to be executed for mortaring a Vietnamese district headquarters during the revolt. But of course, I didn't know about those things yet. Knowing Nay Re though, it was predictable that something similar would happen. It was also predictable that a convoy of government troops would be ambushed on the same road where I used to drive a jeep alone and unmolested, because they didn't understand the principle of not setting a pattern. Six Americans were killed on that ambush, and it wouldn't have happened if even one member of our team had been there.

We were being withdrawn because of a peculiarity of the Department of Defense joint travel regulations which only permitted us to stay for six months. Don't ask why; that would only lead to thirty-two pages of bureaucratic gobbledygook that would still make no sense. The Old Man had volunteered to extend us, which we all wanted, and been turned down.

I had to come back, not just this time to get my stuff, but because we had led the Montagnards way out on a limb and shouldn't have quit until they were safe. When you fight with people there is an implied obligation to stand with them until the fight is over. It was something we all felt keenly, personally, but our government felt not at all.

The U.S. didn't do that, but we stuck with them another nine years, and without that, their culture wouldn't have survived *either* Vietnamese regime.

I'd keep coming back as long as it was there to come back to.

I moved close to the door and took the wind blast full in my face. Down below was the canopy of trees to the left of Highway 14, and back on the other side of the highway were the Chudleya Mountains. And below the tree canopy, on the small trails, were little skinny guys in black shortie pajamas and tire sandals, with wicker helmets and captured American weapons, or the new family of Chinese weapons which were just beginning to appear.

I became conscious of Chief McKee there beside me, a worried frown on his face. He kept his balance by hanging onto the cable. We passed over some more green mountains, the camp, and the town of Cheo Reo on the left. We came up on the Cheo Reo airstrip, more than three-quarters completed now, but still with a great clutter of ill-maintained construction equipment at the unfinished end. I grinned, fired up and ready to go, and the AWOL bag flapped against my legs as the pilot turned to make his downwind leg.

When we got past the construction equipment at the other end, he turned again and started his approach run.

I leaned way out the door and caught the wind blast full in the face. I squinted and my eyes watered, but I could make out the red cross on top of the ambulance. We were about four hundred and fifty yards from the desired exit point.

"Sir," said Chief McKee, beside me. "I don't see any smoke on that DZ."

"I didn't ask for smoke, Chief," I yelled. They'd only put out red smoke for no drop.

"You can't hardly judge the wind without smoke, Sir. I don't think you better jump." In his mind's eye he probably saw me slamming into the runway at about thirty knots and being dragged to death before I could get the chute collapsed. All this time we were steadily eating up DZ. I leaned way back in the door, with my fingers hooked around the outside.

"You got a point there, Chief," I said, jumping up and out. The blast whirled me away as I shouted, "One-thousand, two-thousand, three-thousand, four-thousand." I was away and free.

# 23

# Peace For Galilee

The Israeli tank, a Centurion, lay about forty feet off the winding mountain road, its right track blown off by an anti-tank mine. That should have told me something.

There is a particular mindset you need for combat, but we were a day behind the point of Operation Peace for Galilee and I felt quite safe.

"Peace for Galilee" was the official name for the 1982 Israeli invasion of Lebanon. Kat and I had flown into Tel Aviv ten days before, to do a couple of small stories on the Israeli Defense Force before going on to Beirut for the Lebanese Forces Commando Course. We had spent about a week getting our press credentials, touring Jerusalem, Jericho and the site of the Dead Sea Scrolls while we waited for approval. The preceding Friday, Major Irit Atsmoun, the very attractive press liasion officer in the IDF Spokesman's office, had told us to come back Monday. "I think we may have something for you." That Sunday they invaded Lebanon.

Now we were part of a convoy of journalists in rented cars, each car accompanied by an Israeli officer from the Spokesman's office. Our little convoy of civilian cars was stopped in the middle of a dun-colored column of tanks and armored personnel carriers. The mountains were beautiful, the air crisp and clean. What's to worry?

For a close-up of what this particular mine had done to this particular tank, I stepped over a piece of engineer's tape, and walked toward it.

"Jim, *STOP!*" Bill Gross yelled before I had gone two steps. He ran down the road, Uzi slapping against his side, an Incredible Hulk in flak jacket and billowing afro. "There are anti-personnel mines out there. We had to send another vehicle out to retrieve the crew."

Bill had moved from Minneapolis to Tel Aviv a few years before, to go into the diamond business. He was a lieutenant in the Israeli reserve, called up for the Galilee operations.

After I left the minefield, we were still stalled in the road, waiting for a Caterpillar tractor to smooth off a bend that two days of tank columns had made impassable.

I climbed up a dirt bank and scrambled onto an armored personnel carrier. The infantry squad, who rode into combat inside, now lounged on top, with the insolent idleness of young soldiers who had nothing to do but bitch and make bum jokes while they waited for the order to move out.

Thoroughly bored, they made me immediately welcome, and showed me their vehicular-mounted machine guns and personal weapons.

"Are you getting a good story?" one collegiate-looking blond kid asked.

I laughed and told him I had come to do a story on Israeli airborne training. "This is a bonus."

From their fearsome reputation, I had expected the Israelis to be an army of smartly turned out, gung-ho troops. I soon learned that military courtesy and spit and polish were far down on a list of priorities headed by tactics and training.

I was told that the more elite the unit, the sloppier it is. Boots are bloused or not, at the whim of the individual. Berets are worn folded, shoved through an epaulet. They wouldn't fit on the hair anyway; the Israelis see no inverse correlation between hair-length and combat effectiveness.

On my way to Metulla, on the northeast border, on the first day of Operation Galilee, I gave a ride to a young paratrooper on his way to his unit. His boots were unshined, but his SAR was spotless.

Israeli soldiers carry their personal weapons everywhere, and I never saw an obvious demerit on one. They were lightly oiled and perfectly cleaned, with all the creases, cracks and crevices immaculate. "It's like a second wife," one Israeli lieutenant said.

The Israeli Defense Force consists of every man with four limbs and two eyes between the ages of 18 and 55. For women, the ages are 19 to 35. Most battalion commanders are under thirty. But beyond that, the entire nation is part of the defense effort.

Israel, in the best of times, is a nation on alert. The Israeli Army, as far as I know, is the only one that hitchhikes to combat. All reservists keep personal weapons and web gear at home, and upon mobilization, troops hitchhike to designated points, ready to fight. Any Israeli travelers, military or civilian, will give them a ride.

Their basic fighting unit is the tank infantry team. In 1973, during the Yom Kippur War, the Israelis became temporarily infatuated with the notion they could fight with tanks alone—and lost a bunch of them. Now they fight with each tank paired with an infantry squad in an APC—except for their own Merkava, which has room for a squad in it, and is, therefore, both a tank and an APC.

The infantry carried Galil assault rifles. The Galil SARs are for paratroops and commandos, the M16s for artillery and support troops. Rumor has it the Israelis captured so many AKs in Lebanon that they planned to start making ammo for them and issue them to troops.

The Israeli Defense Force is informal, but because of their training and discipline, they don't take many casualties. They can't afford to; there aren't that many of them. They were taken by surprise in 1973 and had two thousand casualties, their worst to date. It seems as though everybody in Israel lost a member of his immediate family in that war.

One of the kids we gave a ride told me, "If one of us kills twenty PLO and gets killed himself, he has failed, because he was more valuable to us than those twenty were to them."

After heavy losses in 1973, the Israelis set out to revamp their military force. They built a bigger and better military, with more sophisticated weapons, more troops, better equipment, and new tactics.

In 1973 the IDF had only 2,000 tanks; in 1982 it had 3,500. APC's had increased from 3,000 to 8,000. The few dated anti-tank missiles it had in 1973 were replaced with thousands of state-of-the-art weapons. Similar improvements were made in the air force.

More than 600 combat aircraft were available in 1982, including many American-built F-16 Fighting Falcons and F-15 Eagle fighters. "Smart" weapons, television-guided for pinpoint accuracy, and electronic anti-radar devices had greatly improved the Israeli Air Force. The Israelis had amassed an awesome military force, one in which they were very confident.

"Motivation," one soldier explained to me, "is the key to the Israeli Army."

I thought I knew what he meant, but later I saw a perfect example.

One morning in Metulla, on the fourth day of the operation, kids were going to school. Metulla is Israel's northernmost city, and looks like a suburb of Phoenix, except that every house has immediate access to a bomb shelter. Metulla and Kiryat Shemona, the first city south, had taken plenty of Katyusha rockets from the PLO in Lebanon. They had lost a few people, and were in constant jeopardy. That was part of the original rationale for the invasion.

The kids looked like American school children. Mothers escorted young children along streets clogged with olive drab APC's, half-tracks, and trucks.

At one corner, a young mother and her daughter, about seven, stood waiting to cross while a three-quarter-ton truck drove by. The two soldiers in front were tired, bearded and dirty, maybe four hours out of the fighting, and maybe the same before going back in.

The little girl squealed and jumped on the running board of the truck to give the driver a big hug. Dust from southern Lebanon smeared her school dress; his dirty, bearded face scraped the soft skin of her neck. He was a reservist from Metulla; she was his daughter.


Nabatiye, about thirty miles into Lebanon, a beautiful hillside town of maybe a hundred thousand, had been a major southern base for the PFLP (Popular Force for the Liberation of Palestine), a radical PLO faction. For seven years the PFLP had occupied Nabatiye. People spoke of them with fear, recalling forced evictions, looting, rapes, and senseless killings.

The Israelis hadn't shelled in Nabatiye; they didn't have to. The PFLP pulled out rather than defend. The Israelis were greeted by open shops, fresh fruit and vegetable vendors, and joyous people; some of them said they were smiling for the first time in years.

In Nabatiye the Israelis captured three times as much PFLP ammo as their own intelligence estimates had indicated, all Soviet. I saw cache after cache of it, in houses and garages. As in Tyre and Sidon, the entire town was an ammo dump. It made me wonder how much of the damage to these cities, for which the Israelis were being consistently denounced in the press, was caused by secondary explosions of PLO ammo.

Bookshelves in PFLP-occupied houses were full of Marxist propaganda, on the walls were hammer and sickle posters of Lenin, Marx, and Ho. It reminded me of the stuff Coyne and I had seen at Surat Thani in Thailand, also all Soviet. When you see the same stuff in lots of different places, it tells you something.

I was reminded of the doctrine proclaimed at a party congress in 1976, to support "Wars of National Liberation" wherever they might arise, worldwide. I was beginning to see that these small wars, funded, armed, and trained by the same source, were coordinated; therefore, they must have a common objective.

If a "War of National Liberation," backed by the Soviet Union, were successfully waged in every vulnerable Third World country, and at present there was very little to prevent that; the result would be a chain of wretched Marxist-Leninist Soviet client states controlling enough of the world's vital resources to lock the United States out of Twenty-first Century technology, and control enough sea lanes to prevent our deployment of military forces to strategic areas.

This strategy alone, successfully pursued, could relegate the United States to the status of a second-rank power, leaving one and only one superpower, the Union of Soviet Socialist Republics. That would leave only one thing between the Soviet Union and world domination, the U.S. nuclear deterrent; and I did not think we would destroy the world to prevent them from taking it.

If the Katyn Massacre in Poland after WWII, in which all non-Communist Polish officers were simply slaughtered by the Soviets, the genocide in Cambodia, the "re-education" camps in Indochina, and the executions in Cuba after the Castro takeover were any indication, it was also their objective to line me, these Israeli troops, and everybody like us up against a wall and silence us forever.

The taking of the ruins of Beaufort, the old Crusader castle high on a mountain, was the first objective of the operation. For years Beaufort had been the symbol of PLO domination of southern Lebanon. From the square, jagged peaks of Beaufort, on a clear day, you can see the Litani River, Nabatiye and Marjayoun in Lebanon, and the Israeli cities of Metulla and Kiryat Shemona. It was such a clear shot with a Katyusha rocket that all forward observation and fire-direction functions had been handled by the gunner.

The mountain on which the castle sat was extremely steep, almost straight up, with a clear field of fire down the slopes.

With enough food, ammo, and water, a well-trained and motivated squad could defend it forever against anybody.

In Beaufort's 800 year history, with the exception of a couple of starve-outs, and a negotiated peace, it had never been taken. The Israelis took it on the second day, at the price of six killed in action.

Staring down the slopes from its summit, overlooking the broad, green agricultural valley, I asked Bill Gross, "Who did this?"

"A two-hundred-man commando unit of the Golani brigade, one of our best units," he answered. "Heliborne to the mountain's base, then a night assault straight up the hill. It took from one in the morning until seven to do it. Night operations are a specialty of ours. The Palestinians don't like them, and they aren't very good at them."

Only a highly trained and disciplined force could have done it at night. If the slope had been ten degrees steeper, it would have been a cliff.

# 24

# High Adventure

The lobby of the Arazim Hotel in Metulla, Israel, was filled with Israeli soldiers and an international smorgasbord of correspondents. Most of the Israelis wore fatigues or the olive drab, zippered jump-suits favored by some of the tankers. A variety of pistols hung from their hips; from their shoulders hung Galils, Uzis, and M-16s. Most of the Israelis were covered by a fine khaki dust, except for the pink raccoon mask where their goggles had been, with dark-rimmed, blood-shot eyes peering out from those ghost goggles.

The Israeli way of playing the role is to underplay it, and these guys were really tired, anyway. The only people acting heavily macho were the correspondents. They swaggered around in their camera vests and safari jackets, affecting a bored and knowledgeable air, chain-smoking their cigarettes overhand, demonstrating that, even though they were noncombatants, they were *real guys*.

The most macho of them all were the female correspondents, many of whom appeared to be working up a Chesty Puller imitation for the Marine Corps birthday ball.

The major exception to this rule was Kat, quietly amused in her safari suit, with red, heart-shaped sunglasses on her forehead.

The glasses were a gift from me, and a lucky one, for while the Israeli GIs had little use for macho noncombatants, they were all suckers for a cute girl in Lolita glasses and a Cambodian bush hat. That day, on the road to Beaufort Castle, which two days before had been the PLO stronghold in southern Lebanon, and today was an Israeli tourist attraction, an Israeli armored personnel carrier had clanked past thirty clamoring photographers to stop in front of Kat, who dangled from the back of a three-quarter-ton truck. But she couldn't get them to look grim and warlike. All they wanted to do was grin and give her the thumbs up.

Into the lobby of the Arazim strode a grinning trucker from any truck stop in America. He wore bluejeans, cowboy boots, a blue Kentucky Wildcats windbreaker and matching baseball cap. Blond hair curled out from under the cap, which was pushed back on his head. Stocky and muscular, he appeared to be in his late-thirties/early-forties, but his face was so unlined, the concept of "worry" seemed entirely alien to him. He looked as though he had just won the Publisher's Clearinghouse Sweepstakes.

"We took the tail-fin off one of them Syrian MIGs you guys shot down in the field today," he announced to the Israelis at large. "I had a farmer drag it back to the station. That thang was brand-spankin' new, built in 1981," he drawled. I caught his eye and waved him over.

"Where you from?" I grinned.

"Lexington, Kentucky," he replied as we shook hands. "Why?"

"I'm Jim Morris, and this's my wife, Kathy. I'm from Oklahoma, and she's from Arkansas. We've been chasing the wars for almost six months now. You're the first person in a long time we've heard talk right."

He laughed and sat down. "I'm Harold Cox," he said.

"What are you doing in the middle of this war?" I asked.

He laughed again. "I'm with High Adventure," he said, and pointed toward a flag-sized banner on the wall over the serving counter that led back into the kitchen. It was a navy-blue banner, with a white dove very like Picasso's, except it seemed to be flying faster and wasn't carrying an olive branch. The lettering read, *High Adventure Broadcasting—the Voice of Hope.*

When Kat and I first arrived at the Arazim three days before, Bill Gross had told us that there were some American Christian broadcasters who maintained an office in this hotel, living in Israel and operating a radio and TV station three klicks over the border in Lebanon. "They're just super people," he said.

The idea had seemed so bizarre that I had erased it from my mind. But here was Harold Cox, smiling and immensely likable.

"Don't write nothin' bad about these Jews," he said. "God loves 'em."

I laughed. "I haven't seen them do anything bad," I said. "They're good folks, and I'm no fan of the PLO.

"You're easy enough to spot as a Pentecostal Christian," I went on, "but you don't look like a broadcaster."

"I'm a truck driver," he said.

I was about to ask him what a Jesus-freak truck driver was doing in Metulla when the cook opened the doors to the dining room. Dinner was served.

Kat and I shared a glance of agreement, and I said, "Join us for dinner?"

"Sure." He grinned.

"Meat or dairy?" the young lady in jeans and black blouse asked as we walked through the door. You can find any kind of restaurant in Israel, but by law the hotel restaurants are kosher; no cheeseburgers, no BLT's. There were no menus, because the Arazim served only one entree in each category. Half the time we didn't know what we were eating, but it was always wonderful.

We took our seats and Kat and I ordered a bottle of Carmel Avdat, a local red wine, and Harold asked for water. Around us the crowd was seating itself in revealing groups. The correspondents all sat with correspondents, and the Israeli soldiers always sat with each other.

Kathy and I were the only correspondents who sat with the soldiers, which we preferred to do most of the time.

Sometimes we sat with the correspondents. Except for Terry Anderson, who was a veteran, they were mostly quiet around me, but they were more open with Kat when I wasn't there. She got to watch a process I never saw. She got to watch them all get together and decide what was news and what was not. The facts were never in dispute, but even in so-called objective reporting, the order in which those facts are presented, the weight given them, and the connotations of the words used to describe them, can slant the story. The invisible subhead on every story these guys were writing was, "Get the Yids."

"So what brings you here?" I asked Harold, when we were

comfortably seated.

"Well," he said, "I was livin' in California, drivin' my truck. One day I was on my way home when a voice said, 'Harold, you can't go on livin' the way you have been.'

"Nothin' like that had ever happened to me before, but I knew Who it was, and what He was talkin' about. 'What you want me to do, Lord?' I asked.

"'Turn left at the next block. About two blocks down, on the left-hand side, there's a little church. Go in there and talk to the pastor.'

"Which I did. We talked for quite a while, and I made an appointment to talk to him again. He gave me his card.

"When I got home, my wife was all packed up, and she was going to leave me. I told her what happened.

"'You've told so many lies,' she said. 'Why should I believe this one?'

"So I whipped out the preacher's card and gave it to her. 'Call him,' I said.

"He told her to wait a few days and she'd know by then. She saw I was serious and she stayed.

"Then the Lord told me to quit my job and put the house up for sale. She figured I'd gone nuts and started to leave again. I told her she could go where she wanted, and she could have everything. When she saw I was serious, she decided to stick it out.

"I quit my job and put the house up for sale. We had to wait eighteen months and that was a strange time. My neighbor next door played for the '49ers, and I built him a hot tub. We became friends and I spent some time with the team, went on a couple of road trips. I was just waitin.'"

Something about his shoulders and the way he walked made me ask, "Were you ever an athlete?"

He nodded. "Boxed middleweight. I was good enough that for a year nobody would fight me but light-heavies. Then they discovered I had a soft head. A good blow to the center of the forehead and I was out like a light."

"Ever been in the service?"

"Air Force communications. Korea."

"So you were awaiting instructions?"

"Yeah. Long before the house sold I knew I was going to come to the Holy Land and be in television. My neighbors and my in-laws figured I was crazy." He laughed. "Anyway, for about a year and a half we didn't get a single call on the house. Then one day this Jewish couple from New York came and offered me $165,000 for it. That wasn't what I was asking, so I said, 'I'll have to pray on it.' The Lord said, 'Don't be greedy, Harold. I doubled your investment.' So I took it.

"Everybody thought I was nuts."

This statement kept cropping up in Harold's conversation. They said it again when Harold told them he was going to Israel to work in television, pointing out that all he knew about television was how to wiggle the rabbit ears.

It was not until he got to Israel that he even heard of George Otis.

George Otis was a former vice-president of the LearJet Corporation who had produced and hosted a television show about the romance of aviation, called, *High Adventure*. When he became a Pentecostal Christian, divine inspiration led him to raise the money to found a radio station in the seemingly inhospitable religious climate of southern Lebanon. Everybody within range of his broadcasts was already either a Jew, Muslim, or Maronite Christian. There were no Protestants, and certainly no Pentecostals. But everybody liked the music, and at least the news wasn't slanted in favor of any one of their rivals. The station was an instant success.

In fact it was such a success that Otis decided to expand into television, and to that end, a remote studio fitted into a motor home had been purchased.

"It was still on the docks when I arrived," Harold said, "sitting on the floor of the crate it was shipped in. They'd tried to back it off, and did eleven thousand dollars' worth of damage to the transmission."

Nobody in Israel could drive the mobile studio. It had six forward gears and four reverse gears. It was the same transmission as had been in Harold's semi.

On his first day in Israel he met George Otis in a hotel lobby and moved the mobile studio that afternoon. He ploughed most of his profits from the house into High Adventure, sent for his wife, and learned to engineer the TV remote system. "I'm doing fill-in shifts for the other engineers now," he said.

"That's a pretty miraculous chain of events," I interjected. "But why does God want a TV station in southern Lebanon?"

Harold nodded. "Well," he said, "the Israelis have just built the most modern air base in the world in the Valley of Megiddo. All the hangers are underground, and the planes are brought up on elevators, like an aircraft carrier. Anyhow, the Israelis are going to win this war here. The Syrians aren't going to come into it. Then, for the first time, the Israelis are going to be at peace for years. Then the Russians are going to attack, with some of the Arab countries as allies. It's all in the 38th Chapter of Ezekial. Where it says Gog and Magog, that's Russia.

"Anyway the Russians are gonna sweep down right through Lebanon, in just too great a number for the Israelis to handle them. That's when they're gonna turn to God and get in the synagogues and start praying.

"The Russians are going to stop to consolidate right there in the valley of Megiddo, and God's gonna destroy 'em there."

"How?" I asked.

"Bible says fire, earthquake, pestilence, the whole nine yards."

I made a mental note to look up Ezekial 38 when I got back to the room. "Okay," I said, "that's all very interesting, but what's it got to do with you?"

Harold nodded. "Up in the mountains overlooking the valley there's a flat concrete slab with a road leading to it. I've never seen it, but I know it's there. There's a millionaire oilman from Denver who's a Christian and owns the land. He called and told me God told him to build the slab. Anyhow, when God destroys the Russians in the valley of Megiddo, I'm gonna have a TV camera on it and you'll see it live in your living room via satellite."

"Okay."

"The networks will be ringing their hands and not knowing what to make of it, but the Christian stations will know, and that will be our witness."

That was kind of hard to take at one sitting, but when we got back to our room that night I looked up the passage in the beat up old copy of the *Living Bible* that Crews McCulloch, my first CO in Vietnam, gave me just before I went to Cambodia in 1973.

In that version, Ezekial 38 says, *"The Lord God says to Gog: When*

*my people are living in peace in their land then you will rouse yourself.*
*You will come from all over the north with your vast host of cavalry*
*and cover the land like a cloud. This will happen in the distant future*
*in the latter days of history. I will bring you against my land, and*
*my holiness will be vindicated in your terrible destruction before their*
*eyes, so that all the nations will know that I am God.*

*"The Lord God says: You are the one I spoke of long ago through*
*the prophets of Israel, saying that after many years had passed I would*
*bring you against my people. But when you come to destroy the land*
*of Israel my fury will rise. For in my jealously and blazing wrath I*
*promise a mighty shaking of the land of Israel on that day. All living*
*things will quake in terror at my presence; mountains shall be thrown*
*down, cliffs shall tumble; walls shall crumble to the earth. I shall*
*summon every kind of terror against you, says the Lord God, and*
*you will fight against yourselves in mortal combat. I will fight you*
*with sword, disease, torrential floods, great hailstones, fire and*
*brimstone! Thus I will show my greatness and bring honor upon my*
*name, and all the nations of the world will hear what I have done*
*and know that I am God!"*

Harold came in again the following evening at supper. He suggested
that we get permission from the IDF to go in with him the next day.
They didn't like journalists running around with no escort all over
southern Lebanon, especially not since Mosi's Italian TV crew had
stumbled into the PLO and been held prisoner for a day.

Harold reckoned that if he asked them they'd give us a pass to go
in with him.


The next day, while we were at his radio station, Harold got a call
that the generator on their transmitter, on a mountaintop thirty miles
east, had quit, and his expert hand was called for. We headed back
to the TV remote van to await the station's Lebanese engineer.

The motor home remote unit was parked just on the Lebanese side
of the Good Fence, as it was called, that marked the border, opposite
an Israeli observation platform. They had set up a couple of machine
gun positions there, but primarily it was a place for tourists to look
over into Lebanon. There was a restaurant and a gift shop back behind
the platform, both closed now. There was a sandbagged M60
machinegun emplacement atop the restaurant.

Waiting for the engineer, we witnessed the arrival of the first load of tourists since the war started. Just days before, artillery had boomed across the valley all night; now there were tourists, sunburned and giggling, taking each other's pictures in shorts, fat thighs, and funny white hats with 'I (little red heart) Israel' inscribed on them.

When the engineer arrived, he gave us a handy-talkie to put on the dashboard of our rented Autobianchi. We followed Harold for almost an hour over the twisting mountain roads of southern Lebanon. It was beautiful country, fairly big hills, rocky, sandy-brown, with little vegetation, sparsely-populated. The towns were old, and there were stooped and stolid elderly people in the streets and on the roadside. It was easy to get a feel of what Galilee must have been like in Biblical times. That feeling was frequently interrupted by a dusty new Mercedes booming over the hill with ten or fifteen Lebanese inside.

Under the PLO, southern Lebanon had been a collection point for stolen autos from all over Europe. It was possible to buy a car there that would have cost $25,000 in the States for $600, but there was no way to get it out after you bought it.

Finally we reached the transmitter. Harold grabbed his tools and went into the shed to work on the generator. He worked swiftly and efficiently. Harold was not an average guy, but one thing he was not was nuts. I didn't really know what to make of his story about the Russian Army in the Valley of Megiddo, but I would not have bet anything *against* its happening.

A young man in boots and a fatigue uniform wandered over while Harold worked. He was introduced to us as Fares, a fighter in Major Saad Haddad's Army of Southern Lebanon, a predominantly Christian militia, although it contained many Moslems, Fares among them. Fares was assigned to guard the transmitter. The surprising thing about Fares was that, although he had an olive complexion, he was blond and had European features. Then I remembered that the crusaders had been in this area for centuries.

Fares had news. Not an hour before, a Syrian jet had roared in low, dropped a 500-pound bomb on a house in the nearby town, and killed every member of the family, a mother, father, and two children. He asked whether we wanted to go to take pictures of the damage, which, of course, we did. We went in our car, leaving Harold to work on the transmitter.

The funeral was already underway when we reached the town. Not having any embalmers there, these people didn't mess around before they buried their dead. We drove in on a rocky road. The funeral was taking place further on down the hill to our right. A fairly large crowd that must have been half the town was gathered around the grave site. They were just lowering a tiny coffin into the ground as we drove by.

I started to take a picture, but Kathy put her hand on my arm. She had covered plenty of car wrecks for the Arkansas *Gazette*, and a fat woman from Illinois, with her hair in curlers, called her a "ghoul" at Elvis Presley's funeral, but something about these simple people's tragedy was just too personal to film.

The town was built of ancient moorish buildings, terraced into hillsides. We drove through, twisting and turning on the narrow streets as we wound up the hillside to the house where the bomb had fallen.

Soon we came to it, a flat-topped, two-story concrete house smashed, with the roof collapsed at an angle, debris scattered for a hundred feet around. A smaller crowd was gathered around the house, mostly young men in slacks and shirts that fit tight around the waist. They were mostly poor, and wore cheap, shoddy clothing, but the look they aspired to was Vegas dealer.

Kathy went to work with her camera. I decided to wander on up the hill and see whether I could get a good shot from above. There were other houses on up the hillside, but they were surrounded by shrubbery, and it was hard to get a clear shot. I wandered out into a yard, but to get a clear view I had to step into the garden.

I walked very carefully between rows and tried not to step on any plants, but that didn't seem to make any difference to the two angry women, probably mother and daughter, heads covered with kerchiefs, who stormed out of the house.

I pointed to my camera and smiled. They poured forth a torrent of verbal abuse. I don't think they really objected to the camera. I was just a representative of the outside world who had come into their village and done this terrible thing. Almost everybody in Lebanon speaks French. *"Merci, merci, pardonez moi,"* I said and started edging out of the garden. I had already taken a couple of shots anyway, and I could tell they would be lousy. *"Merci, merci,"* I muttered.

Then a strange thing happened. When they saw I was genuinely contrite, they smiled and invited me back. I took two more photos, just to be polite.

When I got back down the hill the crowd had grown. Two of the young men angrily demanded of Fares to know who in the hell we were and what in the hell we were doing there. He patiently explained that we were good people who were here to help.

Some of them looked like they were buying it, and others did not. The nonbuyers were the most vocal. I had faced down a couple of Vietnamese mini-mutinies, but I couldn't read these people. I looked at Kat, just checking to see that nobody threatening was near her, and prepared to start smiling and jiving. I wondered just how far this might go.

Harold arrived at that moment, parked on the road, and walked up to the crowd. Apparently they knew him, because they immediately led him to where fragments of the bomb had landed.

"They say a Syrian jet came over heading south, chased by two Israeli jets," he said. "Nobody knows which side dropped the bomb." He dusted off the fragments to see whether they were of Russian or American manufacture, but he couldn't tell.

Two of the boys brought me a black and white photo of the man who had been killed. In the photo he was a nice-looking, smiling, smallish man, about thirty-five, in a dark suit and tie, walking on one of the roads of the village.

Harold still had some work to do on the generator, so we went back to the transmitter site.

Fares and the Lebanese engineer were concerned lest we be bored, standing around on the barren hilltop while Harold fiddled with the machinery, so he led us over to the little shack that housed the transmitter and gave us a tour. Floor to ceiling banks of grey-metal cabinets, covered with lights and dials. There was one tiny monitor that showed what the station was broadcasting.

A tiny lady in leotards was going through a series of leg raises, showing the ladies of northern Israel and southern Lebanon how to reduce the size of their thighs.

# 25

# Cheeseburgers In Nazareth

It was not until the Israelis surrounded West Beirut on June 8 that reporters were allowed to catch up to the actual combat. Even so, IDF policy required that we be back in Israel by nightfall.

The practical effect of this rule was to send us each morning hell-bent, in convoys of uninsured rental cars, over rutted and shell-pocked highways, through the blasted, shattered cities of Sidon, Tyre and Damour, a Christian city which had been destroyed and its populace massacred by the PLO in 1976, past a blasted and shattered seaside amusement park, to Beirut, a bigger blasted and shattered city. In the evenings we returned separately, at the last minute, racing the sunset down sniper alley.

When we crossed the Israeli border in the evening it was like entering the U.S. from revolutionary Mexico. We kicked back, Kathy and I, and teased each other in our respective hick accents, maintaining our roots.

Since Thailand, we had maintained a running argument about women in combat. I have no reservations about women's courage or intelligence. But I maintain that much of an infantryman's job is to be a beast of burden, and women are not suited to that.

"God!" she said once, as we slowed to pass a column of tanks, parked beside the Metulla-Tel Aviv highway. "It kills me to look at these kids, wondering which ones aren't going to live out the week."

"You get used to it."

She shook her head. "I don't think women are supposed to get used to it. Maybe you're right about women and combat. I'm beginning to feel that women's true role is to nurture. Without that there'd be no society to defend."

We passed a pole posted with road signs, one to Megiddo. A bit later we passed the Sea of Galilee to our left. Far out on calm blue water a guy skied behind a boat. Beyond were the hills of Jordan. We stopped for a cheeseburger, fries and a shake at an Arab restaurant in Nazareth, and checked back into the Plaza in Tel Aviv that night.


In Lebanon, CBS alone lost five Peugeot 504's on the roads. One was run over by a tank, another hit by a PLO rocket; the others, I don't know.

Lebanon was the first story Kathy and I covered as a team. She became a partner, as cool as Coyne and more diligent. This was not her idea of a good time; she was there to work. She seemed to lapse only once, as we roared past a bombed-out shopping center in East Beirut. Her head whipped around to read a sign. "Oh, Charles Jourdan sandals!" she cried. Then she smiled wryly.

As we drove into the city of Tyre the first day, rubble and shattered buildings lay everywhere. The only thing untouched on that stretch of road was a mosque. Obviously Israeli gunners had been ordered not to hit it, for public relations purposes if nothing else. But with the entire city blanketed by artillery, it had taken tremendous skill to miss it.

The smell was horrific. Kathy was thinking, *'Did they leave every refrigerator door in this town open?'* when Roy Uaval, the ginger-bearded, English-born Israeli photographer who was driving, asked, "Anybody want to see the mass grave?"

"God, no!" I blurted.

In Sidon, the next town up the road, a PLO terrorist academy was found in the underground floor of a United Nations-administered vocational school, complete with cutaway models of rockets and machine guns, and a dormitory set up like a barracks, with uniforms in wall lockers and double-decker bunks. The U.N. had taken sides, voluntarily or through coercion, in this conflict.

There was disagreement over civilian casualty figures in southern Lebanon. The International Red Cross's initial estimate was 1,541 deaths—no differentiation between civilians and terrorists—in Tyre alone, and 300,000 homeless. In contrast, Israeli estimates were 450 civilian fatalities in the two cities, and no more then 20,000 homeless in southern Lebanon.

Nearing Beirut we encountered a long line of refugee traffic moving south. People were leaving West Beirut before the Israelis moved in on the PLO. They came down that dusty alley of destruction, a single column of Okies going to California in Mercedes. We slowed now to a crawl, past a huge tractor hauling a demolished tank, moving around APCs parked outside a store. Dusty GIs leaned against them, smoking and drinking warm Coke.

Finally we pulled up behind a three-quarter-ton truck and stopped. We'd be moving in a minute.

I looked to the left. Israeli GIs had established a roadblock and were thoroughly searching a black Mercedes with a very large family in it. I felt a blast of the sheerest hate, and did a take into a pair of blazing almond eyes. In the back seat were four people. The two in the middle, one staring lasers through me, were well-built young men of military age, in civilian clothes, but with military haircuts.

We moved on again. Now I carefully watched the backseats of oncoming cars. Every second or third one had what I was sure was a PLO fighter in it. They were so obvious that I wondered why the Israelis were letting them through. Later I learned they had collected about 700 of them further south.

There was a bad run after we left the main road, before we got to the Israeli headquarters at Ba'abda. It was in the winding hills south of Beirut, surrounded by stone fences and olive groves.

On this road we were in range of PLO gunners. A barrage of high explosive 82-millimeter mortar rounds crashed into the grove to our left. Arnold Sherman, our IDF escort, a red-haired transplanted New York author and Israeli reservist, took off his steel helmet and made Kat wear it. It looked great with her Lolita shades.

Our first day in Beirut we had a gourmet lunch at Emil's atop a high hill overlooking the city, and watched artillery and rockets exchanged between East and West Beirut, while a waiter in black pants and a red mess jacket poured the wine. During the dessert course a flight of F-15s smoked down out of the sky directly over our heads and poured rockets into West Beirut.

After lunch I found a pay phone and called Fouad to tell him we were in town and would be by to see him.

The Lebanese Forces command was in a new headquarters, set up in a row of buildings in a military compound. As we pulled into the parking lot I saw a familiar walk, yelled, "Sam!" and bailed out of the car before it came to a stop.

We grabbed each other and hugged. "Jim!" he exclaimed. "We were expecting you to come in from Jounieh."

I quickly explained what had happened, and introduced Kathy, Arnold, and Roy.

"Come inside," he said. "Rick will want to see you." In a small room Rick sat at a desk, talking to correspondents, very official-looking in pressed, tailored fatigues, with a cammo T-shirt underneath, clean-shaven, hair neatly combed. The picture of a young staff officer.

"Jesus!" I said, barging through the door at the head of my troops. "I never thought they'd get you into uniform."

"Jim!" he grinned, and came from behind the desk. His fatigue pants were jean cut, and under them he wore his old roughout cowboy boots. They hadn't quite got him into uniform yet.

Sam quickly explained that we were here with the Israelis. "Why don't you just blow them off and stay here?" Rick asked.

I looked at Arnold.

His brow furrowed. "I can't stop you," he said. "But if you do, I'll be in terrible trouble."

This was the man who had put his own helmet on Kathy as we drove through a mortar barrage. I looked at Rick and shrugged. "No can do," I said.

Sam gave me one of his more mournful looks. "We have a house for you two," he said.

I shook my head.

We watched, with about two dozen other correspondents, as Fouad explained why the Lebanese Forces weren't going to attack West Beirut, as the Israelis wanted. The Israeli notion was that they had fought their way up the highway and given the "Phalangists" their chance to settle all scores. Now it was up to them.

"This is our city," Fouad said, standing in uniform beside a map, pointer in hand. "We have relatives over there. Our boys are not going in to kill their relatives." Either his English had improved in the past year or he had rehearsed this briefing.

In fact the Israeli battle to surround the city had been a cakewalk compared to the nightmare of casualties they would incur going into West Beirut. The PLO had fought only to delay as they fell back, assuming that the Israelis would stop when they came to their announced objective, 25 kilometers into Lebanon.

I'm still not convinced that the original objective was to go further than that. I think maybe it was just too easy not to drive on north.

But now the Israelis were confronted by the chilling prospect of having to root out thousands of PLO fighters, who would be fighting for their lives with their backs to the sea, from superb defensive positions.

Nobody wanted to do it. It would be block to block, house to house, room to room, hunting cornered fighters who were armed with AKs and RPGs, with artillery and tanks at their backs, determined that if they had to go, they were going to take as many with them as they could.

The Lebanese Forces' volunteers hadn't signed on for anything like that. They volunteered on a mission by mission basis, mostly to defend their own neighborhoods. Only a few commandos and elite units fought offensive actions, and most of those were raids. No one was up for a frontal assault into what looked like, and probably was, almost certain death.

After you, my dear Alphonse.

So for three days we toured a static front, kidding around with the militia kids, going into gutted apartments to peer through holes Katyushas had left in the walls, PLO fighters sunbathing on a balcony a hundred meters away, photographing Israeli artillerists, and dining splendidly.

On the third day the incoming held your attention, and there was machine gun fire about two blocks away. Driving out was the worst, with the incoming very close, right at the same place we had taken mortar fire two days before. This time we screamed and slewed down the dirt road like Grand Prix racers, mortar rounds and artillery coming in all around us, although nothing hit the car.

On the last hill overlooking the city, the air was shattered by the crack of outgoing 155s; then there was a noise as though the sky were made of silk and had suddenly been ripped from horizon to horizon. We stopped and got out.

In the distance, we heard a muffled WHOOM, WHOOM, and two grey puffs billowed out of the dark haze that overlay the Burj Al Barajneh Palestinian camp, just north of the airport.

The press habitually called it a refugee camp, but it could just as accurately have been called, Fort Burj Al Barajneh. By then I had come to think of my press colleagues as so many Eskimos at the Super Bowl.

We got out of the car and walked to a shelled apartment house on the point of the hill. A couple of guys with a big battery commander scope sat on a third-floor balcony, adjusting fire. I gradually became aware of a cracking roar overhead that swept from the south up the Mediterranean coast and then turned in to a high, keening shriek over the airport.

The sound of anti-aircraft fire came drifting up from the valley...pom-pom-pom...pom-pom-pom.

A series of loud crumps followed as the bombs hit and the shriek ascended and disappeared. For all we could see of the airplanes, we might as well have been listening to the radio, but bright flashes came from the center of the smoky haze over Burj Al Barajneh. Twice there were ballooning orange and black secondary explosions—ammunition caches.

The minutes of dead silence followed. Way below, the smoke drifted. Then the whole sequence of aerial attack repeated itself, and after that, once more. The papers the next day did not mention the secondary explosions, just a helpless refugee camp, vandalized by naughty Jews.

I decided it was getting too hot to take Kathy in. I broke the news at dinner that night, after a day of dodging mortars and snipers, as we ate in the dining room of a luxury hotel on the Mediterranean.

"I have to go in," she said in almost desperate exasperation. "It's my job. You're the one that's always going on about 'professionalism.'"

"Yeah," I insisted. "But that's not what's going on here. What's happening here is that my baby's gettin' shot at. You're doing your job, but I'm not doing mine. All I'm doing is watching to see if you're okay. That's the final argument against women in combat. The men won't be worrying about the enemy. They'll be worrying about the women."

"But..."

"You're not going in," I said calmly.

The next morning at the kibbutz on the border where the correspondents gathered, I found the IDF Spokesman's office had reached the same conclusion No female correspondents allowed in the forseeable future.

Nonetheless, it was a light day. I saw nothing that was newsworthy.

That night Kat and I talked it over. We had everything we needed for the *SOF* invasion special, and were both bone-deep tired from a month on the road, eight to twelve hours every day. I decided on one more run to say good-bye to Sam, Rick, and Fouad. Who knew when, or if, we'd ever see them again?

But when I got to the kibbutz the IDF was permitting runs only to the Bekaa Valley. I could not convince the major in charge to let me go to Beirut, so I wrote Sam a letter, which the major promised to deliver, and the next day we flew out of Tel Aviv.

That day, June 27, was our first anniversary. The stewardess brought Kathy a rose and served champagne with our meal.

When we collapsed into the bed at our London hotel, I called our friend, Graeme, to see whether he and Caroline were free for dinner the following evening.

"Oh, Jim," he said, "pity you didn't arrive yesterday. We had two extra tickets for the Stones concert."

I managed a weak smile into the receiver. "That's okay, Graeme. We weren't looking for excitement yesterday."

# 26

# El Salvador

A week back from Israel, sick and soul-weary of death and the smell of death, I walked into Brown's office. He sat with his beat-up shitkickers on his desk, howling into one phone while he held the other a foot from his face.

In thirty second intervals between frantic overseas phone calls, people bursting in and out of his office, we talked.

"Brown, I've been in three wars in the last six months..."

"I know. I sent you."

"Everywhere I go the bad guys went to the same schools, use the same gear, exchange personnel, and read the same books. When we dumped Vietnam, they decided they had a winning strategy, and now Vietnam is measles. It's everywhere, and it's all the same war."

"Everybody knows that." He spat a glob of Skol into a clear glass.

"No, they don't, Bob. Nobody knows it but people who've seen it firsthand, because it ain't in the papers, and it ain't on TV.

"I want to do a book about it. To make it convincing, I need to go to one more area. Africa, Central America—it doesn't matter."

I had seen ample evidence of Soviet involvement in Lebanon—no surprise, since they do not conceal their backing for Syria—but it really came home when I saw those posters with Lenin and Ho on them, hammer and sickle, and the writing in Arabic.

The Soviets backed the Vietnamese in Laos and Cambodia; the Soviets also backed Libya, which was backing Muslim separatists in

Thailand and Malaysia and the Philippines, for that matter. At Surat Thani, Coyne and I had seen an entire arsenal of Communist Party of Malaysia weapons, and they were all Soviet, as was their communications equipment and their mines and booby traps. They backed Syria, which armed international terrorists, threatened Israel, and had occupied most of Lebanon.

I wanted to see it with my own eyes in one other theater of operations. That wouldn't constitute proof, but the proof was well-known to foreign policy and military professionals; it was just not widely publicized. I wanted to tell the story in a popular format, one that would be widely read and, I hoped, believed.

I intended to hang around Boulder for a couple of months, get some of my Lebanon and Thailand stuff written, rest up, run, lift weights, eat some American food for a change. I was still jetlagged; my ears still rang from self-propelled 105mm howitzers. But I wanted to get my bid for another expedition in early. Sometimes it takes a while to set these things up.

"Fine," he said, "you can go to El Salvador Friday."

He was sending a reporter with a congressional delegation led by congressman Bob Dornan of California, and including Major General Jack Singlaub and Andy Messing of the National Defense Council. No way could I pass that up.

"As long as you're down there you might as well stick around for a couple of weeks, try to get in some combat, then go to Honduras and Guatemala."

That night Kat and I had one of our few really bad fights. She knew I was in no shape to go. Her face showed real anguish. "Look," she said, "we're just moving into a new apartment. I need you here now."

"Ah, bullshit!" I said. "If you were going, you'd be champing at the bit."

"Maybe so," she admitted. "But I'll be scared to death with you down there."

I shrugged. "Can't help it," I said. "If I don't do this one, the book won't get written, and Thailand and Lebanon will be wasted. Stories in *SOF* won't accomplish anything; that's preaching to the choir."

My first week in El Salvador, August 1982, we traveled to briefings and cocktail parties in air conditioned vans. I went from one air conditioned environment to another, half the time with a drink in my hand. It was only toward the end of the week that I noticed the van was bulletproofed. A year before I would have picked that up immediately. I had become so jaded, and tired, that now I did not see the obvious.

We were wined and dined by people who desperately wanted our help. The Salvadorean Right wanted U.S. support; the U.S. Special Forces trainers wanted to know that the people they were risking their lives for cared.

The trainers felt betrayed by the recent ruling that they could not carry rifles, only pistols. A New York *Times* reporter, Ray Bonner, had run a story that he had seen a U.S. lieutenant colonel, an engineer advisor, carrying an M-16 while working with a bridge crew in guerrilla territory. Bonner cited the M-16 as proof that the trainers were leading combat ops, something they were forbidden by law to do.

Against assault rifles, the pistol is nothing. Not without reason, the trainers felt ill-used by their country, that nobody in the States cared about them. Not the army, not the government, and certainly not the people.

What kept them going was professionalism and a belief they would be vindicated in the end.

I mentioned to General Singlaub my thesis that we were *in* a *Third World* war, WWIII in two meanings, a worldwide conflict being waged in the underdeveloped nations. General Singlaub is a kind of cross between Mickey Rooney and Buster Keaton, a grown up All-American kid with a deadpan manner. He seldom makes a joke, and when he does it's usually so dry it's easy to miss. He's about 5'7", maybe 150 pounds. I once told him that I had this image of him as the smallest guy on his college basketball team, who lettered by outhustling everybody. "UCLA Football," he said. "Third string guard and center."

To my assertion that we were in a worldwide guerrilla war, he replied, "Yes, of course. That's quite correct."

General Singlaub became famous when he was fired for publicizing his displeasure at the Carter Administration's plan to withdraw two divisions of troops from South Korea, but his real field of expertise is guerrilla warfare. He fought with the Maquis, the anti-Nazi underground in France and was in training to go in as an advisor to Ho Chi Minh's guerrillas, whom the allies backed in WWII, when the war ended. He ran guerrillas into North Korea during the war there, and ran the Special Operations Group in Vietnam—where Hiney Aderholt had been his deputy for air—where he had run cross-border ops and other secret missions.

He also has a significant intelligence background. Since his retirement he had toured the world, visiting anti-communist guerrillas and visiting countries threatened by "Wars of National Liberation."

General Singlaub, Andy Messing, and I spent an evening with officials of the ARENA Party, the ultra-conservative group blamed for the Death Squads. The meeting was held at the stately, three-story home of Billy Sol, a Salvadorean businessman, graduate of Texas A&M. He had been a huge landowner before the land reform program went into effect. After his land was confiscated he went into the insurance business. He wasn't living on the scale he had, but he was doing all right. He had his home and servants to staff it.

On the other hand, our dinner was carry-out chicken and beer. Good chicken and great beer, but not in the style of old.

"I flew over my rancho week before last," said Sr. Sol, a chubby man with heavily-framed glasses, gesturing with a drumstick. He walked with a slight limp, recovering from an assassination attempt by the insurgents. Almost every official of the ARENA Party carried scars or fragments. The Death Squads in El Salvador weren't all right-wing.

He went on, "The jungle had grown up around all our modern, concrete loading pens.

"When the peasants took over our land, the first thing they did was kill and eat the breeding stock. Now they are barely making a subsistence.

"They are good people, very hard-working, but they do not have the knowledge to run a modern cattle ranch. They are much worse off economically than they were before."

This seemed to distress him as much as the loss of his own holdings.

A short time after dinner the doorbell rang.

Major Roberto D'Aubisson, president of the ARENA Party, later a candidate for President of El Salvador, and his entourage swept through the front door. D'Aubisson had been a major in the National Guard prior to a preceding change of regimes, then he had been a fugitive, and a prisoner condemned to death.

He was a small man; physically he reminded me of Joel Gray, the actor, but with a cocky air and military bearing. He was dressed in a Swiss Army shirt and slacks, very self-possessed, but did not speak English. His translation was handled by Ricardo Valdivieso, a Salvadorean who had grown up in the U.S. and been a U.S. paratrooper in Germany during Vietnam.

Later I got to know Valdivieso. He was a very likable man, a burly, handsome Latin, full of good will and charm. A leftist journalist described him to me as a "fascist with a heart of gold," but he was no fascist; he was just a guy fighting for his life and the lives of his family, and his property. He had only come back from the States to settle his grandfather's estate. He figured he'd be there at the most six weeks. That had been sixteen years before. He fell in love with the country, but more than that he fell in love with his wife, Patricia. Together they had fought and farmed and been fugitives with D'Aubisson.

"We lived in Guatemala and made runs in and out of the country. Sometimes we changed cars three times a day; we wore disguises. We could never spend more than three hours in any one place."

Finally they gained legitimacy and set up as a political party, only to become targets of leftist guerrillas.

"We were in jail with Roberto—Billy and I and the rest," he said. He leaned forward earnestly. "We were put against the wall in front of a firing squad. Roberto said, 'These men are guilty of nothing. They are only my friends. If you must kill somebody, kill me, and let them go.' The officer in charge was so impressed he dismissed the firing squad and had them put us back in our cells.

"Then one of the guards offered to open the doors and provide us with weapons. It sounded like a set-up to us, so we stayed put." Finally, they were released.

I was entranced with D'Aubisson's bodyguards. There seemed to
be a dozen of them. They wore mustaches and carried pistols, submachine guns, and shotguns. They brandished their weapons. They
were...perfect.

Also with D'Aubisson and Ricardo were a couple of men in suits,
one a lean, scholarly type, the other a stocky, Zapata-mustachioed
goon, in a suit made of a fabric that looked like burnished aluminum.

D'Aubisson sat at the coffee table and spread out a map of Central
America. General Singlaub and I leaned over the map as D'Aubisson
explained how guerrilla supplies were delivered. Roads in central
America are few and bad, so there is a lot of civil aviation. Guerrilla
supplies were flown in from Nicaragua in light aircraft at night and
landed on roads in guerrilla territory. Some stuff also came across
the Gulf of Fonseca in boats.

The goon in the suit lolled, legs crossed, in a Louis XIV chair,
jiving with the other goons. He let out a burst of laughter and gestured,
working his trigger finger.

We chatted about Salvadorean politics and guerrilla warfare. Ricardo
translated one of D'Aubisson's questions as, "What's the big deal about
the nuns?" He referred to four American women, three nuns and a
lay worker, who had recently been killed by four drunks guarding
a roadblock near the airport.

"Respect for women, respect for the Church," I said.

His look held no comprehension. They were Maryknoll sisters.
*Subversivos* had been seen going in and out of the Maryknoll Chapter
House. As far as he was concerned that made them Communist spies,
fair game.


Congressman Dornan didn't arrive until three days after we did.
Dornan was another believer in the *Third World* War theory. As a
congressman he had traveled the world on fact-finding missions, and
the War was what he had seen. He came directly to El Salvador from
Beirut.

A Catholic, he said, "There is nothing the Communists would like
more than to take over a country named for Jesus Christ." Dornan,
a redheaded, former TV newsman from California, was ebullient;

I think the Salvos found his personality a little overwhelming.

He was very proud of having been an Air Force fighter jock and having flown every jet aircraft in the U.S. inventory. "Nothing I like better than to get an F-16 up to about forty thousand feet, find a rock 'n' roll station on the radio, and just...rock 'n' roll," he said.

Our delegation was given a tour of Salvadorean military installations. Since the trainers couldn't carry anything heavier than pistols, Andy and I were pressed into service as Dornan's and Singlaub's bodyguards.

The second-in-command of the U.S. army trainers, Lieutenant Colonel John Boykin, a big, darkhaired man who wears a moustache and is built like a weightlifter, gave us a couple of old Danish Madsen submachine guns to carry, and showed us how to work the safeties. Andy and I slung the SMG's over our shoulders.

Since he worked out of the embassy, John wore civilian clothes, polo shirt stretched tight over bodybuilder's muscles, designer jeans and dingo boots, .45 tucked into the small of his back. We were all dressed pretty much the same, except that Andy and I were better armed.

Standing there chatting, I explained my *Third World* War theory to him. He gave me a look as though I had just grown two heads, and said, "Where the fuck have you been?" He had gone in the army after I had, but had been in during the years since I had got out, most of that time in Special Forces. Having spent his life in the *Third World* War, and among others who lived the same life, it was incomprehensible to him that most civilians don't realize what is going on.

Starting from such a world view, our foreign policy, to the extent we have one, must have seemed insane to him.

To me it seemed strange that there was common acceptance by everyone I met in the field that war was being waged against the United States, while the American public was *totally unaware* of it.

One evening, after we had been there a week, I called Kathy. She had been badly scared and was angry that I wasn't home. A man in the next block had gone crazy and was shooting people from an upstairs window. Police advised everyone in that block, and ours, to stay indoors, while they lay siege to his house.

Great! I'd been in El Salvador a week, hadn't heard a shot fired, and Kathy was pinned down by a sniper in Denver.

We met the archbishop, and we met the acting president, and the Congressional delegation went home, leaving me to try for a combat story with the best set of introductions I could have asked for.

By the end of a week there, I was sure El Salvador would be the next domino to fall. The hapless government, the oligarchy entrenched and vulnerable, had so obviously been a straight-out fascist dictatorship until recently that I was convinced only a miracle could save them.

But now, six years later the situation in El Salvador has improved wonderfully. The army is more professional and the government more compassionate. The death squads have all but disappeared. I credit that to the patience and professionalism of our army trainers, and to the fact that the Salvadoreans, both sides, are among the gutsiest people on Earth. They don't do things very well by our standards, but they keep going.

# 27

# Two Days With The Paracaidistas

One of the advisors, Tony, a compact, almost criminally handsome Puerto Rican sergeant, worked in the military training group's headquarters at the embassy. He had also volunteered to train the Salvadorean paratroops, on the side—a job that would normally be full time for a six or twelve-man detachment.

With only fifty-five men in-country, the trainers met themselves coming and going. They voluntarily worked nights and weekends to make up for the congressionally imposed lack of personnel.

Tony arranged a jump with the *paracaidistas* for me. The night before the jump he called.

"No go," he said. "Over seven hundred insurgents have been reported near Tenango. We got one company that just completed training going in as a blocking force. The jump's off."

"I'd rather go on an operation anyway. Is it possible?"

"Probable," he said. "I'll pick you up at 0600. We'll go out to the airbase and see."

Since U.S. advisors aren't allowed in combat, Tony wanted an evaluation of the paras from me.

At the airbase, Major Turcios, the paras' commander, told Tony it was fine with him if I went along, but he would rather I got out of civvies and into a suit of fatigues. He didn't want his men to have to sneak through the jungle with a huge, redheaded gringo in civilian clothes.

I had met Turcios before, with General Singlaub. He was a compactly built young officer, and, although starched and spit-shined, a relaxed and friendly man. His troops both liked and respected him.

"Good," I said. "How about a weapon?"

"You want to carry a weapon?"

Oh, yes I did. By putting on a green suit I was dealing myself into the game, and the game in El Salvador was played under a very rough set of rules.

The custom was to keep your last round for yourself.

They gave me the largest suit of fatigues they had—a bit snug, but I could move—and a Heckler and Koch G-3 assault rifle, with four loaded magazines and 300 loose rounds in a pack. I could see myself burrowing into the dirt while trying to reclip those mags in a firefight.

Having carried an M-16 for years, my G-3 seemed as heavy as an artillery piece. And this one, although immaculate and well-oiled, was old enough to have most of the bluing knocked off. How accurate could it be? How prone to malfunction? I asked one of the paras to show me how the selector switch worked before we climbed aboard the chopper.


We lifted off the main runway at Ilopango and soon were where it's high and cold and your pant legs flutter frantically in the blast from the door. I looked at the Salvadorean paratrooper beside me. Ripples from the wind ran through his cheeks.

Flying over Vietnam, I had believed it was the most beautiful place on earth. Now, fifteen years later, I felt the same about El Salvador. The fields were smaller, without rice paddies. There were huge lakes and volcanoes. Everywhere the land was flat, there were houses: farmhouses, ranch houses, haciendas. But the tropical vegetation and the feel of danger were like Vietnam.

Our choppers flew in two V's in trail. By craning my neck, I could see another Huey rising and falling through the windshield over the co-pilot's shoulder. It had been a long time, fourteen years, since I sat in the open door of a helicopter at 3,000 feet. I gripped the edge of the door and hoped the kid with his knee in my back wouldn't decide to shift his weight.

We flew for about fifteen minutes. The door gunner pulled the pin that held his M60 down and brought it up, ready to fire. There were no gunships.

We circled and landed without contact.

The paras deployed around the grassy clearing to provide security for the next two lifts, but they tended to bunch up at the perimeter.

The Salvadorean army was a young army, and only since the insurgency had it tried to develop into a modern force. Until recently, everything technical, complicated or difficult had to be supervised by an officer.

John Hoagland, an ex-G.I. *Newsweek* photographer, told me he had been astonished to see a .57mm recoilless rifle set up by two grunts, then a lieutenant come up to fire it.

Julian Harrison, a British television reporter, told me of having seen a Salvadorean accidentally kill two of his own men with a rifle grenade. He was called over by his commander, who made him bend over and grab his ankles, then proceeded to beat his ass with a swagger stick.

Hoagland said that until the last couple of years, an NCO in El Salvador was somebody who got too old and fat to hack it in the field; so they gave him three stripes and a clipboard and set him out front of the headquarters to write down names.

They still lacked an infrastructure of experienced leaders.

It was the first week of August, noon, and very close to the equator. Going from the chopper to the perimeter of the LZ, my head buzzed from the suffocating heat. Sundazzle spots drifted before my eyes, and I broke out in a sick, feverish sweat. I was in trouble, even before we got off the LZ. Maybe I'll be okay once we get moving, I thought.

I melted into the minimal shade on the edge of the LZ. The men were bunching up, and once satisfied they weren't taking fire, most of them sat down and lit up. There was a low buzz of Spanish conversation.

Perdomo, the commander, stood with his radio headset pressed into one ear, hand over the other, calling in the next lift.

He looked up. "They put us too far from the objective," he said.

"We must walk five kilometers, not two."

I nodded. Five klicks. How bad can it be? In Denver I ran further than that every day.

When all the troops had landed, we walked single-file across the open jungle, going almost straight down toward a rushing creek below.

It was the worst five klicks of my life. In the Rockies it would have been a workout, but not much of a challenge, yet here in this heat, it was murder. All of it was either straight up or straight down. Stretched out it would have been about twelve klicks. Years before, I had scrambled over worse terrain in heat as bad all day every day, for weeks at a time, but even then it took a few days to get used to it.

We slid down slick mountain trails and slipped up them. All the wait-a-minute vines that the Salvos passed through caught me square in the face.

We went slowly; the point was moving cautiously, and when we stopped the paras sat quietly. I flopped on my back in the trail and panted like an old dog.

I wondered, very seriously, whether they knew the treatment for heatstroke.

Crawling over a stone fence, I tripped, fell six feet straight down, smashing my jaw on a rock. I didn't feel it, just dragged myself back to my feet and lurched ahead to catch up.

The next to last hill, one para had my rifle and another had my pack, and I crawled up it, using both hands.

Perdomo took a break at the top. "I'm slowing you down," I said.

He shrugged. "It's no problem."

"Well, I made it this far."

He stubbed his cigarette and grinned. "Come on," he said. "We are going to the *chingada*," the whorehouse.

I grinned too, but it was a bluff. We moved out.

At the top of the hill I found Perdomo sitting, totally alert.

"That's it," he said softly, pointing to a small stone house with a red tile roof on top of the next hill. He scanned it for signs of occupation. We sat there for a long time. The shadows lengthened; the land cooled. I found my strength returning.

When Perdomo was satisfied, we moved out again. This time he was pretty sure there were guerrillas in the area. The stone house had been an observation post/way station. He figured they had vacated it when his column appeared, but he also assumed they had kept it under observation.

We cut down a little draw and up another long, steep hill, single file on the narrow trail. Shadows were starting to lengthen. The temperature had dropped a few degrees; I had no trouble at all.

When I reached the top of the hill Perdomo held out something like an adhesive-wrapped tennis ball. *"Bomba contact,"* he said. It was guerrilla ordnance; they had been here, recently. It looked like an overgrown cherry bomb, and I didn't take it too seriously.

Perdomo set up his CP at the stone house. It occurred to me that if I were a guerrilla I'd already have a mortar concentration on it. But Perdomo wasn't worried about that, and we didn't get mortared.

Perdomo told Elga, his radio operator, to set the radio on a low stone fence about six feet from the house. He picked up the handset and gave instructions to his troops. "I am putting ambushes at the four cardinal compass points," he told me. One squad moved by us heading into the bush to the north, carrying an M60. Another moved back down the hill to the west, taking up a position in a smaller stone house at the base of the hill.

Since we seemed to be settling in for the night, I laid down my G-3 and started to take off my shirt. Around the corner of the house a couple of Perdomo's soldiers started building a small fire.

Elga, a tall, likable kid, eyed my camera with an admiring glint in his eye. He had been a tour guide in civilian life, and after Perdomo, he spoke the best English in the company. "If you get killed, can I have your camera?" he asked.

I grinned. One of his buddies lurked nearby, eyeing me. "You can't both have it," I said.

"He wants your watch."

I laughed out loud. That stuff would never get back with me if I bought it, and these kids might as well have it as anybody. "Sure," I said. But I didn't like being on combat patrol with people who would profit if I got killed. I stripped off my shirt. I was soaked through with sweat: T-shirt, shirt, lapels, epaulets, pockets, everything. Pants the same way.

A six-round burst from an M-16 snapped over my head and I found myself flat on the ground by the stone house. *You may just earn your money this time, my boy,* I thought.

G-3s returned fire from the north and east, none from the other two directions, as far as I could tell. Everybody in the CP was cool and collected. Perdomo was on the radio, too fast to follow, but I heard the word "putas" several times. A few rounds still snapped overhead, and there was a lot of outgoing. I slithered over to my weapon and took up a position facing down the hill to the west. It was the only field of fire available where I wouldn't hit one of his men. "The north ambush killed one insurgent," he said, looking up from his radio.

The firing died and there was a series of insults shouted in Spanish. The paras answered in kind.

When that died down Perdomo said, "I want a cup of coffee. Would you like some?" A few rounds were still passing back and forth. One ricocheted over our heads.

"Yes," I replied. "That would be nice."

"Eh, Guatemala," he called to one of his troopers, under the lean-to at the side of the house. *"Cafe."*

*"Capitan!"* Elga said. *"Una columna de putas."* He pointed across the valley to the west. Putas, whores, was what they called the guerrillas.

Perdomo and I faced to the west. The shadows were very long and I couldn't pick out any movement in the jungle across the valley. In rapid-fire Spanish, Elga gave Perdomo directions as to where he had seen the guerrillas.

Perdomo placed six single shots from his G-3 into where he thought they were, and since we were already facing that way, we paused to enjoy the sunset. The sky turned a vivid mauve behind the mountains across the jungle below. The breeze grew cool and night sounds started.

Guatemala brought Perdomo a blackened canteen cup of coffee. He took a sip and handed it to me. It was hot, sweet, and killer strong. I took a long sip. Perdomo handed me a paper sack and said, "Eat!"

Oatmeal cookies. We sat as the last of the sun went down, drinking coffee and eating oatmeal cookies.

Something flew by. Perdomo snagged it out of the air and popped it into his mouth.

"This captain eats insects," Elga said, choosing his words carefully. Perdomo had picked up insect-eating at the Columbian "Lancero" school, their version of our Ranger school.

"We will get you a nice fat butterfly for breakfast," said Perdomo.

"My Montagnards used to scrape locusts off window screens and eat 'em like cocktail peanuts," I said.

They wearied of the search for foreign words and the conversation drifted into Spanish. I dropped out and tried to listen. The young troopers talked and chuckled, talked and chuckled. They were at an age where everything is a joke.

I wanted very badly to wander off in the bushes and urinate, but every time I tried to move, my leg cramped. I devoted almost an hour and a half to taking a piss.

By then it was pitch black. When I got back to my seat on the wet ground, one of the troopies asked another, "Who was that?" in Spanish.

"El Gringo," was the response, followed by the sound of panting like an old dog, the sound I had made on the trail that day. *Fuck you, kid,* I thought. *If you went where I live, all the clothes you own wouldn't keep you warm.*

I had hoped my clothes would dry by the time it got cold, but they didn't. I had no poncho, and I started to shake. What a letdown, sleeping in a muddy ditch in wet clothes without even a poncho.

It started to rain. Nice fat drops fell on my face. Perfect, I thought. I wondered whether I would die.

"Go in the house," I heard Perdomo say. Even in a semi-sleep that seemed like a good idea. I staggered into the house, carrying my rifle and dragging my pack. Inside the house I lay with my head on the pack, head cradled on 300 loose 7.62 rounds. I shook for another hour and a half. Finally I shook my clothes dry and went to sleep.

I awoke the next morning feeling looser and better than I had for weeks, a little tired from lack of sleep, but good.

I shuffled and limped around until I found Perdomo just waking up under a poncho liner, using a folded, grey issue blanket for a pillow.

"Where's the body of the guerrilla?" I asked. "I want to get a picture of it."

"They drag it away," he said, sitting up.

I nodded. Everybody wants their dead back. He handed me a cup of his killer coffee.

Just before we left that morning he hollered down the hill to make sure his outpost in the little stone house below had pulled in, then hurled the contact bomb we had captured down the hill. The throw was about twenty-five meters out and at least fifty down; it couldn't have dropped into the wet jungle with much impact. But it exploded violently and smoke rolled out of the valley for two minutes, finally building to a grey column about thirty-five feet high.

At the bottom of the hill we connected with a level dirt road leading due north. Perdomo put a squad out on both flanks and we headed right up the road. *Easy day,* I thought.

The roadside was a museum of guerrilla life. As we advanced north I collected several samples of propaganda leaflets from both sides. Perdomo handed me a homemade ammo pouch he found, a small blue denim pouch with a half-dozen .223 rounds in it.

The road was a pleasant, tree-shaded lane, lined on either side by stone houses with red tile roofs. Behind them lay fields of corn and pasture land. There was plenty of evidence that the houses had been occupied by guerrillas. We found a one-room schoolhouse, set up to teach drill and squad tactics to the tiniest children, with little wooden rifles. But no people.

The troops attempted to destroy everything, but it was largely a futile effort. Stone and tile don't burn. They booted a few tiles out of roofs and kicked down a few corrugated tin walls.

The paras brought whatever they found novel or interesting out of the houses. They pushed a wooden-wheeled cart until it fell apart on the rocks in the road. One of them found an ornately framed print of the Virgin Mary, and carried it from then on, probably to take home to his mother.

There was a festive air; we moved up the road, eating fruit from the trees, telling jokes, kicking down walls.

Until the firing started.

Perdomo was immediately on the radio. I unslung my G-3 and dropped three feet off the road into the yard of the house his troops were attempting to kick apart. The left flank security must have made contact. I put my selector on semi-auto and peered around the corner of the house to see where the firing came from.

When I first started running combat patrols in 1964, I experienced an elation which surpassed anything I had felt before. Then I got badly hit.

After that, combat caused a sour feeling in the pit of my stomach. I did my work, but I didn't like it. Only pride and determination not to let my friends down kept me going. Then I got hit again, worse than before.

I've been shot at a few times since, mostly while working for *SOF*, but this patrol was my first as a participant. I felt no elation and no fear; I was just doing a job. I might have been taking out the garbage.

"They are killing cows," Perdomo called.

"What?"

"They found guerrilla cows. They are killing them."

"Son of a bitch!" I put the G-3 on safe, slung it and went back to the road.

Gutierrez, Perdomo's second-in-command, screamed into the radio in Spanish. "Your guns are for men, not for animals," followed by a long burst I couldn't translate, but it got quiet quickly.

The paras and the Third Brigade were closing in on each other's positions; sporadic gunfire on all sides, but too far out to be coming at us. Perdomo was busy on the radio.

Finally we came to a large, open, barbed-wire-fenced field to the right of the road. Paras fanned out inside it, taking up defensive positions. They weren't bunching up as much as they had; they were taking this pretty seriously. Perdomo stayed on the radio. Both Gutierrez and Ordonez hustled around, trying to be everywhere at once.

Suddenly a Huey appeared over the horizon and circled the LZ.

Ordonez popped yellow smoke out on the LZ, and from across the road eight paras dragged three bodies, hastily slung in ponchos. The soldiers had handkerchiefs over their noses. The corpses were in their underwear, but from their haircuts they seemed to be government troops. One wore macho maroon bikini briefs, and one black sock. They were dead limp and bloated in the ponchos. But they couldn't have been paras, because if we had lost anybody, it would have been in the past ten minutes, and these bodies had been dead for a while.

I went over to Perdomo and asked, "Who are those guys?"

"Soldiers of the Third Brigade," he said. "They were killed by mortars." No wonder our guys had quit bunching up.

The chopper crew was quick to get handkerchiefs over their noses. The soldiers dumped the bodies in a random pile on the floor of the chopper and got out as quickly as possible. The rotors whirled and the chopper lifted off.

There was intermittent helicopter activity for the rest of the morning. The next flight brought in huge gunny sacks of rations. I took mine over the shade by the road. Swilling down a small can of pineapple juice at a gulp, I opened up a can of tamales. Not as bad as you might think, under the circumstances.

I was almost through when an explosion shattered the calm. It came from about a hundred meters away, in the woodline to the northeast. A half-dozen guys ran toward the sound.

I hung back until the medics had gone into the treeline and then followed them in.

Down a slight depression in the woods a soldier lay. He looked dead. A cluster of maybe eight men stood around him. One of them threw a jungle boot, with the canvas top completely ripped down to the leather, into the bush. They quickly got an IV into him—he wasn't dead after all—and dragged him across the clearing back into the shade where I had been sitting. One soldier held a plasma bottle over the kid as they moved him.

He became conscious then, moaning. The medic drew a clear liquid into a hypodermic and knelt to give him a shot. He got quiet very quickly.

They didn't bother to throw smoke this time. The chopper knew where to go. He just came in and landed, and they ran the wounded man out. I wasn't sure but I think he was one of the new kids on his first patrol.

"He stepped on a mine?" I asked Perdomo.

He nodded. "Contact bomb, under a rock."

"He'll live, but he'll lose the leg, right?"

He nodded. "He will lose the foot."

We waited around the LZ for another hour. Some troops led five or six apprehensively mooing cattle onto the field. Perdomo had told me earlier that they had captured 22 cattle and were taking them back to the mess hall.

They led a fat Guernsey into the center of the field. She and Perdomo circled each other for a few minutes.

The two soldiers holding her rope scurried around to get out of Perdomo's way while he tried to line up a clear shot. The cow had become frisky, and Perdomo had to be more nimble as a result. Finally he dropped her with one shot.

She jerked and flopped over on her side.

The sun was high again.

Three choppers came in. Troops loaded onto two of them, and eight or ten guys managed to load the cow onto the deck of the chopper. Three paras hopped on with her.

Perdomo turned and yelled to me, "Time to go home."

I grabbed my pack and rifle and jogged to the ship, ducking under the rotor blades, hitching my butt up onto the floor of the Huey. The dead cow's eyes looked at me blankly. She was still warm to the touch. I leaned back against the warm, dead cow and the chopper lifted off.

# 28

# Diving Into Brooklyn

My physical incapacity on that patrol hit me hard. I went to Honduras sick. In my hotel room I lay near delirium, time after time watching Bo Derek's *Tarzan* without sound, waiting for phone calls that never came, rising occasionally to throw my guts up. I had never before been so depressed.

I was sure that with thirty days of training, I could outwalk most of the *paracaidistas*. Later, Brown sent more reporters and also financed a couple of training teams. In those mountains they all had a rough go at first, no matter what their age or how good their physical condition.

But in my feverish depression I wondered why I should kill myself to be mediocre at something I had been good at twenty years before. Especially when there were young guys coming up who were in great shape and still possessed of a sense of wonder.

Pride, of course. Pride only.

Perhaps my proper mission was to use my writing and editorial skills to explain the *Third World* War, rather than roam the jungle, looking for a firefight with people younger and quicker than I was. It was time for subjective journalism.

I fought in the Tet Offensive, so I don't even want to hear the term, "objective journalism." It's one of those joke oxymorons, like "Military Intelligence" or "Business Ethics."

Not only had the press not covered the war in Lebanon objectively, but no one had done the story of how or why the war was not covered objectively. "Objective" reporters don't fink on each other, not even in the interest of objective journalism.

Consider this. Almost all the foreign news in this country goes through about fifteen editors—New York *Times*, Washington *Post*, the three networks, *Time, Newsweek, U.S. News*, AP, UPI. There's not much more than that. And for that matter, the networks follow the *Times*.

Network producers read the *Times* on the way to work in the morning, and whatever the lead story is, that's what they want film on. Cover a war and you'll find TV guys sucking up to the *Times* correspondent to find out what he's going to write so they can cover it. Whatever the foreign editor of the *Times* says is news *is* what's foreign news in the U.S., and if the KGB finds some way to get to that guy, then they control what you learn about what goes on in the world.

I don't know whether they have such a way or not, but I do know that one Vietnam vet who worked for the *Times* finally quit because he could no longer stomach seeing stories which supported a "progressive" view played out of proportion, and important stories that supported a "reactionary" view spiked. At one point I tried to shame him into doing a book about it. "It's your duty," I insisted.

"Yeah, well, I've got four kids, and if I do that book I'll never work as a journalist again," he replied. "What about my duty to them?"

As a journalist, and as a former Special Forces officer who has had his nose rubbed in the *Third World* War, I felt it was my duty to do as much as one person could to correct that imbalance.

Shortly after returning from Central America, I left *SOF* for New York, to become editor of their main competition, *Eagle*. I sat behind a desk in a swivel chair, half the day at a typewriter or with a blue pencil in my hand, half a day with a telephone mashed to my ear.

I had reporters on five continents, and everything they found served to reinforce my belief that most of the wars in the Third World were part of a global conflict directed by Moscow; their ultimate target being the U.S., and their principle weapon—disinformation.

One of my reporters went through IRA Provo roadblocks in *West Beirut*. Another discovered a Sandinista recruiting booth at a street fair in *Mexico*. Recruits were sent to Nicaragua for thirty days of guerrilla warfare training. After that they simply returned to Mexico, to their regular jobs.

But, of course, their names were on a computer in Managua, ready to be activated when the time came to start the revolution in Mexico.

About a year after I came to *Eagle*, the regular newspapers began to acknowledge that guerrilla weapons in El Salvador came from U.S. stocks in *Vietnam*. Even then they didn't draw the obvious conclusion, that they came by way of the Soviet Union, Cuba, and Nicaragua.

A statement one hears often, "We don't want another Vietnam." From a strategic standpoint it's not "another" Vietnam. It's the *same* one. We've just got in the habit of naming wars after the patient rather than the disease. The war is not "Vietnam." It's us against the strategy of the "War of National Liberation." Once the U.S. abandoned Vietnam, the other guys decided they had found the winning formula and extended it to the *entire Third World*.

Almost every nation in the world has had its Vietnam now. France, the U.S., and China have had their Vietnams in Vietnam. Vietnam has her Vietnam in Cambodia. England has her Vietnam in Northern Ireland. Israel has her Vietnam in Lebanon. The Soviet Union has her Vietnam in Afghanistan. The U.S. has a new Vietnam in Central America. Want it or not, that's the deal.

The press used to talk about the Domino Theory, and how it failed. But the Domino Effect rolled up three countries immediately; Vietnam, Laos, and Cambodia. It stopped at Thailand, because the Thais: a) have never been colonized by anybody, and aren't about to start now; b) have in the King a unifying national symbol who is universally loved; and c) really practice the counterinsurgency principles that we taught them.

But if the Domino Effect failed in Thailand, it still jumped to three other theaters of operations: Africa, Central America, and the Middle East.

Whether capitalist or socialist, the factor which makes a country subject to such a war is a rigid class structure. Anywhere a society is rigidly stratified, whether by race, religion, or class, it becomes vulnerable to subversion.

This is obvious in South Africa. It was also obvious in El Salvador. A poor kid there was destined to spend his life chopping cane or picking coffee beans, watching his wife grow old quickly and his kids die of easily curable diseases.

Then the Communists came along and provided another option. In the guerrillas, a man could rise as fast as his talent could carry him. And if they succeeded in taking over the country, he could really be somebody.

If your kids were dying of some easily curable disease, you'd kill anybody who stood between you and the medicine that would cure them. In the Third World there's always disease, and the medicine is always controlled by a monopoly. You can't afford it...unless you become a Communist guerrilla, or unless the Americans come along and make the government change the rules.

Those of our allies who have successfully resisted the War of National Liberation have been those who have succeeded in opening their societies so that capable people from the ranks of the *Outs* have been allowed *In*. Two examples that come immediately to mind are Thailand and Malaysia.

It does not particularly concern me that Congress has kept our aid to El Salvador and the Contras down to a thin trickle, although it would concern me deeply if it stopped altogether. Our experience in Indochina indicates that aid given too lavishly leads to an indigenous leadership diverted from fighting the war to slicing the pie. Careful control of the thin trickle of aid gives us the leverage we need to require the oligarchy to reform its own society.

The Thais and the Guatemalans, for two, have done better without or with little aid than the Vietnamese and the Laotians did with lavish backing.

It's time for the *Right* in this country to accept that our problems in the Third World are in many ways of our own making, because we have supported governments that were antithetical to our own principles. It's time for the *Left* to acknowledge that while the roots of these insurgencies come from within, the rain, the sunshine, and the fertilizer come from the Soviet Union. Their ultimate objective is to wipe democracy, personal freedom, and human dignity from the planet.

It takes a generation of counterinsurgency work to teach the ruling classes in these countries that they will have to share the wealth to survive. In Vietnam, we were halfway through with that task when we quit, and we lost. You have to start with second lieutenants, and low-level bureaucrats, and hold on until these people become generals and presidents. We could have won in Vietnam with one-tenth, or even one one-hundredth the people we sent, but with professional people: experts, committed for a twenty- to thirty-year period.

War is being waged primarily in the Third World now, but it would require only a policy decision on the part of the Soviets to expand it. They now encourage limited terrorism in western Europe, but withhold funding for any terrorist group that wants to operate in the United States, because they don't want to raise public awareness here. They want America asleep until they have a lock on the Third World's raw materials, without which a technological society cannot survive.

People talk about how they don't want another Vietnam, as though the choice were between that and some sort of wonderful Eisenhower America. The choice may be that we have to fight Vietnam over and over again in every little ceiling fan, rat-and-fly infested Third World country, until we get it right—or face the prospect of seeing the U.S. turned into an oversized version of Lebanon.

If this narrative has not convinced the reader that we are at war, I recommend the following experiment. Every day for three months read in the New York *Times* every article about guerrilla warfare anywhere in the world. You have to read all of it, particularly the last three paragraphs where the really significant information is buried. It would help to underline every time the word "Soviet," or any synonym appears.


For myself, I found New York jungle enough, and a challenge of a different kind. Kat found us a great apartment in Brooklyn, top two floors in an old brownstone, huge living room with a cathedral ceiling. In Manhattan the rent would have been three times what we paid. But it was in a neighborhood which strongly resembles Calcutta. We have a storefront Shiite Mosque backing our place, on the next street over.

These Shiites are black guys who hate Whitey so much they joined the Ayatollah's religion.

To the front we are across from the Patrice Lumumba School for Wayward Girls. Working the nearest corner one can usually find the second, fourth, fifth and seventh ugliest hookers I have ever seen.

Six blocks over is a Haitian neighborhood that looks like Hiroshima.

But we've never been bothered in our own neighborhood. I once had a guy pull a knife on me on the fashionable Upper West Side; Kat pulled me off him before either of us did the other any damage. Once a guy hassled her on the subway; she clipped him in the nuts with her attache case.

I wasn't in very good shape psychologically when we first came to New York. Several times on the subway I hallucinated that the passengers were all dead. I saw their skin go waxy and they didn't seem to move. This sometimes happened when the light changed as we came out of the tunnel to cross the Manhattan Bridge.

I usually looked out the window and watched the illusion of the Statue of Liberty moving across the Brooklyn Bridge in the distance. It looked as though the statue, actually way off in the distance, was mounted on the bridge and crossing as we did. Then we hit the top of the arc of the bridge and started gathering speed as we approached the tunnel, diving into Brooklyn.

Rick, my friend from Lebanon, has come to visit several times. Things deteriorated in Lebanon, and his brother had been killed shortly before his first visit. Outwardly he projected his old suave manner, but at lunch, when a waiter dropped a tray of dishes behind him, he winced, and almost went under the table.

He and Christine had split up. She wanted marriage and a family; he couldn't see bringing a kid into the world he knew.

He stayed in the States several months, dividing his time between New York and Washington. Christine came to visit. She and Kathy had not met, but they became close friends almost immediately. But she seemed drawn and sad. Shortly after she left, Rick returned to Europe. They have since married and Christine became pregnant.

Between my writing the second and third drafts of this book, Rick called. He and Christine have a "three kilo, two hundred" baby girl.

Fouad, the Lebanese Forces press officer, came to New York on official business about a year after I started with *Eagle*. He brought a new girl friend, a sweet young lady named Nadia, who had been French-language anchor on the Beirut evening news.

At dinner I asked Fouad how his brother Teddy was. His face fell. Teddy had finally decided on an operation to restore partial use of his leg and had died under anesthetic on an operating table in Dallas six months before.

Later Fouad got caught on the wrong side of a Christian intramural squabble and left Lebanon. He and Nadia have married and he practices law in Indianapolis.

Sam, our other Lebanese friend, who looked like either a mad monk or a tong killer, had been scheduled to lead a detachment of troops into the Sabra Refugee Camp the night of the massacre. He and his men got off to a late start, and when they reached the main gate the firing didn't sound right. It wasn't like a firefight, too sporadic, too one-sided. He took his detachment and left. Since then he has left the militia altogether. I understand he has taken up with a beautiful Italian lady with children and lives in Byblos, where he is cultivating a magnificent tan.

The Lebanese Christians who did enter those camps were all volunteers from towns that had been massacred by Palestinians.

Of the 460 people killed in that "massacre," more than four hundred were men of military age, and more than half of them were not Palestinians at all, but free-lance terrorists from countries other than Lebanon. This information comes from the official Lebanese investigation of the massacre, which has never been seriously challenged.

But you could search the headlines and lead paragraphs of every story on that issue in every newspaper in the U.S. without learning that fact.

Larry Dring went back to Lebanon twice. Once, in a car with a couple of Lebanese Forces press bureau guys, a French woman photographer, and a Druze driver, their car was attacked and shot full of holes by Druze militiamen. The French lady screamed, and Larry hurt his arm when the car turned over.

The driver crawled out, shrieking curses at their attackers, who then realized they had hit the wrong car, apologized, and asked everybody in for coffee.

When he got back from that trip, Larry reported in to the *SOF* office with a duffelbag full of bombs, rockets, and grenades he had collected. They weren't just souvenirs. Larry was fully conversant with the Army technical manuals on Soviet weapons, and this was new stuff that wasn't in them. He had strolled blithely through customs with it, and his duffel had never been touched. *SOF* did a piece about it, and Brown turned the stuff over to the DIA.

Larry was preparing for his fourth trip to Lebanon for *SOF.* One Sunday afternoon at a cookout in his backyard in Summerville, SC, he complained of not feeling well. He lay down on the couch in his living room and died of a massive heart failure. He was forty-three. I believe his heart had been weakened by fifteen years of painkillers. I know several guys like that, who finally succumbed to wounds incurred in Vietnam.

Haney Howell went back to CBS in New York as a producer, and then to produce an overseas news feed for CONUS Communications in Minneapolis. He now teaches communications at Winthrop College in South Carolina and has written a novel set during the war in Cambodia. Al Rockoff gained a measure of fame when John Malkovich played him in "The Killing Fields" and is still one of the best combat photographers in the world. Captain America is a multimillionaire commodities broker who buys and sells with the same killer instinct that made him so happy in Cambodia.

I recently received word that my friend, Kpa Doh, was not, as we all thought, killed right after the Khmer Rouge took over Cambodia. Probably because he was not a Cambodian national, they offered him a job fighting the Vietnamese on the border. It has been reported that he fought on for another two years before finally being killed in combat. He had finally found another backer for his war with the Vietnamese.

I was shocked when I heard that he had collaborated with the KR. Then I realized that this was his only means to keep his family alive. To whom did he owe not to do that? The Americans who deserted him twice; the Cambodians who sold him out over and over again? Of his family there is no news.

In Bangkok, Dawson, my correspondent friend from the Bangkok *Post*, and his girlfriend, Tuk, have married and have a son, Patrick Michael, I call him Sluggo. Dawson has left the *Post* and is free-lancing and working as technical advisor on Vietnam movies being made in Thailand.

Roger Warner has also returned to the States, married, fathered a child, and written two excellent books.

Brigadier General Hiney Aderholt is back in Florida, developing an autogyro as a cheap alternative to helicopters for Third World countries with a counterinsurgency problem.

Coyne has also married. His wife, Thuy, is an intelligence analyst for the U.S. government. They live in Washington with their daughter, Tricia. Coyne is writing a novel.

Mme. Suon, the KPNLF press liaison officer, is no longer with the resistance. She is raising her children in Paris.

Neil Davis, the CBS correspondent who went into Cambodia with Kat and T.R., was killed in '85, in a little Mickey Mouse coup attempt in Bangkok. He filmed his own death, and it was shown on the NBC Nightly News.

Bill Gross, our first escort officer, is still in Tel Aviv, off active duty and back in the diamond business. Arnold Sherman was forced to retire from the IDF reserves when he reached fifty-five. He has moved to Athens and is writing a thriller.

Terry Anderson, the best friend we made among the American correspondents in Lebanon, a Marine combat vet from Vietnam, has been hostage in Lebanon for several years now. Oliver North and company were a week away from getting him out when Terry's colleague, Jack Anderson, printed the Iranscam story.

Ironic indeed. I have been angry at the press for continually printing stories that jeopardize the lives and slander the accomplishments of American servicemen. But what are we to think of an institution that eats its own?

Roberto D'Aubisson was narrowly elected president of El Salvador; they like macho men there. But the vote count was rigged by the CIA to give the election to Duarte. D'Aubisson's right-wing views are so unpalatable to Congress that it would rather let the Communists win than support him.

The day after I left El Salvador, Julian Harrison, my British friend, was shot in the chest. A very able Salvadorean army doctor saved his life, but he'll never fully recover. About a year later John Hoagland, the American who filled me in on background in El Salvador, was killed in an ambush.

# 29

# The Montagnards

Cambodia, 1984, Colonel Y Guk Hlom lay almost naked, his face pressed into the dark jungle earth. The one piece of clothing he wore was an old pair of tiger suit cutoffs, bleached white with repeated washings, then recamouflaged by months in the jungle. Slowly he raised his shaggy head and looked in hatred at the six PAVN *bo doi*, Vietnamese communist soldiers, ahead of them on the trail.

He had meticulously planned a route that circumvented all enemy troop concentrations, but nothing could prevent the occasional encounter with a recon team. Y Guk was not much impressed with their quality. As a young man, he had run recons with B-50, a U.S. Special Forces reconnaissance project.

They were so sure of being alone out here that they had no security out. He looked with contempt at the *bo doi* as they sat cooking rice beside the trail. The unrestrained sing-song lilt of their conversation made him shudder. He had hated these people all his life, and for the first half of it he had feared them. Then the Americans had taught him he was as good as any man, and they had treated him and his Rhade brothers, all his Montagnard brothers, as though they were equals.

On his first leave to Ban Me Thuot after his Mike Force training, he and two of his friends went into town in their new slacks and jeans, in polo shirts and flip-flops, feeling very good. They had just earned American parachute wings; they were somebody.

Coming down the street a South Vietnamese Ranger, a sniveling, limpwristed pfc, his beret ironed into a coxcomb, a cigarette dangling from his lip, broke off holding hands with one of his buddies long enough to shoulder Y Guk off the sidewalk and into the street.

Y Guk had heard stories from his Jarai friends about ARVN Rangers coming into the Mike Force villages near Pleiku, raping women, stealing chickens and goats, killing some of them for no reason, not even for food. Since the Montagnard Revolt in 1964, the Mike Force had been forbidden to take their weapons home, but Vietnamese Rangers carried theirs wherever they willed. If Montagnard men were in those villages, they were held at gunpoint while the Rangers did what they wanted. The Americans stopped it by staying in the villages with their own weapons.

"You die now," Y Guk muttered in his gutteral tribal language to the ARVN who had pushed him, but his buddies held him back.

"You never leave ARVN jail," Y Blik muttered.

"Wait!" Ksor Drong had whispered in his ear.

Y Guk had fought with the Americans for four years, but then they left. His unit was itself made an ARVN Ranger outfit, and Y Guk wouldn't be an ARVN Ranger, so he joined FULRO in the jungle. He had fought in the defense of Ban Me Thuot when South Vietnam fell—word had gone out that the Americans had sent for the Montagnards to fight there—and then he had run raids and ambushes until their ammo ran out and their weapons all broke.

They took fewer casualties than the PAVN, but the PAVN had replacements. They lost fewer weapons, but the PAVN had more.

For five years they had lived on the myth that the Americans would come back. He had believed that; he had preached it to his men.

But he could not preach it when he did not believe it anymore. In 1980, FULRO had sent a delegation that got as far as Bangkok, to talk to two Americans who would say only that they "worked for the government." The delegation was not permitted to see the Ambassador. They were sent to the Khmer Rouge for help—to the Khmer Rouge, who had slaughtered a third-to-half of their own countrymen.

They realized then that there was no way they could win, and so sent everybody who could go safely back to the village. But for four thousand of them that was not an option. They were marked for death by name. In four groups they set out for Thailand, to find their friends, their only hope, the Americans.

So Y Guk was still fighting now, eleven years later, though he had nothing left to fight with.

Strung out on the trail behind him, lying quiet next to the jungle floor, were eight hundred people, mostly men of military age; there were only about fifty women. Almost everyone was sick—malaria, scurvy, tuberculosis, yaws—and all of them were slowly starving to death. In his entire column Y Guk had only seventy-three men who were fit to fight, and they were weak. They had foraged their way halfway across Cambodia, and the pickings had been slim. He had last eaten meat two weeks before, an iguanid lizard called a Tokay. He ate grass and roots and the bark off trees. You could live on it, barely, but you lacked an energy reserve. Intense hunger pangs came and went, as did cramps, fever, dysentery.

On top of that there were only six working weapons in the column. Without ordnance support, their delicate M-16s had fallen apart within two years after the Americans left. What they had were three ancient M-1 Carbines, an M-1 rifle, which he carried himself, and two captured AKs. They had five or six rounds for each weapon.

He remembered being on patrol with the Green Berets, flying in, sitting in the cool wind at the door of a helicopter, the adrenal thrill building in the cold air above small arms' range, then slamming into the LZ and running through the prop blast to the perimeter, ammo thudding against his pelvis, so much ammo that he complained of the weight of it. He wished he had some of it now. Some choppers to get the hell out of here wouldn't be bad either.

He looked briefly at the Khmer Rouge guide beside him in the dirt. As it had turned out they would help, to the degree it suited their purposes. This one was strange, not bright, but with moody fanatic eyes. His solution to almost every problem was to kill somebody. This time he was right, however. No way could Y Guk sneak this entire column of people past these *bo doi*.

He signaled for four more men with weapons. He wanted this quick and final. One by one the men came down the trail. They moved silently. When they were in close behind him he gave a sudden gesture with his arm that meant to move on line through the jungle, and fire only on his command. These guys had been at this a long time.

It took more than two hours for each man to pick and crawl his way through the jungle without making a sound, vines pulled aside, branches parted and replaced carefully.

When he was sure everybody was in position, he slowly brought the ancient M-1 to his shoulder. He got a good sight picture on the leader of the *bo doi* and squeezed off a round. The man jerked backwards and went down as more shots rang out.

Y Guk waited a while and then went forward.

Six good weapons for his impoverished command. And some food. His decision was to give half of the *bo doi* rations to the armed men, and half to the sickest in the column. For himself he took nothing. He was a good leader.

About six months after I left *Eagle* to do this book, my phone rang. It was a guy named Peter Geismar, from "West 57th," the CBS magazine program. He wanted to know about the 220 Montagnards who had fought their way across Cambodia and were now in a refugee camp in Thailand.

These people were the remnants of FULRO, the Montagnard revolutionary organization. After the Americans left they had fought on alone until 1980, when they recognized that without outside support their cause was hopeless.

A force of four thousand of them set out for Thailand in six groups. Many of them had to leave their wives and children behind; they had no illusions about their chances of crossing Cambodia successfully. They were betting on an almost certain death against an absolutely certain one.

It took them two years to cross Cambodia. When they arrived at the Thai-Cambodian border, instead of turning them loose, the Khmer Rouge interned them in a camp in the jungle, eight klicks from Thailand.

Finally, they escaped in February 1985, when the Vietnamese hit the Khmer Rouge in that year's dry season offensive and destroyed all the Cambodian Resistance's bases on the border.

Only two hundred and twenty made it to Thailand. Some were interviewed by Barbara Crossette of the New York *Times*. After all they had been through, they said they wanted to emigrate to the U.S., but they were determined to stay together. They wanted to immigrate as a tribe, and the Immigration and Naturalization Service had no provisions for that.

Having spent two of three tours working with Montagnards, I wanted to help them. But how?

Then the call from CBS. "West 57th" wanted to do a story on them, and that story could only work in their favor. Regardless of any personal bias I might feel toward General Westmoreland and his lawsuit against the network, CBS was the only handle I had. I gave them every name I knew, every telephone number of people who had worked with the Montagnards, who had a deep affection for them. Among them was that of Don Scott.

Don Scott had been the in-country chief of Project Concern, a civilian nondenominational charitable foundation that ran a hospital in Tuyen Duc province, about an hour and a half from Dalat, and also ran schools, well-digging projects, and much more.

Once Scott, alone in a jeep, stormed into a village that had been occupied by an NVA battalion and confronted its commander. God knows what this guy thought when an enraged American civilian appeared and screamed in his face, "You can't stay in this village. The Americans will come out and bomb it flat. Get these people out of here!"

But he took his battalion and left.

Their headquarters was in an abandoned Special Forces camp, but they flew no flag, and their hospital took all comers. It was not unusual to find a wounded NVA trooper in bed next to a wounded South Vietnamese GI from the same battle. At one point, Scott got an invitation from an NVA general to visit Hanoi, because the hospital had saved his son's life.

Scott also formed a personal friendship with General Westmoreland, and once took him, alone and in civilian clothes, into a village that was "VC controlled." It was a Montagnard village, and the general had such a good time that he didn't get back until very late. He and

Scott paused and leaned against a fence and looked at the stars for a long time on their way back to the Project Concern compound. "You know, I don't get many moments like this," the general said wistfully.

The general's aide gave them both hell when they returned. "Sir, you can't do this. You can't just disappear like that."

"They pay me to take this," the general muttered to Don.


In December, 1968, Don Scott found out about the group at Site II in Thailand. He also found out that one of them had been his friend and interpreter, Ha Doi.

Don had been informed by a reliable source that Ha Doi had been assassinated. He had to go to see for himself. Accompanied by his fourteen-year-old adopted son, Bryn, who is Vietnamese; by Ha Kin Lienghot, a Koho Montagnard who has lived in the States since he was thirteen; and by Hugh Brown, a *Time-Life* photographer and Vietnam combat veteran, Scott set out for Thailand to find Ha Doi.

He found more than Ha Doi. Several of the Montagnards in the camp were people who had worked for him. Fourteen of them were in jail in Bangkok, charged with illegal entry. Our embassy had done nothing for them.

Don hit the ceiling. He paid all their fines. Then he called the U.S. Embassy. Normally he would have had a hard time getting through to a high-level official, but, as it happened, he called at lunchtime, so the Deputy Chief of Mission's secretary was out. This official, one Charles Freeman, answered the phone himself. He told Don, "The Vietnam War was a long time ago. There is no reason these Montagnards should have any higher priority than anybody else. If they're on the agenda at all, they're at the bottom, and personally, I don't think they're on the agenda at all."

Scott slammed the phone down and muttered an expletive that he has asked me not to quote, as he is trying to teach his kids not to talk like that.

Having done all he could, he returned home to Brunswick, Maine, to get in direct contact with his Senator, Bill Cohen. He intended to devote himself, full time if necessary, to getting the Montagnards to this country.

Don had kept contact with almost all the Montagnards in the U.S. It was not hard to do; there were only twenty-four of them. After he got back he called Pierre-Marie K'briuh, in Bakersfield, California. K'briuh claimed to be in possession of the minutes of a meeting that took place at the U.S. Embassy in Saigon in 1975, during the waning days of the Thieu regime, at which the Montagnards were specifically empowered to form a resistance movement, in the name of the United States.

A week later, Rob Hershman, the producer of this "West 57th" segment, had struck a deal with Scott. "If you return to Thailand to see the Montagnards, we'll bring a crew and film the reunion, as well as all the by-play with the State Department and the Montagnards in the refugee camp."

When he told me that, I immediately called Brown, who gave me an assignment to cover the trip for *Soldier of Fortune.*

On the plane over I read all the paperwork Don had brought. There were no "minutes" of the meeting, only a memorandum of record that the meeting had taken place. It was extremely vague as to what was said. Certainly there was nothing we could use to prove the U.S. had reneged on an agreement.

But one thing that was there was a list of who was present, and one of those was Ed Sprague, my friend from the 1973 trip to Vietnam and Cambodia. If I could find Ed, and the U.S. had made such a commitment, I had no doubt he would testify to it.

The first thing I did in Bangkok was to go down Patpong Road, looking for a journalist friend of mine. He was at his usual spot at the bar when I arrived.

He laughed when I explained to him what I wanted and why. An old Indochina hand, he is a member in good standing of the Montagnard Mafia. "There were two guys from the embassy here last night," he said. "I told them they better do what they could to get those 'Yards out of here as a group, and right away, or they'd have veterans' groups and congressional inquiries out the ass, and I'd personally see to it."

I grinned at that. "Do they know the Special Operations Association is having their annual reunion in Bangkok in December?" I asked.

He laughed. "No shit! That's great. If they don't have those guys out of there by then it's going to be like the last scene in *Rambo* with two hundred Rambos."

He told me, though, that it would take at least a week to get a pass to enter the camp. I didn't have a week to get the pass. I had to be back in the States within ten days.

He had been in the camps the week before and had a pass with his name on it that had two days to run. "The Thais won't ask to see your passport," he said. "Just give them my name and go on in."

I put his phony pass in my pocket and rented a car.

That night I told Don about my friend's conversation with the guys from the embassy. He laughed. "They received a letter from Senator Cohen. That probably happened the day after he threatened them. Then today I called and got an appointment with the ambassador. They know this CBS crew is here. Couldn't be more cooperative."

We talked for a long time that evening. I told him about the daughter of my Montagnard friend, Philippe, a.k.a. "the Cowboy," whom I had worried about for years.

Phil had been my patrol buddy. On more than one occasion he had risked his life for me. And the best operation I ever ran was one where I gave him the mission and went along for the ride. We ambushed a VC battalion headquarters, killed the commander and most of his staff, captured all their gear and a load of valuable documents.

I got a Bronze Star with "V," and he got a $25.00 bonus and a three-day pass.

We put him in for a U.S. medal, but, as a civilian, he was ineligible, and he wouldn't take a medal from the Vietnamese.

His daughter, Marina, had been only two when I last saw her. She was a kind of rusty blonde; some Montagnards are. There had been a rumor that she had not been Phil's daughter at all, but the daughter of one of the CIA guys who set up the Special Forces program in the Central Highlands. Easy to believe, because Philippe's woman was absolutely stunning, with rusty, reddish-black hair. Allegedly the Agency man had persuaded Phil to take over the woman and the baby when he left.

To be a good-looking half-American, half-Montagnard girl in Vietnam is just about the least enviable situation I can think of. What's more, her Montagnard father had been the most famous Cong-killer in the Highlands.

Don said that there was indeed such a girl in the camp. A rusty blond, not classically beautiful, but very striking; she was the best weaver they had.

Don and I agreed that he would stay in Bangkok for a couple of days and come down with the CBS crew. I would go ahead, spend a couple of days with the 'Yards, and try to negotiate a fraudulent extension on my phony pass.

The next morning at four o'clock I was on the road from Bangkok to Aranyapathet. It had been four years since I'd driven on the left side of the road, and even longer since I'd been someplace where the cops don't particularly care how fast you go. I managed to cut about two hours off the average time for the trip, Pink Floyd blasting from my cassette recorder, driving like a kamikaze, as I winged in and out of maniacal Thai traffic.


I stopped in Aran and picked up seven cartons of cigarettes and four big jars of instant coffee. Then I headed for Site II, five kilometers from the Vietnamese army in Cambodia, well within range of their artillery.

It was another 45 minute drive to the camps, through six or seven Royal Thai Army checkpoints, the road progressively more full of potholes, until finally it became a nightmare. I crawled along at five miles an hour behind convoys of tanker trucks carrying water to the refugees.

The camps were well back from the road; you could only dimly perceive them through the dust and the trees, huge cities of small thatch and rattan buildings.

Site II is the second largest city of Cambodians, after Phnom Penh, in the world. These regularly spaced buildings stretched for more than a mile before I came to the road leading to the camp entrance.

I missed the entrance to the small checkpoint I'd been directed to, and turned in at the main checkpoint, where the headquarters for the guard detachment was located. The barrier pole came down, and I stopped. A guard in black jungle fatigues came out and his eyes quickly locked on my jacket, which I had thrown over the coffee and cigarettes.

I had dealt with the Thai Rangers at Khoa Kor, and found them to be good people. But I'd been warned in Bangkok that this was a special unit, slapped together quickly by a raid on the Bangkok jail.

The guard whisked the jacket aside and smiled, then gestured for me to turn in at the headquarters.

"They're chicken thieves," I'd been told. "You have to make friends with them. Then, instead of stealing your chicken, they'll steal chickens for you."

But I didn't have time for that. Very nervously I got out of the car, confronted by the commander of the checkpoint, a Southeast Asian Burt Reynolds lookalike in black fatigues, with a very large service .45 on his hip. Smiling, he led me to his interpreter.

The interpreter, a smarmy wisp, was all smiles too. He held out his hand for my pass. "You cannot take anything into the camp," he said. "You will have to leave this material here with us." He examined my pass curiously. He looked at the name. "I will have to see your passport!" he demanded.

I patted the pocket where it was. "I, uh, seem to have forgotten it," I muttered. No way was I going to let him see that the name on the passport was not the same as the one on the pass. "Er-You must give me receipt for coffee and cigarettes."

He carefully wrote the amount of stuff he had taken on the back of my pass, but it was just a list. It didn't say he had taken it, and he didn't sign it.

We were at an impasse. If they didn't let me go in they had no excuse for not giving me my stuff back. If I demanded he sign a receipt, he would throw me out of the camp.

I smiled. He smiled. I got back in the car and drove in.

After a half-hour of driving around, trying to find somebody who spoke English or French to ask whether anybody knew where the Montagnards were, I found a dispensary staffed by European medics with an organization called, *Physicians Sans Frontieres*. I stopped a good-looking blonde German nurse in the parking lot of their bamboo headquarters. "Do you know where the Montagnard camp is?" I asked.

She said I had to go back out the gate and to the one across the road, the one I'd missed the first time.

Surprise! When I went back through the gate my coffee and cigarettes had disappeared, and nobody seemed to know what I was talking about when I asked for them.

The kids at the other gate accepted my pass without a second look. I could have breezed through with a couple of RPGs and an AK with no problem.

Now the Montagnards were easy to find. I drove straight down the road until I found a building with a sign on it that said, "ILOT DEGA." Mountain people. I parked the car and got out, feeling not a few belly flutters. Some kids came out to see who it was. Then a few elders. They weren't wearing traditional Montagnard dress, of course. They wore western pants and shirts. But I recognized them at once. There is something distinctive about them, something straight, that you don't see in other cultures in the Far East. These were my people.

A short man with stiff hair came out, surrounded by others, small brown men in pants, shirts and flip-flops. When he recognized me as an American, he smiled. We shook hands. He shook in the diffident Montagnard manner, pressing my hand softly. It amuses me that these people have developed a reputation for ferocity. They were always brave, but we taught them ferocity.

"Is Y Tlur Eban here?" I asked. Y Tlur's was the name I had been given as the man who had worked longest with Special Forces. He went all the way back to the first camp at Buon Enao. He had also worked for Chuck Darnell, now president of the Special Operations Association, and for the B-50 (Project Omega) Mike Force.

"No, he is at Ban Thai Samat. They are interviewing us. He is the interpreter."

I smiled. The embassy had started the interview process already. The presence of that CBS crew had certainly jerked their chain. This was no cause for complaisance though. This process could take months, and stop dead at any point. It would not be smart to let up until the Montagnards arrived in the States.

My informant introduced himself as R'mah Doc. We went inside the Ilot Dega headquarters and sat down. I was served a glass of hot water, which I received gratefully. They had no tea or coffee. Doc and I talked, and other Montagnards gathered. This group was made up of members of four tribes, although most of them were Rhade. But they called themselves "The Dega People." Montagnard, after all, is a French word. These folks had claimed the right to name and define themselves. From this and other clues I began to recognize that these were not the simple primitives who had first slipped their bracelet on my wrist on December of 1963. They had taken the grand tour of hell, and learned.

R'mah Doc was a Jarai from Pleiku. My people had been from Cheo Reo. I asked him whether he knew what had happened to them. He did; they were all dead, except maybe Nay Phin.

I asked him about Philippe's daughter. Marina. I knew Phil was dead, and I supposed his wife as well. But their daughter would be 24 now. R'mah Doc told me that he had heard she had married and had a child, but she had not come on this trek.

There was one person there from my old camp, a girl. She was in her twenties now, married, and with a baby of her own. She had been one of two sisters whose parents had been killed in the war. She had been "adopted" by an American SF captain. This was a couple of years after I left the camp, and I wasn't able to figure out who that captain was. She couldn't remember his name; she had only been two or so at the time. They told me how it had been in the Highlands when the North Vietnamese took over.


H'bia's small brown feet padded on the packed cool earth of the trail back to Plei M'nang. She paused and adjusted the weight of the wicker rice basket on her back. She had walked two hours to a small stand of corn that grew by the river. She put fifteen or twenty ears of corn and a couple of hands of stubby green bananas into the basket. They were for her wedding tomorrow, to Ksor Blem, the warrior who had come home.

Her heart beat a little faster at the thought. They couldn't afford to sacrifice a water buffalo as they had in the old days, but there would be rice wine—the men would sip it from crocks through reeds and grow morose or jolly, depending on their natures— and corn and bananas. All the old wives would tell stories of their own wedding days, in the guise of advise, and the younger girls would look at H'bia in awe.

She swung the basket off her shoulders and felt the breeze in the shady spot she had chosen to cool the perspiration on her budding fourteen-year-old breasts. She could remember when the American missionaries had made her mother wear a cotton blouse, and was glad she didn't have to. She filled a crooked pipe with harsh, homegrown tobacco and took a pull through the brass mouthpiece. Checking the tuck on her black sarong and another on the loose turban that kept her long hair off her neck and back, she repressed a giggle at the thought of undoing them for Ksor Blem. Then she set off down the trail, singing a song from the days before the Americans left. "Oh helicopters, you came and took my man away. Helicopters, please bring my man back to me."

Something didn't feel right as she approached the village. The birds weren't singing; they were twittering excitedly, and as she got closer to home they were dead quiet. Then she heard two gunshots and an excited jabber of Vietnamese.

A big American truck was parked at the gate, half-full of unhappy Montagnard men. Two excited *bo doi* in khakis and pith helmets were angrily shoving more men toward the truck. A ring of *bo doi* with AKs stood around all the men in the village, who stood dejectedly, submissively, in their loincloths.

She gasped. Ksor Blem was one of them.

The leader of the *bo doi* called out names from a clipboard, and he called out Ksor Blem's.

One of the soldiers started to shove him toward the truck, but the leader demurred. "Not that one. Kill him with the others." It was only then that she saw the corpses across the road from the truck. Roughly they led Ksor Blem to the edge of the field. A downy-cheeked *bo doi*, too young to have been in the fighting, fired directly into Ksor Blem's stomach, and, as Ksor Blem lay screaming on the ground, looked at his buddies to see whether they were impressed with his toughness.

"Quit screwing around with that *moi*," the one with the clipboard called. "We got work to do!"

One of the older ones sighed and blew Ksor Blem's brains out. They went back to their work.

Her hand flew to her mouth. Eyes wide, she fled back into the jungle. She'd heard of a village deep in the forest where the men still wore tiger suits and carried M-16s. They went out at night and attacked small Vietnamese outposts and ambushed truck columns. With Ksor Blem gone, she needed a man like that.

R'mah Doc told me how it had been. How they went into the villages with lists, and put some people in Re-education Camps, but many were just shot on the spot. He had been in a Re-education Camp for three years, then escaped by simply wandering off one day when the guard wasn't paying much attention.

He joined the Resistance in the jungle; he had never been a fighter before, but he became one, because he had no choice.

Next he introduced me to Y Bhuat Eban, who was acting as civilian leader of this group. He was an intensely sincere and decent person, but his most marked feature was the suffering that showed in his eyes.

We went to Y Bhuat's hooch. The striking, rusty blonde weaver was there, working at her loom. She was his wife; she wasn't Marina.

I stayed for a couple of hours, photographing, touring the area, then headed back to Aran for a shower and to buy some more coffee and cigarettes.

Next day I went back out and had no trouble smuggling my stuff in. Coffee and cigarettes for all. It was Sunday, no interviews. Y Tlur was there.

Not what I expected, a thin, middle-aged man with a receding hairline and a thin mustache. He introduced himself as Thoraban, a name many of the Americans had called him. We had a couple of laughs talking about Special Forces, jump stories and all that, and I asked him how it had been after the Americans left.

His face became grave. It had been bad. The North Vietnamese had been so bad in the mountains that even lowland Vietnamese had joined in the fight. "They were brave," he said. "But they could not live on grass and bark from the trees as we did."

Finally they had nothing. Not enough weapons, no ammo for what they had. The miniscule amount of help they got from Beijing disappeared in a policy change. They were left alone out there with nothing but the grass and the bark.

"We never lost a battle," he said, "but we never gained a thing. Everybody that was wounded died, and we came out of every victory with less than we had before."

The miracle was that they weren't bitter at the Americans.

The next day Don Scott and the TV crew arrived. Rob Hershman, the producer, was a no-nonsense get-the-story type of journalist. Meredith Vieira, the reporter, was warm and friendly from the start. But it's fair to say that they began with a cool, professional approach.

Thirty minutes after they arrived the 'Yards were singing hymns in Rhade in their church, and Hershman was all over the camp in his khaki shorts, sunglasses pushed up on top of his head, rubbing his hands, saying, "This is great! This is great!" Not only because it was a great story but because he had fallen in love with the people.

Later we went to Ban Thai Samat to cover the interviews. Young American refugee workers doing the screening were 100% behind the Dega people. One young lady led me aside and said, "Make all the noise you can when you get home. That's the only way to get them there."

I laughed. "Don't worry," I said. "That's the plan."

Don had an appointment with the ambassador in Bangkok for the following day, so we left before the crew. As we pulled away they were all wreathed in smiles, Meredith standing there with a baby on each hip.

That night, after a hellish ride around Bangkok trying to find our hotel in a city where we couldn't read the signs and nobody spoke English, Lacy Wright, who handles refugee problems at the embassy, came over for a drink. It was a cordial talk. There was no question that Don's congressional inquiry and the CBS crew had changed things. But I got the impression that what we had done was give the old Asia hands in the embassy ammunition to make the case for us. They had wanted to help the 'Yards all along. So far the only serious opposition had come from the dyspeptic Mr. Freeman.

Lacy visibly paled, however, when I told him about the SOA Reunion being in Bangkok. "I think we'll have them out of here by then," he said nervously.

The embassy insisted that there be no press present for Don's interview with the ambassador, especially not CBS, but not me, either. I could go as an interested party, but if I went I had to agree not to write about it. He went alone.

The interview couldn't have been more cordial. The ambassador turned out to be an old paratrooper. When he found out that more than thirty of the Dega people were qualified to wear U.S. wings, and that some of them had earned the 101st Airborne Division combat patch during Tet, he said, "I've got to get up there and meet those people."

Back in the States, Peter Geismar of CBS found Ed Sprague, my friend who had been at the meeting at the embassy in Saigon, the one where the 'Yards were allegedly promised support for their revolution. As soon as we returned I called him. He confirmed that the meeting had been held. "Did the embassy promise to get the resistance out?" I asked.

"Look, they dazzled them with footwork. The 'Yards left with the impression that certain promises had been made. But they weren't really. They were flimflammed."

After that conversation I went back to the original memorandum and looked at it more closely. K'briuh, who was at the meeting as Secretary General of the Ministry of Ethnic Minorities, states unequivocally that a Montagnard resistance was established at that meeting. The memo quotes Nay Luette, the Minister, as having proposed such a Resistance Movement, or to have Montagnard forces start moving toward Saigon for the last-ditch defense of the city. There are no quotes for G.D. Jacobson, the American who chaired the meeting, a curious omission in view of the gravity of the situation, but this sentence does appear: "Mr. Jacobson said that all our information indicated that the GVN intended to defend Saigon and he was confident they would consolidate their forces to do so."

In the Montagnard culture there are no weasel-words, no diplomatic language. If you ask a man a straight yes or no question, and he nods and smiles and says something that sounds positive, that means yes. It was obvious to me that whether the U.S. had authorized a Montagnard uprising or not, the Montagnards thought it had. They had fought on for five more years in the full belief that they were acting as our agents.

I called Sprague back. "I know that's what they thought," he said. "That's why I was so pissed off. That's why they threw me out of the country. I told them what the Montagnards thought, but they didn't care about Montagnards. They were getting ready to get out."

Our two hundred and twenty Montagnards are in the United States now. It took Don and me and several others eight months of hard work to get them here. Eight months of jet travel, meetings, and telephone calls. The only real action we saw during that time was running down a jetway with suit bags over our shoulders.

I have a new Montagnard bracelet to replace the one I gave Sam in Lebanon. It was made in North Carolina by a Montagnard I helped get there. It is the VIP model, like John Wayne had, and like him, I intend to wear it to my grave.

# Index